Action

Action
(1893)

Essay on a Critique of Life and
a Science of Practice

by
MAURICE BLONDEL

Translated by
Oliva Blanchette

University of Notre Dame Press
Notre Dame, Indiana

Copyright © 1984 by
Oliva Blanchette

A Translation of
L'Action (1893)
© 1950 by
Presses Universitaires de France

The publication of this volume was
assisted by a grant from the
Ministry of Culture of France,
which is gratefully acknowledged.

Library of Congress Cataloging in Publication Data

Blondel, Maurice, 1861-1949.
  Action : essay on a critique of life and a science of
practice.

  Translation of: L'action,
  1. Act (Philosophy) 2. Ethics. 3. Life. I. Title.
B2430.B583A2713 1984   128'.4   83-40113
ISBN 0-268-00605-9

Contents

v

THE NATURAL ORIENTATION OF THE WILL
Does the problem of action allow for a positive solution?
51

Part III
The Phenomenon of Action
——————

**How we try to define action through science alone
and to restrict it to the natural order**
54

Stage One
FROM SENSE INTUITION TO SUBJECTIVE SCIENCE
The scientific conditions and the unconscious sources of action
56

CHAPTER 1
The Inconsistency of Sensation and Scientific Activity
56

CHAPTER 2
*The Incoherence of the Positive Sciences
and the Mediation of Action*
62

CHAPTER 3
*The Elements of Consciousness and the Subjective
Science of Action*
94

Stage Two
FROM THE THRESHOLD OF CONSCIOUSNESS
TO THE VOLUNTARY OPERATION
The conscious elements of action
109

CHAPTER 1
The Conception of Action
111

CHAPTER 2
The Reason of Action
121

Maurice Blondel's Philosophy of Action

Translator's Preface

Action was once a prominent theme in philosophical reflection. It figured prominently in Aristotelian philosophy (ενεργεια), and the medieval Scholastics built some of their key adages around it, such as *actiones sunt suppositorum* and *operari sequitur esse*. But by the time Maurice Blondel came to focus on it for his own philosophical reflection, it had all but disappeared from the philosophical vocabulary. As one of his fellow students at the École Normale in Paris remarked, when he noticed that Blondel was contemplating a dissertation on action, the word "action" did not even appear in Adolph Franck's *Dictionnaire des sciences philosophiques*, the only one available in France at the time. And when Blondel came to have the subject officially inscribed at the Sorbonne for his dissertation, he was at first turned down, on the grounds that action did not offer matter for a philosophical thesis.[1] It was only with the support and at the insistence of Emile Boutroux, who was to be the *patron* for the thesis, that the subject was finally admitted.

But it was the same Boutroux who was later to remark, in his summation of the results of the First International Congress of Philosophy in 1900, that "the philosophy of action, life properly so-called, the social and individual destinies of humanity," all terms that clearly reflect Blondel's approach to action, had become a real and legitimate part of philosophy.[2] Since then the word has found its way back into the philosophical vocabulary, in the *Vocabulaire technique et critique de la philosophie* of André Lalande, for example, where Blondel had a good deal to say in the discussions about how it should be defined,[3] and in almost any other standard philosophical reference work. It is no longer possible or legitimate to ignore action in philosophy as it was in France when Blondel appeared on the scene in 1882, when at the age of 21 he first began to focus on action as a dissertation subject, and in 1893, when he defended and published the dissertation now presented here for the English reader for the first time in its entirety, 90 years after its original publication in French.

Blondel later published a second work entitled *L'Action* in two volumes in the context of a systematic trilogy on thought, being, and action.[4] The relation and the difference between these two works, which came more than forty years apart and each of which is systematic, has been a matter of controversy among interpreters of Blondel, a controversy which is intimately connected with the interpretation of Blondel's approach to the question of religion.[5] But it is enough for us to note here that *L'Action II* takes up more or less the same theme and the same method as had been worked out in *L'Action (1893)*, though with some important modifications due in part to the new context in which it was being presented. Some have argued that these modifications were due to some of the opposition that Blondel had encountered in his earlier work and constituted a watering down of the original thesis. But Blondel himself argued that the more comprehensive and technical framework which the trilogy afforded for his philosophy of action had been a part of his intention from the beginning.[6] He did not like being identified merely as "the philosopher of action," especially when action was seen as opposed to thought and the philosophy of action as anti-intellectual. His intention from the start had been to bring out the intellectual aspect of action[7] and to reopen the realm of action as an integral part of philosophy as a whole. Once the more technical aspects of his thought on thought, being, and pure act had been formulated, he was able to present his original philosophy of action in a new light, without some of the apparatus that had been necessary in the original version of 1893.

Blondel himself called attention to the fact that the first provisional subtitle for his thesis on action had been: *Essai d'une métaphysique commune de la nature, de la science et de la morale religieuse*, essay on a metaphysics common to nature, science and religious morality.[8] But in order to meet the rational exigencies of his contemporaries and to stay within the limits of a scholarly exercise such as a doctoral dissertation,[9] he had to place artificial restraints on such a vast subject and adopted a strategy of focusing primarily on the question of human destiny: Yes or no, does human life make sense? The method he adopted was one of accepting only the least possible answer to the question and seeing whether one could stay with such an answer. Thus the first answer to be examined was the dilettante's reply to the effect that the question itself is not worth considering. After showing that this answer could not stand, the next one to come up was that of nihilism: if there is a question of human destiny, the answer lies in nothingness. Blondel argued against this answer as well and went on to argue progressively that the answer lies in something, the something of positive science, the something of national life, and even the something of humanity as a whole, until he had exhausted the whole of what he called "the phenomenon of action." But since the question of human destiny found no satisfactory answer even in that, he then went on to argue about the "necessary being" of action and how that entered into the question of human destiny. But in the end, at the defense of his thesis, which was at once an ordeal and a triumph for Blondel,[10] he noticed that many, if not most, had missed the metaphysical import of his philosophy of action, and so he tried to remedy the situation by adding, rather hurriedly, a long chapter on "the bond of knowledge and action in being" to the end of the thesis he had submitted to the Sorbonne.[11]

Eventually, however, the additional chapter, though it constitutes a veritable philosophical *tour de force*, proved satisfactory to very few people, not even to Blondel himself, which explains why it did not appear again in *L'Action II*. But in this later version it was no longer deemed necessary since the metaphysical point had already been made in the preceding volumes of the trilogy. Other changes were also made between the two published versions of *L'Action* which we cannot go into here, though the question of human destiny and the general cast of the argument were preserved as a necessary complement to the integral philosophy Blondel wanted to develop, changes which reflect a greater concern to develop and follow his own language and train of thought, rather than espousing the language and thought of adversaries at every turn, in order to bring out the truth that is in them and leads beyond them, but changes which also did not maintain all the verve and force of the original version.

In defense of the second published version of *L'Action*, it should be noted that Blondel had been blind some five or six years by the time he got around to working on it with the help of Nathalie Panis, who became an invaluable assistant in the production of all of his later works. In his revision Blondel reformulated the old outline of the work and kept many sections of it intact while inserting new paragraphs of transition and touching up the language, thus giving the work a somewhat different, less "phenomenological" tone and making it somewhat disjointed in style and less easy to read. But even those who think that this second version of *L'Action* may still be truer to Blondel's original and fundamental intention, in spite of its difficulties, as this writer does, will still agree that the first version offers a much more ready access to the thought of its author in whatever mode. According to Mlle Panis, Blondel spoke of this early monumental work as his cathedral, and he was loathe to see it parceled out in *morceaux choisis*, or selected passages, which lost the eloquent and moving force of the whole.

L'Action (1893) was meditated on for some ten years by Blondel[12] and was put in writing in a final burst of activity beginning in 1889, when Blondel took a leave of absence from teaching in order to work full-time on his two doctoral dissertations.[13] These were times of both intellectual torment and inspiration for the young Blondel as he worked to give his

thought a systematic and dialectical form. He wrote two or three outlines, dictated one short version to a secretary, changed his subtitle sev-
eral times before settling on *Essay on a Critique of Life and a Science of
Practice*, and rewrote many parts of it six or seven times, as he told one
of his examiners,[14] in order to make himself clear and forestall any accu-
sation of obscurity, knowing that this thesis on action would come as
an intellectual bomb not only for the examiners but for the intellectual
milieu of France at the time. Blondel showed remarkable confidence for
someone in his position, and the anticipated explosion did not fail to
materialize. When Blondel arrived in Paris to defend his thesis, Boutroux
warned him that the other members of the board of Examiners were
furious, and he advised Blondel to go call on them privately so that they
could vent some of their anger before the public defense. The galleries
were packed for the defense, which lasted from 3:00 to 7:15 p.m., and
Blondel was awarded the *Docteur ès Lettres* by the sheer force of his
method, even though his examiners felt compelled to express a total disagreement with his conclusions, especially those concerning the necessity
of a supernatural religion. It was only a few days later that Blondel
learned he would be refused a university teaching post for arriving at
such conclusions, a refusal that would be overcome only two years later
through a direct appeal to a new Minister of Education of France related
to Boutroux, who had by this time himself become a sort of intellectual
martyr in university circles in the cause of Blondel.[15]

It must not be supposed, however, that in order to follow the dialectic
of action one must first have gone through the more technical parts of
Blondel's work. As Blondel remarked even of *L'Action II*, which came at
the end of the trilogy on thought, being, and pure act, the way or the
method that it follows "does not require any technical preparation or any
special competence since it deals with the itinerary to be followed by the
most simple as well as by the most adept as long as they are looking for
the rectitude of intention in all the byways that human existence can offer
amidst the current ideas and the passions that intersect one another. In
many respects such an aim can more readily be understood by minds free
of any preconceived system than by those accustomed to a particular ter-
minology and doctrinaire attitude."[16] Even though the philosophy of human action in the concrete comes as a necessary complement to the rest
of philosophy, as Blondel resolutely maintained, it can still be read as "a
relatively autonomous investigation into what can serve and suffice for
all those unfamiliar with the other technical disciplines of philosophy
who feel the need to rationally illuminate and vitally assure their road
toward the inescapable term of their destiny."[17]

The reason for this is that the relation between philosophy and life is not a one-way street. Just as life stands to learn from philosophy, so also philosophy stands to learn from life. Hence the importance of "a critique of life and a science of practice" for philosophy as such. In some respects *L'Action* can be likened to Hegel's *Phenomenology of Spirit* in its relation to Hegel's system. It is a systematic introduction to a philosophy of spirit, especially in the 1893 version, and it follows its own phenomenological method. But it is not an introduction that can be left behind once one has entered the realm of systematic thought. For Blondel, who insisted on being a systematic philosopher, systematic thought can never close in upon itself. Even the idea of action is never equal to action itself, as Blondel repeatedly maintained. In all his systematic work he argued to keep philosophy systematically open and integral so that it would always have to return to action for its necessary complement. Theory cannot do without practice any more than human practice can do without theory. This is why at the end of his trilogy he had to return to his initial philosophy of action. It is a conclusion as well as an introduction, but a conclusion that opens the way to a completely new set of questions. Each one of his volumes on thought, being, and act called for this return to action. Thought and action must mutually enrich one another by taking turns in being principle and consequence in a sort of cycloidal motion.[18]

Nor must it be thought that this philosophy of human action in the concrete is meant to be simply an edifying and elevating moral discourse filled with instructions for leading the good life, as one of the examiners had mistakenly expected in reading the phrase "science of practice" in the subtitle of the original dissertation.[19] To be sure, there are elevating passages in *L'Action* and there are pages of moral exhortation in this long dialectic on human action, but ethics is by no means the principal concern of the dialectic. It appears as one stage in the dialectic, while the dialectic itself is aiming at a much higher and much broader goal, an understanding of the metaphysical and religious foundation of human action as a whole. Given the kind of thinker he was, Blondel could hardly eschew all moral exhortation along the way, but his ultimate aim was to show that no natural ethic, no separate philosophy, could be grounded apart from the religious and the supernatural, and he aimed to do so philosophically, not theologically, as he tried to make clear not only to his examiners in 1893 but also to all who would continue to misinterpret his intentions as a philosopher of religion later on. His science of practice was meant to be critical of action as a whole, "a critique of life," and to encompass all that makes human action what it is, from the lowest stirrings in the nature of man to the highest aspirations of the human spirit and the ontological and divine foundations on which these aspirations are grounded.

To achieve his purpose, Blondel had to distinguish clearly between *practical science*, which comes with life and constitutes a veritable experimentation, but an experimentation that cannot be completed until the end of life, and the *science of practice*, which starts from that practical science but attempts to anticipate its conclusions in a rational and methodical way by examining the contents of action as it now presents itself concretely.[20] As a science of practice, therefore, it had to be a philosophy of the *concrete*,[21] and, as a philosophy, it had to be *universal* in its scope, leaving out nothing of what might affect human action and trying to harmonize and unify everything which an abstract and notional reflection left in a state of exclusive separation. This is why it focused on action as the concrete universal. Action appeared to Blondel as "that 'substantial bond' which constitutes the concrete unity of each being while assuring its communion with all. Is it not, indeed, the confluence in us of thought and life, of individual originality and of the social and even the total order, of science and of faith? . . . It comes from the universal, it returns to it, but by introducing something decisive into it: It is the geometric locus where the natural, the human, the divine all meet."[22]

This already suggests some of the richness of meaning which Blondel attaches to this short word "action," a meaning which can only be articulated more precisely in the course of the dialectic. But there is one more aspect of the idea which should be brought out more clearly to assure that the dialectic will be followed critically. If the philosophy of action is to be critical, as it claims to be, it must proceed from a principle that is critically established. This principle, to anticipate for a moment something that will also be established in the course of the dialectic,[23] can be expressed in terms of a certain inadequation which appears in action itself where we find a mixture "of obscure virtualities, conscious tendencies, and implicit anticipations," for, as Blondel writes, the term "action" includes at once "the latent power, the known achievement, the confused presentiment of all that, in us, produces, illuminates and attracts the movement of life." This is why for him "philosophy begins when it turns expressly to the study of this internal disequilibrium in order to aim at a progressive coincidence between the implicit and the explicit; its proper object is action."[24] But if such a philosophy is not to remain anarchical, without principle, it must seek an adequation, not of an abstract speculation with reality (*adaequatio speculativa rei et intellectus*), but of thought with real life (*adaequatio realis mentis et vitae*),[25] by first recognizing as its point of departure "the systematic affirmation of our actual inadequation and of the solidarity of all the problems that concern our being and beings."[26] In some respects this could be seen as a conclusion of the dialectic of action as well as its operative principle, since its aim is not to close off but to open up philosophy in its endeavor to embrace all that is real.

This is not the place to go into any elaborate explanation of Blondel's dialectic. Like any good systematic work in philosophy, it must be allowed to speak for itself and to develop according to its own logic and method. But we could mention that there have been many accounts and summations written on this dialectic of action.[27] Among them is an extensive one in English, the only one, written in anticipation of a translation of *L'Action (1893)* as an "initial approach to the Philosophy of Action for the American reader" by James Somerville—*Total Commitment: Blondel's L'Action*.[28] The book is the most complete and detailed analysis of the work translated here, and it contains a good introduction to Blondel and his work. Somerville taught Blondel for years at Fordham University when Blondel was otherwise little known in the English-speaking world. The only other comparable introduction to Blondel in English is the one by Alexander Dru and Illtyd Trethowan given with their translation of *The Letter on Apologetics* and *History and Dogma*,[29] two long early articles by Blondel, one in 1896 and the other in 1904, in which he took issue with developments in Catholic thought on both the right and left and which embroiled him in long and bitter controversies over the Modernist crisis among Catholic theologians, controversies which kept Blondel for a long time from doing the work he should have been doing as a philosopher. Dru and Trethowan give a good account of this theological turmoil and of Blondel's involvement in it in an introduction of over one hundred pages.

We should mention also some of Blondel's many ties with modern and contemporary philosophy. One of these was with William James and American Pragmatism, though no strong relationship ever developed there. Blondel's philosophy of action did not escape the notice of James's ever-roving eye. James refers to Blondel in the preface to *Pragmatism* as a kindred spirit in philosophy. The relation between pragmatism and action seems obvious enough at first glance, and Blondel did speak of his philosophy as a "practicing philosophy." He may even have been willing to refer to it as a form of "pragmatism" at one time, but not after he discovered what the term meant to James and others in England and America.[30] The criterion of truth remained too extrinsic and utilitarian in pragmatism, whereas for Blondel action was more intrinsic to knowledge itself. Pragmatism also saw itself as opposed to intellectualism, whereas Blondel admitted of no such opposition between thought and action. Beyond pluralism, he sought a more unitary view of life, but one which did not reduce religious life to the uniform level of empirically observable facts.[31]

For his part James tried to read *L'Action (1893)* in 1907, which he had to borrow from Blondel himself since he could not find it in print anywhere, but he had to admit that he could not follow the argument or agree with it.[32] What stood in the way seems to have been precisely the method of implication, or disimplication, as some now prefer to say, which he saw Blondel make so much of in the formulation of his point of departure and operative principle.[33] In spite of this disparity, however, James could still write to Blondel, "you belong for me to the race of absolutely original, probably prophetic, thinkers with whom one feels that one must some day settle one's accounts," and he could go on citing Blondel at least implicitly in speaking of how philosophy affects reality in the pluralistic universe and the cycloidal relations between theory and action.[34]

Blondel was also, of course, a contemporary of Bergson, who had just left the École Normale Supérieure when Blondel came there in 1881. He was critical of Bergsonism, if not of Bergson himself, for wanting to rely too exclusively on intuition[35] and for being only a futurism instead of an eternism.[36] But along with Bergson he was largely influential in helping French philosophy break out of the narrow positivism and rationalism in which it found itself at the turn of the century. While Bergson was the more elegant writer, Blondel was the more systematic one. While Bergson spoke of the *élan vital*, Blondel spoke of the *élan spirituel*. While Bergson used a method more closely related to the observational sciences, Blondel developed a more critical and dialectical method.

Blondel is also said to have been an existentialist philosopher long before the era of such philosophy. Anyone who reads the first few pages of his introduction to *L'Action* written in 1893 will readily see why this can be said. Moreover, Blondel surely had an influence on existential philosophers like Marcel and Merleau-Ponty, who is reported to have acknowledged an important debt to Blondel one day, and he spoke of freedom and subjectivity in a language quite similar to Sartre, though with diametrically opposed conclusions with regard to the existence of God and the significance of religion. But unlike most of these existentialist thinkers, Blondel was resolutely systematic in his pursuit of the existential question of human destiny. In this way, it has been argued, he was able to overcome the opposition between "existence" and "truth" that is often found in existentialism.[37] He was also able to answer the arguments of existential atheism, so to speak, as found in Sartre and Polin, for example, long before they were formulated.[38]

William James was quick to note a resemblance in formula at least, if not in substance, between Blondel and Kierkegaard as well as with himself,[39] while others have brought out similarities with Hegel and Fichte. But the latter must not be unduly exaggerated. Blondel was not unacquainted with the German Idealists, but his acquaintance was mediated more by his close friend Victor Delbos, the historian of philosophy, than by any prolonged meditation of these authors. The similarity with Hegel is obvious enough in that both were systematic and dialectical thinkers, both had a "phenomenology of spirit," and both saw religion as an essential part of human life. In some respects Blondel was to French Catholicism what Hegel had been to German Protestantism. At least he reintroduced into a recalcitrant French philosophy the theme of religion as a legitimate realm of investigation. Blondel himself made this point early on, using the parallel with Hegel, in a letter to the *Revue de Métaphysique et de Morale* in defense of the legitimacy of his concern with religion as a philosopher.[40]

But the similarity with Hegel may end there. When it came to the supernatural as such, Blondel took a view that was quite different from that of Hegel. Far from trying to absorb religion into philosophy, Blondel argued philosophically for the necessity of a supernatural with a positivity of content and precepts which philosophy could not attain, let alone absorb. This is what came as a shock to his examiners in 1893, and it would have come as a shock to Hegel as well because it was presented as a philosophical claim of the highest order. If both Blondel and Hegel treat of the same themes when it comes to religion, they do not treat of them in the same way be any means. The difference that separates them is like the difference that separates the cycloid from the circle.

It is true that at the end of part V, chapter III, Blondel refers to Goethe's saying *Im Anfang war die That* (In the beginning was the act), which could be read as tying him into the German idealist tradition and its philosophy of act.[41] But he immediately corrects or complements it by a quotation from St. John, *In principio erat Verbum* (In the beginning was the Word), to bring out an equal primacy of truth with action. Blondel was intent on overcoming the Kantian dichotomy between theoretical reason and practical reason, and in *L'Action (1893)* he espoused the Kantian language of determinism and freedom to the hilt to do so. But his effort was not so much one of digging down into the subject in idealist fashion, as Fichte did, to find where reason is common to both theory and practice or to reduce truth to practice, but rather one of going over the top of the dichotomy, so to speak, back into the concrete where the two are already one. This is why he chose to do a philosophy of action rather than merely a philosophy of act. As he writes, "The word 'action,' more concrete than 'act,' expresses what is at once principle, means, and end of an operation that can remain immanent to itself."[42] To illustrate its meaning he preferred referring to the Greek distinction between ποιειν, πραττειν, and θεωρειν, with the idea of including all three of these in his meaning, rather than to a German theory of act. Though he is very careful to distinguish between act and fact in making the passage from objective phenomena to the phenomenon of consciousness, thus establishing the necessity of a distinct science of the subject,[43] he does so only to move on to the more comprehensive phenomenon of action as a whole. To be sure, as he writes, "the least *act* has a reality, an importance, a dignity, so to speak, infinitely higher than the fact of the universe," but that act must be seen as encompassing the universe. Action is a function of the whole, and, before it can reach completion, the initial act must reach out to encompass the whole of reality as a necessary means to its end. It is the purpose of the dialectic of action to show how far this can and had to go.

Hence Blondel's philosophy is as closely related to the theory of action and even decision making as it is to the theory of act. To the extent that it places before us an option to be taken before God, it is also related to Kierkegaard's dialectic of existence and faith, except that where Kierkegaard insists on faith by reason of the absurd, Blondel will try to show how the necessity of the supernatural itself implies some form of positive manifestation of the eternal in time and some form of religious practice for this world, beyond all superstition and false worship, even if it be of reason itself.

With regard to Thomism it should be noted that Blondel, though a Catholic, received his philosophical formation entirely within the state university system, which was quite impervious, not to say directly opposed, to that way of thinking, and he resolutely pursued his own philosophical career within that same system. This was to be a source of some resentment among certain clerics later on when he would comment on Thomism and intervene in matters that affected theology. Christian influences on Blondel go back to writers that antedate the great medieval systems, to St. Bernard, the only medieval quoted in *L'Action (1893)*, to St. Augustine, and to St. Paul. To be sure, Blondel was a devoted and faithful Catholic, but not because he was a Thomist. In fact, he was severely critical of Thomism when he first encountered it and of the way it was trying to deal with the question of religion. That was the burden of the misnamed "Letter on Apologetics" of 1896, which caused no less of a stir in church circles as his dissertation of 1893 had caused in university circles. The real title was *A Letter on the Requirements of Contemporary Thought and on Philosophical Method in the Study of the Religious Problem.*[44] The "Letter" was a prolonged reflection on the development of modern philosophy and its exigencies. It was written as an attempt to set the record straight as to his intention and his philosophical method, and it dealt with apologetics, a theological category, only tangentially inasmuch as it presupposes some kind of philosophy. Blondel's argument was that if philosophy is to intervene in the study of the religious problem, it must do so according to the exigencies of modern philosophy, and Thomism was not doing that at the time. Later on he changed his view on Thomism when he encountered authors like Rousselot and Maréchal who had in fact themselves been influenced by him, and when he began to read more of St. Thomas himself. But he never felt compelled to become a Thomist, even though he came to see a common interest between Thomas and himself, which was to think the unity of his life as both human and Christian at the same time.

A philosophy of action such as Blondel conceives it is bound to contain a wide diversity of interests along the various stages of its development. Besides dilettantism and nihilism, both of which it must overcome in order to get underway, it must deal with the sciences of nature and the positivism that frequently underlies them. At this stage of the development[45] Blondel shows remarkable insight into the nature of the mathematico-physical sciences and the kind of action they require on the part of the scientists to bridge the gap between calculus and observation and to make them work. The analysis is something that would interest both scientists and philosophers of science even to this day, even though the analysis antedates most of the revolutions in modern post-Newtonian physics. For his own part, however, Blondel uses the analysis to show that one cannot stop at merely objective science in the study of action, but one must move on to a science of the subject as such according to a method that is appropriate to this subject. In other words, Blondel demonstrates an objective necessity for a subjective science of human action.

It is at this point that Blondel enters into his own insight as to how to pursue such a science in a rigorous fashion. He begins with a reflection on the dynamics of consciousness, or what he calls "the conception of action," and goes on to demonstrate the necessity of freedom, or that the very notion of determinism presupposes the notion of freedom. He shows how freedom necessarily arises in consciousness and how it necessarily exercises itself as freedom, that is, freely, and in so doing gives rise to a whole new order of determinism, an order that is no longer prior to the exercise of the will but consequent to it and an order which the science of action must now unfold stage by stage. In the first free exercise of his will, the subject finds a certain emptiness in his transcendence, a need to make himself equal to the fulness of himself in his willed action, and so he is launched into the pursuit of equality with himself in his body, in his psyche, in language, in action with others, and on to the confines of the phenomenal universe. In this systematic reflection on the experience of the subject the young Blondel shows himself at his best form, inviting every objection and ready to overcome it and move on, a form he was not able to maintain in the later version of *L'Action*.

The entire thrust of the argument, however, was not just to develop each stage along the way with all its exigencies as rigorously as possible, but at the same time to reach to the very confines of the phenomenal universe of action where the question of religion appears along with that of the necessary being of action. In a letter to Lalande for the *Vocabulaire technique et critique de la philosophie*, Blondel writes as follows of his twofold intention in *L'Action (1893)*: "It focused on the following two problems and with the attitude defined as follows: 1. A study of the relations between thought and action conducted in such a way as to constitute a critique of life and a science of practice, with the aim of arbitrating the contention between intellectualism and pragmatism through a 'philosophy of action' that includes a 'philosophy of the idea' instead of excluding it or limiting itself to it. 2. A study of the relations between science and belief and between the most autonomous philosophy and the most positive religion conducted in such a way as to avoid rationalism as well as fideism and with the aim of uncovering through a rational investigation the intrinsic claims of religion to be heard by all minds."[46] Thus, Blondel's philosophy of action was meant to be a philosophy of religion from the start and to raise the question of religion which was being excluded from academic philosophy in his day or simply dismissed out of hand. It was with this purpose that he had originally decided to focus on action.[47] His intention had been to extend the domain of philosophy both at the bottom and at the top and to reach deeper into the hidden sources of human action in order to bring philosophy higher to the question of religion.

In *L'Action* the question is approached first through a radical critique of religion in all its superstitious forms, including the superstition of the enemies of superstition and of those trying to do without religion in an attitude of self-sufficiency.[48] The outcome of this critique is not an elimination but a reinstatement of the question in its true meaning, a question which Blondel then goes on to pursue, not just in the sense of "religion within the limits of reason," but in the sense of a strictly supernatural religion with positive revelation, precepts, and practices. The ambition of the project seems daring and almost excessive even to this day, but Blondel was quite serious about it precisely as a philosopher. What he came up with was an unparalleled argument in the philosophy of religion that is worthy of the most serious consideration, one that managed to impress his most hostile examiners even as they still rejected its conclusion.

Part of Blondel's purpose was to put an end to the idea of an autonomous philosophy separated from religion, a philosophy which even many Thomists had long accepted and still often cling to. For him, as we saw, even the most autonomous of philosophies could not prescind from religion, even from positive religion, and his argument was to show that integral and comprehensive thought had to be systematically open not only to the teaching of action in the concrete but to whatever new or supernatural intervention of God that might come through this action.

From the other side, this also meant that religion itself could no longer consider itself "autonomous" or separated from action and philosophy. Religion had never much enjoyed being ignored or dismissed by philosophy, but it found something disquieting in Blondel's claim to include religion in his philosophy of action, especially when its critical aspect became more manifest. As a philosophical champion of religion Blondel did not bring theologians an easy comfort. Many of them felt threatened by what seemed to them an illegitimate intrusion into their domain, which according to them had to be separate and apart from the domain of philosophy, and they reacted no less violently to his efforts than philosophers had done on the other side of the division. In fact Blondel, who remained a faithful son of the church, suffered much more from the violence coming from this quarter over the years than he did from any other source. There were never any official condemnations of his work. Indeed, there were expressions of official approval at various times. But there was always a certain fear of condemnation, especially in the early years of the Modernist controversy, and the hounding threats of certain theologians that lasted until Blondel's death. Ironically, it was Blondel who first began to notice the unorthodox tendencies of writers like Loisy, long before most clerics, and to write in opposition to these tendencies.[49] What he wrote proved to be very successful for the renewal of the idea of tradition and the development of dogma and was to have a significant impact on theology, but it offered little comfort to those who remained his foes, since it was as critical of the "old" way of thinking, which it characterized as excessively extrinsicist, as it was of the new, which it characterized as falsely immanentist.

But in the end, in spite of these long and painful adversities, Blondel's philosophy of the supernatural was to have a significant impact, not only on the development of the theology of the act of faith but on the conception of the relation between the natural and the supernatural in both philosophy and theology. For those who believe in the supernatural, as he did, he marks in many ways the end of the idea of a layered, or two-storied, universe, one natural and another supernatural, the latter simply superimposed on the other in purely extrinsic fashion. For those who do not believe, he marks the end of a philosophy that ignores religion or refuses to treat of the strictly supernatural as such, the secular, or one-storied, version of the layered universe. Blondel was well aware of the difference between philosophy and theology as intellectual disciplines, but he did not think the competence of the one excluded the competence of the other even in religious subjects. Without infringing on the competence of theology as to the content of the idea, he thought the idea of the supernatural could be determined philosophically, and he argued for its necessity in his dissertation of 1893.

The argument which he presented then was never reproduced in any of his later works in precisely the same form. In *L'Action II* he only leads up to such an argument but does not develop it, and in his last major work, which he was still working on at the end of his life, *Philosophy and the Christian Spirit*, a work which he had begun to plan forty years before at the turn of the century,[50] he treats of some of the same themes but not in the same rigorous, closely knit fashion. It is this philosophy of the supernatural as such of *L'Action (1893)* which makes the work one of permanent interest along with some of the other features which we noted earlier. A translation of it into English has long been overdue. Now let us let the work speak for itself by accepting Blondel's invitation to explore with him: "Yes or no, does human life make sense, and does man have a destiny?"

Oliva Blanchette
Boston College

Notes

1. *L'Itinéraire philosophique de Maurice Blondel*. Propos receillis par Frédéric Lefèvre. 2nd ed. (Paris: Aubier-Montaigne, 1966). Blondel is the author of the questions as well as the answers for this work published in the form of a long interview in 1928.

2. *Revue de Métaphysique et de Morale* 8 (1900): 697-98. At the congress Blondel himself had read a paper entitled "Principe élémentaire d'une logique de la vie morale." Cf. *Congrès Intern. de Philosophie* (Paris: Colin, 1903), II, pp. 51-85.

3. Cf. 4th ed. (Paris: Alcan, 1932), pp. 16-19.

4. Cf. *La pensée*, 2 vols. (Paris: Alcan, 1934), *L'Etre et les êtres* (Paris: Alcan, 1935), *L'Action I: Le problème des causes secondes et le pur agir* (Paris: Alcan, 1936), and *L'Action II: L'Action humaine et les conditions de son aboutissement* (Paris: Alcan, 1937). To distinguish the earlier work here translated from this

later work, it is usually referred to as *L'Action (1893)*. It was reedited in offset printing, only in 1950, shortly after Blondel's death, and again in 1973 by the Presses Universitaires de France.

5. Cf. especially Henry Duméry, *Blondel et la religion: essai critique sur la "Lettre" de 1896* (Paris: Presses Universitaires de France, 1954) and *Raison et religion dans la philosophie de l'action* (Paris: Seuil, 1963) vs. Henri Bouillard, *Blondel et le christianisme* (Paris: Seuil, 1961). The latter has been translated into English by James Somerville: *Blondel and Christianity* (Washington, D.C.: Corpus, 1969).

6. Cf. *L'Itinéraire philosophique*, pp. 63-64, and texts written by Blondel in view of a preface for a reedition of *L'Action (1893)* in *Etudes Blondéliennes* I (Paris: Presses Universitaires de France, 1951), pp. 7-21.

7. Henry Duméry has shown how this is done in *L'Action (1893)* in his first important work on Blondel, *La philosophie de l'action: Essai sur l'intellectuelisme blondélien* (Paris: Aubier-Montaigne, 1948), for which Blondel wrote a preface underlining the importance of this integral intellectualism which includes action as well as thought.

8. Cf. *Etudes Blondéliennes* I, p. 11.

9. Cf. ibid., pp. 12, 16, 19.

10. Cf. the account given by Jean Wehrlé, "Une soutenance de thèse," *Annales de Philosophie chrétienne*, May 1907, reproduced in *Etudes Blondéliennes* I, pp. 79-98. The account is based on notes of Blondel himself taken during the defense and pulled together immediately after.

11. Cf. below, Part V, ch. 3. There were actually two editions of *L'Action* in 1893, one which was submitted for the defense, of which 200 copies were printed but to which Blondel had reserved the right to add from page 401 on, and one intended for general publication, of which 750 copies wre printed, soon to be exhausted to the surprise of the publisher and not to be reprinted again until 1950. A critical edition of this controversial chapter was established and published by Henri Bouillard, "Le dernier chapitre de 'L'Action' (1893)," *Archives de Philosophie* 24 (1961): 29-113.

12. For a running account of these meditations, cf. Blondel's *Carnets intines (1883-1894)* (Paris: Cerf, 1961).

13. Blondel's Latin dissertation was on the idea of a substantial bond in Leibniz: *De Vinculo substantiali et de substantia composita apud Leibnitium, hanc thesim Facultati Litterarum Parisiensi proponebat Mauritius Blondel* (Paris: Alcan, 1893). This Latin thesis on an idea which had an important role in the development of Blondel's thought has since been published again with a French translation and a commentary by Claude Troisfontaines, the director of the Centre d'Archives Maurice Blondel at Louvain-la-Neuve in Belgium as the first volume of the series emanating from that centre. Cf. Maurice Blondel, *Le lien substantiel et la substance composée d'après Leibniz* (Louvain: Nauwelaerts, 1972). Blondel himself had earlier published a sort of commentary in French on

his Latin thesis under the title *Une énigme historique. Le "Vinculum Substantiale" d'après Leibniz et l'ébauche d'un réalisme supérieur* ("Bibliothèque des Archives de Philosophie"; Paris: Beauchesne, 1930). Needless to say, it was the French dissertation on *Action* which got the bulk of attention in 1893.

14. Cf. "Soutenance . . . ," *Etudes Blondéliennes* I, p. 88.

15. Cf. *L'Itinéraire philosophique*, pp. 48-52.

16. *L'Action II*, pp. 12-13.

17. Ibid., p. 10.

18. This image of a point on the circumference of a moving wheel tracing a pattern is first suggested by Blondel in "Le Point de départ de la recherche philosophique," *Annales de Philosophie Chrétienne* 152 (1906): 241, and used again in *L'Action II*, p. 130. Note that the cycloid can never become a circle, which was Hegel's favorite symbol for "Philosophy," the circle of circles.

19. Cf. "Soutenance . . . ," *Etudes Blondéliennes* I, p. 90.

20. The distinction is worked out in the introduction given below which Blondel wrote for *L'Action* in 1893 and which he simply repeated in 1937.

21. Cf. *L'Itinéraire philosophique*, pp. 26-45.

22. Ibid., p. 36.

23. Cf. below, part III, stage 1, ch. 3, and stage 2 *in toto*.

24. "Le point de départ," pp. 234-35.

25. This formula, which brought many critics having a fixed conception of truth down on Blondel, is already adumbrated in 1893. Cf. below, at the end of part V, stage 5, ch. 2. We refer to it here as it is given in "Le point de départ," pp. 234-35.

26. "Le point de départ," p. 236.

27. Cf. René Virgoulay and Claude Troisfontaines, *Maurice Blondel: Bibliographie analytique et critique*, 2 vols. ("Centre d'Archives Maurice Blondel"; Louvain: Institut Supérieur de Philosophie, 1975 and 1976).

28. Washington, D.C.: Corpus Books, 1968. The book is now available through the Philosophers' Book Exchange, Box 11144, Winston-Salem, N.C. 27116.

29. Cf. Maurice Blondel, *The Letter on Apologetics and History and Dogma*, tr. Alexander Dru and Illtyd Trethowan (New York: Holt, Rinehart and Winston, 1964).

30. Cf. M. Blondel, Lettres Philosophiques (Paris: Aubier-Montaigne, 1961), p. 82; Frederick J.D. Scott, S.J., "William James and Maurice Blondel," *New Scholasticism* 32 (1958): 37.

31. Cf. *L'Itinéraire philosophique*, p. 24.

32. Cf. the letters to Blondel in Frederick Scott, "William James and Maurice Blondel," pp. 42-43.

33. Cf. the marginal notes of James on the article by Blondel which he refers to in *Pragmatism* as also given by F. Scott, ibid., pp. 35f, 39.

34. Cf. *A Pluralistic Universe*, pp. 317-318, 329-31, as quoted in F. Scott, "William James and Maurice Blondel," who also completes James's quotations and shows where they come from in Blondel.

35. Cf. "Le point de départ," pp. 353ff.

36. Cf. *L'Itinéraire philosophique*, p. 25.

37. Cf. Albert Cartier, *Existence et vérité: Philosophie blondélienne de l'action et problématique existentielle* (Paris: Presses Universitaires de France, 1955).

38. Cf. Henry Duméry, "Blondel et la philosophie contemporaine (Etude critique)," *Etudes Blondéliennes* II (Paris: Presses Universitaires de France, 1952), pp. 71-141.

39. Cf. F. Scott, "William James and Maurice Blondel," p. 34.

40. Cf. *Revue de Métaphysique et de Morale* 2 (1894): 5-8, reprinted in *Etudes Blondéliennes* I, pp. 100-104.

41. Cf. John J. McNeill, *The Blondelian Synthesis: A Study of the Influence of German Philosophical Sources on the Formation of Blondel's Method and Thought* (Leiden: E.J. Brill, 1966).

42. Cf. *Vocabulaire technique et critique de la philosophie*, 4ᵉ éd., p. 17. See also the footnote at the beginning of part III, stage 2, ch. 2 below.

43. Cf. below part III, stage 1, ch. 3.

44. Cf. *Annales de Philosophie Chrétienne* (1896): vol. 131, pp. 337-47, 467-82, 599-616; vol. 132, pp. 131-47, 225-67, 337-50. Reprinted in *Les premiers écrits de Maurice Blondel* (Paris, Presses Universitaires de France, 1956), pp. 5-95 and translated into English by Dru and Trethowan (cf. note 29 above).

45. Part III, stage 1.

46. *Vocabulaire* . . . , 4ᵉ ed., p. 19.

47. Cf. *L'Itinéraire philosophique*, pp. 20-22.

48. Cf. Part III, stage 5, ch. 3.

49. Cf. "Histoire et Dogme: Les lacunes philosophique de l'exégèse moderne," *Quinzaine* 56 (1904): 145-67, 349-73, 435-58. Reprinted in *Les premiers écrits de Maurice Blondel* (Paris: Presses Universitaires de France, 1956), pp. 149-228 and translated into English by Dru and Trethowan (cf. note 29 above). For a recent comprehensive account of the role of Blondel in the whole Modernist controversy, cf. René Virgoulay, *Blondel et le modernisme* (Paris: Cerf, 1980).

50. *La philosophie et l'esprit chrétien*, t.I: *Autonomie essentielle et connection indéclinable* (Paris: Presses Universitaires de France, 1944); t. II: *Conditions de la symbiose seule normale et salutaire* (Paris: Presses Universitaires de France, 1946). A third volume had been planned but was never completed. It would have dealt with "the outlooks for human civilization and spiritual unity in terms of the ongoing crisis of development" (cf. *L'Action I*, p. 328, note 1).

Acknowledgments

I would like to acknowledge the encouragement and support of all those who have made the appearance of this translation possible. First and foremost I must thank Mademoiselle Nathalie Panis, whose persistence over years of communication finally led to my undertaking this task and whose cheering helped me to see it through to completion. To her this translation is dedicated in the hope that she will live to see it finally in print. Thanks also are due to the Camargo Foundation in Cassis, France, whose congenial hospitality provided the atmosphere in which most of this work was done. Thanks also to Boston College for the sabbatical leave during which this work was undertaken and, more particularly, to Dean J. Donald White of the Graduate School of Arts and Sciences, who provided financial assistance for typing and preparing the final copy of the manuscript. And thanks to Clare Crawford who did such a magnificent job of typing such a long manuscript. Thanks to John Ehmann, associate director at the University of Notre Dame Press, who took the publication of this work under his wing when no one else would and found funding for it from the Ministry of Culture in France. Very special thanks to James Somerville, whose knowledge of the original and whose careful and meticulous work of editing and suggesting alternative renditions has contributed in making this translation much better than it could have been without him. Thanks to Brian Shea and Joe Carrig, who helped with proofreading. And last, but not least, thanks to Dorothy Kennedy, my wife, who came to Cassis with our two small children and who since then has facilitated in countless ways the searching and the work that has finally led to seeing this translation to press.

O.B.

Note on the Translation

L'Action is a carefully written, systematic work in philosophy. Many parts of it were revised and rewritten as many as seven times. It was given its final form in a burst of energy that lasted about a year and a half, after having been preceded by two other preparatory versions and numerous partial drafts. There was even a "last minute" revision between the version originally submitted to the Sorbonne for the defense of June 1893 and the version eventually published in November of the same year, in which the final chapter was reworked and greatly expanded in an effort to counteract an antimetaphysical impression left on the first readers of the work.

All of this adds up to a carefully elaborated work where an argument is carefully laid out and a precise language created to support that argument. A translation of such a work must try to be as consistent as possible with both the argument and the language, while trying to be as readable as possible in English. However, it should be kept in mind that Blondel is not easy to read even in French. *L'Action* is a demanding book in any language. In spite of the many reworkings, the style remains abrupt in many places, apparently deliberately so. I have tried to convey the same kind of abruptness in English, as part and parcel of the argument and the rhetoric of the book.

In order to preserve as much of the systematic aspect of the work as possible, certain principles have been followed in translating key terms that present some difficulty in going from French to English. The first of these was that of *conscience*, in French, which can mean either "consciousness" or "conscience" in English. The double meaning expressed in the English distinction is sometimes intended by Blondel, but the more basic meaning is that of "consciousness." This is clear from the nature of the work, which is not restricted to morality, but purports rather to be a science of action as a whole, with a special emphasis on the scientific validity of subjectivity. Hence, in principle, I have translated *conscience* by "consciousness" in all cases, except those where the more restricted idea of moral conscience was clearly intended in the text, in which cases I rendered it as "conscience" simply, without qualification and without quotation marks.

Another term that presented special difficulty in translation was the

French impersonal pronoun *on*, which is used throughout the argument. As an impersonal pronoun, *on* can be rendered either by "one," as in "one expects that," or by "they," as in "they say that." But anyone who speaks French knows that *on* is also used as a sort of alternative to *nous*, in which cases it should be rendered by "we," as in "we went to the movies last night." Thus, the impersonal *on* can also be quite personal. Much of *L'Action* is written with *on* as principal pronoun. The concrete and reflexive nature of the argument suggests that it should be translated by "we," especially in the main part of the book, where Blondel is speaking in his own name. The only exceptions to this principle, which occurred principally in the early parts of the book, are those places where Blondel is clearly rehearsing views he does not espouse and speaking quite impersonally. In those cases I resorted to the use of "one" or "they."

Then there are terms which, while presenting no special difficulty in translating, require special systematic attention because they are central to the argument. These center around the idea of the will. Blondel uses the terms *volonté*, *volontaire*, and *vouloir*. I was able simply to transliterate the first two of these. I translated the infinitive form of the verb either with "to will" or "willing," depending on what the context called for. Blondel also distinguishes between *volonté voulante* and *volonté voulue*, expressions that become technical in the argument and that appear as barbarisms in French as well as in English, rendered as "willing will" and "willed will." The precise meaning of the distinction is elaborated in the text and had to be translated literally.

Less crucial, but still requiring some interpretation in translation, is the term *esprit*, which is similar to the German term *Geist*. English translators, for example, of Hegel, used to eschew the term "spirit" and use the term "mind" to render this term. In doing so they were sacrificing a very rich meaning for a more depleted one. More recently, however, the term "spirit" has become more acceptable to convey what the French and the German have in mind. Yet the French term *esprit*, more than the German term *Geist*, has both connotations of "mind" and "spirit," depending on the context. In some cases it can refer only to a particular frame of mind, and in others it can refer to a profound principle of spiritual life. Hence *esprit* has been rendered by either "mind" or "spirit," as the context seemed to call for.

Finally, I should perhaps mention that the term "ground" has been used systematically throughout to translate *fonder* or *fondement*. In the context of contemporary philosophy that seemed to convey more of Blondel's meaning than a more literal translation might have done.

O.B.

Action

Introduction

Yes or no, does human life make sense, and does man have a destiny? vii¹
I act, but without even knowing what action is, without having wished
to live, without knowing exactly either who I am or even if I am. This
appearance of being which flutters about within me, these light and
evanescent actions of a shadow, bear in them, I am told, an eternally
weighty responsibility, and that, even at the price of blood, I cannot buy
nothingness because for me it is no longer. Supposedly, then, I am condemned to life, condemned to death, condemned to eternity! Why and
by what right, if I did not know it and did not will it?

I shall make a clean breast of it. If there is something to be seen, I need
to see it. Perhaps I will learn whether or not this phantom I am to myself,
with this universe I bear in my gaze, with science and its magic, with the
strange dream of consciousness, has any solidity. I shall no doubt
discover what is hidden in my acts, at that very depth where, without
myself, in spite of myself, I undergo being and become attached to it. I
will know whether I have a sufficient knowledge and will concerning the
present and the future never to sense any tyranny in them, whatever they
may be.

The problem is inevitable; man resolves it inevitably; and this solution, viii
true or false, but voluntary at the same time as necessary, each one bears
it in his actions. That is why we must study *action*: the very meaning of
the word and the richness of its contents will unfold little by little. It is
good to propose to man all the exigencies of life, all the hidden fulness
of his works, to strengthen within him, along with the force to affirm and
to believe, the courage to act.

I

To take stock of the immediate evidence, action, in my life, is a fact,
the most general and the most constant of all, the expression within me
of a universal determinism; it is produced even without me. More than

1. The numbers in the margins indicate the pagination of the French edition.

3

a fact, it is a necessity, which no doctrine denies since such a denial would require a supreme effort, which no man avoids since suicide is still an act; action is produced even in spite of me. More than a necessity, action often appears to me as an obligation; it has to be produced by me, even when it requires of me a painful choice, a sacrifice, a death. Not only do I use up my bodily life in action, but I am forever putting down feelings and desires that would lay claim to everything, each for itself. We do not go forward, we do not learn, we do not enrich ourselves except by closing off for ourselves all roads but one and by impoverishing ourselves of all that we might have known or gained otherwise. Is there a more subtle regret than that of the adolescent obliged, on entering life, to limit his curiosity as if with blinders? Each determination cuts off an infinity of possible acts. No one escapes this natural mortification.

ix   Will I at least have the power to stop? No, we have to go forward. To suspend my decision in order to renounce nothing? No, I must commit myself under pain of losing everything; I must compromise myself. I have no right to wait or else I no longer have the power to choose. If I do not act out of my own movement, there is something in me or outside of me that acts without me; and what acts without me ordinarily acts against me. Peace is a defeat; action leaves no more room for delay than death. Head, heart and hands, I must therefore give them over willingly or else they are taken from me. If I withhold my free dedication, I fall into slavery; no one gets along without idols: neither pious folk nor even the most libertine. A scholastic or partisan prejudice, a watch-word, a worldly compromise, a sensual delight, and it is enough for all repose to be lost, all freedom to be sacrificed. And that is often the reason why we live and why we die!

Will I be left the hope of guiding myself, if I will to, in the fulness of light, and of governing myself only according to my ideas? No. Practice, which tolerates no delay, never entails a perfect clarity; the complete analysis of it is not possible for a finite mind. Any rule of life that would be grounded only on a philosophical theory and abstract principles would be temerarious. I cannot put off acting until all the evidence has appeared, and all evidence that shines before the mind is partial. Pure knowledge is never enough to move us because it does not take hold of us in our entirety. In every act, there is an act of faith.

Will I at least be able to accomplish what I have resolved, whatever it be, as I have resolved it? No. Between what I know, what I will and what I do there is always an inexplicable and disconcerting disproportion. My decisions often go beyond my thoughts, and my acts beyond my intentions. Sometimes I do not do all that I will; sometimes I do, almost without knowing, what I do not will. And these actions that I did not completely foresee, that I did not entirely order, once they are accomplished, weigh on all of my life and act upon me, seemingly, more than I acted upon them. I find I am like their prisoner; they sometimes turn against me, like an insubordinate son before his father. They have fixed the past, they encroach on the future.

Impossibility of abstaining and of holding myself in reserve, inability to satisfy myself, to be self-sufficient and to cut myself loose, that is what a first look at my condition reveals to me. That there is constraint and a kind of oppression in my life is not an illusion, then, nor a dialectical game, it is a brute fact of daily experience. At the principle of my acts, in the use and after the exercise of what I call my freedom, I seem to feel all the weight of necessity. Nothing in me escapes it. If I try to evade decisive initiatives, I am enslaved for not having acted. If I go ahead, I am subjugated to what I have done. In practice, no one eludes the problem of practice; and not only does each one raise it, but each, in his own way, inevitably resolves it.

It is this very necessity that has to be justified. And what would it mean to justify it, if not to show that it is in conformity with the most intimate aspiration of man? For I am conscious of my servitude only in conceiving, in wishing for a complete emancipation. The terms of the problem, then, are sharply opposed. On one side, all that dominates and oppresses the will; on the other, the will to dominate all or to be able to ratify all, for there is no being where there is only constraint. How then resolve the conflict? Of the two terms of the problem, which is the unknown to start from? Is it goodwill that will show trust, as if it were betting on something sure and infinite, without being able to find out before the end whether, in seeming to sacrifice everything to this something, it has really given up nothing to acquire it? Or must we consider first only what is inevitable and forced, by refusing to make any concession, by repelling all that can be repelled, in order to find out, with the necessity of science, where this necessity of action leads in the end, except to show simply, in the name of determinism itself, that good will is right?

The first way is unavoidable and can suffice for all. It is the practical way. We must define it first, if only to set aside the part of those, the majority and often the better ones, who can only act without discussing action. Besides, as we shall show, no one is exempt from entering on this direct route. But it will be good to prove how another method becomes legitimate to confirm the first and to anticipate the final revelations of life, and how it is necessary for a scientific solution of the problem. The object of this work must be this very science of practice.

II

Before discussing the exigencies of life, even in order to discuss them, we must have submitted to them. Can this first verification suffice to justify them, and will it be possible, without any effort of thought, through experience alone, for all equally, to find the certain solution that will absolve life of all tyranny and satisfy every conscience?

I am and I act, even in spite of myself; I find myself bound, it seems, to answer for all that I am and do. I will submit without rebellion then to this constraint which I cannot suppress because this effective docility is the only direct method of verification. Whatever apparent resistance I may offer in opposition to it, nothing, in fact, can exempt me from obeying it. Hence, I have no other recourse but to have confidence; every attempt at insubordination, while failing to rescue me from the necessity of action, would be a lack of consistency as contrary to science as to conscience. It can never be said too often: no factual difficulty, no speculative doubt, can legitimately dispense anyone whatsoever from this practical method which I am forced and resolved to apply first.

I am asked for head and heart and hands: I am ready; let us experiment. Action is a necessity; I will act. Action often appears as an obligation; I will obey. So much the worse if it is an illusion, a hereditary prejudice, a residue of Christian education. I need a personal verification, and I will verify at whatever cost. No one else can exercise this control for me and in my place. The issue concerns me and my all; it is myself and my all that I put into the experiment. One has only oneself; and the true proofs, the true certitudes are those that cannot be communicated. One lives alone as one dies alone; others have nothing to do with it.

"But if it is impossible to attempt a trial by proxy, would it not be enough to do so by projection, in the mind's eye?" Amusing people, all these theoreticians of practice who observe, deduce, discuss, legislate on what they do not do. The chemist makes no claim to produce water without hydrogen and oxygen. I will not claim to know myself and to test myself, to acquire certitude or to appreciate the destiny of man, without having thrown into the crucible all the man I bear in myself. The organism of flesh, of appetites, of desires, of thoughts whose obscure workings I feel perpetually is a living laboratory. That is where my science of life must first be performed. All the deductions of moralists based on the most complete facts, on mores and social life, are ordinarily artificial, narrow, meagre. Let us act, and leave aside their alchemy.

"But there is doubt, darkness, difficulty." Again, so much the worse; we have to go ahead just the same if we are to know what is at issue. The true reproach that is addressed to conscience is not that it does not

xii

xiii

say enough; it is that it demands too much. Besides, for each step there is enough room; there is enough light, enough of a faint call for me to go where I have anticipated something of what I am looking for, a sense of fulness, an illumination on the role I have to play, a confirmation of my conscience. One does not stop at midnight in an open field. Were I to use the darkness in which practical necessities and obligations seem wrapped as a pretext for not trusting them or not making any sacrifice, I would be failing in my method and, instead of finding an excuse for myself, I would be condemning myself if I dared to blame what this obscurity conceals or to cloak myself rashly with it in order to abandon the experiment. — The scientist, too, is often forced to be daring and to risk the possibly precious material he has in hand. He does not know in advance what he is looking for, and yet he looks for it. It is by anticipating the facts that he reaches them and discovers them. What he finds, he did not always foresee, nor does he ever entirely explain it to himself, because he never goes into the workshops of nature down to their last depth. — This precious material I have to expose is myself, since I cannot carry on the science of man without man. Life abounds with ready-made experiments, hypotheses, traditions, precepts, duties we have only to verify. Action is that method of precision, that laboratory test, where, without ever understanding the details of the operations, I receive the sure answer no dialectical artifice can replace. That is where competence is to be found, no matter if it costs dearly.

"But still, is there not equivocation and lack of consistency in this rule of life? If we are faced with many options, why sacrifice this or that? Do we not have the right, almost the duty, to experiment with everything?" No, there is neither ambiguity nor lack of consistency when, faithful to   xiv
the enterprise and putting the goodness of living ahead of the pride of thinking, we dedicate ourselves without haggling with conscience and its simple testimony. Moral experimentation, like every other, must be a method of analysis and synthesis: sacrifice is that real analysis which, by mortifying the all too imperious and too familiar appetites, brings into evidence a higher will that is only in resisting them; it does not impoverish, it develops and brings the human person to completion. Is it those who have tried heroism who complain? Would we want life always to be good to the wicked? That is when it would be evil, if for them it remained sweet, serene, savory, and if there were as much light in deviance as on the straight path. It is not a question of speculative satisfaction, but of empirical verification. If I already have the solution, I would be inexcusable if I were to lose it while waiting to understand it; it would be to run away from it in order to reach it. The curiosity of the mind does not suppress practical necessities under pretext of studying them; and, in

order to think, I am not dispensed from living. I need at least the shelter
of a provisional morality, because the obligation to act is of another
order than the need to know. Every derogation from the dictates of conscience is founded on a speculative prejudice, and every critique of life
that relies on an incomplete experience is radically incompetent. A thin
ray of light does not suffice to illumine the immensity of practice. What
we see does not destroy what we do not see. And as long as we have not
been able to make a perfect connection between action and thought, and
between conscience and science, all, unlettered or philosophers, have
only to remain, like children, docile, naively docile to the empiricism of
duty.

Thus, in the absence of all theoretical discussion, as also during the
course of all speculative investigation into action, a direct and quite practical method is offered me. This unique means of judging the constraints
of life and appreciating the exigencies of conscience is to lend myself
simply to everything that conscience and life require of me. Only in this
way will I maintain an accord between the necessity that forces me to act
and the movement of my own will. Only in this way will I find out
whether, in the last analysis, I can ratify, through a definitive acknowledgement of my free reason, this preliminary necessity, and whether
all that had seemed obscure, despotic, evil, I can find clear and good.
Hence, on the condition of not leaving the straight path of practice which
we would abandon only through a lack of consistency, practice itself
contains a complete method and surely prepares a valid solution to the
problem it imposes on all men.

Do we understand what this method of direct experimentation is, and
do we have the courage to apply it? Are we ready to pay for moral competence at the price of all that we have and all that we are? If not, there
is no admissible judgment. For life to be condemned, life itself, once we
have experienced what it has to offer that is most painful, would have
to warrant our regretting all the sacrifices and the efforts made to render
it good. Is that the way it is? And if we have not tried the test, are we
in a position to complain?

III

Yes, these complaints have to be accepted. It is possible that the
straight road leads where no other does, it is possible too that one be
guilty of leaving it. But if one has left it, if one has not entered into it,
if one falls along the way, does one cease to count? Science must be as
broad as charity and not ignore even what morality frowns upon. Notwithstanding the sufficiency of practice, another method, destined

perhaps to enlighten and justify the first, but quite different from it, xvi
becomes legitimate and even necessary. For what reasons? Here are some
of the principal ones.

To be sure, no one is forced to debate with his conscience, to haggle
about his submission and to speculate on practice. But, then, who escapes the curiosity of the mind, who has not doubted the goodness of his
task and has never asked himself why he does what he does? When traditions are shattered, as they are, when the rule of mores is subverted
on almost every score, when, through a strange corruption of nature,
the lure of what popular consciousness calls evil exercises on all a sort
of fascination, is it possible to act always with the happy and courageous simplicity that no uncertainty undermines and that no sacrifice
disheartens? No, if the method of the simple and the generous is good,
we should at least be able to show why. Such an *apologia* could only be
the supreme effort of speculation, while proving the supremacy of action.

Besides, even when we have no hesitation as to what is to be done, do
we always do what we know and what we will? And if repeated failings
spoil the experiment of life, if the first sincerity is lost, if there rises across
our path the irreparable past of an act, will we not have to have recourse
to an indirect way? And is not reflexion, roused by the obstacle itself,
necessary, like a light, to find once again the lost way? Often born of a
proud or sensual curiosity, the presence of evil, even in the most naive
consciousness, produces in turn for it a need for discussion and science.
This complement or this supplement of moral spontaneity must, therefore, be sought in ideas as scientific as possible.

But let us be careful. Nothing is more perilous and less scientific than
to govern ourselves, in practice, according to incomplete ideas. Action
cannot be partial or provisional, as knowledge can be. Hence, when one
has begun to discuss the principles of human conduct, one must not take xvii
the examination into account as long as the examination has not been
brought to completion, because we have to have something principal,
something central, something total to illumine and regulate acts. Now,
if it is true that no one is obliged to speculate on practice, still there is
almost no one who does not have *his own ideas* on life and does not think
himself authorized to apply them. Hence, it is essential to push this examination to the end, since only at the end will the authority that speculation often usurps over action become legitimate.

It is therefore a science of action that must be constituted, a science
that will be such only insofar as it will be total, because every way of
thinking and deliberate living implies a complete solution of the problem
of existence, a science that will be such only insofar as it will determine
for all a single solution to the exclusion of all others. For *my* reasons,
if they are scientific, must not have any more value for me than for

others, nor must they leave room for other conclusions than mine. In this also the direct method of practical verification needs to be completed; but this remains to be shown.

Entirely personal and incommunicable, the teachings of moral experimentation are valid in effect only for the one who instigates them in himself. No doubt, he has succeeded in learning where one acquires true charity of soul and in grounding in himself an intimate certainty that surpasses, in its own sense, every other assurance. But what he knows because he does it he cannot communicate to others who do not do it. In the eyes of strangers, it is only opinion, belief, or faith; for himself *his* science does not have the universal, impersonal and imperious character of *science*. But it is good for each one to be able to justify as fully as possible, against the sophisms of passion, the reasons for his conduct. It is good for each to be able to transmit and demonstrate to all the solution he knows to be certain for the problem imposed on all. It is good that, if our life is to judge us with a sovereign rigor, we should already be able, if we will to do so, to judge it with sufficient clarity.

xviii

Why it is legitimate and even becomes necessary to raise the speculative problem of practice is therefore manifest. How it is raised, we must now look into.

IV

In what way, in the study of reality, do truly scientific methods proceed? They exclude all false explanations of a fact, all fortuitous coincidences, all accessory circumstances so as to place the mind before the necessary and sufficient conditions, and to constrain it to affirm the law. This indirect way alone is that of science, because, starting from doubt and systematically eliminating every chance of error and every cause of illusion, it closes every way out but one. Hence, truth imposes itself, it is demonstrated.

Now there will be science of action, properly speaking, only insofar as we shall succeed in transporting into the critique of life what is essential about this indirect method. For we must not make believe that men are other than what they are for the most part, especially men of thought. They only do as they please, that is, they like to choose and to know where they are going; and to know with certainty, they will go down blind alleys. Without a complete investigation, there is no conclusive and constraining demonstration. If in the sciences of nature the mind surrenders only before the impossibility of doubting, all the more, in the world of his passions, of his sufferings, and of his intimate struggles, does man hang on and remain where he is, as long as he is not dislodged from the position, whatever it may be, where self-love, in the absence of any other interest, keeps him. Ask no one to make the first step. Science _{xix} has nothing to concede.

It would be to take the first step and the decisive step to accept, be it only by way of a trial or a simple postulate, moral obligation or even the natural necessity to act. This is the constraint, these are the practical exigencies that are in question and that must be justified in the least indulgent eyes and through the effort of the very ones who try to run away from them with all their might. The moment I raise the theoretical problem of action and set out to discover a scientific solution for it, I no longer admit, at least provisionally and from this different viewpoint, the value of any practical solution. The usual words, good, evil, duty, culpability, which I had used are, from this moment on, bereft of meaning, until, if occasion arises, I can restore to them all their plenitude. In the face of necessity itself which, to speak the language of appearances, forces me to be and to act, I refuse to ratify, in the order of thought, what, in the order of practice, I have resolved to practice. And since we must first eliminate all false ways of being and acting, instead of seeing only the straight way, I will explore all those that are furthest away from it.

My situation, then, is quite clear. On one side, in action, complete and absolute submission to the dictates of conscience, and immediate docility. My provisional morality is all of morality, without any objection in the intellectual or sensual order authorizing me to break this pact with duty. On the other side, in the scientific realm, complete and absolute independence. This does not mean, according to a common understanding, the immediate emancipation of the whole of life with regard to any regulating idea, any moral yoke, any positive faith: that would be to draw conclusions before having justified the premises, and to let thought usurp a premature authority, at the very point where we are recognizing _{xx} its incompetence. Whatever the scientific result of the examination underway will be, only in the end must it return to and illumine the practical discipline of life. The independence necessary for the science of action must therefore be understood this way. This research itself will manifest more clearly the fundamental importance and the unique originality of the problem.

What is at issue in effect? To find out whether notwithstanding the obvious constraints that oppress us, whether through the darkness where we must walk, whether in the depths of unconscious life whence emerges the mystery of action as an enigma whose word will perhaps be dreadful, whether in all the aberrations of the spirit, there does not subsist, in spite of it all, the seed of a science and the principle of an intimate revelation such that nothing will appear arbitrary or unexplained in the destiny of each, such that there will be a definitive consent of man to his fate, whatever it may be, such finally that this clarity unmasking consciences will not change in their depth even those it will overwhelm as if by surprise. At the root of the most insolent negations or the most foolish extravagances of the will, we must inquire whether there is not an initial movement that persists always, that we love and we will, even when we deny it or when we abuse of it. The principle of the judgment to be passed on each individual must be found within each. And the independence of the mind becomes indispensible in this research, not only because it is important to admit first, without prejudice of any sort, all the infinite diversity of human consciences, but especially because in each consciousness, under all the unrecognized sophisms and the unavowed failings, we must find the primitive aspiration, so as to lead all, in full sincerity, to the very end of their voluntary *élan*. Thus, instead of starting from a single point whence would spread the doctrine peculiar to one mind, it is necessary for us to place ourselves at the extremities of the most divergent spokes in order to lay hold, at the very center, of the truth essential to every consciousness and the movement common to all wills.

xxi

As I approach the science of action, then, I can take nothing for granted, no facts, no principles, no duties. It is to strip myself of every precarious support that I have been working. Let us not pretend, like Descartes through an artifice that smacks of the schools with all its seriousness, to extract from doubt and illusion the very reality of being; for I do not sense any consistency in that reality of dreaming, it is empty and remains outside of me. I will not hear, with Pascal, of playing heads or tails over nothingness and eternity; for to wager would be already to ratify the alternative. Let no one, following Kant, pull out from I-know-not-what darkness I-know-not-what categorical imperative; for I would treat it as suspect and as an intruder. We must, on the contrary, take in all the negations that destroy one another, as if it were possible to admit them all together. We must enter into all prejudices, as if they were legitimate, into all errors, as if they were sincere, into all passions, as if they had the generosity they boast of, into all philosophical systems, as if each one held in its grip the infinite truth it thinks it has cornered. We must, taking within ourselves all consciousnesses, become the intimate accomplice of all, in order to see if they bear within themselves their own justification or condemnation. They have to become arbiters of themselves; they have to see where their most frank and their most interior will would lead them; they have to learn what they do without knowing it, and what they already know without willing it and without doing it.

Thus, for the problem of action to be raised scientifically, we should not have any moral postulate or intellectual given to accept. It is not *a* particular question, then, a question like any other, that presents itself before us. It is *the* question, the one without which there is none other. It is so primary that any preliminary concession would be a *petitio principii*. Just as every fact contains all of its law, so also every consciousness hides within itself the secret and the law of life. There is no hypothesis to be made; we cannot suppose either that the problem is resolved, or even that it is imposed or simply posited. It must be enough, for the most intimate orientation of hearts to be revealed, to let the will and action unfold in each individual down to the final agreement or to the contradiction between the primitive movement and the end in which it terminates. The difficulty is to introduce nothing external or artificial into this profound drama of life; it is, if need be, to correct reason and the will through reason and the will themselves; it is, through a methodical progress, to make errors, negations, and failings of every nature produce the hidden truth that souls live by and that they may perhaps die of for eternity.

xxii

V

Thus everything is called into question, even whether there is a question. The spring for the entire investigation must come from the investigation itself; and the movement of thought will sustain itself without any external artifice. What is this internal mechanism? It is this. For it is good in advance, not for the sake of validity, but for the sake of clarity of exposition, to indicate the moving thought and, calling into question along with the value of life the very reality of being, to underscore the common intertwining of science, morality and metaphysics. Among these, there are no contradictions, because where people have seen incompatible realities, there are still only heterogeneous and solidary phenomena. And if some have burdened themselves with inextricable difficulties where there are none, it is for having failed to recognize the one question where the difficulty lies. In question is the whole of man; it is not in thought alone then that we must seek him out. It is into action that we shall have to transport the center of philosophy, because there is also to be found the center of life.

xxiii

If I am not what I will to be—what I will, not with my lips, not in desire or in project, but with all my heart, with all my strength, in all my acts—I am not. In the depth of my being, there is a willing and a love for being, or else there is nothing. This necessity that appeared to me as a tyrannical constraint, this obligation which at first seemed despotic, must in the last analysis be seen as manifesting and exercising the profound action of my will; otherwise they would destroy me. The whole nature of things and the chain of necessities that weigh on my life is only the series of means I have to will, that I do will in effect, to accomplish my destiny. Involuntary and constrained being would no longer be being, so true is it that the last word of all is goodness, and that to be is to will and to love. Pessimism stops too soon in the philosophy of the will; for, in spite of pain and despair, we will still be right in admitting the truth and the excellence of being if we will it of ourselves in all sincerity and in all spontaneity. To suffer from being, to hate *my being,* I have to admit and to love *being.* Evil and hatred are only by becoming a homage to love.

Also, whatever apparent disproportion there may be between what I know, what I will and what I do, however fearful the consequences of my acts may be, even if, able to lose myself, but not to escape myself, I am, to the point that it would be better for me not to be, still I must, in order to be, always will to be, even if I have to bear within myself the painful contradiction of what I will and of what I am. There is nothing arbitrary or tyrannical in my destiny; for the least external pressure would be enough to strip being of all value, all beauty, all consistency. I have nothing I have not received; and yet at the same time everything has to arise from me, even the being that I have received and seems imposed on me. Whatever I do and whatever I undergo, I have to sanction this being and engender it anew, so to speak, by a personal adherence, without my most sincere freedom ever disavowing it. This is the will, the most intimate and the most free, that it is important to find in all my endeavors and to bring finally to its perfect fulfillment. What is most important is to bring the reflected movement of my willing into equation with its spontaneous movement. But it is in action that this relation of either equality or discordance is determined. Hence the importance of studying action, for it manifests at once the double will of man; it constructs all his destiny within him, like a world that is his original work and is to contain the complete explanation of his history.

The ultimate effort of art is to make men do what they will, as it is to make them realize what they know. That is the ambition of this work. Not that we would violate here the protective obscurities that insure the disinterestedness of love and the merit of goodness. But if there is a salvation it cannot be tied to the learned solution of an obscure problem, nor denied to the perseverance of a rigorous speech. It can only be offered clearly to all. This clarity must be borne to those who have turned away from it, perhaps unknowingly, into the night they make for themselves, a night where the full revelation of their obscure state will not change them if they do not first contribute to change themselves willingly. The only supposition we will not make initially is to think they go astray knowingly and willingly, that they refuse the light while they sense that it envelops them, and that they curse being while admitting its goodness. And yet perhaps we shall have to come to this very excess, since there xxv is nothing, in all the attitudes possible for the will or in all the illusions of consciousness, that is not to enter into the science of action: fictions and absurdities if you will, but real absurdities. There is, in the illusory, the imaginary, even the false, a reality, something living and substantial that is embodied in human acts, a creation which no philosophy has sufficiently taken into account. How important it is to accept, to unify and bring to completion, so many scattered aspirations, like members perishing through their divisions, in order to build up, through the infinity of errors and by them, the universal truth, a truth that lives in the secret of every consciousness and from which no man ever frees himself.

But let us forget now this anticipated look at the road to be taken. Let us give ourselves without afterthought and without distrust, precisely because no side has been taken nor any act of confidence asked. Even the point of departure, "there is nothing," could not be admitted, because it would still be an external given and like an arbitrary and subjugating concession. The ground has been completely cleared.

Part I
Is There a Problem of Action?

CHAPTER 1
How We Claim the Moral Problem
Does Not Exist

There are no problems more insoluble than those that do not exist.
1 Would that be the case with the problem of action, and would not the surest means of resolving it, the only one, be to suppress it? To unburden consciences and to give life back its grace, its buoyancy and cheerfulness, wouldn't it be good to unload human acts of their incomprehensible seriousness and their mysterious reality? The question of our destiny is terrifying, even painful, when we have the naïveté of believing in it, of looking for an answer to it, whatever it may be, Epicurean, Buddhist or Christian. We should not raise it at all.

Granted, it is not all as simple as we imagine it to be at first; for abstention or negation is still a solution; and nimble minds have long since recognized the trickery of neutral or free thought. — To pronounce oneself for or against is equally to let oneself get caught in the gears and be crushed in them completely. It matters little what one is, what one thinks and what one does, if one is, if one thinks and if one acts; one has not made the weighty illusion vanish. There remains a subject before an object; the idol may have changed, but the cult and the adorer remain. —
2 To avoid taking a stand, believing one can succeed in doing so, is another shortsighted illusion. We must in effect reckon with this constraint which, as a matter of experience, perpetually forces us to act. There is no hope of escaping it, even by fighting against it, even through inertia; for a prodigious energy is spent in asceticism, more than in the violent movements of passion; and activity takes advantage of all oversights and abdications as well as all efforts made to reduce it. Inaction is a difficult craft: *otium* (idleness)! How much delicacy and skillfulness it requires; and can one ever arrive at it completely?

Will there really be a wisdom refined enough to disentangle the subtleties of nature and give in to it in appearance, since we have to give in, while at the same time liberating itself from its cunning lies?

To be duped without knowing it, that is the ludicrous misfortune of the earnest, the passionate, the barbaric. But to be duped knowing that one is, while lending oneself to the illusion, while enjoying everything as a vain and amusing farce; to act, as it is necessary to do so, but all the while killing action with the dryness of science, and science through the fecundity of dreaming, without ever finding contentment even in the shadow of a shadow; to annihilate oneself with erudition and delight, will that not be the salvation known and possessed by the better and the more informed minds, the only ones who will have the right to say they have resolved the great problem, because they will have seen that there is none?

What an enticing tour de force and a useful tactic! It is good to have a close look at it and appreciate its end. For to suppress everything, it is important and apparently sufficient to be all science, all sensation and all action. In making one's thought and one's life equal to the universal vanity, one seems to fill oneself only to become more empty. And if in effect there is no problem and no destiny, is not the simplest and the surest way of finding out, to abandon oneself to the free flow of nature by stepping out of the fictions and the confining prejudices in order to rejoin the movement of universal life and to attain, through all the powers of reflexion, the fruitful peace of unconsciousness?[1]

I

To begin with, let us gather from the fine flower of thought all the subtle and deadly essence it distills.   3

There is no error, it is said, that does not have a soul of truth; there is no truth, it seems, that does not carry a weight of error. To stop at any particular judgment and hold fast to it would be pedantry and naïveté. To maintain a clear and fixed attitude, to believe that "it has happened," to dirty one's hands, to tangle with men, to contend for position, to do that nasty thing expressed by that nasty phrase: assert oneself, conscientiously to introduce a rigid unity into the organism of one's thought or the conduct of one's life, bah! What a ridiculous narrowness, how enormously boorish! All the philosophical systems, even those most opposed to one another, have been caught in the same trap: they have always looked for the relation between being and knowing, between the

---

1. Many of the expressions in this chapter are taken from some contemporary writers. I have chosen not to quote them, in order not to appear to impute to them indiscreetly intentions they may not have. I refer to states of soul and vague tendencies from which I try to draw out here the doctrine that mutely inspires them.

real and the ideal, and they thought they could define it. The ontological argument is found at the heart of every dogmatism, even the one that is sceptical: about the Unknown it is known that it cannot be known. About Pessimism one can say that it is still an optimism since it has a doctrine and offers a goal. To affirm that nothingness is, what a pleasant joke, and how happy one must be when one knows that being is not, and that not to be is the supreme good! Blessed hopeless people who have met their ideal, without seeing that, if it is, it is no longer and that, by rushing toward it, they play the game of that ironic nature which they boast they have confounded. Not only is every monism an error, that is, every doctrine that claims to reduce the principle of intelligibility and the principle of existence to a unity, but so too is every system, by the simple fact that it is a system, just as every action inspired by a fixed conviction is an illusion.

Hence there is truth only in contradiction, and opinions are certain only if we change them. But one must not make of contradiction itself and of indifference a new idol. In openmindedness, one will even practice intolerance in order to savor the charms of narrowness of mind. At one time, one will be enchanted with the acrobatics of a transcendental dialectic, at another, disdaining the weight of even a light armor, one will mock those clods who, with their helmets on, do battle according to the book in hand to hand combat with the wind. Through history, to belong to all times and to all races; through science, to be in all space and to be the equal of the universe; through philosophy, to become the field for the interminable battle of systems, to bear in oneself idealism and positivism, criticism and evolutionism, and to feast on the carnage of ideas; through art, to be initiated to the divine grace of serious frivolities, to the fetichism of advanced civilizations; what pleasant efforts to give oneself to everything without giving anything, to hold in reserve this inexhaustible power of a spirit now sympathetic now destructive, to weave and to unravel without cease, like Penelope, the living garment of a God who will never be! One kneels before all altars, and one gets up smiling to run off to new loves; for a moment one subjects oneself to the letter in order to penetrate into the sanctuary of the spirit. If, before the grandeur of the mystery that covers everything, one feels something like a chill of religious dread, quickly one runs for cover behind the thick certitudes of the senses. One uses brute certitudes to dissipate dreams, dreams to sublimate science, and all becomes nothing more than figures drawn in air. One knows that there are inevitable reactions against any abuse of the positive, and one lends oneself to it devoutly, neither more nor less disposed to venerate the retort of the chemist than to prostrate oneself before the ineffable splendor of the nothingness disclosed to the soul. Some take pleasure in mixing the extremes and in bringing together in one single state of consciousness eroticism and mystical asceticism; some, by means of sealed compartments, develop along parallel lines the double role of alcoholic and idealist. One after the other, or at one and the same time, one tastes, one loves, one practices different religions and one savors all the conceptions of heaven through a dilettantism of the future life.

At times even this undulating and diverse wisdom feigns to overlook itself in order better to dispel the odious appearance of a system, in order to keep, through its incurable nimbleness, the pleasure of anxiety or risk. One flatters oneself, but without contention and blithely hopeful, for having avoided forever the troubling questions, the tormenting answers, the menacing sanctions. One does not assert nothingness to be more certain of not encountering being, and one lives in the phenomenon which is and is not. Don't try to tell these clever people that underneath their free play and the suppleness of their fleeting attitudes is hidden a prejudice, an original method, an answer to the problem of destiny, and certain involuntary preoccupations: that's false, one does not run away from what is not. Don't repeat for them the banal objection that the absence of a solution is still a solution: that's false. Do not question them, do not press them: no question makes sense, because every response is false, if one does not sense in it the inevitable lie. What shade is a pigeon's neck? The thought expressed is already a deceit. If they entertain all curiosities it is to be freer to steer clear of any indiscrete questioning; long since have they seen through the vanity of discussions, and have learned always to agree with whoever contradicts: to refute anyone or anything whatsoever is a Philistinism of the worst kind. To be neither offensive nor defensive, for one playing at loser-wins that is the art of being unbeatable.

And that is the true panacea. It counterbalances the rigor of the positive sciences with mystical effusion and, mixing into one and the same crucible the old idol of clear ideas and the fresher beauty of the noumenon, the unconscious and the unknowable, it anoints the classical spirit with the oil of suppleness. To arid minds, it provides a varied abundance; to the narrow, breadth; to the doctrinaire, doubt; to the fanatics, irony; to cold impiety, an aroma of incense; to materialism, an ideal. Thanks to this panacea, admire how our time, after having kissed one cheek of centuries past, slaps them on the other. Give it credit for treating with proper contempt some of those inanely witty objections that charmed Voltaire, for accepting and surpassing all the reversals of opinion, for wearing out its cults so fast that some now revert to those of India and, before the end of the century, some will claim to turn even

Catholicism itself into a new and fashionable adornment, for expecting a kind of perpetual renaissance, and for making the need for a flexible and firm rule grow out of the taste for anarchy. Take pleasure in seeing rise, as once in Alexandria, amidst the confusion of ideas and bazaars and from under the oppression of material pleasures and sufferings, an intense breath of mysticism and a passion for the marvelous. Be proud of your brow, enlarged to comprehend more than one beauty, to embrace all the infinite variety of thoughts, the logic of contraries, the new geometry, nature conquered. But behind this glitter, this generosity, this display, you will take pleasure in considering the vanity of a science that enjoys vanity, you will be amused at the ridiculous spectacle of ambitions, of business, of systems. And in the midst of all the entertaining follies of the world, you will exult as you feel in your heart, as you size up with your eye the infinite emptiness of what is called living and acting.

Thus thought, through the double weapon of universal sympathy and
6 pitiless analysis, manages to play with nature as it plays with us. *Beati qui ludunt* (blessed are those who play): a game, that is the wisdom of life; a game, but a noble and poignant one, which is sometimes to be taken seriously so that it may be a better game, and more, of an illusion winning against all illusions. You, Poor Nature with the thousand faces, you seem to cast about ingeniously to vary the bait for all credulities through a perpetual generation of contraries; it is enough to nibble at every lure and give ourselves over to all your Protean caprices for you to be poisoned by your own tricks and vanquished in your triumph. The more we embrace you, the better we escape you; by becoming all that you are, we place a gnawing worm at the heart of everything; we volatilize ourselves along with all the rest, squeezing between heaven and hell in a crisscross of contradictions. With the same respect and the same disdain for the yes and for the no, it is good to lodge them together and let them devour one another; irony and goodwill, it is all the same, the universal master-key, the universal solvent. One cannot know and affirm everything without denying everything; and the perfect science of the aesthete vanishes of itself in the absolute vanity of all.

The speculative problem of action seems well eliminated. Will the practical problem be equally suppressed?

II

By itself the dilettantism of art and science does not suffice for long; it is soon complemented by the dilettantism of sensation and action. For it is generally not enough anymore for the head to reveal to the imagination the universe of sentimental experience; indeed, there is nothing like a man devoted to the ideal for paving the way for the practitioner of the senses and to end up envying him and following him. But is there not in calculated depravity the principle of an art and even of a science that no speculative fiction could equal? And if a desire for unknown emotions seems to be the common law of literary intoxication, there is, on the other hand, also hidden in practical dissoluteness, a source of dissolving discoveries and thoughts. Is not the best way of making the mind flexible and emancipating it from the narrow prejudices that limit its horizon on life to go beyond them and, in order to understand everything, to come to feel everything? One less depraved is thought to be less intelligent.

Not that one should ruin the superstition of shame or even of piety. The damage would be great because the fun and the love of evil are perfect only thanks to the tang of internal contradiction and to the savor of the forbidden fruit, as for those courtesans who preserve the spice of a prie-Dieu. It enlivens enjoyment when we make of it a synthesis of op-posed feelings and experience therein, through the variety of contacts and contrasts, something like the multiple caress of a fine and volumi-nous hair. "His soul elevated to the seventh heaven, his body more hum-ble under the table," the mystical libertine, "a Christian poet with the flanks of a faun," he it is who will discover how purifying adultery can be, or savor all the voluptuousness there is in corrupting a virgin soul.

But these learned contrasts of sensation serve not only to refine it; they decompose it and kindle it only to consume it. By insinuating the most exquisite delicacy and the most impure ardor at one and the same time into the same heart, they hasten the dispersion and, so to speak, the agony of the moral person. No more simple and sincere feelings: nothing real, indeed nothing either good or bad. If to know everything an-nihilates in one blow the object and the subject of knowledge, to feel everything brings this marvelous work of science to completion in practice.

How, then, vary and multiply our sensations enough to escape the disappointing truth of simple impressions and the deceiving lucidity of life? A less well advised wisdom no doubt would recommend the ataraxy of the universal dreamer, who does not engage in action in order to scoff while renewing himself more freely, and who enjoys the world like a grain of opium whence he draws the smoke of his dreams, and life like the shimmering shadow of mist by moonlight. If he had to choose be-tween irony and fanaticism according to the abundance of pleasure he can expect from one or the other, he would perhaps listen to the call of that voluptuous laziness that dreads the stains and the transports of ac-tion. A false wisdom that, still too timid, and outmoded! See how today, with infinitely powerful gifts for analysis, the more delicate aspire to action, as if they sought "to reconcile the practices of interior life with the necessities of active life"; see even how, without renouncing the supreme irony of criticism, people applaud whoever seems to be daring enough to have a trenchant opinion and gives the impression of one about to penetrate minds like a sharp wedge through a rigorous clarity and a vigor of conviction!

8   The fact is that there is in practice an inexhaustible source of new sensations, contradictions, and disappointments; the most generous action can be a deprivation, one more destruction. The essential then is to "mechanize" one's soul so that it will produce at will all known emotions, to be relentlessly agitated with the most interesting and passing enthusiasms, and to light up each night with new universes like happy circuses where one performs for oneself decked out in high style: a superior form of vagabondage where one takes pride in feeling a whole life going to waste in contemptible occupations, a science of self-liquidation that one is happy to possess by finding it admirable and shameful.

To tell the truth, to act this way is less to act than to set up experiences of practical scepticism and, through this "essayism in action,"[1] to become drunk on the powerful poison that kills, not individual life, since it is not real, but the illusion of life. Sensual egoism keeps everything for itself, it is the last word of a past that is dying; fanaticism, on the other hand, represents the first word of the future. It is this double state that the voluptuous ascetic sums up in his present: for him, action as a whole is the end of a world and the beginning of a new world. In all his palinodes, he is always dying only to rise again, and rises only to die again, to destroy better the variety of his own artistic emotions and to construct more different worlds, to feel more how everything is unrealizable, everything is unreal, and to adore, in these very chimera, the eternity of what is forever dying in him and through him. Always ready to reverse his judgment, always busy at moving and fragmenting himself, all routes are equally good and certain to him, even the ill-famed roads that lead to Damascus; all meetings are to him equally attractive and instructive. He sinks deeper into his dream without fearing that little by little a regular sequence of images or a sudden impulse born of the dream itself will wake him up. What does he have to fear, since the more he collides with the real and learns from it, the more he experiences its nullity?

1. "Essayism" here refers to a philosophical attitude which consisted more in trying different experiences of life than in taking any of them seriously. It was called an "essayism in action" because the object of its experimentation was human life as such, and not something that could be set apart and examined abstractly. But, as Blondel explains, it set store only by the experimenting itself, the essaying, and not by any outcome of the experiment (Translator's note).

Also, immediately after the aesthete seemed, with a sort of sensual irritation, to want to hold his dear idols tight in his arms, to preserve them from destruction and "to enjoy with a sensation stronger than the centuries what is in the process of dying," he looks for a new formula through new experiences; and when he appears "raised on high to that total of emotions that is his self, that is his God," when he succeeds "in living all his being, all past, present and future Being, by grasping it as Eternal," then, no longer able, no longer willing to aspire to the absolute alone, he comes back down to those violent movements which are what he likes, because one thing remains which alone he cares about, that is to be fortified against disgust and atony, to still have needs, "to be carried off, through the divine Unconscious, by the gentle tug of desires which, propagated from an unlimited past toward an unlimited future, indiscriminately animates all those moving forms characterized as errors or truths by our shortsighted judgments."

To turn to pessimism, to suicide? Come now! That would be to believe there is something serious about the world. Ardent and skeptical, taking pleasure in the means without care for the end, feeling that there are only ways of seeing, that each one contradicts the other and that with a little cleverness one can have them all on the same object, the essayist[1] looks for peace, quiet and happiness with the conviction that he will never find them; and "in order to escape the uneasiness of proper children which is born of a disproportion between the object they were dreaming of and the one they attain," he places his felicity in the vain experiences he sets up, not in the results they seemed to promise.

To experience thus the perfect serenity of absolute detachment at the same time as the troubled ardor of a militant soul, to unite all the charms of the learned, artistic, voluptuous and religious life with the peaceful security of death, to maintain with the agility of a clown the inertia of a corpse, *perinde ac cadaver* (in the manner of a cadaver), to penetrate oneself with the Exercises of Saint Ignatius while jumping into the fray of political intrigues, isn't that the perfection and the very sanctity of perversion?

Look now for the problem. The challenge is indeed to find it. The means of salvation, the object of the new cult, is talent, the inestimable virtuosity of the fencer who, everywhere and nowhere, is never where we strike. But can one get angry with Harlequin? Like the converted clown who, not knowing how to sing psalms in choir, during the office would

---

1. "Essayist" here refers, not to one who writes essays, but to one whose philosophy it is to essay or to try different experiments with life and, as Blondel makes clear, to value the experience itself rather than any result that may come from it (Translator's note).

go entertain the statues of the cloister with his tricks, one has only to
frolic with life to be in good conscience. After having always been the
advocate of God and of the devil, what fear could the buffoon of the
Eternal have? He has respected, despised; filled, emptied; incensed, blas-
10   phemed; divinized, destroyed everything, and himself more than all the
rest: that is his reward. Poe imagines a dying person being hypnotized
at the moment of his passing: it is at precisely that point of unstable
balance that we must live. And even an instantaneous photograph of
death would not capture us; we would no longer be there; we would
never have been there. Go and keep on talking, then, of those good old
words like duty and virtue; talk of an examination of conscience,
without conscience; of a judgment, without code or due process or judge;
of a destiny and a will reaching its ends, when one has neither will to be
nor will not to be, a pure nolition (*nolonté*); when underneath the surface
movements or in the body of life there are no intentions and no heart;
when actions, without soul, are always stillborn!

How far removed we are now from that simplicity of conscience and
from that practical candor which pulls together into one sheaf all the
energies of man. It is no longer a simple accidental doubling of the personality; it is complete frittering away of it, the decomposition of death
in life itself. Isn't that what we wanted: the annihilation of thought and
being through multiplication and dissociation; the disorganization of all
elementary mechanisms, as if each cell of the organism played its own
little tune apart; a complete liquidation, a huge burst of laughter, a
mournful joke, a mystification and, that's the word, a hoax, nothing,
that is what a man and his destiny have become.

That is admittedly an extreme state. But, how many there are in our
day who, without penetrating into this subtle conception of life, without
doing any more than apply the common adage: "we have to try
everything," without being conscious of the attitude they take in the face
of practical necessities and obligations, go in the direction of that solution: "There isn't even any question: the only mistake is to look for a
meaning where there is none." If thought and life are nothing, it must be
enough to think and to act for illusion to appear; it appears, it would
seem, through the complete use of thought and of life. Against the naive
people who have taken their conscience seriously, and who believe they
can find in their personal experience of duty a certain confirmation of the
infinite value they attach to their being, against their acts and their
sacrifices, it is objected, in the name of a fuller experience and a more
open science, that all absolute certitude is born of a lack of intelligence
11   and a partial ignorance, that all practical rigidity is the sign of a narrow

heart and an obtuse sensibility. To affirm any reality whatsoever with certainty, to raise the moral problem resolutely, one has to have a degree of inexperience and of simplicity which, like the gaucherie of the peasant, so amuses the smart set. The well-mannered society of the bright lives by pleasant fictions, lies and truth both together. All is light and charming, since all is empty. The emancipation of the aesthete seems complete.

It was not without value perhaps to take note of this state of many contemporary minds. As it is sometimes enough to write out a word whose spelling is in doubt or to narrate a nightmare to see the mistake or the foolishness in it, simply to expose certain subtle dreams is to dissipate them and to strip them of their prestige, especially in the eyes of those young people who are ordinarily infatuated by them only insofar as they appear unheard of, incomplete, and mysterious to them, and who create for themselves "a literary soul" by unconsciously modeling their heart in the image of the perversions of a novelist and of poetic passions. Certain traits may seem excessive. But it is good to look at what we are all too ready to hide from ourselves in the face, namely, the conception of life that follows from an attitude whose delicate comfort and grace we like to taste, and no more. And yet, as would have been said in former times, we must pull the cushions from under the elbows of sinners.

Chapter two tries to show that the aesthete fails to dodge the problem of action, that he raises it voluntarily by this very pretention, and that he solves it in a certain way. I show there how the fleeting and elusive attitude of the dilettante or the "essayist" results from a double movement. The profound and hidden tendency of which their nolition is made up is what they themselves call the divine Egoism. The contrary will which their endless games declare is the desire and like the hope for nothingness. I conclude by analysing the secret lie, the inevitable contradiction of this entire state of soul; and taking the will, involuntarily made manifest by acts, as the imperfect but truthful expression of a sincere tendency, I attempt to set it on its way toward its end.

CHAPTER 2
That We Fail to Suppress
the Moral Problem and How

12   The aesthete scoffs at refutations that aim at a heart but even miss an agile shadow. Maybe he is right. But let this mighty analyst look, with the attention he gives to so many other spectacles, and observe this play of infinitesimal oscillations through which he makes himself elusive. In his very nolition, he will discern a voluntary duplicity.

To will nothing, simply nothing, would be well and good, if it were a simple state; the spontaneous *élan* of life and of curiosity that no reflexion would disturb would go straight, who knows where, without any return or looking back by conscience. But this simplicity and this candor, this ignorance and this self-abnegation are not the ordinary virtues of the refined; they cannot be, once these people start enjoying their own subtlety. For, thanks to that scientific law they pick up from the associationists and name discrimination, every distinct knowledge of an interior disposition supposes the consciousness of a contrasting state. To know we will nothing is to will nothing. And "I do not will to will," *nolo velle*, in the language of reflexion translates immediately into these two words: "I will not to will," *volo nolle*. Unless we do violence to the laws of consciousness, not moral conscience, but psychological consciousness, unless we cover up the truth of things with a subtlety that is quite verbal, the mere sense of an absence of will implies the idea of a will that does not will and abdicates. The learned precautions, the game of an unstable

13   equilibrium, all this dialectical refinement through which our spiritual acrobats make their escape manifests an intellectual duality. In the name of their law of universal relativity, we must lay bare the ambiguity they cover themselves with. They know there is a problem, and they do not want to know it. A deliberate ignorance is no longer an ignorance; they artificially limit their natural curiosity and fake their sincerity. Hence it is where their experience is incomplete and deceiving, indeed by reason

of this internal dissension itself, that they preserve the consciousness and the enjoyment of their ambiguous disposition.

Nor is this all. This necessary duality of the mind must be shown to proceed from a duplicity of the will; for it is always in the depths of consciences, at the very principle of active sincerity, that we must uncover in each the secret of the judgment to be passed on each. What then is this double voluntary movement of which the equivocal attitude of the aesthete is made up, and how resolve its internal contradictions?

I

To be every thought, every sensation and every experience is a beautiful method of universal disillusionment; and it would be easy to jeer, from the height of this full science of vanity, at the shortsightedness of those barbarians who still give each thing a name and believe in life. There remains only one small difficulty, namely, that this science is never full, namely, that the experience is never finished nor conclusive, namely, that to begin the test, to persevere in it, to complete it by anticipation, a hypothesis without definitive control remains always indispensable. Once he has recognized the decisive obstacles of his method, the aesthete-ascetic seeks in vain, by multiplying his experiments, to try out many contrary lives at once; he senses that at every instant, while he is enchanted with his own emotions, an admirable but incomplete artist is dying in himself to be reborn always perishable and always immortal. He will never know the vanity of everything if he has not exhausted everything, and never will he nor anyone else exhaust everything to the last drop.

The man of sacrifice, for his part, can, by depriving himself, have a total experience, carry out a complete verification and receive an interior confirmation of his conception of life; whereas the conception of the aesthete who enjoys everything remains a fiction without any proof possible. Between the naive and the jaded, it is the naive person who is more experienced; at least he is the one whose attitude is founded on a positive experience, and he may be the less deceived because he does not entertain the unjustified pretension of being duped by nothing in knowing the deception of everything.

If there is no need for any postulate to first accept and to resolve courageously in practice the problem of duty, there is need for one, if one is to contradict conscience and try out the experiences which, without our knowing why, conscience disapproves of. What is this secret hypothesis, and on what profound will is it constructed?

To play and to enjoy as if we knew, as if we experienced the vanity of all, while we have not experienced it and while we do not know it, because it is impossible to experience it and know it, is to prejudge every question on the pretext of suppressing every question, and to admit by an arbitrary anticipation that there is neither reality nor truth.

Where the artifice shows, where the mask falls, is in the face of what is called intolerance, a painful and sensitive spot in contemporary consciousness, a sign of contradiction and a stumbling block. You broad and liberated spirits, you want to exclude nothing; you therefore exclude dogma, which (whatever be its value, a question held in reserve) is only insofar as it is exclusive. Everything depends on whether what you embrace in your most vast syntheses is not infinitely little in comparison with what you give up, and on whether you do not take everything for yourselves, except the truth that is. For you can claim to grasp the whole soul of absolute doctrines all you want, to understand their relative interest and to appreciate their symbolic beauty; in leaving aside, in pushing away what makes up their unity and their life, you are left only with the inert and torn body. The spirit without the letter is no longer the spirit. You have claimed to discover a pass that does not exist between these two inescapable sayings: "he who is not for me is against me; he who is not against me is for me." Something has reared up that you cannot admit because it rejects what you admit, something you cannot understand because it is closed to pure curiosity, something you deny and you hate without any admixture of doubt and love because one loves it only without any admixture of hatred. Such a disposition of soul, entire and simple, does not exist for you, you do not have any knowledge of it. The fact is, then, that you have resolutely taken a resolute attitude and that, like the common run of men, barbaric on this point, you have your decided way of being, of thinking, of willing and of excluding.

15

"To be intolerant of intolerance," the saying goes. What does that mean? It signifies that one does not admit that there should be *one* truth recognizable by man, useful for social harmony as well as for the life of each; it signifies that one admits that all opinions have an equal right to respect, that if none is absolutely false, none is absolutely true either. How many problems are prejudged when we avoid resolving any or raising any!

And when dogma does not limit itself to presenting your reason with an intransigent ultimatum, all or nothing at all, when, by laying claim to the will and the whole machine, it pretends to govern the inside and the outside of acts, you who will nothing, will you will to go along or to resist? If there is within you a movement of protestation and rebellion, if you become indignant at the violence that seems done to you since you cannot keep either from going ahead under a yoke or from sustaining a war you did not want to declare, that is already a defensive act which regroups your artfully dispersed forces and which, concentrating them into a common thrust, manifests the most intimate, the most personal foundation, the solid and resisting center to which are anchored aestheticism's most wanton caprices and freest fantasies. I am not blaming, I am not explaining, I am only making an observation. In the face of what would force you to act, you act. The party is interrupted, the plan in disarray. In fashioning a science and rule of neutrality, you become militants, and under pretext of peace, you cross bayonettes. You have taken sides; and you now feign surprise that facts no longer correspond to your theory aimed against the facts. Your hypothesis is that there is nothing either real or false, as if everything were a matter of indifference, as if everything were equivalent. But if truth is, it is: a supposition that appears simple and legitimate, and it is the only one you forbid yourself. What is it that keeps you from making that supposition; and why, after having made life so insignificant and vain by taking pleasure in being duped, do you make it so noble, so full of itself, so loving of its comforts, so self-sufficient that you no longer consent to surrender any part of it?

II

If, in the face of a truth that claims to be exclusive and before the despotic imposition of action, one balks or one steals away, it is that one has of oneself, of one's rights, of one's independence an ideal one loves and wills; one wills to be, since one is already laying down one's conditions. When Magali[1] runs away from an offensive pursuit, now as bird, now as breeze, flower, or wave, she has a love at heart; when the dilettante slips through the stone fingers of all idols, it is that he has another cult, autolatry: looking at everything from the height of the star Sirius, everything becomes petty and mean to him, everything and everyone; all that remains important is the self-love of one alone, *me*: "Ut sim!" (That I may be). That is the basic aspiration which, like a quite spontaneous and heartfelt *fiat* (so be it), sanctions in him the being received and produces it freely, lovingly. And is that not the tacit motto of many: "Nothing before me, nothing after me, nothing outside of me."

1. Magali was the heroine of a very popular song in France, especially in Provence, written by the Provençal poet, Mistral (Translator's note).

Thus, nolition itself harbors a subjective end. To will nothing is to turn away from every object, in order to hold oneself entirely in reserve and to forbid oneself all gifts, all dedication, and all abnegation.[1] One wills that being not be, but it is a pleasure to be in order to deny being: a radical egoism that would destroy everything in order to remain alone like a god. This is a subjective pantheism whose precise characteristics it is interesting to determine better than has been done up to now, since it is only recently that it has refined itself into a subtle doctrine. The time has come to classify it; that will be to take away some of its prestige.

Under the apparent indetermination of its fluctuating forms, and in spite of the care it takes to avoid the pretentious color of a system in order to preserve the grace of supple attitudes and of shaded nuances, aestheticism hides a very settled philosophy. It is a system like all the others by the very pretention it makes of being outside of or above all the others. To discern its original inspiration, it is necessary to refer it back to its origins, to German pantheism, whose forms it has made more supple in order to adapt it to the French mind.

For the pantheist, the spirit is an indefinite and unlimited power; it is only by manifesting itself, but none of its manifestations contains it entirely; it does not go without symbols, but it is not satisfied with them, all are true and all false, all necessary and all inadequate. Spirit and matter or, from another viewpoint, subject and object, are nothing without one another, and are nothing for each other. To produce himself, the subject *becomes* object, without *being* it originally, but he is object only for himself; he is nothing for everything outside of himself. The subjective whole, then, is objective nothingness, and inversely, without the solidarity ever coming to an end between the two compatible terms. They can never completely annihilate themselves nor realize themselves purely, though they tend toward that by progressive approximations, as they oscillate from nothingness to the whole in the infinitesimal undulations of consciousness.

Once the way is open for deductions, abstract reason can pursue without assignable limit the series of its turns and its contradictions. It should not stop. In fact, it does stop always; it ends up admitting that

1. To what is irony in the speculative realm corresponds a singular virtuosity in practice. Irony is the sign of a kind of sovereignty of the *self* that emancipates itself from all external rules to deploy its power freely while being detached from any work done, without any other object than its own satisfaction and enjoyment. It makes itself master, so to speak, of laws and of things. This exaltation of the person always ready to take hold of itself and to dominate what is highest outside of it is the theoretical form of this transcendent egoism that looks for the pleasure of play in action.

the inexhaustible is exhausted and taking the letter for the spirit. It belongs to pantheism to subsist only by a lack of consistency with its method. It professes to contradict itself and to surpass itself endlessly. After denying personality, it would have to restore it. After ruining the distinction between beings and the substantial reality of the action proper to each, it would have to affirm it. After putting God everywhere except in God, that is, nowhere, it would have to restore Him to Himself and place Him only in Himself, that is, everywhere, for immanence is conceivable only through transcendence. It would have to do all this, if instead of remaining tied to the literal doctrines it declares dead as soon as we embrace them, it obeyed the internal law of renewal and of progress that inspired it at the outset. It does not do so. It remains obstinate in its principle without seeing that this obstinacy condemns it; it is inconsequent with its inconsequence, for there is a way of sophisticating even sophistry.

It is this fundamental weakness of pantheism that "aesthetism" tries to make up for (and that is its philosophical originality), without perhaps having a clear consciousness of doing so. By reason of the variety of its forms, of the concrete and free character of its manifestations, of the ease and the number of the entrances and exits it opens up for the coming and going of intelligences, no doubt it represents one more stage in the development of intellectual and moral *anomy*. Breaking out of the always too narrow framework of technical dialectics, and spreading out over all the realms of philosophy, science and religion, it understands marvelously well that the time of scholastic questions and partial heresies is past, that it is no longer a question of exploring abstract theories like a bottomless pit, but of a whole attitude to be taken, one infinitely complex. 18

Hence its doctrine is not to have one; and it is one. In spite of itself it bears the stamp of a system, and in spite of its reluctance, it is labeled. Its aim, since it has one, is to substitute an aesthetic anarchy for intellectual dogmatism, an infinite fantasy for the moral imperative, for the compact unity of action an embroidery where the fulness of science brings out the emptiness of the universal dream; it is (to use the technical terms we must also inflict on it) to subtilize the subject and the object by bursts of alternating and direct current which, going from one to the other, annihilates each by turn without ever succeeding in eliminating both and yet without ever ceasing to admit that it always achieves this impossible destruction. The logical imperfection of the system, for being difficult to unearth, subsists nonetheless. It remains for us to see that this vice is no more than the sign of an internal contradiction of the will and of a moral failure.

III

From the moment when the aesthete, in the face of intellectual and practical constraints that would oblige him to believe and to act, but that only reveal in him antecedent dispositions, takes hold of himself in some way in a sincere and profound movement of egoism, what is it that results, for the system of his thought and the orientation of his life, from this sudden hitch and through what compensatory rhythm does he recover his disconcerted nolition, if he persists in it?

19   What results from it? Either one of two things.

Either, giving in to this *élan* of sincerity and this love of self that no artifice can destroy, he perseveres in his will for emancipation and absolute sovereignty. (And we shall see later on at what cost he will arrive, through the sacrifice of his egoism, at a generous and sincere love of self.)

Or else, stubbornly holding fast to the attitude that does not correspond to his most sincere will, he maintains himself in it only by a contrary will. And this will he wants to have perverts the one he has. In truth, even without reflexion to shed light on this subtle mechanism, without needing to know the theory of it, nolition could not subsist if it were not composed of a two-fold willing; and in convicting it of duplicity, we are only revealing what it is, unwittingly perhaps, but without this ignorance suppressing the voluntary character of the double movement that forms it.

It is this hidden contradiction between what we would call the voluntary (*le volontaire*) and the willed (*le voulu*) that we must consider for a moment, in order to determine the meaning of the acts that express it. For it is always acts that manifest the agreement or the discord of the double will, voluntary and willed, that every reflected movement, every deliberate attitude of man implies: they result from both one and the other at the same time. And when these two wills are at odds with one another, acts declare the will that is willed, that which is lacking in profound sincerity; or rather they are the synthesis of these two incompatible orientations, a hybrid synthesis, bad acts, because, as in a mathematical operation where the least error of detail vitiates all the result, as in a syllogism where the conclusions always follow the weakest part, action draws its character from the willed-will it realizes, without thereby ceasing to be founded on the primitive willing it perverts.

What, then, in the aesthete, are these antagonistic movements, whose agreement is impossible precisely because the first *élan* is absolutely and sincerely voluntary, because it dominates all others, because it persists intransigently, always whole in all of them?

1. This first movement of the immanent will is disclosed in the very

effort the dilettante makes to renew himself and to go on escaping endlessly, in order to be, and to be more than all, alone of all. Underneath the most persistent indifference and in the most subtle doubt there is an established doctrine, there is a positive resolution, there is a willing of *self*.

2. It is a necessary law of reflected thought: we cannot, from a subjective viewpoint, suppress the will, *nolle* (not-to-will), without immediately assigning nothingness to it as object and as end. This is an intellectual necessity that only translates into psychological language the equivocation of the artificial attitude wherein the aesthete takes pleasure. To unmask this magic, it is good to remember that, according to whether they belong to the speech (*langue*) of the *subject* or the language (*language*) of the *object,* all words have an opposed double meaning that opens up for thought innumerable subterfuges. Thus it is that none of the dilettante's negations could have a simple meaning, απλως, because each one of them always contains its contrary. What is nothing for the senses will appear to be all for the mind, and inversely. But underneath this sophistical interplay, we must come to see finally the seriousness of the wills involved. While he wills to be, to the point of annihilating everything in the face of his sovereign capriciousness, how can the aesthete succeed in willing nothing? By annihilating himself in turn, so to speak, before what he was just despising, and by treating himself as nothing while he considers the degraded object of his thought or of his enjoyment as his all. He has spit upon life only to make himself drunk with it or with self. He loves himself enough to sacrifice everything to his egoism; he loves himself poorly enough to disperse himself, to sacrifice himself and to lose himself in all the rest.

And when, on these fictitious ruins, he takes pleasure in the phenomenon in order to experience the nothingness of things with a strangely refined Epicureanism or when he acts to exalt himself in the nothingness of self, with the delight of a kind of mystical atheism, everything in his attitude is only a lie. And what is a lie, in effect, if not the intimate opposition of two wills, one sincere and upright whose permanent and inviolable presence serves as an incorruptible witness, the other failing and fallacious which is embodied in the evil reality of acts? It is not an issue, then, of legitimate or necessary contradictions, nor of involuntary errors: there is falsehood. The intellectual vice of the system which is difficult to unmask is the sign and the penalty for the lack of consistency or the moral duplicity into which the will easily falls. The condemnation and the punishment for this willed state must be this state itself, clearly known; for in the light of full knowledge the voluntary contradictions of action become the necessary contradictions of suffering.

And through an inevitable revenge of the voluntary against the willed, it is from the very depths of sincerity and of the primitive love of the being for being that will have to arise the reprisals of sanction.

The moral problem of action and of human destiny does not exist, it was said, and to solve it, it seemed, is to suppress it. But lo and behold, thinking that we slip out from under it, we raise it in its entirety.

We cannot, because we do not will to dispense ourselves from being and acting; no more than metaphysical abstention, is moral abdication either possible or honest. In vain through art and science and subtle experiences do we decompose the spiritual organism, in order to disconcert all the elementary mechanisms of life and to convince ourselves that nothing of it subsists: the more profound willing of being survives the nothingness of willing. In vain do we persist in a systematic nolition, as if the subject and the object, taking arms against one another, succeeded in destroying one another: attached to the nothingness of willing there remains the artificial but positive willing of nothingness. In vain does the subject, to triumph over his power of destruction and his own indestructibility, throw himself into the object: he looks for the enjoyment of the senses and action, he exteriorizes himself in the phenomenon, he annihilates himself in it only by bringing the being he is to it, and by finding himself in it, but lost, as he willed it, and condemned by the inner contradictions of a perverted will. To will nothing, then, is at one and the same time: to admit being, by looking in it for that infinite virtuosity that always enters into the game and always runs off; — to affirm nothingness while investing in it the vague hope of a refuge; — to keep to phenomena and be enchanted with the universal fairy-land, in order to enjoy being in the security of nothingness. It is the abuse of everything.

It was claimed that we could suppress all primary or ultimate questions, take all meaning away from life, and close off every exit for man. — All exits are now open for him. And since he has to will and to pursue an end, for what end will he act and what will his acts be? Where will they lead? To nothingness? This way seems open, we must look into it first.

---

22   After the absence of a solution with which we cannot stay, it is appropriate therefore to examine the negative solution to the problem of action, as the one that is least onerous. After the fruitless effort of a subjective annihilation, it is, so to speak, the attempt at an objective annihilation of man that we must study. Entering first as always into the design of those who affirm, who think they ex-

perience and prove, who seem to will the definitive nothingness of man and of his acts, I try to discern what this declared resolve contains; and here again I show that under this apparent will there subsists another willing and another thought. Thus, of the three ways that seemed to be open, that of nothingness will be closed off, it does not exist, no one wills it to be.

Chapter one briefly exposes what, in practice or in theory, inclines beliefs and human desires toward the solution of nothingness as to the single and necessary conclusion of experience, science and metaphysics. There we shall speak in the name of the very ones whose attitude we shall have to discuss, in order to be penetrated by their sentiments, and we strengthen as much as possible their reasons for thinking and acting as they do, justifying them as they seem to justify themselves before their own tribunal, before showing them, as the occasion arises, how in fact they condemn themselves at this same tribunal.

Part II

Is the Solution to the Problem of Action Negative?

CHAPTER 1
How We Claim to Make Nothingness the Conclusion of Experience, the End of Science and the End of Human Ambition

23   What idea of action do a very great number of men have, of action that hardly anyone has thought of defining in a concrete way? And for what end do they act most ordinarily?

Action for them is a system of spontaneous or willed movements, a setting of the organism into motion, a determinate use of one's vital strengths, in view of some pleasure or interest, under the influence of a need, an idea or a dream. Nothing more; no disquieting layers underneath the surface. Our acts are without threat; they all fall into nothingness, as do the organic unity and the living system of which they are the function. Of what use all those manoeuvers to set aside a chimerical problem? A frank and brutal negation is worth more than all the hypocritical subterfuges and all the sophistications of thought. To taste death in all that is perishable before being buried in it oneself forever, to know that we will be annihilated and to will to be so, that is the last word in emancipation, in courage, and in experimental certitude for spirits that are clear, free and strong: on to death, all is dead.

Or if the practice of life is not enough to dissipate the inveterate illu-
24   sions of a superstitious hope or fear, nor to detach man from the foolish love of being forever, then positive science and metaphysical criticism will exorcise once and for all this phantom of hidden being from his thought and from his will. And what in the eyes of pessimism seems to confirm this conclusion even more is that evil and suffering rise precisely from the fact that we rebel against this happy annihilation, so that nothingness has in its favor even the witness of those who have a horror of it, and it is felt, known, admitted even by those who do not know yet how to will it. It is certain that in desiring it, in fearing it, we admit it equally.

Let us listen, then, to these fearful ones and these apologetes of nothingness who render it an equal homage.

I

The nothingness of life: how many false ideas and depressing images these two salutary words arouse! They seem to lay out before the eyes a bankruptcy made more painful by the very progress of desires and pleasures. Do we need to unroll another bit of the canvas? "The great multitude of men, which is governed by the senses, suffers and complains; and yet all that has been said of the immensity of human pains is perhaps nothing in comparison to the disappointments, the betrayals, the degradations of pleasure. There are lives where everything seems to be full, but in this fulness there is nothing. The happy ones are often the saddest ones; in abundance is hidden a strange poverty; and those who have gone through many states of soul know that they felt perhaps the most subtle bitterness in well-being, a condition for which there is no consolation! Make everything the best it could be, the cry is the more sharp. We get used to everything except being well off and we grow tired of life in the happiness it has to offer. Blessed are those who can weep; they are not the pessimists; misfortune is not as bad as we think and it is darker from far away than from close up, for there it still has hopes and illusions; you are the rich ones, you poor avid and envious ones, because not having had the chance to feel the vanity of possessions, your desires are attached to them with a frenzied eagerness. But from satiety and plenitude, as those who have exhausted the test of life know, come only disgust and nothingness. Fortune, ambitions, success, what is all that? Two dogs fighting over a pile of rubbish where the winner will find nothing. And the disenchanted ones are not just those who grow old and die in the bewitchment of trifles without ever having penetrated beneath the surface of their senses; they are the better ones, the most tested, the most competent, men of triumphant action or of ardent thought, artists and sensitive types who have suffered from living in a world where there is not one straight line and where even a ray of light is broken."

What then must follow from this universal experience of the universal vanity? These two conclusions. If life is as bad as it seems, it is because we ask it for something it does not have to give, because we take it for what it is not, and because in pressing it we hear from it a despairing answer of death while it pronounces a serene and consoling word of nothingness. Life will be as good as it can be when, emancipated from all chimerical pretentions about it, and convinced that it never goes bankrupt because it never takes anything from us or gives anything, we look at it peacefully as it is. That is the brutal reality; it is also the true deliverance. There is nothing in our acts, there is nothing beyond: nothingness.

II

Nothingness of life and of human acts, that was the conclusion of clearsighted senses and of experience; and it is also that of science. But listen once more to what artificial sentiments people ordinarily mix into this certitude, and how they interpret, through a prism of hereditary illusions, the doctrine that dissipates them: "The nothingness of man, we must acquire a conviction of it, not only because in the face of the horizons open before the mind and the ever receding depths of thought, before the general history of humanity and the universe, we become detached from our narrow perspective in order to feel invaded by a grand and sad admiration; but also because the progress of knowledge analyses and reduces its object to an abstraction, because reflexion destroys instincts and natural inclinations, because it creates new needs faster than it can satisfy them. If the life of the senses leaves us with an infinite lassitude, scientific research leads to a more profound emptiness, to a collapse without remedy. To know is vain, is painful, because knowledge brings to light an unsatisfied and inexplicable desire, the unknowable and the vanity in human being. Through its very development, science multiplies our contacts with the mystery as an expanding sphere touches at more and more points the void into which it is plunging. What is even a simple fact? Can we place ourselves in the presence of any positive, palpable, complete fact? No, every fact is already a complex fiction, an organic integration, a mental construction, almost the conclusion of a reasoning process, an action of spirit. And what is spirit, what is action? To find out wait until physiology has finished dismantling the cerebral mechanism, chemistry has discovered the last divisions of matter, mathematics has found the one formula that will apply from atomic crystallography all the way to social functioning! Science leaves an enormous amount unknown in the world; in vain do we seek from it reasons for acting, a rule for concerting acts, a complete explanation of the human dynamism, a law of pleasure, of interest and of happiness. It cannot furnish us with a single motive for action, nor render an account for any one of them; it could not even justify itself, nor posit itself as real and necessary. What use is it that the world should be given over to the disputes and the discoveries of men? Science does not prescribe science and, if we act to acquire it, it is through a motive power independent of science. In the domain where it is competent, it sees in action only nothingness, it sees in itself only nothingness."

These observations are certain, it is insisted, but they must be defended against the acquired strength of mental habits and the lack of consistency in artificial sentiments. Science knows what it knows and does not know what it does not know, without our having either to complain about it or to be alarmed by it. No doubt, it will always have an unknowable before it; that can be granted, but this unknowable is only an unknown, and the unknown is of the same order as the known. What remains to be known does not weaken what is already known; and if the scientific analysis of human acts, without being completed, has decomposed their organic unity, if we have begun to dissolve the intellectual mechanism into its elements like the physiological machine, it is enough to enable the pacifying certitude of a truth that is neither so sad nor gray, but that is what it is, to relieve and to calm consciousness. To create an illusion   27 about man's nothingness, some considered the nothingness of science; we must, on the contrary, exalt science because it demonstrates to man that nothingness is the end of what he calls his person, his life, his acts and his destiny. And instead of considering the nothingness of the object, instead of being afflicted because of our personal nothingness, we must, indifferent to the ephemeral illusion of what goes on and disappears in us, rejoice in the eternity of what remains outside of us, by consenting to the extinction of individual will.

III

Nothingness of action: that was also the conclusion of metaphysical criticism, the end toward which it directs man's thought and will. But here again, here especially, how many prejudices have to be overcome to have access to the bliss of nothingness just as pessimism offers it to our desires! It is useful to recall briefly the progress of this philosophy of action, from the point where it begins by making man despair, so as to purify him of his false attachment to life, to the term where the will, converted to its ultimate depths, aspires to non-being and is swallowed up in it.

The pressures of pain and the more disgusting deceits of delight would never justify pessimism by themselves and would not be enough to cure man of his fanatic love of being. See how the experience of life or the clarity of the sciences remove few illusions since we still suffer from losing them, and since in undeceiving us more or less on what we are, they let subsist in us a kind of regret and bitterness about what we are not. The origin of illusion is more radical: all the more radical must be the cure for the will. Let us consider its history and its forward march.

It was the great achievement of Critical Philosophy to bring to light the conflicts between speculative reason and practical reason. Now action pertains at once to all the powers in man alien and hostile to one another: through thought, which illumines its origin and accomplishment, it is of an intellectual order; through intention and good will, it belongs to the moral world; through execution, to the world of science. At one and the same time, it is an absolute, a noumenon, a phenomenon. If, then, there is an antinomy between the determinism of movements and the freedom of intentions; if moral formalism is without relation to the laws of sensibility and of the understanding; if all union is broken between thought, the senses, and voluntary activity; if the body of acts is separated from the spirit that inspires them and if, in this world that is presented as the theatre of morality, man dispossessed of all metaphysical power, excluded from being, and fragmented feels surrounded by impenetrable realities where the most absurd illogicality can reign, then the will to live is broken along with the daring to think. Under pretext of raising and strengthening practical reason, they have ruined it with the same blow that kills pure reason. For all, whether they know it or not, the problem of life is a question of metaphysics, of morality and of science all at once. Action is that synthesis of willing, knowing and being, that bond of the human composite that cannot be cut without destroying what has been torn apart; it is the precise point where the world of thought, the moral world, and the world of science converge; and if these worlds do not unite in it, everything comes apart. If to think, if to will is not to be; if to be is neither to will nor to think, what is this nightmare? Every doctrine, then, for which metaphysics, science, and morality remain alien or become hostile, makes being evil, makes it unintelligible, makes it uncertain; if the three are not solidary, there is nothing.

From the day criticism broke up the fruitful unity of action, pessimism, which had been as yet only a disposition of soul among some, took on the form of a system and has been able to chant the metaphysical hymn of nothingness. What does sense wretchedness matter? What does physical suicide matter? It only proves an attachment to being among those people who kill themselves because they find life too short: simply a *petitio principii*. It is not from external obstacles nor from sufferings involuntarily endured that detachment and deliverance must come, that they can come; often they only irritate and exasperate the appetite for living. To be sure, the incurable lassitude of delights, the disappointments of knowing, and the crying immorality of the world contribute in us to an interior work of dispossession; but it is from the intimate will and from it alone that the disavowal of and the emancipation from being will rise.

For we live and we are only through an illusion, we want to be whereas we cannot be; and that is the evil, the inexplicable pain, the pure absurd- ity we must be cured of. It is not being that is evil, it is the consciousness of being, the will for being, the illusion of being. And as "the notion of nothingness is always relative, referring to a determinate subject which is to be denied (that is the very admission of Schopenhauer), as the actual world does not exclude the possibility of another existence, and as there remains a wide margin for what we designate only negatively through the very negation of wanting to live," a completely consequent pessimism, then, is a radical optimism. In the face of the evil of everything, it seems to say, there is no longer any subtlety that holds up: I would rather be- lieve in nothingness than to accuse Being, whatever it is. Nothingness is the good, it is; being is evil, it is not.

Thus the will, stripped of illusions and the bonds that held it captive, comes back to its essence; dying to the world of passions and of egoism, it is born again to a new being, it engenders itself through the voluntary destruction and the abnegation of self. The tendency of every being to persevere in being, the struggle for existence, all this instinct for preserva- tion and conquest is not only deceiving, it is deceived, it is the illusion of an illusion; if it existed, it would be good, because in spite of the suf- fering and the despairing, the will to be which would succeed in being would be an infinite good the value of which would make any crossing of little account. All the immense oppression of hearts come, not from the fact that those who suffer are, but from the fact that, not being, they think they are and will to be. Are not evil and being in effect the fear of nothingness, whereas truth and goodness is the desire, the will not to be?

Also, since the will to be does not succeed in being, and therein lies the supreme pain, and since the will not to be, by entering into the truth, brings infinite relief to souls, what is called for, then, is to kill within ourselves not the being that is not, but the chimerical will to be, to con- sent to the non-being of the human person, to crush even the deepest roots of desire and all love for life. To unmask the deceit of every instinct for preservation and survival is to procure salvation for humanity and the world in nothingness, that nothingness that must be defined as the ab- sence of willing.

Nothingness of sensible life, nothingness of scientific research, nothing- ness of philosophical speculation, nothingness of moral activity: this is the universal conclusion and the only end in which pessimism leads us

30   to bury the deceiving appearances of reality and all the unhappy velleities for existence. Its originality and strength is to consider that the suicide of sensibility and of thought is entirely insufficient for or even contrary to our aim, if we do not turn the will from its attachment to the error of being and if we do not obtain from it the supreme abdication that alone suppresses evil and suffering in their cause by opening nothingness up for it, by making it desire and love nothingness.

That, then, is the perspective offered me. Does it not succeed in making me feel nothingness, in demonstrating it to me, in making it lovable to me, in making me will it as an unfathomable beatitude? It had seemed to me, it seems to me now more than ever that I cannot be, for myself, in spite of myself: if then my most sincere and profound will aspires to annihilation as to a sure refuge, as to a fact of experience, as to a scientific truth, as to the ultimate conquest of philosophical wisdom, who then can close this avenue before me and tell me without absurdity: "We can't get through, we have to be!"

The following chapter will establish that there is neither a proper conception of nor a deliberate and frank will for nothingness. The action that seems to aspire to it is composite and like a hybrid. First, regarding this double will that concurs in nothingness, we show a lack of consistency in the attitude of the disillusioned man of the world or of the laboratory materialist who are mistaken about the meaning both of their affirmations and of their negations; then, pushing on to the very metaphysical root of pessimism, we uncover, in the annihilation of willing it requires of man, the conflict of two diverging movements, one that inclines the will toward a great idea and a lofty love of being, and another that hands it over to a desire for, a curiosity about, an obsession with the phenomenon.

CHAPTER 2

That There is No Negative Solution to the Problem of Action; and What the Consciousness of or the Will for Nothingness Harbors

To anyone persuaded that he conceives and wills nothingness as the end 31 of his personal action, we must answer: one does not conceive it, one does not will it. And the impossibility of having a simple and distinct idea of it is only a translation into the intellectual order of a sincere and sovereign decision of the will. The artificial conception of and desire for nothingness, then, derive from a lack of consistency and from a deficiency in willed action. That is what we must try to show clearly by sorting out the internal contradictions of what we could call nihilism, if this name had not been given another meaning, and by uncovering the secret movements of sincerity in those who, in the name of experience, of science, or of metaphysical criticism, believe in and aspire to the destruction of the human person.

The idea of nothingness is not a simple state any more than any other state of reflected consciousness; logical analysis as well as experimental laws and the organic rhythm of mental life reveal in it a necessary complexity. Under very different forms and from very divergent points of view, from Plato and Descartes to Hamilton, Schopenhauer, Spencer and Büchner, we can affirm these diverse propositions with equal justice and an equivalent meaning: "I think of nothingness, therefore there is a thinking subject and an object thought, nothingness is being." — "To think is 32 to condition; the concept of nothingness is subordinated to the positive idea of being." — "There is consciousness only through discrimination and syntheses; nothingness is a symbolic representation." — "In the idea of nothingness, the only thing real is the cerebral labor it is tied to; and what must be understood by this word is the dissolution of the organism reduced to its elements." Thus, in every way, to conceive nothingness, we must begin by affirming and denying something else, so that the very thought we have of it maintains itself outside of nothingness and posits it only by escaping it invincibly, and by wrapping it in a kind of eternal presence. Since we cannot conceive it simply, it might be legitimate to conclude that we cannot will it absolutely. But this impossibility itself is what we must account for, by looking here as everywhere for the secret of intellectual necessities in the most intimate movements of the will. If we do not conceive of nothingness, it is because we do not will it; and if it seems that we might will it, what lies behind these words, and what is this willing?

I

Whether we listen to the suffering and sorrowful sincerity of the great multitude of naive lovers of life and of joy, or whether we consult the most discerning of those who have lived what is called living, and ask if they think they have acquired an experimental certitude of nothingness, and if they are persuaded they aspire fully to the abolition of their being, in all cases here is what they do and here is what they would have to do.

To will and to experience nothingness, what does that mean ordinarily? It means unscrupulous passion for pleasures, attachment to the life of the senses, an ardent search for well-being, levity in seriousness and gravity in the frivolous, contempt for man and exaltation of myself. One wills nothingness, and one enjoys everything possible: a forced will, a fictitious experience, a lie. Does one realize what this desire harbors, shameful because of its self-interest? A disordered love of being and well-being.

To will and to experience nothingness, what would that truly be? It would be to be detached from the apparent goods through renunciation; it would be to mutilate natural desires through a rigorous method of sacrifices and to suppress little by little the spontaneous energies of life; it would be, through the gradual extinction of the self, to die bit by bit, and through this mortification to have the decisive experience of non-being. Is it still not understood that, whatever has been said, there is one metaphysical experimentation, only one, it is death, which resolves the question still pending, to be or not to be; that we anticipate this death, have a feeling for it, wrench its secret from it by being able to deprive ourselves in order to possess a certitude only it gives, to diminish ourselves in order to see what dead things hide, to mortify ourselves in order to penetrate into the truth of life? Do we perform this experiment which, in practice, corresponds to the scientific methods of absence and suppression? And seriously, what is it then that we wanted, if already we no longer will it in act?

Let those pronounce their own condemnation, then, who, without generosity and without honesty, shelter their passions under the shadow which they hope will be a refuge, and yet which they fear because of a foreboding of light in it. There are enough of the others, to be sure, who are frankly persuaded they have found the proof of their annihilation in the experience of life or in the certitudes of science. They are sincere; but there is the sincerity of theories and thoughts; and there is the sincerity of sentiments, desires, practical resolutions, which the intervention of learned reflexion and of verbal logic can often cover over with a superficial veil without abolishing it. This veil has to be pushed aside.

II

What allows the man of the world or the laboratory scientist to affirm, through sensible enjoyment or the physiological phenomenon, the nothingness of man? At the root of his reasonings or even of his observations, what is the tacit premise whence all his conclusions follow? — It is the idea of, it is the need for a better satisfaction and a reality other than the one he tastes and touches. Violating the first law of experimentation, the most essential rule of the scientific method, he concludes, without counterproof, from what he has observed against what he could not observe. From the phenomenon he argues against being, even though he senses the insufficiency of the phenomenon only because he is first penetrated with the greatness of being: he affirms it before denying it and in order to deny it. It is in this inconsequence that the contradictions of his will will be uncovered.

Is it in the name of experimentation or of science that I can affirm 34 nothingness? No. Let these two multiply their analyses and their destructions, always they come to a stop and their competence comes to an end. What are sensible qualities, indeed what is movement and all that mechanism to which science reduces the universe? It is at least the expression of an unknown in the function of the mind. And if the mind that strips itself of its modalities to put on the nature of this mechanism is itself unknown in its depth, will not all the rest be even more so? Yes, but all the rest, sensible qualities, movement, and nature, cannot be affirmed without mind also being affirmed at the same time. Much more, if I were to deny nature and mind, if I were to deny all that I have been able to, there always remains something else to deny, an infinite that escapes me and into which all my successive destructions fall. Element by element, analysis has dissociated, exhausted, sublimated the apparent reality; there is no more activity, no more qualities; there remains only a pure indetermination, something that can be added to anything passive, that cannot be conceived alone, that the ancients called prime matter, and less still, being as it were without being, το ομενον. But behind, behold something that grows, an unknown, a real mystery that haunts the thought of a Pascal, a Littré, a Spencer, and before which the understanding no longer acts, stunned by the grandeur of what it sees and knowing only one thing, that is, that it cannot understand it, also that nothing can be understood, denied, called into doubt, admitted without this mysterious affirmation.

What does it mean then to believe in and aspire to the nothingness of every object of thought or desire? It means that, through an admission and an act of spontaneous faith that surpasses science, through an original decision that manifests the initiative of the will, one acknowledges the Great All about which especially those who promise themselves annihilation love to talk. All and Nothingness are for them two equivalent terms. What does that mean, if not that deep within these consciousnesses there subsists the profound and obscure sentiment that what will not be or is no longer has never truly been; that being in its fulness escapes duration and destruction; that the phenomenon appearing in order to disappear does not correspond to their infinite expectation; and that the life which dies is absurd. A lofty idea and a kind of eternal desire for being bursts out everywhere in them; what they deny reveals the greatness of what they will. Dogmatic or practising materialism therefore is a mysticism which, in matter, adores the invisible reality of what it sees and offers a cult to being under the species of the phenomenon. Here there is nothing scientific left; it is no longer even a matter of being satisfied with the ontological argument of the metaphysicians. For even in this nothingness into which it seemed to be fleeing, the mind finds what it did not appear to be looking for, some being and perhaps Being. And we must not be surprised at the spontaneous and universal development of religious thought, whether among Australian aborigines or in the United States, whether in a state of ignorance or in the most advanced civilization, since even underneath this reflected affirmation of nothingness there is a hidden belief and a distorted homage to the unknown Being.

Hence the will that tends toward the annihilation of the human person is founded, whether it knows it itself or not, on a singular esteem and an absolute love for being. What is the value of anything, one asks, if it is not eternal? The vanishing of individual appearances, of ephemeral passions, of all capacity for suffering and enjoying into the immense reality that does not know death, that is the coveted end. But at the same time see how a contrary will arises. At the moment one declares the insufficiency of the phenomenon, one becomes attached to it as to the only solid and real being; one persists in being content with what thought and desire recognized to be vain, disappointing and null; one places one's all where one otherwise admits there is nothing; one acts not only as if this life were all there is, but also as if it had an absolute value and a divine importance; and when one wants to fill oneself with this material science, enjoyment and existence, one condemns oneself by instituting in oneself a merciless conflict between the primitive will for nothingness that is inspired by a true love of being and this appetite for the phenomenon which, through the sophisms of sensuality or the proud perversion of the mind, propels the faltering will to the very place from which it had excluded itself.

To thus will nothingness, beguiled by words we fool ourselves with, is in effect to render homage both to the vanity of what we give as nourishment for action and to the greatness of what we willed with all the strength, all the sincerity of the first and intimate desire: a lie, because we take advantage of an equivocation. We do not will to, we are not able to deny at once both the phenomenon and being; and yet, as need arises, we deny them by turns as if we were annihilating them both at one stroke, without noticing that through this very alternative we posit them just as well.

III

This total destruction, can it not be willed sincerely? And when pessimism detaches the will both from the illusions of painful delight and from the great fraud of *wanting-to-live (vouloir-vivre)*, does it not kill in one stroke the phenomenon and being itself? Does it not succeed in destroying what is alone important for us, ourselves, and in us all power of suffering, through the abolition of personal will? No.

If physical suicide manifests a disordered attachment to the sensible life, because, according to a remark of Pascal, the will never takes the least step except toward happiness and because that is the motive of all actions of all men, even those who go and hang themselves, does not this attempt at metaphysical suicide also reveal a mad and impassioned love of being, but a love that in its native sincerity is good, a love stronger than suffering and death and even the eternity it claims to get the better of? Hence, it would be enough to will to be for the evil of existence and

36

all its retinue of crushing phantoms to rise from nothingness! Hence, it would be enough not to will being for being to be destroyed; and the will that creates and annihilates all the rest at will would have the supreme power of annihilating itself! Pessimism, if one reflects on it, lets loose an immense and invincible confidence in the omnipotence of the will since the will appears both necessary and sufficient to produce the pain of existence as well as to create the happy annihilation that would not be without it. And beyond this willed and proclaimed end, there is a full faith, there is a hymn to the sovereign and creative action of willing.

Let us break through all this inextricable network of illusions and disillusionments, as pessimism weaves it; here is what we can assuredly untangle: (1) the universe is the illusory and evil phenomenon of a fundamental will to be; (2) the evil of existence, the illusion of life is destroyed by a will not to be that annihilates the phenomenon of the first willing and constitutes blessed non-being; (3) in order not to be, in order to resist the invasion of the subtle illusions, it is not enough to extinguish in oneself all apparent and mortal life, this will not to be has to embrace eternity, it needs to be infinitely in order not to be any more and in order to deny itself perpetually without weakening, and it is because it is omnipotent enough to create the evil and the error of being that it has to be omnipotent enough to annihilate its own work and undo itself. — But we can goad thought and desire as much as we like: in *willing-to-be,* in *willing-not-to-be*, in *willing-not-to-will,* there subsists always that common term, *willing*, which dominates with its inevitable presence all the forms of existence or of annihilation and sovereignly disposes of the contraries.

There is, then, a double ambiguity in the meaning of the words, *being* and *nothing*. At times being has to be taken as meaning this disappointing life that the torrent of chimerical movers and the painful magic of the universal phenomenon sweeps along; and then in willing-to-be it is willing that is nothing, it is being that is the evil and the real illusion: *Si fallor, non sum* (If I am mistaken, I am not). At other times being has to be taken as meaning that profound will that does not possess and emancipate itself except by detaching itself from all individual forms, from all distinct thought, from all life of its own; and then in willing-to-be, it is being that is not, it is willing that alone has infinite reality: *Si non fallor, sum* (If I am not mistaken, I am). For once the passions are put down and desires mortified, the will, disengaged from the object that captivated it, returns to its pure essence; and dying to the world of the senses, it is born to impersonality.

But see how incoherence and the ineluctable contradictions of the will come out of this equivocation: if it wills to be, it loses itself; in order to be, it must not will itself, and yet it cannot deny itself thus unless it started by positing itself first; that is to say that, before not willing, it is necessary for it to have willed, it is necessary that evil and illusion be the conditions of final liberation, that the phenomenon be indispensable for the conception, for the conquest, for the will of nothingness, and that in wishing for complete annihilation one requires both the phenomenon and being at the same time, to oppose them to one another and to suppress them alternately one after the other. On the one hand, the *willing-to-be* is not efficacious, whereas on the contrary the *willing-not-to-be* is; and yet it has to be efficacious only if the former has produced some real effect which has to be overcome. On the other hand, it is not being (since it is not) that is evil, it is the will to live; and in the meantime it is not of willing, but of being and living that one has to be cured; as if the will were at one time the phenomenon of being and at another time the being of the phenomenon, here placing itself above and outside of everything, there subordinating itself passively to illusions and to external influences! It seemed that it should withdraw into its pure essence, and now in order to judge life it takes into account the first suffering that crosses its path, without noticing that either one of two things has to be the case: either this suffering is illusory, since it derives from a willing-to-live that is an illusion, or it is serious, worthy of being taken into account in the balance-sheet of life, and then it is the real consequence of a real will that has attained being. Hence, either suffering is not, or it proceeds from a fund of love of being.

Thus, pessimism gets lost in insoluble contradictions, because it proceeds from a double willing, the willing of the phenomenon, and the willing of being. Now attributing reality only to the magic of shifting appearances, now reserving it only for that mysterious abyss where illusion is dead, it takes the phenomenal will into account as if it were noumenal, and vice versa. By its very negations, it posits a double reality, one individual, one impersonal, thus placing before one another the two terms whose dramatic opposition makes for all the seriousness of moral conflict.

Here then is a first result, of extreme importance, though quite negative in appearance: there is neither a simple and distinct conception of nor a frank and homogeneous will for nothingness; in the action that seems to be reduced to it or to tend to it there always subsists an intimate and implacable contradiction. Some, no doubt, can deny the phenomenon through the pure idea they have of being, others can deny being through the obsessive image they have of the phenomenon. But the symbolic representation of nothingness is born always of a double synthesis:

the subject affirmed without object, along with the object affirmed without subject. In this concept, therefore, there is the alternating union and opposition of the phenomenon and of being, of sensible reality and of the invisible.

To posit nothingness is to affirm in a single stroke this entire system of co-ordinates; to deny one of the terms is, by an inescapable compensation, to put forward the other, without forasmuch ridding oneself of the contrasting term, which remains indispensible to the very one affirmed. Thus the will for nothingness is necessarily incoherent and it harbors in itself a struggle wherein it cannot succumb in spite of the lie and the error; for error is not nothing, it is nothingness that is the error, since we cannot deny everything except by affirming the infinite, and since nothingness is not nothingness without the absolute, veiled perhaps but present.

And how the secret of hearts is revealed through these ambiguities! In thinking we aspire to nothingness, it is at once the phenomenon in being and being in the phenomenon that we are pursuing. See how passion mixes a strange mysticism in with the delirium of the senses and seems to absorb into an instant of stillborn delight the eternity of being and to make it die with the delight; but see also how quietism adds to mortifying abnegation a desire for indifference, a need to feel the immolation, a joy of abdication, and all the refined sensuality of a false asceticism that manifests a self-will, a subtle and ambitious egoism: a lie on both sides, since the will always ends up willing what it wanted to exclude, and since it is already inflicting on itself, since it seems to be preparing for itself in this way, the torture of intestinal discord, where, armed against itself, it will tear itself apart with all its force.

It seemed to be a violent paradox to maintain that we could not have either a conception of or a will for nothingness, that we can no longer buy this nothingness even at the price of our blood, because it is no longer for us and because from the moment we posit the problem of action the fact is that we already have a positive solution for it. Nevertheless, it is so. Where can we turn now that the way we thought we could take is like a dead end with a double access? What is the least we can affirm and will? It seems to be the phenomenon as it is studied by the Positive Sciences. And when we were pretending that man aims at nothingness, was that not in effect affirming in an inappropriate way that his person and his works are reducible to phenomena? Could not thinking so be called, in the double meaning of the word, the *positive* solution of the problem? We must therefore examine whether the phenomenon is sufficient unto itself, or whether in admitting it we do not implicitly posit something other than it.

THE NATURAL ORIENTATION OF THE WILL
Does the problem of action
allow for a positive solution?

The way of nothingness is closed: we cannot, we do not will to enter it; 40 there is no such way. While seeming to be swallowed up in it, one left open behind one two other routes: the way of the phenomenon and the life of the senses, the way of being and the life of sacrifice. And the will got lost in its contrary movements. Its lack of coherence condemned it.

I. — How attain in the will the intimate accord that will give action its sufficiency and its perfect cohesiveness? — Will we be able to live at one and the same time this double life where the ambiguous will for nothingness would seem to lead? But apart from the fact that we might not find any means of reconciling these two divergent directions, is it not scientific first to have recourse to the least onerous hypothesis; and will we not be more sure of finally finding in action a perfect homogeneity of the will by following only one way? — Since we can opt, then, what shall we choose: being in the nothingness of the rest, in a contempt for any object of the senses or of science; the rest possessed in the nothingness of being, in a contempt for the invisible and the "supernatural"?

But what is this mysterious and troubling being that seems to escape our grasp without our being able to escape it? Is it not this that we want to set aside, especially this, this alone? "There is nothing," we said; and now this radical negation has become filled with a menacing and accusing unknown: "You would not be turning away if you were not facing me." What we will, then, is that there be something, and that this something be self-sufficient; we want the phenomenon to be; we want sense life, science, we want all this immensity of the universe known and yet to be known which fills our eyes and our heart to be, and to be all for us. And behind this screen of the phenomenon, we hope life will be lucid, complete, and satisfying, and we want action to unfold and be

51

completed in it. *There is something:* this simple and vague proposition that did not seem very difficult to conquer, but wherein it is not easy to uncover a sincere admission of the will,[1] thus ends up becoming all the more evident and reassuring even as that other ambiguous and terrible word is not: "There is nothing." There is something in our sensations and our pleasures, in our knowledge and in our acts: most people live with this conviction; it is the wide and long road on which the greater part of humanity goes forward. These words undoubtedly have no philosophical precision: they come prior to any profession of phenomenalism, of criticism, or of idealism; they translate the naive movement of life taken up with itself and all that sustains it without knowing what it is. In my acts, in the world, inside of me, outside of me, I know not where or what, *there is something.*

II. — From this admitted given will arise, through a hidden initiative that will appear more and more clearly, all the sensible, scientific, moral and social order. Thus we will see entering into the voluntary plan of our life the very thing that seems prior, foreign and consequent to the will. And by following to the end of its exigencies the *élan* of our willing, we will learn whether man's action can be defined and limited within this natural realm.

Since the will, never tending toward nothingness, ordinarily goes toward the object of sensation or of knowledge, we must therefore inquire now as to whether action can be adequately defined in function of this object which it proposes as an end for itself, and whether it is really restricted to phenomena; whether, in a word, it is not itself only a fact like other facts, and whether, in the narrow sense of the term, the problem of life allows for a *positive* solution.

If there is anything new in the method of this investigation, this, it seems, is what it is: from the first awakening of sensible life all the way to the highest forms of social activity, a continuous movement is unfolded in us whose rigorous concatenation and fundamentally voluntary character it is possible to manifest at one and the same time. Thus, as we make our way through the long inquiry we must institute, we shall have to take note that the apparent necessity of each stage results from an implicit willing. On the one hand, the successive terms of action will

1. This way of showing that "the phenomenon is willed" as well as undergone, artificial and provisional to be sure, expresses for distinct thought the natural movement of a will which, as we shall see, takes on its own account all that goes before it and produces it, and which does not have to know all it wills in order to will effectively all that it is.

be tied together in such a way that scientific rigor will be communicated from one stage to the next to studies that hitherto have not received it. On the other hand, as we discover how our acts irresistibly expand and by what hidden impulse they surpass themselves ceaselessly like the eddies of a stone fallen into deep water, we will be prepared little by little for the ultimate question: Yes or no, for one who limits himself to the natural order, is there any concordance between the willing will and the willed will; and does action, which is the synthesis of this double willing, finally find in itself the wherewithal to be self-sufficient and to define itself? Yes or no, will man's life be restricted to what is from man and from nature, without recourse to anything transcendent?

We are going to study the phenomenon of action, then, from its most elementary origins to its broadest development possible. Since this search is complex and since the movement of expansion goes on throughout the immense organism of life, we will consider many stages successively. We shall see action germinate from the conditions whence it draws its nourishment, then we will follow its natural vegetation and its expansion in the milieu where it had its birth and where it fructifies.

It is by analysing first the most immediate data of sensation and of science that we shall draw out in one sweep the elements of action, just as in discussing the conditions of knowledge we shall find the very principles of the reality known. For in the order of phenomena and in the sciences which are limited to it, the ontological distinction between being and knowing makes no sense: the phenomena is at once something known and something knowing. We can and we must show how the subject results from the object and how the subject returns to act and live in the object, without prejudging thereby any ontological question. In this very way the problem of the originality of thought will be brought back to its true terms and be resolved with certainty; for if it is positively established that the object of sensation and of the sciences is posited only in function of something else, it becomes manifest that we cannot isolate at its source what cannot be conceived in isolation: there is no need of any speculation to prove it; it is a fact. One of the essential results of this inquiry must therefore be to confer a properly scientific character (the character of a distinct and original science) on studies which the positive sciences and metaphysics claim as their domain with pretentions equally illegitimate.

Thus, we shall provide as a basis for the science of action the widest field possible, the whole field of human knowing; for action is the knot of sense experience as well as of scientific knowledge and philosophical speculation. On the way, then, we shall encounter the most diverse mentalities, and if they are prematurely stopped on the road, we shall try to make them go all the way to the end of their hidden aspiration.

Part III

The Phenomenon of Action

How we try to define action through science
alone and to restrict it to the natural order.

43   There is something. This given that even those who concede the least
grant, this admission of naive experience is not imposed on me in spite
of me: I have willed that there be something.[1] Indeed, while we were
pretending to elude the anxiety of the moral problem, we were positing
this very problem through a hidden movement of the will. While we were
pretending to discover in nothingness a sure solution and expedient, we
were setting up a double way out for ourselves. We opted for this
something that is immediately felt, known, desired by all, that offers an
immense field for human activity, that the very progress of the positive
sciences hardly allows us, it seems, to deny or to fear; we did so in a spirit
of defiance against the other alternative we had raised for ourselves, and
whose unknown seemed filled with troubling superstitions. I will remain
44   faithful to this aim; and with the help of all the means that the senses,
science and consciousness offer me, I will construct on this simple foundation all that it will be able to support.

Perhaps the edifice will be self-sufficient; perhaps, without leaving the
phenomenon and considering it as all there is, I will have a complete idea
of my action and a satisfying solution to the problem of life. If man
comes entirely from nature, if his acts are only systems of facts like the
others, if the movement of his will is restricted to the very limits of
positive science, will we not be justified in exorcising once and for all the

1. It is important to forestall every misunderstanding. It is not the will that
makes what is be; far from it, merely by willing, it implies something that it does
not make; it wants to be what it is not yet. Hence, it is not a question of considering this *something* either as exterior or as interior or reducible to the representation we have of it. It is a question of analysing the content of willed action, in
order to see wrapped in it all the diversity of objects that seem to be alien ends,
but that are in reality only means to fill out the interval between what we are and
what we will to be.

phantom of hidden being? To bring into the field of human knowledge and power all that at first seems least accessible (nature's energies, occult forces, even apparent miracles), to base individual or social life on Science alone, to be self-sufficient, that is indeed the ambition of the modern mind. In its desire for universal conquest, it wants the phenomenon to be, and to be as it knows it and disposes of it; it admits that observing facts and their interconnection is to explain them completely; it takes as half proved any hypothesis that allows it to avoid the intervention of what used to be called the First Cause? Is not the fear of metaphysics the beginning of wisdom? The modern mind works at determining "the genesis" of man, the origin of consciousness and the whole evolution of moral activity as rigorously as for astronomical movements, because for it the whole world is only one problem and the only problem and because, it seems, there is a unity and a continuity in the scientific method.

The ambition is splendid. Is it justified, and is the declared will to restrict man and satisfy him within the natural order of facts, whatever they may be, in accord with the more profound will whence proceed, as we shall see, the entire movement of his knowledge and all his intellectual activity? Decisive questions that must be explored at all costs before we can have any right to pronounce with scientific competence on the bearing of action and on the meaning of human destiny. But if the difficulty is great, the method for resolving it appears quite simple. Let us consider, then, starting from the first sensible given, how we endeavor to confer upon the phenomenon all possible consistency and sufficiency, and how, failing always to do so, we shall perhaps be led endlessly further, not than we will, but than we imagined willing.

Stage One
FROM SENSE INTUITION TO SUBJECTIVE SCIENCE

The scientific conditions and the unconscious sources of action

---

CHAPTER 1
The Inconsistency of Sensation and Scientific Activity

45   Sense intuition appears quite clear and coherent, of an absolute simplicity. Why then did man not stay with this first given of life, with this rudimentary knowledge which seems perfect from the start, and what is natural, what is necessary about the need for science? To what secret ambition does this recurring desire for research correspond, and by what provisional satisfactions do we seem to put it to sleep?

I

At first glance, the sense impression is for each one all that it can be, the only point we can never discuss because we never communicate the very reality of what we feel. The quality of the sensation I experience is unique in its kind, of an incomparable species, without analogy; and what is proper to this intuition could not be analysed, or measured, or described: we do not argue about tastes and colors. In this order of pure quality, there is only heterogeneity. I am what I sense, at the moment I sense it.

But for me to sense, does there not have to be in sensation itself something more than sensation? Sensible quality is not the only im-
46   mediate given of intuition; if it were, it would vanish, because, being discontinuous, self-sufficient, incomparable, always perfect and always disappeared, it would never be anything more than a dream without remembrance, without past, present, or future. Why is this not so? Because from the moment sensation appears, it harbors an incoherence

and as it were an internal antinomy. For it is only inasmuch as it is felt; and it is felt only insofar as it is represented at the same time as present, imagined at the same time as experienced; so that in it are necessarily contained these two apparently irreconcilable affirmations: "I am what I sense, I sense what is." The duality is prior even to the laws that govern the succession and the contrast of states of consciousness and in it nevertheless some have claimed to discover the primitive form of all intuition; for even supposing that sensations are perceived only through "discrimination," still it is necessary that in each of the contrasting states there be something to make it possible. At issue then here is what in the sensible phenomenon makes it a *phenomenon*, at the same time as it is *sensible*. Now between these two terms there is a fundamental opposition that has not been sufficiently taken into account although it is the point of departure for all scientific or philosophical investigation.

To see this, let us reflect on this strange and universal curious fact: in what we see and what we hear, at the very moment we are persuaded that the sensed impression is the absolute and complete reality, we look for something other than what we hear and what we see. Pascal, as a child, wanted to grasp the sound he perceived as if the sound were at once other and the same as he perceived it. Unknowingly, we are all invincibly in the same situation. I have sensations only under this double condition: on the one hand, what I experience has to be all mine, on the other, what I experience has to appear to me entirely exterior to me and foreign to my own action. Isn't that the popular belief and wish? People imagine that the visible is nothing more than what is seen, as if sensation were in effect the measure of all things, and people remain convinced that what is seen is the thing itself, as if sensation were nothing and the object were everything. This is a constant lack of coherence found in the most minute details of life. Are we not equally inclined, and almost at the same moment, to will that all sense as we do, penetrated as we are with the universal truth of our tastes, and to will to be alone in sensing, in enjoy-   47 ing, in suffering as we do, persuaded that others would be incapable or unworthy to feel as we do? And when critical reflexion applies itself to demonstrate that the immediate data and the necessary forms of sensibility cannot have their own subsistence outside of ourselves, to be sure it rightly establishes that human perception could not be independent of man, but it does not entirely escape the belief that it claims to be fighting; for it rises up against what it calls the metaphysical illusion only on the condition of thinking that behind the sensible given there is a given different from it, whatever it may be.

And the issue is not one merely of a simple logical duality; no, but of a real incoherence and a factual instability. At the very principle of the most elementary intuition, there is as it were a loss of equilibrium that does not allow us to stay with it, because we actually have this intuition only in surpassing it already and in implicitly affirming that it is in some way more than it is; for, in order for it to be, we must lend it a consistency it does not have without us, and it begins to be itself only at the moment when we look for, when we place in it something else than ourselves and in ourselves something other than it.

Can we ever succeed in resolving these difficulties, and in spite of its incoherence can we ground the reality of the sensible phenomenon? We will be able to make up our minds about this only at the end of this investigation. What deserves attention even now is this very ambiguity, the necessity we find ourselves in of representing the visible for ourselves at once as it is seen and yet other than what we see it to be. To be sure, practice, in teaching us through a multiple experience how to decipher our sensations fluently and how to use them, neglects the equivocation that disconcerts reflexion; and it is a wonder indeed that the least action decides, without worrying about it, a problem which no philosophy has completely overcome, because none has done a complete study of action. The fact remains that, behind brute sensation, as it is impressed on us, we are led by a natural movement to search for what it is. Even when we believe it to be as it appears, and we naively admit the identity of what we sense with what is sensed, there is in the simplest intuition a duality and an opposition that cannot fail to break out. That is the origin of all need to know.

II

48   As long as we take sensation for the object itself, no speculative curiosity is awakened; this curiosity is born only from the moment when, through the contradictions that experience seems to inflict on itself, through the conflict of individual tastes, through the movement of reflexion, the idea arises that what we sense is not the only, the true, and the total reality of what we sense.

This simple discovery for many centuries was responsible for confused discussions of philosophy and science. Indeed, in the sensible, people have claimed to discern the real, independent of sensation itself, though similar to it, unless it were its contrary; they have searched for the universal principle of things, the element of which they are composed, the number or the idea they participate in, the genus of which they are the species, the substantial form they hide under their sensible accidents, the primary qualities that constitute them, their mathematical characteristic, the equivalents of the force whose unity is manifested by the diversity of physical phenomena. From the moment when we place underneath sensation another knowledge, it seems that this new world of facts imperceptible to the senses gives back to thought its lost equilibrium and finally satisfies the natural need for a hidden being to be discovered. How many contemporary minds remain convinced of it! Behind the immediate perceptions which plain folk will long continue to take at face value, reality appears to be such to certain scientists, absolutely such as the positive sciences present them, and for them the universe is in sum a system of varied and rhythmic movements into which our actions are inserted. What they cannot perceive directly, they imagine through analogy with the sensible; and because their eyes have claimed a kind of double vision, they think that this visible reality they do not see is in the end the true reality, which, it is admitted, cannot be what we see.

How did this phenomenist realism develop? It is interesting to show how, in order to prepare ourselves to see whether the sciences are truly sufficient for us in every respect and self-sufficient in themselves.

Science and criticism have ruined the value of the ancient metaphysical distinctions; the primary qualities signify nothing more nor less than the 49 secondary qualities of matter; and it is an unmasked illusion to take one set of qualities as the real reverse side of sensible appearance or to make the two sets play mutually the role of phenomenon and of substance. But this relation, whose inanity has been recognized in the ontological order between two terms as disproportionate as the sensible qualities and an alleged substantial reality, is reconstituted, in the realm of science, between mathematical calculus and nature. Here is how and with what pretentions.

The mathematical sciences, the most ancient, the most rigorous, the most closely linked of all, have for a long time, in the ideal and abstract order where they seem to be confined, appeared to have independence and a complete self-sufficiency. If certain applications were drawn from them, it was without any thought of connecting this concrete use of abstract truths with the principles themselves and without seeing therein a properly scientific consequence of the calculus. They were used in practice, but they were not considered as constitutive of experience and immanent to nature. From the mathematical to the sensible the distance was too great for anyone to take it into his head to see in the sensible itself an object of science and in nature a realized mathematical calculus.

But when knowledge through observation, thanks to the precision of a method distinct from the ancient forms of demonstration, laid claim to the rank of science, a new problem arose. Can we link mathematical deduction to facts of experience, and must we not consider as a double aspect of one and the same solution the formula of the analyst and the law of the physicist? The hypothesis proved fruitful and success gave it the seal of approval. Through their parallel and solidary developments, the exact sciences and the experimental sciences seem in a way to grasp nature by both ends at the same time; and in coming together in the common good fortune of their mutual applications, they appear to close the circle where man's life naturally unfolds. They rule at once over numbers and over phenomena, and they rule the one by the other. Consequently, action itself becomes exact and scientific and, without going beyond this order of positive knowledge, it seems to find a stability, a certitude, and an absolute self-sufficiency. And if it is true that the analysis of the real is not completed and can never be, far from being anxious about it, it takes pride in it, for even in the face of the unknown, science does not have to fear encountering nothingness, or being, or the unknowable; what it does not know yet, it can know one day; what it does not know does not destroy what it knows already and does not prevent it from exploiting each one of its successive conquests.

Thus two equally scientific perspectives are opened up on things, two quite different perspectives, two perspectives that agree in fact, we know not how, and compenetrate one another to the point of appearing to be only one and of concurring by their very duality in the unity and the universal sufficiency of Science. And the association becomes so inseparable that we no longer notice its strangeness, but we take advantage of this implicit duality to admit that they account for one another reciprocally, that they satisfy the ever recurring need for an enigma to be explained or for an underside to be attained, and that, while one serves as unknown and limit for the other, and inversely, there is everywhere a scientific problem and everywhere a scientific solution. Also, it is thought, there is no need to look beyond the double and only explanation, since it has a practical efficacity; as a matter of fact, it succeeds, it is enough for action, it is enough for life.

That, then, is how the positive sciences (and by these words one understands especially experimental certitudes, precisely because one presupposes mathematics, which, since Comte ranked all the sciences in a continuous series, seems implied in the other sciences) appear to satisfy all our speculative and practical needs. Hence, it is necessary to see as closely as possible if this claim is justified. Yes or no, is there in science that coherence and that sufficiency which finally establishes the mind and the will in the full peace of certitude and in the fulness of practical success? Or, might we not find as a solution a new given in the question itself? Is it science that explains all of action, or action which still furnishes science with the means of subsisting?

I now propose to show that, between the mathematical and the experimental sciences, at the origin, in the course and at the end of their development, there is at once a break and a solidarity. This tacit and constant collaboration, this unity, this very existence of the sciences is possible only through a mediation on which, far from explaining it, they depend. It will remain, then, for us to define this mediating fact, a point of departure and the matter for further investigation; so that, after having underscored the insufficiency of sensation and the very inconsistency of the explanations offered by the positive sciences, we will move on, through an inevitable progression, from the exterior phenomenon to the interior phenomenon of consciousness and from the science of facts to the science of action, by establishing the necessity and the originality of subjective study.

CHAPTER 2

The Incoherence of the Positive Sciences and the Mediation of Action[1]

51 It is a fact that between the deductive sciences and the experimental sciences there is a fruitful commerce. Science itself seems to have no reason for being nor power for progress except through this assiduous exchange; it is the unity that makes up its strength and assures its dominion. But does science itself account for this real and uncontested unity? Let us look at its double point of departure.

1. I summarize here the investigation that will occupy this long chapter because its inevitably technical character makes it inaccessible to certain minds. And as this investigation is necessary for the continuity of our thought, it is useful to offer an approximate equivalent of it. Here then is what it tends to establish.

We cannot stop at this *something* whose immediate revelation is given us by sense intuition; and there is need for us to search, behind these appearances, for the very secret of their appearing. — Now it has been claimed, it is claimed more than ever that positive science is enough to enlighten this mystery, to suppress it; it is claimed that the element called *subjective* can be completely reduced; supposedly, it would precede scientific knowledge, it would not survive after it. — I show on the contrary that in this primitive given there are three elements to be taken into account: (1) what the exact or *a priori* sciences determine; (2) what the observational sciences describe; (3) something indeterminate which will be the object of a new science, one properly subjective or philosophical. Hence the subjective that comes before is found once again, delimited and enlightened, after the positive sciences. For in indicating what mathematics presupposes to constitute itself without explaining or accounting for this indispensable postulate, I underscore the sides of the hiatus it bridges. Similarly I indicate what the experimental sciences require to subsist and I underscore also the borders of their realm. Thus I arrive, through a double approach, at negatively defining the field of what remains to be learned in the primitive *something*. — I do more: for I show that this field, whose study the sciences do not undertake, is the point where from both sides they converge and ally themselves with one another (they do not sub-

On one side mathematics, thanks to a fiction that works, supposes that   52
the analysis of the real is finished; but since in fact the analysis is never
finished and never can be, it is in this sense that they have an ideal and
transcendent character with regard to empirical knowledge. Hence,
without going on indefinitely in an infinite regression, mathematics is
grounded in the one, as if experience reached the atom or the point, and
in the homogeneous and the continuum of space, size, and number, as
if these were the realizable or verified limit of sensible discontinuity and
heterogeneity. The antinomy of the simple and the multiple, of in-
divisibility and of indefinite divisibility is presupposed as resolved in
mathematics; that is the very principle of all calculation; and through this
daring artifice of thought which success justifies, we act as if we had in
hand what will always escape our grasp, unity and the homogeneous
continuum.

On the other side, while the deductive sciences, presupposing at the
outset the analysis to be finished, proceed by *a priori* synthesis to determine the necessary bond that forms a perfect continuity, the sciences of
nature, in describing beings or in determining the facts as they observe
them or as they produce them, always presuppose the original reality, the
relative perfection, the sufficiency of each synthesis as synthesis. The
concrete unity is considered in them as a total which, though divisible,
is not reducible to its parts. Only on this condition are these sciences
possible and valid; for, inasmuch as we do not know the whole of
anything, we would not know anything of the whole, if we could not
latch firmly on to each degree that the order of compositions and decompositions enables us to reach. Thus, the true property of any science
grounded in experience is precisely that which we shall never deduce,
namely, the complex nature, the discontinuity and the heterogeneity of
the objects it takes as the matter of its research. And the quantitative   53
determinations it succeeds in making use of (as, for example, in the study
of chemical compounds) serve only to make evident the precise distinction, the hiatus, the specific and irreducible differences that separate the
closest relatives of the same families and the combinations of the same

sist in effect except through mutual borrowings). —Better still, I bring out that
it is in this reserved field that each science by itself draws its own inspiration and
finds its intimate cohesion. Far then from reducing or suppressing the subjective
element, they are subordinated to it and hang from it. Also neither would it be
enough to recognize that there is present in these positive sciences such an element, without determining its role; for thereby we would only be weakening and
restricting their value, without preserving for the mind access to another
knowledge, to the true subjective science, which is, we shall see how and why,
the science of action.

elements. No, the perfect theory of nature would not resolve it into something purely intellectual, no more than the full knowledge our senses might have of it would reveal it in the fulness of its truth.

There is then in science, indeed in its very principle, a manifest duality.[1] At one time it looks outside the immediately perceived phenomena for what is abstract generality and necessary interconnection. When the nature of compounds and the proper qualities of the elements is left out, mathematical calculus appears as the continuous form of the universe. At another time, the unity of composition being left out, science applies itself to giving the synthetic intuition a quantitative precision and a definite individuality.

Reducing everything to the homogeneous, recognizing and defining heterogeneity everywhere, these two tendencies are equally scientific, these two methods are equally complete and self-sufficient each in its own sense. Both the one and the other use analysis and synthesis; for the first, analysis, for the second, synthesis is hypothetical. For the first, synthesis is, so to speak, analytical *a priori*; for the second, analysis is synthetic *a posteriori*, that is to say, one is built up with the elements of an ideal analysis and the other in its decompositions reaches only real syntheses. For the first, action is an integration whose rigorous formula a perfect calculus would provide; for the second, action is a *sui generis* fact, whose originality no mathematical approximation reveals and which, like every other synthesis, can be known only by direct observation. The positivist conception, the dominant conception of today, according to which the sciences are supposed to follow one another in a unilinear series according to an order of growing complication, is therefore radically wrong.

And at the same time, each of the forms of science has meaning and a reason for being only inasmuch as one duplicates the other in a way and equals the other. Although in the style of mathematics the whole and the part are homogeneous, mathematics constitutes specific syntheses and symbolizes with the heterogeneity of sense knowledge. Although the sciences of nature are grounded on the *quid proprium* of intuition, they claim to introduce into it causal continuity and the law of number. Thus each seems to be a matter, a method and an end for the other.

1. This necessary ambiguity is underlined by the double meaning of *unity*: for one thing, unity is divisible, though not resolvable; for (as Leibniz notes, *Gerhardt* III, 583) fractions, which are the parts of unity, have less simple notions, because whole numbers (less simple than unity) always enter into the notion of fractions. But the parts are not always more simple than the whole, although they are less than the whole: the whole is resolvable, but not divisible. And yet these two functions of *unity* are constantly solidary in fact.

Suffice it to indicate in this way, between the two general forms of science, this solution of continuity, this parallelism and this cooperation. What has been less noticed and is perhaps more worthy of note is that, inside each scientific discipline, in the detail of the procedures of calculus or of experience, in the constitution of positive truths is hidden a similar discordance and is established a similar accord not justified by science. Hence, it is not only as a whole that science is, so to speak, split into two trunks which yet live only in being brought together; it is in the detail of the construction of each one of the sciences that will be revealed both the same incoherence and the same solidarity. At the principle, in the course and at the ideal end of every science, there is an antinomy, and an antinomy resolved in fact.

It is important, then, to examine to what indirect and tacit borrowings each one of them owes its existence and its progress, how finally a mediation is necessary for this perpetual transposition of elements foreign to one another and for this constant collaboration of irreducible methods. For to show that what is transcendent and strange to them in the positive sciences is the very thing that makes them possible and applicable will be to bring to light what, in science itself, requires that science be surpassed. If each one had a sort of independence or self-sufficiency, we would have a right to stop with it and to be content with even its provisional successes. But that is not the way it is; and this imperfection does not come from the defect of its results, which in any event is always partial, but from the nature itself of the truths it reaches and the method it uses. Not only is the science on the way to being completely insufficient, but even supposed as complete and perfect, it is still so: an initial and 55
final weakness of each taken separately and all taken together in their mutual commerce, that is the truth. The positive sciences are not sufficient for us, because they are not self-sufficient.

I

From the simple and the homogeneous, which they suppose from the start as the end of their analysis and which they posit in the principle of their constructions, the exact sciences derive their *a priori* syntheses. But whence comes the very idea of this synthetic procedure that is essential to them; how do we come to consider the construction as a whole in which the materials have determinate relations, an order, a value they did not have before becoming part of it? No doubt, nothing is empirical properly speaking either in the elements or in the plan itself of the mathematical edifice; but nothing is conceivable in it without a primitive borrowing, without a disguised plagiarism, without a continual limitation of the concrete. For it is the proper character of infinitesimal calculus, of that calculation which is the eminent form of every other, of the calculation that inserts mathematics into the very heart of physics and of practice itself, to be at once a fiction and a useful fiction, to remain in the ideal and to be adapted to the concrete, in short to suit the nature of things without claiming to account for the nature of things.[1] Do we

56   not see in effect that the deeper abstract science buries itself into calculations where it seems to flee reality, the more it tends to come back to it, and the better it can be applied to it?

From its origins, indeed, to make it possible, there is in exact science an unnoticed insertion of something other than itself. As Helmholtz remarks, by taking as an experimental basis this simple fact, this simple "sentiment" that in our interior life a fact retained by memory has preceded the actual fact, we can rationally construct all the vast edifice of modern Analysis. What does this mean, if not that all successive syntheses are *a priori*, but that the idea itself of synthesis and the existence of every mathematical relation is grounded in a real experience, on the "sentiment" of a complex unity, as is that of a state of consciousness or of a mental action? The ambition of the exact sciences is to produce from

---

1. To be sure, it can be objected, "the results of calculus have only the significance they can have without burdening mathematics either with metaphysical encumbrances or with utilitarian preoccupations; only experience, it seems, can enable us to give a practical interpretation to abstract formulas." Nevertheless, if we should not subordinate calculus to considerations foreign to calculus, it would be equally wrong to think of it as entirely independent and autonomous. The object of this analysis is to show precisely that, in spite of their ideal and detached character, the exact sciences have no reason for being and no possibility of existence unless, from the beginning, they implicitly tend to become what they are more and more, a substitute for experimental knowledge and an auxiliary of practical activity. The application made of them is not therefore an accessory or derived use, it is an extension in conformity with their original nature and their true destination. The real use they lend themselves to is not extrinsic, it is intrinsic to their very constitution. And in discovering this secret virtue that permeates them from their origin, we will see better how all their progress only manifests, through the interconnection of intellectual necessities, the more profound movement of the will: for it is because they have as their end a practical interest and an efficacious operation that these sciences arise from the very depth of our activity and are organized spontaneously under the influence of the same interior law that presides over our entire life. Thus mathematics itself will appear as a form of the development of willing; it will find its place in the series of means we use to resolve the problem of action; it will become, in the learned knowledge we will have of our acts, what it is in the living reality of our operations, an element of the solution.

the continuous and homogeneous they dispose of at the start all the diversity of the formulas and theorems that more and more equal the multiplicity of the forms of life. From the elements they combine they constitute as it were ideal species whose properties and generic individuality, so to speak, they consider. But if at the heart of each of these analytical groupings a unity is formed, if there is a distinct integration of the integrated elements, it is through a daring which mathematics takes advantage of without justifying it in any degree. A synthesis constituted *a priori*, a system of homogeneous elements considered as heterogeneous to them, a whole analytically formed and seen as non-decomposable into its component parts, that is strangeness itself, and it is not even wondered at. Thanks to a schematism, borrowed by way of transposition and analogy from sensible intuition, and which is like a perception of the unreal or an imagination of the imaginary, thought is exercised on a fictitious matter abstracted from positive experience; and having eliminated the sensible quality, *vinculum perceptionis* (the bond of perception), it relies, in this sort of analytical synthesis, on a pure experience and on a world of intellectualized phenomena.

If from this point of view we examine for a moment the development 57 of the exact sciences, we will see in them the image of the evolution which the sciences of nature will claim to give as a description of the organic world; and through this parallelism worthy of attention, we will find in mathematics the constant and indispensable influence of a conception foreign to mathematics.

They were born, these sciences, only from the moment when, in the homogeneous and the continuous, they supposed a differentiation and possible relations of size and number; that is the ideal matter on which they will impose the form of their deductions. Possessing only this pure abstract at the beginning, they look on the element at first as isolated and inert, even within composition and spontaneity. It is through this abstract simplicity that they have access to rigorousness, to clarity, and to exactness; single element is juxtaposed to single element in the whole; and according to this first mechanistic conception, the universal system and each particular synthesis is nothing more than an elementary relation and an order of the constitutive parts; any problem can be reduced by analysis to what is simple, without any need for looking at the intrinsic organization itself of the composite. Thus is constituted the quite abstract and quite homogeneous first milieu wherein will be deployed, like a hierarchy of more and more organized forms, the growing complications of science; thus, through an original elaboration, the fundamental principles of rational mechanics emerge from experience. That is a necessary fulcrum, but it is only a point of departure.

"Composites symbolize with simples," as Leibniz notes; that is to say that in turn they can be considered as unities, but as complex unities, and that between the element and the whole a hierarchy of definite constructions is inserted. Always, then, the same postulate reappears: a mathematical construction is constituted, without having recourse to and without ever reaching the *quid proprium* (something proper) of empirical intuition, through the force of analysis alone as an original novelty and an *a priori* synthesis. And in this rational world are formed closed systems and a whole set of subordinate functions, just as are established, in the world of living beings, multiple relations, an organization of parts, and an accumulation of vital force.

58   The composite, then, behaves like a single center, like a whole; and in the unity of its development there is a world of internal movements, intimate echoes and repercussions of energy. Thus, dynamism is added to mechanism or even substituted for it, without suppressing it. The progress of calculus (from Descartes to Leibniz) was to grasp this complex unity along with the infinite it harbors, the effort it envelops, the action it produces. It is in this way that sensible qualities themselves, through this mediating notion of the infinite, are reducible to or rather convertible with mathematical expressions. What does that mean here again, if not that the deductive sciences go beyond and advance only by accepting a notion that contradicts them and by inserting within themselves as it were an admission of their incoherence? Leibniz, at the very moment when he sees to what extent the concept of an actual infinite number is contradictory, admits that every finite reality contains an actual infinite; this is to say that calculus can reach empirical data only by bringing the real and the zero together with the data in the infinite, in the mathematical infinite whose character is quite negative since it is proper to the limit never to be reached. Here, then, it is the fiction itself which enables us to reach reality. Descartes surely had a vivid sense of this difficulty; it was even the springboard for his entire metaphysical enterprise; but he tied experimental knowledge to deduction only with an artificial bond. Totally sacrificing one of the aspects of the problem and subordinating sense intuition to the universal mathematics he dreamed of establishing, he did not have the idea of a true and original science of nature. It is through an intimate and intrinsic relation that Leibniz embeds calculus into the very heart of physical reality and subordinates to it even the spontaneity of force.

Each system becomes in turn an element in higher syntheses. Once it has been considered as closed and independent for the sake of the deductive progression, it is made to enter into composition with others in order to bring the entire hierarchy of these synthetic constructions into participation with the universal system. If this system of the universe in turn is considered in its unity as a determinate whole, it is possible to make the homogeneity of indefinite space express the unlimited hetero-geneity of the relations it contains, and to formulate in the language of the relations of quantity all the variations of quality. Thus, by consider-ing a space with n dimensions, higher geometry introduces into the study of movements the character of direction and quality, the quality that is $\alpha\pi\epsilon\iota\rho\sigma\varsigma$, not indeterminate, not indeterminable, but entailing an infinity of particular determinations or directions. Contingency itself is therefore brought back to determinism and to mathematical necessity, without los-ing anything of its character.[1]

59

Nor is this all. From the moment we conceive the unity of the universal system, we are led, by a new initiative of that rational imagination that conducts its experiments in the *a priori*, to conceive the possibility of other systems, to look upon the first as only one particular instance of a geometry more general than the common one, as an element for new combinations or for ulterior syntheses. That is the meaning of those new attempts made by thought to emancipate itself from the postulates or even from the laws that had always seemed most necessary for it. The world, as the progress of mathematics leads us to understand it, is not a closed system; it is unlimited, $\alpha\sigma\rho\iota\sigma\tau\sigma\varsigma$. What we call life and freedom can intervene in it without disturbing the calculus. Is it disorder or a vio-

---

1. "Not only does nothing happen in the world that would be absolutely ir-regular, but we could not even imagine anything of the sort. For let us suppose, for example, that someone makes a number of points on a paper haphazardly, as do those who practice the ridiculous art of Geomancy; I say it is possible to find a geometrical line whose notion would be constant and uniform according to a certain rule, so that this line would pass through all these points, and in the same order as the hand had made them. And if someone were to trace in a single stroke a line that would be now straight, now circular, now of another nature, it is possible to find a notion or a rule or an equation common to all the points of this line in virtue of which these same changes are supposed to take place." (Leibniz, *Gerhardt,* vol. IV, p. 431; cf. VI, 262, 629; IV, 569). — Some contem-porary mathematicians have developed and applied these views. Reimann's theory of cuts developed in the work of M. Hermite on definite integrals makes it possible to give the formula not only of a continuous development, but of a series of lines which, at some arbitrary point with regard to coordinates, take whatever position and inaugurate whatever process one may wish. At the limit, the necessary and the contingent coincide, each remaining what it is. Or rather, the exact sciences have no reason for distinguishing one from the other; that is why they are radically incompetent regarding the problem of freedom. What is called the necessity of mathematical deductions is therefore without any analogy, without any relation whatsoever to what could be said about the internal deter-minism of acts.

60 lation of the law of conservation of energy that something new should be incessantly produced in it and, so to speak, something miraculous? No, it is a more complete order. Already broader formulas of a general algebra enable the mind to express rigorously this improvisation of movement and this arbitrary aspect of spontaneity. Indetermination thus enters into line with determinism itself; and it is conceivable that a perfect mathematics could give an absolutely singular solution for each point. Thus, it would be the image of the sensibility which reproduces under an infinity of individual forms one same reality and a single life, or the symbol of a special Providence which would make of each atom a whole world and a center of perspective, or again the expression of that charity which gives itself entirely to all and which realizes the perfection of calculus.

What could be more beautiful and more solid, it would seem, than this triumphant construction of a science able to erect a universe and to imprison the world, all possible worlds, in its formulas! But it is only a spell to be broken. — Mathematics can be adapted to experience, but it does not start from it. — It borrows from experience something to subsist by, but it does not arrive at it. — It seems to find a confirmation of its reality in facts, but by nature it has no relation to facts. And while it appears necessary as the only form of phenomena which it serves to determine and govern, its symbols are arbitrary; it is an act of the mind that posits them. To grasp this act in the quick, think of the mathematical limit which is never reached, but which we must begin by admitting as given in fact; that is to say that at the end we must still presuppose the point of departure, that the final certitude remains grounded on the initial fiction, and that the highest guaranty of calculus is outside of calculus. We do not reach the limit, we start from it in order to be able to come back to it while inserting under the fact the whole world of mathematical determinations. Or rather, we come back to it as if we started from it; we start from it as if we were coming back to it. External to science, the limit is necessary for science. And this fiction which makes infinitesimal calculus possible is identical to the simple operation that posits unity. Everywhere the same cut and the same suture. Everywhere the same arbitrary and necessary character of the symbols.

The exact sciences, then, remain marked with this triple stigma, and that even down to their most tenuous tissue:

61 1. They render no account either of the way they are disengaged from reality or of the way they come back to it and adjust to it. The efficacity they have, they do not explain; what they effect, they do not know.

2. Though they seem grounded in reality and to rule in it, they are foreign to it; they cannot account for the simplest sensation, nor for the

least act. In quality, which as quality escapes their grasp, in the hierarchy of each synthesis that forms a new world, there is an element that is absolutely refractory to them, something, for example, that will remain proper to chemical compounds when we shall have succeeded in translating their combinations into the spirit and the language of mathematical physics, something that is given in the first intuition, προτερον προς ημας (what is first with regard to us). What they reveal to us, they do not reveal as we know it.

3. In their work of continuous integration, they are constantly appealing to a synthetic procedure alone capable of offering them a matter that is, so to speak, completely formal; but this very initiative of thought escapes them; they are strangers even in their own realm. In these sciences where everything seems penetrated with light and where the distinction of ideas reaches its perfection, the competence of the science does not belong to the science; *what* they know, they do not *know* as they know *it*.

— Hence, at the origin, in the course and at the end of the exact sciences, in their internal constitution as in their natural relations with the other sciences, everywhere in them there subsists a tacit postulate and a kind of permanent hiatus. To be sure, this is the point at which the experimental sciences enter into commerce with them,[1] and it is through this commerce that science can lay claim to unity and to the sufficiency of a universal explanation. But, from the side of mathematics at least, the gap is not bridged, it will never be, it cannot be bridged by them anymore than in them. No matter how developed we suppose them to be, they do not exhaust, they do not attain perceived reality; they always bear in them even down to their furthest deductions the unsoundness of their principle, the fictitious character of their initial postulate; and if

62

---

1. A simple example will bring to light this useful incoherence of scientific procedures. Let us suppose we have to find the expression of the intensity of a sound. To analyse the phenomenon under study, to define the very intensity of the sound and represent it as the sum of the lively semi-forces of the air molecules of a whole vibratory wave, we suppose matter as discontinuous and formed of separate points. But by remaining faithful to this conception about the molecular constitution of air, the only conception that enables us to determine with precision the proper object of the operation and even of enunciating it, to add up these lively semi-forces, we would have to know the number of molecules, their mass and the speed that animates each one of them at the moment in question. There is no way out. Therefore, to effect the synthesis and evaluate this intensity of sound, it becomes necessary to do an about-face: setting aside the first hypothesis in order to apply the mathematical procedures to the phenomenon it served to define, we will reason as if matter were continuous.

they succeed in practice, it is without justifying this success nor even this use. Also, contrary to the Pythagoreans and even to Descartes, who saw in mathematics the most real foundation of things in opposition to sensible appearance, people seem inclined henceforth to find this more solid reality in experimental truths; for, since they have taken on a scientific rigor, they appear to play, *vis-à-vis* their mathematical substitute, the role that mathematics seemed to play *vis-à-vis* sensible phenomena. Is it then in these positive sciences that we finally shall find a stopping place for the mind, the limit of our voluntary curiosity and the definition of our action?

II

The point of departure of the experimental sciences is not easy to discern with precision; hence it was late that these sciences truly had their inception and grew. But even from this origin on, an incoherence will appear analogous to the one that remains fixed at the heart of mathematics, a secret postulate that will insinuate itself in all their developments, and from which, at the very end of what they tend to, they will not be emancipated.

The complex simplicity of immediate perception and the irreducible intuition of the senses seem to be the foundation of all experimental knowledge, since every ulterior attempt at analysis disfigures this concrete given without giving any account for it.

But this first given is absolutely confused; and in the midst of this confusion, differentiation is infinite: the sensible universe is for the senses a chaos; and it is in this disorder that analytical observation endeavors to discover some order and laws.

But, whence do we learn to consider the world as a whole where there are distinct parts? Whence comes the idea of this analytical procedure which, under the primitive indetermination of quality, introduces numerical clarity and distinction? No experimental knowledge is conceivable without a fictitious analysis and without an initial abstraction that artificially delimits the very matter of observation. Every perceived fact, however vague it may be, thus presupposes an effort of elaboration for which experience has no account at the very moment it observes it. The synthetic character of sensible data is therefore the result of an analysis foreign to these data themselves: the possibility of observation is already a postulate.[1]

1. To say that observation is not self-sufficient and that experience implies a postulate is not to speak of an *a priori* or of innateness; the question pertains to

And now let us follow the progress of the inductive sciences. We shall see that they seek, on the one hand, to bind together in a rigorous determinism all the discontinuous forms which the analysis of reality presents, and on the other hand, to define in precise terms these distinct and original forms within the universal continuity itself. But always, for their analyses and their syntheses, they need to take a step where they are no longer treading on their own ground.

I. — Indeed, it was not without delay or difficulty that we began again to consider the sensible fact (that phenomenon which the first scientific step had been to contradict in a certain way) as the proper and direct object of science. There is science only of the general, antiquity had thought. Henceforth the perspective seems almost reversed, and it seems that there is science only of the concrete, the positive, the particular. As much as the fact and the individual were scorned, so now we like to look for a precious lesson in singularity and anomaly; and we know how to make the monstrous exception produce an abundance of new truths. How, then, have we managed to introduce into the study of the qualitative and discontinuous phenomenon an order, a precision, a determination which have made or will make possible a true science of experience?

It was by the concurrence of these two conceptions which developed separately, and which have not yet to this day succeeded in coming together on all points: on one side, the idea of a necessary succession of phenomena; on the other, a numerical characteristic for the diverse sensible species: — science of the concatenation of facts; — science of the real forms and of their relations.

1. What first appeared to take on the character of universality and scientific necessity amid the infinite confusion of singular facts is the constancy of the relations and the fixity of their concatenation. Now, to establish these long sequences of facts integrated into laws analogous to the long series of deductive truths, not only is it necessary to have recourse always to the artificial analysis whose indispensable role we took note of for any observation of facts, but also, through a new effort which sensible intuition does not justify, we must provisionally abstract from the original content of each contingent phenomenon to consider only its necessary form. Thus it is that, in affirming universal determin-

another order entirely, for it has to do, not with the origin, but with the originality of our knowledge. It is to say simply that, as the previous chapter had indicated, to observe we have to see and sense otherwise than we do immediately. Besides, before we can arrive at numerical precision, there is first a difficult effort to achieve a qualitative precision: consider how in the *Philebus* Plato describes the invention of letters and of musical notations.

ism, the physicist, through a redirected borrowing from mathematical conceptions, is only designating with a symbolic expression that single formula which governs and determines the immense concatenation of phenomena with their growing complication; that is how the hypothesis of the unity of forces expresses what in observation is foreign or even contrary to observation, which never grasps the homogeneous and continuous. This is to say that, without being a mathematic of nature, since they do not go back to the pure and fictitious unity which ideal analysis alone reaches, these sciences are nevertheless like a "mathematization" of experience; for, starting from the concrete unity they borrow from observation, they assume the "mathematoid" form, so to speak, of the exact sciences. Fundamentally independent from them, they still live and develop only by incorporating into themselves, in a subalternate and subsidiary role, all the resources of mathematical calculation. *Scire est mensurare* (to know is to measure), according to the saying of Kepler.

The introduction of mathematics into the sciences of nature does not therefore constitute an autonomous mathematic; there they are only an instrument subordinated to a method opposed to their own. The calculations in them are not strictly calculation; so that, to study the simplest measure of physics closely, one has to squint somehow.[1] And yet the convergence of these divergent rays seems natural and perfect. It is enough for the physicist to set up a coherent relation between the intuitions of experience that entail no direct measure and certain symbols submitted only to the double condition of being measurable and of conventionally representing empirical data. What he is looking for is a manageable summary and a systematic coordination, not an explanation, of experimental laws. And what is arbitrary in his initial convention persists in all developments and even in the best verified results of science.

2. But mathematical physics is not the whole of the science of nature. Parallel to it, and even prior to it, another form of scientific experience has developed. Indeed, while some were discovering the laws that ex-

---

1. This uneasiness we experience in analysing certain scientific procedures comes from bringing together two orders which, even united, remain separate. Thus, for example, to study hydrostatic pressure, we define a quantity which we call the pressure at one *point*; but as soon as we borrow this expression from the abstract ideal of mathematics we find ourselves obliged to return to the concrete, as we hasten to say that pressure P at point A will represent the pressure on the *unity of surface* taken around the point and smaller, it is true, than any conceivable dimension. This fleeting unity, therefore, must refer to the concrete, to make sense and be of some use in physics, and to the abstract, for the mathematical deduction to be possible: it seems to be a question neither of the geometric point, it is too small, nor of the physical point, it is too large.

press the constant succession of phenomena, others were endeavoring to determine the sensible species and the living forms, without suspecting at first that there might be a real solidarity and continuity between these sciences of *facts* and these sciences of *beings*.[1]

And already, to discern the distinctive and hierarchical characters of each of the syntheses realized in nature, a difficult effort of analysis was necessary. All the ancient classifications exhausted themselves in the effort. Indeed, how can we substitute fixed conceptions and precise definitions for the fleeting data of intuition? Besides, it would be wrong to imagine that definitions *per genus proximum et differentiam specificam* (through proximate genus and specific difference), like those of Aristotle and the scholastics, or even that the methodical classifications of modern naturalists are sufficiently rigorous. Their value is neither properly philosophical, because they bear only on the relations of subordinated phenomena without attaining the depth of beings, nor properly scientific, because these descriptions, however precise they may be, these classifications, however natural they may seem, only note down, in detail it is true, but with a "literary" precision that calls only for a spirit of finesse, sensible characteristics and complex qualities whose internal composition or law of production or numerical equivalents have not been penetrated. Thus, the zoologist, to establish his distinctions, constantly needs to appeal to notions of subjective psychology.

How then introduce, into the study of the real syntheses whose diverse qualities experience reveals to us, the precision necessary for mathematics to have something to work on? It is chemistry, it is well known how, that began to discover what we could call the quantitative histology of bodies. And not only does it define the numerical relations of the elements in the compounds, but it also establishes general laws, the law of definite equivalents and of multiple proportions, which enable us to extend mathematics to all the variety of combinations. Now, if the first observation that isolates a fact in the universal milieu already supposes an artificial analysis, then chemical experimentation, which decomposes a qualitative synthesis into quantitative elements, transposes by the very fact one order of phenomena into a completely heterogeneous order, without any explanation for this passage. In order to introduce the scale into the laboratory, and to express in function of a unity of weight the body submitted to experimentation, one had to have in view something other than a banal weighing (a weighing which besides implies a mental operation analogous to the association of a continuous duration with the

----

1. It goes without saying that the words *being, reality* here have no metaphysical value; so far they designate only a system of given phenomena.

divisions of a space measured by a regular movement); one had to be looking for a way of translating the quality of a synthesis into definite quantities of its elements. This initiative whence chemistry was born chemistry lives by without justifying it: the cohesion of the science is not scientific within the science.

3. But after mathematics has penetrated into the physical sciences, after it has become implanted in the natural sciences, a new problem arises. Can we tie together the knowledge of concatenated facts and that of coordinated forms? And do we grasp well enough the bearing of this question? To reduce the diversity of "the beings perceived" to the concatenation of "the integrated phenomena" would be, in effect, to express sensible nature in function of those abstract symbols mathematics has at their disposal; it would be to make it such that, in the *a posteriori* itself, everything would be subject in a certain way to *a priori* calculation; it would be to represent with a precise formula the order of production of the phenomena and the possible or real transformations of the natural species. But how, in a common alliance with the exact sciences, can we connect in this way the study of classifications with the study of genetic or mechanical laws?

The recent advances in chemical notation and in crystallography appear to be a double progression toward the solution to this problem.

—On the one hand, in effect, using the double idea of *analogy* and of *substitution* that serves to determine a *chemical type* as a foundation, we succeed in bringing into evidence, through a progressive elimination of the arbitrary element which the appreciation of these purely qualitative characteristics introduces, all the types with which it is possible to connect a single compound, and in establishing what is called *the formula of constitution*. Thanks to the latter, we can classify and even foresee the reactions a body will give rise to; we can reproduce this body by means of other bodies by way of substitution; we can effect a synthesis. The numerical secret of the combination seems to become in this way a practical secret of production.

—On the other hand, crystallography manages to institute a determinate relation between the disposition of the systems it studies and the very structure of molecules. And if, to define chemical analogies, isomorphism is an essential characteristic, is that not to admit that between the qualitative nature of the combinations and the geometric constitution of the elements there is a fixed relation to be discovered? The formula of constitution and that other formula, no longer chemical, but mathematical, which expresses the architectural plan of the atoms[1] in the

1. The ambiguity we have already noted in the use of the word *unity* reappears here. The atom seems to be considered as an element now quantitative,

molecule, can therefore be connected through a system of coherent symbols; and in this point the physical sciences were welded to the natural sciences, inasmuch as they are both mutually inserted into mathematics.

But let us take note. The great highways from abstract terms to the most complex syntheses may well open up wider and wider before conquering Science; we must not let ourselves be taken in by its very success. To be sure, the symbols set up by the scientist end up being so coherent among themselves, having such an efficacity, being realized so visibly in his hands, that the temptation becomes great for him to look upon all this symbolism as the faithful image of reality, as reality itself. It is projected outside with the conviction that the laws of rational mechanics, the constructions of the crystallographer or the paradigms of the chemist are the expression of a real mechanism to which, under the guise of scientific certitude, it is appropriate to attribute an objective and truly metaphysical bearing. Therein lies the fundamental error to be overcome. 68

For the point of departure of each science harbors a germ whose arbitrary nature a successful growth may hide but does not suppress. Everywhere at the origin of scientific procedures, an artifice has to mask the unexplained passage from the order of quality to the order of measure; everywhere a decree intervenes to set up a fictitious relation which alone enables one to symbolize with the other. But because new conventions will join science to science in a way each day more complete and more efficacious, will the arbitrary character of the first set-up disappear? Far from it. It is not the convergence, itself also artificial, of all these fictions that will empower science to express reality itself and make of it the last word.

Also, whether it is a matter of mathematical constructions, of physical theories, of crystalline forms and molecular arrangements, of atomic combinations, or of biological laws, in all cases it could only be a question of coherent symbols, without our ever having to project these symbols themselves into a reality distinct from them. To suppose some intermediary entity and a subsistent mechanism between empirical data and scientific symbolism is to impose a quite gratuitous hindrance; it is to give rise to complications that restrain the fruitfulness of science by depriving it of the diversity of useful theories that can be developed at one and the same time from the moment when, instead of seeing explanations of things in them, we look only for a means of coordinating experimental laws; it is to run the risk of illusions able to warp at once the spirit of science and the spirit of philosophy through a confusion of competences. 69

now qualitative; here unsplittable and yet composite, there divisible and yet irreducible.

To be sure, theories and calculations always have to be referred to an experimental verification: based on fact initially, they return to fact, which remains the arbiter. But the theories are not homogeneous with the initial data, nor do the practical consequences which analysis deduces have the least natural relation to the theories they serve to control. The bridge between the two does not come under science, although science has to cross it. The whole of science, then, is to coordinate the facts and the laws which experience reveals to us, but which only the help of mathematics enables us to enunciate with precision. It does not worry about knowing whether its symbolic fictions are true absolutely, nor even whether they have verisimilitude, as long as they establish a relation as coherent as possible between the calculation and the facts. If there be any need to set up many conventions at the same time, it does so, with only the condition that, between these diversely useful hypotheses, there be found no formal incompatibility.

Also must we not, under the cover of science, reinstate the false mysticism of sensibility by giving back to the data of intuition a consistency they do not have. No more than mathematics do the experimental sciences exhaust the simplest knowledge. They may well ally themselves among themselves; their very alliance remains a problem. Each one apart offers an explanation that seems complete, that seems even to absorb the other correlative explanation, but that remains distinct from it. And each subsists truly only to the extent that it becomes a function of the other. But it is not because they correspond to one another that the two series, the one or the other, or the one and the other, are real. Also, in opposition to current prejudices, physical and chemical laws are symbols that have neither more nor less subsistence than geometrical formulas.

Continuity and discontinuity, then, are not the incompatible theses of a metaphysical antinomy, but the solidary terms of scientific symbolism. The role of experimental science is to bring out discontinuity in continuity itself. For in it mathematical deduction remains and will always remain subordinated to the knowledge of what each synthesis has that is irreducible to the elements of the analysis. To suppose, for example, as Kekule does, that the combination of atoms takes place by virtue of their specific properties according to the simplest numbers, is that not to recognize that the intuition of a qualitative datum must precede any application of mechanics and that the intervention of mathematics, far from suppressing the originality of the sensible species, serves to highlight it?

Also the ambition of the sciences of nature must be, without attributing to their results the value of a real history of nature, to find at the very heart of continuity and determinism a new method for individualizing bodies, by considering them as polyzoarial species. Formed from the same elements, combined according to uniform laws, compounds constitute a new form, quite different from the sum of their parts, and whose physiognomy no formula can predict. Water is water and nothing else, it is not oxygen or hydrogen.

As experimental science necessarily starts from an empirical given, it therefore returns necessarily to the empirical intuition. As it develops, it recognizes, along with a more profound unity of composition and more general laws, a more radical and more precise distinction of compounds. Thus it is that, at the last boundaries reached by analysis, we find always the same definite diversity among the data of experience; in spectrum analysis, the characteristic bands of each element have their specific arrangement or, so to speak, organization; and never is one system of such spectral bands transformed into a system by imperceptible transitions, no matter how small the difference. A state of equilibrium is changed only to move to another equally precise state of equilibrium. And far from the progress of chemistry consisting in reducing everything to a homogeneous determinism, it consists in grounding the heterogeneity of the discontinuous syntheses in determinism, in focusing on them precisely, and in defining them.

This point is so important that it is good to insist on it a bit more by examining the recent moves of the sciences of nature. Avoiding the temerity of their new pretentions, we shall see to what conditions their progress and their very existence remains subordinated; and we shall prepare the way for discovering their irremediable lacunae.

II. — The place where today perhaps the greatest effort is being made   71
to unite and to subordinate the descriptive study of beings to the rigorous determination of interconnected facts is in the field of biology. The claim of transformism is to substitute for the apparent distinction of living forms the continuity of a progressive evolution; it is to discover the formula of the total concert and to erect the system of relations defined in time and space as a real explanation of nature. What is scientific about this endeavor, and what will it bring about in the general development of experimental science?

Transformism is an *alchemy* of nature. That is to point out in a word both what is useful and fruitful about it, and what is transitory and incomplete. Its usefulness, first, consists in this: to suppose, underneath the brute diversity and the apparent independence of beings that coexist or succeed one another, a continuous bond; and in this way to prepare the ground for a new extension of mathematical determinism and to suggest that, even in the most supple organisms, there is still a law of numbers to be found, *mensura et pondere* (measure and weight). It senses that the living relations that make up the unity of the world have their equivalent in other, abstract relations which deduction will establish in its technical language. Going from the homogeneous to the heterogeneous, cosmic, physical, biological, social actions result from an adaptation to the universal milieu. Thus every fact, like every being, is an expression of the total continuity, solidarity and unity, a product of the common history of all, a particular and passing solution to the general problem of the world. And this problem grows more complex as the successive solutions enrich it with new data through the incessant search for an equilibrium that is always being upset. Great and fruitful is the idea of a sympathetic solidarity among all beings that, as it were, build one another up, just as the members of a perpetually growing organism complement one another; a prophetic hypothesis that symbolizes, but without scientific rigor, the precise formula of the concert composed by the universe; a presentiment of truths that a more advanced science will have to define and limit by completing them.

Indeed, what is lacking in transformism, what makes it fiction rather than a science of nature, is the following. As the alchemist, starting from the transmutations he saw taking place before his eyes, made pretense of finally extracting the gold from all the bodies which he thought he was leading to their perfection, so also the transformist is persuaded he will discover the progression of the rudimentary beginnings of life toward the higher forms and toward humanity. Must not the reproach made against one be applied, by analogy, to the other? In what, then, does alchemy merit the discredit of false science that has been associated with its name? Satisfied ordinarily with resemblances or superficial verisimilitudes, it mixed the most temerarious views in with its positive experiments, without discerning the part played by the imaginary in the perception of the real. Lacking a method able to eliminate the chances of error and to determine the precise object of its inquiries, out of its curiosity it sought a goal external to science itself; and, prescinding from all the irreducible qualities of the bodies that direct experience offered it, it endeavored nevertheless, through a lack of coherence that went unnoticed, to reduce all of them to one and the same quality.

So it is with the transformist: allowing for differences, he seems to be at the point where, not knowing the positive laws of chemical compounding, people still believed in the transmutation of elements. When he appeals to the struggle for survival or natural selection, when amidst the anomalies of heredity he seizes upon certain visible transformations to construct a thesis which he hastens to declare scientific, is that not still to be persuaded that, in science, verisimilitudes and descriptive approximations are enough? Is it not to proceed by half measures, without being careful first to define and delimit the affirmations through the negative method of counter-proof, which alone can eliminate the causes of illusion and impose rigorous conclusions and confer upon them a demonstrative value? If he judges according to the mere observation of favorable appearances that the living species issued from one another through imperceptible transformations, he is behaving, if not like the alchemist who calls mercury quick-silver, at least like the chemist who would imagine, between carbon monoxide and carbonic acid, a gradation of more or less oxygenated states wherein we could pass from one to the other.

To judge roughly about organic modifications or resemblances, to presume imperceptible transitions, to hope that, by pulling the stages of the universal metamorphosis infinitely close together, we shall cause all difficulty and all discontinuity to vanish, like a housekeeper who disperses a pile of dust to make it invisible to less observant eyes, is therefore to make illegitimate use of mathematical analogies and of the illusions of the imagination in opposition to the method and the originality of the natural sciences. As legitimate and scientific as it is to establish the close dependence of parts that sustain one another, and to have the same elements and the same laws of composition circulating from one end of the world to the other, it is no less temerarious and inconsistent to misrepresent, in the midst of a certain homogeneity, an equally certain heterogeneity.

For even supposing that in the laboratory of nature we were to see a new species come from a determinate species under the influence of complex causes, as unforeseen combinations are formed in a retort where many substances are mixed together, the problem of the transmission and the transformation of the organism would not thereby be resolved. If the alchemist was inconsequential in suppressing all the specific qualities of bodies to look for one final quality, the transformist is equally inconsequential when he prescinds from the derived species, as if it did not have its irreducible quality, in order to concentrate on the original species, on the primitive cell which he considers as a fixed datum. The former did not believe in the specificity of metals, and yet he was looking for a fixed species, gold; the latter does not believe in the specificity of organisms, and he claims to reduce all beings to one type; that is to say, in abstracting from the heterogeneous quality, he misuses homogeneous continuity to definitively set up one initial or final quality, as if there could be one unique type from which the others would come through combination, in the same way as quantities come from numerical unities.

Therefore, we must admit from the start, and beginning with the first germ of life, an infinitesimal coordination of parts, a specific system, a combination of the organized elements that is quite *sui generis*. Otherwise there would be no biological chemistry, nor any science possible about life, because everything would be amorphous in life. If a definite synthesis changes, it can only form another definite synthesis, just as a distinct individual comes from a distinct individual. Whatever the origin of the living species, the question of their fundamental difference therefore remains intact: there is an essential distinction on which the positive character of the sciences of nature depends. The problem of the real origin and of the constitution of beings is quite different from the problem of the historical descent and the organic composition of living forms; and in order not to do metaphysics without knowing it, we must separate these problems, since science is forever incompetent regarding the first.

Under what condition will phylogeny and ontogeny take on a properly scientific character; and what will remain of transformism when, after ceasing to be a doctrine and to aspire to pronounce the last word and hold the great secret of things, it takes its place in the system of the experimental sciences, which will preserve and surpass the truth of this hypothesis, as of so many others, after having avoided and condemned its excesses?

To the extent that one can look into the future, no doubt this much will remain. We shall know scientifically that, from the last always provisional element that analysis will reach to the most complex syntheses of life, there circulates one and the same sap and the same formula of composition. Already crystallography is studying the architectural plan of the atoms in the molecule. If it succeeds in determining how the elements combine and are composed, how they are juxtaposed in crystallizing according to mechanical laws which mathematics will be able to grasp, then organic compounds will themselves be able to be defined rigorously in function of their histological structure; then we shall no doubt know how the connexion of organs and the correlation of forms, whose harmony among higher beings seems to obey more a law of aesthetic finality than a geometric order, depends upon the specific nature of the elementary combinations that are expressed in the whole of the living being; we shall know how the organic synthesis is subject to the precise laws of a crystallization,[1] how even the variety of races according to milieus is a case of polymorphism. Thus the unity of composition in nature and the universal concatenation of facts, forms and beings would no longer be an indeterminate hypothesis or a vague approximation

---

1. We must in effect distinguish between the constitution of the organic elements and the composition or the arrangement of the organs: to effect the synthesis of gallic acid is not to produce a nutgall. Do we appreciate the difficulty of defining the law of this assemblage *exactly*?

based on verisimilitudes or generalities; it would be a formula that deduction could exploit, and which would verify in rigorous detail the old
saying: *Homo de limo terrae* (man is from the slime of the earth). That   75
is how not only astronomy, but also physics, and chemistry, and now
biology, and perhaps soon sociology no longer appear to hinge on a
problem of rational mechanics. An obviously fanciful result; but it is
useful to suppose science as perfected, in order to see that even then
scientific cohesion would not exist.

But how can this real continuity be thus mathematically determined?
Will it be on condition that among all the forms of the organization there
will be imperceptible gradations and confused indetermination as in a
mass of dough ready to be molded little by little by all sorts of vague influences? In no way. For, quite on the contrary, the determinism of the
mathematical continuity in nature requires that at each stage, as close as
we suppose them to be, in each of the particular syntheses, as analogous
as they may be, there be a precise determination and an intrinsic organization of the original composite. In the experimental sciences, therefore,
the use of continuous deduction is subordinated to the discontinuity of
the real syntheses; and quantity is appropriate in it only to bring out
what is always proper to and irreducible in quality. Once numbers have
been introduced into them, the sensible data are maintained by the precision and the rigid fixity of mathematics against mathematics itself.

Hence, when we study the architectural structure of atoms in the
genesis of molecules, under what conditions can the problem be conceived, raised and resolved? It is under the condition of considering that
the diversity of the cooperating parts forms a systematic arrangement.
Now every disposition, $\tau\alpha\xi\iota\varsigma$, every complex unity, every intelligible
form, every system as an organic system, exists only as perception and
quality. Far from its being reducible integrally to its elements, the elements have their name, on the contrary, and play their role only in function of the whole on which they depend. It is all the more so when it is
a question, not just of the combinations of organic chemistry, but of the
organs themselves and of their assemblage. If the elementary parts in a
living body are determined rigorously as in the crystal, the whole is not
of indefinite malleability; it is, on the contrary, from its total quality,
from its specific originality, that all the detail of the biological chemistry   76
proper to each organism results. Experimental science is a science only
to the extent that, in determining the precise laws of the combinations
and of the universal solidarity with a mathematical continuity, it fixes by
that very fact the distinction and the proper quality of the syntheses of
which the first experience gives an indeterminate perception.

Also, in the study of the hierarchy of forms, henceforth united to that of the concatenation of facts, a two-fold danger must be avoided. On the one hand, among the species that nature presents for observation, it would be wrong to see only relations of juxtaposition, as if, realizing a very ideal plan by their diversity, their analogies did not reveal any kinship or mutual dependence. On the other hand, it would be wrong, on the basis of observations always gross and incompetent when they bear on the purely apparent characteristics of living forms, to believe in an indeterminate transformation of beings. As in inorganic combinations there are genera and natural families, so in the world of life there are organic systems, which, whatever their origin and filiation, constitute instances of definite equilibrium and original syntheses.

To be sure, the same elements can be found in the whole series; but the diversity of their assemblage is, in a sense, something more real and more essential than the very unity of their composition: that is the fact that resists all reduction, even after deduction has determined its infinitesimal generation, or even after observation has recognized its historical dependence. No composite is reducible to components; while it does not get by without them, it always gets beyond them. That is why the relation of cause to effects cannot be analytical; and whoever recognizes this truth no longer has the right to reduce everything in nature to the determinism of facts.

In short, the bond between the closest states is never perceived by direct experience, even when we know their conditions, their relation and their connections. Analysis necessarily omits the x whose action presided over the internal organization; even the recomposition does not reveal to the observer the profound operation that takes place below the sense level and unknown to his calculations. Once the elements are placed in the presence of one another and the conditions have come together, it is up to nature to complete the rest secretly; every generation takes place in the night. We may well discover intermediary types and transitory species, but empirical continuity will always be an approximation, and will represent only in a symbolic way the mathematical continuity which alone has an absolute rigor. The error of transformism is to think that all the forms of science are tied to one another of themselves, without seeing that there is in them and among them a perpetual incoherence. By attributing the value of a universal explanation to the very thing that needs to be explained, it falsifies what scientific truths it has to offer through the illegitimate extension it gives them. It is therefore only a hybrid construction; and the true science of nature is the one that, knowing how to determine rigorously the continuous interconnection of discontinuous beings, focuses on what is proper to each synthesis, τοδε τι (this here), without mistaking relations for beings nor even a historical succession for a real explanation.

Thus, a hierarchy of quite distinct and quite solidary forms appears, no longer just to the first inspection of the untutored senses, but also to the most enlightened look of the scientist. The explanation of the world by the observational sciences, while basing itself on an abstract continuity, must be and will remain discontinuous; and regarding the whole as well as the detail of the objects of experience, diverse viewpoints are open, diverse forms and, so to speak, diverse degrees of explanation are equally legitimate. Mechanics, physics, or chemistry, while tying in more and more closely with one another, preserve their special competence; they grasp phenomena which in other respects escape their grasp. Neither does the study of the synthesis dispense from determining the elementary conditions, nor does the knowledge of the elements take the place of a direct study of the synthesis itself.

Thus it is that the inertia of brute bodies already manifests an internal dynamism without which the shock that drew the moving thing from its state of rest would not produce its effect. Similarly the living germ effects, with the materials it gathers, a veritable creation, and as long as there is life, there is a phenomenon of surplus production. Between the excitation of external circumstances and the stimulus of its organism, it is the organism that the animal undergoes (*subit*) most forcefully. In the nervous system, each cell is, so to speak, a heart which, receiving a current, discharges it with an increase of strength. Psychophysics brings out the victorious progression of effort over the resistance to be overcome and the intensity of what it calls the psychic reflexes. Consciousness emerges from the organic functions, without being conscious of it and without letting itself be reduced to them. In reflexion a power of inhibition and impulsion appears that popular experience calls freedom and which it thinks able to dominate the energies of nature or to regulate the instincts of animal life. Voluntary operation in turn proceeds from thought, from the organism, from the world, without relating itself to the confused multiplicity of unknown seeds of which it is the completion. Each degree, then, has a proper characteristic, without any measure in common with any other. A summation of the whole, while it is at the same time an excelling novelty, it cannot be known scientifically unless it is tied into the universal determinism through the continuity of deduction, at the same time as it is perceived by direct observation in its synthetic unity.

Now this is the cooperation for which experimental science offers no account; it subsists only by admitting the joining of two orders which, from its viewpoint, are incoherent. The relation between calculus and intuition, between the intelligible determinism of facts and the sensible discontinuity of the data of observation escapes it at the beginning, in the course, and at the ideal end of its development; and yet it lives by this very relation.

Here then, in all their starkness, are the conclusions that result from a clear view of scientific procedures: — there is true science of phenomena only if their laws are determined by mathematics; — there is true science of species only if their internal constitution can be defined with numerical precision; — there is a real unity of these sciences only if mathematical continuity is implanted into them and ties them together, because from their viewpoint beings are only a system of integrated phenomena. But, if it has appeared that the application of the exact sciences to reality was not justified by them, it appears equally that the necessary recourse to mathematics by the experimental sciences is not justified either. Among the sciences, within them, there is a flaw that, whatever degree of progress we suppose them to have reached, will not disappear. Mathematics can insert itself into nature, physics can arm itself with mathematics, as if they each played in turn the role of container and of contained; in spite of this double coincidence and this mutual insertion, there is in the apparent unity of scientific explanation an invisible fissure. Science cannot stop with science.

III

79   How then does the rapprochement between these two separate segments take place in fact? And whence does science draw, with the coherence it does not have and yet without which it is not, the life and the efficacity it has, since it is?

Let us pull together in a single view the results of the preceding analyses: we shall discern the final postulate, the precise point where, in the whole as well as in the least detail of knowledge, the connection is made on which all positive certitude depends.

On the one hand, mathematical analysis never really reaches sensible reality at the end of its abstractions. On the other, direct observation may try as it will to make scientific the concrete, the particular, quality, by inserting a world of quantitative determinations under the intuition of the senses; far from making the qualitative phenomenon disappear inside an abstract formula, it makes its irreducible originality stand out. Neither experience can furnish the pure abstract, nor mathematics, the true concrete; for mathematics is based precisely on the idea that real analysis goes to infinity, and experimentation, on the idea that mathematical constructions do not produce the real synthesis. To be sure, due to a subtle illusion, we are persuaded that, from the moment the exact sciences, starting from the abstract, arrive at practical applications, from the moment the experimental sciences, basing themselves on sense intuition, succeed in discovering therein numerical determinations, there is a coincidence and a welding of these two inversely symmetrical methods of calculus and experience. Yet there is nothing of the sort; for the meaning of unity, of analysis, or of synthesis is by no means the same on both sides. In *its* calculation, experimental science never attains *the* calculus, because for it unity is not the abstract principle of ideal analysis, but a concrete element. Moreover, there is no scientific truth of any order whatsoever where this duality is not to be found; for every mathematical construction presupposes, so to speak, an imaginary experience of synthesis as synthesis; and every distinct observation requires an effort of abstraction which, in the confused mass of intuition, determines a unity and numerical relations, to which sensible quality remains irreducible.

Now, to define the difficulty in this way is to say that it is resolved in fact, but that, far from seeing in the effective success a solution, we should see in it a problem.

80

I. — It is resolved in fact. All the antinomies some have claimed to find in the realm of speculation reside in science itself. Seen from the depth of things, they do not have a bearing on being, and it is not ontology that is at issue. Under the guise of combatting the metaphysical illusion, Kant, by force of acquired habit, was still subject to a metaphysical illusion when he transposed the question: continuity and discontinuity, determinism and contingency, analysis and synthesis, deduction and production of effects distinct from their conditions, those are the terms of the conflict, and the conflict arises at the heart of positive knowledge.[1] Hence it is science itself that is compromised, and no one is alarmed by it, no one notices it. Why? Because the problem is resolved before anyone has to formulate it; it is resolved practically, which is to say that action,

1. Kant makes metaphysics depend on the possibility of synthetic *a priori* judgments. In other words what is at issue is the possible agreement between the *a priori* of the analytical syntheses and the *a posteriori* of the synthetic analyses. But it is in the sphere of the sciences that the duel and the reconciliation takes place, without our having to consider phenomena otherwise than as phenomena or to suppose anything else beside or underneath them. And from this pacified antagonism only one thing becomes evident, namely that the sciences called positive cannot know all the phenomena.

whence the sciences proceed, is not exhausted in them, that in supporting them it surpasses and overflows them, that in fostering their growth and their success it proves that there is in them more than the sciences know and attain.

Thus it is that all the subtleties of Zeno do not prevent Achilles from catching up with the tortoise. All the incoherences of science do not prevent the scientist from dominating the phenomena and from actualizing, thanks to the industrious activity of the man whom recent classifications decorate with the name *Homo industriosus,* the conceptions and the abstract calculations of the mind. He is a magician in his own way, in making his own work penetiate into the universal work. Our power always goes further than our science, because our science, risen from our power, needs that power still to find in it its support and its end. There is more at the point of arrival because there was more from the beginning.

81   It is therefore impossible for science to limit itself to what it knows, since it is already more than it knows. By reason of the will that posits and sustains it, there is in science something that some might claim to exclude as short of it or beyond it. Hence, in this *something* which we first admitted with the hope that positive knowledge would exhaust it, there subsists an irreducible element which, from the viewpoint of the positive sciences, remains transcendent without ceasing to be immanent to them.

If we wish to see the presence and as it were the imprint of this mediating action in all knowledge, we have only to recall how at the beginning of mathematical analysis a fact was necessary, an experience as simple as one could wish, merely a succession of two states of consciousness, the bare given of an effective synthesis: a generative action which, necessary at the entrance to science, makes its final success possible at the issue. Also, if we inquire into how, from the combination of numbers, one could derive the laws of musical arithmetic or of chemical proportions, without borrowing from experience, or how, from higher algebra, the engineer could extract quite *a priori* a knowledge of resisting materials, without the combined initiative of thought and of observation, everywhere we find the necessity of an action to furnish each of the sciences with what is lacking in it from the other, of an indispensable intervention for each to arrive at its point of departure and for each to ground itself in its point of arrival, justifying itself through its practical success. This is to say that every scientific discipline requires the postulate of action to subsist, and that action itself must become, if the will remains consistent with the initial movement of knowing, the object of a proper science. It does not resolve the antinomy of the positive sciences except by raising a problem of another order.

II. — Science succeeds: hence we must render an account of this success. In vain would we try to be satisfied with it, to enclose ourselves within it, to draw strength from it against every higher desire, curiosity, and faith. Since what we would like to exclude from it is already included in it, since we can neither get along without it, nor stop with it, we must go beyond, by studying what in science is ulterior to science itself.

Here is a fact that is not explained, a fact that will never be explained in the eyes of the scientist, but a fact certain and positive which he cannot fail to admit implicitly from the moment he admits science. To be sure, at times he is persuaded that, in spite of this fundamental insufficiency, positive knowledge sufficiently supplies the wants of individual and social life; but if he affirms this, it is in the name of an arbitrary belief, through a decree that does not find in science its motive and its justification. He has done nothing to resolve the real problem; and he presupposes it as resolved at the very moment he falls back under the common law of naive consciousness. Is it by knowing the Abelian functions or the classes of gasteropods that we will acquire a greater clarity about life? If then we are sincerely looking for a light in science, it is not with the sciences that we can stop, since in them the vital point remains obscure; on the contrary, focusing on this x which sums up in its indetermination all that remains to be known, we must make of it the object of a new science, different but equally positive. The indeterminate, as Aristotle remarks, is the category of action. It is not that we must leap rashly into the contested realm of metaphysical speculation; our entire effort must on the contrary, be to keep to the fact, to determine the unknown with precision, and to discover its scientific characteristic. That will be the object of our coming chapter.

82

From the preceding analyses follow considerable consequences.

1. The positive sciences, in the whole of their extension, result from a constant association of two irreducible orders.

2. By reason of this very incoherence and solidarity, they constitute simply a symbolism, arbitrary in its principle, coherent and related in its continuous development, verified by its applications.

3. But neither do the theories have any essential relation with the experimental consequences they seem to arrive at, nor does the given of experience have any essential relation with the mathematics that seems to be realized in it. Moreover, both the one and the other, without any natural relation between them, are without natural relation to any third term whatsoever. No intermediary reality must intervene, in science, between the two functional series of its symbols. Each series finds in the

other its matter and its apparent reality. Each series, though irreducible to the other, has to symbolize with the other. There is, then, in sum, a double reciprocal symbolism which gives positive disciplines their relative solidity. They are all the more true as they adapt to one another with greater ease, precision, and coherence. But in themselves they are not more true one than the other.

4. It follows from this that the sciences do not have to preoccupy themselves with explaining the basis of things. They have only to consitute a system of coherent relations, starting from different conventions and to the extent that each of their different hypotheses is verified in fact. As there are many ways of demonstrating and expressing a known truth, so also there are many ways of reaching an unknown truth and many ways of knowing it. Thus the variety, the fruitfulness and, so to speak, the freedom of science is unlimited.

5. Thus are removed the shackles that once subjected the sciences to the fictitious necessity of faithfully representing and entirely constructing an objective world, a world they were able to present to minds charmed by the certitude and the precision of their results as if it were reality itself, a world of prestigious mechanisms where one could not tell whether it was the work of the senses or of reason, of physics or of metaphysics. Thus, instead of trying to realize the schemata of crystallography or the construction of metageometry, we must guard against attributing a substantial truth even to the space of Euclidian geometry or to the atomistic hypotheses of chemistry.

6. Thus are equally removed the ancient chains that seemed to rivet science to philosophy. Every speculative construction that takes scientific symbols and positive truths for materials is ruinous. To science belongs the notion of invariable sequences and of unconditional causality; but from the necessity of the truths it establishes we must not conclude to any necessity of nature. For in it there is no nature, there are only relations; and the arbitrary character of the initial definitions and conventions limits the necessity of scientific relations to these relations themselves.

7. But does this mean that the sciences are to see their relations with philosophy fall apart, and that they are no longer an integral part of the human problem? By no means. These bonds that must be broken from the viewpoint of knowledge are restored from the viewpoint of action. Hypotheses, symbols, explanations may change, indeed they will surely change. What will remain is the activity of the mind in the construction and the mutual adaptation of these theories, as well as the very significance of scientific research. Positive knowledge is not exhausted in its own work; and what makes it be does not restrict it to what it does

and knows. We cannot believe that the sciences do not have a real bearing; they have one indeed, but otherwise than what we ordinarily suppose and contrary to what we imagine. For it is in what is scientifically and, so to speak, objectively determined that the arbitrary part and the subjective mark of human intervention resides. And we must look for what reality they do have in what determines them, and not in what they determine.

8. Thus the vice of the positivist or evolutionist conception becomes manifest: "The *subject,*" it is said, "is not of itself *object* of science; it is known only through the other scientific methods, in function of positive facts; it is an *epiphenomenon* entirely reducible to the external side, a reverse side." Surely an error: subjective knowledge has a proper object, since its reason for being is precisely to be what the other sciences are not and that without which the other sciences would not be.

9. Thus moreover is resolved, from a positive viewpoint, one of the essential problems Critical Philosophy had left on another ground. Instead of taking the immediate intuitions of sensibility as point of departure, why not take advantage of the felicitous effort which science makes to shed light on this first given of life? The usefulness of the preceding analyses is to introduce all the achievement of science as a contribution to the critical study of knowledge. It is to show, by merely looking at the procedures and results of science, that this entire part of our intellectual richness and our practical efficacity bears only on the relations of phenomena.

10. Thus, the old question of the originality or the innateness of our thought is reduced to its positive terms. What the senses and the sciences grasp of their object, far from explaining the rest, can subsist only in function of something left over. If it was of any use to insist on the incoherence of the most certain methods and truths, it was to bring out at the same time the certitude of what maintains their solidarity. Thus are established at once two conclusions apparently contrary, but in reality   85
correlative: the sciences give us no light on the foundation of things; the sciences require the mediation of an act irreducible to them. They are not absorbed in their object and never bring knowledge back to the known.

11. It is not necessary to have penetrated all this subtle mechanism to be emancipated from fascination with the positive sciences. To yield to this illusion is, on the contrary, to prove by the effect that the will, stopping at a premature term, is lacking in consistency with its own exigencies and that it is surrendering to something unworthy of it.

12. The final result of this research, then, is to bring to light what justifies one who is less tutored and to authorize him to resolve the prob-

lem of his destiny without all this luxury of knowledge. The science of life remains accessible to one who has no other.

It was claimed that man and his acts can be reduced to just the phenomena that positive knowledge determines, or what comes down to the same thing under a different form, it was claimed that the positive phenomenon can subsist without man and his action; and now we see that this claim cannot hold up. It is contradictory, since to exclude what makes the sciences possible and valid is to deny them at the moment one admits them or exploits them. By merely positing them we require something more than they; we admit that the complete solution to the enigma is not in them; they are themselves enigmatic. Thus falls, along with the superstition of *Science*, the unworthy presumption of whoever abuses of the prestige of a magic word before simple folk and makes himself their guide, as if the scientist knew more about the secret of life than the least of the humble. No matter what we do, we shall never live only by scientific ideas; and notwithstanding so many recent advances, we have not taken along this way, we shall not take a step toward the intimate depths of beings and their operations.

It must be said emphatically; and it is not a personal opinion to affirm it, nor a speculative fiction, but an acquired truth, κτημα εις αει (a possession forever): the sciences have before them an immense but restrained career; and it is in what they know that, without recourse to any metaphysical critique, is to be found the certitude of what they will never be able to know. They will grow indefinitely without encroaching one bit on the mystery they bear within them. The time when it could have seemed that mathematics, physics, or biology had a properly philosophical bearing has passed. To be sure, a certain confusion of competences was useful to pull the fragments of science together and mutually fecundate them. But that is done with; the split is accomplished for good, an era of thought is closed; and it is precisely starting from the day when the efficacious union of the sciences reveals their solidarity and their strength that it becomes possible to appreciate their weakness and their lacunae. An unlimited field is open to them, an infinite realm escapes them; and these two truths are tied together, for by its very success, the action from which they proceed proves all the more that it surpasses them and that it cannot expect any further clarity from them. We could render thought no greater service than to underline thus this boundless power in this irremediable weakness.

In vain, then, would we hope to resolve, from a *positivist* viewpoint, the problem of life: there would be incompetence, there would be inconsequence in doing so. The positive sciences are only the partial and subalternate expression of an activity that envelops, sustains, and overflows them. There remains only one way out, it is to follow the movement from which they proceed, and to look for its equation, so to speak, by seeing whether, in what surpasses and grounds them, there is matter for a true science, a science which perhaps may be self-sufficient.

―――――――――

What does the next chapter aim at? To show that the subjective study of action involves a scientific rigor and that it necessarily prolongs the positive sciences; it ties into them, and it surpasses them. The aim, then, is to determine the bond which, starting from mathematical or experimental knowledge, maintains scientific continuity up to the facts of consciousness; to define the proper characteristics of these subjective facts; and on this foundation to constitute a science of consciousness. — Thus, I start by establishing the dependence and the solidarity between the subjective phenomena and those the positive sciences deal with, so that the movement of the inquiry is unbroken. — Then I indicate how the internal facts, far from being an *epiphenomenon* or a translation, simply equivalent or even inadequate, of the external facts that accompany them, contain, along with the summation of all their antecedent conditions, an originality and efficacity of their own. — Finally, I take advantage of the relative transcendence of these facts, at once scientifically determined and independent, to justify the subjective study of action and to define the conditions of a science of consciousness, — of a science which, tied to the others, nevertheless will inaugurate a quite new order of inquiry, the one ordinarily designated by the premature name of "moral sciences." Hence it is from the positive science of the object to the otherwise but equally positive science of the subject that this chapter leads us.

CHAPTER 3

The Elements of Consciousness and the
Subjective Science of Action

87 The positive sciences subsist only thanks to a permanent postulate. They
have a continual need to admit that the intelligible or organic systems
they consider are distinct from the elements they are formed of, and that
synthesis and analysis are not reciprocal. For, as we saw, not knowing
the whole of anything, we would not know anything of the whole if in
the given phenomenon there were only a mechanical complex, and if the
synthesis, constructed *a priori* or observed *a posteriori*, were not a
distinct whole and a new unity. This is to say that in every scientific truth
and in every known reality we must suppose, for it to be known, an internal principle of unity, a center of grouping imperceptible to the senses
or to the mathematical imagination, an operation immanent to the diversity of the parts, an organic idea, an original action that escapes positive
knowledge at the moment it makes it possible, and, to say it all in one
word which needs to be defined better, a *subjectivity*.

How can we determine this unknown that has been refractory to the
explanations of the sciences, but whose presence is necessary and fruitful
in them? The question is doubly delicate; for it is a matter of defining
88 what the subjective is as seen from the outside,[1] as it appears in the object

---

1. To speak this way is to adapt to the common habits of language and
thought. But in truth we can say with equal exactness either that the internal fact
is a concentration or an expression of the whole exterior, or that the
phenomenon, whatever it may be, is wholly interior to consciousness; for scientific truths, psychological facts, metaphysical affirmations are all at first a subjective state. Instead of searching for how it is possible to extract the notion of a
subject from positive knowledge, therefore, we could show how, even from inside, we are led to distinguish an inside and an outside. In this last form, more
precise perhaps but more paradoxical, the question now under discussion would
come down to the following: in any state of consciousness, how do we separate
what is objective representation and what is subjective act? How do we bring out

94

of knowledge, and what it is as seen from the inside by the subject himself. Better still, it is the passage from this objective interiority, so to speak, to this subjective interiority that we must study, in order to underline at once how there is a continuity from the science of the object to the science of the subject, and how the originality of this science of consciousness remains entire. What is difficult, then, is to maintain the relation and the independence of these two orders of knowledge while showing that one is subordinated to the other and that both follow from one and the same willing.

I

This is the very formula from which the existence of the positive sciences is suspended: "The multiple composite has, as composite, an internal unity; and the bond of the elements has a reality distinct from the elements themselves." Indeed, it is under this condition alone that the mathematical synthesis is possible and useful, under this condition also that experimental knowledge succeeds in focusing on the successive forms of sensible reality, under this condition finally that there is a fruitful commerce between mathematics and observation, which finds unity in multiplicity and multiplicity in unity.

Now the unity of a synthesis does not consist only of an internal rela-   89
tion of the parts; it is the ideal projection of the whole into a center of perception. The *vinculum* (bond) is of an intelligible and, in truth, a *subjective* nature; but if this indivisible union of a multiplicity interior to itself already surpasses the domain of the positive sciences, it is nevertheless, even in the eyes of the scientist, their first postulate; and to reach it is to have ascended to the summit from which another slope is

and define, alongside positive facts, this internal act enveloped in every phenomenon? — To be able thus to reverse or scramble with impunity the two forms of the question, realist or idealist, is proof that in effect every metaphysical or critical prejudice has been set aside. Kant himself stopped halfway: transcendental or subjective idealism could only be a reverse realism, since by reason of the revolution of thought it attempts, it is still looking for a center of gravitation; the value it takes away from one of the terms is to be attributed to the other. Also, far from being worried about the necessary confusion which this chapter entertains, we must see in it the only simple and true way of describing and adjusting the two aspects of the universal phenomenon without adding to it any presupposition. Besides, it is proper to an organic system that the parts be for one another and even one through one another: such is the very organization of phenomena in consciousness. That is all we claim to be proving in showing here that action (not the fact, but action), the scientific condition for the sciences, becomes itself matter for science.

discovered. What we must look at now, therefore, is how phenomena *are interiorized*, and how from objective knowledge itself we are led to extract a more and more precise notion of the subjective.

— In considering right from their point of departure the homogeneity of a solidary whole so as to introduce into it the abstract differentiation and the relations of the parts, the exact sciences recognize a principle of unity at the heart of the universal solidarity and suppose an invisible bond in the diffuse multiplicity, since without this unity neither whole, nor parts, nor relation, nor knowledge would be possible. The whole, merely by being considered as a whole, is more than the sum of its elements; for it appears as it appears only by being brought back to the unity of a system. The part, merely by being a part, is more than itself alone for it expresses its relation with all the rest. If we reflect on the development of the exact sciences and on the architecture of their abstract constructions, we shall discover that in their successive syntheses they insinuate a growing character of subjective ideality.

If on the other hand it is true, as the sciences of nature have recognized, that all real unity from their viewpoint is synthetic and symbolic, there is therefore, even in the most subtle element that experimental analysis can attain, the implicit affirmation of an *inside*, of an internal center of projection to which a virtual multiplicity is related. And in all the hierarchy of organic combinations and forms, systematic unity is more and more marked, as the sign of an immanent principle of perception and organization.

Thus on both sides, in the field of mathematical construction as well as among the living productions of nature, the phenomenon is the better perceived and is all the more intelligible, and seems all the more objective, as, manifesting a more complex intrinsic organization, it reveals a growing subjectivity. What is for us the principle of the knowledge we have of it, is what seems in it the principle of its synthetic reality and of its internal perceptions. In one sense, it is known in the same way that it is; it seems to be in us to the extent that it is in itself. Prescinding from all ontological preoccupation, then, the phenomenon is neither more nor less a perceiving than it is a perceived; and from this viewpoint, the ancient formulation of Parmenides is exactly right, knowledge is identical with its object.

— But that is still only an exterior way of defining the presence of a subjective element at the heart of all positive data. To arrive at determining, in the continuity of the universal phenomenon, the relation of the external facts and of the internal facts whose double irreducible and solidary process has always seemed an enigma, we must advance further. It is in analysing the very constitution and formation of the phenomenon, as the sciences have taken it in and exploited it, that the unconscious sources of conscious life will be discovered.

For it has appeared that the sciences are not constituted and consolidated, that their principles, their methods and their results have no coherence and efficacity, that the phenomena which they make the matter of their study do not have any consistency and reality except inasmuch as a mediating action intervenes at the origin, in the course, at the end of their development. Hence it is not enough, in the detail of each scientific truth, to unravel the subjective element that hides in it; we must, in the whole of positive knowledge and in the total system of phenomena, grasp in act the very progress of subjective life. Thus, after having passed from the external fact and from the object of the sciences to the notion of an interior or of an inside, we shall now penetrate from the notion of the subjective into the very consciousness of the subject, *a vinculo perceptionis ad vinculum percipientis* (from the bond of perception to the bond of the perceiver).

Without parting ways with the positive sciences, we shall see rising from them then what they seem inclined to deny or to exclude, the psychological fact. — By a sort of internal evolution, consciousness emerges from the surrounding universe whence it draws its nourishment; — but it distinguishes itself from it and emancipates itself from it; and why? — because, if it is true that it sums up in itself all the rest, it is not as a product, it is as an original synthesis that gives more than it borrows from its conditions: a triple relation that it is important to make more precise by sketching out mental embryogeny.

II

To consider the phenomenon as a first given, from which we would only have to draw the notion of a subjective element, would be to reverse the most certain relations. In truth the phenomenon is what it is only in function of an activity that contributes in engendering it; we perceive only according to the very order of its production; and the constituting action of the subject is essential to it.

If in effect the phenomenon is conceived only in relation to universal determinism, if all scientific knowledge focuses on a distinct synthesis of its elementary conditions, if the necessary cohesion of the sciences implies a mediation which they do not explain, what does that mean? It means that, even after we have considered the least fact as the expression and the product of all the others, there always remains an irreducible surplus, a kind of virtuality and a power, infinitesimal it is true, but

91

thanks to which the effected synthesis contains and surpasses everything from which it is formed.

Hence there is no phenomenon which, to subsist as such, does not imply an infinite, transcending the fact of the entire universe. And is it not on the condition of supposing this infinite that calculus has worked in practice? Every object known by science is a synthetic unity. Now each object is tied to the total system. If therefore the synthesis is something more than the immense multitude of its conditions, there has to be in it something to contain and dominate this very immensity: a remainder that no doubt is as little as nothing and which the sciences take into account only to eliminate it; but it is this nothing which, from an interior viewpoint, is everything, since it is the invisible principle of the synthesis, the soul of all positive knowledge and of every efficacious operation.

The simplest fillip raises and answers in fact a problem which no abstraction will ever account for. Thus are resolved the antinomies whose presence the analysis of the operations of science revealed: in every positive fact there is a complexity that defies all enumeration. And at the same time the effective production of any phenomenon whatsoever requires that this innumerable multiplicity be understood and actually dominated. On the one hand, the imagination is overcome by the infinite richness of the universally intertwined phenomena; on the other hand, this infinite of the total phenomenon is overcome by the least act inserted into it, by the least of its particular aspects. There is, so to speak, an apparent infinite that is the projection and the expression of the infinite interior to every operation of nature or of thought. It is what appears immense on the outside that is truly limited; it is in what seems finite and particular like a being or like a singular fact that an infinite resides, on the inside.

And this *inside*, whence all the positive proceeds, thus has the characteristic of escaping positive knowledge at the moment it makes it possible by furnishing it with a matter. That is why infinitesimal calculus works only on the condition of first using the mediation of this infinite without which it would not reach operative reality and would lack all efficacity. But if it supposes it, it is only to eliminate it immediately, because there is no place for the subjective in the positive order. Or rather the precise place of this transcendent is the ambiguous locus that seems still to belong and no longer to belong to science, the interval between the smallest assignable magnitude and the zero that is its inaccessible limit.

There is *inside*, therefore, only where we find, no longer the subjugation of a part to the whole, but the victory of a point over the entire universe. The subject is not part of a series, but he is constantly represented in one; he does not appear in the total determinism, but he is, in every detail, the principle of variety and of action. We must see him in that principle.

Already in the most abstract, the most mechanical and, in a way, the most exterior conception we can have of things, something of a subject is manifest in them. It is a truth at once mathematical and experimental that everything is solidary: deductive continuity, cosmic concert, and conjunction. Now in the mere idea, in the mere fact of solidarity there appears a general and internal action of the organic system. Indeed, from the moment when the presence of the universe is expressed in a point, and when the point is impressed on all the universe, there is a break in the balance of the homogeneous, and a disproportion between the proper action and passion of each part of the general system: there is, if one cares to use a comparison, the interval between the blow received and the blow returned, and a kind of mechanical *reflex*. In this sense we can, without recourse to any metaphysics, interpret the term Leibniz applied to the monads of bare matter, *"mentes momentaneae"* (momentary minds); for in the world, as the scientific knowledge of phenomena first [93] proposes it to us as a set of determined movements, what goes back to the whole from the part is not identical with what came to the part from the whole. This always singular reaction is like a beginning of a subject, a sort of refractive milieu, a more or less *natured* middle term, an inside. And what we thus call "interior" is the presence of the whole to its part and of the part to its whole, without there being an exact symmetry between the passion and the action. That is how force appears.

Force therefore implies a proper action which, no doubt derived from the universal mechanism, reacts on it and has to be considered apart as an empire within an empire. The direct influence of the elementary parts one on the other is complicated in effect by the influence of the totality on the part; the reaction of the one part on the others is not equal to the action directly undergone. A dynamic spontaneity appears: the new and, so to speak, unforeseen way in which the response is made to the exterior excitations is properly speaking the scientific *acting* or *being* of the subjective phenomenon.

From this natural subordination of the parts what results are not only detached elements *vis-à-vis* the whole and the other detached elements, but centers of partial equilibrium are formed, more or less stable groupings, systems more apt for representing through their multiple unity the unity and the multiplicity of the whole. Each one of these centers of nutrition or of perception, so to speak, expresses and mirrors from its viewpoint all the isolated parts, then all the groups, then all the representations of these particular systems that endlessly reflect back to one another their actions and their perspectives, just as a hundred spherical mirrors would criss-cross and superimpose *ad infinitum* the growing complication of their images. Now as soon as the universal concatenation is revealed no longer only by the set as a whole, or in each detail, but in those solidary groupings that become like a new universe with their proper and internal evolution at the heart of the total system, life appears along with individuality.

94   Life therefore is the organization of a little world that reflects the big one and manifests, even by its internal disposition, the dissymmetry and the variety of the universe.[1] Behaving as a whole in relation to its parts and as a part in the whole, it supposes a double exchange from the outside to the inside and from the inside to the outside. But how does it interiorize the general system within the individual system it forms, if not through sensibility? That is to say, it finds within its own organization the reflexion and the repercussion of all the forces that act upon it. Thus it is that there is a perpetual doubling and true integration of life which is illuminated and vivified, so to speak, by reflecting itself from one center of focus to the other. It has its nourishment in the universe as a whole; and each perception is accompanied by an increase in energy. Every spontaneous action supposes an internal organization of movements, multiple relations, echoes and repercussions of forces. Also wherever a natural spontaneity is manifest, there is composition and organism; *actiones et passiones sunt compositi* (actions and passions are of the composite).

In the diffuse infinity of its determining conditions, what is living thus appears as a concentrated system of coordinated forces; and the infinite of its act is more interior to it than exterior. For the influences it undergoes, instead of bearing it along passively, accumulate and express themselves through special functions, through a progressive adaptation of the being to its milieu and of the parts among themselves. Instinct is, like the organization whose internal principle it is, a very condensed and very elaborate response to the multitude of exterior excitations, a particular case and a partial solution to the cosmic problem; its narrow scope does not prevent it from being tied to the forms of life most different from those where it moves; we see that from the difficulties of acclimatization. What psychological activity the animal has is a reduced

---

1. This dissymmetry may not always be the necessary and sufficient condition that enables us to define the living, and to determine the objective criterion of what is biological. Nonetheless it indicates, even if it be in brute bodies, the representation and the particular influence of the general ordonnance within a closed system.

projection and a determinate concentration of the rest; and its acts are particular conclusions whose general premises remain outside of it in the total ordonnance. Finally, reason develops in the measure that it becomes more adequate to the universe and that it knows how to concentrate, understand, use a greater variety of phenomena; it is thus that civilization tends to equal, to enrich, and to surpass the nature from which it emerges. The field of becoming is without assignable limit; and new perspectives will always open up, with new theories that will not exhaust the object to be known since they constitute it in part.

What seemed chimerical to claim becomes scientific truth: external   95
finality itself recovers once again the characteristic of definite certitude that only internal finality had maintained. Man is a "microcosm," *summa mundi et compendium* (a summation of the world and a compendium), the summary of all the experiences, of all the inventions and of all the ingenuities of nature, an extract and an original product of the whole; the universe concentrates all its rays in him. Subjective life is the substitute and the synthesis of all other phenomena whatever they may be.

That is how the fact of consciousness is built up little by little. The relation of the subject to the elementary conditions by which he is nourished is manifest, but he can contain and sum up his antecedents only by dominating them. It remains for us to understand this properly.

III

If it is true that external phenomena are not of a different stuff than internal phenomena,[1] nevertheless there is this fundamental difference

1. But in recognizing this, it is important to be on guard against this triple error: first, we must not forget that the ontological question has been put off, and would be premature at this point; but it is forgotten if from the defined relation between these two orders of phenomena one draws any idealist or materialist conclusion whatsoever. — Secondly, we must not reverse the order of relations as analysis has just determined it; for the subjective appeared as a higher synthesis, and even as an antecedent condition of the phenomena whence it was taken. — Finally, it would not be enough to recognize a relation of two parallel processes, a "progressive adaptation of the internal to the external," nor even to add with the new school of scientific psychology that "the adjustment of the organism as a whole to its milieu is precisely what is meant the *psychic*;" for in opposing what is called the external face of reality, one is led to declare their relation inaccessible to science and to take the phenomena studied by positive science as the equivalent of the subjective facts; and consequently these "psychic" facts would appear as only an unexplainable leftover and a useless luxury.

that the former are only a particular aspect and as it were an abstract slice of the total determinism and the latter are like a concentration of the universe in one point whence every concrete operation of thought or of nature proceeds. Between them there is an infinite that enters in, not to divide them, but to tie them together. The synthetic unity of every real fact envelops and dominates the whole world; for, existing in the world, it also bears it within itself. In the same way our knowledge, which has a plurality of representations as a condition, raises itself by the unity it constitutes above this plurality; it emancipates itself from its content since it contains it. In either case, the bond, *vinculum percepti et percipientis,* is of a subjective nature; there is solidarity, there is distinction between these two orders: a reciprocal relation, ascending and descending, which it would be good to consider a moment longer.

96

The least glimmer of organization and of subjective life presupposes a prodigious integration of elementary actions and reactions already systematized and more and more *natured (naturées),* an interweaving of all the threads that necessity spins out to form the growing complexity of forms, of instincts and of sensibilities. The fact of consciousness then is the product, not merely of the last, but of all the antecedent acts, conscious or unconscious, that converge and are summed up in it. Also it is not isolated from the other phenomena, but it maintains a double relation with all the others: — on one side, the subjective fact is the condition of all the phenomena that are the object of the positive sciences, so that the knowledge of these phenomena depends on it and is possible only through its unnoticed presence in every sensible intuition and in every scientific affirmation; — on the other hand, the subjective fact has as its conditions all these same phenomena so that the very reality of this fact depends on them and the most obscure consciousness bears within it and represents all the determinism of its antecedents.

Thus light is shed upon the law that we have had to observe, without explaining it, in the course of every positive science: each synthesis is an originality irreducible to its components; indeed, it is in its subjective reality itself that the excelling newness of each degree of composition resides. In this order of phenomena, the progress of existence and of knowledge are solidary, whence this double formula:

— The elements are such that the composite draws from them its reality and does not exist without them: they have a necessary role in it, while at the same time preserving their proper being and while participating in the total solidarity. *Omnia quanquam diversis gradibus animata sunt* (all things, no matter how diverse their degrees, are animated). A more complex form, where interiority is more in evidence, is therefore a reflexion of the subalternate forms that served as nourishment for it; and in this sense the subjective is a concentrated objective. There is no life in the universe that can do without the elementary conditions in which the organism is immersed, and man remains subject to the laws of brute matter.

—Composites are such that each one is quite other than its components and constitutes a new world with its own laws, independent energy, needs, resources, and end. In a very true sense, the components exist only for the composites, and they even exist only through them; for wherever there is synthesis, there has to be a center of perception for the synthesis to be expressed, there in the unity of its composition. The sensible, the positive, the objective, or whatever other name we may wish to use to designate what differs from the phenomenon of consciousness, would crumble and fall into dissolution if there were not, to support and realize the progress of its forms of existence, a simultaneous progression of subjective knowledge.[1]

What we were proposing to establish, then, is grounded: the subject is scientifically tied to the object, and contains it, and surpasses it. Facts of consciousness are as real as all the others, since all the others communicate with them at once and borrow from them what reality they have. They remain distinct and they are solidary. How these internal phenomena entail a scientific characteristic is what remains to be defined.

IV

Seen from the outside by the scientist, the subjective is precisely that which cannot be known either in function of mathematics or in function

---

1. Idealism and realism, therefore, are equally vain without one another, and equally founded both the one and the other, if instead of seeing in them two incompatible metaphysical conceptions, we consider them as the expression of two orders of solidary facts. Similarly also the doctrine of evolution, whose allegorical and novelesque character has been shown as long as it gives itself off as the real history of *beings*, takes on a precise meaning and a new exactness: the most complex forms derive in effect from the inferior forms through a continuous determinism; but the discontinuity of phenomena is no less scientific than this very continuity. Each synthesis forms a degree which supposes the preceding ones, but which harbors an irreducible subjectivity. What is higher bears within itself and represents by itself all its antecedents, without what is lower, alongside, underneath, or inside, ceasing to keep its nature and its place. Thus, man, according to the word of Pascal, is "all nature," but nature is not all elevated, nor all apt for life and for consciousness. What is known is not equal to what knows; for to know a thing is to be that thing, to be by that thing, to be in a sense more than that thing.

of sensible observation, because it is that which constitutes their bond and introduces unity amid the multiplicity. As the sciences determine the mathematical relations and the experimental laws more precisely, they define at the same time what they leave unexplained; from the moment the two extreme terms are rigorously fixed, it follows that the intermediary equally entails a determination which, for being negative, is no less precise.

Here a second characteristic is seen, but one already quite positive. As we were led by an inevitable progress from the sensible intuition to science, so also from science a new fact emerges from which all the others hang. If the subjective is nothing from the positive viewpoint, still it is that without which the positive itself would be nothing, the principle invisible and present in every object of knowledge.

Now what is given as a multiple unity, what is *everything at once*, could not be perceived except by an internal intuition. And it is even to define the subjective fact to call it the perception of the indivisible unity in irreducible multiplicity. Also, even when we know that there are indispensable conditions for the production of conscious life, it remains impossible to determine these elements of the act that constitute it; as Aristotle had already noted before Leibniz, we cannot analyse the ingredients of action, τα στοιχεια του ποιειν.

It is, therefore, a matter of science that the subjective fact, though tied to all its objective conditions by a rigorous determinism, cannot be sufficiently defined through even a complete knowledge of its antecedents. For it constitutes with reference to them an indeterminate synthesis, and only from the inside is it perceived, or rather it is this inside itself. Far from claiming to substitute the study of the external face of phenomena for that of their internal face, it is necessary to take the phenomenon of consciousness in itself, to abstract it from the objective representations it is mixed up with and of which it is the soul, and to take hold of it in all its purity.

How arrive at this and, once we have separated from consciousness the phenomena that serve as matter for the positive sciences, what remains that is properly subjective in the subject himself? What remains is what distinguishes the conscious subject from the elements of his consciousness and from the objects that nourish it, what enables it to transubstantiate them and to achieve their synthesis, what brings it to respond by original reactions to the determinism of its conditions. We have shown that, seen from the outside, the subjective is precisely that which, indeterminate and inaccessible to mathematical or sensible knowledge, yet constitutes by its precise action the particular reality of each synthesis. Seen from the inside, then, it is what is determining, efficacious, active, singular, — the spring of mental dynamism. Thus it is that the true science of consciousness could only be a science of action.

Indeed, we must avoid representing the phenomena of consciousness in function of objective phenomena and reducing *action* to *fact*. That would be to act like the miller who, to get to know his mill better and the force that moves it, would examine the course of the river downstream. In this study, the danger is always, so to speak, to objectify the subjective, and to imagine that the conscious is composed of abstract elements and of general data like the universal and necessary notions the positive sciences live on. For in the eyes of consciousness and also in themselves interior facts are always singular; they do not result from a *sum,* they are not a permanent possibility or a simple extract of the representations that people the stage of consciousness; they are not even the result or the expression of a synthesis; for they are what forms this living synthesis of elements that are themselves living. There is nothing then in properly subjective life that is not as an individual initiative and as a unique case, ἀπαξ λεγομενον; nothing that is not an act.

Thus, then, we begin to enter into the intimate truth of action and to distinguish it radically from what is represented phenomenon, a product detached from its cause, a fact perceived and undergone. In this sense, the least *act* has a reality, an importance, a dignity, so to speak, infinitely higher than the *fact* of the universe. This is what explains in the adolescent, in the scientist or the philosopher the first rapture or the obstinate pride of thought: whoever begins nourishing himself on his reflexion imagines he discovers what was not known beforehand, a new sun all his own. This is what causes in everyone the dreadful illusion of egoism: the most fleeting interior light has more value and more charm than all the brightness from outside; the least personal sense that reveals us to ourselves as by an intimate caress has more sweetness and force than all that comes to us from the world.

What is properly subjective, therefore, is not just what is conscious and known from the inside (properly understood, that is the case for every phenomenon); it is what makes the fact of consciousness be; it is   100
the act, internal and always singular, of thought. A science of the subjective will inevitably be a mental dynamics.

V

But how can we constitute a science of what is thus singular and indeterminable, of what escapes all measurement and all representation, of what is on the way to becoming? How determine what has neither quantity nor quality, since we cannot analyse its elements nor even consider its complex whole as a definite unity, for the character of each is produced and modified with each successive state?

Perhaps this embarrassment is born of a confusion and an abuse of analogy. Forestalled and penetrated by the idea he habitually has of the methods of positive science as of the only type of a truly scientific method, the psychologist is anxious to apply their procedures to subjective science, without noticing that it is a distinct science only insofar as it has a distinct method. In attempting what he calls psychological analyses, in discussing the possibility and the use of synthesis or of mental experimentation, he perverts the meaning of the words and succeeds in outlining only a pseudo-science, because in the very use of his "subjective method" he considers the subjective as fact and not as act; he disfigures it under pretext of studying it. For we enter into its living reality only by taking, not the static viewpoint of the understanding, but the dynamic viewpoint of the will. We must not try to imagine action, since it is precisely that which creates the symbols and the world of the imagination.

The true science of the subject is the one which, considering the act of consciousness from the beginning as an act, discovers through a continuous progress its inevitable expansion. It seeks the equation of action, that is to say that, setting out to develop all its content, its aim is to determine what is its necessary end according to the very strength of the initial movement from which the act proceeds and which is to be noted at each effort of its development. Hence it is in the very work of the will that the law and the end of willing will have to be revealed. For even where man seems to be subject to antecedent and subsequent necessities, these conditions are still only means subordinate to his hidden desire.

101   No doubt, by reason of the intimate and always singular character of the act, subjective science does not at first seem to have the abstract and impersonal generality of the other ones. For it supposes an initiative and an experience proper to each of those who create it anew for themselves, and from which no artifice of exposition could dispense them. And yet this science has a character of universality and precision higher than the exactitude and the generality of every other. There is no one not subject to the necessity of practical experimentation; not an act that does not bear in its unfolding a hidden concatenation, a rigorousness and a logic higher than that of the most subtle reasonings. Consequently, what is approximate and really indeterminate is the formula or the fact as the positive sciences, necessarily partial and abstract, try to define it; whereas what is complete, systematic, precise, living, is action, pregnant with its consequences and solidary with them.

That alone is a true science where nothing is communicated from the outside, where everything grows from the inside, where we learn only what we make be, where the consequences are deduced with infallible certainty from the premises entrusted to the labor of life, and where the rigorous necessity of the conclusions only gives birth to the fruit of the first initiative. For the issue is to determine not what is outside the will like a more or less fictitious object, but what is in it, what it is already by merely willing *as such* and not by *what* it wills.

Let us look at the road covered in this first stage from the point where we willed that there be *something*. From the first sense intuition, which appears simple only because it is confused and which necessarily remains inconsistent, was born the need for science. But positive science does not find within itself the unity and the cohesion it avails itself of without explaining it; just as in brute sensation there is already the awakening of a curiosity without which there would not even be any sensation, so also every positive truth requires the mediation of an act, the presence of a subject, without which there would not be any positive truth.

We have shown how this subject arises from the phenomena that are its conditions, and how it distinguishes itself from them totally. The subjective is tied to its antecedents by a continuous bond; and it is in discovering this scientific relation that we see at the same time the ir- 102 reducible originality of the internal act. From the still exterior unity of the perceived we passed to the intimate unity of the perceiver, and we restored to the subjective phenomenon its true character of act. But in defining its relations with the other facts, in maintaining its relative independence, we justified this conclusion: far from being a mere *epiphenomenon* or a duplicate of physical or physiological phenomena, the act of consciousness harbors and concentrates the entire milieu it has fed upon, — it is a universal receptivity; it has a degree of reality and of precision higher than the objects of the positive sciences that would not exist without it, — it is a radical originality. For the fact is only by the act; and without the subjective phenomenon there would be no other. Whoever posits something, therefore, requires a subject. The positive sciences converge in a science of action.

Hence consciousness drains and concentrates all the forces of nature. Through what it represents it dominates all that is represented in it. Also in studying the conditions of subjective knowledge we have at the same time determined the antecedent conditions of action, but by emancipating it from scientific determinism and by showing that these conditions themselves enter into the series of means through which the will sets itself to work.

Let no one, then, go on reproaching subjective science with being a vain and completely chimerical speculation, as if all that is essential in internal phenomena pertained to cerebral physiology, or as if the true equivalent of thought were the neural function. Henceforth we have the right to take the act of consciousness as a reality as rich as, as positive as, as definite as, as precise as, even more rich than any other phenomenon: the road to the interior world is open to science.

Stage Two
FROM THE THRESHOLD OF CONSCIOUSNESS
TO THE VOLUNTARY OPERATION

The conscious elements of action

It is a matter of science that consciousness is, and that it is not enough to study it in function of the exterior states to which it is tied as to its natural conditions, but to which it still cannot be reduced. It has to be so, for the positive sciences to subsist; it has to be so, since in willing that there be *something*, through the very admission, we were already implying the subjective phenomenon. Hence it is no longer a verbal subtlety to say that in taking the object we posit the subject, and in affirming the phenomenon we put thought in it. The internal act is certain, precise, positive, scientific, as much as and more than any physical fact, any mathematical truth.

Consciousness takes its nourishment from the immense milieu that it sums up in itself; but it sums it up and contains it only by surpassing it, only by forming an original synthesis, only by becoming the *act* of all its conditions and of its subalternate *powers*. Also, once it appears under the form of appetite or instinctive desire, there is a victorious spontaneity of the mechanical determinism, an already quite psychological automatism.

To be sure, these internal stimulants depend on more profound and, so to speak, subterranean causes as unconscious germs of consciousness; but from the moment they arise and open up into subjective life, they dominate, by what they manifest, all that they harbor. Thus the very principle of every conscious phenomenon is a dynamism; and the higher the clarity rises, the better it concentrates the forces and the rays of nature. To speak the language of scientific appearances, in the fulness of the world, under the oppression of the physical energies and amid the gears of the universal machine, do not movements follow the impulses of desire? That the image or the tendency derives from the ignored determinism that precedes or prepares the awakening of consciousness is possible, is true; but the image or the idea finds in what arouses it and in what it is, the power of producing its own movement. There is then a moving spontaneity that depends on subjective spontaneity: psychological determinism absorbs physical determinism and, without suppressing it, substitutes itself for it and superimposes itself in using it. Therefore, it is in consciousness alone that we must now look for the internal principle, the determining principle of action.

What enters into the illuminated field of consciousness can only cross it, and necessarily returns to operate beyond; but in passing thus through the intimacy of the subject and in reflecting on itself therein, the act, issued from nature, transforms itself and, becoming master over is original conditions, which it takes up again on its own terms after a fashion, it creates the voluntary intention that will animate all the subsequent history of its expansion. Hence we are touching here on the central point of the natural development of action. For, on the one hand, we show that to this voluntary determination of the act all the "preconscious" antecedents are tied; on the other hand, we indicate how this free decision is inevitably embodied in a sequence of "post-conscious" acts that remain implied in it and suspended from it. Earlier we saw consciousness higher than scientific determinism; here we shall see a new initiative emerge from the internal determinism which, on the other hand, will preserve its relative freedom only by ceasing to restrict the voluntary movement to a purely formal intention and by looking beyond clear consciousness for an end of its development. — Thus, to study the conscious integration of action, I describe the automatic dynamism of internal life. I show the necessary appearance of freedom in it at the heart of psychological determinism. I establish that this freedom preserves itself only by going out of itself to submit to a heteronomy, to conquer for the will what escapes it and to throw itself into operative action. In short, the subjective will keep itself intact, complete, and sincere only by "objectifying itself."

The aim of the next chapter is to show how the consciousness of psychological determinism arrives naturally at suppressing the automatism and at suspending the fatality of action. — Studying first the mechanism of spontaneous subjectivity in what is necessary about it, I then examine how this fatal development of interior activity can produce the very idea of determinism; and finally I indicate how the existence and the knowledge of internal determinism presuppose that subjective life has been radically emancipated from it. Hence this determinism itself is subordinated to a more internal freedom.

CHAPTER 1
The Conception of Action

Desire or the image has appeared. No need, no way of knowing whence or how the point of instinct or the clarity of the idea has revealed itself. The birth of what is most admirable and least admired, the interior light, remains impenetrable. Like those plants that for ten years gather the perfumes and the precious sap with which they nourish the lone flower that exhausts them in a day, a hidden labor drains all the forces of life to feed the source of consciousness: there is no water that comes to augment it unless it has taken these subterranean passages where distinct knowledge does not penetrate. And when it springs forth it is with an all virgin vigor and purity, as if it owed nothing except to itself. What is its virtue? Where is it distributed?

I

Nothing acts upon us or through us, unless it is truly subjective, unless it has been digested, vivified, organized in us. It is not an abstract representation that is enough to move the psychological automatism. Consciousness is a closed world; it opens up only thanks to the intermediation of the unconscious influences of life. That is why suggestions need to be understood in order to be followed, and why the same teachings do not grow the same wherever they fall. For every thought is autochthonous; and there are no true truths for us except indigenous truths. Our desires are and are worth what we are and what we make them; the idea passes through feeling or else it remains a dead letter.

Intellectual light thus bears vital force within it and exploits it: the motive is in effect only the repercussion and the synthesis of a thousand mute activities; that is the reason for its natural efficacity. The motive does not appear suddenly, up in the air, so to speak, and as if by spontaneous generation; it is the deputy of a crowd of elementary tendencies that back it and push it; it results from causes further removed and more general; it is the conclusion of a whole prior system and serves as an intermediary between habitual dispositions and the particular circumstances that are the occasion for it. At the moment of its birth it has a flower of newness, a freshness, a magic grace, because, secretly inspired and as if penetrated by the fecund energies of which it is a first completion and a living commentary, it is all act. Its efficacious charm therefore comes from its expressing and representing precisely that which it moves; and the power by which it rises to consciousness is precisely that by which it is also able to act on the unconscious forces from which it emerges. This natural magic, which in the animal gives to instinct, in the sleepwalker gives to the image, its sovereign fascination, is equally the one that vivifies the most abstract idea with a feeling without which it would remain inert. — A motive is not a motive without something that moves, without "a mobile" (un mobile).

— But "a mobile" is not "a mobile" either without a motive. What does that mean? It means that, in order to become an efficacious principle of action, the diffused energies need to be gathered into a mental synthesis and represented under the unique form of an end to be realized; they are confirmed and vivified by the very effort that expresses them, as attention is strengthened by tensing up the organs. No doubt, by themselves, the excitations of the senses exalt the power of the one undergoing them, and increase the intensity of his nervous strength; but this dynamogenic influence exerts itself only by being embodied in a definite representation and even in a determinate movement, so that the final cause becomes the moving cause and ideas and signs are the indispensable conditions of the dispositions they manifest.

Thus it is that the study of mental combinations and compensations in hypnotic automatism shows that every sensation (such as a tactile impression), apparently destroyed by the anesthesia induced by suggestion, tries to express itself in a system of analogous images and ideas (such as visual representations), and tends, through transposition, to set in motion another sensory apparatus under the influence of an hallucination at once corresponding and foreign to the primitive excitation. The diffusion of reflexes reaches action, therefore, only on the condition of being translated into an ideal synthesis.

This necessary transformation, whose mechanism certain exceptional cases enable us to analyse, always takes place also in the normal interplay of psychological functions. The obscure forces of sense life have all their efficacity only from the moment when, as if to illuminate them and to fix an aim for them, a representation arises which appears to abstract and to detach itself from them: thus finality is at first only the subjective expression of antecedent necessities. But from the moment when the confused and incoherent impulses of desire have taken shape in the instinctive image or in the clear conception of an act, they are indebted to the systematic unity of the internal representation for a firmness, a precision, an efficaciousness that are quite new. In consciousness, always, at every moment, states are produced that are tied to one another and unified into organic systems; and what effects their synthesis is what confers an original power on the system. Introspective analysis therefore confirms what, from the viewpoint of the positive sciences, we showed to be true of every synthesis, i.e., it is irreducible to its elements and master of its own conditions. — "Mobiles" are valid only through the motive they prepare and propose for themselves.

— But the motive itself is no longer a motive, if it does not in turn become a "mobile." Again what does that mean? It means that, from the moment when the deep causes of the moving emotion have provided themselves with the goal of their tendency, they cease to be confused with the total current of life, in order to constitute a distinct end. They were *ourselves*; they become simply *ours*; and the motive would remain as it were the abstract and ideal term, as it were only the objective production of the action of these causes, if it contained nothing more than the complete summation of the subalternate determinism that bore them to the light of consciousness.

Hence this motive, to be efficacious, to exist, to effect the concentration of the diffuse energies and launch them to the attack, must bring some new perspective and the promise of an unknown to be conquered. When we act without knowing entirely why (and it is always so), when the reasons we give ourselves are neither the only ones nor the truest ones, it is no doubt because in this approximative explanation of our behavior there always subsists, alongside some clear ideas, a vague sense wherein are summed up the natural inclinations, the hereditary habits, the slowly constructed desires, the entire organism and the entire universe; but it is especially because the known motive dominating all prior energies, exploits them for ulterior ends that always surpass experience and even foresight. Better still, the actual motive of our act is never the same as at the origin of the choice that inclined toward it. There is no imperative mandate: the deputy is not a simple spokesman; if he has the power of the members, he also enjoys the initiative and the direction of the chief, he has the *élan* of the improvisor; for at the decisive moment it is always something unforeseen that carries us off. Thus, born of force, the interior light is a source of force; the image that results from movements is cause of movements, and thought constantly fecundated

108

by nature fecundates it in turn, like an organism that digests and vivifies everything it takes in.

Having come from an impenetrable origin, the conceived act then crosses the illuminated field of consciousness, in order to tend toward a goal again still impenetrable. We live, it is said, only by hope; we labor only in view of the better. Whether we have a clear understanding of it or not, we belong to a world higher than sense phenomena and the science of facts; nothing of what is exterior determines us, and in what we desire outside of ourselves, it is still ourselves that we are looking for. If the idea is nothing without the sentiment, neither does the real have any purchase on us without the ideal; and we do not act, if we do not draw from ourselves the principle of our action, if this principle does not surpass past experiences, if we do not sense in it something else, if we do not make of it a kind of transcendent reality. One is never interested in one's own acts unless they are mixed in with some passionate ideology. The clear idea is inert; all that is demonstrated and fixed as mathematical certitude does not elicit active devotion. We die, as we live, only for a belief,—when, in what we know, we expect more than we know, when we have placed ourselves at stake, when we love this mysterious known both for what it contains and for what it promises.

109   Thus it is that even instinct seems to work in view of ends foreign to the individual whose life it crushes; thus again it is that in the actual incertitude about his destiny, man sometimes has the obscure and intense feeling that, in the hands of a blind fatality, or of an almighty cunning, or of an unfathomable providence, he contributes to the great work he does not know. Through the very interplay of the internal determinism, then, action hangs from an effective finality;[1] and far from reducing subjective dynamism to the mechanism of brute forces, it is unconscious activity that serves the nascent life of consciousness by supporting it.

The study of mental dynamogenics establishes, therefore, in the very name of determinism, these interconnected conclusions:—consciousness results from a series of elementary and unconscious acts, not just from the last;—it constitutes a synthesis and a distinct act;—it prepares and

---

1. No doubt all the movements of life in us do not end up in consciousness, nor does consciousness once awakened equal all its antecedents. For one thing, there are reflex reactions, and a diffusion that uses up a part of the unconscious force along the way. For another, we shall see through the study of the obstacles which stand in the way of willed action that not all the diffused energies are systematized through even the most comprehensive reflexion. But the issue here is first to show how the intervention of the conscious cause is an integrating and vital element of certain actions, even when these actions proceed at the same time from unknown powers that contribute in determining them.

begins a series of new acts whose end it does not foresee, but which it proposes for itself at least as provisional. To conceive is to have acted, to be acting still, and to be about to act further. Prior to any reflexion, these diverse moments that analysis succeeds in distinguishing are mixed in together, in instinct, for example, or in passion. When an idea suddenly takes hold of a hothead or an ardent heart, are there any obstacles, are there any hesitations, is there even consciousness, so close upon conception does execution follow? How quickly the work is detached from the worker! And with what speed action, perhaps slowly elaborated, slow to have come to consciousness, comes out of it after a few phenomena of refraction and mental amplification! And if our French genius is more active than any other, more dedicated to ideas, more ready to live by them and to define them through practice, it is not a singular or abnormal trait, it is the law of the truly human character: we think (it is in the order of things) only after having acted, and in acting, and in order to act.

Yet the proverb remains true: to say and to do, to conceive and to execute, are two things. Why? And whence is it that ordinarily we hesitate, we deliberate, we seem to choose, when it should be enough quite simply to be carried away with the immediate certitude of instinct, without hindrance and without obstruction? And once we have acted with that sort of imperturbable unity as if under the domination of a suggestion, why is it, if we come to notice it, that we think we were determined, while in the course of the action itself we were able to believe we were free?

110

II

A motive is not a motive if it is alone. If it is alone, it is an animal desire, an instinctual image. If it appears alone before consciousness, it is an impulse of spontaneity or of mechanical habit, the delirium of one sick or deranged, the suggestion of a sleepwalker, the automatism of one distracted or dreaming; it is a fixation, it is not an idea.

Every idea, every state of distinct consciousness implies a contrast and an internal opposition. Just as the eye spontaneously brings up the color complimentary to one it grows weary of perceiving to make them both live by one another, so also the mental organism is constituted in such a way that every representation evokes contraries and antagonists, as so many harmonics meant to highlight them through a subdued accompaniment. Consciousness, as we recalled, is born only of discrimination, it develops under the dominion of a law of relativity. The study of what is called psychic polarization shows that, under every perception apparently simple and frank, is hidden the image of another fictitious perception quite ready to supplant the first one. This also explains why, in cases of hysteria, there is a need for simulating and an appetite for lying, which, incidentally, has haunted certain touchy but still sane organizations. For alongside real memories, appears and grows a system of adverse associations; and through the momentum of a strange giddiness, one comes to the point, as if in spite of oneself, of saying the opposite of what one was thinking, of reduplicating one's conscious life, of falling into illusion, as if the false representations, precisely because they are quite subjective, had more authority over the subject than those whose real impressions he underwent. In the same way the regular mechanism of negation sets in motion a pair of rival affirmations, one of which manages to exclude the other, but without ever destroying it. Whence the spirit of contradiction; whence the danger in awakening doubt or disobedience in the child through some premature question. Whence, on the opposite side of the coin, the usefulness of the temptation overcome, to strengthen the very vigor of the moral sense. In short, to conceive an act distinctly is to imagine at the same time at least the vague possibility of different acts, which play the role of a foil and serve to add precision through elimination and through approximation to the primitive conception. Every conception, then, is like a fraction that makes sense only in relation to the total unity and that calls for the complement of another fraction.

Here are the facts: man's animal automatism and the determinism of his life, at once physiological and psychological, is penetrated by this law of simultaneous or alternating contrasts.[1] The internal mechanism is such that, down to the very vitals of our brute life, the monotonous and unperceived unity of the organic process is shot through, divided, torn by internal struggles. Hence if it is true, as we saw in studying subjective spontaneity, that *every act of consciousness* is a synthesis of forces and a new principle of force, it is no less true that *every consciousness of an act* (an idea or a sentiment) results from a conflict, from a disturbance and from a halt in the mental dynamism, from an at least partial "inhibition." It is necessary to study its causes and its effects.

1. Thus it is that man's animal and instinctual life is not that of the animal. Intelligence manifests itself, not where automatism is prolonged in instinct, but where there is choice of means and discernment of the favorable milieu. The sureness with which instinct solves problems insoluble to reasoning shows that, if the unconscious representations are a faithful image of the world, the consciousness representations are an image of it deformed by the exigencies of contrast. Reflected consciousness is the state of maximum contrast for the unconscious representations.

As images and ideas arise in greater abundance, more numerous ways open up for activity; for the unconscious labor of psychological life translates itself spontaneously into the form of ends to be realized. Determinism projects the goal it assigns itself and, with the aid of the antecedent conditions, it constitutes the ideal to be pursued. That is how, among the different tendencies that manifest themselves in us through an unknown necessity, contrasting systems of known ends are formed which bear, each within itself, a power of realization. And through the attraction of diverse conscious motives, the diffuse forces of the interior life group themselves under a law of finality into antagonistic syntheses. Now, how is it that there is opposition among these heterogeneous groups? How, from this intestinal struggle, does there come to be a more distinct knowledge and a new power of attention? How is reflexion born from consciousness itself? How does the divergence of tendencies ordinarily unequal and disproportionate come to end up in "inhibition"? Here is how.

If the antagonistic systems are opposed in consciousness, it is because, in spite of this antagonism itself, they are contained in the complex unity of one and the same organism; it is because they depend equally on a higher power of contraries; it is because, rather than being isolated fragments, they are the parts of a whole. The multiplicity of images and motives no doubt prepares, but it first supposes a unity able to comprehend and produce them all. Moreover, in the presence of adverse motives there is a third which intervenes to oppose them. Even in the face of a single motive, from the moment it is conceived distinctly, it is the case that we consider it as only one of the possible solutions in its relation to the sum of actual impressions and tendencies. This relation, in consciousness, of the parts contrasting with one another and with the whole is, properly speaking, reflexion. It results from the partial character of the antagonistic states; but this plurality of the solidary and opposed states is possible only through the immanent action of a power able to embrace all the multiplicity of the contraries in a higher unity, and which we have to call reason.

Thus, as soon as there are internal contrarieties and a halt of tendencies, consciousness, finding one more force within itself, becomes reflexion. From the conflict of energies and desires held in suspense, affective states are born that serve as matter and nourishment for new intellectual states. Instead of remaining obscure and incoherent, the diverse motives of action come to confront one another; it is Reason that contains in it the entire system of the rival reasons. It is none of them in particular; it contains them all, it distinguishes itself from them all, and sets them all in balance, because it sees that each one of them, a portion in a whole, is only one motive among others and like others, *una e multis* (one of many). That is why, whatever the inequality of the forces present, reflexion paralyses them equally; for it supposes, not just the power of one of the hostile fractions, but the reunion of all the virtual energies. It draws off from these spontaneous energies all their promotive force and uses it to bring them to a stop.

Here moreover is found the way in which the consciousness of determinism is formed in us. For we conceive the necessity of an act under the fascinating influence of a mental representation only by imagining that the system of victorious motives has eliminated every adverse tendency and has become, so to speak, a total part; this is to say that, considering this dominant motive by abstraction as the only real and effective one, we maintain in the face of it, in order to understand its dominant strength, the idea that it could be only a part in a whole. Hence determinism is known only inasmuch as we find in ourselves the wherewithal to surpass it.

Finally, this analysis enables us to explain why, inversely, certain suggestions that end up as act under the influence of a fatality leave the agent with the illusion of freedom. Actually, when the suggested action appears with all the retinue of motives that can reinforce it, the effect of the suggestion itself is to chase away from the field of consciousness the obstacles and the contrary velleities. Without any real suppression of antagonistic tendencies, there is a subjective anesthesia. A moment ago, through a fiction, we were imagining that a partial motive had absorbed the total activity, and we concluded to determinism. Now it seems to the patient who executes the suggestion that a goal presents itself to him in the absence of any other motive and, in tending toward it, he thinks himself free, as he would be if he were acting with the habitual fulness of his discernment.

Reflected knowledge is therefore like a synthesis on two levels; it is representation of representations. What it is sums up what is in us, and what is in us sums up all the rest. But after we have gone up these tiered levels through a necessary progress, if we look back, how will we explain that *more* seems to come out of *less* in this way? Why this victorious power of the derived states? Whence is it that, at one and the same time, reflexion narrows the breadth of spontaneous life, since it introduces limits and contrasts into it, while it broadens the power of particular motives, since it makes one or the other of them able to thwart all the others?

The reason is that this ascending movement is itself predetermined by a secret aspiration which, from the beginning, sowed the seed of these unforeseen growths. Seen from the bottom up, according to the series of means, everything seems necessary; but there is constraint only in the appearances. Seen from the top down, so to speak, and in the order of the ends sought, everything is born of an initiative which each new effort is bound to reveal better. And that is why each later synthesis contains more than its already determined antecedents; that is why the transcription into consciousness of unconscious states creates a new energy; that is why, moreover, reflexion, in concentrating the diffuse light onto one point, in a way multiplies it; that is why, finally, even this accumulated light is already no longer enough to bring us to action if beyond it we do not still perceive the attraction of some obscurity and something unknown.

Hence it is not from the perspective of a single moment of the interior life that we can resolve at a stroke the problem of freedom and determinism. For what is at first necessitating becomes necessitated in turn; only at the end, if we attain it, will we discover the true character of this total movement of life. Let it suffice, then, to show, at each growth of the act, the forced sequence of this development itself and the victory of the new state over its own conditions. But we must guard against reversing or confusing the levels of this rigorous progression. Otherwise we would betray the scientific character of this concatenation and we would run the risk of taking the necessary production of freedom[1] (the aspect of the problem ordinarily neglected) for an absorption of freedom itself into necessity.

Such is the genesis, such is the efficacity of reflexion: it derives from spontaneity, and it emancipates itself from it by explaining it; it proceeds from determinism, and it surpasses it by knowing it. Born of an internal differentiation and from an inhibition, it is itself (as Positivism had already noted rightly) this inhibiting and perturbing power. From the moment reflexion appears, every tendency is held in check; it suspends, not the knowledge that it fixes, but the immediate activity, through a power which it borrows from the antagonistic tendencies and which is higher than each and all. Has it not often been noted in fact that a too close attention disconcerts what is natural and hinders the ease of the most habitual movements, that curious and learned analysis kills the

115

---

1. As earlier I spoke of objective phenomena or of subjective life without giving these words any idealist, realist or phenomenalist bearing, I will deal with freedom without worrying about knowing whether I am speaking of a reality, an idea or an illusion. Again, it is not here that the question is resolved, it is much farther down the line than the determinists or their adversaries have ordinarily supposed.

élan, the naive sense of happiness, the fecundity of life, and even love? And do we not see instincts and traditional mores sometimes crumble in the face of the progress of this dissolving force, reflexion?

From the determinism of "mobiles" and motives, then, a power arises that holds it in check. Thanks to it, no suggestion of nature keeps the magic charm that made it sovereign; before it, nothing has a decisive influence, an absolute value; no one thing, so to speak, merits any longer to be done. There is a halt, there is indifference. Isn't that the death of action, and is not action conceived only to be aborted?

The aim of chapter two is to show how the power of inhibition that is enough to hold in check all the play of spontaneous tendencies inevitably has its own activity. First I study the necessary genesis of freedom (for it does not depend on us to be free, in our own eyes, or not to be free); and I indicate how, through this popular and ineluctable belief, each individual, persuading himself that he is in some way his own point of departure, ratifies and assumes responsibility for all the antecedent conditions of this at least apparent freedom. Then, from the *necessary idea* I go on to show the *necessary exercise* of freedom amid internal phenomena, and the role, no longer inhibitive, but active and propulsive of liberating reflexion; and I call attention to how this act of free will embraces the whole series of consequences, even unforeseen and in appearance involuntary, that are due to result from it. We are therefore at a culminating point here, which serves as a divide between the waters of determinism flowing up and the waters flowing down from personal determination, but where we see that, whether in the past or in the future, this double movement of concentration and expansion has its reason in actual willing.

CHAPTER 2
The Reason of Action

From the moment when the conception of an act is accompanied by contrary conceptions, and when, through the antagonism of these rival forces, reflexion has appeared, the simplicity of the primitive automatism is lost. Brought to the fore by the very functioning of the internal determinism, a new power holds the entire movement of spontaneity in suspense. But what is this power for both understanding a system of complementary ideas and paralysing its immediate influence in order to reflect and deliberate on it? It is what we commonly call reason; and the act that will proceed from this interior labor is the one we ordinarily call, without sufficiently distinguishing what deserves to be called by that name, the human act,[1] the reasonable act, the voluntary act, the free act, or simply the act or action. But how is it that, in spite of what seems to be murderous for activity in reflexion, there is a truly reflected energy? How is reason engendered? And does it have its own action, without be- ing detached from its conditions; a necessary action, without its being necessitating; a decisive action, without its being determined?

1. The very precise differences noted by the Scholastics between an *act of man* and a *human act* are well known, as are also those between the *voluntary* and the *free*. Similarly a fairly sharp nuance separates *act* and *action*. *Act* (barring particular usages) refers rather to the first initiative of the internal effort, whether by nature everything had to be confirmed within the bounds of this spiritual operation or whether we consider, in the work itself, the entirely subjective part of the agent. The word *action* refers rather to the passage from the intention to the execution that embodies it, and often, consequently, to the result or the work itself of this transitive operation. Between act and action, then, an analogous difference subsists, but one contrary to the one there is between *work* (*oeuvre*) and *operation*.

121

I

In what way is reason constituted before consciousness; and how does it furnish, along with the regulative notions of reflected life, the necessary idea of freedom? That this idea appears fatally in us is something certain, and it is something no one has thought of explaining. That it sums up and represents by itself all the prior history of determinism is a truth equally misunderstood and equally essential. For from this it follows that (wrongly or rightly, —the absolute value of phenomena actually matters little; the issue is simply to study their mutual relations) the agent, substituting himself for all the antecedent conditions of his actions, attributes their paternity to himself.

I. —If the motives and the "mobiles" are the repercussion in us of all the world and the expression of our own nature, the consciousness that perceives them is the perception of the universe and of the total solidarity from a particular point of view. But to know the universe, a new relation has to be established by this knowledge itself; the more we understand the greatness of the world and this immense duration where we are as though lost, the higher we are above it. To know is to possess and to rule. *Intellectus fit omnia, sed, ut fiat, superat* (intelligence becomes everything, but for it to become so, it overcomes). To grasp its object, the understanding transforms it into its own substance.

We can really understand the parts only through the idea of the whole; we know the whole only by distinguishing oneself from the *universe* through the perception of the *universal*. The consciousness of a motive did not occur without the presence of other motives; the consciousness of the multiple reasons for acting did not occur without at least a confused view of their opposition and of the system they form; the consciousness of these contrasts in the midst of an organic unity does not occur without the thought of what is inaccessible to relation and to limitation, without the known and possessed presence of an absolute, without the regulative idea of the infinite.

About the presence of these rational notions in consciousness, about the role they play in the very way we look at our personal conduct, we can have no doubt. If some have denied them, it is out of fear of the absolute reality we could be tempted to attribute to them from the start. But here there is nothing of the sort. The issue is simply to determine the mutual generation of these ideas and to explain their appearing in consciousness. And so little should we worry about attributing to them an objective value that, far from raising them to the absolute, we shall define their reciprocal and hierarchical relations. They call one another

118

forth and produce one another, like simple solidary phenomena, in the thought of the subject. As Leibniz had noted for mathematics, there are in the mental dynamism "many degrees of infinite." *Directive ideas* of reason and *freedom* are the names of two of these tiered levels. Also to account for the generation of these rational notions will be at the same time to explain the production of the consciousness of our free willing.

In two words: the consciousness of action implies the notion of infinite; and this notion of infinite explains the consciousness of free action.

What does it mean to act, according to the common idea people have of it? It means, in the immensity of things that everywhere and always contain an actual infinite, in the midst of the determinism that encircles all the complexity of phenomena, to insert and to add something of one's own. No one thinks he is acting if he does not attribute to himself the principle of his action and if he does not believe he is someone or something, like an empire within an empire.

This interior persuasion only translates and confirms the scientific definition, as we gave it earlier, of what is properly subjective. There is no effective synthesis, no internal act, no state of consciousness, however obscure it may be, that is not transcendent regarding its conditions, and where the infinite is not present, — the infinite, that means here what surpasses every distinct representation and every determinate motive, what is without common measure with the object of knowledge and the stimulants of spontaneity. The light of each idea sums up a whole system of forces; and through the ideal action they exert on one another, the motives take over the powers they represent: that is how we can transform into internal freedom the exterior necessities of the world. Reflexion is not sterile, it is the force of forces; and like a lever leaning   119
on the idea of the infinite, it can raise the universe. That is why theory acts on practice; for thought is a form of action which it makes into a free will. This is why also the speculative doctrines of moralists are events in the formation of general morality.

The decisive reason for an act, then, never seems to reside in any one of the partial tendencies that contributed in making it possible; in our eyes it resides in this power which none of the particular determinations could exhaust and which, absorbing all the piecemeal reasons, seems naturally able to dominate the whole of the defined forces: physical energies, appetites, tendencies, motives, determinism of nature and of spirit. Conscious action finds its explanation and its total reason only in a principle irreducible to the facts of consciousness as well as to sensible phenomena; it is conscious of its own initiative only by attributing a character of infinitude and transcendence to itself.

Now it belongs to reflexion to place the resources of spontaneity at the disposal of its own advantage. What the agent has done by instinct, he can, by taking advantage of invention, renew by art; what was contained in the natural expansion of his energy, he can dominate and exploit; what resulted from an indeliberate force, he knows how to make into the goal of a new effort; and imitating himself, he puts all the power of the efficient causes he bears within himself at the service of a final cause. From the moment when conscious action appears to him as a result irreducible to the determinate conditions from which it proceeds, he makes of this result itself the principle of his eventual decisions; and the inifinite virtuality that the nature of the acting subject harbored becomes a sense of free will.

Hence it is because we find in our acts a kind of creative sovereignty that we have a consciousness of ourselves and reason; it is because we are reasonable and conscious of ourselves that we judge ourselves capable of voluntary initiative. Thus the reciprocity of means and ends which had already manifested itself in a still extrinsic way in the dynamism of nature is illuminated within the intimacy of reason. As the higher syntheses earlier explained the lower forms, which are nevertheless their antecedent conditions, so also here the relations between immanent determinism and transcendent finality reappear. Reason would not be in us, would not know itself in us, without this rhythm of the unconscious or spontaneous life whose necessary laws we have traced up to here; and this whole organic process would not be, would not develop, without the latent intervention of a directive idea, since it is under the hidden influence of this finality that all the motives and states of consciousness, calling to one another, associating themselves with one another, opposing themselves to one another, brought forth reflexion and, with it, the consciousness of a free power.

The role of action in the constitution of reason and in the idea of freedom is therefore essential as well as little attended to. Indeed, what reveals to consciousness this apparent infinite of a power proper to the agent? It is the very action that is accomplished in him and by him. And what inspires him with the desire and the sense of a power proper to himself? It is the idea of that infinite of action which he makes the origin of his voluntary decisions: a reflexion and freedom that would be impossible in one who, instead of acting, would be *acted upon*. For there is reason and reflected consciousness and a sense of the infinite only where there is a free activity, and there is free activity only where there is consciousness of acting. To take phenomena for what they are, neither more nor less, there is a solidarity between reason and freedom, between consciousness and the power of the infinite. The *real* idea becomes *ideal*, that is, reflected, only through this mediation; for if the infinite is present to every subject, not every subject is present to the infinite and knows how to use it.

The voluntary act, then, goes from the infinite to the infinite, because in it the infinite is efficient cause and final cause. Freedom, far from excluding determinism, comes from it and uses it; determinism, far from excluding freedom, prepares it and produces it. The chronological order matters little; time is only a way of representing the subjective unity in the multiplicity of subordinate phenomena; and the necessity immanent to the sequence of these phenomena is only the objective projection and, so to speak, the project of the transcendent finality from which reason draws its inspiration.

Thus it is that reflexion, scanning the series of efficient causes and final causes in all directions and seeing whence the act comes, knows how to go back to it and to reproduce it; it equally goes down or goes back up the double sequence of spontaneous operations for which it is alternately end and point of departure; it goes into nature to take up the thread of causes that lead to its goal; it predetermines the sequence of the means proper to its ends. To the determinism of brute force or of animal instinct   121
or of mental spontaneity is added, not to suppress it, but to use it, the voluntary determination of the act.

In short, in order to act we have to participate in an infinite power; to be conscious of acting we have to have the idea of this infinite power. But it is in the reasonable act that there is a synthesis of the power and of the idea of infinite; and this synthesis is what we call freedom.

II.—Here, then, is freedom, that scandal of science, affirmed by science itself, by a science more complete and more consistent with the law of its progress. It is, since the movement of science and of consciousness are unexplainable without it. It is, since at the point where we posit what is true about determinism, we escape from it. But let us make no mistake about the meaning and the bearing of this affirmation; it contains a triple truth: (1) nothing in the determinism of nature and of thought, nothing in phenomena nor in the science of phenomena contradicts the consciousness of a force exempt from necessity, *immunitas a necessitate* (immunity from necessity); (2) it is the movement of spontaneity and the progress of determinism that produces the necessary and inevitable consciousness of freedom, *necessitas libertatis* (necessity of freedom); (3) the very interplay of this determinism is explained and consecrated by freedom, *necessitas a libertate* (necessity from freedom). It is on this last point that it is especially important to forestall any misunderstanding.

All our proper action appears to rest on a primitive foundation of passivity, and it would be absurd to pretend that it is our doing to have come through all the forms of unconscious life and finally arrive at the dawn of consciousness and the clarity of reason. Far from proving that we have the say about being reasonable and free, we have just seen on the contrary why we are so inevitably. Is this to imply that this necessary freedom is absorbed in determinism? Not at all. We must also maintain these two assertions at the same time: on the one hand, determinism has necessarily led to the consciousness of freedom; on the other hand, freedom, in becoming conscious of itself, ratifies all that goes before and wills all that enables it to will.

From the moment, then, when the reasonable agent attributes to himself a power higher than the conditions from which his consciousness, his reason and his freedom all derive, he could not, in willing, disavow these origins of his will; and if he could discover a motive for denying what he is, it is not in the antecedents of his act that he would find it. Thus is legitimated this entire process that seemed foreign to human willing; thus do we see that all the movement of science rests on a profound will; thus, when, through a decision which could have seemed artificial and arbitrary, we were opting for that *something*, for that phenomenon of which there is immediate intuition and scientific knowledge, we were expressing in an extrinsic form this essential truth, namely, that the whole system of objective and subjective phenomena, the entire organism of positive knowledge, is subordinated to and suspended from the phenomenon of freedom.

We must say the *phenomenon* of freedom as a matter of fact, in order to stress once again that no ulterior question is being prejudged at this point. If at times the determinism of nature and thought has appeared to contradict freedom, it is only because people attached an ontological value to it, and because people treated positive facts and states of consciousness as absolute beings to which the principle of contradiction applied. Henceforth no objection from mechanics, from physics, from psychophysics, from experimental psychology, makes any sense against this free choice. For scientific affirmations, always made from different viewpoints, could neither cross one another nor conflict with one another, since among phenomena, in spite of the very solidarity we have recognized everywhere in them, there is heterogeneity. It is through an illusion as contrary as could be to the spirit of science that, in affirming the truth of determinism, one thinks he is denying freedom, as if diverse forms of phenomena were not compatible, or as if, for example, the laws of gravity could exclude the spontaneity of vital functions!

Here, therefore, we must resolutely cut the web of invisible roots that tie us to the subterranean origins of our conduct. Action has its own proper vital sap. It is always a *beyond*. If it was indispensable, lest any intelligence tarry amid sterile difficulties, to determine the antecedents of the reasonable and free decision, henceforth it is from this decision that we must start as from the true and solid origin of the movement that bears man toward known and willed ends. Once he acts, knowingly and willingly, he is not preoccupied ordinarily with the efficient causes of his decision; and he is right. For he really substitutes himself for the entire mechanism of unconscious life. The light enlightens him no less, without his searching for where it comes from; and besides it is never by looking where it is coming from that he discovers the decisive reason for his resolution, since he is never conscious of acting without having transformed the immanent necessity into a transcendent finality. He dominates all that goes before without needing to know it distinctly, because it is enough for him to know where he is tending. For in what he knows, he understands and surpasses what he does not know in this way; in what he wills, he ratifies what he had not yet been able to will.

123

This is why the analytical reflexion of the psychologist, by looking back to the conditions of the act, runs the risk of denaturing what it claims to be studying. True knowledge is that reflexion which turns the interior look forward toward the ends that solicit the will because there alone is to be found the sufficient reason of free determinations. Whoever is born for action looks in front of him; or if he looks back to where he comes from, it is only to know better where he is going, without ever closing himself up in the tomb of a dead past. Onward, and upward. Action is action only in that way. It is a matter of science that the final cause is more than the efficient cause; and it was to show this that it was necessary to define the relation that unites them.

It happens thus that the popular sense is in agreement with the conclusions of subjective science. The scientific notion of freedom remains quite close to naive consciousness and to practical experience. Voluntary action appears as a creation in creation; it is an infinite gathered up in one point, and it triumphs over universal oppression and lifts the world up, because there is in the subject a power in comparison with which the weight of the entire object that knowledge expressed no longer counts. To move my little finger by myself, I have to disturb the fulness of this system of phenomena. Yes, at the moment I undergo its impression I have to be stronger than all that is known to me. I walk under the weight of the infinite.

To conceive the unity of the universe, to affirm that this universe is not a closed system, is that not in effect to admit that the spirit, with regard to the world, is like an infinite capable of dominating all natural forces?

Do we not sense, has it not been noted a hundred times, that we are stronger than everything, not always through the vigor of the human animal, but through the direction of the will, through the internal energy and the central action of the spirit? Emancipation through science will always be incomplete; liberation through moral initiative, through patience, even through death heroically confronted and accepted always remains possible. Scientific knowledge never releases us; on the contrary, it is from scientific knowledge that we are liberated, through this simple feeling.

No doubt, along with the mysterious power he experiences within himself, man feels assailed and often vanquished by obscure tyrannies; and this mixture of strength and weakness is the great enigma of his nature. But if he is at times like a toy in unknown hands, it always remains that nothing on the side of the positive sciences, nothing in the determinism of phenomena, menaces his sovereignty. And if it is true that his effort often runs up against miserable perils, it is never for causes that science can define nor in the name of the general laws of nature or of thought. It was essential, then, amidst the confusion into which we are thrown by the vague consciousness of our strength and subjection, to sort out this first freedom and defend it against the groundless objections which positive science has often showered upon it in order to reinforce the entanglement of our real bonds. Nevertheless, there remain enough obstacles to the exercise of this freedom, as we shall see in studying the natural expansion of voluntary action.

Let us hold on to these interconnected conclusions firmly then. Freedom is postulated by science. It appears before consciousness through the very interplay of determinism. There is consciousness of determinism only through freedom. Freedom adopts all its antecedent conditions. But it does not find in them its reason for being. It becomes necessary to find the true reason for action in an end transcending nature or science.

II

Necessarily produced before consciousness, freedom is necessarily exercised. Do we grasp the extent of this new determinism which embraces, no longer just the past in its entirety, but is valid for all the future? Once this liberating reason has shone through reflexion, it is done forever; it has shone. But let us be careful: this ulterior necessity is still enveloped in the actual determination. Hence, attentive to this double relation, we must now investigate how freedom has an inevitable influence, and how nevertheless it does not disavow either this inevitable use or anything that can result from it. It does not escape the necessity of being and of remaining the reason for action; and at the heart of its sincerity it consents to it.

I. — What we have seen we cannot help having seen. When reflexion has awakened the sense of a free power within us, and has placed us in the hands of our own counsel, it is too late: not to want to use this power is still to use it. Freedom is not, as it has too often been represented, and quite wrongly, like a simple arbitral power, always the master over lending or refusing the mediation of reason; it has issued from the dynamism of spontaneous action, that is why it necessarily tends toward the dynamism of reflected action. In this it bears the indelible mark of its origin and in a way continues the movement, accepted and legitimated as well, of determinism.

Not to will to will is therefore always to will. And when the will, apparently running away from the difficult circumstances where it is summoned to struggle, turns its back on the importunate beam of light that is troubling its quiet, it does not cease being the accomplice of the tendencies that carry it away while it makes a pretense of remaining neutral. It would be convenient for it to wash its hands of everything! But what happens before it, without it, happens through it, since being conscious of finding only in itself the true reason for the act, it places the reason for the act elsewhere than in itself. *Adversus rationem, non absque ratione velle est* (it is to will against reason, not without reason). And when in fact we do not will to will, the fact is that we will to abstain from willing as we act, the fact is that we will to act. Always, then, it is from the will that conscious action fetches up, not all the conditions from which it draws its sap, to be sure, but that "unconditional" cause without which it would not be.

To understand this complicity of abstention better, let us think of the invincible strength in resistance; for the freedom not to do is infinite, sovereign and definitive from the beginning. To get a man to act, neither external power nor internal violence has any hold on his reason held in reserve; he may be killed, but that is the triumph of this will not to act, since death, in destroying the freedom to do, consecrates the freedom not to do.

What the heroic freedom to die thus confers forever on the past, the equal and contrary power of living and acting sows in the future forever. Even when the will seems to restrict itself to the proximate occasions and to the passing "mobiles" to place them in itself without giving itself to them, it places itself in them and, instead of having them serve it, it serves them. Every motive that is efficacious over us is more than this motive. For example, whoever proposes science for himself as the goal of his life

126

already makes of it an end transcending science, a moral reality. Similarly, universal determinism is not an object of science; hence we could not fall back on it to excuse an act except by virtue of a belief, and an illegitimate belief. The willed act always infinitely surpasses what is known, analysed, determined. Beyond what he covets, man is interested in what covets and enjoys in himself; he prefers himself to the world, because he is indeed worth more than the world. He acts, then, according to the idea of action he has, only inasmuch as he is principle and end of his acts.

II.—Free will has necessarily arisen in us and it has adopted all its origins.—Free will is necessarily involved in all our reflected acts and it ratifies all the consequences of its intervention or its abstention. It is not just a necessary *possibility*; it is a necessary *fact*.

It is a delicate task to show that freedom, in exercising itself necessarily, conserves the voluntary property of all this forced appurtenance with which the future encumbers it. Determinism seems to go before freedom, to accompany it, and to follow it, since freedom germinates, grows and fructifies inevitably; and yet, as freedom consented to the necessity of willing and acting, it ratifies this new necessity which results from it. Or rather, this double constraint is but the form under which it reveals itself to itself and imposes its own conditions on itself. For, since it finds only in itself the sufficient reason for its conduct, it could only blame itself for the consequences that derive directly from what it willed or excluded.

And it is this determinism which alone authorizes the science of free action, or that even constitutes its object. For in the infinite variety of decisions and possible acts, thought remains lost as in a chaos; there is no science of the particular. But if this undetermined power is defined only in *that* it wills, and not by *what* it wills, better still, if in the mere act of willing must be revealed the end it is tending to and the means it is using, then this rigorous concatenation entails a scientific determination: there is a necessary logic of freedom.

What we have to do henceforth is to develop the content of the will consistent with the very movement it impresses on itself in its first *élan*. If it has a rule to observe, an operation to produce, moral and social relations to institute, it is through this expansion itself that it will discover them, thanks to a method whose originality is incomparable. For it is the *a priori* initiative of this free activity which, in deploying itself, must reconstitute the necessity it is subject to, so to speak, *a posteriori*; thus the heteronomy of law will correspond to its interior autonomy. So that, when we do truly what we will in all sincerity, we are obeying an obligation which, far from depending on a decree of ours, is for us an imperative end. Therein lies the unique character of practical experimentation: action in a way provokes a response and the teachings from the outside; and these teachings that are imposed on the will are nevertheless wrapped up in this will itself. Everything that follows will shed light on this view and justify it.

The reason for the act, in the eyes of consciousness, could reside only in a freedom able to sum up, exploit and surpass all the determinism from which it issued and which it accepts; and this power is not free to steal away from its role; it cannot, it does not will to run away. It remains always the true reason for the reflected act and that which legitimately bears its weight. But do we not see this double reef against which all these first appearances of freedom are in danger of being shattered? — Necessarily produced, necessarily active and efficacious, is not freedom another name for determinism, a simple spiritual automatism whose spring, instead of being a blind force, would be an idea, the strongest of forces? — Inevitably sovereign, and alone able to bring the act to a resolution, able to resolve it by itself, is freedom not arbitrariness itself? Caught between pure indifference and a determinism which, for seeming less brutal, is nonetheless absolute, that seems to be the alternative before me. Slave or despot, nothing or everything, depending on the viewpoint from which we look at this nascent freedom, is that all there is to the *reason* of action?

128

Freedom, necessarily produced and necessarily exercised in us, keeps itself free only under the form of a determination, an obligation and an action. Hence for the will to remain sincere, we must pass from autonomy to heteronomy, and from the formalism of intention to the production of action; in this it goes beyond the domain of consciousness. The object of the next chapter is to establish this. — In it we first examine how freedom, instead of having an assured efficaciousness and sovereignly dominating all the subalternate motives, mixes itself in with them and needs to determine itself among them. — Then we define the character of the goal which free willing thus assigns itself; and we show how this end which the will proposes for itself is irreducible to this will itself, and appears to it as an obligatory law. — Finally we see that this conception of duty takes on a practical form, that is, that the intention is sincere and complete only to the extent that it passes into action. In short, once the will has been interiorized in reflected consciousness, it can no longer confine itself therein; coming from the outside, where it draws its nourishment, it returns to the outside to operate in it. — At one and the same time, then, we shall do away with the chimerical conception of a freedom of indifference, the contrary illusion of a determinism of the good, and the error of moral formalism.

CHAPTER 3
The Determination of Freedom and the Production of Action

To be conscious of determinism it has appeared that we must be free; for the awareness of any definite state supposes and constitutes a higher state. To be conscious of freedom, must we not fall back on a new necessity? Will not the knowledge of it we acquire neutralize this very freedom? Will it not be exposed to the peril of arbitrariness, to the vertigo of indifferent immobility or to the tyranny of a new determinism? It appears called to be the whole of action; and yet by itself it seems to be still nothing. Is it possible then for freedom to exercise itself? If it can, will it inaugurate in man another form of necessity; and from the moment when, like a power higher than every other, it emerges from its obscure conditions, will it not in fact always be the strongest power, necessarily sovereign and determining? — No. Fatally produced, it preserves itself only freely. This we must show.

I

Here then is the state of the difficulty. On the one hand, we are conscious of an interior power that alone gives our decisions, whatever they be, their true reason. On the other hand, this power is not defined, and seems to be only an absolute indifference, a blind and arbitrary force, and so to speak, an unreason (*déraison*). How then find in it a principle of discernment and of choice?

I. — The mental dynamism raises contrasting images and ideas: hence it is impossible that in the eyes of reflected consciousness any motive, whatever it may be, should appear unique and total; and that is the very condition of our emancipation. Freedom itself is not any more than any other a motive apart or wholly formal; it necessarily embodies itself in

132

the particular motives; and when it distinguishes itself from them, it does not suppress them. If there is a universal good, it can only present itself to us under a singular form, *portio*; and if we must live *sub specie totius* (under the aspect of the whole), the whole question will be precisely to make a whole, *unum et totum* (the one and the whole), of what seems to be only a fragment.

Among the diverse reasons that vie within us, how then will free will be able to intervene, lend itself to one of them, and thus become the true reason for the final resolution by choosing that one among the determinisms to which it will, as it were, prefer to give itself over? — In each of the tendencies that solicit activity resides in its entirety the power of contraries that embraces them all; and somehow not having any particular expression, it particularizes itself in each one. Simultaneously with the attraction of a "mobile," then, this power experiences its own virtuality; that is to say that, through an apparent absurdity, it is conscious of determining, if that be its pleasure, the triumph of the weakest one, for no other reason than this very will to affirm its despotism. It finds in all the wherewithal to place itself in each; and inevitably it places itself in one of them.

Thus it is that, necessarily immanent at first in some motive or other among other motives equally determined, freedom distinguishes itself from all and confers upon the object of its preferences a character of transcendence. Submitting to a heteronomy to maintain its own sovereignty, it brings to the service of one elected tendency the very forces of the rival tendencies; it does what it does with all the power it would have used in doing what it does not do. That is how it proposes *a reason* as an end for itself, although it must itself be *the reason* for its decision. To what is insufficient to determine it, it adds its own sufficiency to determine itself; and the resolutely voluntary act thus inevitably becomes expressive of an initiative other than the impulse of the triumphant motive.

Now, in this synthesis which the will constitutes with the motive it espouses, is it the motive that is the true reason for the choice? If so, it means that we give in and that, in willing, we will what the sincerity of willing, left to its own initiative and liberated from all temptation, would not will. Free freedom, then, is the one that wills to will, the one which, first suppressing the natural efficacy of the spontaneous tendencies, consents to undergo the attraction of one of them only to the extent that it places in it the reason for its resolution. For the moment it is enough to note that this distinction, whose terms can appear subtle, is made by consciousness with great simplicity and great force: we all know the difference there is between the willed concession and the voluntary initiative, between what seems to drag us along and what we seem to pro-

131

duce. This appearance is sharp enough so that among our decisions some are in our eyes the consented result of a movement of passion, and others, the exact and sincere manifestation of what we call *our willing*.

And that is enough already to make us now, in avoiding the peril of indetermination and of indifference, have to beware of an opposite peril, what we could call the determinism of freedom or the modern form of the Socratic paradox. For if we know what we will when we truly will, if we are conscious that only therein is found the efficacious reason for our decision, and if this conviction, dominating all the suggestions of the psychological automatism, is stronger than any other tendency, why is this true will not always the only victorious one in fact, as it is in potency? How do we come to will and to do what at bottom we do not will, to contradict ourselves and to enslave ourselves freely? It is important to be attentive to this decisive point.

II. — As every other motive, in manifesting itself to reflexion, takes on an objective character that strips it of its immediate energy, because nothing acts upon us that is not subjective, so also for freedom: it subsists only by knowing itself, and in knowing itself it annihilates its necessary efficacity. It posits itself before itself as object, as goal, as particular end, above the other motives by right, among the other motives in fact, *una ex multis* (one of many); it is mine, it is no longer myself.

That is why, in proposing freedom as our end, we feel a disproportion between the willing will, *quod procedit ex voluntate* (what proceeds from the will), and the willed will, *quod voluntatis objectum fit* (what becomes the object of the will). We experience the difficulty of a choice and a sacrifice. That infinite power of contraries that enveloped and dominated all our ways of being and desiring has to impose a determination on itself. It has to cut back and curtail some of the members of the organism it was animating. *Omnis determinatio negatio est* (every determination is a negation). What we would like, it seems, is the full blossoming of all our natural tendencies; but it so happens that, in the opposition of the motives inside reflexion, none of them, not even freedom, rallies and contents them all. Or rather it is especially freedom, taken as an end, which seems to require of us the greatest effort and curtailment; for through a singular effect of interior optics, after being so full of itself and so seducing in the first *élan* of consciousness, freedom appears empty and inert when we have to make of it a goal for the will.

Thus the willed action is not initially adequate to the will itself. It seems that what we will, we can never will all at once, and that the reason for the free act is not all the possible reason; certain tendencies have to appear to abort, and abort in a definitive way through an irreparable sacrifice. There is an inevitable partiality of the will in action. Hence the reason for the act is never completely clear and totalized in the eyes of consciousness; and that is why duty will always appear with an aspect of risk and mortifying obscurity.

Far then from acting in us as by an invincible grace, the idea of what we will the most meets, in the interior struggle, the toughest opposition. Amid the division of the hostile factions that the mental automatism raises, it is often enough for freedom to appear for all the factions to coalesce against it. As much as it seemed all-powerful, seen from the intimacy of the subject, because it summed up in itself all the energies of life and of thought, considered as object and as goal, it appears as nothing. It is not surprising, then, that if we look for it among the positive ends that inspire our determinations, we do not find it; for it becomes real only in willing to be so. Necessarily produced, it remains itself only by reproducing itself. No one is forced to remain free therefore. Even those who abuse freedom will what they have received from it; the abuse includes the use.

Also freedom is not distinct from the use we make of it. If it abdicates and enslaves itself, it is immanent to its own forfeiture. If it emancipates itself and develops, it is immanent to its own transcendence. In any case the reflected will is always twofold because it is at once a principle of action and an end to be attained. The whole art of living, the whole effort of sincerity, will be to bring about as perfect a conformity as possible between the initial will and the positive will. After the antecedent conditions of necessary freedom, it is the vivifying conditions of free freedom that we must study; for, as it is posed, it is not imposed on itself, but is exposed to the danger of losing itself.

But how easy it is to foresee the practical difficulties of this task! for the tendencies whose fascination draws us away from our own willing have in them the power of the subjective spontaneity; whereas in proposing itself to itself as an ideal to be realized, freedom seems to be only an inert object and like an abstract fiction. Henceforth the enunciation of the problem is quite clear: what do we will, when we will truly all that we will? And how find an end adequate to the integrity of the primitive movement? How, in spite of the partiality it seems condemned to, does freedom preserve its total sincerity?

II

We must therefore make willing equal to itself. What does that mean? It means that we must restore to this apparent nothingness of objective freedom the infinitude of that interior power of which reflexion has given us clear consciousness. This is to say that we must transport the life of the subject into the object he proposes as an end for himself. It is to say that the strength and the freedom we know of in ourselves is only a means for attaining the fulness of what we will. It is to say, finally, that, not being yet what we will, we are in a relation of dependence with regard to our true end. In short, what we really will is, not what is already realized in us, but what surpasses us and commands us. Whatever we will, we will what we are not. In fact, there is always a heteronomy that imposes itself on consciousness.

I.—True subjective freedom, therefore, can be taken as the end, without being denatured, only inasmuch as, considering it as object, we attribute an ideal, absolute, imperative character to it; and what our most sincere will looks for and confesses is a law that requires more of it than it is as yet. Consequently, to propose actual freedom as our end, as moral formalism does, is to stop definitively at the autonomy of willing, to misunderstand our first duty and, in it, all other duties; it is, under pretext of preserving the purity and the integrity of freedom, to restrict it to the poverty of its first form and to keep only a dead image of it.

Thus it is a first duty to acknowledge duty; and to acknowledge it is to recognize that it imposes on interior freedom, not only interior respect and submission, but an effort and effective sacrifices, not only a trust and a generosity whose origin is not just in the knowledge we have of the law, but a positive act which inevitably surpasses a purely formal conformity of the intention with duty. To will what we truly will is to submit to a practical rule.

Hence it is by one and the same act that we conceive the true nature of moral law and that we begin to practice it. For moral law requires more of freedom than this freedom is as yet, a first effort that assigns as the object for our real life the infinite virtuality of the subject. In taking itself as ulterior goal, free will ceases to *appear* autonomous, because there is no adequation between what we are and what we will to be; but it truly *is* autonomous, because it remains itself only by not remaining what it is. For reflexion and resolution, in redoubling the initial movement of reason and in sanctioning the primitive wish of the spontaneous willing, confer upon it a new character and an added reality. It is this new reality, a synthesis of the voluntary and the willed, which is posited as the rule; it becomes the transcendent end of our actual freedom, of that freedom that cannot look at itself from the start as an absolute, since, with regard to the ideal object wherein he projects all that he can and wills to be, the subject is no longer anything but an imperfect becoming in his own eyes.

So far moral obligation establishes only relations between acts of consciousness, then, without authorizing us from the start to confer upon duty a mystical character. We have just discerned its origins and seen how, having necessarily appeared to consciousness in the very order of phenomena, it has an equally necessary influence. But far from reducing its value, the knowledge of this brings out its sovereign importance, its scientific certitude and its higher bearing. Moral law, by just being represented in us, envelops in itself a certain reality. It is not simply an *ought to be* (*devoir être*) which could not be; it *is* already because it is to be (*doit être*). Reason is practical only on the condition of not being just a pure reason. In what it can violate, therefore, the will posits what it cannot suppress. Thus defined, heteronomy is not contrary to the profound wish of freedom; it only consecrates it and responds to it.

Thus here again is found that instability which has not allowed us to stop at anything: it is impossible to fix at any point the continuous movement that carries us through the entire domain of the senses, of science, and of consciousness. At each level we discover that we always have to go further, to be sure not further than we will, but further than we foresaw; at each level, there is a new synthesis, a higher end to attain. Thus it is that sensible and scientific knowledge tied into the subjective phenomena. Thus it is that, in the internal dynamism, we noted the heterogeneity of the motive and of the true goal; for if the intention is at once the end we are tending toward and the effort we make to attain it, if the final cause is the complete expression of the efficient causes, it nonetheless constitutes an original newness. Thus it is, finally, that freedom becomes for itself a transcendent end. If it pretends to keep itself completely to itself and to find satisfaction in its potency, this pretense alone begins to denature and to pervert it; so that moral heteronomy is the necessary complement of the autonomy of the will. For what counts on the whole is not to will what we are, it is to be what we will, separated as we are from ourselves, so to speak, by an immense abyss; and this abyss we must cross over before finally being such, absolutely such, as what we require of ourselves.

II. — Moral law is indispensable to freedom therefore. Duty is thus erected into a positive fact, a scientific truth. To emancipate ourselves from it, under pretext that it is obscure, ill founded, or painful to bear, is to be radically inconsequent with science and with consciousness; it is no longer to will what we will.

But do we ever emancipate ourselves from it to the point of not even conceiving it anymore? And whether we observe it or steal away from it, once we have conceived it, does nothing result from this for all the ulterior development of action? Can we make it so that it will not have been? — No, we must not think that in practice we denature what we explain poorly, that we suppress what we deny, that we destroy what we violate. If moral obligation inevitably appears to us with an imperative character, this necessity, understood or misunderstood, consented to or rejected, nonetheless has a necessary repercussion of its own in our life. In fact, a heteronomy is imposed on consciousness. In fact, the impossibility of an immediate autonomy leads to action as to an inevitable exodus. In fact, the sense of an obligation, the necessity of a choice in the resolution and of a partiality in the action, confers upon all of our behavior the inevitable newness of a moral aspect. The presence of duty in us is a principle of internal antagonism; consequently, it is a principle of strength and the point of departure for a new dynamism. Feign as we will to dispel it, try as we will to muzzle it or to annihilate it, never again will it be a matter of indifference for the subsequent unfolding of action that this witness has appeared.

Also, after this consciousness of obligation has arisen, it is over with. Whatever we will, according to it or against it, there results from the will alone (prescinding from what it wills), an immense concatenation of necessary consequences. Henceforth, therefore, the issue is not, while condemning moral formalism, to offer the will some matter and to pour into action some content from the outside. Far from it. Whatever the formulas, the prescriptions or the falşifications of morality may be, whatever the deviations or the illusions of conscience, whatever the practical failings or negligences, the issue is to determine the element common to every use of freedom and, under what is arbitrary and variable, to take hold of what remains necessary and inevitable. In what we will freely, there is a latent determinism: a necessity whose rigor alone allows for a true science of action, a necessity whose development reveals to the will little by little the series of means it imposes on itself, a necessity which alone is of sovereign importance for man, since it discloses to him what he cannot avoid being sooner or later and since, through an inexorable logic, it draws from his willed actions all that they already contain.

Thus, it is impossible for the intention not to particularize itself, impossible for the decision to express the total will and assure it a full autonomy from the start, impossible again for this partiality of the resolution not to look in an effective action for the precise confirmation and the progress it aspires to. Hence far from believing that the intention is isolated from its conditions and far from considering it as an empire in an empire, we must understand how it contributes in constituting the milieu where it has to orient itself; we must determine what serves in determining intention itself. From the mere fact that man wills deliberately, there will result a sequence of acts and necessary relations that little by little will form the very framework of his life and the natural theater of his morality. Thus, before we can give any content to the intention, all of nature will be reintegrated into morality.

Henceforth the outlook seems reversed; and the movement, which up to now appeared centripetal, becomes in a way centrifugal. After having absorbed and dominated the entire object of knowledge and all the dynamism of nature, the subject finds himself obliged to go out of himself and to submit to a law of detachment, precisely in order not to keep himself chained to an imperfect form of his own development. It is, it seems, outside of ourselves that we must seek the perfection of the interior life. We are called now to live and to operate in a region higher than distinct consciousness; we are entering in a still mysterious domain, the one where the will will be united to its object. It seeks its completion therein; it awaits from it, as through an experimentation provoked *a priori*, the clarity it needs and the answer from which it hopes to find rest. Apparent contradictions: the will is only tending to equal its internal *élan* and it seems to be begging and seeking from the outside the satisfaction it can only appreciate within itself; it claims to be emancipating itself from all the obstacles that stand in the way of its expansion and it goes off to commit itself to the determinism of external powers. It is this necessity of action that we must explain and justify. Under this apparent fatality is hidden instinctively the ambition of a will avid to expand. 138

III

It is a fact that every image and every idea, expressing a system of forces, tends to pass into act; and in effect it is the act that is the popular sign of sincere convictions and of tested sentiments. But, it will be said, "does the effort by which we conceive and affirm the moral law still need to be manifested? Is it not already a complete act that gains in value only through the energy and the purity of the sentiment that is entirely interior, like a faith which, even without works, would be necessary and sufficient for salvation? Will it not be enough, whatever happens otherwise in the human machine, to raise and to direct the intention? And besides, how could the moral worth of resolutions depend on the material execution of a few movements? Is it even intelligible that the all pure conception of duty could be truly translated through the body of an action? In short, isn't formalism the truth?"

On the contrary, the truth is that action itself is an integrating part of the intention, that it vivifies it and sheds light on it, and that it orients the will toward its ends by defining its ideal little by little and by realizing it. To use and dominate the lower motives, we must place ourselves on the terrain where they are; we must conquer them down to their material origin. We do not triumph over them by a simple preference or by an ideal decree. To will what we will is to do it with the whole of ourselves. Execution, beyond the intention it realizes, is an original power and a new end.

—We must not forget, indeed, that we became conscious of our freedom only in acting. It is therefore necessary for us to act to develop our freedom and know it better; for the unreflected will is of the same nature as the one we are most conscious of and, by illuminating us on what comes after it, reflexion enables us to produce what goes before it. —We must not forget that freedom revealed itself, in the conflict of motives, only by taking on the figure of one of the particular motives and by playing an efficacious role in the midst of them. It is therefore necessary for it to continue acting to maintain its independence; otherwise the basis on which it rests will come to fail it. —We must not forget that this freedom, drawn, through the progress of action, from the determinism of nature, does not preserve and complete itself except to the extent that it objectifies itself in some way and puts in itself all that it wills should be there. It is therefore necessary that, through action, it insinuate, down to the springs from which it proceeds itself, the waters that will come back to it more abundant.

Thus born of action, kept up through action, perfected by action, the consciousness of freedom and moral obligation tends to action, αει ενεργει (it is always in act). It is always in the form of a motive, that is, of a tendency to action, that duty takes on consistency and a concrete shape. *Bonum semper in actu* (the good is always in the act). Εν τω εργω δοκει ειναι το αγαθον και το εν (the good and the one appears to be in the act). To imagine that one can determine duty by a deduction of reason is an illusion. It is not by a deductive method that we bring a content to the formal law.

We see, then, that practical obligation, still indefinite, receives a first determination here. As freedom, which at first had seemed pure and arbitrary indifference, had taken shape in the conception of duty, so now the consciousness of duty already bears with it a necessity that is defined and justified: "We must put in practice, it is necessary to act."

It would also be to err totally to pretend to isolate the free intention from the determinism of actions. For, no more than freedom is detached from its necessary antecedents, is it detached from its necessary consequents. People have hardly attended to this determinism that is consecutive to decision; and yet, as the rest of this study will show, this is the great business of man, the one on which his personal and social life depends. For the moment the essential was to understand how the will is faithful to its intention only by awakening, through the spontaneous life it emerges from, needs, motives and energies more and more coherent and conspiring with its aim, whatever it may be. It can do so only by inquiring of action the hidden way through which thoughts, desires and habits are born. It is actually through action that the moral intention insinuates itself into our members, makes our heart beat, and pours its own life into our veins; through action that it unfolds into the immense milieu we plunge into; through action that it comes back to consciousness fuller, more clear, laden with its conquests; for the mechanism of determinism gives back what we give it, but through what transformations   140 and with what enrichments!

It appears then that what is necessary in the obligation to act corresponds to the sincerity of the primitive willing: this necessity itself contributes to realizing the plenitude of our freedom. What is really at issue? It is to get to the point where what we will proceeds spontaneously from ourselves and where there is as perfect an agreement as possible between the *élan* and the result of our effort, equality between the amplitude of the voluntary aspirations and the magnitude of the willed ends. Now, from what we are to what we will to be, the interval seems immense. And what then is this distance from ourselves to ourselves? What keeps our own will from being simple, full and complete? It is the presence within us of hostile desires, it is the interior division of our most vital tendencies, it is the intestinal war that the natural movement of automatism brings about in us. Also must we little by little penetrate this entire psychological mechanism with pacifying and liberating influences, in order that the seeds of unity lying at the sources of unconscious life may grow and fructify, thus furnishing the reflected will with a more and more faithful image of its proper nature, a life more and more in conformity with its proper aspiration.

No doubt, the sincere intention is already an act by itself and, in certain cases, there is no material operation, it would seem, to translate it to the outside. Nevertheless, it cannot be doubted that every act of consciousness expresses itself through an action, that is to say, through a particular state and a systematic disposition of the organs; it cannot be doubted that this intimate act, if it becomes the object of a decided attention and an express will that consents to it and doubles it in a way by adhering to it, determines an organic tension which sustains and rein-

forces the intention itself. Nowhere then can we isolate either freedom
or obligation from their antecedents and their consequents; and it is not
through an unintelligible bond of necessity that they are tied to them; it
is because the will finds in this close relation a means, the only means,
of pursuing its free development. The new synthesis we have to arrive at
is necessary and transcendent with respect to its own elements.

Thus action precedes and follows moral freedom, like a doubly indispensable condition for it to be born and to survive. Even when it takes
itself as end, free will wills something other than itself; it does not will
itself objectively as it is subjectively. It becomes, it makes itself; it is never
without changing and keeps itself only by giving itself. Having come out
of the lower determinism, it needs to draw from it a perpetual nourishment, as it also needs to elaborate and transform without cease that incoherent spontaneity which it must bring to participate in the moral
unity and activity.

There is therefore a double exchange from the object to the subject and
from the subject to the object; and it is this exchange that constitutes the
voluntary operation. After it has separated itself from the animal suggestions and from the psychological automatism, the will returns to irreflex-
ion; the intention blindly throws itself into the movement that executes
it, as if, at the moment we begin to accomplish it, we were entering into
the night of a hypnotic sleep. Do we not admire how the grasshopper
leaps with all its strength, headlong? In giving ourselves to action, do we
ever know where we shall come down? And if we knew clearly where,
would we act? At least we see clearly already that we will to act and why;
we see even that in acting we bring light into the obscurity we are entering, and that there is a luminescence accompanying each step we take,
lucerna pedibus et lex lux (the light is a lamp to guide my steps and a
law). That is sufficient for duty to be illuminated as occasion and the
need to know arises; somehow it produces this light that guides it and
justifies it. And thus it is that the tiny seed of moral consciousness sown
in us can raise the entire mass of the indifferent or rebellious forces.

Narrow then and factitious is every philosophy and especially every
morality which, limiting itself to what the gaze of interior observation
reaches immediately, or which, even pushing on to penumbral
phenomena that precede reflexion, still does not go so far as to penetrate
the darkness which goes before, accompanies and follows all subjective
knowledge. Before and after, below and above the consciousness of action, there is something to be known about action, and not the least important. Consciousness is not the whole of science, no more than it is the
whole person. And what we must now try to do is to study, no longer
phenomena perceived as objects nor realities that are quite subjective,

but action properly speaking inasmuch as it sums up the object in the life of the subject and makes the subject live in the object itself. The interior life subsists only through perpetual expansion and fruitfulness. 142

This action, nourished on unconscious forces, spontaneous sentiments, and reflected desires, this action, which is a concrete and fecundating definition, not an abstract and dissolving analysis of the idea it realizes, we are therefore led to consider as a living seed, which, endowed with an evolutionary power, enjoys, as soon as it is conceived and planted in the human organism, a natural growth, an internal development, and, so to speak, functions of nutrition, of relation, and of reproduction.

We must now follow the organic progress of this germination. For if in concentrating within itself the infinity of the milieu whence it draws its sap, action is the end of a world, it is at the same time the beginning of a new world. It appears suddenly like a trenchant blow that separates the past from the future and the possible from the real, without any possibility of turning back. Through its synthetic character, it is the connecting link between scientific determinism and practical determinism, one following, the other preceding the voluntary decision, but both suspended from the initiative of willing. Through it we restore to the universe all that we seemed to borrow from it, and more; for we moralize our animal nature by sinking into our vitals the operative virtue of duty; and we learn, in acting, what we have to do, that is to say, our will succeeds more and more in knowing itself and becoming the equal of itself.

Thus the system of moral obligations will take shape little by little through the very deployment of life. For in tending toward its truly voluntary ends, action goes through, regulates, orients, all our personal and social inclinations. Before finding ourselves as we will to be, we must therefore concert in ourselves the universal life of which our thinking organism is the receptacle. We must even construct within ourselves a kind of new universe; for the sense of the moral law, in symbolically summing up all that aspires to grow deep within us, is the spring for our total development. What cannot be violated in duty organizes in our consciousness the system of the obligations that can be violated. Also, through its immense expansion in the midst of the organic, intellectual, and moral world, it is always the same will that is in search of itself and finds itself little by little.

In short, freedom maintains itself and develops only by surpassing itself: actual autonomy would in truth be heteronomy. There is no question then of proposing a duty for freedom from the outside; it is a question of discovering duty in freedom itself and of finding in what it is not 143 yet the secret wish for what it is already. And as the antecedent determinism appeared indispensable for the manifestation of free will, so also the consequent determinism is an integrating condition of freedom. This twofold aspect is but a single truth; for the way of dividing and ordering things in time is often only an artifice of analysis. Action, always in part blind, envelops, in that obscure part that is the operation properly speaking, all the series of its scientific conditions and its moral relations. It is this obscure part of the act that all the rest of what follows must elucidate.

— Some ground has been gained. In affirming *something*, and in willing that there be positive science, we were postulating the subjective phenomenon. In recognizing the scientific reality of the fact of consciousness, and in studying the laws of psychological automatism, we became conscious of the internal determinism. In positing determinism, we draw freedom from it. In willing freedom, we require duty. In conceiving the moral law, there is the necessity of producing it in action in order to know it and determine it by practising it.

To follow the progress of the voluntary decision within the confines of the organism where it germinates and for which, through an obscure labor, it constitutes the cooperative unity; to study this interior growth, from the point where the act begins to spread out in the organs and to fashion the system of human individuality up to the moment where the moving operation, inevitably going beyond the borders of the individual, is born after this gestation to a more complete expansion: that is the aim of the following investigation.

Stage Three
FROM THE INTENTIONAL EFFORT TO THE FIRST EXTERIOR EXPANSION OF ACTION

The organic growth of willed action

Action is the intention living in the organism and fashioning the obscure energies from which it had emerged. Freedom, in effect, has to unfold and embody itself in order to preserve itself and develop. Acclimatizing the life of the spirit in brute determinism, it induces spontaneous life to produce motives and movements more and more in conformity with its profound aspiration. All the progress of science and of consciousness proceeds from action, but only to tend once again to action, which alone sustains and animates it.

Also we must now determine the living content of the voluntary operation. For the willed action is not just what we know of it in advance, as though it were enough to have decided to act in order to have already acted; we have willed the action precisely for what in it has to surpass the actual will. Hence, it is not enough to decree it nor even to produce it; we must study both its production amidst obstacles and resistances and the product itself, along with all the results of the operation, πραττειν, πραξιν, πραγμα (to do, the doing, what is done). After we have brought the willed action into being by a sort of *a priori* synthesis, it can only be truly known by an *a posteriori* analysis; for what it brings is instruction and increment.

But before going on, two preliminary difficulties arise. — How, without introducing into the free initiative of willing an unexplainable disturbance and without betraying the method which alone has appeared good up to now, can we explain that there should be lessons from the outside, resistance or organic passivity? — Besides, amidst the infinite diversity of possible decisions, how will we manage to eliminate the variable element in order to do a science of action? These two problems have an answer.

I. — If there exists a disproportion between what we are and what we tend to be, does it follow that this disproportion is definitive, that we are subject to a perpetual, an intolerable denial, and that feeling the "distress of the would-be great lord" justifies pessimism? No; it means that there is something in us to be conquered, that we are still partially and for the best part strangers to ourselves, and that we must treat ourselves, not as an end, but as an instrument of conquest.

Since we are still only a means and a kind of object with regard to the subject we will to be, we therefore become passive to our own activity. The shocks from the outside, the obstacles, even sufferings themselves can thus enter into the voluntary plan of our life. What seems *a posteriori* in the lessons of experience ties into the *a priori* movement of the most fundamental will; it is the solicited and provoked response. We act, in fact, only because action always brings some new element beyond or short of what is foreseen; the effect can never be deduced from its cause, nor what we shall be from what we will. And not only are there unexpected losses or plus-values as a consequence of the normal exercise of activity; but one encounters disorders, irregularities, a strange disturbance, a breakdown in the ordinary interplay of our powers which are condemned to effort, to labor, to sufferings that are, so to speak, unintelligible, *quod operor non intellego* (what I do I do not understand). People have ordinarily tripped on the speculative difficulty there is in tying together these three terms: *knowing, being* and *doing;* a minor embarrassment in comparison with the quite practical difficulty of willing and doing what we know, of knowing and doing what we will. But if our life is shot through with painfully and obscurely instructive trials, if it is no longer enough to act, but we must labor, that is to say, produce more than we can and exert ourselves if we have even an unforeseen lesson to take in, a perhaps unpleasant and distressing discovery to make, an illusion on our nature to avoid, this is a good place for the lesson to be introduced.

To *undergo (pâtir)*: we see how this passivity, how this suffering even, is included in *acting (agir)*. Because it needs to develop and spread itself out, the will exiles itself into a domain where it seems still a stranger, though it brings to it its conquering intention and the ambition of reigning. Does it not make pretense of being everywhere at home, and do not our desires embrace the world? We must therefore follow this willed expansion by studying the *self (le moi)*, not as it is concentrated in interior analysis, but as action alone constitutes it through the collaboration or through the antagonism of the term of its unfolding.

II.—But how reduce to the unity necessary for science the infinite multiplicity of empirical teachings? It seems impossible for theory to make up for what is lacking in practice; isn't it moral experimentation alone which enables us to know in ourselves what is not from ourselves? And yet isn't that the whole difficulty? For if the answer we get can vary infinitely, it is because the question raised by voluntary initiative can also differ infinitely by reason of the very inexhaustible variety of free decisions. Does not the science of action seem threatened with losing itself in chaos?

No. This is where the virtue of the method which alone has scientific rigor for solving the problem appears more clearly; for it enables us to eliminate the variable. Its strength is, after following the thread of the antecedent determinism, to pick up once more the chain of the determinism consecutive to the willed actions and to study its necessary unfolding.

Perhaps. it seems that between these two series there is a lacuna or a gap. Isn't it to denature the problem to prescind from the in-between since the arbitral decision is the one point of convergence which everything leads up to or takes off from? — But let us not be led astray. There is a sure continuity between these two forms of determinism; and here are the intermediary links: there is a necessity that reflexion should arise; there is a necessity again that freedom should be exercised; a necessity that freedom be not necessary; a necessity, finally, that it be not necessary to produce determined acts and that these acts, once freely determined, should have necessary consequences. In short, even in what can be violated, in what is perhaps violated, there is always something that is not violated. It is enough for science to be grounded on this very impossibility.

Also, in the act of freedom and in the consciousness of the moral law, what has to be determined is not what is changing and even arbitrary, but that whose definitive triumph is assured sooner or later. Whether we steal away from duty or submit to it, there is a common element: we must focus on this fixed end. Why, as is ordinarily done, should we stick to the provisional deviations, to the apparent denials, to passing and superficial assaults that the will can inflict on practical obligations? Do we not see that, whatever we might do otherwise, we do not emancipate ourselves from everything, and that we always remain in a certain order? Even egotistical voluptuousness cannot always avoid being fruitful. If there is in the antecedent conditions of action a determinism that brings the will to know itself, in what follows there is a new determinism that makes the free decision bear its natural fruits and that draws the framework wherein it unfolds. Does not what we posit in this way, merely by willing, deserve to be studied? And perhaps from this fact *that* we will, analysis will draw out little by little what we will.

For, we must not forget, man's persevering ambition is to equal his desires. From the beginning of this inquiry the only agreement concluded was to ask no concession of the will, to accept only its own avowals, to record only the results of its own initiative. What is more in conformity with this aim than to prescind, in moral obligation, from everything that seems to require an effort and a sacrifice, that is to say, from everything we can violate? Will that not be truly a morality without obligation, the scientific morality, the one which no longer has to bother with the indeterminable fantasies of freedom, and which excludes that variable of which there could be no science? In what is free, it will focus only on what is necessary; and thereby it will be a science without ceasing to be a morality.

To be sure, through its very progress, voluntary action is led to encounter resistances, to undergo lessons and trials. But these will be spoken of at first only to the extent that we succeed in overcoming them, remedying them, and profiting by them. Perhaps with enough firmness, intelligence and goodness man will arrive at satisfying his aspiration and settle (*conclure*) his destiny. Perhaps he will be able to do alone what he does, to heal by himself what he suffers, to undo alone what he has done poorly. Who knows whether the apparently most cruel contradictions will not reveal to him the primitive meaning and the perfect form of his will? Who knows whether this often costly experimentation will not be for him the true means of attaining and of reconquering the full cohesion of *willing*, of *being* and of *doing*? Finally, will not action, through its own virtue, be mediating and unitive, redemptive and perfective? — And when we shall have thrown into the open abyss of willing all the magnitude and generosity of human acts, works, and sufferings, will it be filled? That will be the decisive question.

For the moment suffice it to hand ourselves over to the current of determinism, since it bears willed action toward its natural ends; let us abandon ourselves to it, as if there were no freedom to exercise, no obligation to respect, no reprisals to fear. Thus will be developed the series of the necessary means that the will raises in its quest for itself and its desire to possess itself fully. The sun shines on the evil as on the good; I mean that life seems to impose on all equivalent obligations. We must therefore see how these common conditions are naturally organized. Moral relations do not stay up in the air; it is important above all to trace the framework wherein they constitute themselves.

The intention needs to realize itself through action, and action enriches it: it is the nature and the progress of this increase that we must henceforth study. In descending to operate in the unconscious, freedom no doubt raises to itself what it fashions; but first it gives itself up to it. Subjective life spreads into the object only to complete itself therein; it gives and it receives. *Nemo agit qui non agatur* (no one acts who is not acted upon). Thus the question of the objective value of our ideas is brought back to its scientific meaning. — From one viewpoint, the phenomenon of the idea, the mental synthesis, is something else and something more than what it represents; the subjective is more real than the positive facts whose general laws science reveals to us, since it implies them and overflows them. — But from a higher viewpoint, the act of consciousness, in embodying itself in action, penetrates the object and insinuates into it its own reality, to make of the whole an original synthesis. Therein lies the principle of the solidity of practical knowledge. We know well only what we have done. This is because we bring light where we act. This brightness is neither in ourselves alone, nor in things alone; we have to move for it to glow. The interior life, which earlier seemed to absorb all that nourishes its knowledge, finds itself incomplete and dead if it does not spend itself and spread itself; surpassing the universe of facts, it is surpassed by an unknown into which action alone enables it to penetrate. It engages itself invincibly in action; and if some secret instinct inclines it to do so, it is in order to shed light on this obscure aspect of things by shedding light on itself. *Qui facit veritatem venit ad lucem* (the one who does the truth comes to the light).

149

The first field where the intention unfolds is the organism. How does the body appear in consciousness? How does even this resistance enter into the development of willing? How do passivity, passion, and organic labor derive from the subjective causes? That is the triple object of the study we must undertake by renewing the analysis of muscular effort to uncover its true significance. In this way, all the active and passive forms of physical life, to the extent that this organic life mixes in with the consciousness of the willed and accomplished operation, will be reintegrated into the science of action, and included in the series of the means subordinated to the search for our destiny.

CHAPTER 1

The Body of Action and Subjective Physiology

150   Just as we ascended the steps that rise to the light of consciousness, we must now follow the degradation of reflected thought and the voluntary intention into the organic operation which is its first expression. But is it appropriate to say degradation? No. If there is some shadow after as well as before the illuminated domain of the interior life, it is because action penetrates above as well as below the region where the limited view of the spirit is distinct, going ahead of the light that it brings little by little. The unconscious is not found underneath only, it is above and beyond deliberate resolutions.

How then does the voluntary intention need to embody itself, and how does it encounter organic resistance? What does it have to gain in suffering? And what does this necessity of effort or of labor in action reveal to us? This is the threefold question to be resolved. To become passive, to be contradicted and constrained, to toil, that, it seems, is a strange way for the will to get to its ends. And yet it is the only way for it to progress. This is the paradox that has to be justified.

No sooner resolved upon, the act in effect throws itself into the execution; or at least the execution appears as the natural consecration of the intention. Without it, action is not action. The first concern of whoever studies action, then, must be to consider this material operation which is its immediate condition. In what way do we encounter the *body*, and does this organic life, which, without being alien to us, still is not *us*, mix

151   the feeling of a passivity into activity? The problem is often discussed, but it can be resolved only from a different viewpoint than the one commonly taken. No doubt it is good to first analyse the aggregate of apparently heterogeneous data that form the consciousness of muscular effort; but, to shed light on the obscurities of this labyrinth, we shall have to lay hold of the meaning of physical resistances and understand the role they play in the growth of the will. For action in a way displaces man's center of gravity, to transport it from the ideal intention into the total

operation. And this aspect of the problem, the most important, is also the most neglected one. In order to unravel the complications of subjective physiology, it is therefore essential to see how the very presence of the body is tied to the progress of willing and in what way it is of moral interest.

I

To describe the origins of the organic sense and the consciousness of muscular effort, to account for both normal impressions and quite varied pathological cases, we must expose and combine into three solidary couples the following certain observations.

(1) There is a first afferent action of the organism that is unconscious in its mode, conscious in its results. — Indeed, the automatism that spontaneously brings images and desires to the threshold of distinct thought, escapes the thought that takes in its productions. There is no light to play on the organic activity on which, as is said today, ideation or ideogeny depends. Even when we know from science where empirical consciousness finds its nourishment and how it is tied to the cerebral functions, consciousness itself is no less ignorant of where its interior visions come from. Also, in studying the scientific conditions and the unconscious elements of action, we did not even have to raise the question of the agent's own proper body. As Descartes notes, we can feign to be without a body, even if it be to think of bodies. The physiological origin of consciousness is unconscious.

(2) There is a first afferent action of thought which is perceived only in its subjective essence. — Once the threshold of consciousness is crossed, the interior life develops within reflexion according to an original law of finality which is not reducible to the simple concatenation of the efficient causes. The mental syntheses that are operated in consciousness reveal a new initiative. Through what is conscious about them, they constitute a proper force. The feeling of power which resides in ideas and which reflexion dispenses is not illusory. Not everything in the interior is an *effect;* the most essential part of the subjective act is a *cause* in turn; it determines its own conditions. If one wishes a symbolic translation of this truth in physiological language, it is acknowledged that the cerebral hemispheres are at once a terminal functional apparatus and an initial functional apparatus; this is to say that, in every circuit of voluntary activity, there is not only a simple arc, as in automatic reactions, but a double reflex arc, one ending in the hemispheres and the other starting from them after an original elaboration. There are, therefore, organic phe-

152

nomena that are no longer the antecedent condition, but the concomitant and consequent condition of the conscious energies.

(3) There is an efferent action of the will that remains unperceived in its physical effects. — To the series of internal determinations that lead up to the decision and the voluntary pursuit of an end, corresponds, in the cerebral mechanism, a parallel sequence of dependent movements. Of these organic operations that make this subjective activity possible, no direct knowledge is brought before reflexion. This is because the mental synthesis carries in it and dominates through a quite spontaneous ascendency the elementary forces that contributed to its emergence. And in determining itself, the will *ipso facto* brings about the determination of all that serves to sustain it. Also, to the extent that sensible nature and even the body are immanent to reflective life, the production of the active intention carries along with it the organic conditions tied to it. It is not perceived, because there is neither contrariety nor inhibition in it yet. Only the resolution is conscious up to now; but the first operation of the will in the organs that makes it possible escapes the interior view. — Besides, to discern this action of thought on its own conditions, we would have not only to sort out all the immense complexity of the objective phenomena, but also to penetrate into the nature of the subjective and synthetic element which, as we saw, serves as a bond for all our knowledge. As Maine de Biran noted, if we knew how we move the members of our body, we would know everything. Concentrating within ourselves the forces of the universe in order to govern this microcosm, we need a power and a multiplicity of action that analysis will never completely unravel, no more through consciousness than through sensible observation.

(4) There is at the same time an efferent action of the will which, at first unperceived in its subjective nature, is perceived only in its organic effects. — Here is the decisive point, the point where the body appears to consciousness and where passivity enters into action itself, the point where, from the interior conflict of the tendencies, emerges the feeling of the organism, the point, finally, where the transcription of the spiritual into the physical is effected.

The will could not find its entire completion in the intention alone; that is why it turns to action; to equal itself, it needs to produce itself. This willed act, therefore, is completed outside and, so to speak, beyond the present will. It is real because it is first ideal; but it is not real only to the extent that it is ideal. There is no equation between the preliminary knowledge and the effective operation, nor between the willing and the acting; also, from the moment when the subject becomes object for himself, he projects a *matter* before himself, he bears a *matter* within himself. Seen through the interior gaze, the body is a consequence and like a prolongation of our subjective nature: we will it to be. For if at first it appears as a veil that hides us from ourselves, as an obstacle which reduces us to the necessity of conquering ourselves and which separates the will from what it wills, it is at the same time the means of the conquest, the passage from the initial willing to the perfect willing, and the terrain of the victory.

Thus, without having to go out of himself, the subject finds in his depths a passivity which, no doubt, is not impenetrable to his action, but which is not immediately rallied to it. *Omne agens agendo repatitur* (every agent in acting is passive in turn.) There is in me something that is *mine,* that must be tied to me more and more closely, and that yet is not *me.* And this *mine* first appears to me only in a form distinct from me, as the consciousness of a material resistance or of a term of exterior unfolding. Here then is how the original notion of the agent's own proper body is engendered. There is consciousness of a subjective initiative; for without the primitive feeling of this production, we would never attribute the result of the efficacious operation to ourselves. But in the growth of the will the new element that action brings appears to consciousness as alien, even at the moment it enables it to progress; for this actual term is never entirely docile to the willing. And what must be understood by *the body of action* is everything, in ourselves and outside, that still separates us from ourselves.

154

Onto this direct perception of the organism come to be grafted all the derived notions we acquire of our body and of alien bodies. No doubt, in the very complex representation we have of our organs, there is a part, not the most important, but the most clear, which we owe to quite extrinsic associations of perceptions and images. The experimental solidarity of the intentions, known from the inside, and of the movement, perceived from the outside, brings precision to and singularly fortifies our consciousness of the organism and of its docility; but this empirical connection is not the origin of the feeling every man has of his members and of his power over them and over things. Over the very principle of the common experience and over the organization of positive knowledge presides an effective action, since only this action furnishes the sciences with, and projects before us, the matter of their research. If there is a given exterior to knowledge, an unknown to be penetrated, an effort to be made, it is because always, from the beginnings of life, a disproportion presents itself between the willing will and the willed will. And it is under the form of an organic resistance or a passivity to be overcome that the one appears to the other.

(5) There is an efferent action of the will which, imagined under an

organic form, is unperceived in its organic effects and is perceived only in a motor representation.

Actually, the feeling of the material obstacle is, like every other, a state of consciousness. The organism appears only under the form of subjective act; it is in thought before thought puts itself in it. Physical resistance offers itself to us, then, not like an extended and inert mass that gives way in reacting against a single and sudden shock, but through the mediation of an image that works little by little in us with the secret complicity of our members, members that we would hardly be able to lift if they were detached and yet which seem to move as if by themselves.

155 Thus the very consciousness of the organism and the feeling or the prevision of material resistance is a new source of spontaneous action. In the way we know effort, we already produce an effective operation. The afferent sensations therefore become the nourishment of the motor energy. It is useless to know how the operation reaches completion to the extent that it follows thought; it is useful to know it to the extent that there is disproportion and resistance. Often our movements are only a means of thinking and willing, like signs which, instead of simply manifesting the ideas we already have, give rise to new ones. The consciousness of the continuous and multiple effort is therefore founded on the stimulating perception of a multiple and continuous opposition. In this way, the organic sensation, the intermediary for all the others, is brought back to a synthesis of infinitesimal actions which, all of them realizing a degree of the willing, progressively compose, through a series of repercussions and partial initiatives, the total operation. That is how the very representation of the body becomes, through the mediation of the motor image, a spontaneous power that operates secretly in the members and serves to map out its interior topography, without our knowing the detail of the operation.

Thereby is explained the common notion of the body or even of matter in general. What is the immediate feeling we have of our organism, and what does matter mean to us? If I understand what I am saying with this word, it is because I find matter within me. Yes, I find within me something which neither my will nor my knowledge completely penetrates, which I do not understand and which does not understand itself any better, which others, if they exist, understand as little, since, without being me, this something at least is mine. And what distinguishes what is mine from me? It is that continual multiplicity of a resistance, which is nevertheless mobile and accessible to my action, although it remains impenetrable to my interior gaze and irreducible to my actual willing. Thus, the organism which earlier seemed outside of my consciousness and my reach now appears reintegrated in a certain way into the consciousness

I have of it; and this subjective physiology has an unconscious efficacity: the image stigmatizes and moves the body, without our having the least knowledge of how.

(6) There is, finally, an afferent action of the organism which properly constitutes the provoked and expected response, the verification of the project of the will, the instruction we were looking for from the act done, the foreseen unforeseen. What it really furnishes is the consciousness of the disproportions between the willing and the fact, the representation of the physical reactions, the teaching of the empirical disillusionments. Around this given are grouped and organized all the other elements that analysis has just sorted out in the feeling of effort. But what is proper to it is less the organic impression itself than the increase of subjective light and experience of which it is the source. For in the conscious image of this organic resistance it is the obstacle that is embodied, it is the stake of the actual will that is determined in a set form, it is the conquest to be made that is precisely manifested. And the clarity, the very solidity of this precise obstacle is already a first advantage gained. By reason of the power of every image, the determinate representation of resistance is the result of a first development, but also the instrument and the goal of an ulterior growth of willing.

The consciousness of organic effort, then, is a conglomerate of very complex data. As an effect of habit, these different contributions melt into one another and form only a single whole, tied to the initiative of conscious action. Even the reaction of the organs that make us truly passive of our activity is included in the primitive project of action, however disconcerting this obstacle may appear. That is why, when we are about to lift a known weight, we seem to measure in advance the intensity of the force necessary to carry it, whereas in reality we are only imagining the habitual resistance whose exact extent the earlier attempts alone were able to teach us.

Thus the preliminary notion of effort is like the framework prepared to receive all the precise lessons of effective experience. What is afferent in real perception is perceived as such only as a result of a still indeterminate initiative and thanks to the *a priori* acceptance of the expected *a posteriori*. According to whether we envisage the form or the content of organic sensation, we must therefore say that everything in it is the effect of the subjective initiative or that everything in it expresses the passive impression of the physical reaction. As a result we perceive the effort truly both immediately in its origin and immediately in its exercise and unfolding; and also we are more clearly aware of our movements through the reaction of the parts than through direct innervation; and, finally, the most varied illusions and the most contrasting pathological cases can be explained through the complexity of the transmissions, through the criss-cross of actions and reactions, through the progress of the nervous diffusion, through the multiplicity of the successive degradations where the initial light and will are dispersed. Reflected consciousness sees the motor operation only globally through the projection of all this infinite detail: it is a repercussion of integrated repercussions. The imagination could not have any distinct representation of it; and we can dispense our effort only by force of habit when, through repeated exercises and the verification of the totals of these elementary actions, we have trained the subalternate powers, opened up the ways, established the habitual connexions, and succeeded in proportioning the energy to the resistance.

II

It is not enough to perform the anatomy of an abstractly isolated effort; we must study its living complexity and its concrete physiology. For in the movement of life there is a circuit perpetually being closed, only to be reopened and grow further. Every point of arrival is but a point of departure. We may well affirm these three propositions separately: the consciousness of organic effort results from the antagonism of the subjective tendencies; — this internal antagonism, the principle of which is not perceived at first, presents itself to us in the form of physical resistance; — and this material aspect of the obstacle proposed to the will as a term of deployment inaugurates a new transcription from the physical to the mental, while revealing the diversity of the tendencies and translating itself into subjective effects. — But the important thing is to see how, in act, these functions combine with one another.

To focus principally on the study of organic effort as if it were the whole or the principal aspect of action would therefore be to misconstrue the true meaning of the voluntary operation and preclude any understanding of this effort at the very moment we were claiming to be studying it exclusively. The popular sense is not mistaken about this. The problem of action does not bear on this obscure question of muscular sensation: to stop at it would be to turn back toward an order of knowledge that is surpassed; it would be to express in positive language and sensible images the reality of the operating will; it would be to bring the new development of the victorious determinism that follows and governs the operation produced back to the vanquished determinism that goes before the conscious decision. We must not let the investigation lose its way. It would deviate from it the moment we would become preoccupied principally with the physical means that seem hidden to us, precisely because they are subordinated to moral ends. Whatever the physiological paths of the operation may be, the manner in which it sets the organs in motion and in which it is brought to consciousness does not have any influence on the progress of our voluntary growth. The great difficulty of effort resides, not in the more or less complete triumph over material inertia, but in the concert of tendencies, in the harmony and the acquired pacification of internal desires. The organic obstacle is only the symbol and the expression of already psychological activities. Suffering is known only to the extent that there is disproportion between the perceived and the willed, between the fact and the imagined ideal; therein lies the profound cause even of physiological distress.

Also, at the same time as we see how the initiative of an imperfect and divided will brings about the consciousness of an organic passivity, we must note equally how the feeling of this physical resistance reveals an interior dissension, and a conflict of tendencies that cut across the unfolding of our action. For once we have acted, there is a new perspective and a kind of alien life that has been incorporated in the agent; the will is other than it was before; knowledge has changed.[1] Proof indeed that the true contribution of the operation willed and performed through the organs is this change itself, rather than the means that obtain it. Now under what condition does this renewal of the interior life depend on the organic effort and the material execution of the act? Here it is.

In the eyes of consciousness, the body is a beginning of subjective life. 159 It is what resists the immediate expansion and the ideal reality of willing, but it is also what submits and lends itself to it. It would be radically beyond the agent if it did not enclose something of the agent on the way to realizing himself. This is why action is instructive: it manifests to the subject a subjective life other than his own, a life he conquers by degrees, a life that already belongs to him more than he knows, but which he does not yet possess completely and which often escapes him more than he thinks.

There is then a perpetual circuit. Through voluntary operation we draw from ourselves power to move and to determine ourselves. The

---

1. "I think I am in a position to prove," writes Maine de Biran, "that there is no intellectual idea, no distinct perception, nor any knowledge properly speaking that is not originally tied to an action of the will." But if it is to misunderstand the true significance of muscular effort to focus principally on its organic character, we would also be perverting its meaning in subordinating it to its intellectual results and in halting the development which it sets in motion at the increase in knowledge whose source it is. If the understanding is a transformed will, it is to be transformed in turn into action and to contribute to the progress of willing.

feeling of effort and the organic reactions (whatever their initial occasion, exterior impressions or motor initiative) only feed in an unconscious way our conscious life. It is this new consciousness which acts in turn on its subalternate conditions. We consume the different forces in us to digest them into ideas and new motives for acting. Whence the ambiguous character of this passive activity, since, in this very passivity, it is looking for a higher form of activity and, in this unconscious, a means of shedding light upon itself. This circle does not therefore turn on itself without advancing. Through action, it seems that we get a grasp on ourselves from as far away as possible and that, underpinning the very foundations of our personal life, we move ourselves forward as a whole.

That is why in enriching us action tires us and taxes us; it is a kind of digestion we benefit from only by first serving as food. Sovereign insofar as the natural magic of the image instinctively works on the instinctive forces, the will, in the prevision and the apprehension of effort, in the sense of what it puts into effort, and in the very idea of the unknown to which action commits itself, the will, I say, encounters a disconcerting obstacle which it does not triumph over without toil and without struggle. Also these two affirmations, though contrary, are equally grounded. —We can act, force our members, bend the machine, while we cannot always master our feelings, our thoughts, and our beliefs. —Nothing gives us pause more than action; and it is superhumanly difficult to conform our conduct to our most firm convictions or to our most decided resolutions. Organic resistance therefore has a double meaning: sometimes it appears as the instrument of a desirable gain and of an increase of subjective life, sometimes as an impoverishment and a weariness. In both cases it is the translation in consciousness of tendencies and actions which, more or less refractory to the will, rally to it or run away from it. It is this internal division that reveals the painful feeling of fatigue and the consciousness of *labor* (*travail*).

III

It is not enough, now, to discover the origin of the consciousness we have of an organic passivity. It is not even enough to explain how the feeling of physical resistances works against or stimulates our action: we must go further. We do not have a complete idea of the vital effort, we do not have the right idea of properly human action, if we do not see in it a hard labor (*labeur*).

Let us not make ourselves other than we all are: we all like rest, that is, the liberation and the anarchy of our powers. For all of us it is taxing to labor; no act of any importance reaches completion without some labor; and labor is passion in action, a suffering, an intimate contradiction. While I am concentrating my thought on the subject I am studying, I sense something like a spring that is trying to unwind, an attention ready to slip away, a bundle whose strands pull against the grasp of reflexion. Thus again, the members of the laborer, always subject to the same movements and compressed into the same mechanism, cry fatigue and pain. False and hateful, those slogans of a new morality, obviously meant to form to hard labor a people deprived of any higher encouragement: labor, to hear these optimists, is alone agreeable, alone natural. No; to discipline our powers, a simple willing is not enough, nor even a single effort of our central energy; there has to be toil. Besides, labor has been looked on as a punishment, as an expiation, as ennobling for whoever has the courage to persevere in it freely without the constraint of need. And whatever may have been said, it is not the universal law in any degree, it is a properly human law. Only man does violence to himself, fights himself, makes himself suffer, kills himself, labors in acting.

What is the origin in us of this suffering that afflicts our action? Even as physical, it is born, if one may say so, of causes that are already moral. However straightforward, simple, and full the directing intention may be, it does not enclose the totality of possible resolutions, it does not use the universality of the actual tendencies. This interior division of thoughts and spontaneous desires has been the condition of reflected life. If at least the reasoned decision could concert into the single action it inspires all this incoherent multiplicity from which it issued! But no; this agreement does not take place or no longer takes place. Neither does the will dominate and concentrate into a single act the contrary movements that have exclusive exigencies, nor do the hostile tendencies lend themselves to a peaceful conciliation. Moreover, whatever we do, in acting we crush as it were a part of ourselves. And what we afflict in this way we do not suppress by as much. Toil, then, is born of a partial action that exercises only certain available energies and sometimes exercises them to excess, at the same time as of a sacrifice of the repressed tendencies.

Thus, conscious suffering supposes the presence in us of unconscious energies that do not rally forthwith to the will, whatever it may be, of energies that contradict one another and seek to exclude one another, of energies that cut into the organic synthesis as it is formed by actual action. It seemed that through the executed act the will should become more and more sure of its integrity; and yet all we have to do is to will and act for unforeseen contradictions to arise, as if rebels and traitors

161

were revealed among our servants at the hour of need. Diverging tendencies that hardly allow us to persevere in our best intentions without a kind of interior dismemberment. Men of action too often pass for having a dulled sensibility and a narrow understanding; for it seems that, in order to push on straight ahead with confidence and stubbornness, we have to trample underfoot, without looking, a multitude of feelings that throw themselves down in our path as suppliants. Whom do we call practical people if not those who, not knowing how to attribute a soul to things, latch on to that tough bark of truth on which only minds without imagination and without sympathy focus? It is as though, in order to affirm and to act, it were necessary to ignore those needs of the head and of the heart, the usual source of the faults and the follies that make the life of the ardent and the passionate enigmatic to the calculating and the ambitious.

162

This is a deceptive prejudice, but one which is only the incomplete expression of a fact of constant experience. There is in us an inconstancy of will, a plurality of desires that make of every act an interior tearing apart: a hidden antagonism which is the source of the struggles of practical life and which often causes our firmest decisions to abort. For to will and to do are two things. If it is much for us to know what we truly will, *nosse* (to know), if it is much more still to will this very willing, *velle* (to will), it is infinitely more to execute it, *perficere* (to bring to perfection). There was already an interval between conception and determination; now between decision and execution there is an abyss to be crossed over. That is the critical passage and the decisive point in action. And if, in the struggles of asceticism, practitioners have felt it vividly, theoreticians have not paid attention to it. They have often seen the difficulty where it is not, without seeing it where it truly is. In the problem of human freedom which we should not pretend to resolve all at once, because the obstacles are spread out on successive levels, it is not over the determinism of the antecedents, it is not over organic resistance nor over the effort of the motor operation, that we must especially delay, but over these interior conflicts of the will, over the surprises and the often fortuitous revolts of the subalternate activity.

Shall we succeed in resolving these intimate contradictions and in pacifying this war through the triumph of the integral will? Let us try to do so at least. The important thing now is to understand how the resistances and the sufferings, even those contrary to our most vivid aspirations, can serve as instruction and as a way to our profound willing. They tell us about ourselves the secrets we would perhaps like to keep from ourselves. They open up perspectives hitherto closed off on the mysterious drama of life and break down the artificial system of our clearest conceptions. Nothing, we said, is known to us with certainty that we have not acted out. Nothing, we must add, enters into us that we have not suffered. It is this domain of the oppositions, the passions, the rebellions in action that we must explore, in order to follow therein the very growth of the will.

Three points seem to be certain. — What engenders the consciousness of organic effort, and what is the subjective notion of the body? It is the idea of a progress of willing to be realized. — How are the nature of the resistance to be overcome and the cause of physical passivities to be explained? Through the presence of energies still foreign but accessible to the will. — To what are the toils of labor and the difficulties or the painful failures of action due? To the division of these tendencies, whose antagonism is aroused by every declared resolution. Thus we cannot have a sufficient understanding of muscular effort and even of physical fatigue, unless we can see, at the principle, this need for expansion of a will divided and contradicted within itself. There are within us powers that act with us or without us or against us; and what is suffering, if not the intestine division of these living things that stick to one another, if not something like the intrusion of a stranger within us? We must study the proper tendencies, the appetites, the pretensions of these energies. Consciousness is ceaselessly warned of these sudden exigencies or these revolutionary currents that threaten the work of our interior unity. In *the body of action,* therefore, it is not enough to look to the intention that is its soul, nor to the operation that produces it; but, considering the organism as an often anarchical and belligerent federation of elementary lives and of tendencies capable of forming systems or factions, we must study *the action of the body.*

There is therefore a psychology of the body to be studied; and this law of the members that is revealed through this very struggle with the law of the spirit tries to mingle with it and to replace it. Thus, to show that voluntary action, whatever its orientation, encounters within itself and arouses against itself hostile powers; to establish that these tendencies can take away from, supplant and counterfeit the will; to bring out, finally, that in any case the willed act takes on one and the same rational character, that is the aim of the next chapter. Thereby all possible variety of deliberate actions and of human passions will come down to a single type, subject to a single determinism. In all cases the operating operation inevitably ends up with a new grouping of the forces, and the operated operation is a synthesis that includes more than we thought we were putting into it. In unfolding, the will therefore transports the center of its equilibrium further and further away from its first perspectives.

CHAPTER 2

The Action of the Body and the Psychology of the Organism

164 When organic life, concentrating itself in the focus of reflected consciousness, has represented in it the needs and the desires of our universal nature, and when, once the decision has been taken in the liberating light of reason, the *fiat* has been pronounced, it might have seemed that all was said and that the higher power of reflexion quite spontaneously had an immediate empire over the material execution of the act. But we have had to recognize that the ideal causality does not immediately become efficient causality. And after seeing how the resolution remains emancipated and becomes master over all the antecedent determinism, we encountered new obstacles, less noticed though more real than all others. The adversaries of freedom, in wrongly denying the truth of the principle, have not always seen what they would have had good reason to see, namely, the practical difficulty of its applications.

Already, in studying the effort necessary for the execution of every act resolved upon, we recognized in ourselves the presence of forces hostile to any action whatever initiated by the will; but forces that are not a pure inertia, nor a brutal and blind weight; multiple forces that express themselves in us through an instinctive tendency toward glimpsed ends, through appetites, through solicitations that resound in our thought; forces, in a

165 word, that reveal to us, below the level of reflexion, a subjective life and the constant intervention of obscure consciousnesses. There is then a psychology of the body to be examined, a complex action of the organism to sort out.

It is no longer a question of analysing "the elements of the spirit" here. No doubt, this is one of the newest truths, it seems for some, but it is also one of those established in ancient times among the truths contemporary psychology has rejuvenated, thinking it was discovering them. If our organism is formed of elementary organisms, veritable infusoria that live and die and renew themselves each in its own way; if the body is an unstable system of innumerable living things of different species, it is the image of the very composition of subjective life. And as an enlightened physiology studies the polyzoism of the individual, it has been also necessary to discern in consciousness the "polypsychism" that forms its multiple unity. That has already been seen.

What is in question now is less to show this anonymous collaboration of the subalternate consciousness melted together in the central life than to look at what goes on in the midst of this confused multitude when one throws an action into it, like a stone cast into a pool filled with fish. It matters little here whence the act was conceived, determined, and resolved. What is interesting is to see how, in penetrating into the system of our habits, it upsets the equilibrium, provokes a new coalition of the thoughts and desires, summons forth from the psychological organism a response to its call, and reveals the secret movements which, without this penetrating blow from the decision, would have remained hidden in the depths. As though it were sowing dissension, action therefore seems to arouse against itself a new determinism before which it is in danger of falling prey. Through its own *élan*, the will discovers its imperfection; it imposes on itself an internal struggle that is the test of its sincerity and the condition of its development.

I

Let us reflect now on this strange truth commonly experienced: if I will to move my hand, my arm, my head, my other more heavy parts, which I would hardly be able to carry if they were separated, the commanded movements are carried out *as if* by themselves without my knowing any of the springs of this admirable machine; they are carried out precisely because in the members there are associated energies and cooperative 166 consciousnesses. But this docility that I get from the organs subject to the will, I do not get from the will itself. I move my finger, but I do not manage to change a desire. I lead my members about like a living and active animal whose disciplined strength I dominate; and as soon as I have to overcome a feeling, flee an occasion, impose a sacrifice on myself, I remain forgetful, negligent, disarmed. I will to act, and I act any which way; I will to will, but at the moment of *executing* and of passing on to the effect, I do not will. The spirit commands the body, and it obeys; the spirit commands itself, and it resists. It commands to will what it would not command if it did not will, and yet what it commands is not done. We more easily govern the material than the moral in our acts.

I. — The fact is that the willing is not integral and that it remains divided in itself. It is that, in the face of every definite and decided attitude, by a spirit of contradiction, there rises the faction of the malcontents. It is that there is a law of the members whose entire role is to resist, more than the members themselves, the law of the spirit. It is that every initial effort is like a declaration of war on the softness and the dissipation of the living forces, which also have in themselves the instinct for survival and independence. In a word, it is that, as the true initiative of the will surpasses the unconscious automatism and the psychological conditions of the act, so also organic resistance, far from being restricted to brute inertia, keeps especially on the alert within us states of consciousness alien or hostile to consciousness, new wills that rise up against the will. There is an already psychological life diffused in the body; and when the voluntary effort groups the offensive forces into a partial bundle, then the dormant powers and the hidden desires are revealed.

For in the face of the declared resolution, which absorbs in itself, in their ideal form, all the representations projected from the body into consciousness, there subsists the reality of the tendencies, abstractly eliminated, but still living and truly acting. They do not go dead by themselves. The concert of willed ends, then, provokes a coalition of the hostile powers which no longer limit themselves to having their little effect in the common consciousness, or to remaining in a state of virtuality. They group themselves and, from the defensive, they move to the offensive.

167   Also, in constantly upsetting the interior equilibrium of life, voluntary activity discovers what is at work confusedly under the surface of the apparent sentiments. No doubt automatism, already guided by an obscure reason, is enough to provoke in us these contrasts of images and desires that make the exercise of reflexion possible; but it is the initiative of thought and the effort of determinate action that force the ignored tendencies to manifest themselves, through the tenacious protestation of the very ones we would like to ignore or destroy. That is why the masters of the interior life advise us to provoke, as in single combat, the passions we have to learn to know and to defeat. Thus it is that action, like a sharp sword, opens up the way for a look down into dark depths where the great currents of the interior life begin. Through the narrow slit of consciousness it reveals to us, underneath this complicated world that we are, infinite perspectives; it constantly renews, with the contrasts and the internal struggles, the source of thought and of freedom.

It is also often difficult to discern what we truly want; and sometimes even the ardor of the will brings about, as if by a phenomenon of interference, impotence and indecision. Who has not known, in the most critical of circumstances, that pain of inactive uncertainty which makes all the possible sufferings of a confident action desirable like a cherished relief! One could say that it is enough to will, for us immediately not to be willing anymore; and that, by means of an ostensible decision, there develop in the background an occult power and hypocritical influences clever at directing us without our knowing it. Has it not been noted how often our speech and our conduct are tacitly inspired by aims we are least aware of, as if, through a perfidious reduplication and a kind of diversion, the will fooled itself in order to allow, on the side, more license to the unacknowledged desires? What a strange organ to play on, this interior life where the truest notes seem at times to touch off very false harmonics! There are cases where we cannot take one step without having a thousand enemies waiting in ambush rise before us and assail us. And our deepest feelings are also those that divide us and surprise us the most like strangers: certain intimate joys tear us apart and, in a mysterious happiness, are identical with the very excess of pain. What we have desired most frightens us as soon as we have to lay hold of it. We are afraid to leave our miseries, as in the sweetness of spring when a sadness slips in with the first rays of the sun playing on the flame of the smoldering fireplace. And sometimes it is enough to be in fear of an act for a sudden dizziness to draw us into it, like those fearful children to whom the seriousness of places and persons suggests the craziest irreverences. 168

A bizarre circle: the will cannot reach its plenitude except in action; and action, sometimes even the thought of action, splits, disconcerts, and represses the will. Freedom seemed triumphant and it was; but no sooner does it appear than it is no longer triumphant. And as if the resolution had exhausted the available strength, the difficulties come to life, again unforeseen and grown greater in the face of the enterprise set in motion, to the point of making the will doubt itself. To preserve intact their dearest aims, to avoid commiting them to a struggle that impoverishes and deforms them, observe those delicate souls who avoid expressing them, as if action were to smother even these victorious dreams and as if, in realizing them, they were about to spoil their infinite charm! For fear of not doing what they love and will, they do what they do not will and do not love. — But observe especially that great multitude of men who cover themselves with the flowers of intention and who never bear the fruit of acts, without noticing themselves this perpetual aborting! Yet it is worth the trouble of looking at this, for, after expecting a plus-value from action, it seems we find in it only deficit and loss.

II. — Every act is a system of concurring powers; but among these allies there are tepid ones, there are inert ones, there are perfidious ones: these are forces that hinder and neutralize one another. Man is like a painting, with the sword always raised on high over the enemy, and never delivering the blow. When does he ever do what he wills, going to the end of his firmest and most persevering resolutions, without deviation or delay? We could all apply this word of a child to ourselves: "I would like always to make you happy; but tell me, mother, why can't I always be good?" And how explain the fact that the very thing we are fearful of doing when we don't do it, we like so much doing when we do do it? Do we even know to what point we delude ourselves about the ordinary inconsequence of projects and effects? It is a strange ignorance, this blindness each one remains in regarding himself; and the beginning of philosophy is to have noticed this. In spite of the daily experience of our failures, we can never believe in our impotence, nor foresee it, nor heal it. Even when we have recognized it, we rarely manage to keep it in view or to reckon with it in our most circumspect aims. We do not know the extent of this infirmity, and we ignore our habitual forgetfulness of the little we do, of the little we can do.

Whence is it that, without attending to it, we get used to this perpetual bankruptcy of life? And what is the secret of these false judgments we pass on ourselves and on others? The fact is that we attend only to our projects and to the consequences that we deduced from them, as if our ideas and our aims were already the facts themselves. As for the results, we look at them only through the logical needs of our intellectual nature or the illusions of vanity. Whatever the word may seem to signify, reflexion projects itself much more toward the future or, at least in the past, turns toward fictions and desires sooner than it comes back to the truth of acts. We often think we have done what we did not even begin; and the severity of our judgments on others ordinarily comes from our taking our ideal for our practice and their practice for their ideal. How many people submit all of reality to their dreams and use their reason only to mis-reason more logically and to take no notice of themselves!

Otherwise, how understand that we do exactly what we have just sincerely criticized in our neighbor? Contrary to the common opinion, we are much more ignorant of our notorious and, so to speak, palpable actions than of our invisible thoughts or our most fleeting fantasies; we do not know how, we do not will, to connect the former with the latter to discover their disproportions. The more resolutions are numerous, broad, elevated, above the humble detail of practicable means and precise reforms, the more dangerous they are; for we think we are bettering ourselves by as much when we are only looking at ourselves in a more and more illusory fiction. Also, when we discuss the principles of human conduct, we should almost always ask: "Do you mean that in theory, abstractly; or else are you talking about ordinary practice and common actions?" Foolish people these authors of morality who have no concern for and no sense of these constant inconsequences, and who go straight on reasoning on the things that should come to pass when they never do in fact. "You must, therefore you can": that is false. It would perhaps be true only if we did what we believe we are doing.

In our action, then, there is a habitual waste. Never, so to speak, do we do all that we will as we will it: unforeseen resistances, frictions, collisions wear down, diminish, deviate the will. We know ourselves well in general, but we are ignorant of ourselves at each moment; and it is this moment that is decisive for acts. Our desires often hide from us our true desires. There are two hearts in the human heart; and the one does not know the thoughts of the other. But by the fact alone that a decision has been taken and an effort has been made, the interior situation has changed; the hidden guest in us is unmasked; and in order to continue willing as we were willing, we have to will more and in another way. After the resolution, the abandoned motives and the unacknowledged tendencies are no longer the same as before; and at the moment we thought we were destroying their empire, it seems as though we had restored it. How so?

II

Not only do we not do all that we will; but often we even do what we do not will. Besides the parasite activity that subsists outside or alongside or inside of action itself, there is a directly contrary activity which often substitutes itself for the will itself and leads it to transmigrate into it. Before any intervention of reflexion, there already subsist in the elements of subjective life strange concupiscences whose exigencies know very well how to make themselves felt; but reflexion itself, in intervening, confers upon the repressed impulses a redoubling of violence. It is the progress of this subtle substitution, it is this imperceptible change of wills, that must be noted.

Sometimes, while we lay down the nicest general rules, we never notice 171 that they apply to the particular case to be resolved at the very moment. Sometimes, while we feel capable of the most generous sacrifices and of a heroic firmness, we trip over trifles; for it is easier at times to overcome in great matters than to conquer oneself in the littlest ones, easier to endure ruin than to patiently lose a penny. Sometimes, as desires become purified and aspirations appear sublimated, the beast takes advantage of the fact that the angel behaves as an angel and adjusts to the situation, in subtle consciences, through a system of double entry where the solidarity of the passive and the active seems broken up. Sometimes, even before we have noticed it and without our knowing how, we have already done what we were promising ourselves not to do; and as if the waters backed up by the resistance had more force, once the dam is broken the flood breaks loose.

Thus, the surprises of the subalternate powers, the felicitous revolts, the revolutionary impulses threaten our intimate willing; and we remain imprisoned in ourselves at times, walled in spectators of our own fall, or even accomplices of the seditious movement to which the will rallies like the chief who follows his soldiers. One has to have seen and heard the tumult of a riot, the disorders and the clamors of the mob, to discern in oneself the often furious movements of this rabble making an assault on the declared will! If the will allows one concession to be extracted from it, if it hesitates, "if it gives an inch of rope," it is done with. Whoever does not struggle is already beaten; whoever does not act is acted upon and undone. No sooner do we stop disciplining these rebels, than we find in us ferment, plots, an explosion of desires, and disorder of appetites. Who then is strong enough to stop and recapture the escaped animal?

We readily imagine that reflexion unmasks and kills passion by throwing light on the absurdity it falls into, and we are persuaded that a moral theory is enough to govern man, as if it were simply a matter of handling cardboard dolls or of toning down Epinal images.[1] But when the barrier is crossed over, is not the will, which perhaps at first made believe it did not consent, tempted to accept what was done, so to speak, without it, to consider what is done as done, to take as a new point of departure what it was unable to prevent, to profit from the situation arrived at
172 rather than go back courageously beyond the point where it deviated, even if to do so meant disconcerting all the equilibrium re-established on another foundation? Do we not on the contrary find that one practical inconsequence almost inevitably brings new ones in its wake, because in appearance a lie appears to be saved only by a lie? Does not the consciousness of an absurd anger, while irritating us more, arouse us to the point of exasperation, like the capricious child who throws himself into his silliness, precisely because he feels its foolishness.

Also how many men, knowing only the obvious and superficial parts of their nature seen through the illusions of an egotistic and vain heart,

---

1. "Epinal images" referred to illustrations in popular magazines that often bordered on the immoral. The expression was quite common, but has disappeared from use along with the illustrations that have been replaced by photographs. Epinal is the town in Lorraine where the "images" originated (translator's note).

find a cruel enigma where there is only a growing tyranny of the senses let loose! It is easier to remain chaste than to become so again. And there is a falsity and a danger in that abstract simplicity and relative independence of the most complicated resolutions or passions deployed in dreamy representations, as if they did not draw after them a whole retinue of their compensations and natural impediments. Admirable feelings are made to spring up in them without seed and without cultivation. Heroism comes up as if out of a trap door. Pure, naive, and new love is prepared for by lust; adultery becomes purifying. One has the benefit of vice and the charm of virtue. — To be sure, in "the old man" there are contrary passions that make up in the end and go along in company with one another. But if Don Quixote and Sancho are the living critique of that literature of illusion which does not admit of the test of life, what a new kind of hero the conscientious practice of contemporary novels would spawn!

Thus, not only does the will not reach all the forces it would like to have serve its ends, so that its action is always more or less hindered or diminished; but in addition it arouses, alongside and against itself, powers which tend to and even succeed in supplanting it, in substituting themselves for it, and in holding it in tutelage. We often end up acting willingly against our will; it is the origin of this passionate movement which it is important to recognize.

III

If there is a pain and a suffering in laborious effort, it is, as we have shown, because in the organism itself there is a life that is already psychological and a world of undisciplined tendencies. If there is a waste and a habitual disproportion in action, it is, as we have also shown, because these subalternate activities subsist and resist even in the face of the firmest decision. But if these rebellious powers are able to lead the will on and suborn it, it is because there is in them (it has to be brought to light) an energy analogous to that of the will itself and, so to speak, a rational character.

Whatever we may have decided or done, we are always inclined to justify it and to think of it as reasonable, even when it is contrary to a prior will or to an impartial evaluation. But this impartiality we reserve for other analogous cases. In practice a perpetual sophism is committed: "the general rules never apply to my particular case; but my case, exceptional as it is, seems to me to have universal reason in its favor." How then is it possible that, in acting according to the reverse of what we were

173

willing, the act should be really willed and find within it its own reason?

The fact is that in us animal life is already penetrated with a sort of rational virtuality; it is that, once they have attained reflected consciousness, the spontaneous tendencies find there, along with a new light, more strength and more exigencies; it is that, in the face of the will which placed them in the balance and which, weighing them against its own weight, communicated to them a redoubled energy, they bear henceforth, even after being ousted, the stamp of the reason that paused in them to examine them, as if they could at any moment satisfy it and be enough for it. Also, once we have done what we did not will through the pull of a passionate movement, since it is what we might have willed, the act we once thought unreasonable seems to contain all of a sudden an unforeseen reason, a reason, it is feigned, whence it had received a part of its triumphant force, a reason capable of rallying to it the consent of the weakening will.

That there should be underneath reflected life and even down to the last confines of the psychological automatism a kind of reason which presides over the most obscure functions and which first prepares the way for voluntary activity before defeating it, is something that can seem strange; nevertheless it is beyond doubt. Besides, is it not proper to a real synthesis that the elements of which it is formed participate in its original qualities and in appearance lose their own in it? Thus the higher form of consciousness and of the will is reflected down into its most elementary conditions.

It would be wrong, therefore, to talk of man's animal life as if it could be purely animal. Even where reflexion does not intervene, where the free decision of the spirit does not penetrate, there is still within us an immanent dialectic which presides over our sensible operations, which inspires our perceptions and our immediate conclusions. Sensations themselves have a rational character and a logical contexture: they result from acquired inferences and primitive integrations where the synthetic strength and even, so to speak, the syllogistic aptitude of our mental life manifest themselves. There is a kind of implicit reasoning and an unconscious arithmetic that governs all our steps. The porter who walks faster under a heavier load, the dancer or the musician, do not know that they are geometers and mathematicians. It is thus, moreover, that the mistakes of the senses reveal the logical initiative of a rational mechanism that comes into play even unknown to reason and consciousness. One has only to analyse, for example, the causes that make stars appear larger at the horizon, or that bring about false visual projections and parasite images in those who have been operated on for strabismus. There is, therefore, in our least perceptions and in our most insignificant acts, a rigor and concatenation that confound the most learned reflexion, because in spontaneous practice none of the solidary data is ever omitted; all have their compensating effect. Also let us beware of the principles voluntarily sown in this fertile ground: there is a natural growth and a fructification of the consequences that later sophisms or self-serving palliatives will no longer stop.

Where this dispersion of an immanent reason down to the organic functions themselves and where the initiative of the secondary centers appear with the greatest exterior and the most convincing evidence is in pathological states, notably in the phenomena of hypnotism and suggestion. In these states a dissociation of the elements of the mind takes place, 175 an experimental analysis of the mental automatism, which manifests at once the relative independence and the virtual reason of each fragment of our mental organism. It seems that in such cases, thanks to a subjective fiction or an unconscious simulation, each portion of the system can play the principal and total role, as in a play where the extras would take the leading role at will.

These subalternate powers, able to reap the education of reason, can also supplant it and mimic it, like those children who give you back the lesson you have just given them. If someone hypnotized can become master over his physiological life as well as we are in control of our relational life in a waking state, it is because in him all activity withdraws into one organ and is used for one function, as if the will had transmigrated into it and concentrated itself in it: a surprising power which nevertheless is not of another kind than the normal activity of the physiological functions; for it is through it that, according to an ancient dictum to which we must give a scientific interpretation, "the rational soul is the substantial form of the organized body," puts its stamp on all details, finds echo in it, is contained in it, and is obeyed.

Thus, in hypnotism, as also in passion, though to a lesser degree, the ordinary hierarchy of the vital forces and of the elementary consciousness is disconcerted, but only to be re-established artificially under the usurped domination of a power usually subordinated. Reflexion seems emptied of all proper content, through a sort of tacit abdication; and thanks to this partial suspension of the multiple activities whose opposition and union form reason, this spontaneity of a simple state absorbs and uses all available energies. Not that total consciousness is absolutely abolished for a time, however short we may suppose it, for the one hypnotized knows ordinarily that he does not know. And in most cases of split personality, what proves the unperceived persistence of abstract reason and general consciousness is that the subject preserves enough of a notion of the *self* to know that he is no longer *himself*. He has a veiled science of his disclosed ignorance; and if he is docile to the successive suggestions, it is because, in the vague field of his dulled consciousness, he can follow the leading light the experimenter is playing on it. Sometimes 176 people even succeed in moving about at will the sealed partitions that seem to make of one life two fragments alien to one another: proof that, in spite of this interior split, there subsists a hidden commissure, and something like an invisible network that catches up in its transparent meshes the most disparate forms of activity, because in all of them there is a sufficiency, a quality of universality, and an immanent reason.

What goes on below the level of reflexion goes on also in the most illuminated domain of the interior life: other powers substitute themselves for reason and the will, with all the characteristics, all the exigencies, all the efficacity of reason and the will. And this action that comes out of us, against our willing, as if it were voluntary, this unreasonable action which we use to give ourselves a new reason, is, properly speaking, *passion*.

By what sign, then, do we recognize the act of reason and the voluntary decision? By this one: the diverse motives spontaneously offered to consciousness are conceived as parts of one and the same total system, and the free resolution appears as a synthesis that envelops these partial tendencies and uses the strength of all the others to realize the privileged ones; hence it is on the whole that judgment comes to bear and it is the whole that action embraces. Now, when ascendency is achieved by the coalition of the powers on which the will, in determining itself, has declared war or which take advantage of its inaction to deploy themselves, then the counterfeiting of the voluntary act becomes complete. This is seen well enough in what passionate men display.

The object of their passion is their all. To act only in view of the whole and for the whole, to enjoy doing so, is reasonable, free, happy. They think themselves reasonable, free, happy; in their total submission and their complete renunciation, they think they have found emancipation and perfect joy. It is not only *their* whole, they want it to be *the* whole: as they see things, then, there are no longer any duties, except toward this one and all, nor any freedom, except in slavery to it, nor any love and veneration and adoration, except in its cult. Apart from that, everything else is as nothing for them; that is the center, they relate everything to it, the price of things and the meaning of words; it is the god, they sacrifice everything to it, the universe and even their life. But also they want to be everything for it, know everything about it and relate all that it is to themselves. They have severed their bonds with the rest; and the rest is as if annihilated for them. Nothing living, human, 177 sacred, subsists any longer, it seems, which might make some claim of devotion and respect on them; there is nothing, outside of their passion, to pass judgment on it and condemn it. All alone with what they love, united to this one and all, the passionate one feels himself, so to speak, absolute, independent, self-sufficient, infinite. If he is still conscious that outside of himself, that inside of himself, he is misunderstanding what he feigns to annihilate, if the spectacle of other passions like his surprises him and offends him, because he does not admit that there might be other worlds apart from his, if the memory of reason irritates him and embitters him, because he does not want there to be only *one* universe (and he would prefer even to accept the thought of a partitioning rather than believe in the one reason that condemns and excludes him), if he experiences a kind of remorse, then he absolves himself by placing what he feels is out of order outside the common rules. Convinced that, since he has been in love, he is quite different from what he was before, he is also persuaded he is no longer like the others; he thinks he is of a different and higher nature; he glorifies himself, he justifies himself through the very enormity of the passion. And as each one presumes he has as much wit as anyone else and more, each believes he is the first to love as he loves: isolated on unknown heights, standing over the human crowd and despising it, he has no affection, no duty, no honor, no strength, no life, except for the one thing loved, but he thinks he has all that to the highest degree. He would wound, despoil, annihilate his idol in order to have to heal it, enrich it, create it. He becomes cruel in order to manifest his omnipotence and his omnigoodness.

Hence human needs and appetites, as analogous as they are to those of the brute, differ from them profoundly. The animal has no passion; what is animal in man, on the contrary, lays claim to all that reason and will require, an infinite satisfaction. Human sensuality is insatiable and unreasonable only because it is shot through with a force alien to and higher than the senses; and this reason immanent to passion itself acquires such ascendency that it can take the place of reasonable reason (*la raison raisonable*), that it confiscates its infinite aspirations and that it usurps the inexhaustible resources of thought. Willed action under the dominance of passion is brought to completion only if it has captured freedom, to drag it along as prisoner, as accomplice, as instigator.

We are therefore forced by the most ordinary and the most universal of experiences to admit that we do not do all that we have willed and that we did not will all that we do even voluntarily. Whoever has not seen this has never once looked inside himself. And yet is there a truth more forgotten? Is it possible that it be ignored by the common lot of mankind who do not pay any attention to the constant inconsequence of their firmest resolves and of their daily practice, ignored by philosophers

178

and moralists who have not penetrated to the heart of human life, into the mysteries of the carnal will, into this closed dungeon whence reason, at once queen and captive, deals with the mutinous powers of nature, ignored even by those who forget this infirmity no sooner than they have recognized it and fall prey to it unwittingly, ready always to point the finger at the alien obstacles rather than at these intestine rebellions, so that the old maxim, "we have no greater enemy than ourselves," remains a dead letter or seems a pious paradox?

Three degrees mark the growing ascendency of these adversaries of the will. — They are invading aliens or disguised enemies; — they are grudging losers; — they are conquerors we accept and flatter. All the inconsequences of action can be summed up thus: we almost never do all that we will; we often do what we do not will; we end up willing what we did not will. At first it is almost without our knowing it that the action contrary to our willing arises; then we consent to the knowledge we have of it; and what we were doing without seeing it, what we did without willing it, we end up willing as we do it. In consciousness, in decision, and even in execution, how quickly we are outwitted, and what ingenious variety of sophisms we are ready for! The possible disorders and reversals of action seem infinite: but because of this, is not the science of action we claim to be establishing once again compromised?

Let us be reassured. The usefulness of the foregoing analyses is less to underline certain moral weaknesses whose extent is never well enough known than to establish how the same rational character, the same systematic unity, is to be found in every reflected operation. The meaning or the quality of the action matters little for now; in showing that, even involuntarily willed, it is the exact counterfeit of the completely opposite acts, we have prepared the way for abstracting at least provisionally from the immense diversity of possible aberrations and deviations, because in the abuse as well as in the use there is an element that is the same. Or to put it better, this talk of abuse does not have any meaning yet; for it is simply a question here of determining the necessary growth of facts whatever they be. We must therefore bring into line with the common law even those that appear furthest removed, and bring back to the same determinism the most disparate or the most abnormal forms of human conduct. Let us not be concerned then with finding out which of the wills wins in the internal struggle. Does not voluptuous debauchery, as well as chaste love, engender and have offspring? Though less fruitful than chaste love, it cannot forever cheat the wish of nature. Thus, failing or victorious, willing deposits in action fecundating seeds. This germ, sometimes thrown down negligently in youthful fantasy, can insensibly absorb all the will's sap by entangling future acts in the pro-

179

gress of its irresistible vegetation. How many men, having become prisoners of themselves, have borne the fatality of an early fault, or have been caught up in a role they had started playing jokingly! It can never be said of a willed act that it will be insignificant.

The declared will and the nascent effort of the intention realizing itself encounter a new opposition in the appetites, the rebellions, and the concupiscences of the body. It is no longer through their ideal projection into consciousness, in the form of motives or temptations, that these act in this way; it is after the judgment has been pronounced in the real mêlée of the desires and antagonistic tendencies. For what the decision has neglected or set aside is not suppressed forasmuch; and the forces of spontaneous life that had solicited reflexion, when the time comes to operate effectively, reappear with a changed character: they were solicitors, they are now enemies. Now this counter-will, which gels all the excluded powers into a system, often manages, as a matter of fact, to supplant the will itself; but it succeeds in governing action in this way only to the extent that it becomes itself reason and will. This clearly shows that in man everything is marked with this rational character, since it is found in him even in the follies of passion. This also most manifestly reveals how many elements alien to the relative simplicity of the first intention action sums up and gathers in itself: for it can reach completion only on the condition of dominating all these resistances which it awakens and adds to itself. The perpetually unstable equilibrium of the will always has to come down on one side and, forming a unique system of vanquished and vanquishers, this synergy necessarily builds up the person.

How action thus becomes a living conciliation of contraries, how it is the cement of the organic synthesis and of conscious individuality, how it fashions character, is therefore what remains to be discerned better.

180

Action is the cement of organic life and the bond of individual consciousness: in the act there is more than the act itself; there is the unity of the agent, the systematic conciliation of his forces, the cohesion of his tendencies. — I note first how in the body itself the organic synergy is established; but the education of the members cannot be separated from that of thought and of the inclinations themselves; for it is action that forms a single natural whole of physical and spiritual life. — Then I study the synthetic role of action in the conflict of feelings and in the incoherence of interior dispositions; I show that it effects a conciliation of the contraries, and that it coordinates and subordinates all the forces it uses. — I therefore establish how, within the confines of the individual, action constitutes a closed circuit; how it fashions body and soul for us; how it effects our interior homogeneity, by expressing, by confirming, by completing the will. However, this moving circle closes in on itself only to open up again once more and to become the point of departure for a new expansion; thus the center of gravity of the will and of the action that realizes it will transport itself beyond the individuality itself.

CHAPTER 3

The Interior Synergy and the Constitution of Individual Life through Action

Whatever power takes the initiative in us, from the moment an act is con- 181 sented to, from the moment it is accomplished, an intimate cooperation pulls even the opposed tendencies into line and establishes an effective solidarity among all the parts of the physical and mental mechanism.

By dispersing the central effort of thought and freedom into the confusion of the organism, it may have seemed that action diminishes the intention in a way and scatters it, without any compensation for this obscure diffusion. That is what all those who consider only the initial decision in their conduct would grant, as they show no interest in the material execution and the consequences of their resolutions. It appears to them that the will falls into a bad alliance and loses itself in the obscurity of the lower movements; it even seems to them that it impoverishes and enslaves itself as it encounters in the consummated action a close-off point, a determination that excludes the infinite richness of its primitive virtuality. To believe them, one diminishes oneself, one mechanizes oneself, one dirties oneself, in acting.

How, on the contrary, action unites into one flow the dispersed forces of life, to constitute the organic synthesis and to serve as mediator between all the forms of physical and spiritual activity, how it enriches the will by responding to the first movement of centrifugal expansion through a centripetal movement whose return composes the vital rhythm 182 and closes the circuit of individual life, that is what will result from an analysis, where we shall have to see also how much all these apparent amplifications of the initial willing were already implied in it, without prejudice to a still broader expansion that will carry action outside individuality.

I

There is unity in our complex organism only through cohesion, and cohesion only through cooperation. Are not the members pulled together better, is not the flesh more invulnerable in a state of tension and in energetic use than in a state of repose and softness? Action is the cement with which we are fashioned; we subsist only to the extent that we act. Idleness is a dissolution, death, a decomposition. The *fiat* of the will is not just the decisive blow that cuts through all the hesitations of thought, that gives to a still floating and multiple representation a definitive unity, solidity and precision, that radically separates the present from the past and the real from the possible; it is also, in a particular and determinate form, the general and, so to speak, the generative function of organized life. For in an action, there is more than this action; there is the cohesion, the solidarity, the real union of all that it uses and all that collaborates in it. This explains the unity of the synthesis and marks the true individuality which the positive sciences were able to consider only from the outside as a postulate, but whose intimate constitution we now penetrate. Εν τω εργω δοκει ειναι το εν (the one seems to be in action).

The fact is that real action could not really be partial, divided, multiple, as thought or dreams can be. What is done is done. And in the operation that moves the organs, there is an unavoidable conjunction among the members. It matters little that I am still hesitant and torn, if I act, I pull the entire machine to one side; and everything follows along, through persuasion or through violence, but in any case through necessity. The organic system is involved in the least conscious and willed act, without any possible duplicity in the operation itself.

Hence action quite naturally envelops and sweeps along the most opposed tendencies; it makes of them a single body, it makes of them the 183 body. And since it forms a concerted system of all that it favors or sacrifices in us, it could not be confined to one organ, restricted to one function, partial to one member, without being biased and unjust against the others. There is only one way, then, to contain, regulate and use the diffused energies in us and even the rebellious impulses of concupiscence; it is to catch them up into the system of a general activity and to make them converge, through labor, toward the integrity of the individual life. Thus it is that the child conquers his organism and brings rhythm to his physical life only through a harmonious exercise of his members. To dominate his senses and to prevent the monstrosities of an uneven formation where the equilibrium of the nervous functions is upset at will, he needs to act by giving his young powers the regulated expansion that maintains them in their natural hierarchy. Nor does the school child form his intelligence or mobilize his mental activity except through an exercise, and a systematic exercise of his faculties.

The important thing is therefore not just to take note of the usefulness or the necessity of action; it is to see the unity that presides over it and that it produces necessarily. No doubt, it is efficacious and normal only if it is a synthesis, and that is why physical and intellectual education should be general. "Specialized, bestialized," an old school proverb used to say. Man is man only by what universal life there is in him. What is to be clearly understood is that for better or worse, action has this universal character, and that, as restricted as we suppose it to be, it is always exercised *sub specie universi* (under the species of the universal).

Through the diffusion and the connection of the reflexes, the act reverberates throughout the organic synergy. Hence there is no partial gymnastics any more than there is a special education. This is to say that any particular activity we would pretend to limit to the part concerned becomes the center of the total grouping. Where we were hoping to develop a part in the whole, we would tend to make of this part the whole itself. If "specialty" remained specialty, it would not be so bad; but the unfortunate thing is that we inevitably make the accessory the principal by exposing ourselves to mistake a candle for a star or an atom for the universe.

Even to look first at only the equilibrium of the physiological functions, the truth of the old and banal adage, *"Mens sana in corpore sano"* (sound mind in sound body), can be given a true demonstration, in spite of the apparent exceptions. Biologists like Preyer think that in the newborn there are diverse principles of action cohabiting and, as it were, many souls that have to be subordinated to the "cerebral soul." And how could the perfect harmony of the nervous centers be established, if not through a regulated exercise of all the organs? To work only with the head, like "cerebral" people, is often to let the animal live and grow below, and not just an animal, but a pack of unsavory appetites and degenerate tastes. The less we are able to act, the more unbridled the intemperance of desires becomes, because the balance between dreams and daily practice is thrown off more and more. "What does the body matter," some will say; "it makes no sense to interrogate this plaything! and whatever foolishness it involves me in, it is up to it to blush before me!" Stupid contempt. Homogeneity is established sooner or later, and in one direction or the other; and it is a dangerous illusion to pretend to form tight compartments within oneself.

Also, no more than we were able, in studying effort and organic resistance, to separate material inertia from the psychological opposition which is its true explanation, no more can we here, in studying action

184

and the role it plays in the formation of the individual, isolate the synergy of the organs from the harmony of the psychological functions. The physical phenomena that accompany and execute our resolutions are, in a sense, more than the signs or the symbols of the properly subjective states to which they correspond; we can say, with the proper understanding, that they are their very reality.

Thus, attention becomes more intense only if there is really a greater tension of the organs. While in consciousness there is diffusion, in many directions and in many layers, of images, desires, and incipient movements, it is an action that, in concentrating these energies sometimes violently, subordinates them all to a single system and obtains the convergence of thoughts through the concurrence of the organic operations, draining off all available activity in this way in order to form of body and spirit but one expressive whole. Why is it that the effort of intellectual production is sometimes so painful, more than the labor that tears the womb, to the point that it can seem that thinking is against nature? It is because, in order to live and grow, our thought has to be communicated to all the rebellious parts whose concurrence is necessary to express it; it is because, in order to assemble its elements as though to manifest its complete life, we must extract it from all our members and produce it through our pores.

Thus again, a feeling, a passion, does not become vivid except by involving the whole moral and physical organism more broadly and more deeply. Memory is tied to the functions of nutrition; the mechanism of thought is a mover: it acts through muscles and on muscles. What is real in states of consciousness consists in the acts they make us aware of and enable us to shed light on and produce.

It is therefore absurd to pretend to isolate the education of the body from that of the will or of the spirit. As much as thought which remains apart from the militant practice of life remains empty and illusory, so much does sport which is only sport destroy the natural equilibrium and the integrity of human development. As gymnastics would produce monsters by exercising only one member, so also the most scientific cultivation of the mind and of the body would only result in the bankruptcy of the one and the other, if it cared for the one and the other separately. In play, it is the play more than the exercise that is salutary and quickens the depleted energy. In labor, physical endurance is the sign, the price, the support of the interior courage of a will accustomed to make little of difficulties. The rough life of the peasant is useful for the upkeep of the nation, less by reason of the food it provides than by reason of the strong sap for temperament and character that contact with the earth gives man. And if we must venerate these active members who courageously busy themselves with the necessary tasks, it is because, in the strength, the beauty and the salubrity of physical labor, they express and effect at once the moral purification, the interior pacification, the vigor, of the will.

It is not by saving our strength, therefore, that we keep it up the best and that we get the most out of it. We must not reason about this as about a beast of burden limited to the movements of its instinct, or as about a field that is exhausted by nourishing the plant it bears. No doubt, in animal life, every expenditure wears out and impoverishes the organism; and the exhaustion of the senses overstimulates their susceptibility and their unwholesome requirements; also there is a bitterness in feeling that the movements of the higher life remain subject to the rhythm of the organic functions. Yet, as voluntary activity penetrates and dominates the powers of the body, it receives more from them; it finds an echo there in that immanent reason that can provoke the infinite exigencies of passion, but that can also respond with an inexhaustible generosity to the call of heroism. False tactics, to give in to softness, to listen to oneself, to baby oneself; it is in using our energy, in appearing to sacrifice and to mortify it, that we repair and amplify it. In this domain of voluntary action, the more we give out the more we possess. *Caro operando deficit; spiritus operando proficit* (in operating the flesh decreases; in operating the spirit increases). And as the surgeon, impassible during the bloody operation because he is acting, sometimes might not be able to stand the sight of it if he were only a passive spectator, as the soldier who in the ardor of the fight does not feel that he has already received many mortal blows, as the scientist or the ecstatic, lost in the contemplation from which his whole life is suspended, seems a physiological paradox, as he absorbs all animal functions into the unity of a thought or a feeling, so there is no assignable limit to the cooperation of the body, to its power of resistance, to its moral force, because action unites and raises it to the inexhaustible fecundity of reason and of freedom. The best hygiene is not to care for the body with the body alone; and in asceticism itself one finds a principle of rejuvenation, of health and of vigor. *Arcum frangit intentio, corpus remissio* (straining breaks the bow, slackening breaks the body).

Hence, then, if a resolution is complete and subsistent only by taking and fashioning the whole of ourselves, action in turn, through a progress of the initial will in the organism, participates in the integrity and the vigor of the higher intention from which it proceeds. To use here, without any metaphysical claim, the good old fashioned words, and in spite of the artificial distinctions they have lent themselves to, it is through action that the soul gets a body and the body gets a soul; it is

186

their substantial bond; it makes of them a natural whole. In us transcendence implies immanence. People are right, then, when quite naively they speak materially of moral affections, when for them the person is the indistinct unity of a life at once physical and spiritual. "The heart, the head," these are not just appropriate metaphors to designate generosity of character or firmness of spirit; they are the expression of a reality experienced each day. Let no one be surprised at the cult given a loving heart. The incarnation of thought and feeling is a human truth, and truth is human only by becoming incarnate.

187

In short, action, whatever it be, sets the whole machine in motion and draws it on. The moment the willed operation comes to completion in us, there is *de facto* synergy and concurrence. It is a living synthesis. How many ideas and feelings we can put into a quite simple and rapid act, in a handshake! Now this unity of the acts has as an inevitable corollary the solidarity of the physical and the moral life. Action makes the material organism participate in the intention that animates it, as it also makes the habits of the body reverberate in our states of consciousness; this body itself it closely associates with the efforts of thought, to the point of making of it an instrument more and more vibrant and docile to the secret touches of the will. But now we must understand how this determinism, brutal in appearance, that seems to exclude all possible acts except the one accomplished and that seems to condemn the will to a rigorous subjection, is on the contrary for it a means of conciliation and emancipation.

II

From the moment when the free decision was taken, it found itself immediately caught up in a mechanism that transformed it little by little. To remain sincere, the intention had to throw itself in fact into execution; the execution required effort; and in the effort indispensable for voluntary operation, one more new necessity appeared: action can be produced only by arousing an intestine struggle and by overcoming from the start the antagonistic system that has formed against its initiative. Hence the operation inevitably bears on the organic and mental whole at the moment it comes to completion; and if it is true that this total and exclusive unity of the act contributes to the mutual dependence of "body and soul," is it not to the detriment of the rich variety of thought or the infinite power of freedom? No. In subjecting the will to the narrow simplicity of a single way out, action is for it the way of expansion and enrichment.

The need to make a great effort or to sustain a courageous decision brings a sense of alertness and keener concentration. As long as we do not act, we do not know ourselves. To live and to think as if in a dream, as if in a brief moment of lucidity between two naps, without enough resilience to get up, to open our eyes, to see and to walk, is that not the one attitude we had to condemn resolutely from the beginning, because it is contrary to the most sincere and the most fundamental movement of our nature? Now, how can we know all that is at work in our interior universe, how can we tell if our attention is sharp enough, our intention precise enough, our ardor lively enough, our will true? But the point is that we do not need to know it in advance. The guaranty and the criterion of sincerity is the act, which settles uncertainties and manifests the most intimate secrets we ignore or hide from ourselves. If is for us, then, a revelation of our profound state. By manifesting the evil we are inclined to, failings themselves can serve as a premonitory and reinforcing warning. Every fall ought to be an advance. Actions are usually in advance of the good they seem to reveal in us which is not yet acclimated there, and they lag behind the evil depths of which they seem to be an exceptional manifestation even when the evil is habitual: a discovery all the more important since it is in contradiction with the feigned idea of our merit. Hence it is by observing our acts more than our thoughts that we must hope to see ourselves as we are and to make ourselves as we will. As the log is heaved into the dark water to measure the speed of the ship, so also the actions which emerge from the depths of unconscious life should help us to study the currents that sometimes bear us along without our knowing it.

In giving us a precise consciousness of what we will and what we are, the act is a sign and a help to us, as geometric figures support abstract thought through the material representation. It provides us with a concrete definition of the idea it expresses; and as every distinct perception is a sort of nourishment that adds to our strength, the sight of what we do is an encouragement for us, even sometimes an impulse and an intoxication as Scaevola's strange act of heroism was for him. *Prole audacior actus* (the act is more daring than the offspring). One could say there is an action of action. If we find timid people whom the mere sound of their voice lays low, others never think as well or hardly think at all, except by talking loud and clear. Sometimes it is even a useful remedy for those who no longer have any other to act for the sake of acting, as the care that might be superfluous for the dying person could be salutary for those around him.

Not only does action serve to reveal what is stronger in us or even at times what is stronger than ourselves, but it also often constitutes, amidst the indifference and the disarray of our interior states, a solid center that becomes like the core of our character. How often we will only after having acted and because we have acted! The child has an alternating life of opposed desires and of capricious movements; he constructs and destroys, soon bored with everything: he is a living anarchy. For a system to be organized in him and for his forces to be grouped into a flow, he has to learn to follow decidedly one of his tendencies while excluding the others. Education is supposed to help him in this crystallization, like the thread dipped in the solution of candied sugar. To give in to him always, to hinder or to repress him in nothing, is to undo him ceaselessly, it is to make his own desires incomprehensible to him. He ends up not knowing what he wants; he has a desire for desire; he gets irritated at not having to desire any more and at not being able to any longer.

The act is sovereignly efficacious for obtaining this interior unanimity. In order to really know, amidst the turmoil of our feelings, the firm resolution on which our will takes its stand, we might ask ourselves in the calm of reflexion whether we would perform a very simple action, on which would depend what we have resolved, by abandoning ourselves, for example, to one whom we are willing to obey and entrust ourselves to by a vow of submission or a blank signature.

It is because action manifests, fixes, confirms and even produces the will, that it serves as a guaranty for promises and that it is like the substance of irrevocable commitments. What seals the contract, what ties the nuptial knot, what consecrates the deacon, is a signature, an utterance, a step, always an act, which by its decisive unity dominates all the intestine divisions, and which engages for good all the perhaps still uncertain or hestitating powers. It is properly to burn one's ships. We can always act, as little as it might be and as embattled as we might feel. This small beginning of initiative, which, if we will, is invincible, becomes the lever for our emancipation; for leaning on the solidity of what is done, and as if with our back to the wall scaled, we have passed from the defensive to the offensive. Action is a conquest.

Also, in acting, we come to will what, it seems, we could not will at first, what we did not truly will for lack of courage and strength, what we would like to will. For in determining to will we do not always follow the final judgment of the understanding; but in willing we always undergo the influence of all our inclinations and our habits. To speak precisely, we do not will to will, because we could also say that we will to will to will, and it would go on *ad infinitum*; we will to act and do, that is, the will presents itself to itself only in the figure of a determinate use. We must therefore use subterfuges and skill; and it is through willed action that ordinarily we indirectly contribute to other voluntary actions.

Moreover, although we are not always able either to judge or to will what we will, we can always hope to succeed in judging and willing in time what we would wish to be able to will and judge today. In this imperceptible labor of conversion or perversion, a thousand enterprises busy themselves with driving a dominant motive of action down to the point where we rediscover it quite naturally in ourselves. As in the case of Francis Borgia who, wishing to cure himself of drinking, used to let fall into his cup each day an added drop of wax, even puerile ruses, tiny means, enticing promises, threats, diversions, flight, everything, makes for a good war, according to circumstances, to rule the beast, the child and the man which each one carries within. We must not speak the same language to all our powers, no more than the head of the family commands in the same way brute animals, servants, sons, spouse. But from all, the same concurrence must be required, because in action we must be able to rely on all.

To will to act is then to let the bridle go for all these infinitesimal forces that direct us more than we direct them. As in the affairs of a state, much business is carried on in us through agents not recognized as such. And it is a hard thing to take when we see that, in spite of all our circumspection, we are led by fleeting dispositions which it is impossible to assess with certainty in advance: after the longest deliberations, the decision is always the work of a moment. Then, once this critical point is crossed, the act unfurls its consequences without end and without return, whatever the fluctuations were that may have preceded it. Moreover, how important it is, since the will proposes not to will but to act, for this *acting* itself to be already a sincere form of the willing! This is why it is prudent to train in advance for the struggle, to challenge these hidden adversaries to combat while they seem deadened and unmasked, and to 191 get used to seeing them as they are, before the hour of surprises and illusions. It is good to foresee, to analyse, and to play all the passions and vices—save one, the very one which becomes the principal or the only nourishment for curiosity, for novels or for plays!

Thus, while we are forcing ourselves to form generous sentiments or to face resolutions that are repugnant to pusillanimity, we are pressing them down little by little into the organic machine through a sort of hypnotism and insistent suggestion. Even when we do not feel all that we say and do, when we have only a desire for true desires, when words and acts flow less from an abundance of the heart than from a dry and distasteful constraint, it has an effect, it goes down little by little into the reality of consciousness, it becomes our life. It seems at times that there is a lack of sincerity in asking for what we fear, and in doing what is still odious. But as long as the will, from the height of its lofty impassibility, ratifies the expression of the desire we do not feel or the violent brutality of the act it finds repugnant, that is all that is called for; it is enough for this higher will to find opposite it a docile echo in what is most mechanical and most brutal for it to close in on little by little and to reduce all the rebellions of average life. We can force our members when we cannot focus our thoughts and our desires. As we surround a fortress with convergent trenches to lay siege to it, so also the will, seeking to reach the perfection of its free movement amid the accumulated resistances, uses the tactic of a double approach: since it is easier to control the gears of the animal mechanism than our intimate dispositions, it is often through a material operation that the spontaneous generosity of feeling will insinuate itself into the heart, and that once the corpse is stirred, life will come back to the spirit.

It was wrong, therefore, to oppose at times two methods of human formation, one which makes the fruit of acts grow from the hidden and intimate affections, as if that were the only fertile root, the other which makes the interior dispositions germinate from actions themselves as from a seed. It is one and the same method, just as the fruit is only the seed. To be sure, the intention has first to have drawn its sap from the deepest folds of the subjective life. But we have already seen through what underground canals flows the water that springs forth to the light of reflexion; and willed action contributes precisely to water these distant sources.

For if we waited for interior harmony and peace to come of itself, we would be going directly against the sincerest wish of the will. Whoever does not do is undone. It is not enough, then, to will only when we can and as we can; for we would not will for long. Inasmuch as every action executed necessarily uses constraint to rally and discipline the scattered forces, inasmuch as it is the signal for a civil war where there are dead and wounded casualties, inasmuch as we march ahead only by crushing within us and under our feet legions of lives, the battle is declared, whatever we do; and if we do not take the offensive against the enemies of the will, they are the ones who form a coalition against it. We must fight: whoever runs from the combat will necessarily lose his freedom along with his life. Even in the best, there are hoards of malice, of impurity, and of petty passions.

Let no one allow these hostile powers to group themselves into habits and systems; let them be divided by attacking them; let the effort be to unite the faithful forces against anarchy before the time of coalitions, complicities and treasons. Ahead of time everything seems so easy! We think ourselves armed against the dangerous impulses. But do we ever encounter precisely what we had anticipated? And it is the unexpected which almost always decides everything. Also, to protect ourselves against the giddiness of the last second and the sophisms of a travestied conscience which prove that such and such an act is allowed or such and such a pleasure legitimate, we must get into the habit of taking the offensive and of doing more than avoid what we must not do. We have to be able to respond with the strength of earlier experience: "Even if it is legitimate, I will to deprive myself of it." Against involuntary movements, it is not enough to will, for we would be taken by surprise and the will itself would defect; it is not enough to resist, we would be overcome. Without waiting for him, we must act directly against the adversary, provoke him and, through the struggle, awaken new states of consciousness, in order to subdue him in advance and capture even at its very origin the source of the revolutionary impulses. *Agere contra* (act against). Willed action is the principle of more and more voluntary and free action.

And the work is never done, nor the conquest made firm. This living construction is ceaselessly unstable, and as if ready to come apart. 193 Always then, we must rekindle with a new breath these allies prompt to defect, and concentrate the ardor of the soul as in a hearth, in order to melt into one all the elements necessary for the act which can be poured only as a single block. To have acted does not dispense from acting: there is no retirement from the moral life.

Thus we understand that, in willing to act, it is, in a roundabout way, the progress of the will itself we are seeking. By placing the hard grain of action brutally commanded under the stone, we obtain the fine and nourishing flower of freedom.

III

Superficially it seemed that the necessity of enclosing the intention within the narrow letter of an act and of excluding all the other avenues open to the beautiful agility of thought was only hindrance and servitude. But a more penetrating look finds in this monopolizing jealousy of action only a secret instinct of the will and an aim of peace, concord, and unity. It gently helps us, through an imperceptible infiltration, to will what we will to will; it coordinates and disciplines all our energies, rallies the contrary tendencies into a composite force, and orients toward the willed end everything in us that can be converted to it; it makes even what is opposed to the declared will pass into the act. Omitting nothing of all the elements of our complex life in the synthesis it forms, it envelops them and carries them along as in an invisible network.

At the very moment it appears to materialize and restrict the will, the voluntary act, on the contrary, broadens it and in a way puts weight on it: *anima operantium impinguabitur* (the soul of those who act will grow fat). Practice succeeds, without ceasing and without pretention, in this wonder where abstract speculations fail: it unites into a new synthesis the opposed tendencies in which both the victorious and the vanquished are all represented, reformed, transformed, in the act performed, because there is an inevitable solidarity, a solidarity in conformity with the wish of the will, between parts that could be independent only in an imaginary state of complete indifference and absolute repose. To act is no doubt to hold certain desires in check, to bruise certain organs, in order to satisfy and vivify others; but the movement fought down and repressed is not lost forasmuch. It serves to modify and add precision to the movement produced; it especially contributes to enriching, as with conquered . spoils, the triumphant will. Earlier we showed the apparent sacrifice that the effort, the struggle, even the victory require; finally, we must understand the real profit of mortification, even for what is vanquished.

194

In effect, action is not like a logical analysis of motives where, through the exclusive choice of the free decision, we would consider the separate ideas in their purity and their irreducible opposition; nor is it an abstract conciliation of contraries in the region of possibles; still less is it a deployment of incoherent forces that would scatter as they spread out in the organism and sink into the unconscious; it is a systematic concentration of the diffuse life in us; it is a taking possession of oneself. Revealing what is obscurely at work in the unknown depths of life, it brings to light and gathers into a visible bundle those impalpable threads that form the network of the individuality. It is like the casting of a net thrown into deep water; and the links of the net come back tightening up, becoming more and more laden. Through action, then, the unity of the vital mechanism is kept up and tightened, a unity which, formed from an assembling of factions, finds cohesion only through the ideal concert of functions; through action the diversity of the antagonistic tendencies, without being abolished, melts into at least a passing agreement; through it is effected what the natural sciences call ontogeny, that is, the particular and, so to speak, circular and closed evolution of each individual.

What is to be understood then by this conciliation of the contraries whose principle action becomes; and what are the contraries present? Here is what seems to be the case. Of the *different* motives which had emerged with reflexion from the psychological automatism, the decision, which has to adopt one to the exclusion of the others, has made apparently irreconcilable *adversaries*, since all must succumb before the preferred one. Now what does the will propose for itself and what brings it to action? It is the aim of finding itself through the obstacles which, separating us for ourselves, so to speak, keep it from being already what it wills, and from going freely to what it would will to will and attain. The tendencies contrary to the actual will therefore represent in us that provisional and mobile barrier that we hope to put down and push back little by little before the advances of accrued freedom. And if action car- 195 ries the recalcitrant powers off in its violent unity, it is precisely because they are the stakes for this future will; it is so that they will gradually rally to it. Thus, in what seems most opposed to our present willing, there is a secret element of conformity with this willing itself. What stands in the way and contradicts the incipient action will find in the consummated action a new use; and from the apparent sacrifice which the natural mortification of the desires held in check requires, will result the real gain which the conversion of the rebellious movements brings to the will.

The initially paradoxical form of voluntary growth thus becomes intelligible. It seemed that, to exercise itself, the will necessarily had to restrict itself: the meaning of this determinism is disclosed. And it should be noted well, the orientation of the intentions we call good or bad makes little difference here. For, good or bad, the act follows its course in all sincerity. No one escapes the consequences of a decision that goes against his sense of justice. Will it be the man himself who will judge later on? Yes, the same man, but changed by his conduct, clever at absolving himself, usually unable to accuse himself or to make reparations. What a shame it is indeed that the consequences of our initiative should be determined by facts and not by excuses! If only life were a calculation that could be started over a second time, but we may as well believe that we can correct a false subtraction by making a correct addition. There is in deficient action a terrible constraint which can first change an honest man into a cheat, and then reconcile him to this very change, with the reasoning that another fault presents itself to his conscience henceforth as the only good thing for him. — A determinism that is the same both in the work of perversion and that of conversion: it is upon this necessity inherent to acts that we must focus.

"Contraries," therefore, are the price offered and the stakes proposed to the will. In acting, it is not just the declared will which triumphs in what it has willed, and which grows more firm in manifesting what it was; it is also the will triumphant in what it did not will, and which extracts from the resistances themselves the obscure desire that was conspiring with it. Therefore, it does not nourish itself only with its own substance and in its acquired domain, but also with the substance of its adversaries and on the conquered lands. By bringing back to spon- 196 taneous life foods already digested and vivified, it effects a kind of transubstantiation, to the extent that, thanks to it, the law of the spirit penetrates the law of the members. Also the best and the most profound forward movements are often the least seen, because they become truly of a piece bodily with us. We must be diligent in regulating the sense of the ordinary detail, the daily course of life, for in the decisive circumstances we are what we have been, exchanging then the small change we have had to accumulate coin by coin for the big bills.

Hence human individuality is a synthesis at once organic and psychological, and this synthesis results from a synergy. That is how individual life is determined, character is shaped, and the person receives its substantial form, since sometimes even a single act is enough to transform it. By penetrating, through action, into this objective world which he bears within himself, the subject communicates his own life to it; and going over his own work, so to speak, as one sews the underside of a cloth to strengthen the weave, he ties the still exterior and floating phenomena to the intimate reality of the will; he enables them to participate in the solidity of reflexion and freedom. So every act is, in its origin, an indivisible unity wherein human initiative and the contribution of the universe meet. Thus the two forms of phenomena whose scientific relation we have already shown, the facts which consciousness represents to itself as objective, the facts whose flow makes up the properly subjective life, unite to constitute a new reality. Mutually completing one another, the will embodies itself and grows in the object wherein it operates, and the phenomena, still foreign to the interior life, receive a soul and become conscious in the will that uses them for action. Freedom, which initially was only an exemption from antecedent necessity, *immunitas a necessitate* (immunity from necessity), becomes a full will and master of itself, a will that knows how to and can will, a will emancipated little by little from what keeps it from seeing, from willing and from doing, a more free freedom, *immunitas a servitute, liberum consilium* (immunity from servitude, free counsel).

It is in the indistinct sense of this enriching conciliation that we must find the secret of pleasure, a fruit of action. There is pleasure when a foreign element is incorporated into the organism, when the organism itself participates more in subjective life, when, through a movement of concentration from the outside to the inside, the central energy and the will are increased, understood, obeyed. That is why pleasure is added to the act, not to perfect it, but to give witness that it is perfect. It means that we have gone full circle, that there is a return or a completion in the activity. That is why also, while it serves as a reward, it serves as an encouragement as well, as a force and as an attraction toward action. For in pleasure it is the will that finds itself, it seems; it recollects itself through the object it assimilates, as if, everywhere at home it had to be

197

the universal bond and to make the entire world that it summed up in our life submissive and immanent to it.

But at this very point is revealed the necessary inconsistency and the incurable insufficiency of this individual life, no matter how tightly knit its circular development may appear. If action conciliates the still incoherent tendencies and procures that well-being which comes from a growing harmony, this feeling itself is the sign and the principle of a resurgent movement; it is an end, but also a beginning over again. The determinism of action always carries it beyond. For in the passive state that follows the voluntary initiative, reappear the often painful contrarieties and the incompatibility of the desires and affections which, already before, had evoked the decision and the effort. Action does not in effect unify everything, convert everything, pacify everything in us all at once. The equilibrium it had established it upsets of its own accord, by becoming conscious of it. The severed roots grow again; the satisfied needs live on; the will, more strong and more ample, not only aspires to remain master over the ground gained, but to extend its successes. Whoever does not go forward goes backward. One does not dismantle a machine while it is working; thus, for the unity of the individual to be kept up and confirmed, a constant cooperation has to pull his powers together and the ever threatened equilibrium must ceaselessly be reestablished, as in walking which is actually only a fall perpetually being stopped. The idea of substance has been discussed at great length: reduced to what our analysis disclosed about it here, the substance of man is action, he is what he does. $E\nu$ $\tau\omega$ $\epsilon\rho\gamma\omega$ τo $o\nu$ (being is in action). We are, we know, we live, only *sub specie actionis* (under the species of action). Not only does action manifest what we were already, but it also makes us grow and go out of ourselves, so to speak; so that, after having studied the progress of action in being, and the progress of the being in action, we will have to transport the center of gravity of the will consistent with the law of its progress beyond individual life.

198

Within the confines of the universe we bear within ourselves, in the midst of this internal struggle of the tendencies refractory to full consciousness and the will, action is not adequate to its total conditions. It is not the integral and definitive expression of life unified, employed, concerted in its entirety. Now, the disproportion of action with the efficient cause is precisely what brings up and explains the final cause: we go forward only if, looking back or where we are, we are not secure or satisifed. Hence it is the fulness of our original will which accounts for our insatiable exigency and projects us always further on. Αναγκη μη στηναι (it is necessary not to stand still).

Also we do not act simply for the sake of acting, and without proposing a goal for ourselves. In the immense variety of the objects that it will seem to pursue as an exterior and superior end, but which in reality it envelops and dominates, always it is the will that is looking for itself. As formal freedom had saved its autonomy only by imposing on itself the heteronomy of a practical obligation and an effort, so also the person is born in the individual, is constituted and preserved, only by assigning itself an impersonal end: a great truth adumbrated in what people feel. Man is not sufficient unto himself; he has to act for others, with others, through others. We cannot manage the affairs of our own lives by ourselves. Our existences are so tied together that it is impossible to conceive a single action which does not extend itself in infinite waves, well beyond the goal it seemed to aim at. The most insignificant actions can go quite far, to trouble an obscure life, to draw some unknown person from his egoism, and to provoke faults or dedications that all together concur in the human tragedy. The individual consciousness, whether it knows it or not, is a consciousness of the universal.

Thus, after having shown that duty is and that the will must act, οτι εστιν (that it is), it will appear little by little what the will must be and do, ο εστιν (what it is). Not that we now have to appeal to good will: here again we claim to be simply disclosing the determinism of voluntary action. The premises having been laid down as they have been, the issue is to direct it to its necessary end. The tares grow like the good grain. Egoism and disinterestedness follow the same law, though they apply diversely. We can never be sufficient unto ourselves. To succeed in being better and more completely one, we must not, we cannot remain *alone*.

The will therefore normally tends toward an end that *seems* exterior to it; it spreads itself out. From being already a synthesis, it becomes the element of a society broader than ourselves. The fact is that we encounter in ourselves a multiplicity and a contrariety of desires not all of which can be brought into agreement, because, like unmatched pieces in a mosaic, in order to be fitted together they await the complementary pieces. How work for the whole of ourselves, then, especially for what in us escapes distinct consciousness or explicit resolutions, if not by consecrating ourselves to some work whose concern is too general not to surpass our reflected calculations? The complete love of self has to lose its footing and drown in the ocean of the self (*l'océan du moi*). There is within us an obscure and permanent sense of all the lives alien to our own, of those lives which, through knowledge, have been concentrated into it to nourish and sustain our own activity. We would like to believe that from these depths rises the mist which always half enshrouds consciousness; we would like to judge that, breaking all ties with our origins, we would belong more to ourselves; and it seems to us that we would gain by refusing to give of ourselves to anybody. No, without this vaguely perceived impersonal, we would be unable to see, as in a mirror without foil. Egoism blinds us. It is by stepping out of the individual life, by focusing elsewhere than in ourselves, that we shall possess ourselves the best. The child still lives only for himself; and that is why he is not in himself. There is no concern for others, for their judgments or their pleasures. Reason appears in him, he becomes a person from the day he knows enough to concede, against himself, a self to strangers, from the day he begins to participate, be it at his own expense, in the person of another, and when he makes an effort over himself not to be naively the center of everything. There is indeed a central place to be taken within us: it cannot belong to us; to whom shall we give it? The illusion of egoism is to lay claim to it.

The triumph of the will, therefore, could not lie in a sort of jealous reserve or sacrilegious apotheosis, but rather in an apparent abdication; it tends toward impersonal and unconscious ends. To act, we must in a way alienate ourselves to others, hand ourselves over to forces we shall no longer dominate. No sooner did we seem, as we emerged from slow formations, to rise to reflexion and freedom than we find ourselves caught up again in a mechanism capable, it seems, of shattering the nascent individuality: a little noticed determinism this, which takes hold of acts at the moment they arise to carry them far beyond our previsions and our intentions, but a determinism which nevertheless great men of action have been keenly aware of, most of them convinced that the breath of fatality was passing through them and carrying their destiny with it. 200

Thus our life is the concurrence of all the rest; our person is our expansion and our dedication to all; our action is the collaboration of the universe and the triumph of impersonality. In alienating itself this way, is the will preparing itself to be enriched? And is this implacable determinism yet another road to emancipation and conquest?

To follow the road that goes from one consciousness to another consciousness; to pursue the progress of action from the confines of the individual to the point where the will, which still animates this movement of expansion, expects and demands the intimate concurrence of others; to transport the center of equilibrium of human activity beyond the individual synergy into a real community of life and action, that is my present aim. — First, in pouring itself out into the surrounding milieu, the voluntary operation there constitutes an expressive phenomenon and pursues an end. — In this final cause itself we look for an efficient response and a cooperation: the will tries, then, to submit and to assimilate the exterior universe to itself, as it had already attempted to conquer and penetrate the organism. — Through this collaboration itself, the initial will grows and expands: considered as a synthesis of concurring energies and as a fecund creature in turn, action will become the cement of a social federation. — Not that it is as yet a question of works born of the intimate union of wills and produced from lives already melted together; it is a question of the works that make this union come to be and that allow a closer cooperation. How do we come to reach and to will other ourselves? What we must study now, then, is the in between (*l'entre-deux*) of consciousnesses and of human actions.

Stage Four
FROM INDIVIDUAL ACTION TO SOCIAL ACTION

Generation, fecundation, and reproduction of human actions

Action is not restricted within the confines of individual life. There is no 201
efficient cause in us that does not aim at a final cause and is not an implicit admission of insufficiency and request for help. After it has taken
from the universal milieu the wherewithal to produce itself, it does not
shut itself up within itself. Born of nature, it seems to have to return to
nature and receive from it its necessary complement. If at the beginning
of our own activity there appeared a kind of spontaneous egoism, now
in the course of personal growth a need for expansion is revealed, a
necessary disinterestedness, a giving of ourselves that calls for a reciprocal giving and an alien intervention. We are forced to give because
necessarily we have to receive. As the individual adapts more and more
to his milieu, he becomes richer; that is the truth which the utilitarian
doctrine contains: a keen insight into his true interests, a precise sense
of the infinite and universal collaboration, keeps man from being nar-
rowly egotistic and leads him to let go of himself.

Hence no resolution can be realized in the intimacy of the person
without involving the surrounding world, without looking for help in it,
without provoking a corresponding action in it. It is this criss-crossing
or this federation of acts that we must examine now, before coming to
society and the union of the agents themselves. We shall see, then, how
through the mediation of individual life, the will organizes a world outside more and more in conformity with its wish. The action which it 202
stamps with its mark, which it detaches from itself like a distinct
creature, and which it hands over to circulation, like the living being who
blossoms into puberty to attract suitors, contracts an alliance with the
object of its desire and loses its virginity only to become fruitful in turn.

In the study of this collaboration there appears a double movement to
be described, a convergence starting from a plan of symmetry. The operation that proceeds from me and, through the material execution and the
sensible phenomena, goes out to fall under the brute determinism of dead
facts, needs, in order to reach completion, to follow an inverse channel

and serve as nourishment for other forces that regenerate its hidden life and more or less second its intentions. Thus, I shall study successively the propagation of the initial act down to the body of the sign which is its natural expression, then, the mechanism of the phenomena that are the material bond of every exchange and every collaboration, finally, the influence that action exerts where it operates, the echo it raises outside of itself, the response it receives in return for its advances. But even where we solicit an alien cooperation and a response from the outside that supposes a movement born elsewhere than from ourselves, this return movement is itself also contained in the primitive ambition of the will. As broad as the field of our action may be, the initiative of the forces exterior to individuality itself are still immanent to the first desire. *Qui agit semper idem est* (the one who acts is always the same).

CHAPTER 1

The Immediate Expansion and the Sensible Expression of Action

Planted into the organism, the act, through a natural push, is produced 203 on the outside. Here we must assume once again the language of sensible phenomena because, through the voluntary operation and the organic execution, the intention falls back into the domain and under the law of mechanical determinism. There is no thought, as purified as we suppose it to be of every image, that is not tied to a cerebral modification; no elementary movement which, in the full system of the body, does not involve the interconnected organs; no physiological function that does not reach out beyond the periphery. Through our presence, through our action, we spread ourselves out around us; and we cannot move, breathe, live, and think without impressing ourselves on the outside. The atmosphere of individuality itself is unlimited.

We must now account for this apparent necessity. Individual life is an inevitable expansion. What does this going out, or what might be called this *exergy*, mean? Why does the human person go out beyond its confines? Does this brutal expression of the inner activity, which throws the work of our thought into the promiscuity of mechanical phenomena, conceal yet another secret aspiration and does it keep an imprint of the initial will? How are *actions* distinguished from the ordinary *facts* and the common phenomena to which this word does not seem to apply?

New questions to be resolved and whose original character we shall have to determine in order to approach them from a viewpoint that is 204 neither physical nor metaphysical. It is a question of the sensible generation of *action*, not of the *phenomenon*. Before all reflexion and every end deliberatly pursued, there is an immediate and total expression of the actual operation, an action of action, which is like its primary sign and spontaneous imprint. It constitutes its initial production and its first work, the origin and the means for all the others.

I

It is a fact: we are perpetually stamping our imprint on the milieu where we live. Every impression on our machine provokes a state of systematic reaction in our organs. We are like a vibrant apparatus that resounds to the least shock, to every wind to come along. But it is not simply a recording apparatus. The current of power that goes through us does not come out without being modified and organized. It is of this internal transformation that there is a more or less clear consciousness; it is this new organization and this system of movements that constitutes the apparent fact of action. Hence it is no longer the movements themselves, but their coordination and their sense that we must now study.

And let us not look just to the more apparent signs of the language of action, nor to the spontaneous or intentional expression of emotions and thoughts. It is a question of a more general, a more precise, and a more profound truth. There is no mental state that does not have its determinate trace. The Greeks used to distinguish between πραττειν (doing) and ποιειν (making) according to whether the act fashions a material or preserves in appearance a completely ideal character. But even in the most "contemplative" form of activity, θεωρειν (contemplating), there is a material fashioned: and this material we sculpt in thinking and willing, is our members and, through them, the milieu where they make their impression. Every act that comes out of the human organism is, even outside of ourselves, an organism of signs and a symbol expressive of subjective life.

Hence, not only does man act within the universal determinism through his mass, like all brute bodies, not only does he exert the in-
205   fluence of a source of heat around him and produce all the ordinary effects of natural agents that contribute to vital functions, not only does he perhaps limit, as some observers have thought, a force distinct from the physical agents already known, but also the determinate action of each individual expresses itself in a determinate way. That is, independent of the physical means that serve to represent it to the senses, independent of the works wherein it realizes itself, action has its expression and, so to speak, its own trace or physiognomy. Thus I write these words under the influence of a preoccupation and through the effect of an aim which they try to manifest. But the perceptible and conscious signs express only a part of the reflected activity and form only a part of the total and spontaneous sign. Besides the phenomena that are the instruments of my decision, besides the material result of my operation, there is produced in me a synthesis of images, internal states, and expressive

movements, where the particular acts that manifest the decision are only a more or less direct derivation and a more or less partial and superficial application. At each moment, the total system I form and which is my actual *self* expresses itself in its very totality.

Also we must be on our guard against letting the investigation stray. It is not a matter of opening up again the physical question of the production and transmission of the signs. Still less is it a matter of approaching the problem of the communication between consciousnesses through metaphysical paths: this problem has been rendered unreal by the way it has been raised. To come back to phenomena that come under the positive sciences would be to misconstrue precisely what distinguishes action, and its always particular physiognomy, from common facts and from their always abstract generality; worse still, it would be to imagine falsely that the milieu, wherein the senses and the sciences appear to be following the birth and the development of the sign, has a reality identical with the knowledge we have of it; it would be to forget the fictitious character of scientific symbolism. A surprising wonder, it seems, this apparition in the world of an act that comes down to it as if from on high, since it seems to express reason and freedom directly, without following the channel of nature. — Yet it does follow it: once the intention, by penetrating into the members, has moved the organs, it is done with; what appeared to be outside the concatenation of the physical forces has gone back into the mechanism. The body and its servitudes, these are the intermediary of a freedom that naturalizes itself in them in order to speak the language of brutes to the brutes on the outside. 206

Hence, there is no need to concern ourselves with the way in which the expression of the act is manifested on the outside, as if this outside had a defined subsistence, or as if scientific determinism were a law of being, the law of a metaphysical physics which is a phantom. We have seen how, in the system of phenomena, subjective decisions entail their objective conditions. That is what is important: for the science of the relations positively determined among phenomena establishes that this apparent determinism is absorbed by the very knowledge we have of it. The sensible sign is a natural consequence of the operation interior to the agent; and in what is sensible or material in this expression there is nothing more to be explained.

Here then is what remains to be discovered. It is the meaning of this continual expansion which brings the agent to the apparent necessity of expressing himself; it is the inspiration and the role and the goal of the signs, even when invisible, that make of the individual a center of radiation; it is the reason for the scientific need itself. For everything hangs together in the deployment of our acts; and we must understand what deep aspiration the institution of signs, of language, and of the very symbolism of positive science corresponds to, and on what hidden wish it is grounded.

A science of the working out of empirical and scientific knowledge therefore has to be developed. Not that we should construct a theory of human labor and of the advances of technology, as what has been called *praxeology* attempts to do. For the study of practical procedures or of scientific methods presupposes a prior investigation. How does it happen that man inserts himself efficaciously into the world of phenomena? By what means does his mediating action operate, with the help of the arbitrarily constructed symbolisms whose practical usefulness it exploits? In short, what is the profound reason for its entire unfolding in the world we refer to as exterior to ourselves?

To answer this question we must scrutinize the nature and the bearing of the sign inherent in every operation of man, no matter how interior we suppose it to be. Nothing in the expansion of the will is superfluous and remains outside the series of the means that direct it to its ends. It might seem that the quite spontaneous and quite impalpable expression
207   of organic and mental labor could be neglected; would not undertaking such a study be to enter into an impasse where only the curious have any interest in going? It will without doubt appear, on the contrary, that this is the natural and necessary passage through which willing spreads itself out into the universe and tends to absorb it.

II

If we were to consider only the *material* of the sign that manifests action, we would be falling back into the study of the phenomena which the positive sciences submit to their general laws and to mechanical determinism. But what brings it about that action, even while being a fact or a phenomenon, is no longer a phenomenon like those others, is precisely the expressive value in it, the subjective meaning, the organized system to which it owes its ever singular physiognomy. In being produced outside, it keeps the coherent and ordered character of the individual synthesis whose prolongation it is. In all our productions there subsists an image and something like a soul of intimate life and of subjective organization. It is in this profound sense that to produce, τικτειν, is to beget an animated being and to detach from self a new creature that continues to grow as a separate organism.

Also man's first work is to fashion for himself, so to speak, his own matter, and through this operation to produce an immediate trace which, ordinarily unknown to him, organizes outside the confines of the individual an image or, better, an expression of the act, an expression which is the proper stamp of the whole agent and like his inimitable signature. What is unique and incomparable in each sign is the precise point on which the effort of the present study must concentrate. The singular and the concrete, that is, what is ignored by the positive sciences, necessarily limited to the abstract and the general, such is ever the object of the science of action.

For example, a gesture is the material construction of a feeling whose infinite complexity is revealed through the infinite details of an original structure. A saying is a thought garbed in rhythmic and nuanced sounds. Even a thought is a system of vibrations which, produced by cerebral labor, undoubtedly offer a type as distinct as the timbre of a voice or the appearance of a face. Think of the paradox of the phonograph: there is in each articulated sound a quite special quality whose very particularities can be gathered, preserved, and reproduced. The same is true of all the sensible signs that translate the presence and the absolutely singular action of the individual. Perhaps it is in these infinitesimal traces of the act and of thought itself that we must look for the secret of the lucidity peculiar to hypnotic hyperesthesia. Produced in an unconscious way, the primitive signs of life can be received and interpreted in an unconscious way; it is somewhat like one who is deaf, thinking aloud without hearing his voice, would be surprised to see those near him docile to his desires and informed of his feelings. In any event, perceptible or not, these traces have their original physiognomy; and as the dog picks out the step of his master among a thousand others, as the hand of the worker or the manner of the artist can be discerned with certitude, there is no act within us that does not constitute outside of us a tenuous and fragile, but organized and expressive network, a complex system of movements and something like an animated creature.

What then constitutes the incomparable originality of each act in the very fact that manifests it? It is the unity of the intelligible relations that form the synthesis or the very organism of the sign. We must not think that in the sign there is nothing more than in the organic operation itself and that it is only a feeble echo of it. No, there is already in it, to make it possible and to realize it, a commerce between the agent and something other than the agent, a new synthesis of the individual life and the milieu in which it unfolds. Thus we do not speak in a vacuum; and it is an alien cooperation *a parte acti* (from the side of the one acted upon) that enables the most rudimentary expansion *a parte agentis* (from the side of the one acting). Every sign is already a work. It is not simply the internal operation as it had organized itself in the intimacy of the living body,

208

nor some phenomenon or other, a banal *fact* the study of which could be handed over to the positive sciences. It is, if we dare say so, a secondary subject, detached in appearance from the acting subject, and rather like an intention embodied and vivified. It is a real idea in nature, almost with the same claim as the other living beings.

But before studying this alien concurrence and the very synthesis that results from it, we still have to see better what the agent brings, and what the profound aspiration is for which the sign produced and the work effected serve as provisional ends and natural means.

III

209   In the sensible body of the invisible act there is an ideal unity. And this interior unity of the expressive phenomenon is the intention, but the intention already on the way to being realized. The sign, which we might perhaps be tempted to take as an accessory appendage, especially where it is involuntary and imperceptible, marks an effective progress of the will; it responds to a real need; it is in conformity with the primitive intention and useful to it, by orienting it toward its completion.

Hence there is a relation between the natural expression of the act and the more or less intentional end it proposes for itself. The language of emotions is a spontaneous sketch of the suitable movements for satisfying needs or fending off dangers; a gesture often outlines a whole drama in action. What is true of a mime, of a facial play, of a whole attitude is equally so of the least traces of operative activity. The immediate expression of the interior life is the matter and as it were the sensible substance of the invisible desires and states which, taken up by reflexion, will lead us to pursue distinct ends and produce particular works. This necessary expansion has a meaning therefore; and this meaning is found in the aim of the will in quest of its growth. There is nothing, then, that does not enter into the voluntary plan of our life, nothing that does not serve it, not even the spontaneous manifestation of our innermost operations and the expressive unity of the act.

Indeed, from the moment the willed operation set just in motion stamps its imprint on the determinism of facts, from the moment it tends to determine the total system according to its own orientation, the will little by little unveils its power and its ambition. It begins to penetrate the world with its intentions as it had already penetrated the organism with them. It aspires to become as it were the soul of all that surrounds it and serves it. It ambitions gaining the universe and dominating it by absorbing it. Is not the natural movement of egoism to make itself the center and refer everything only to itself? Does it not ask to possess all of the exterior object as the complement and the dependency of its sovereign caprice? Thus the sign that expresses the motor operation on the outside is, at least in germ, a conquering invasion and an absorption of the universe by the will.

Hence, just as willing, in spreading into the individual organism, was instinctively seeking to enrich itself and to find itself more complete, so also, in penetrating into what we call the exterior world and in pouring itself out into the sign, it assimilates new food. It spends itself only to concentrate itself and to take in more, as if in the end the entire universe were to become immanent to it and no longer be anything more than a prolongation of the body quite docile to thought. Is this not the marvel that every day the advances of the sciences enable us to achieve more perfectly? Through them the world of phenomena is submitted to man; it is penetrated by the spirit; it is opened up to the circulation of the interior life. Having become truly an adjunct of the organism for transmitting or fixing, without fear of time or space, the speech and all the signs of human activity, it seems to be summed up in the unity of a thought that bears it within itself and is everywhere present in it, as in an animated system where life, in spite of its invisible unity, is everywhere at once. Everything in it communicates, circulates, is exchanged, without our having to know the how. And spontaneously the forces of nature seem to have become an organ of the will: such is the beauty of scientific civilization!

But the primitive sign of the inner operation, by projecting our spontaneous aim before us, proposes it to distinct knowledge; it makes of it a partial object for reflexion. And as, in the deliberation over the act, the conceived end is always determined under a singular aspect, so also in the execution the end willed and realized always has a determinate and partial character. At the origin of reflexion and of free decision, it was the disproportion between the elementary conditions and exigencies of the willing and the willed activity that gave rise to the idea of finality. Here it is no longer the idea of an end, it is the end itself that the operating will continues to pursue and begins to assimilate to itself as it manifests itself on the outside. The sensible expression of the act therefore points to a tendency of willing toward an ulterior goal. That is why action always appears as transitive, that is, it seems to be in a perpetual becoming. We cannot, except by abstraction, consider it as absolutely closed, for its consequences and increases are virtually unlimited in time and space. And each end, as soon as it appears reached, is already only a stepping-stone for going beyond.

If in acting the individual seems to go out of himself, it is therefore

precisely because there is in him insufficiency, penury, imbalance between the initiative and the results of his internal operation. Through this
expansion the agent obeys the need created by the very development of
his will; he is seeking his completion and his equation. This exodus does
not prove that he already has surplus and superabundance, far from it;
it shows that individual life cannot restrict itself to itself, that a complement is indispensable for it, that between what it is and what we will,
there is a lack of equilibrium. This is the reason why the internal finality
must not be isolated from the external finality; for the system of the individuality and of the organic operation that manifests it is not a closed
circuit. This synthesis of life maintains itself only by stepping out into an
exterior end of unfolding and by organizing it according to itself while
organizing itself according to it. Action is action only inasmuch as it constitutes an organism, by making a diversity of phenomena concur in a
single end. The more this finality is realized in the complex whole, so as
to be like its soul, the more also the action is manifest and clear, the more
the act is act. Thus it is that a beautiful machine or a statue are real ideas,
active intentions in turn: the developed image of the first production
which embodies the act in the natural sign.

Thus, to regain the perpetually broken accord between the realized
and the willed, we have to make ourselves the efficient cause of a final
cause and draw it to us. Just as we found powers favorable or rebellious
to our operation within our little interior world, there must also subsist
in the exterior world, forces that are no doubt alien at first or hostile to
our aims, but forces that, with an energy of their own, can be converted
to the initiative of the will to be submitted to it like the docile members
of one and the same organism.

To will, to act, to operate, to produce: we are thus drawn little by little
toward developments perhaps unforeseen, but surely in conformity with
the profound aspiration of our primitive willing. The expression of the
act, as imperceptible as it may be at the beginning, is the germ of an immense growth. This primary sign of life, which is produced with the in-
212   fallible ease of an unconscious spontaneity, becomes the principle of the
signs more or less natural or willed, of the works more or less artificial
and difficult that will develop man's thought and dominion. But henceforth, even in what will seem to come from elsewhere than ourselves, we
will have to recall always this initiative which dominates all future increases. The double movement, centripetal and centrifugal, that composes the rhythm of vital expansion is equally contained in one and the
same aim of conquest. Efficient cause and final cause, then, are, through
an alternative progress, the mobile forms of one and the same tendency
of the will toward a new extension of its empire.

But how subordinate the alien forces whose cooperation seems indispensable for any production and for the most rudimentary of natural signs? We have already had to study the inner struggles of the voluntary operation against organic resistances. And we recall with what difficulties, but also with what results, the will concerts the diffused or rebellious forces to compose the individual out of them. Now the obstacle seems still greater; for action is no longer setting in motion only the organism in its depths, it has to involve the ambient universe in its work. No doubt, through the teachings of experience and science, it manages to dominate these mysterious powers that surround it. But we must account for this very success. Under what conditions is this outcome possible, and what does it suppose both in the *agent* who brings it about and in the *acted upon* that allows or seconds it? — Is it not the case that there are, around us as well as within us, *subjects* virtually conformed to our aims and accessible to the influence of the natural signs of our acts? Every action is a request for concurrence, and already an obtaining of help. What follows will show this.

Also the *sign* deserves this name doubly. First, under the system of organized phenomena that constitute it, it manifests an aim to increase. Then, for it to have its efficaciousness, even to succeed in constituting itself, it needs to be received, taken in, given back by the milieu where it appears. Action produces itself in the atmosphere that envelops it only by involving in its very appearing what it does not know and what it does not yet attain. From the viewpoint of the individual, it seems that its spontaneous expansion peters out here; for it is starting from this point that, going back from the brute phenomena which clothe the sign to the 213 forces able to restore its signification, we shall see little by little auxiliaries lending themselves to our initial action. But this collaboration itself, this active concurrence of alien and apparently independent allies remains included in the original meaning of the sign. That is enough to make us appreciate the ideal ambition of the will over the whole world. But how it realizes itself, by obtaining an effective cooperation, remains to be seen.

Few truths have been less noted and are more worthy of attention than these: — (1) Every action necessarily involves the alien milieu in which it expresses itself, and this very expression is possible only through an immediate complaisance of something other than the agent. — (2) This natural trace of the operation is an intelligible system of phenomena on which the subjective intention is stamped and which constitutes its first increase; it relates less to the efficient cause than to the final cause, toward which it is already on the way. — (3) Every production is thus, not just an arrangement of sensible facts, but a concurrence and a synthesis of operations coming from alien agents. And yet these operations, whose origins seem independent or even divergent, are enveloped in one and the same willing.

The intention on the way to realizing itself therefore descends to the terrain of brute phenomena only to find there, and only by finding there already, an echo, a complicity, a cooperation. It is a fact that action necessarily expresses itself through a sign, and that it takes its place in the total determinism. We have had to understand this fact; and what is understanding it, if not bringing it back to the normal and consequent development of the will by showing that under this apparent constraint is hidden the germ of all its future expansion.

It pertains to the next chapter to study the response provoked by the agent, the brute and forced concurrence that necessarily completes his initiative, in a word, *coaction,* at once in the etymological sense and in the usual sense of the word. After what we called *exergy,* we must therefore analyse what could be called *allergy,* "the action of others," but an action that remains entirely suspended from the initiative of the agent. The conclusion of this study will be to show how the will is always present to the work which nevertheless it does not seem to have produced by itself, is always busy about a broader extension, is always in quest of a more intimate and more docile collaboration.

CHAPTER 2
Coaction

There is no act, however interior it may be, but always forced to express 214 itself, that does not call for a sort of complaisance and collaboration outside the individual. A gesture, a word are possible only through the milieu where they manifest themselves. The phenomenon is neither from ourselves alone nor from the surrounding world alone; it is from both and, as it were, indivisibly so. Every act comes from the *agent* (*l'agent*), but to go directly to what is *acted upon* (*l'agi*), without which it is not. Not only are we not able to create or make anything from nothing — that is, some matter, whatever it may be, is indispensable for the exercise of our activity as a prior condition — but also our operations, our very intentions will be molded in some way on the object they tend toward in order to receive their form there.

It is therefore in all truth that, in order to act, one must accommodate oneself to one's milieu, and that this milieu contributes to the way of being and of doing of whoever unfolds into it. Thus architectural forms are commanded both by the purpose of the edifice and the nature itself of the materials, that is, by the idea of the worker and by the corresponding action of the object to which the operation is applied. The sign is fashioned in part by the body it expresses itself in, and the letter of the symbol is active on the very spirit that inspires and animates it. If in sense perception we react by coloring the impression felt with our subjective character, reciprocally our initiative, in implanting itself in the object, receives from it an imprint that is from it and not from us.

Our action then is never only our action. It is not enough for it to be 215 led to go out of the individual confines, it must also arouse, through a sort of natural affinity and through *coaction*, powers alien to ourselves; and its work or its phenomenon has to result from a convergence and from a synthesis of operations coming from different origins. How then does another's action, "allergy," one might say, enter into the movement of our personal will? How do we obtain this necessary concurrence? And what is the result or the consequence of this coaction?

I

The idea of a determinate end to be pursued already supposes the immediate expression of the ideal intention in the real sign which is its first work. In producing itself and in order to produce itself, action determines itself according to its own tendency and according to the very occasion for its expansion.

Whatever direction we may wish to give our activity, we always have to take into account the term of unfolding in which it is applied, because it is from this term that will result in part the physiognomy of the work pursued and wished for. What we call the formal cause, then, is not exclusively proper to the initiative of the efficient cause; it depends as much on the object toward which the operation tends as on the subject from which it starts. For the moment an object serves as a goal for an act as subsequent condition, we expect from it something more than what we bring to it. Truly there is no final cause for our will, in truth, except one where we foresee an efficient cause, where we look for one, where we require one.

It would be wrong, therefore, in studying intentional finality, to look only to the will aiming at a goal, as if alone, through its own resources and its isolated efforts, it could succeed in attaining it. The final cause is in part its efficient cause. It furnishes not only the end, but the accompaniment of the action that leads to it and calls for it. It would be wrong also to limit our gaze to the foreseen and predetermined goal; for in imagining that we will this end alone for its own sake, it is something else again that we are seeking, its effect, its gift, its incorporation into our willing, often without our knowing it; that is, if the end seems to be a final cause, with respect to which we play the role of efficient cause, it is on the reciprocal condition and with the secret intention that it will be an efficient cause for which we shall be the final cause. Thus the true goal of the egotist is not what he wants and conquers, but himself. We aspire only to what we do not have, only if that something is supposed to produce with us or for us a new synthesis into which the apparently coveted end enters only as an element and a means.

Whether I know it or not, then, my action, taken in or taken over by those very forces I intended it for and where I was seeking a completion, has to be profoundly transformed. And I have willed this transformation at times unforeseen and out of proportion with my plans: it is implicitly understood in the free decision and in the operation that was its point of departure. What in effect does the will propose for itself? It is to adapt everything to itself. And as the tool is a kind of organ added to our organs, action is an extension of willing outside of us. It goes out, but only in order to bring into itself and assimilate that wherein it seems to alienate itself.[1]

Also, whatever we have to do, we have to draw on forces alien to ours: this is a coalition required for the production of the least work, of the least sign of our activity. We must therefore complete the ancient Peripatetic definition and say that an act is more than the passage from a potency to completion under the dominion of a potency already in act: it is the synthesis and the progress of two concurring potencies under the mediation and through the exchange of an efficient cause and a final cause. For each of the two causes at work serves as a relative and provisional end for the other; both have to furnish and to receive something; so that the result obtained will appear for each the product of the determinism or of the efficiency of the other. What does this mean, if not that the will, already realized but still imperfect within us, tends to insert itself and to find its completion in the world as it had already done in the organism? In what it is already, it is only a means; in what it wills to be, it is the true final cause. And between these two terms of its development is placed, as an intermediary that seems at first to be an end but is only a means, the alien cooperation, "allergy." 217

The action of something else is what our personal action requires to enable and to perfect our expansive synergy. But it is also what modifies it profoundly, and it is what complicates the problem of the efficaciousness or the success of our efforts. We produce nothing without extracting it at the same time from often indocile or treacherous powers. It is also ordinary, in the best prepared and most nursed action, to feel disgust, surprise, or anger, because our resolutions are poorly executed, our dreams disappointed, our concerns meagerly remunerated. The impenetrability, the insufficiency, the lack of intelligence of our allies betray our projects as much as the hostility of obstacles conjured up: they make theirs what we willed to be ours. At the sight of the little we can do, in the presence of this infinite we need in order to act, which we must handle gropingly, and which goes against our weak operation, turns it to one

---

1. Unlike knowledge, which transforms its object into thought, action transports the agent into the very end he is seeking. Also what we do outside of ourselves is more essential and more interior, so to speak, than what we concentrate within. *Non quod intrat, sed quod procedit, hoc coinquinat hominem* (it is not what goes into a man, but what comes out of him, that defiles him).

side, or hurls it down, does not a feeling of panic arise in us? What we have to beware of is at once the impotence of the repressed effort and the unforeseen fecundity of an all too supportive intervention. Sometimes more, sometimes less, and never exactly what we willed: that is the reason why some disappointment usually goes with every satisfaction sought after. In what we were hoping for, behind the apparent end of the desire, was hidden an infinitely vaster wish.

It is also a natural aim of man to obtain, with all possible precision and through constraint, the concurrence of alien forces. Effacing himself, so to speak, he tries to spare his own effort in order to let them produce what he has rigorously predetermined and, in order to be, by himself, the will of what has no will. How is this coaction possible? For this word, besides the idea of constraint which it evokes, must keep the meaning of its etymology: convergence and union of activity. It is not anymore a question now of taking note of tendencies or considering projects; it is a question of determining an effective concurrence and an intervention in fact. How then does the human operation succeed, according to its need and its wish, in using and in submitting, in assimilating and in incorporating into itself what seems to be exterior to it?

II

218   We never act alone. In what way can our action provoke and even force the action of something else, and what does this very possibility presuppose? The question is delicate; for instead of looking at the sensible phenomenon or the produced work as the expression of the *agent*, we must now see in it what belongs to what is *acted on*. In this phenomenon itself, then, it is no longer the sensible that counts; it is what makes it sensible. Physical determinism had no doubt already been surpassed and overcome. But it still remains for us to see better how the victorious production of the act is possible only through what is *subjective* outside the agent.

To penetrate into the universal system of phenomena, action in producing itself must become as the nourishment of the milieu where it appears. In order to make itself an object and to manifest itself sensibly, our subjective life evokes subjects still alien to it. To bolster the imagination with the help of an analogy, we must place ourselves again at the point where we were considering the elementary conditions and the unconscious sources of action in ourselves. Thus we can more easily represent to ourselves how our voluntary operation, having descended into the domain of brute facts, becomes in turn the invisible source and the necessary stimulant of other energies and of actions started from elsewhere than ourselves. We go back into the determinism of nature to solicit it in our favor and orient it toward our ends. We solicit it as it solicits us.

Also, to act and to succeed in anything whatsoever, we must know how to go about it. Whether we have to work with granite or with glaze or to handle men, always there is the same need of an instinctive tact or an unperceived suggestion. In spreading out into the surrounding dynamism, action brings to it, through the mechanism of the sign, an intention and an idea. Wrapped in the expressive symbol which, thanks to the constraint of the determinism, it comes to propose and even impose on the total system, action conserves a meaning and an individual physiognomy; it is a subjective virtuality able to organize other spontaneities and make them serve its aims. The finality and the efficacity of that first work produced which is the immediate expression of the operation itself is disclosed better and better: it becomes the instrument of the growing reign of the will. Where we seem to be doing violence to brute matter, our intervention is still only a sign, in the sense that we are calling for a reaction and counting on some assistance.

Thus, when the will is confronted with the efficient cause which, through the vehicle of the sensible phenomenon and under the form of a subjective nourishment, supplies it with an intention and a sort of determining suggestion, the term of its unfolding furnishes the means and, with more or less spontaneity, resistance, and intelligence, this term becomes, for its part, efficient cause of the common end which it would no doubt not have obtained by itself and which nevertheless it had hidden within itself. Every work done presupposes two efficient causes that correspond to one another and complete one another: both the one and the other are mutually the necessary condition for their common success. And the soul of this coaction is an initial intention, a will that proposes for itself, not just the object toward which it was first tending, nor even the concurrence of this objective end, but a community of action and effect. We dominate phenomena only by using them as signs to lead us back to what determines and produces them, that is, we too serve as signs for them in order to stimulate the forces they proceed from.

The mechanical operation that is effected in this world of phenomena with the guidance of sensible appearances therefore implies a more hidden and a more efficacious action, the confrontation of dynamic aptitudes, the trial or the calculation of profound affinities, everything which metaphysicians had prematurely called the communication of substances. The efficacity of the act in the world of phenomena rests in the last analysis on a concurrence of spontaneities perceived through

219

their natural symbols. When the engineer with the help of calculus determines the resistance of the materials he is using, when the physicist
through his experiments determines the conductibility of a body, when
the practitioner applies to his constructions the empirical knowledge that
enables him to do good work, all, perhaps unknown to themselves, try
to penetrate the *quid proprium* (what is proper) and, if we may so speak,
the subjective and active nature of the brute elements from which they
expect a conformity with the proposed goal.

220 In all truth we do nothing, even in the disposition of materials; we
have others do what our thought has conceived and our resolution decided. And as in individual life it is the concurrence of subalternate energies that works in us under the mediation of the initial intention, so also
outside of ourselves the role of the will is less to act than to arouse and
orient the external powers by assimilating them to the act. Even in cases
where the provocation of the author who has the initiative in the work
appears necessitating, he does not act without making act. From the outside he brings the conditions together; only from the inside does the determining and operative cause respond. As Bacon had already noted, we
are limited to placing the natural forces in the presence of one another:
natura intus cetera transigit (nature transacts the rest interiorly). And
even to place them in the presence of one another, already a sign has to
have awakened in them a dormant and sterile energy that lends itself to
the sign's solicitations. Hence not everything is absurd in the pretenses
of magic or occultism: there is a natural incantation which, although inefficacious in normal circumstances, can become the principle of marvelous or miraculous operations.

No doubt it seems strange to say that to act on a stone we must,
through a sort of suggestion, appeal to virtual energies that lie dormant
in it. But it also seems strange that, in somnambulistic hyperesthesia,
the one hypnotized should perceive, without being aware of the intermediaries, the most imperceptible signs and even the unconscious states
of his mesmerizer. Cannot what is produced obscurely through an intelligent activity also be obscurely received and interpreted? Indeed, that
is the ordinary mechanism for the interpretation of even the most distinct
signs. The internal harmony of an expressive and living symbol down to
its lowest parts is never felt except as a whole; and what ends up taking
over is the arbitrary character of the expression. But if artificial convention eclipses, it does not suppress this expressive histology of the natural
sign. There subsists an unconscious language that speaks to unconscious
senses; and like every other language, it can be learned and perfected
through practice. Thus the mesmerizer takes better and better possession
of his subject and makes himself more precisely understood as he speaks

to him more often in his mysterious idiom. What has been called mind reading is perhaps only the delicate perception and the secret interpretation of these imperceptible traces, εἰδωλα (images). Thus, moreover, we can conceive at least the possibility of explaining the oddness of instinctive sympathies or antipathies, and the strangeness of those telepathic communications whose testimony some psychologists are today busy gathering. It seems that unknown to ourselves we live in a perpetual crisscross of impalpable influences.

221

If in the hygiene of animal organisms we are led to make much of the infinitely small, it is no doubt equally necessary, in the unconscious detail of mental operations, to attribute a role to all these imperceptibles. They are like seeds which, buried under the dead letter of the material phenomenon, need only a propitious terrain to germinate amid a spontaneity able to nourish them. Hence, wherever there is a touch of a subjective life, that is, everywhere, it is possible to operate. We intervene in the determinism of phenomena only on this double condition: that we draw our own act from a power that surpasses it, and that we obtain our useful action from a force that is beyond this determinism and behind the phenomena produced.

Also, it is never on directly perceived phenomena that, strictly speaking, we ground our science and our dominion. What actually does the man of action's need for the lessons of experience presuppose; what does scientific investigation presuppose; what does science's power over nature presuppose? All this implies that, to act efficaciously, we must discover and convert to our ends what in the perceived phenomena is their invisible subjective phenomenon and proper action. And in this way, after internal subjectivity and organic subjectivity, *external subjectivity* also becomes a scientific truth.

Between the question of the relations of phenomena among themselves and the problem, still kept in abeyance and perhaps illusory, of the communication of substances, there is room then for the study of relations that are neither physical nor metaphysical, but psychological. Whatever the case seems to be, it is not on positive facts, taken as sole reality, that we act; to operate in them we must, through the signs that they are, reach the obscure forces capable of producing them. Through the interpretation of phenomena it is causes we are addressing ourselves to. The facts experienced are, so to speak, only the echo of the profound resonances where, gropingly, we strive to handle deftly without being able to see. There are many things, and some of the principal ones, where a peasant knows as much and more philosophy than Aristotle.

Here again the bonding together of the experimental and the mathematical methods reappears. What is the object of infinitesimal calculus

222

and how explain the paradoxical and reciprocal adaptation of numbers to observation and of experience to calculus? Infinitesimal calculus presupposes precisely a living and infinite virtuality in nature; it presupposes, in the face of our thought, other energies, other subjects, monads, a dynamism underneath the apparent mechanism. That is the reason why it applies to appearances and enables us to govern them. To act is to penetrate through tact and through divination into the closed intimacy of other subjects and to interest them in ourselves. To calculate is to represent symbolically this infinitude of life and these relations among the concurring forces. That is why, as we showed, calculus supposes action, and why action appeared as natural mediator between numbers and experience.[1]

Thus, finally, we explain better how the positive sciences correspond to a secret inspiration of the will. For that still exterior and, so to speak, artificial desire to know which had already appeared as a solid reason for human learning is grounded, as can be seen, on a more profound need: action, involving outside of itself other agents, in order to be efficacious, seeks to penetrate, by a double labor of approach, *a priori, a posteriori*, the invisible universe whence proceed the facts it claims to bring about. And as in governing our members and our desires we regulated their crude efforts in order to catch as between a crossfire (between the higher will and the passive obedience of the material acts) the rebels on the inside, here again, with an analogous tactic, we use empirical knowledge and mathematical deduction as a vise, to force the elusive forces of nature into our service.

Hence it is action that constitutes the domain of these positive sciences, for in every case they have as their object to study the content of the operation, the concurrence of our knowledge with the internal conditions of phenomena, the coaction in the universal determinism. Moreover they appeared tied to one another only in action. That is why also they are willed as a means of illuminating and developing man's reflected intervention, of augmenting his power and of extending his dominion. In studying the most distant nebula, or in scrutinizing the organism of an insect, the scientist, for one who can understand, is collaborating in the solution to the problem of human destiny. Every question enters into this question. Deep down, the sciences analyse the processes of willing and contribute to serving its intentions; their true reason for existing is

1. There is no question of affirming the substantial reality of these subjects alien to the agent, no more than that of the agent himself. The issue is simply to determine the mutual relations of the subjective order and the objective order, or to adapt all the aspects of the universal phenomenon among themselves.

to assimilate to the will other energies and to add to individual life something of the universal life.

III

In producing itself, action transforms itself. But this transformation is what we were seeking in acting. The agent puts himself into what he does; and what he does fashions him. The center of equilibrium of individual life moves, therefore, and transports itself into the work to which the will consecrates itself. Ενεργεια ο ποιησας το εργον εστι πως (in action one who has produced is somehow the work).

It is this viewpoint that we must take to understand, along with the notion of causality, the relation of external finality to internal finality. Every cause, to be efficacious, supposes an effective synthesis. How can diverse parts of one and the same organic system cooperate so as to become mutually means and end, if not because one, the efficient cause, finds in the other, the final cause, a spontaneity that seconds its own under the influence of one and the same directive idea? So it is with the forces we call exterior to one another, but which in reality are part of one and the same complexus where everything is solidary and where adaptation is everywhere possible, everywhere perfectible.

Thus the causal connection results at once from a subjective disposition and from an empirical association. Its originality is to be at once analytical *a priori* and synthetic *a posteriori*; for in the effect produced each of the subjects that contribute to it is a principal agent. The ideal intention seems entirely taken from the initiator; the response appears to come entirely from the collaborator; but in fact there is reciprocity of form and matter, and in the work there is a double symmetrical operation: each believes he does everything. In intention, the result belongs entirely to each one, though it is never only what each brings to it. No doubt the effect is tied to its causes only through a synthetic relation (whence the impossibility of erecting the determinism of nature into an absolute truth). But the effect is not just a phenomenon placed alongside its antecedent; it presupposes the intervention of a second cause, also itself subjective, and *natured*, if we may so speak (whence the impossibility of seeing in causality a purely arbitrary connection). Between the agent and his cooperators is established a relation analogous to the finality that associates the members of one and the same organism. Also the will becomes as the soul of the determinism it makes serve its ends. Man is truly "all nature," the universal bond.

Inasmuch as the effected work is always a synthesis different from the

224

projected work, nothing could take the place of effective experience. And for what concerns the science of practice, it means a lot to prove thus the irremediable impotence of pure speculation. In the study of economic and social functions, for example, it is inevitably to court error to consider the expansion of human activity and to construct its consequences without looking directly at the movement of return and the natural reactions. Whoever gives receives. But what is received, the *given*, serves as a guide to the *giver*. In the most inventive mind there is always a backdrop of passivity: a discovery does not take place without the juncture of an occasion and a curiosity on the alert. We do not labor any which way, in vagueness and indeterminateness; but the order of things directs our effort, supports our thought, orients our action through indiscernible contradictions.

No doubt, infinite deviations are possible; but whatever violence we may be able to do to the apparent order, always, even in the most disordered acts, there subsists an ordered sequence in the growth of the willed operation. Prescinding from this indeterminable diversity, we must therefore continue to study the necessary development and the natural history of the effected work.

Let us pull together the results of the preceding analyses.

Individual action imposes itself on the outside, be it only through the natural expression and the organic system of phenomena that is its sign.

225   Now this sign, which harbors a tendency toward an end willed ulteriorly, manifests itself, constitutes itself, and *a fortiori* works out its effect only if it already interests something alien to individual life in its production. It has to be; and for it to be, there has to be coaction.

This coaction, whence the phenomenon of the act results, no matter how elementary, is possible only through a correspondence of the milieu wherein it unfolds; the mechanical continuity of the determinate and solidary facts implies an external dynamism. No need to have recourse to metaphysics to establish the truth of this dynamism. That there should be subjects alien to the agent is a phenomenon of the same order as the existence of the subject himself. The connection between these phenomena is necessary; and we can constitute the science of them only by recognizing this determinism.

There is therefore a double movement in every exterior operation; the first, in which the expressive sign imposes itself on the surrounding determinism; and the second, in which, through this sign, the reaction whence will come the work hoped for is solicited, demanded, obtained.

Thus the phenomenon of action supposes the convergence of two series of phenomena, one starting from the agent, the other provoked from elsewhere. Every production requires the concurrence of two actors; and the extorted act, proceeding through the mediation of the sign of the agent who has the initiative in the work, comes in some way to join the sign or the phenomenon whose suggestion it underwent. The exterior operation of the will, then, constitutes a synthesis of phenomena that contain between them an internal energy, a forced cooperation.

In this way the common terrain is constituted where the inevitable exchanges take place and the universal solidarity is consolidated. It does not depend on me, for example, to have heard a word; and yet in the sound that struck me there is an aspect of spontaneity, a natural reaction of my senses. My receptivity is active. And thus it is that perceived phenomena have a double point of leverage or, so to speak, a double reality, in what produces them and in what undergoes them. The consistency they have comes from a cooperation of powers, powers isolated in their intimacy, but for which these phenomena are the knot and the unification. If the positive sciences are suspended from action, then, it is primarily because action furnishes the phenomena that are their object with cohesion and solidity. And thereby the universal determinism, the domain of these sciences, enters, along with the coaction it makes possible, into the broader development of the will. 226

To show how action can exert an influence on agents other than its author and solicit their cooperation while respecting their initiative and their independence, but still tending toward as intimate a union as possible, that is the aim of the next chapter. — First I indicate how the result of coaction, detaching itself from its causes, forms a distinct creature with an evolution of its own and a natural efficaciousness. — I show how it rises again in consciousness where it is taken in as nourishment; how it is interpreted there and accepted with more or less reflexion. — I determine what is attributable to each of the associates in cooperation. And all this investigation is dominated by the thought that, more and more, the profound intention of the agent is to obtain a real conformity with those he reaches, an effective unity, a community of thought, of life and of operation. The study of this spontaneous proselytism will bring us to understand the need for a closer communion of consciousnesses and of wills among themselves.

CHAPTER 3
Influence and Cooperation

227 When coaction has produced its effect, the result seems to form a self-sufficient whole and as it were a creature new to the milieu of phenomena. But by that very fact the work has a necessary "influence;" it is a wheel in the general determinism. Inevitably, action is more than the work itself; and beyond every particular end there is found a more general end. What I have done by myself with the concurrence of another is no longer for me alone or for that other alone. The act brought to completion inevitably has a broader bearing. And in one sense it exists for all others as much as for those who produced it. What does this necessity mean? And is there a secret ambition of the will hidden therein? — Yes; and what is it?

I

At the very moment when the work is born through the concurrence of its causes, it is not yet a spectacle for its own authors.. *In actu, actus nondum est actus* (in the act, the act is not yet done). As we speak we do not hear ourselves speak; and on the phonograph we hardly recognize the sound of our voice; on the sheet on which it comes back to you in print, you are surprised at your own thought. But no sooner than, after the blind operation whence it comes, the work is produced, it becomes, for us as well as for any other, an object wherein we learn to see
228 ourselves. We are unaware of our face as long as a mirror does not reveal it to us: action is the mirror that offers us a visible image of our character. It is performed to be seen. The end knowingly pursued does not shut desire off. What we do, we still do for something other than what we think. There is a hidden surplus in the intention; and it is this enfolded tendency that is found once again in the very result of the operation.

218

Action first flowed over into an immediate sign; then it pursued a determinate end, to make of it a work that appeared to be its complement; but that is not all. Underneath this work referred to this particular goal, subsists a broader need that is already beginning to look for its satisfaction in it. By calling back to himself the result of a collaboration, man is led to evoke, to will, not only the work, but the very intimacy of the worker and the collaborator. What is universal in every subject is what he wants to put into his act; and that is what he wants to find in it.

Hence we must once again displace and broaden the notion we should have of finality. The end was first the preferred motive, then the decision that made the effort to execute the voluntary intention, then the object to which the operation itself led, then the collaboration of this final cause, and finally the product of this coaction, referred back to the primitive intention of the agent. But there is still more: thanks to the contribution of our partner who preserves the heterogeneity of the cause and the effect, the consummated action, differing always from the projected action, detaches itself from us. It begins to behave independently and to enjoy a kind of impersonal life. Our idea, at the same time as it is *ours*, is *an* idea; and in every idea there is a universal principle. Also, in acting, we invincibly propose for ourselves a satisfaction of self-love which is, so to speak, disinterested. What we do, we do (even when it is through egoism) with a kind of luxury, art, and surplus. Do we not find an exaggeration of this inclination even in the criminal who appreciates the beauty of his deed, or in the fop "as foolish as the rooster who imagines that the sun rises to hear him sing"? We never act for ourselves alone, no more than by ourselves.

Where this tendency first finds expression with the greatest sharpness, even in works available to the senses, is through art: and art appears in the first objects worked over by the human hand. The beautiful work   229
seems to have an absolute self-sufficiency; it seems to live, to be not just the reflexion of an idea, but a real idea, to truly have the power of being, of acting, and of loving. Beauty has a charm that goes far beyond and above the one who feels it or is decked out in it. Just as a much more ample significance than was first appreciated is hidden in the works of genius, so also in beauty there resides an impersonal expression we appreciate better as our soul is more noble. This is a feeling which, by its very breadth and radiance, becomes anguish and mystery; as if in what we love, our admiration focused upon a distant and more powerful love, of which the beauty seen would be only a weak symbol.

In every human work, therefore, there is a nascent mysticism. In the beginning it seems that people attached a superstitious intention to the representation of figures and ornaments, as if the image had a reality of its own by taking over the interior life of the object it depicts. It would seem that to express through signs the thought with which the soul is pregnant is to bring to the light of day more than this thought itself, and to make a god. Also art is, by an anticipated view, the mythical summation of all the future development of the will in quest of its perfect completion. Into the sensible work, into the phenomenon, it fictitiously inserts the real, the living, the human, the divine; it instinctively captures and develops by intuition the symbolic equivalent of all the aspirations still implicit in willing.

From this tendency to the aesthetic in even the most egotistic and the most self-centered action, let us retain only this: that the completed work attains a relative independence; that it falls when it is ripe, like a fruit covered with its flower and full of seeds; that, from the moment an intention and a thought has been put into it, it singularly surpasses the individual life where it took root.

If art is the very nature of man, or at least the symbol of the total unfolding of his activity, it is because, in the beauty he expresses, he makes of the beautiful work a detached and impersonal truth; he tends to set it free from time and space so that it will stand above the diversity of particular tastes. By reason of this very impersonality, the work of art is no more for the author than for the spectator; we have to recreate it in ourselves to feel and understand it. Also, in every truly human action, there is what Kant calls "a finality without end," that is, a reality independent of the immediate occasions that were the pretext for it and of the agents who produced it, an undefined virtuality. Engendered by the impersonal power of reason, this work is prolific in its turn by retaining from its origin a need for expansion and propaganda.

Here is how, in fact and without going beyond the relations of phenomena among themselves, the formulations wherein the *Critique of Practical Reason* sought the pure expression of duty are realized of themselves. We cannot, we do not will to close our life up in ourselves. In acting, we act as if for all and in all. This is the reason why we are all naturally inclined to maximize our conduct. At the very moment we are conscious of making an exception in our favor and of treating ourselves as an incomparable personage, outside the common laws, we set ourselves up as a living example by the brute force of the deed done. If we are led to incarnate the intention into the body of a work that stands before us and before others like a new agent, it is therefore because in the initial resolution there was already contained this desire to make of the act a sort of creation distinct from its author, participating in the common reality, subsisting in the eyes of all, infused with the character of universality that everything which falls under the objective determinism of science harbors. Does there not have to be a proportion between the impulse of the force and the effect it produces? If in order to express itself through a sign and through a work, the intention has aroused this determinism, clearly it is in order to mark the work itself with the seal of its power, in order to make of it a real and general truth, χωρίς (apart). And it is this end, implicitly sought, which has sustained the effort; it is the one that procures the efficaciousness of willing. We manage to act voluntarily in the universe only because action has to have a virtually universal bearing.

What is true of material appearance then is true first of the meaning it expresses and for which the sign is the vehicle. If the realized act has an impersonal character and an independent evolution, that is the literal fact whose interior inspiration had to be found. The intention, the operation that executes it, the natural expression that manifests it, the coaction that constructs the work, the influence that comes from it through attraction or through teaching, all that hangs together. The Stoics used to say, nothing is vile in the house of Jupiter; nothing is arbitrary, insignificant, accessory in the deployment of the will. And as we discovered the way that leads directly to the coveted end under the sign that is apparently alien to the intention, so also here, under the work constituted, appears the hidden proselytism and the latent influence that is its reason for existing. Every work produced is a propaganda in act.

A strange illusion it is to think that one can at will restrict or extend the consequences of one's action, that it is a matter of choice to close oneself up within oneself, to do wrong to ourself without doing wrong to anyone else, to drop in or drop out of the surrounding world, the universal life, or morality, as we wish. We are in it; we move in it; we plant our acts and our thoughts in it like seeds that are fruitful to infinity. It would be like saying that the seducer owes nothing to the innocent woman he has burdened with a seed of suffering or of death. By drawing us out of ourselves, action is for others, so that, in return, others may be for us; it gives them our thought; it is the social cement; it is the soul of common life. Why wouldn't it be enough to shut ourselves up in the intention? The fact is that the individual cannot isolate himself, that his acts form the milieu where other works will take root, that in this atmosphere of consciousness new intentions will flourish. Yes, it is a mistake to imagine that we can fall and not harm others. We cannot do evil without causing more prejudice and grief than we would like to believe, like a job ill begun that brings annoyances without end. But also, whatever we do, whether it be to analyse an idea in depth or build a wall, it is a public service to do it well.

Hence, if the material work has a character of universality in the deter-

231

minism of facts where it takes its place, it is because it has an equally universal bearing in thought and in sincere intention to begin with. No doubt, we act for ourselves in the first place; and if we have recourse to the outside, it is because we do not know ourselves as long as we don't measure ourselves against the exterior. But what we do to know ourselves is done to be known by others. It is the spectacle of *our reason*. It is therefore the spectacle of *reason as such*. From the moment the act is willed, it is implicitly addressed to everything that can understand and will. One and the same word is received in its entirety by a thousand hearers. Action is the multiplication of the interior word which, decked out in a body in order to offer itself to all sensibilities, proposes itself in communion to the universe, and spreads in it to infinity its fecundating seed. It is the organ of spiritual reproduction.

232

This is also how we can explain the fact that all the signs, all the works, and all the productions of man or of nature have their living summary in language. Language is the manipulable, animated, intellectualized equivalent of the entire universe. Words carry within them something of all the objects they evoke and all the thoughts that are nourished by them and use them. Full of light and mystery, they never render all of the interior word and they always surpass it. As the cloud is a mixture of shadows and rays, spoken words are not equal to the infinite of thoughts, nor are thoughts equal to the infinite of words. They express the individual and the universal in one another. And that is why they form the intellectual atmosphere of spirits; thanks to them, there is nothing that is not like a nourishment already digested for consciousness; and if every action can be expressed and explained in word, it is because every action is an implicit word to begin with, that is, a need to reveal itself to all. Do we not see with what force, growing each day, man tries to fix his ideas and his feelings, to universalize and to immortalize his acts and his works, to communicate with the whole earth and all times, and to interest the entire universe in his lowly person?

A first point seems made: voluntary action, in constituting a distinct work, manifests an implicit intention, but one that is certain. Beyond the individual act and the particular object wherein it has taken pleasure, it aspires to take on a universal character, to produce itself in such a way as to be understood by all, to create a work valid by itself and capable of exercising an action in its own turn. How does this influence become efficacious?

II

Through the universal character it takes on, action tends to approach and penetrate other consciousnesses. If it becomes visible, one could say, it is in order to be seen: this is a relation that has been little noticed up to now, this continuous progression which, from the material construction of the sign or of the sensible action, leads us to the natural need to   233 be considered, understood, imitated, supported. Without knowing them, we count on the complaisance of other subjects in order to radiate, to will, and to live in them. Detached from its generators whose types it keeps and unites without being their identical reproduction, the work, like the child, lives and grows; it bears within it this spark of a thought that seeks to communicate itself; it is active and generative in its turn.

The idea of influence would retain the superstitious or childish character it had received from astrology, it would be a fatalistic or materialistic prejudice, if we supposed that every thought can directly and properly act on every other, through coaction, as we move a stone. But on the other hand, to suppress, by a sort of spiritual protestantism, all communication between consciousnesses; to pretend that each individual lives for himself (as if, in such a case, we could know that there are other minds to begin with); to judge that every subject is fundamentally original "without windows to the outside," that nothing enters into him unless it comes from him, that individualism and discontinuity are the absolute law of the intellectual world as continuous evolution is that of sensible phenomena; to be convinced that we can remain indifferent or that we are truly alien to the consequences of our acts, our words, our examples, or our teachings, as if nothing entered into us or into others that would not be, upon entering or going out, deliberately controlled and accepted: all that would be to fall into an arbitrary and illusory idealism. And yet how little have we bothered to look closely at all these questions of such lively interest!

What we must do, on the contrary, is consider the work, not just as the product or the effect, but as the instrument and the bond of a more real union between consciousnesses naturally solitary and unknown to one another. And just as the consummated act is for the one who accomplishes it a teaching, a confirmation, and an encouragement, so also the completed and subsistent work is, for whoever feels its presence and is penetrated by it even involuntarily, a nourishment and an incentive. To be sure, it is not by a servile imitation or through a brutal push that this living preaching of the work can truly bring about its effect. Nothing is more stupid or more perilous than the completely exterior fidelity of a clumsy copy or the routine application of recipes and formulae, like the ridiculous affectation of Molière's *Précieuses*. To be fecund, the work,   234 detached from its authors like the grain from the stalk, must in some way die before being ready to be reborn in another soil; it has to be dissolved, like the seed in the ground, to germinate and grow; in order to reach the consciousness of others, it has to take those secret ways where the infiltrations seep drop by drop, invisibly, as they nourish the sources of knowledge and action.

Granted, it is a delicate task to explain the transfusion of thoughts and motives for action from one closed consciousness to another closed consciousness. No doubt, through the interposition of universal determinism, action, as we saw, reaches outside of ourselves as a nourishment proposed to other agents; but that is still only the symbol of a more intimate propagation. For every thought is itself a particular expression of the universal: therein lies the principle of the real communion between intelligences. In the most personal conceptions and works, there is a quality of impersonality that makes them accessible to all and places them in the community of spirits.

Every action, then, where man deposits a parcel of thought, is a living idea, whether he is plowing his field or weaving a tissue or carving stone and marble. But under the determinate form they put on and from which they cannot be separated without perishing, these real ideas maintain their universal value; it is what makes them communicable. Thanks to what is common and universal in them, then, the most singular suggestions and the most eccentric works can be interpreted. Through the double mediation of the particular sign and the general idea, whose union constitutes their life, they are capable of rising again in other consciousnesses, of acting on resolutions, and of growing in their own way in a different soil. Just as a specific type persists throughout all the caprices of nature and all hereditary transformations, so also there are families of spirits, a passing and an evolution of ideas by way of filiation or alliance. And through what is generic in every human act, we all penetrate into one another, bringing with us, along with the impulse of general reason, the habits and the aberrations of our particular cultivation. A living thing is born of a living thing.

And if we were to enter into the detail of the paths of this fecundation, what routes would lie open for these contagious germs! What, after all, is a thought realized in an action that becomes for us a spectacle and a lesson, if not an example and an incentive? Do we know what a scandal is? It is the formula for confused needs that were at work in us perhaps without daring to become distinctly conscious of themselves; it is a redoubling of the secret appetites that finally find their open expression; it is a justification, through the fact, of unavowed tendencies; it is an obstacle set aside and a shame lost. By stripping certain feelings little by little of what is shameful about them when we think we are alone in experiencing them, the teaching of acts engenders the tyranny of human respect. Thus is formed from invisible influences the moral atmosphere and the spirit of a century. The quite material way in which the intention is realized is already a way cleared for the imitators: every act is a discovery; for in order to act it is not enough to feel a vague desire or form an abstract conception; we still have to invent precise means and real satisfactions. Example proposes such inventions ready made.

That is not all: more profoundly, in the influence exerted by action, we must take account of the thought and of the body in which it lives in two ways. After, through coaction, the work of a word or a spectacle has been produced at once by the actor and by the witness, not only does it act to the extent that there is in the spectator a dry and exterior representation of the phenomenon he undergoes while participating in it; but in addition, underneath this distinct viewing which leaves his decision full mastery over itself, an unconscious labor takes place that comes in to fill with secret incitements and confused feelings the abstract framework of cold and empty knowledge. The mute activity which even the passive witness spontaneously unfolds in order to perceive the spectacle offered him is like a first acquired momentum. To feel and to perceive is already to begin doing. For, as Plato remarks, there is a great risk in purchasing knowledge. We cannot place it in any other vessel but the soul; and as soon as it enters in, good or evil is done irretrievably.

There is still more. For the constituted work, while containing more than clear foresight had thought, also includes more than the clear image depicts of it in consciousness. If, on the one hand, the sensible expression of a sentiment never renders all that we feel in our heart, on the other hand, there is always also something else and more in this act of the sign, than the state of soul to which it corresponds; it manifests precisely that 236 which remains obscure in us and escapes us. And inasmuch as action adds an essential complement to thought and the intention, inasmuch as the realized operation is a synthesis enriched further by new elements, it is therefore natural that the act, dressed in its sensible increase, should have on other consciousnesses the double efficaciousness of what is at once intelligible and material about it. Thus, through what is unfaithful, exterior, and inadequate to the spirit in the very letter where it is embodied, the letter completes and in a way surpasses it. What gives the perceived and interpreted world all its action on the one perceiving it, is what needs to be interpreted in it: it bears with it its gangue or its envelope, as in the shell around the germ where there is always a first provision of nourishment.

The profound and durable nature of the influence which a work exerts therefore depends on the way the idea is there united to its matter. The closer this bond is, the more life stamps it with power and fruitfulness. It is proper to genius to discover the distant relations of things, and to effect a more simple and more stable synthesis with more . scattered elements. In this very composite, through what is obscure in it, there subsist latent virtualities which time little by little brings to act. There is no great work in which the crowd does not collaborate. And with the centuries, these anonymous collaborators withdraw and add their part. As human works live longer, we have to find more profound reasons for this survival: not that the author has first seen all that the following ages discover in his own thoughts; the destiny of the great inventors is usually to find something else and more than they realize, to set foot in America thinking one is disembarking in India. But they have nonetheless deposited the fecund germ; what they have caused to be done is still in some sense done by them. They set humanity upon a new path which without them would not have been thus opened up and, serving at the head of the line for the army of human sheep, they give direction, sometimes unawares, to people and civilizations. The variety of means and ends is unlimited in the development of life as well as of science. Each action is a turning point in universal history. We must always act as if we were governing the world: others perhaps will know how to take in and make the least gift confided to them fructify. What we have others do, no doubt we do; but at the same time, what we do, others have us do.

237

Also the great works of science, of art, or of virtue, that surpass individual consciousness belong to all; it is from all that they receive little by little their meaning and their commentary; it depends on all to modify insensibly the judgment given them. Their influence is indeterminate; the work grows richer with what time slowly adds to it; and yet it remains always itself, since nothing has been put into it except what a longer and more diverse practice of life has proved it already actually contained. Is a page of Dante or a gothic cathedral for us, men of the nineteenth century, what it was in the thirteenth? It seems as though, by coming to rest on words, on thoughts, or on stones, human eyes finish sculpting them and penetrate them with new energies that confer on ruins themselves an increase of life. But the first initiator cannot entirely refuse the paternity of this unlimited generation. The bond that perpetuates the continuity of his intervention is never broken. If by nature operative action is like the union of an idea and a body, γαμος, this marriage is indissoluble and fecund to infinity.

No doubt it is possible for the work, out of commission, so to speak, and perverted, to be tossed about by the wind of opinion and the caprice of harmful interpretations. A fable without malice for innocent childhood, as it perhaps was in the eyes of the unsuspecting fellow who narrated it, appears in the eyes of the moralist full of egotism and Epicurean voluptuousness. Inspired by the bigoted and fierce hatred of an aristocrat overcome in political struggles, full of shameful passions, the sayings of

Theognis become a manual of morals for schoolboys in the democracy of the times that followed. But precisely because works always surpass the clear vision of their author, because the most fixed remain malleable, because their generative virtue comes from what is unfinished about them, the initial will remains immanent, by a kind of atavism, to all this proliferation that seems at times to betray or surpass its intentions. There is no need to have distinctly sensed ahead of time all the content of an action, in order to remain tied to the most distant conclusions that flow from the premises and to lend support precisely to the exigencies of the hidden logic which links the decision to all its effects.

Also what reverent precautions are not to be taken as soon as questions arise where the least error is propagated in infinite waves of suffer- 238
ing! What one said, what one could have said otherwise, what one did not say when one should have spoken, what occasions of responsibility for whoever teaches or acts! Concern for being clear and precise is a moral concern. Do not the false applications of a thought graft themselves onto the obscure points? For truth is valid only in the total unity of its expression, whereas objections and heresies always have the easy task of latching on to details. How much evil a partial knowledge can bring about! As long as ideas come to us from the outside, they risk being harmful; they are good and true only if, in the circulation of life, they come up from the depths where personal certitudes are formed. There are premature or out-of-place ideas that must be, not distorted or dissimulated, but offered to minds according to what they can bear. The indifference of laying everything bare and the neutrality of teaching nothing are a two-fold cruel excess in education. For every idea, in every consciousness, there is a period of puberty one cannot skip over without crime. Let us watch over the influence, then, even of what we think is the truth. Whatever we do and whatever we say, there is an art to be practiced, the art of intellectual vaccination.

Action, then, is efficacious both by what is total about it and by what is partial, by what is clear in it and by what is obscure, through its idea and through its body, through the necessity of determinism and through the suggestions of spontaneous life, through the originality of its invention and through the universal principle that makes every idea accessible to every spirit.

—Such are the ways, such is the mechanism of influence. First the voluntary decision projects itself into an act; it creates its expression and embodies itself in a work. This work, which already supposes the effective concurrence of other agents and depicts itself in them through the effect of the very determinism of phenomena, solicits, through what life is infused into it, a labor of interpretation and assimilation. It does not depend on us, for example, to hear a word; that is still a brute necessity, though we do contribute to the subjective impression of the sound. It does not always depend on us not to understand the word: that is a spontaneous elaboration against which it is sometimes impossible to defend ourselves. Now, already into this labor of interior translation, along with the image and the meaning transmitted to thought, there is insinuated an attraction and an impulse. It is from this suggestion that knowledge draws its strength in part; for it is often all the more influential when reflexion does not intervene in it and as a result one cannot be on guard against it. That is why the true action we exercise on others is not always the one they are aware of. Thus it is that education owes its power especially to the invisible network with which it envelops the emerging faculties, to the unspoken inspiration it places in a young man's heart while persuading him that his thoughts all come from him, to the silent habit with which it permeates his judgment and his character.

239

III

Two points seem established. — Human action tends to take on a universal character and to become a living propaganda. — The influence of the effected work exerts itself through multiple ways; it spreads out; but to spread out and in spreading out, it transforms and resurrects the first intention in ever more original ways. — A third problem presents itself then to be resolved: does this fruitful transformation of our thoughts and of our works in other agents enter itself into our primitive ambition? How much of what others do under our inspiration do we will? Where does coaction stop and where does the adherence of a free concurrence begin? How sort out what truly goes back to the initiative of the author and what is the proper operation of the cooperator? What does this need to be seen, understood, imitated tend to?

Action is a social function par excellence. But precisely because it is done for others, it receives a new coefficient from others and, so to speak, a reformation. To act is to evoke other forces, it is to call on other *selves*. Is there in this also a secret aim of willing?

When I act on brute forces, ordinarily what I expect from their operation is a basic modification of my act. To obtain the chemical combination he needs, the industrialist has recourse to energies whose profound nature he ignores; he provokes a response that seems entirely different from his personal initiative; he does not even notice that, if he brings an idea to common production, he also receives one from the outside, and that, if these alien agents furnish him with a matter, he also serves as

240

matter in a way for the power whose concurrence he requisitions. He readily forgets what there is of himself in his work; he does not appear to be what he does. — But as the forces concurring in the common work acquire a more conscious spontaneity, the nature of cooperation seems to change.

When I act on other minds through teaching, or if I give an order, it is my own thought itself which I claim to find as my work in others; I will that the action of my disciple or my worker copy mine; I ask that their initiative submit and substitute itself for my operation. I transmit to them all I can of my own activity, so that their production may be identical with the one which I am thinking of or which I achieve myself. What I look for in them is a perfect conformity to my aim, a complete duplication of my inner life. I raise up another self (*un autre moi*). It was to this end indeed that my action tended from the beginning: for if every work harbors a latent force of expansion, what is more natural than this need to live again in others, this need for disciples, this need for auxiliaries able to operate for us like ourselves? — It seemed a moment ago that I expected some originality of action from brute forces; now it seems that I am asking for a passivity of imitation and obedience from intelligent forces.

And yet what I am truly looking for from the one and the other is a complement for myself, but a complement more and more like me, active also, capable of initiative, such finally as I am myself with regard to it. Let us not be fooled by the apparent inertia of the disciple: the true master knows how to make himself passive and efface himself, so that the child may discover what he is learning; to be the pupil of one's pupil, that is the only way of procuring for him that life whose light no man can kindle in the depth of consciousness. *Hominibus non imperatur nisi parendo* (one does not command men except by obeying them). It is natural to wish that others will conform themselves to us. And in this perfect conformity of souls, it is natural to wish that each preserve his perfect initiative.

Also, for every thought eager to communicate itself, what a struggle there is between the impetuosity of a domineering conviction and a respect for all the inner discretion of others! We wish to place ourselves in others as we are; and we want to find ourselves other than we are in each. We sow what is most precious of what we have, we hand ourselves over; and of the teachings sown nothing apparently remains. But it is because the grain is as if lost in the furrow that no one can any longer remove it and that the harvest is being prepared. Such are the apparent contradictions of human desires: we will that others be ourselves and we will that they remain themselves.

But it is all one and the same desire, namely, to spread ourselves out and to increase. And here is how these two seemingly opposite propositions are equally justified. —(1) The influence of our action is virtually infinite. It contains all the particular effects that are its consequence. And whether these consequences are produced or not, it is pregnant with them, it remains laden with them. —(2) Wherever there is an intentional decision, the accomplice, whatever influence he may have undergone, remains responsible for what he discerned clearly and resolved deliberately. The law punishes him along with the principal author, and that is grounded in reason. Each behaves as if he were acting for himself alone; and each behaves as if he were acting in the other and through the other.

Thus, for example, a writer whose books have corrupted thousands of readers will be held responsible for all the germs which, disseminated, grew or could have developed in consciousnesses, without however ceasing, in his most intimate center and in his fundamental independence, to govern himself, to be able to change himself, to work out his own destiny. The idea we wish to pass on to others is given them under a necessarily symbolic form: this means that there has to be a work of elaboration, indispensable in the one who is to receive it, in order to penetrate under the shell and discover the spirit in the letter; and therein lies the safeguard of our spontaneity and of his. What could be more astounding than to have at once both the impenetrability of a soul fending off the influences that besiege it and the fecundity of the seeds as soon as they have taken root! The organism is touched by a contagion only if it bears within it the morbid germ. But, although the same seeds do not grow the same way in diverse spirits, still, thanks to what is impersonal in the work and common among the different subjects, the individual character of a thought, a desire, an intention, can be grafted onto and nourished by an alien sap. The fruits plucked from this new plant, though drawing their nourishment elsewhere than from their original stock, will keep its savor and nature.

242   Thus are explained the necessity of expansion, and the means of influence, and the very meaning of this fecundity which makes of human actions something like a perpetual planting. From my will to the will of others, by means of the material execution and the sensible phenomena that precede and prepare the spontaneous regeneration of my thought in an alien consciousness, there is a double and inversely symmetrical process. For after the act has propagated itself from my resolution down to the body of the sign, it returns in the opposite direction, though by an analogous route, to the reflected life of my witness in order to solicit from him an initiative and as it were a complicity. My intervention, whatever impulse it otherwise impresses on him, appears to him as a

motive for action, but without chaining his choice. It is at once true that I act in him and that he alone acts in himself.

Hence it is by reason of the universal bearing of action that influence is possible and that there is filiation and transmission in the world of consciousnesses. In fact, the intention I have deliberately put into practice is erected into a universal maxim. What immense consequences the little germ of subjective life deposited at the heart of action harbors, foreign as it is to the laws of time and space, still as living and contagious and salutary a thousand years after or a thousand leagues away as at the point or at the moment of its first production, able always to keep, amid its renaissances and its metempsychoses, the imprint of its author and the mark of its origin!

In passing into action, the intention has inaugurated an exodus and a kind of "procession" in the Alexandrine sense. The work it constitutes marks a new degree of expansion; and underneath the phenomenon it inserts into the universal determinism, the interior need and wish of the will has revealed itself: for what it tends to is to spread itself out, to present its image to the outside, to encounter other consciousnesses, to make of its exterior work the spectacle of reason and the common nourishment of minds, to animate with its inspiration everything that approaches it. Is not the ardor of the adolescent, ready to give himself to everything, to dedicate himself, to pour himself out, really a faithful translation of this secret instinct, as though it cost him nothing and as if he were driven by an egoism whose very naiveté and sincerity carries him beyond the narrowness of his personal life? And are not those spurts of generosity also a mark of this invading and prepossessing ambition, or the sometimes presumptuous confidence, or those melancholic discouragements 243 of a juvenile soul, who thinks he loves a lot because he aspires to being loved a lot and who suffers from not being loved enough because he is the one who is not yet loving enough or disinterested enough?

But underneath these reveries of the adolescent, so full of tenderness that he feels almost melted and poured out like a flow of oil, charming to all, ambitious for genius, for honors and for sovereign power in order to flow more vehemently; underneath the passion of the artist who hopes to see his glory flourish like the smile on his lips or the sunrise on the horizon; in the ardent proselytism of a soul dying to bring light to souls, wherever the superabundance of the heart seeks to spend itself, there is a new and more profound need that makes itself heard. It seems that we no longer pay any attention to all that others are, do, and give, if we do not have these others themselves.

The place where both the force and the impotence of the action of influence can best be gauged, or where the necessity for a more intimate cooperation begins to appear, is in the work of education. What unexpected results follow at times when we know how to handle and shape and exercise the malleable and active soul of the child! But also what would we not give, often without succeeding in giving anything, to overcome invisible resistances, to lower those barriers we nowhere strike against but which we half see everywhere, to light a spark, to pour ourselves out entirely and really touch those we have before us, eye to eye, and from whom we feel separated irremediably! The tiredness of a master is nothing in comparison with the good he feels when he is appreciated better by his nurslings, when he gets them interested a bit more, when he causes a new light and a higher conception of life to rise in them. Let us not judge this eagerness for proselytism alien to the communication of the truth: it is the soul of teaching, because it is all one and the same to love the truth and to love intelligences, to know it and to want to spread it, to look for it in oneself and to elicit it in others, to live by it and to make spirits live by it. Thus the master and the disciple are united to one another under the ascendency of and in a reciprocal love for a truth that is the same and common. It is because science is indigenous to each and impersonal in all that it can rise and bear fruit under the incitement of an instructive word. But this leaven is also necessary, because truth is living, loving, and loved, only in a living spirit; it becomes personal for us when it comes from a person. It would be to lessen the role of the master to see in him only a sterile midwife for intelligences: he brings life and love; and the communication of thoughts is an image of the union that makes the body fruitful, ερως (love).

But are not these very exigencies contradictory? When I act on blind forces, usually I can obtain a total submission through coaction; they are mine. They are still myself. As these docile servants awaken to spontaneity, do they not also rise for insubordination? And when I will to deal with other selves (*d'autres moi-mêmes*), does not coaction disappear to make way for the independent originality of a reason and a freedom? Strange conditions to be conciliated: I will that my partner be as distinct from me as I am from him; and I will that his autonomy follow my law. I have to have with him a union that is full, sure and perfect, without unity, without duality being sacrificed one to the other.

Will it be possible to resolve these difficulties? — Yes; and perhaps we shall even see that it is where the intimate penetration of wills seems fanciful that the unity becomes most real and most efficacious. For it will no longer be a question of acts coming from separate sources to converge in a common work, nor of coaction or influence; it will be a question of an active union, and one that is itself fecund. The acts will no longer be born of distinct origins; they will not be merely the means of a *rapprochement* or the results of a cooperation. Coming from a double and single source, they will result from lives and freedoms melted together.

Action has not reached the end of its natural expansion: it will constitute the different societies of which man becomes a member, but which at heart he sustains and envelops with his personal willing. It seems strange that the fecund union of federated wills should be contained in one and the same will; and yet so it is. Better still, the need for solidarity extends beyond humanity, up to an effective conjunction between man and the universe; it extends beyond the universe, no longer just to what is, but also to what is to be, and up to what we would will to be; still further, it goes all the way to the illusory satisfactions of a disguised autolatry. The will exhausts everything, invents everything, admits everything, even the impossible, in order to be self-sufficient and to content itself: it does not succeed at it; and this very ambition is contrary to its most intimate wish. This will remain to be seen.

Stage Five
FROM SOCIAL ACTION TO SUPERSTITIOUS ACTION

The profound unity of wills and the universal extension of action

---

245   Individual life is forced to open itself up and to spread itself out. It makes other forces concur in its ends. It seeks a complement from the outside. It looks for a confirmation and a kind of doubling of its own energy. Inasmuch as the individual cannot close himself up and does not will to keep to himself alone and wholly within himself, he aspires to live in another. He transports the center of his action, so to speak, no longer just into his external work, nor even into a cooperation which enables him to extend his power and his influence, but into the intimate union that he establishes with another self. Will he not thus somehow multiply and fulfil his own life? He gives himself, therefore, in order to find once again in what he receives in return all that he already was — what he was, but without being able alone to contain the abundance of his own life. And through a substitute for egoism, which seems to be a conditional and reciprocal "altruism," he spreads his radiating ardor, but so that it may be reflected back to him warmer and more concentrated.

    Just as there are nodes in sound waves or, in some instances, virtual foci in the diffusion of light waves, so also action does not spread out without turning back and without further concentration. Thus there is established, by simultaneous actions and reactions, a circulation and an exchange from life to life. From two beings one and the same fecundity is formed; there is constituted, so to speak, a coenergy (*coenergie*). This is no longer a mere cooperation, reduced to producing a work which may

246   seem alive, but which is not really alive. It is like a double substance which is alive and produces life. It is a real society and a single existence in its very multiplicity. It is a community which functions as a proliferating organism and for which the union itself causes the fecundity. The issue is no longer to entrust an intention to the dead letter of a sign. The issue is for man to live anew in his work and to multiply himself in it. What is the meaning of this wonder?

    Even in spreading himself out, man wants to be paid back in return.

If he instinctively takes shelter in a closed system, as if to gather up the outpouring of his life in a double movement of giving and taking back, it is still in order to reach what escapes him within himself. If he looks into another, it is to find himself more. Whether he notices it or not, he belongs to natural groups where his acts are not only allied with other acts to form a common work, but where they proceed from the social federation. They are a vital function of it. Here the union is no longer just an effect, it is a cause. And these truly social acts suppose a kind of hymen already consummated between the beings whose wills they bring into concert. They make use of energies in us, then, which are nothing unless they are fecundated. It is an alliance to be concluded with all the forms of life in order to define within ourselves the yet unknown powers which tend, through action, to insert us into universal life. Thus the center of our interior equilibrium will move once again and stop at more and more broad societies, up to the point where it will be everywhere, so to speak.

These more or less comprehensive societies are indeed defined and limited, as every organism is. They form a collective individuality and, like any living thing, they have a name: family, country, humanity. But, while they are circumscribed and dovetailed into one another, they remain open. They spread out without being deformed. And not only does each individual find his place and play his determinate role in a social group, but each belongs at the same time to those diverse groups that go on growing and broadening without ceasing to be distinct, like the moving circles caused by a ball falling into placid water: πέρας καὶ ἀόριστον (limited and unlimited).

Thus, underneath the spontaneous and even necessary development which establishes human societies as a work of nature, we must uncover the movement of wills, as if each one by itself, espousing all the others, 247 alienated itself to all without ceasing to find only in itself the principle of collective life. It is a delicate task to show how, while the individual will remains coextensive with the total development of common action, each of the diverse social groups constitutes itself, closes itself up, opens itself up, in order to pass on to the next one and to close itself up again.—And one of the first difficulties is to find out how we come to will, to know, or to reach other human lives. How, then, can the subject come into contact with other subjects and become one with them?

Indeed, the issue is no longer what strangers and unknown individuals may have to offer individual egoism. It is no longer a question of all the contributions which the will requires and exploits for the benefit of its work. That is still "the object." What we want now of the subject is the subject himself,—not what he manifests or produces, but his intimacy, what is, so to speak, infinite and incommunicable about him. Until now we have taken him only as a means; we wanted from him only a concurrence, in view of a work which seemed the principal end and for which he was only an instrument. Now we are treating him as "an end in himself"; we desire him and solicit him for himself; we expect from him less what he does and more what he is; and what we want of him, it seems, is, in preference to the work, the worker himself, in order to ally ourselves to him, no longer as end to means or as whole to a part, but as principal to principal and as part to part, within a whole to which the individuality of each is devoted in a truly single life and in a real communion.

How does this movement which bears us toward other wills succeed in penetrating the closed door of consciousnesses? If we believe so spontaneously in the existence of others like ourselves, it is because we need, we will that they be. The issue is not in the signs of sensibility and intelligence which we find calling for interpretation around us. Whoever remains at that level (if it is possible to do so), can well exploit this apparent life of men. But in the strict sense of the terms, he remains isolated in their presence. He has not entered into them. He does not put himself in their place. He has before him only instruments to manipulate with the cleverness and the egoism of his passion, only beasts of burden that are more intelligent and machines that are more precious, that is all. It is a fundamental error to claim to ground social life on an exchange of phenomena, on a contact of sensibilities, or a commerce of interests. No, human society, as limited or as ample as it may be, does not rest on a play of signs, or a calculus of useful forces, or a compensatory equilibrium of economic laws, or the exterior side of facts. It has quite another reality, because it implies the active union of the subjects themselves, a placing in common of energies and lives.

For the common work always more or less escapes our grasp and our precautions. In what we do, there is always what we have done, and in what we have done, there subsists always a hidden fund of energy which skirts our foresight and our governance. In all the most informed calculations of the practical man or of the economist, we must make room for an unknown, which is surely nothing appreciable to the senses or even to the understanding, but which conceals the infinite of a force or of a will. This mysterious and indefinable subject who seems at first refractory to my knowledge as well as to my initiative, this infinite who disconcerts my solitary action by modifying it incessantly, this egoism that I conjure up facing mine and who is as inaccessible in his depths as I am in mine for him, him I wish to penetrate, to annex as a partner. I am tempted to submit him to me and revel in him. I want this unknown force that collaborates with me to be a subject analogous to myself and this subject to be an ally, a helper, a friend. I want to hold him in some way, have him for myself, be him without ceasing to be myself and, in order to be myself better, to bind him to myself as I bind myself to him by the mutual affection in which Aristotle saw the foundation and the first virtue of society. In my eyes, he really is only if he is for me as he is for himself.

For me to recognize a subjective life outside of myself quite like and equal to my own, I must therefore, by an implicit act of will, place under the sensible signs and the apparent works, the invisible presence of another will. That is why avid and needy love is an organ of knowledge. For if every subject is fundamentally reflexion, reason, freedom, he cannot be truly known except as such, and he is known in fact only to the extent that he is willed. The only way to understand him is to love him. This love is still more egotistical than is imagined ordinarily by the apparent generosity and professed devotion of one who loves this way, but it is nonetheless a tendency to disinterestedness and, if it is sincere, it brings the individual to a detachment from self. Sincere and disinterested, these two feelings make only one, so much does the first reflexion condemn exclusive egoism!

"Altruism" is therefore no less natural, necessary, and voluntary than egoism itself. It remains concentric with it. It is in conformity with the intimate wish of my will. And it seems that I cannot be myself, as I will to be, except by placing myself in another. The formulas in which people have claimed to see the pure expression of duty are therefore, no matter what we do, realized in fact. They are realized in fact like natural laws, if not in act like ends willed. For it is the accord between necessary fact and spontaneous will which alone, in order to be willed to the extent that it is voluntary, requires the moral effort whose infinite variations are eliminated by science. If social life is a necessity, because nature commands sympathy and because reason commands the agreement of forces and interests, more profoundly still, therefore, is it a work of freedom. We will it to be. And here, as everywhere else, the spontaneous form, the inevitable character of our action, is only the external translation of a fundamental and original will that comes from the most intimate depths of our person.

Thus, as soon as we turn voluntarily to act, we implicitly require by the very fact that society be, because society is the term of unfolding and the very confirmation of action. We can rely only on the effective and affective concurrence of wills capable of responding to us in the freedom and confidence we have in their regard. And even though it is ever and always *one* will—my personal will—which is in search of itself, it must,

249

to be consequent, defend itself against an immediate return to egoism. The same movement which induces me to want another to be like me leads me to want him to remain other for me, precisely because I wish from him what is incommunicable about him. It is this mystery, this infinite in his life, that draws me all the more because I penetrate him less. I do not really admit that he is in himself as I am in myself, except on the condition of not referring his operation, his life, his person to my individuality, on the condition of respecting these in their integrity, or rather of subordinating myself to him in the measure that I subordinate him to our common action.

Indeed, in view of this reciprocal respect which would seem at first to hold in suspense and keep on their guard the different subjects present, 250 how can a union be sealed and how can their intimacy fecundate them? —Each one must for his part propose for himself an end higher than each taken in isolation, an end good enough to pursue with a common *élan*, an end such that one could sacrifice himself to the other, as in the heroic paradox, where one man dies to save one other, like himself, less than himself. We do not come together simply to come together. We cannot contain between two individuals this torrent which flows from the will. The unity of the lives joined together must be more than the sum of the lives in isolation. This surplus must spill over and the superabundance of the multiple being must engender a work that will become its reason for being.

Thus we see once again, and with more clarity, how the synthesis is always transcendent to the elements which it dissolves and transforms. Thus we understand that, if man is for man "an end in himself," it is in view of a development higher than their mutual solitude. Thus it becomes manifest that there is no such thing as a social *statics*, because in human relations everything is in action, everything is born of action, everything flows into action. Justice, all contrary abstractions notwithstanding, does not reside in a static opposition of rights, in a separation of persons such that everyone would remain by himself and for himself; it is a promoting force which, in conformity with the profound will of each, maintains an equilibrium, but an equilibrium in movement. For if the need we have of another is born of the unfolding of an individual willing, it becomes in turn a cause of action. Among men there could be no real relations and living cooperation except by some progress toward social synthesis.

Here we find demonstrated the at once natural, necessary and free character of society. The intervention of reflexion only sanctions and perfects nature. To the slow formation of social organisms, of traditional institutions, and of spontaneous federations which have brought men together without express agreement or conscious contract, reflexion adds all the work of an enlightened will. In acting men were forced to unite, because they were acting in order to unite. And it is not only in order to arrive at union that they act in concert, but also out of devotion to the unity once it is constituted. For one cannot pursue a common end except by subordinating oneself to it and personifying it to devote oneself to it with others. The expressions of ordinary language, "family spirit, social consciousness, group spirit, body of the nation," do not have only a verbal value. For a whole, like a living synthesis, is not merely equal to the sum of its components. The latter are not parts or arithmetic units, but solidary members who vivify one another.   251

Voluntary action is therefore the bond that builds up the city of man; it is the social function *par excellence*. Action is meant for society and we are held one to the other only by action. Only on this foundation will social science be solidly established, a science that would be incomplete or even false, if it were satisfied with studying the mechanisms of external phenomena and the abstract concert of collective life, a science where one can account for private rights, for civil power and for political organization only by avoiding an impersonal method and the generalities of the positive sciences, in order to consider the always concrete and particular way in which societies came to be. For it is proper to *acts* that they cannot be looked at as *facts* without any singular and subjective character. And just as one is not first a man and then such and such a man in particular, so also society does not exist without being such and such a society, without becoming something like the common heart of those who love one another in it and for it. Sociology has a scientific nature only if it is not a science like the others.

To approach social phenomena only from the viewpoint of the positive sciences is thus to suppress them in fact; for it is to leave out precisely what distinguishes them from other phenomena. For anyone who co-operates in a common life, there is family or country only under a concrete and singular form, one's own par excellence. We must therefore see how each one of these groups comes to be through a particular and precise will. This will be to indicate the way of access to the *social sciences,* while maintaining the double character, *social* and *scientific,* which they must have. Many errors have come about through a failure to note the degrees in the continuous and distinct hierarchy of different human associations. Many have come from taking, as realities absolutely exclusive of one another, diversely compatible phenomena. Many have come from treating the singularities of collective action like general abstractions. We must set the various functions of life in their proper   252
order. And even though, perhaps, a higher individualism may absorb it,

we still have to go through a provisional socialism. To be sure, it is impossible to examine here in detail the constitution and the physiology of each of the sciences based on a cooperation of persons. That is the task of particular disciplines. But at least it is essential to indicate the continuity of the bond between sciences by showing the uninterrupted development of action all the way up to its complete realization. Let us study, therefore, through its social expansion and in the impersonality of its fruitful and indefinite action, the will that is still and ever trying to find its completion, not willing to remain *alone* in order to be more *one*.

Even while forming a closed and exclusive system, each society seeks to spread out and opens itself out to enter into a broader synthesis. We must therefore follow the movement of the will from the most simple and most intimate union of one on one all the way up to a point where this coenergy tends to surpass the limits of social life itself. — First, I study the bond of friendship and, more particularly, of love. — Then I look for the way one passes from family to country and I show that national life is a spontaneous need and a natural construction of the will. — Finally, I bring out how our action, overflowing the confines of the political, enters into solidarity with humanity as a whole, but still without finding in this new dimension the equilibrium and the satisfaction it is looking for. — It must be clearly understood that it is always the progress of voluntary action which engenders and justifies the successive forms of human life, that these forms are superimposed on one another and mutually complete one another, and that each one adds a new perfection to the one that prepares it, but without suppressing thereby the relative independence and the perpetuity of the preceding forms.

CHAPTER 1
The Voluntary Unity and the Fruitful Action
of Common Life

Family, Country, Humanity

We do not need only the help and the works of others. What can all their gifts be, if they do not give themselves and if we do not have them themselves? What we aspire to is their affection, their will, their devoted and loving action, as to a spring capable of refreshing an ardor that cannot be concentrated entirely in ourselves, as to a hearth that warms an activity in danger of dying without fuel. 253

Here, in this need and this will, resides the secret of the mystery of friendship. A vague and general desire of union with men is not enough. We must have a precise point of departure and a very concrete choice. It is by a very unique love that man is brought into life, and that in turn he enters into it himself. But how can we become attached quite particularly to a being that is in no way particular? How can an affection survive the loss of all the qualities that had bound us to the loved one? The fact is that two lives were joined together, not only in what they know of one another or of themselves, but down to the principle of their common actions and their undivided sentiments. And that is why, according to a beautiful saying of Aristotle, a friendship which was able to come to an end never was a true one. That is why, in the most common human nature, there is always something unique deserving of being loved in a unique way.

To love oneself by loving another sincerely, to give oneself and to redouble oneself by the gift, to see oneself as other and to see oneself in another, not to be solitary and to be alone, to unite with one another and to embrace as we distinguish ourselves from one another, to have everything in common without confusing anything and to remain two in order to ceaselessly merge, as in a unique whole and a single more perfect and more fruitful being, to reduce a million rays of glory into the loving 254

241

esteem of one soul, to prefer one who loves fully to a million who love a lot—that is the natural cry of the heart. Is it not apparent that we expect a new life from this coming together and that every full affection is destined for and as though suspended from the intention of engendering a work common to those whose union it consecrates, justifies, and seals? All social action is therefore like a generation because it proceeds from the need we feel to extend our will into another and redouble our life. We will that something other than what we already were should result from the gift: an enrichment, a pledge appropriate for encouraging, tightening, and sanctioning the bond of mutual affection.

This movement of expansion and consolidation pauses at three principal progressive terms within the confines of humanity: the family, the country, the whole of human society. How does the will engender each of these definite syntheses wherein it incorporates its action, and how does it go from one to the other as it opens out?

I

All that it touches, all that it knows, all that it gets from the cooperation of others, all the finite ends that it pursues exteriorly and that it attains, have not been able to satisfy the appetite that projects man out of himself in quest of a response equal to his call. The immensity of the satisfaction he can only get from another self—from another who is incommunicable and impenetrable like himself—is offered him in the intimate and closed unity of a life alien to his own. This life is alien to him: he wants to enter into it to form a separate world with it and to enclose himself in it as in a total and independent universe. That is love, exclusive love, jealous, passionate love, often egotistical way down under. But if we follow its development or unravel its secret aspirations, we will find the serious design of a fecund will under the fascinations of sterile voluptuousness.

First, is it not an initial attraction and a sincere movement that leads us to live doubly by another and for another? The tenderness and devotion that a solitary egoism is incapable of providing for itself, is willed and achieved by the love of one for the other—an egoism-for-two, all the more delicate and rewarding because it loses sight of itself and imagines it is quite the opposite of what it is. To be sure, if one went to the bottom of all this obliging attention, solicitude, and generosity of mutual affection, if, starting from the acts, following the tenuous thread of involuted rationalizations, one went back to the principle of the unseen sentiments, one would be surprised, as most moralists have been, at the disguised

255

self-love that is at play under a surface of goodness and abnegation. Thus, when we weep over a separation, it is over ourselves that we weep. But self-love sees better still than the moralists. It suspects that true affection felt for another brings more satisfaction than an egoism too much in a hurry to enjoy itself. Since the end knowingly sought does not exhaust the desire, since action ordinarily surpasses any definite intention, it follows that the profound causes of an act and even its effects may seem to fall under the law of self-interest, even though the agent himself may not be self-interested.

Naively, therefore, we love to be loved and we love to love. For in a love given there is a generous activity which alone prepares the heart to taste a reciprocal gift. In a love obtained and received there is an exaltation, a confidence, an abundance which gives back, and more, all that the lover seemed to sacrifice to the loved one. When the child talking about himself with an open tenderness expresses surprise at not being able to embrace himself, he is the image of this disinterested egoism which awaits the kiss of another egoism and gives itself in exchange. Each thus has the merit of its total and sweet renunciation; each at the same time has the benefit of a watchful tenderness which the most despicable egoism would not equal in noble solicitude; each has the noble joy of tasting and admiring the devotion he benefits from. To enjoy both one's own disinterestedness and that of the lover while gathering all that the refinements of the most informed and the most subtle self-interest could not procure, is that not the wonder of love?

But to attain this perfect intimacy, what art, we could say, what science of common life would not have to be acquired and practiced! If to suborn and govern the powers of nature, the expert or the practitioner 256 needs such an effort of thought and energy, then in order to enter into a heart, to maintain oneself there, to truly bring into concert the unanimity of two consciousnesses melted into one, what tender ingenuity and what diplomacy in mutual devotion do not become necessary! Nothing seems to cost too much if it is to seal this union which appears as the coveted end and which is yet only a provisional stop. And for this life-for-two, each seems ready to sacrifice all the individual life he has.

Moreover, how could we not want this intimacy to be more, by itself, than the entire exterior world? If for each one of us the least thought that shines inside has more charm and truth than all the radiance from the outside, is it any wonder that, in tasting the interior life of another self, one feels a fullness and something like a rapture? By an extraordinary abstraction which love performs, the loved one is set completely apart from the rest of the world. Only he, in the eyes of the lover, seems to have a real life. He becomes for him the measure of his impressions and his judgments. And just as we do not allow another to seek or to possess the loved one, in a sincere movement of the heart, we do not allow that we could seek another than him. We find lovers quite ridiculous. But it is in revenge, for they are the ones who seem first to expel others from the world, ready to sacrifice all the rest to this nothing that they are in the immensity of their souls, so that this nothing may be for them all the rest.

There is nothing analogous in all of man. Even one who loves cannot understand love in another. Between two loves there is no relation, because down deep there is only one; and each one thinks it exhausts all without thinking it will ever be exhausted. In it nothing is general or common; everything is particular, proper to the one who feels and the one who inspires it, incomparable, infinite. This is the incomprehensible wonder of the enamored heart, so ready to divinize the meagre reality which it thinks it holds alone and entirely for eternity, but which still escapes at that very moment; a tyrannical and voluntary blindness, which transfigures the obscure idol in order to see it, to see it better, by closing its eyes! Bodies are a strange solitude indeed, and all that has been said about union is nothing compared to the separation they cause. You whose arms are weary before your hearts have come together, what you are still looking for, thinking you already have it, is perfect unity, exclusive and indissoluble perpetuity. That is why, when reason and passion speak, they conspire together to require in the very name of the grandeur and sincerity of love, an indivisible, an indefectible, a perfect union. Divorce is contrary to nature. And this unity which the weakness of nature seems to make impossible, this unity which the effort of mutual tenderness, so ingenious in covering up its intermissions and its failings by the renewal of its professions, does not succeed in obtaining, has to be consecrated between the two conjoined by an invisible and permanent bond so as to rejoin them and to lock them together with all the strength of their intimate desire.

Thus it is precisely because of its immense need for love that the will aspires to the unity, the totality, the eternity of the knot it forms from one to the other, *toti totus, unus uni* (whole to whole, one to one). If it is completely consistent with its wish, it aspires to monogamy. It expects a kind consecration of nuptial indissolubility. For what it loves in the loved one is not just what one can see, touch, know, and understand; it is that, but it is also the reality which is obscure, unconscious, impenetrable, the fecund infinite which the loved one hides in himself and which he manifests in the whole of himself. That strange fetishism which clings to a single detail to make it the object of a cult is an unhealthy love; true love embraces the entire person, considering it a living unity of parts that have their beauty from their intimate relation to the whole. It is, so to speak, monotheistic. For it is not enough for it to say, one heart in two bodies. It unites not only loving wills and minds that understand and penetrate one another, but it melts the hidden and unknown parts, those from which acts originate, those where the will has embodied and enriched itself. While respecting the distinction of consciousnesses who continue to enjoy what is proper to each and their willed and felt union, it mingles the substances; it intimately associates actions; it makes the sources of being and life identical; it seals forever, even down to their primordial foundation, the stones of the common edifice: *duo in carne una unum sunt* (two in one flesh are one).

Once it is done, then, it seems that, united in body to form one soul and united in soul to form one body, the two conjoined have found their all. *Tenui eum nec dimittam* (I have held him and will not let him go). And yet, when by a mysterious exchange two beings form but a single being which is more perfect, does their mutual presence, their common action close the circle of their will? Is it full possession? Is it the term where ends the *élan* of desire? No. Two beings are now only one, and it is when they are one that they become three. This wonder of generation indicates by a fact what must be, indeed what is, the profound will even of those who hope to find in their unstable unity a moment of rest, of satisfaction and of sufficiency. In pursuing a loved end, we love this end less than the fruit with which, fecundated by love, it will enrich those who spend themselves for it. Thus the will always seems to surpass itself, as if new waves coming from the center were ceaselessly pushing the widening circles of action — that action which seems at every instant the end and the perfection of a world, but which is always the origin of a new world. It closes in on itself and concentrates itself only to open up broader horizons for the insatiable ambition of desire.

That perpetuity which love required, the indissoluble and surviving unity, is now in the child. The very momentum of passion breaks the magic circle where it perhaps hoped to close itself up forever. In that absolute, that sufficiency, and that eternity of a moment which it was seeking infinitely, the will, at the very moment, is already beyond itself; it wants the soul of the loved one to produce a body. A third appears, as if to make up for the unfruitful attempt at unity; this third is no longer love, *osculum* (a kiss); it is born of love: it manifests love's power and infinity. It seals the love in a tomb, — the cradle, — which does not give back what it has taken from the parents. They are many, that is riches. They are many, that is poverty, they are no longer one. A strange day has dawned: in getting larger the family has to open up and disperse; the common affection has to multiply itself in dividing. The two united no

258

longer can, no longer will to be all for one another. Often their detoured tenderness finds itself again only over the head of the child. And in their life, henceforth parallel, they sometimes encounter only habit, indifference, even hostility. Thus the end of love is not love, but the family, the first natural and necessary group where life is born and grows, as in a warm womb, sheltered from the immensity of the universe.

259   It is in generation that man finds a way of expressing himself, giving himself, of outliving himself as a whole, where he meets the perfection of his act and the first finished response that he hopes for. His first living work is the child, a wondrous synthesis: two and one and three, *non hi tres unum, sed hoc unum tres sunt* (not these three are one, but this one is three). That is the secret reason for the attraction that hands two beings over to one another body and soul; for what the will is seeking, beyond egotistical and voluptuous satisfaction, even beyond the unfathomable loved subject who escapes the loving subject, is the common work of their power and their incarnate love, the visible and real image of their double and unique life, the expression of what in each one seems ineffable and inaccessible.

The progression of the will's ambitions is manifest. Earlier we wanted the useful work, the external concurrence of another: this was a still solitary egoism. Then desire fastened on the worker himself: an egoism-for-two. Now what we will and what we make be is the living work and, in this work, what in each worker is impenetrable and infinite: an egoism-for-three. The child is the substantial action of powers that know themselves well only in him, that are one only by him, and that spend themselves like a fire of tenderness before him. And the will, consistent with its own law and in conformity with the sincere wish of love, transports itself into him as to its natural end.

It is he, therefore, who grounds the indissoluble unity and who reveals the dissolving weakness of the nuptial bond:—dissolving weakness, for we want to outlive ourselves only because we pass away and die, because we cannot capture between two the infinite movement of willing;—indissoluble unity, for the child remains, in his very individuality, the pledge of the irreparable and indivisible union. He is the indelible sign of what was willed by reason in love with unity and eternity, in concert with the sincere passion that wants only to be exclusive and perpetual. Reason has marked the engendered work with its own seal. And as the child has within himself the infinite power of development which he holds from those for whom he is a first fulfillment, he remains for them the permanent means, by the education they give him, of moving on to their destiny. Toward the child they have an unlimited duty, an indefeasible responsibility, an indestructible bond, since it is a matter of forming his reason and of realizing in him, unto infinity, what is best in them. It is still themselves whom they raise in raising him above themselves, for they are both superior and subordinate to the child over whom they have authority, but to whom they themselves are duty bound. Indeed, he receives from them what he must perfect in himself and it is to him as to their end that they relate their own perfecting of self.

260

From this study it is evident that love proceeds from individual will, though it surpasses the individual, that it requires a sometimes heroic generosity and abnegation, but that it is not thereby contrary to the intention of the one sacrificing himself to it, that its reason and its justification is an end higher and further removed than the apparent aim of the first desire, without however making of the attraction which bedecks it a deceiving ruse and a cruel trick of nature. To be sure, if it were the "genius of the species" which, through the fascination of a fragile voluptuousness, fooled the individual by hiding under an immediate response of life and happiness a reality of pain and death, pessimism would be grounded. All that has been said about the hidden calculations of the racial instinct is right. But that impetuous movement starts from further back in order to go further on than has been recognized. The flow of love proceeds from the most interior will in each one. And even while this outflow, by its own impulse, is drawn beyond the term desired at first, this primordial will remains always coextensive with its entire unfolding, even if it is unforeseen. Love goes beyond the person, beyond space, to infinity. But just because it carries individual life to ulterior ends, without ever closing off its expansion, we must not, like pessimism, turn against the mysticism of love, as if it were only a trap.

We are not talking, then, about an impersonal and obscure willing which would not only be alien and unknown to those it moves by an instinctive fatalism, but which would be opposed and hostile to them. We are talking about a profoundly personal will that reflexion can shed light on without changing its nature or rejecting its meaning, a will which is not limited to working blindly only for the species, but which serves at one and the same time the interests of the individual and of the species, because it is not confined to the limits of the species and at the highest term of its expansion it aspires to fuse its personal ends with the universal ends. Thus there is continuity and logical connection in its development. The solitary will has embraced another will: it establishes the family; it wills it, and it wills it to be one, steady, and permanent. There is nothing artificial, therefore, in this first society, the type and the origin for all others. We have still to see how the social family and the human family

261

are equally in conformity with the aim of freedom and how, no matter how ample they may be, these lives in composition fit in also with the ever broadening map of voluntary action.

II

I. — For the child, there is really only one family, his own; it is to him incomparable, unique; and the others exist only in the measure that they relate to his own, or rather they do not yet exist. It is thus within these narrow confines that he first comes to know lives other than his own, lives that are still his and that he barely distinguishes from the interests of his naive egoism. For he is not far wrong in making himself the center of this little world which he vivifies with his presence. Here he really makes his apprenticeship of the *ours* and the *we*; in this way he comes to a consciousness, a will, a devoted love of a more ample society; more-over, it is worth noting that access to social life presupposes filial and fraternal feelings rather than conjugal affection. And it is because the family is a closed and exclusive group that it serves in this way as a school preparing for the collective life of which it is the elemental unity. Closed as it is, it concentrates and brings to completion the feeling of mutual af-fection before it later transports itself, admittedly quite other, into a broader milieu that is equally closed, the city or the country.

It is an important moment in the history of a child's thinking and feel-ing when he becomes clearly conscious that he, which is to say his family, is not alone on earth, that there are others, that all the interests of the world do not gravitate around this unique center, that there are other people who have their own affections, their distinct horizon, their separate life. Of course, he already knows this, before he feels it in this way. But rather than think of men from the inside, so to speak, by con-ferring on them his own need for being a center of viewpoint and action, he saw them still only from the outside without any internal reality. Hap-py childhood, and one that allows a richer development of the heart, when it is prolonged for loving natures and in exceptional families where the illusion that no one is like those who surround the domestic hearth is more justified, until the day when, by an unexpected revelation which takes place in each one in a different way, a bruised heart, but a compas-sionate and broadened one, opens up to other homes and embraces other lives.

It would be a mistake to imagine that, in expanding little by little, the circle of the domestic hearth reforms itself around the altar of the country (*la patrie*). The national spirit does not appear this way, neither in the historical constitution of peoples nor in the awakening of each individual consciousness, because in the depths of our affections, the country is something other than a bigger family and because the movement whence comes the moral organism of the political is quite original. To be sure, the nation gets its members from the family; but as in a chemical reaction, where the elements still present are transfigured into the new unity of the compound, individual life, family life, without losing their natural vigor, are transformed in the heart of the nation where they are lodged. To study society, then, we must not start from the elements; we must start from the group itself. How is a people formed? Why are men led to mingle their thoughts and their affections within the great social community? Why this characteristic of a limited unity and this enclosure of frontiers? How does the profound will of each individual produce this circumscribed extension so as to ratify at once the breadth and the narrowness of national life? That is where the question truly lies.

If the bond that unites the members of one country is not of the same nature as the one that envelops and ties the family together, it follows that the solidarity of citizens is not explained by an extension of domestic relations or of blood ties. It is well known how quickly these relations of the family come undone and how even, not satisfied to just die down, they can easily turn into hostilities and bitterness. In the body of a whole nation there flows one life and one will, as in a single organism, all of whose parts seem tied by a mutual relation of finality. This is to say, then, that if the family is the social element, the nation is still not a mere reflection and a kind of prolongation of domestic society; for it forms, so to speak, a homogeneous society, from the closest relative to the most distant compatriot, so that, as with the outer limits of our body, the most lively sensibility resides in its distant members. What proves quite well that the country is a distinct organism is that the light that goes out from the will, eager to spread itself abroad, instead of spreading beyond the limits of the political whole, begins there to reflect back and to return upon itself as if it had met the term it was tending toward. Patriotism comes before the feeling for humanity and surpasses familial affections, like an original synthesis defined between the two. It even seems contrary to the two at times.

What need does this construction of national unity, this enclosure of the country, respond to? — One could account for the heart to heart in the intimate exchange of two lives that penetrate one another and give warmth to others at their hearth. One could account for the all to all in the immense fraternity of affections learned at the center of the family. But how, in between, can we find a place and justification for this already general federation, though still restricted, that forms a nation?

Isn't it only an artificial construction? And as a surging cosmopolitanism used to maintain, is it not only a prejudice bound to disappear, a secular superstition, a narrowness of mind and heart? Or does this jealous love of country ground itself on a profound will, on a natural and enduring need of our humanity?

To be sure, it is delicate to determine what makes the country (*la patrie*). It is not merely the expanded family, the race, or the common species, nor the configuration of the same land, nor the advantage of the same climate, of the same type, of the same language, of the same law, or of the same tradition. For, besides the fact that certain peoples do not present this concurrence of favorable circumstances without ceasing to be one in the sympathy and the devotion of all for all, these conditions touch only on the external modes of human activity. But social life is not only a regulated exchange of self-interests; it is not limited to economic phenomena; it is not alien to the intimacy of affections and neutral in the reserved domain of consciousnesses. As long as a people is not one in thought, it is not a people but a balanced conflict of appetites and desires. To keep or to reconquer the integrity of its soil is not everything for it. Material cohesion and external solidity in a nation are only an effect whose cause must be found in the will of each one of those who compose it. For, in order for individual action to become truly a homogeneous synthesis and a living organism, it must somehow embrace the common action; the entire people must, so to speak, stir in the heart and in the devoted love of each one in particular; the citizen, participating in authority as well as in obedience, must have a will that coincides with the collective expansion and that perpetually grounds the national synergy.

It is therefore in the intimacy of personal life that, here as everywhere else, we must look for the secret of social life by asking how we are led to will the confines of the political whole, the inviolable boundary of the country. Why these partial societies which, in the human species, form like composite individualities, each with its own physiognomy and its definite character?

No matter how broad action may become, it is always the same will that animates all its unfolding and that spreads itself out in order to find itself better after each new sally. This means that the centrifugal movement finds its meaning and its reason only through the centripetal movement which brings back to the primordial willing what it wished to attain, precisely because it did not have it yet and because it was not it as yet. The first concern of the will, however ample we now suppose it to be, is, after each new conquest, to consolidate itself and to exclude at first precisely what it is destined to pass on to later on. It opens up only to absorb and to close back on itself. It seems that we don't want to have everything at first, so that we may appreciate what we possess better and so that we may still have the need to enrich ourselves, outside of ourselves. What the individual cannot take or keep by himself, he takes, he retains, he assimilates, through the powerful organism of the city. But to realize that he has it, to enjoy his new extension, he must, at least provisionally, repel what he has not yet absorbed into his life.

Thus, the charm, the strength, the incomparable intertwining of the conjugal bond is that it excludes the whole universe from the loving embrace. It is a union that has its value only in isolating those it captivates, in the face of the surrounding multiplicity, a union whose concrete and living reality is to be an abstraction from and something like a protestation against the banality of the crowd. It is quite the same for the national feeling. We do not form a concert with only one sound; for *one* human society to be, there have to be many of them, each having its individual accidents or its specific difference.

265

The plurality of cities is analogous to the plurality of persons, to the repetition in particular of the same life and the same common will, each having it all in itself. And as nature loves to multiply by variation the samples of one and the same type, human actions imitate it on this point. Better still, just as a sincere movement of the will led us to desire that there be outside of ourselves one or many wills that would unite and identify with ours while remaining distinct, so also we will that there be a city and that it be limited and that there be a world foreign to it outside its borders.

The unity of the country, to the exclusion of all other societies, is not then a transitory and artificial state. The pride of the citizen which places his country apart and above the others is a natural feeling. Just as each consciousness keeps the secret of what makes it unique and incomparable to itself, each country, seen and loved from the inside, takes on a charm to which aliens must remain alien. Or rather, there is only one country for each man, and the name has no plural.

Thus the ever singular character of life must be found in social science, for it to be a science. *Omne individuum ineffabile* (every individual is ineffable). The true meaning of history is to define the originality of each of the living syntheses that the movement of general life has engendered. In this way, history ties solidly into all the sciences, already better constituted, which determine the interconnection of facts and the heterogeneity of the beings they study. It is the evolution of a whole which creates races, more even than the races contribute to the formation of nations. How do different cases of definite equilibrium become established? And what is the unique genius, the proper work, the incomparable organization, the entirely new countenance of each nation? That is the historical problem. Let us not, therefore, under pretext of scientific impartiality, talk about prescinding from the feelings that stir the heart of a people. The most patriotic history is the most scientific one.

Every people, then, has an idea and a feeling to bring to life in the world. That is its reason, its mission, its soul. It is a mortal soul, one dying at times for lack of a common action, but one capable of resurrection, one imperishable, if the thought it lives by is one of those that reaches the permanent interests or the sacred consciousness of humanity. A certain people, dispersed and as it were decomposed, maintains its indestructible vitality both through the idea of which it is the keeper and which has woven itself into its flesh, and through the faith that inspires it and whose ardor is mixed with its blood: no matter how bruised it may be, it bears within its torn flank an infinite power of regeneration. The greatness and the duration of peoples depends on the role they have to play; each has its work. Each, like an organ in the great body of humanity, absorbs the thought of other nations according to its own genius, and puts back into circulation as it were a new richness, different in each and common to all.

It is not that this historical development of nations and races goes on with an infallible spontaneity of instinct. The issue is not merely the confused life that vegetates amid the popular masses. Human history is not, in the strict sense of the word, a natural history. That is, besides the unspecified forces that move the great human currents, reflexion and freedom are original powers, capable of penetrating deep into the destiny of peoples as essential factors. As causes that are disturbing or salutary, promoting or dissolving, thoughts and deliberate actions, institutions and revolutions, even in what is arbitrary about them, have a definite influence on the progress of societies. As superficial as it is to think that the acts, the words, and the decrees of the principal actors govern the world, without taking into account the role of anonymous causes, it is no less false to neglect what goes on in the area of deliberate counsels, distinct events, and even caprice. A historical method that, under pretext of not departing from living realities, excludes artificial codifications and the theories of jurists as merely the result of abstraction, falls into the same error as a psychology for which the conscious act is only a useless surplus with reference to its elementary conditions.

National consciousness, then, is a force whose efficaciousness grows as we penetrate more deeply into its profound causes. It is not one of those feelings that we should avoid looking at, as if to see it as it is were to violate or lose it. To be sure, the advances of reflexion or the needs of a broader development have compromised the cult of the city at times;

to some, the form of love, devotion, and heroism we call patriotism seems to rest only on a respectable but obsolete illusion. But a more advanced reflexion restores this spontaneous feeling by justifying the instinct of the heart. Even after we have risen to a more ample communion with humanity as a whole, to a feeling of universal solidarity which antiquity had no idea of and which appeared quite late in the history of moral ideas, it remains true that the frontiers of the nation continue to subsist and must continue. Far from excluding a more liberal need for affection, patriotism prepares the way for it, as attachment to the countryside, to the steeple, the home, prepares and warms the heart for love of the broad country (*la grande patrie*).

Here once again we find the law whose application we have noted in the sequence of syntheses that action forms in unfolding itself and whose meaning becomes clearer little by little. Each time the will placed a new end before itself, it was led to consider the earlier ends where it had stopped as insufficient and even illusory. But as it arrives at the coveted term, it notices that this new end also is transitory; henceforth it understands better how the preceding stages were, in spite of the instability it encountered in them, necessary conditions and relatively fixed points, in the progress of its expansion. Thus it sees that, far from excluding one another, the successive syntheses which ordinarily appear to contradict one another, suppose one another, that each is at once an end and a means, and that in all of them there is an established system, an original character, a precise determination. So we go from one of these syntheses to another only by passing from one definite equilibrium to another definite equilibrium. Indeed, progress in the organization of life or of action is possible only if each successive point offers a solid support and if, at each level of development, the system formed is determined less by the addition of parts than by a new idea of the whole. Hence the need for inserting into each form of personal or collective life an appearance of something absolute: just as we instinctively attribute a sacred char-   268
acter to the nuptial bond in order to assure its solidity, instinctively we also consecrate the country and sanctify the flag, as if the confines of the city enveloped heaven and earth, indeed heaven still more than the earth. There is then a sort of spontaneous mysticism that enables the will to stop at successive stages, as if each were the end; for it places in each, at least provisionally, the illusion of the infinite in the finite itself.

The political is thus constituted, not as an amorphous body or as a transitory organ in the general evolution of social life; it has a relative sufficiency, a necessary organization. That is why, as we shall see better, it does not result from a more or less arbitrary convention, why it does not depend on the caprice of the members who make it up, and why authority is indispensable in it, in order to meet the need whose mission it has to satisfy. Power (*le pouvoir*), which is its synthetic bond and as it were its "substantial form," remains the expression of the profound will that grounds the nation itself. And the political form in which authority is exercised manifests the particular action of circumstances and human liberties in the tradition of national life. A society is therefore never just any society, because it is always grounded on a very particular feeling and on an absolutely concrete will. The first social truth, that on which sociology depends, is to posit in principle the historical originality and the individual character of every national organism. From this, all the general laws that govern the organization of human societies follow; from this, all the abstract principles of public law come.

II. – Through the spontaneous unfolding of collective life, there is constituted, between the individual and the group in which he takes part, one or more systems of balancing forces. As there are organs in the body, in society there are organized and living associations. Nothing brings out better than these elementary organizations what difference in nature subsists between the family and the social body; for these elements of collective life, as they constitute themselves under our eyes at times, reveal a law of formation quite contrary to that of domestic society.

In the one-on-one of love, it is the fruitful unity of a double life that expands and multiplies. In the all-on-all of the association or the country, it is the multiplicity that is concentrated in each, it is the whole synthesis that embodies itself in the least of its elements and communicates its own strength and all its dignity to it. It appeared that patriotic devotion made a means of the individual in the face of a common and higher end. It happens that, fundamentally, the relation is the reverse, and that the whole is a means for each of its members. Do we not understand now to what secret wish of personal willing the immense increase found in social life corresponds, because what social life is, willing becomes? And what proves that society is not an artificial mechanism, is that, far from creating antagonism between the whole and the parts, the progress of social life should broaden both the action of the State and individual initiative. In society each has in himself what all are together. Here again, the idea of the whole determines the nature of the elements. Yet, at the same time, the principle of the synthesis is wholly at the bottom of each personal will. No one has to go out of himself to discover its presence and its efficaciousness. The force that actualizes society and, through it, each citizen, is in each individual.

From this concrete truth come, as necessary corollaries, the very conditions of social justice and of political organization. To be sure, liberty introduces, here as everywhere, infinitely varied perturbations. But it is still possible to set the variable aside and to consider, in what can be violated, what is not violated, and in what is violated, what remains in conformity with the logic of the human will. Under the most revolutionary aberrations, there subsists a latent rule and a principle of order. It is this determinism of willed action that we must take hold of in the distinct development of social justice and of political power.

— From the moment when, to be myself better and to become more *one*, I can no longer remain *alone*, I require that a principle of peace and harmony preside over social cooperation. When one wants the end, one wants the means. In calling collective action forth, then, I institute, however vague or precise the form may be, a central force capable of representing the entire community for which it is something like a consciousness. Since all are for each in society, I need some kind of expression, whatever it may be, for this universal solicitude for me alone. The idea of a penal protection, the feeling of a social sanction, the need of a power armed with jurisdiction and coercive force, all this is essential to common life. And its necessity is grounded on the very exigencies of personal will. Society seems to be constituted under the action of an end transcending the individual only to procure for the individual the reassurance of that higher power from which each derives all the benefit.

But we must be careful not to denature this social justice and not to pervert the essentially relative character of human penalization. Even though it is impossible to succeed in doing so, nothing is more dangerous and less justified than to claim the establishment of an exact proportion between punishment and moral offence. For example, there is a way of justifying capital punishment which, under the guise of justice and morality, makes it bloodthirsty and barbaric. Also, to unravel the confusion of contemporary ideas, it is important not to complicate the problem ineptly and to avoid any consideration foreign to the order wherein human jurisdiction should be confined.

To be sure, alongside the bare *fact* and the material harm caused by the offence, another element must be taken into consideration, which, in opposition, can already be qualified as *moral*. But this qualification itself leads to equivocation. For it is not a question of appraising the absolute value of either the act or the intention; it is a question of the public defense, of the general interest, of the common life. But the collective interest does not depend only on material facts, precisely because society is not a mere system of economic or political phenomena. Also, when we speak of the moral character which penalization should assume, we must understand only that here culpability is merely a function of the social danger, that extenuating, aggravating, or exculpating circumstances can

270

be weighed only from the viewpoint of the common safety, and that, rather than having to do with an absolute justice, an ideal liberty, and a perfect responsibility, we have only to determine in what measure the criminal action, coming from a deliberate decision and thereby touching on what binds the wills together, takes on a character that is contagious, imitable, and detrimental to the collective life. What is essential and legitimate here, therefore, is society's need to preserve itself. There is no point in placing the metaphysical question of freedom before the judge. For if he has the authority to condemn, it is not in the name of a higher equity which he is not charged with upholding. Here especially, the better part would be the worst. No, the internal value of the accused is not to be weighed; this would be a temerarious and culpable and odious kind of justice, since it would not be able to pardon even the most sincere and purifying repentance.

271

What is absolute in human justice, therefore, is that it is relative to the exigencies of conscience and common life, in a civilization and at a determinate epoch. In every form of the social state, a type of honorable man is determined, particular necessities of general defense arise; this is the living and flexible norm which should be applied to the mobility of social phenomena and which does apply more or less, no matter what we do or want.

— Quite similarly, what is absolute in political organization is that it is relative to the historical development and the particular traditions, always still perfectible, of a concrete society. To what profound need does the political ambition of the citizen correspond, and how is civil power constituted, lost, or transmitted?

The will, through its necessary and accepted expansion, creates social life. But no society is possible without an authority able to move and regulate this great machine. Society and authority are therefore above the reach of human arbitrariness. But precisely because they correspond to a fundamental aspiration of man, man determines the exercise of public power. He designates, or he accepts, or he becomes himself the holder of it. Political investiture is a matter of national law. And therein lies the delicate point. For if authority is necessary for every society, it is necessary that power be constituted: a people (*le peuple*) is not free in its holding of this trust; a government has to be determined. And if the constitution of power does rest on a basis of free option, it remains true both that authority remains necessary even in its arbitrary form and that this power is always perfectible, though fundamentally intangible.

Here then are the consequences that follow from one another, in spite of apparent oppositions. Society is willed and necessary. Authority is willed and necessary. They are above every human will. It is up to the concurrence of human wills to recognize and ratify power (*le pouvoir*). It is impossible that the concurrence of human wills not recognize or not ratify some power. Power is at once higher than the nation and subordinate to it. It is constituted for the nation, not the nation for it. Since authority has no other reason for existing than the common good, the nation can transfer into other hands a power that fails in its obligations. Theoretically this right is certain. In fact, however, since social disturbance is the worst of evils, since the right of determining or transmitting authority resides, not partially in each individual, but indivisibly in the unity of the social body, since all the generations are solidary, it follows that tradition is a national inheritance against which violent protests and sudden decisions are dangerous and often perverse. In public as well as in private law, prescription is respectable. And apart from elections, which are the innocent way of establishing power, even usurpation, having lost its odious character, becomes legitimate with the passage of time and the consent of peoples.

It is not the law of numbers that creates law and rights. It is a mistake, then, to think with Rousseau that "the sovereign, by the mere fact that it is, is always what it ought to be." And it is because the need for authority rises from each one that it is higher than all. In a body the head is there for the members without ceasing to be the chief part. In political life, power, by reason of its origin, is above even those who constituted it; for it is not the sum of individual wills or the expression of the common strengths; it is not revocable *ad nutum* (at will); there is no simple delegation, but a regulated and regulating power which remains a property personal to each individual, even when it is exercised by only one. And just as a consistent will requires the unity and indissolubility of domestic life, so also it maintains the always singular fact of public institutions, reformable to be sure and perpetually in movement, but beyond the legitimate reach of each one of those who vivify them with their willing. Thus power is neither a sum of arbitrary wills, nor an abstract formula applicable indifferently to all peoples. Always, it has taken a concrete form, always, it remains grounded on a will prior to artificial and changing conventions.

Thus the political organization and the social justice that compose and assure national life only manifest for their part an intimate and quite personal will. For, through them, all the strength of the public body is at the disposal of each of the lowest members. The State is at first an end with regard to the individual only to be a means afterwards. If each must live and act for all (the rough sketch of society which socialism falsely presents as the perfection of political life), it is because each wants all to busy and to concentrate themselves in each. Just as, in the organic system, one call is an end for all the rest, to the point that a pin prick is enough to arouse the entire machine, there is, in an ordered society, such a solidarity that the humblest citizen bears within him all the dignity, all the power, all the multiple egoism of the social body.

And since the social will is found in each individual, it follows that all political forms can be equally organized and equally justified. Differences in customs, climates and circumstances make variety inevitable, and a concert is not formed with only one sound. Whether it actually resides in only one, in many, or in all, the role of power in the nation is always to insure solidarity and the most intimate communion of the parts; always power must be, it can be in one what it would be in all. Nevertheless, by reason of this multi-presence of the social principle in each will, needs that were long hidden come to light little by little. As social consciousness awakens more clearly in each individual, a profound labor of growth is effected in the popular masses.

To be sure, the common consciousness appears first in the head of the political organism, before it spreads throughout the body. What an immense and heartfelt devotion to one man alone, and what a loving thrill sometimes runs through simple folk at the sight of their beloved chief! What value the least word of the czar seems to have as it comes to a humble muzhik! But note also how the feeling of dignity, esteem for the role, and the height of power expand the outlook, broaden the affections, and add both to the clarity of an intelligence and to the warmth of a soul that knows how to be the brain and the heart of a vast people! And as if the chief alone loved more nobly, more deeply, than all together, from this height the most simple and most calm affection seems to come down with sovereign force.

But it is not merely one man who can inspire and receive the feeling of mutual devotion. It is also each citizen, when in each member of the social body we can see and love the common soul that lives in all. National consciousness is not, then, a sum of fractions. The citizen is the living political whole. In him resides virtually the power and the action of all. That is why each one aspires to be himself the head and the heart of the great body whose entire substance he bears within himself. If an agreement of wills raises him to authority, he does not receive an imperative mandate, he is not the abstract total of an arithmetical operation; he becomes in act what he was in potency. By a sort of natural grace of state and by the echoing of the general life within him, the chief, conscious of being the culmination of a whole people, seems raised above himself. And yet his authority always has another source than the addition of popular votes; his role is to take a personal initiative, to the extent that even the most ordinary man can have a clearer vision, a more enlightened power of decision, a more real continuity of action than that sum of individual wills which it would be wrong to make the expression of social consciousness.

Thus the will of the citizen vivifies and absorbs within itself the whole social organism: it determines its always concrete character; it forms it into an original synthesis as are the living species and the distinct races in the animal kingdom; and whatever be the original unity or the general laws of societies, each one is a singular nation. It is *the* country (*patrie*) because it comes from a love that is personal to each of its members and because love always goes to what is unique. To be sure, national life has its prolongations beyond its borders; for it, as for any organism, the functions of integration and disintegration are a principle of perpetual renewal. It remains nonetheless a definite individuality, even in the face of ulterior syntheses and new extensions of human action.

III

Man's will and his action do not stop at the borders of the country. In swarming outward, the political is the symbol of the interior life of the will that spreads out without any confines to hold back its expansion. The law of active and conquering egoism is to contradict itself and, in a way, to change its mind, to reach out for what it seemed at first to repel. It is no longer enough to bear within oneself a whole nation and to become one soul with it; man aspires, as it were, to espouse humanity itself and to form only one will with it. 275

Individual life, then, tends to become identical with universal life; or rather, it is this general and impersonal will which seems to become concentrated in each consciousness. The very idea of a progress or of an evolution is proof of this growing solidarity. As long as generations and individuals thought themselves independent, it seemed that the world was growing old by wasting away. It still seems that way, to be sure. But in understanding better that humanity is like a single man who does not die, we also get more and more the sense of a growth and a real union. Thus the progress of social life itself develops in men's minds a new feeling of "humanity," a feeling that was almost unheard of in antiquity, whatever certain exceptional actions or a few verses of poets may indicate, a feeling that has now acquired, so to speak, a right of entry. Officially accepted into the concert of motives that influence the conduct of men and people, the feeling has enough control over public opinion to have already inspired a new form of hypocrisy or even a cult.

For ancient philosophy, the supreme effort had been to conceive, to define, to will the city; all is subordinate to it, both morality and religion. The political order is the symbol, or even the reality that contains the infinite object of the devotion of all; and notwithstanding a few heartfelt exceptions, the enemy started at the gates of the republic, just as within the city walls lived the foreigner within, the slave. Perhaps nowhere else can the difference between the ancient and the new spirit be seen more clearly. Even for Aristotle, everything speculative or practical, moral or religious, remains subordinate to politics as to the last end. The city is not a stage in the human edifice; it is the universal consummation. Where we now see only a level or a means, he found the highest term and the perfection of human action.

In only one ancient people, the Jewish people, did the patriotic cult coincide with the religious cult without, in spite of a monopolizing jealousy and a passionate exclusivism of the national spirit which tended to confiscate God, causing this great God to be restricted to the very dimensions of the "Chosen People" or forever reserved for itself alone. But also on what condition was this singular attitude possible? On the condition of anticipating a future of universal expansion, on the condition of considering the present, narrow and closed, as the symbol and the seed for an immense broadening of consciousness, on the condition of bearing in each act of national life the promise of all future humanity.

276

But following this childhood of our age and of history where egoism sees only the individual, where the individual knows only his family, thinking of it as incomparable and unique, where the family limits its horizon to the political life of the city, moral ideas have advanced little by little. Without abandoning patriotism and to preserve its flavor, man has had to learn to be more than a citizen in order to appreciate and love in others, not the relative, the friend, the compatriot, the guest, the stranger, or the ally, but the man whose only title is to be man; an unknown, an enemy perhaps, but a man. It is a great act and an admirable step of reason to have felt that in the slave, in the savage, in the pauper, in the diseased or the crippled, there is humanity itself. And how many remain incapable of seeing this? They say it is so because everyone says it; they know it in an abstract way; they may feel it; but with them this will for humanity does not go all the way to actions, to actions in conformity with the knowledge and the words.

Yet who knows what treasures of peace and unity the future holds! It seemed impossible that the social need for slavery could ever be eliminated: it has been. It seemed impossible that, toward an enemy on the battlefield, any consideration could be given; little by little a law of nations is being established which, violated though it may be, is forcing itself on the judgment of peoples. It seems impossible that war should disappear and that disarmament should come. But without hindrance to the beautiful diversity of national federations within the human confederation, again, who knows what treasures of peace and unity the future holds!

Moreover, under these developments of reflected consciousness, we must always uncover the secret will that vivifies them. They are only a growing effort to equal it. Even without a clear idea of the fact and without wanting to settle a decision on the feeling we may have for it, human action implies, in fact, the solidarity of men and expresses the unity of the species: a unity, moreover, in conformity with the mysterious continuity of generation which makes the same blood flow in all, which realizes in the one life of the child the double life of the parents, which, rather than divide them, draws them closer in multiplying them and perpetuates them both under the same bodily species. 277

Thus, issued at first from the quite personal intention of the agent, action has little by little incorporated the family and the city to take flight into humanity as a whole. In requiring the total solidarity of all men, it becomes what it wills to be; it wills to be, by free choice, what it is already by the impulse of its first *élan*. If, therefore, it seems to have imposed on it as a law the obligation of constituting itself as a universal maxim, if it is commanded that each one must act with the intention of doing what all should do, if we must have the feeling of bearing in our particular action the will and the action of others, that is only a translation, not only of what should be for the deliberate and willed will, but also of what is already for the willing and operative will. Indeed, whatever we do, humanity has an interest in the action of each individual as in a new element of the general equilibrium: the action whose origin man attributes to himself is one which could take place in the name of the entire species.

To be sure, it seems strange to say that in willing and acting we actually go beyond the family, the political, to attain and involve humanity as a whole in our action. But does not the ordinary end of our conscious decisions appear from the start, in the motive that determines them, as superior to all the domestic and political conditions wherein they are made? If the first sense of freedom and duty implies the idea of an end that transcends all the unconscious and conscious elements of action, it is because action itself envelops in its real expansion more than its individual and social conditions. Whether we know it or ignore it, voluntary action has a scope such that from its first flight it escapes the confines of domestic or political society. We cannot, we do not will to live only for ourselves, only for ours, only for our fellow citizens; thus, by the force of the continuous movement that bears it along, action will now cross over the very bounds of the human federation.

---

278   I propose to study the extension of action into the universal milieu that it involves and where it looks for the answers and the sanctions it aspires to; and I show how it goes through the various moral enclosures where some have claimed to contain it one after the other, as if it met there its definitive rule and its satisfying use. — I examine first what one may call naturalist morality, with the aim, not of refuting it, but of showing what is at once correct and insufficient about it. — Then I indicate how action, going beyond the order of nature, seems to require another field and as it were another world in which to unfold and to satisfy itself. — Finally, showing that this metaphysical morality does not yet satisfy the exigencies of the will and does not equal the expanse of action, I study "moral morality," the one which seems concerned only with determining the sufficient and necessary conditions of voluntary action, by seeking what are the postulates or the indispensable beliefs for scientifically grounding human conduct.

These diverse forms of "natural" morality seem, from the viewpoint of intention, irreconcilable and exclusive. Yet, in fact and from the viewpoint of action, they are reconciled and disposed in tiers, so to speak. So, in formulating them before reflected consciousness, we are only analysing more and more completely the content of the operative will, so as to arrive, in this chapter, at showing that the will overflows this moral domain, no matter how purified, how broad, how sublime we suppose it to be. In the operative will the real surpasses the ideal, the actual fact exceeds formal duty.

CHAPTER 2
The Universal Extension of Action

The tiered forms of natural morality

In acting, man does not limit his outlook to the family, to the city, to 279
humanity. He projects his intention still further. As the Stoics said quite
rightly, he inserts himself into the universe as a whole. Indeed, voluntary
action concerns the whole system, from which it has taken its nourishment and in which it claims to rule. Thus it is no wonder to see two apparently diverging tendencies converge in this need for universal solidarity: on the one hand, there is the egoistic aim of the individual will that
seeks always to fulfill and to satisfy itself, on the other, the infinitely
complex movement of general life whose immense apparatus seems to
crush all partial ends and the pretentions of the individual.

But it is all one and the same movement. And in spite of the fluctuations of human freedom, in spite of the diversity of conceptions, of
theories, or of moral habits, here again a determinism derived from the
willed act, whatever this act may be, develops the inevitable consequences of the premises posited by action itself. How then does man rise
to a disposition more and more disinterested and moral, without ceasing,
in losing sight of himself somehow, to work in the true direction of his
destiny, to contribute to his most certain interest, and to support, by the
intention and the science of what he is doing, the hidden aim that inspires
his voluntary actions?

I

To act is in a way to entrust oneself to the universe. Like avarice, 280
which loses everything in wanting to hold on to everything, the most
jealous egoism could not keep everything to itself without impoverishing
and wearing itself out, without ever succeeding in not letting go. For better and for worse, action is in its own way a speculation; that is why the

man of action is often like a gambler who, throughout his most careful calculations, is still only taking a chance. To dare to act, we need something like a love of risk and a forced detachment, even to the point of not talking yet of a free disinterestedness or a sincere abnegation.

Consistent with the necessary law of its development, utilitarianism is therefore forced to go beyond itself in some way. In fact, the individual will can find itself only through an infinite complexity wherein it seems to lose itself. Thus, through the feeling life gives us of the immense and obscure expanse wherein it runs its course, action inevitably takes on a character that we can already call *moral*. For it is not useful, it is not possible, for our conduct to be a pure calculation; it encompasses a field more vast than all reflected combinations. Also, after the ever broadening will has transported the center of its intention into the organic operation, from the organic operation into the exterior work, from the work into the intimacy of an allied will, from a uniquely loved heart into the love of the family and of the city, from exclusive and jealous affections into the universal assembly of human generations, it must still, by a new advance, seek its equilibrium in the whole system of the world. To act is the function of the whole. It is no longer a question of inserting our personal operation into the general determinism. On the contrary, it is an issue of inserting ourselves into it; of willing and admitting the action of this determinism into ourselves; of accepting and embracing what surpasses our foresight, our comprehension, our free disposition; of recognizing, under the interplay of phenomena, the inaccessible forces that produce them; and of consenting to receive from this mysterious power, which the positive sciences admit but do not encroach upon, the obscure dictates and the inspirations of moral experience.

Thus, even in what seems voluntary morality, we must find once again the necessary expansion and the natural result of the initial willing. The merit of determinist and utilitarian doctrines is to show that, where others saw only an ideal duty, there is already an inevitable fact. To bring this naturalist morality back to its true meaning, it is appropriate then to consider it under the following twofold aspect. — From one side, through the effect of an experimentation which nothing can replace and which nothing can suppress or prevent, action receives *a posteriori* the lessons of the milieu wherein it unfolds. It undergoes the reactions of the universal milieu and, by the very interplay of this living organism, conscience forms itself little by little, the secular tradition of practical rules is established, the fact of human morality rises perforce. — On the other hand, this fact becomes the consciousness of a duty; this constrained detachment is the way to an intentional disinterestedness; this *a posteriori* necessity results from the *a priori* movement of the will. For we interpret the lessons of experience only in the measure that we provoke them. We must therefore find out how the fact of the moral ideal inevitably emerges from practical empiricism under the influence of an inner aspiration.

I. —It is impossible to place abnegation at the end of self-interested calculation; it is no less impossible to find pleasure and profit without fail at the term of a real self-sacrifice. This world is too complicated for us not to lose, in this labyrinth, the thread of our practical deductions. Utilitarian arithmetic is an illusion; and the egoist usually goes against his aim. Our action is never ours alone; we have to cast our acts, like our dearest treasure, before strangers, before ingrates, before robbers. Good and evil mixed together, indifference and apparent disorder in the chaos of universal life, that is the evidence of the facts: it is immorality itself.

And yet, through a system of obscure compensations and by the confused reaction of all the intermingled forces, broad lines are drawn in the consciousness of humanity; a conception and a meaning of life arises within us. It seems that only the beginning of our actions is in our power and, in running their course, they envelop within the tissue of their consequences even the future use of our apparent freedom. But from this fatal concatenation, nothing comes out which was not germinally in the act originally planted. Circumstances modify our nature less than they pull it out of its original indetermination; and without creating anything new in us, they reveal to us what, unknown to us, we bore within ourselves. The longer the web of acts becomes, the more rigidly a tighter determinism envelops us; and this exterior constraint still proceeds from ourselves, even when, turning against our aims, the responsibility hidden at the heart of concessions or our apparently most insignificant failings robs us of our independence, peace, honor, in usurious payment for our secret debts.

In this way, from the trial of life come maxims, empirical precepts, and folk "moralities" that seem to sum up the wisdom of centuries and nations. To determine more precisely and rigorously the law of necessary repercussions and the consequences of human actions, to explain the formation of moral notions that hold sway at a given time and in a country, to regulate their movement and hasten their progress through the consciousness of them it brings forth, that seems to be the object of the science of morals (*science des moeurs*)—a truly scientific morality, which, independent of all recourse to freedom and of every particular view of obligation, is grounded on the determinism of actions and total reactions.

282

And to maintain its scientific character, the science of morals must take the viewpoint, not of the individual, nor even of society, but of the whole. Human conduct does not find its organization within the confines of clear consciousness; individual life is not concerted within the limits of individuality. We must cast our action into the immensity of things, therefore, and await the response from this very immensity. Action is a call and an echo from the infinite. It comes from it and goes to it. Here, science can only be practical, that is, founded on a real experimentation regarding the impenetrable complexity of life. Morals (*les moeurs*) do not in fact have their rule in what we know of ourselves, in what we are clearly conscious of willing and doing, but in themselves.

283 And let no one think either that this universal mechanism gives back exactly what was entrusted to it. To disinterestedness there is no corresponding benefit of nature charged with being interested on our behalf. What foolishness, this so-called immanent justice! What childishness, to think that the world sees to it that natural virtues are rewarded, even within the narrow confines where empirical egoism operates. There is a forced disinterestedness in the source as well as in the results of an act. Moreover, even when we are convinced that only the consequences of actions are important, nothing is more "scientific" than to be detached from the consequences themselves, in order to follow the indications of conscience which are already a lesson provided by action. Face the task, then, without asking in vain eagerness: "To what end, what is it worth?" Acts are like the stones of an unknown edifice, where it is better to be a laborer humbly than to raise ourselves to play the architect, because the overall plan escapes our eyes and the common experiences of practical life remain mysterious to our reason like those worn-out flagstones we do not even look at but on which all our steps rest.

Moreover, how important it is to shelter moral science from empirical sanctions as well as from rationalizing reason (*raison raisonneuse*) and individual fantasies! For if we thought that "conscience" is subject to the court of dialectics, that would be the end of it. Nothing is more perilous here than logical deductions, clear and distinct ideas, over-simplification. The vital beliefs of man result from prolonged probings, from innumerable trials and, so to speak, from a slow accumulation: there is more wisdom and foresight summed up in them than in the systems of the most brilliant geniuses or in the most profound thoughts of an entire academy. What we call the moral ideal is, in one sense, only an extract and an anticipation of experience, a postulate or hypothesis necessary for the interpretation of facts, or rather a real and progressive adaptation of action and of consciousness to the conditions of life. This legitimate appropriation is the empirical rule of practice, for practical reason here does not dogmatize starting from abstract conceptions on which it would pretend to model, once and for all, all consciences and all societies. It takes shape little by little and renews itself interiorly by the very movement of general evolution. So, viewed under this aspect, morality is the summation and the always provisional and changing conclusion not only of humanity, but of the entire universe.

The ideas regulating conduct, then, are not a sudden revelation, but a slow crystallization of the total experience and like the expression of   284 our social sense, of the meaning of universal life in us. After a period of probings and instability, actions become fixed; they seem to be demanded of us by something outside of ourselves, by the common interest, by the truth of real relations, by the total system of the world where they are inserted. Thus, the character of obligation they appear to take on is explained, in fact, by the necessary synthesis and the spontaneous compensations of actions that combine and correspond with one another. Morals (*les moeurs*) are not simply generalized individual habits. If there is an action of the individual on society and of society on the individual, we must especially take the influence of society on society itself into account. This is to say that morals create morals, that one social fact derives from other social and collective facts where feeling has a greater part than clear ideas; and that individual action is not enough to organize the life of the individual, because in practical logic there is always more than abstract analysis can discover in it.

That is why morality is not just an art, a question of tact and delicacy, a virtuosity of consciousness in a few privileged individuals, a matter of taste, or a decree of the proper sense of things. It is a science that develops from age to age according to laws, as real relations and the adjustment of ordinarily solidary actions are established in fact and are recognized by reflexion. The true role of the science of morals is to make man see that he is not a whole, but the part of a whole; it is to study the conditions of the immense society wherein he mixes his life, and to formulate what is necessary for partial and total existence. It is a science of the social composite, in order to be a science of the individual composite. For action seeks out, from the law of the whole, the secret of the rhythm of the parts: it is the projection, into one point, of the complex unity.

Thus we can explain how the science of morals, without leaving the real somehow, proposes a kind of ideal, and without recourse to the intervention of freedom, justifies its own existence and its usefulness by showing the positive conditions of social functioning; through this very knowledge it influences individual consciousness. Thus also we can see to what extent economic organization escapes or lends itself to reflected reforms: society is not a machine moved from the outside, but a living

285 thing that moves itself from the inside; not an automaton constructed by force of calculation and reflexion, but an organism wherein is found a mutual reaction of clear ideas and unconscious influences, a balancing of social functions and individual habits. Consequently, in the perpetual work of maintaining and reforming moral and social "virtues," room must be made at once for reason and for nature, for morals and for law, for private initiative and for public action. To be sure, we cannot radically transform what is necessary and natural in the play of human life; and yet these rules have a flexibility and, so to speak, an indefinite elasticity. To the point that, with our brutal violations, we never hit against brutal impossibilities or immediate denials.

Hence, since the springs of this immense mechanism are too numerous for the most penetrating look, for the most powerful hand to discern and manipulate all of them; since we reach only the nearer consequences of our actions and not all their ramifications in the depths of the organized body; since it would take a miraculous perspicacity to unravel in detail, for example, how egoism is its own enemy; since acts, diffused and amplified in the universal organism, return to consciousness charged with a new richness the complete inventory of which is impossible to make, it follows that the sincere and consistent will has no other recourse, in order to have an intimation of and to attain the hidden goal it aims at, but to hand itself over in a way blindfolded to this great flow of ideas, feelings, moral rules that have emerged little by little from human actions through the strength of tradition and the accumulation of experiences. Already repudiated in the name of practical sincerity, man's revolt against his "conscience" must therefore be condemned in the name of science itself.

II. — From the fact itself the conception of law arises. But is it the fact that engenders it? No. If the dark lessons of experience teach us that the search of egotistic self-interest appears as the worst of calculations and that the best way to attain happiness is not to pursue it because the direct way does not work, disinterestedness remains no less real from the mo-
286 ment when, no matter what we do, we must hand ourselves over to the universal machinery without knowing exactly what it will give us back. Let intention bring more or less free generosity to it, it remains always true that to act we must begin by being detached from ourselves. In any human enterprise, there is an element of forced abnegation.

But let no one be mistaken about the necessary generation of this disinterestedness which confers an already moral character on the act: nothing is more delicate than this light but infinitely complex web of emerging morality. And as awakening each morning is mysterious, the rise of conscience in each one of us seems as elusive as the changing light in the dawning of day. Yet, as it was possible to explain the inevitable genesis of freedom, it is equally possible and necessary to explain the inevitable production of this minimum of morality, which, in spite of all abuses and all possible abdications, remains one of the specific characteristics of what has been called the human Kingdom.

If in the consciousness of action there is more than in action itself, if the reason for a voluntary operation is found only in the conception of an end distinct from its efficient causes, then, this end must itself also in turn appear as higher than the practical experiences it inspires. In the realized ideal an ulterior ideal is perpetually reborn, like the mirage of water that recedes as we go forward. That is how the positive practice of life unceasingly projects before it a *should* (*devoir*) at once ideal and real, real because, grounded in already constituted experience, it draws from it its operative force, but truly ideal because within action itself it sets off what is never reducible to the simple fact.

Here then are the terms of the problem: from merely pulling them together the solution will result.

(1) In acting, the will quite spontaneously is seeking itself; that is the impulse of its first sincerity; that is the reason for its expansion.

(2) In pursuing a goal, whatever it may be, action is forced to abandon itself to the immense, to the impenetrable power of the entire universe. Whatever precautions he may take, whatever science he may have, the man of action, by an anonymous devotedness, hands himself over to the great universal experience from which he may not profit.

(3) In searching for itself, the will is therefore constrained to become more or less detached from itself. It can serve itself and rule only by seeming to abdicate, by truly abdicating. The most intense life is the one with the greatest extension. And the only way to bear individual action up to its highest degree of force and fecundity is not to insulate it by itself, but to spread it out and to sacrifice it to all: a generosity which is neither a blind and foolish passion for risk, nor a calculation of foresight, but which expresses, under a still incomplete form, man's most profound, his most reasonable aim. The normal will is therefore an impersonal and universal will which tends to identify with the common life and to bring to it, without afterthought, its own disinterested contingent.

(4) Between what wills and what is willed, between what acts and what is done, therefore, there is really a world that passes. That is why what starts from us and what comes back to us are incommensurable things. Seen from the origin, the movement of action proceeds from a self-love; seen at the return, it takes on the contrary aspect. And it is because he tends to come back toward himself from the beginning that

287

man inevitably recognizes to what extent what comes back to him did not start from him. The consciousness of and the necessity for disinterestedness presuppose, therefore, a first impulse of self-love, a need for growth, a naive search for self.

(5) From this it results that self-interest and disinterestedness are equally real and equally grounded in the determinism of moral life. It is quite true that the primitive basis in every action is a love of the agent for the agent. And it is quite true that, to act according to this very love, we must expose and give ourselves. People have tried in vain to reduce all apparent endeavors of the heart to secret ingenuities of egoism: subtleties of moralists! No one can succeed in bringing the reduction to term. And even if one could ever succeed, it would still remain true that even the illusory consciousness of disinterestedness consecrates a real disinterestedness. For it is in the impossibility of connecting the point of arrival back to the point of departure with certainty that a principle of detachment resides. Even supposing that we had demonstrated in an abstract and general way that devoted abnegation coincides with utility (a conclusion moreover that is as illusory as the proof), we would not thereby have persuaded the consciousness of everyone that it will be so for every encounter and for every detail of life. In fact, even egotistical action remains a risk and a speculation.

288 (6) Thus we can explain how it is that disinterested maxims have a purchase on the will, that the ideal motive has a real efficaciousness, that, without denaturing it, an attractive mover joins itself to this apparently quite arid motive, and that moral autonomy allows for a heteronomy. It is true at once that nature deceives us and that virtue is not a trickery; grounded in fact, disinterestedness needs nothing from the fact. Our spiritual richness is formed beyond the order of nature. It seemed impossible to understand why and how the universality of a purely formal precept could interest and move us. Here is the explanation. Under the most absolute and most sincere disinterestedness subsists always, not to vitiate it, but to render it possible and active, the fundamental ambition of the personal will.

(7) Moreover, though sprung from a primitive self-love, detachment remains no less genuine; though tied into the reality of facts, the necessary conception of an ideal presents consciousness nonetheless with a duty higher than the facts. Just as the determinism of efficient causes, at the first awakening of reflexion, had projected before us an end to be pursued, here again with greater force, the mechanism of life brings forth a motive higher than the very facts that prepare the knowledge of it. Action, therefore, hangs from an effective finality without which the preliminary concatenation of means would not even be intelligible.

(8) In this way the will takes up within itself and ratifies, not just the appearances of the universal determinism, but the universal reality that is its source. It had already accepted its objective truth, to the extent that science takes it over and rules therein; henceforth it accepts its intimate and inaccessible power, to the extent that this universe fashions and hammers the individual himself, his thought and his weak action. So, it is no longer an issue of simply consenting to the elementary conditions of reflexive knowledge and of freedom, therefore, nor even of admitting the action of other concurring forces and of a milieu whose cooperation contributes to the success of personal initiative. We must somehow become this determinism and this very milieu, in order to conspire as a whole with the whole immensity of the mystery of nature. The center of individual action thus seems to be transported to infinity. In this way the will, whose development despite its growing amplitude seemed to remain always concentric, becomes so to speak eccentric to itself; as if the circumference, going beyond its limit, which is the straight line, turned to form itself around another infinitely distant point.

289

(9) No need to delude ourselves with the vain illusion of a "universal consciousness," or lend a living and rational soul to the "Great Whole." It is to give the necessary disinterestedness of the human act a false interpretation to imagine that it must be profitable to others. Of course, there is grandeur in handing ourselves over to the forces of the universe, with the feeling that one and the same law governs the movement of the stars and the secret dispositions of the heart; of course, it is generous to be resigned to nature's hidden reason; it is grand to consent to absolve all its apparent cruelties and to love all its work by reason of the magnanimity it affords man as he throws his own life in as fodder for it; of course, the Stoic sage, ready to die for a virtue that is not to be recompensed, can find the joy of dying well, even if it lasts only as long as a flash, which is preferable to the mediocrity of a long and dull existence; of course, to satisfy noble and tender and proud hearts, the haughty pleasure of a renewed quietism that wants no sanction is already a sanction. Yet all that is illusion. The pleasure of being tricked, of knowing that we are, of wanting to be, does not prevent the fact that we are. Moral disinterestedness does not gravitate around all these beautiful, subtle, and pretentious fantasies. The reason for it is not found outside ourselves; it is in the personal will and by it that, in each one of us, is effected the immense synthesis which arrives at this inevitable detachment. But the sense or the term of this disinterested movement has not yet been found.

(10) Thus little by little the profound aspiration of man is unveiled; thus the series of means by which he seeks his end is laid out. The entire order of nature enters into the field of his experience. All that he receives

from it *a posteriori*, he was already soliciting *a priori*. What he is looking
for is the very definition of his own self-interest. Indeed, what must he
understand by his self-interest? He crosses the universe without meeting
it. Therefore, he loses interest in the universe. The world has an ambiguous character; conscience is not at home in it. Something above it
is required to explain it and to add a meaning to it. Naturalist morality,
useful in underlining the continuity of life's progress and the awakening
of conscience, hangs therefore from a new form of thought and action,
a metaphysical morality. By an original initiative, the human spirit, beyond the actual world, quite naturally supposes another one, an ideal
world.

290

II

As in the least sensation we are inclined to seek beyond for what it is,
always also, in one form or another, we attribute an ulterior meaning to
our own life. What experience does not give us, we claim to find or to
place in it. We seem to borrow from the whole of reality something to
help us see that it is not what it ought to be, that it is not what we will
it to be. From facts, therefore, man inevitably rises to rights, even when
he seems to identify or subordinate the one to the other. This necessary
generation of at least an implicit metaphysics is what we must now explain. Even where we have the most complete experience possible, there
is always something which, for illuminating and regulating action, surpasses experience itself.

Whence do these metaphysical conceptions arise? How do they intervene in the organism of human life? What is their role and their bearing? — It is actually a property of man to create universal notions, in
order to conform his feelings and his conduct to them, in order to adapt
the facts to them. But this metaphysics with which we ordinarily claim
to constitute a separate order, a sovereign and absolute order, perhaps
an illusory order, must at this point be forced, so to speak, back into the
ranks. The originality of its position is to be, not a more or less definitive
or fictitious end, but a rung in the series of ends sought after. The
idolatry of the understanding is all too ready to make of it the whole, the
god; metaphysics is not *everything*; it is *something* in the dynamic progress of the will; it forms a level in the determinism of action and is like
a new phenomenon which, tied to the others, has its own efficaciousness.
It is a passageway which allows the movement of life, by moving itself.

What is true, original, and efficacious in metaphysics can be summed
up, then, in the following three propositions that we will have to justify
briefly. (1) Metaphysics has an experimental ground; it is nourished from

291

the whole of reality. (2) It subordinates actual facts to facts which *are not*, in the positive sense that the former *are*; it prolongs the world of nature into a world of thought that becomes for it the reason and the law. (3) What is not, it affirms and practices so that it will be; the act thus becomes a naturalization of the possible in the real. Metaphysics, therefore, is a dynamic. It starts from facts, to return to facts, but to facts of a higher order. It leads man inevitably to draw the principle of his conduct elsewhere than from the universe. Into the rhythm of life that goes from action to action, it inserts thought, a fruit and a seed of a more perfect will. Thus the ideas that metaphysics organizes into systems are at once — real, because they express to consciousness the multiple reactions which sight does not reach at the heart of the universal life in us; — ideal, because as they shed light on actual experience, and surpass it, they prepare the coming decisions; — practical, because they have an indubitable influence on the orientation of voluntary acts.

(1) That these metaphysical ideas are real and grounded in fact has to be understood properly. Thought is not isolated from the world of phenomena wherein consciousness draws its nourishment. What was true of images and quite spontaneous desires, must be repeated with greater force and in a fuller sense with regard to the highest conceptions of reflected thought. Enriched as it is by all the growth of organic, social, and universal life, this thought gathers in the teaching of this immense experimentation. Thus, in this focus of the idea born of action, is found a concentration of all the scattered rays and a kind of summary of the whole of reality. But how are we brought to conceive, beyond the facts, something else again? Whence this necessity for projecting outside ourself, outside the world, what is not in them? And if it is true that there is in metaphysics an experimental truth, by what determinism are we led to extract from what is not given in fact a principle of total explanation for the facts themselves?

In the spontaneous life of consciousness, the very mechanism of efficient causes brings up, as we saw, a final cause, a cause which by its synthetic character is in advance of the still blind powers which it takes over for its own benefit. In the reflected development of voluntary action, a similar labor takes place in a more distinct way: from the very interplay of life comes a conception that seems higher than life, like an objective ideal. If it is true that human practice furnishes the material for a positive science of morals and constitutes an experimentation without which the most subtle deductions would remain in a vacuum, it becomes necessary to add that our conduct organizes itself only in the light of a total idea and by projecting the complete reason for its production in the form of a final end to be attained.

Why this need of unity in the total explanation? And why this "objective" projection of the conceived ideal? It is because action cannot be partial, abstract, or provisional, as science can be. We act really *sub specie totius* (under the aspect of the whole). As we achieve a more clear consciousness and a freer possession of our acts, we tie them to a more universal principle. Activity and sociability are in direct proportion to one another; and whether we see personal life as a synthesis pregnant with the mysterious dynamism of nature, or look on the universe as a vast society on the way to being formed, as a federation of consciousnesses that are awakening or a concurrence of wills seeking themselves and finding themselves little by little, always action seems inspired by and referred, not to what there is of each in all, but to what there is of all in each. This total unity of an action inserted into the whole must be found finally in the consciousness of it which we come to more and more clearly; and that is why any deliberate way of living contains at least the beginning of a metaphysics. Action is, if we may so speak, universalist; the consciousness that expresses it and the thought that claims to govern it become equally universalist.

And because action always brings new nourishment to thought, as thought brings new lights to action, this moving circle does not stop and does not close in on itself. Speculation and practice are always at once in advance and in arrears of one another, but with the perpetual pretense of coming together and equalling one another. They do not succeed in doing so, and this necessary disproportion has a necessary repercussion in the system of our thoughts. For if life is the true school of life, in the same way that all the waters of the river already come from the Ocean
293 where they return again and always, then the center of equilibrium on which depends all this movement of thought and action can only be found higher, it seems, as it is the sun which raises the waters of the sea up to the summit from which fecundity comes down. Thus man quite naturally projects above himself a kind of "unmoved mover."

And the conception of this ideal finality manifests, not the insufficiency or the penury of a needy will, but the superabundance of an interior life which does not find in the entire universe the wherewithal to spend the whole of itself. This metaphysical order is not outside the will like an alien end to be reached; it is in it like a means to go beyond. It does not represent a truth already constituted in fact, but it sets up what we could will to will as an ideal object before thought. It does not express an absolute and universal reality, but the universal aspiration of a particular will. Every human thought, therefore, is a metaphysics, indeed a singular and unique metaphysics.

To be sure, these directive ideas of life are not constituted in each individual or for each individual; they are formed in society and by the communion of all with everything. Nevertheless, as each human personality is organized through determinations that are more and more a result of reflexion, the transcription of these determinate and organized actions into an at least implicit metaphysics becomes more and more personal for each one. As reflexion comes to govern the system of acts and thoughts more, it seems that the abstract principles acquire more efficaciousness and that life is conformed better to an absolute rule; men of thought are persuaded of it; but, at the same time, the principles themselves reflect more faithfully the spontaneous tendencies and the moral habits of the one applying them. We think we are submitting to truth: but also we are submitting it to ourselves; we make ourselves our own truth. And the more ideas influence practice, still more does practice influence ideas.

In life, everyone finds what he puts into it: reality is ambiguous. If you scandalize one, you edify another; one is enlightened and another is blinded or hardened by the same lessons. To understand events, we must find within ourselves something to interpret them by. *Omnia sana sanis* (everything is healthy for the healthy). Inclined as we are to maximize our conduct and to justify what we have done because we did it, we are all, in our judgments on ourselves and on others, great idealists. In the light of conscience, then, through feeling and the immediate effect of action, there is something more real than the real.   294

(2) Whatever may be the origin, whatever may be the particular form of the master-ideas man places over his life, each one of us necessarily has his own metaphysics; and this metaphysics, no matter how futile we imagine it, has a necessary influence, a proper efficaciousness.

Even though, unknown to us, our seemingly most theoretical and most impersonal conceptions derive from hidden moral dispositions, speculation nevertheless maintains a certain independence: its development is autonomous. The system engendered by learned reflexion has an original evolution according to the laws of a quite rational dialectic. It is true that this transcendent character of metaphysics should not make us forget its experimental origins; for, under the pretense of cutting it loose and purifying it, to sever the bond that ties it to lived life would be to weaken it. It would be like hoping the kite will stay up better without the tight string that keeps it tied to the mobile hand of the child. But if the ideas with which metaphysics forms its synthesis have their roots in practice, they do grow above the ground out of which they come; they serve to disengage the will from its shackles; they express its initiative and its progress; they present to the will, under the figure of regulative and "objective" notions, the summary of the conquests made, the symbol of conquests to be made, what it wills already and what it wills to will, what it aspires to be and to acclimatize in the growing spontaneity of moral life. From this viewpoint, knowledge seems one step ahead of reality, and that is the reason why, beyond the given and known facts, we are led to construct that ideal order which explains them and which is like the *a priori* truth of all things.

Let no one remain indifferent, therefore, or even hostile to the often-times complicated labor of dialectics. Underneath their abstract formulas, these meditators keep a profound sense of life, undaunted as they are by any subtlety when it is a question of making more precise their reasons for affirming and for believing. They know there is no durable influence, no penetrating lesson, no directive teaching, unless one has dug deep for subterranean foundations at the risk of sinking into darkness, as if one had to pierce through the earth all the way in order to find light on the other side. Man loves abstractions: he speaks evil of them, he scoffs at them, but he does not get along without them. While he is chasing them away and exterminating them, they still govern him.

No doubt, there is an infinity of ways to carry on this abstract dialectic, and this reasoning reason (*raison raisonnante*) can become a terrifying power of dissolution, if it does not become a force for building up. Inasmuch as it is the fruit and the expression, in the order of thought, of an entire intellectual, moral, and social state, all the imperfections of an incomplete and halting life ordinarily vitiate it in its source; and perhaps already compromised by this sort of original sin, it is further exposed to the risks of its own growth. Thus, divided in life, men are often more so in thought. There has to be a practical unity of belief and action, in spite of the inevitable divergences and the necessary variety of what is living and what is free, for minds to rally together and enter into concert with one another in the intellectual unity of a "School." For those who are already united, thought then becomes a principle of more perfect union. But the issue here is not to explain the chaos of metaphysical systems, nor to determine the principles of a true dialectic, nor to seek for the conditions of agreement between intelligences.

The issue is, on the contrary, leaving aside as always the variables science does not have to be concerned with, to discern the element common to every metaphysical enterprise, whatever it be. What is the result for man of having formed these regulative ideas and what is the necessary role of these conceptions in his life?

(3) From the moment when we have conceived the unity of a universal explanation and when behind the fact we posit something else, be it the fact itself redoubled in some way by a negative reflexion (as Positivism tried to do in prohibiting all investigation into causes and facts), our life

too is tied into this explanation of things. If in voluntary action there is something principal, central, or total that a metaphysical transcription presents to reflected thought, in return every conception that takes on a character of universality embraces action and ends up in practice. A complete system becomes an ethic. In one sense, to be sure, action goes from thought to thought; but at the same time, speculative knowledge is only a form of transition in the progress of voluntary living; for thought starts from action to go to action.

Thus do we enter little by little more deeply into the secret laboratory 296 where the ever enriching exchange takes place from thought to life and from life to thought. Every great philosophy, far from being simply a construction of the mind, has its principle and its end in a conception of human destiny: practice directs it and in turn it directs practice. Every idea that does not proceed from a real experimentation of the will is dead and mere word; dead especially and fictitious, all knowledge that does not turn to acting. And if every deliberate form of conduct implies within us a solution to the human problem, more truly still every metaphysics prepares and postulates in some way a practice which is its fruit. We are led by our ideas, more than we lead them; and that is as it ought to be, because they enter into the determinism chosen by the will and contribute to developing its consequences.

The originality of metaphysics, therefore, is to prepare action to draw its true motive outside of everything already realized in nature or in the agent himself. It proposes to thought what is neither positive nor real, and proposes it as more real than the real, because that is what should be done, what is already included in the ambition of human willing. Not that we should conclude that metaphysics is the category of the unreal; that would be to misconstrue everything. For metaphysics bears in itself all that is objective and all that is subjective, as the necessary elements of the ulterior synthesis it forms. It is a new phenomenon, but pregnant with all the others. It has a double foundation, then, in what is done and in what is not yet done.

Thus, in grasping all the natural order in his development, man gathers from it, in the form of a more comprehensive thought, the notion of an ideal order which, grounded relatively on universal reality, seems to ground it absolutely in surpassing it. We must not separate thought from the life that sustains its fecundity; nor must we reduce metaphysics to being only a prolongation of the empirical order and a kind of superfluous luxury or an impasse, far removed from the general current of voluntary activity; nor must we make of it a substantial absolute, a definitive and fixed object. Ideas are efficacious only because they come from where life is laboring obscurely; but they would have no effica-

297 ciousness if they did not contain something other, than that of which
they are the expression. Issued from practice, speculative reason tends to
become a practical reason, but remaining still a reason, that is, by adding
to the facts a principle capable of explaining and directing them. It is one
and the same will that leads man to involve in his action the whole of
the real order, the same will that brings him to posit over the given reality
a new reality, and still the same will that inclines him to seek in this new
order a direction and a practical rule.

Such is the rank, such is the necessary role of speculative conceptions.
They are a particular synthesis of the universal reality digested and incorporated into thought by action. They express for distinct consciousness
the intimate sense and the profound orientation of the will. We must consider them, then, not as a world of fixed and separate entities, χωρίς
(apart), but as the eminent truth of what is already realized and as the
moving reason of what is on the way to being done. Metaphysics has its
substance in the acting will. It has truth only under this experimental and
dynamic aspect. It is a science less of what is than of what causes to be
and to become. The ideal of today can be the real of tomorrow. But the
ideal lives on always, and it is always the same one, more or less
misunderstood, that rises as humanity grows.

Moreover, although metaphysics remains mobile, although it is simply
transitive, like all the phenomena of life and of thought studied up to
now, we can say that it determines what, in the real, already surpasses
the fact, indeed what is relatively fixed, absolute, and transcendent, what
voluntary action necessarily adds to the given reality to constitute itself,
what in a word composes the permanent contribution of thought and
reason in the knowledge of the world and in the organization of human
life.

III

Undoubtedly, the science that determines the ideas without which the
real order would not be intelligible or possible has a sufficiency and a certitude of its own. But it is not limited to be the regulative science of the
298 understanding. In establishing that given reality does not explain or sustain itself by itself, that it is in fact suspended from an order higher than
the facts, that it does not exhaust the movement of thought because it
does not equal the content of human action, metaphysics is led to become
itself also a moving science; it requires a new form of action.

Indeed, these ideas that emerge from scientific or practical experience,
precisely because they cannot be contained therein and because they

overflow the actual, express what does not come from nature in voluntary action, what the will still wills once it has assimilated the real order in its entirety, what it aspires to be and to realize, because *that is not* and because *that must be* for it to become what the movement of sincerity imperiously inclines it to desire. The issue, then, is to incorporate into voluntary action this ideal order that is the transcendent end of the natural order. This is to say that the will is led to place the center of its equilibrium outside of all reality given in fact, to live somehow on its own, and to look within itself alone for the purely formal reason for its act. Thus it is by what is unreal in it that it will increase its fecundity.

There is, then, in voluntary action more than scientific knowledge, more than subjective life as it is revealed by consciousness, more than the universal reality which naturalist morality or metaphyics itself feed upon. And it is this additional element which we must now conquer for reflexion by analysing the conditions and the exigencies of properly moral action.

I. — How does a moral consciousness inevitably arise in man? The natural science of morals can prepare the way for it; but such an independent morality does not even begin to produce it. Metaphysical conceptions may serve as antecedent conditions by fixing an ideal and raising the right above the fact; but such a rational morality is not moral. How then will there come to be a *moral* Morality?

The moral fact, even in its most embryonic form, is not a fact like others. For the first notion of morality to be a phenomenon of consciousness, for the very idea of right to be a fact, for the sense of practical obligation to rise as an imperative before the will, we must first have learned to place the true motive of our conduct elsewhere than in the facts. It is through the mediation of an implicit metaphysics that duty appears to consciousness as a reality. In the phenomenon of a conscious obligation (whether put in practice or not, it matters little), a synthesis of the real and the ideal is effected. 299

But this synthesis itself becomes something other and independent. In practice illuminated by reason, there is a new mystery, as there was one in thought in relation to nature. It is a mistake then to try to ruin metaphysics in order to build morality up; the solidarity of phenomena remains as indissoluble as their heterogeneity is certain. They have among them determinate and hierarchical relations. Thus it is right to enthrone morality on metaphysics, like a queen. It is right to think that there is no need to know the obscure origins of this practical consciousness to be obliged by it. It is right to suspect that, under the subtleties of intellectual errors, is often hidden the simplicity of willful failings. It is right to maintain that, in a state of doubt, it is not justified to abstain and that, in the face of obvious honesty, there is no speculative objection that holds. It is right to think that the great regulative truths of life are required by morality rather than have morality required by them. It is right to recognize that there is more in the system of practical postulates than in the system of metaphysical hypotheses, for action always reaches further than speculation.

However enlightened consciousness may be by the lessons of practical experimentation, however rich we may suppose it to be with empirical data and metaphysical clarities, knowledge stops short then, sooner or later, but always inevitably, before the mystery which the eye of the mind does not penetrate. Beyond the most ample horizons of thought there are unknown terrains; our ideas always fall short in some fashion; the best knit systems, far from ever succeeding in cornering infinite truth, let fall back into the night something of what they claimed to enclose in their light. But where vision ends, does action also end? Not at all. And if man launches out into the uncertain, if it is for what is uncertain that he sometimes gives his life, it is in order to draw from action itself a new certitude. Action always crosses a dark region; it enters into the cloud to find more light beyond. Obscurity, even unconsciousness, is a principle of movement; and that is why the most generous, the ones most enamored of infinity and mystery, are not, regardless of what we think ordinarily, the great dreamers, but rather the dedicated and the active, who are more mystical than the mystics themselves. To act morally, we can, without neglecting anything vital, prescind from all human science other than conscience. The light is not in back, it is in front. The method of discovery and progress resides more in action than in thought.

Metaphysics thus serves to open up an abyss between nature and morality. For, once reflexion, through the initiative of spontaneous life itself, rises to the conception of an ideal order, once we have understood that there is more in human action than all of nature can offer, once the will takes over what is autonomous and transcendent within it, it is no longer in the real facts, nor even in the ideas that regulate the understanding, that man seeks support and finds the end for his conduct. It is in practice alone that he aspires to equal the amplitude of his acting will. And henceforth, action (far from seeming a phenomenon conditioned by an infinity of other antecedents, whether objective or subjective matters little) appears as conditioning all the rest. Considered in all its purity apart from facts and ideas, action commands and produces the ideas and the facts; it organizes itself freely; it creates the organs of its necessary functions.

Let no one speak, then, of the supremacy of action and of the sovereign autonomy of the will as if, in order to maintain this primacy of practical reason, we had to isolate voluntary action from nature and break the bond of speculative thought with moral practice. The opposite is the truth; there is a correlation between what has too often been opposed. It is by operating in nature and in looking for itself therein that the will is led to place outside the real order a system of metaphysical truths; and it is because these conceptions still harbor an impenetrable virtuality — impenetrable to thought which stops there, but accessible to the movement of action — that the will sets itself free, without denying its origins, and freely pursues in this new domain its moral *a priori* syntheses.

Thus the distinction and the solidarity of the positive order, the metaphysical order, and the moral order are a direct function of one another. We have to find our duties in what happens to us and not in what we imagine might have been. The down-to-earth of daily life, that is the field to be fecundated. And here, as everywhere else, it is effective action that is the great mediator; it manages to reconcile what, from the static viewpoint of knowledge, for a critical or idealist philosophy, is mutually exclusive in a formal way. On the one hand, indeed, it is action that draws, from nature worked over and digested, the ideal order in which all the surplus of the will expresses itself; on the other hand, it is action still which digs the tunnel between the ideas regulating the understanding and moral truths. From nature to pure thought, from thought to practice, then, there is an uninterrupted passage. They are heterogeneous but solidary phenomena. And what should be surprising about that? In dealing with metaphysical conceptions or practical obligations, did we not consider them, like all the rest, in relation to the consciousness where they are engendered and the action which produces them in the interior light as phenomena of the will? One side expresses more completely than the other what we will. Both sides are but means subordinated to an end which we cannot yet distinctly recognize or deliberately will.

II. — Because moral action finds within itself something that comes neither from nature nor from thought, in proportion as it feeds on itself through practice, it becomes more acutely conscious of its relative autonomy. The issue, then, is no longer to explain the consciousness of obligation, much less to ground it on an absolute; the issue is to discover what this sense of duty implies and grounds, and to develop the determinism of practical reason. It is no wonder, then, that the will, henceforth more fully in possession of itself, creates and projects before it, under the form of postulates, new phenomena, original phenomena that are known, not as integrating elements or determining causes, but as final causes and subsequent conditions of moral action. They are its necessary sequel and production.

Of these practical truths required by voluntary action, the first is the very definition of duty. To define it is not to step out of determinism nor to appeal to the variable intervention of any free decision. It is to recognize and to describe the phenomena just as they necessarily appear before consciousness. We can construct practical morality without appealing to free will; it is something to be practised: it is necessary, that is all. Whether it be practised or not, whether it be this or that, whether it be even practicable in fact, that is not the question. To be sure, according to customs and ideas, the notion of what is good has varied infinitely; nothing is more relative than the moral absolute. But there remains an absolute: always, there is an order to be maintained. How is this order determined? Through the necessary sequence of the successive conquests of the will. There are natural relations and a hierarchy of functions whose law it is, for the sincere and consistent will, to follow the orientation and to respect the gradation. Neither the form nor the matter of moral obligation, then, is the expression of an imperative without roots in real life, of a mysterious and arbitrary commandment. Duty is neither a given fact nor an order blindly imposed on consciousness; it is a necessary postulate of the will, no longer as the will posits itself at the beginning, but as it has unfolded and enriched itself little by little through its continuous expansion; duty is an inevitable production of the will. The multiple and growing heteronomy of primitive freedom is quite in conformity with its most profound wish and serves only to guarantee its real autonomy more and more.

If then, from this culminating point, we turn back toward all that has gone before, what do we see in summary through this reversal of perspective? We discover more and more completely how the will has successively grounded all the forms of thought, how it underpins all the productions of life. Far from the moral truths proceeding from positive facts, it is the phenomena that are linked to the reality of action and hang from it; what makes their solidity is that they are willed as the field where freedom germinates and fructifies. Action has been the ever present bond of the successive syntheses that have constituted this ample system of phenomena whose levels we have just indicated; and what, in this ascending march, appeared as a necessary development of determinism, appears, to the descending look of reflexion, as a hierarchy of obligatory relations and of duties to be consecrated by an accepted practice. Moral freedom is thus the goal and the realizing form of the natural order.

Hence, through the growth of the seed sown by the voluntary act, a 303
more and more complete assimilation takes place from nature to thought
and from thought to will. From the sensible phenomena studied by the
positive sciences, from the interior life of the individual, from the city,
from human society, from the universal solidarity, from the ideal
republic of intelligences, from the moral kingdom of ends, there is produced an organism wherein this will has spread itself to be its soul and
where, in order to equal itself to itself, it has opened itself out to the point
of becoming coextensive with the whole and of placing its center
everywhere. So, instead of being the result or at least the summation of
an antecedent necessity, human action, from this standpoint which is still
provisional, is the reason for all the beautiful ordering. The universal
phenomenon seems to exist only to become the theater of morality or
better still, to be the very body of the will.

Voluntary action, therefore, has absorbed all the rest, in order to
shape organs for itself little by little and to make its own universe. What
it tends to more and more is the accord between the voluntary and the
willed: *mentis et vitae, intelligentis et agentis, volentis et voliti adaequatio* (an adequation of mind and life, of the intelligent and the agent,
of the willing and the willed). In this sense, moral truths are rather the
consequence of voluntary action than the principle. As we determined
the conditions of scientific knowledge through analysis, so we are led to
determine the conditions of moral activity. Undoubtedly the solutions of
this spontaneous or reflected labor are infinitely varied. But we must
eliminate this very diversity to consider only the common trait for all
these attempts. What is it, in sum? It is as follows.

The end from which reflected action seems to feel an imperious need
to suspend itself is an absolute, something independent and definitive
that would be outside the sequence of phenomena, a real outside the real,
a divine something. It would seem that, no more than from all the rest,
we would be unable to draw from the moral phenomena anything other
than phenomena. And yet we *postulate* something else. Postulate, that
is precisely the word; the postulate is a necessary affirmation which is of
a different nature from the premises. Whence is this exigency born, if not
from the circumstance that in the primitive *élan* of the will there is more
than we have yet used? Not to be satisfied with the effect is to admit the
superiority of the cause. Does it not seem as if, bearing within ourselves
an overpowering burden, we were in a hurry to unload it, by throwing
it onto the first prop in sight? It seems as though, in order to make believe
that we do not get out of phenomena and that we find our satisfaction 304
in them, we turn back towards them to make more of them than they
are. A supreme effort, which it is instructive to study, for the very vanity

of this illusory attempt will manifest the voluntary necessity of another satisfaction.

It remains for us to see then how man, in an attempt to perfect himself, tries finally to absorb what escapes him infinitely, to fabricate himself a god in his own fashion and to garner with his own strength alone something to make him self-sufficient. We must study the *phenomenon of superstition:* the *phenomenon,* i.e., the necessary manifestation of a need under whatever form it may try to satisfy itself; *superstition,* i.e., the use of a remainder of human action, outside of the real. If it seemed strange earlier to say that the will fashions its subalternate conditions, is it not still more strange, and yet is it not more clear to say that, in the final analysis, it tries to subjugate the infinite power? Does it not readily imagine it has bent and mastered the mysterious power for which it feels the need? And does the will not pretend to produce, by its own strength, the bond that ties it to the divine and that hands the divine over to it captive and docile?

As ample as the phenomenon of the will has become, a remainder subsists still, whose meaning, whose use, whose equation has not been found. From this, in the attempt to make human action equal to man's will, come the multiple forms of superstitious activity. The determinism of action imperiously gives rise to this need. But, for the sake of disentangling what exigencies we have to satisfy, it is useful to look at what illusory satisfactions this need has seemed to require. The history of the solidary transformations of the object, of the rite, and of the feeling of superstition will enable us to purify the religious aspiration of every admixture. And far from dreading the boldness of critical analysis, we have only to fear stopping its assault prematurely, as if man could be finally content with this "something" he has given himself as an idol.

CHAPTER 3
Superstitious Action

How man attempts to bring his action to completion and to be self-sufficient

Nothing up to now has stopped the initial movement of the will. It has 305
gone through all successive enclosures without meeting a term firm
enough for it to bounce back to its origin in its entirety, with the force
it has developed in the very course of its deployment. And if along the
way it has received some partial satisfactions, it seems to draw from them
only more energy and a greater exigency. *Aliquid superest* (something is
left over). Sprung from the infinite power that the subject harbored in the
depths of his life, action seems able to find support and conclusion only
in an infinite reality. Where can we find such a total use? Where is that
perfect equation which would establish a reciprocity between the necessary expansion and the return of a freedom always in progress.

Since in voluntary action, as it is given in fact, there subsists an element
whose mysterious fecundity is exhausted by none of the forms of personal, social or moral life, since, after having brought into this abyss of
the human will all the grandeurs of science, of consciousness, of affections, of ideas, of duties, there remains a vacuum, since, no matter how
stretched the enveloping lines may be, the circle cannot yet be closed; it
is therefore necessary to push on further still. As a matter of fact, in the
least willed act there is more than we have yet been able to determine.
As a matter of fact, to all that we have just said about the heterogeneous, 306
compatible and solidary phenomena, a belief is added which insinuates
into them a new form of reality and which seems to render them incompatible and exclusive, as if, for example, determinism and freedom,
disinterestedness and love of self, pure morality and metaphysics, could
not be reconciled. As a matter of fact, an ulterior need inevitably comes
to light, and even if it may get only illusory satisfactions, it is still a real
need. The science of action has to account for this fact, this illusion, this
reality.

In spreading out, in realizing itself outside, the will cannot find in its objective work all that it harbors in the sanctuary of its interior life. This infinitude which he obscurely feels within and which he needs in order to be what he wants to be, what he is already in desire and intention, the subject draws from himself; he presents to himself, under the form of a symbol or an idol, his own need for completion and perfection; he adores the incommunicable and inexhaustible life whose latent source he bears within himself. It is at the very heart of voluntary action, then, that a mystery resides, and we do not escape the desire of mastering it. Like the spectrum of the sun, more ample than the colored rays, action is at once light and obscure warmth. It carries farther than our sight can reach.

Strange condition this! What man cannot grasp, express, or produce, is precisely what he projects outside of himself to make it the object of a cult, as if in his inability to touch it within himself, he hoped to reach it better by placing it in the infinite. And, in a reverse movement, but one that is no less surprising, what he sets infinitely above himself is precisely what he pretends to dominate, monopolize, absorb, as if he had divinized it only to require imperiously a satisfying response to the creative call of an avid heart. Thus we want to realize outside what escapes us inside, with the secret aim of somehow imprisoning this infinite in the finite of a real object, with the inward hope that this is the true way of conquering it and of finally having, in a perfect action, the coveted conclusion, security, and repose. Εν τω αυτω περας και απειρον (the finite and the infinite is one and the same). The finite infinite, the infinite possessed and used, that is the meaning and the ambition of the ritual act.

Cult, then, appears as a supreme effort to fill in the immense interval that separates the will from what it wants, and to bring together, as if to join them in prayer and adoration, the arms of complete action opened out to immensity. The object of cult, then, somehow projected and created before the adorer, like a mirror wherein the will can reflect its full image and its whole warmth, is only an occasion for the will to know itself better and to learn to equal itself. Hence it is no wonder that man has tried to suppress or to sublimate little by little this intermediary exterior to the inward wish of the heart. It is this necessary genesis and this progressive purification of superstition that we must now study. With the object, the cult, and the feeling, which seem to be the threefold element of every superstitious act, we shall see each one of these terms melt into the next, as man comes to recognize in it an image of his own nature and a more inward need of his consciousness. Perhaps at the end of this effort the equation between the voluntary and the willed, between the principle and the end of action, will finally be found; perhaps man does end up being self-sufficient.

I

This surplus of the human act that always exceeds sensible facts and social life, this remainder of strength and will which seems not to know what to latch on to, the natural temptation is to assign it an object, an object which, finite and insufficient like the others, would not of itself have the capacity to receive the homage man claims to give it, but which, precisely because of its smallness, satisfies man's double need both to create and to master his god. He wants it to resemble him and to differ infinitely from him. In a singular sort of giddiness, he takes it from the series of things to set it outside the series. Whence this twofold form of primitive superstition where we cannot say which is the more ancient, but which both come from one and the same initiative: the cult of the *double* and the cult of the *fetish*. The double is what outlives man in man, what remains inaccessible to man, what commands and obeys man. The fetish is the visible and mysterious, the incomprehensible and accessible, the menacing and protective object that sums up the divine, as if the finite could become the very reality of the infinite.

Therefore, it is because the idol is not at first naturally in harmony   308
with the role it is charged with that it lends itself to the illusion and corresponds to the requirements of the believer. The appetite for the divine even offers itself stones as nourishment; it acquiesces in what seems furthest removed from the infinite majesty, as if the "sacred object" had to be at once enigmatic by the very absurdity of the choice from which it draws all its mystery, and very easy to manipulate to be at the disposition of human power. Man wants its true grandeur to be something that does not appear to the senses, and he wants it to be something that the senses can still take hold of and feed on. Is it not man's ambition always to invade the secret of things, to disarm and subjugate the occult power with which he feels his acts are woven? And when he is persuaded that in fact he has succeeded by his own initiative alone in this prodigious enterprise; when he vaunts himself for having placed his hand on the infinite forces which nature harbors or which surpass it; when he has measured his conceptions and his heart against the size of the idol he offers himself for adoration, then it is, undoubtedly, that his action seems consummated

to him and he believes himself secure. There is no act, no matter how vile, where man has not placed the divine, no act that has not aroused some idolatry.

What then, in short, is the object of the superstitious cult? Under a borrowed form (for here the need creates the organ and the food that nourishes it), it is the expression of that inexhaustible depth of the interior life which no particular act has equaled, it is a desire that embodies itself, the desire for an infinite response to an infinite tendency. And, since it is the impenetrable secret of his individual consciousness that man adores in this way, he is led, by the very progress of his reflexion, to conceive this mysterious object according to the type of his humanity; but of a humanity such that it cannot be realized in him, and which remains the permanent and mobile advance of his ideal over his real development. This is how the solidary evolution of the idol, the cult and even the mediator can be explained.

As soon as the idol ceases to be a brute and unintelligible mystery, the ritual act is no longer alone in being clothed with the superstitious character. The anthropomorphism that is added to the fetishism entwines the role of the sorcerer with the personage of the priest. The obscure feeling that there is a subjective infinite, θειον τι (something divine), in each one of man's acts, inclines him to spread this divine element itself into the whole of his life. The superstitious act is no longer apart, bereft of any reason other than being superstitious; it tends to envelop all other acts. To the practices of sorcery and magic, then, are joined prayers and sacrifices. For, from the moment when the idol has a consciousness analogous to that of man, from the moment when this consciousness penetrates, in man and in his acts, precisely that which escapes him, is it not to this that he can and that he must address himself, through an imploring mediation, in order to obtain this sovereign concurrence, in order to consecrate all his undertakings, none of which is completed without this omnipotence?

Thus we can explain how cult flows back from the unique object which seemed at first to claim for itself the entire fulness of adoration, to all other actions, in order to complete and sanction them. And thanks to this extension of the ceremonial that corresponds to a clearer consciousness of the unfathomable character of each action, the very idea of the sacred object is also intellectualized; it humanizes itself. Under the literal practice a new spirit insinuates itself, the sense of a god who does not just require a tribute, as an egotistic and fierce tyrant, but who expects of human actions that they be what they should be, as if their perfect and regular execution were necessary for his own perfection.

II

Superstitious action, then, is not limited to constituting a form careful-ly isolated from every other. As the sacred object comes to be conceived more in the image of the spirit itself, it seems that its transcendence can become immanent to each particular action in order to consecrate it and impress upon it the seal of the infinite that human consciousness demands. If it resided entirely in the material symbol that manifests it and places it at man's disposition, it would be enough to take care of the rites that have it directly as their end, without having superstition involved in the rest of life. But when in every action of any note we think we sense its presence and its power, when beside every inspiration of the heart and at the source of every operative force and beyond every partial end, there seems to be room for this unknown and veiled guest, then, as Plato remarks, all those who have a bit of reason have to invoke the 310 divinity at the beginning and at the end of their acts, great or small. Thus we find verified here once again, and explained, the law whose truth all the development of science and of human life has made manifest. Each synthesis, once constituted, takes over its own elements in some fashion in order to mark them with its imprint and to penetrate them with the higher idea that is its principle. Ritual ends up by enveloping all of man and all of his conduct, from birth to death.

Hence, in one sense, the blossoming of the superstitious feeling and of the rites that give it body supposes that man has already crossed the pro-gressive forms of individual and social life. It is not without reason, therefore, that some have claimed that religion is primarily a phenom-enon of solidarity and a corollary of organized society. But in another sense, the seed is sown as early as the most rudimentary form of indi-vidual life; and, as low as the degree of culture which man has reached may be, he always has a superstition, because always he discovers in his action as it were a remainder for which he does not find the use. Always also it is from this higher perspective that he looks on his life and tries to inspire his conduct. For if superstition means to bring action to a full circle and to make of it a closed system, if it tries to "loop" human life in and to organize the perfect city where, hypothetically, everything would be end and means, then the most diverse forms of activity must concur in preparing and nourishing the faith and the cult; and at the same time, once it has been conceived and idolized, the object of the cult must come back to transfigure and perfect all the sketches of action and all the incomplete works.

This is why the superstitious act seems to flow more directly from the most complex forms which a civilization has reached, since it somehow starts where the ground gives way under man's walk. But if it seems to embody itself especially in the highest result of evolution, it is in order to subordinate everything else to it. Hence, in a sense, all other acts precede and prepare superstitious action; and in a more profound sense, ritual penetrates and grounds all other acts. Not only are the individual, the family, the city, the universe, the feeding ground where superstition flourishes like a flower that is at once natural and parasitical, but conversely all these forms of life seem suspended from the sacred art which was their end and becomes their principle, which contained their hidden spirit and which constitutes their seal, their letter, their cornerstone. There is no "ritual" without the family or the city; there is no family or solidly organized city without a consecration, without a mystical thought.

In every human act, then, there is a beginning of budding mysticity. As soon as an act breaks the daily monotony, as soon as we want to think of it as a self-sufficient whole or to complete it like a distinct and viable creature, we sacralize it. If the ordinary flow of things dulls us, the first exception to come up, the most simple event that breaks the chain of habit, quickens reflexion; and the first reflexion, as it opens our eyes to the mystery, launches us into the infinite. Thus it is that, even in private life, every important event arouses, not only a feeling for and a preoccupation with the divine, but a ceremonial. Here the question is no longer that of the mysticism of love or of the enthusiasm of inspiration or of all the successive idolatries of the child, the lover, the citizen, the thinker; it is a question of the positive cult which, by a kind of return, claims to insert into them what all these forms of life could not at first find or retain within them. Birth, solemn decisions, dangers that bring a prayer or a vow to the lips, contracts, words of honor, death, are all high points where rituals take hold. Wherever the individual is led to reflect on what he is doing or on what he can do of his own power, he does not will to be alone, he cannot be alone. For he does not feel himself the master either of all his power or of the results of his striving.

Domestic life is founded on ritual practices. A cult, originally maintained as the exclusive and essential property of the family, watches over it. From its inception, political life is tied to a traditional respect for minute devotions and legal observances: the gods of the ancient city belong to it, as it belongs to them; between them and it there is a rigorous exchange of services and guaranties. And still to this day, under less brutal forms, something of the same feeling is to be found in the passionate susceptibility of the citizen, in whose eyes the cause of the country is unique, incomparable, sacred, jealously protected and loved from on high, as he loves it. The country symbolizes the infinite object of devotion. All well and good, but do we not see that, for some, the State itself becomes an idol for which feasts are required, which admits of no 312 other public cult than its own, and which, rather than consider itself as a level in the universal development of moral and religious life, tolerates nothing outside or above its sovereign fantasy?

Even among those who claim to be liberated from all superstition, let us take note of this need for rituals and this counterfeit of the ceremonies of a real cult; as if we had to enhance at all costs, by a kind of liturgical solemnity, the all too visible poverty of bare actions. For man the marvelous and the occult are a need; he is given a touch of them, even if it be through a Greek word inscribed over the gate of a cemetery. Once a disturbance, a change, or a partial inhibition is produced in social life or in individual habits, and once consciousness quickens in the face of a decision to be made, it seems that it is no longer enough to do only and simply what we are thinking of doing. For if we never act for what is perfectly clear, without expecting from the execution more than there is in the idea and the project, is it not because it seems logical to act even beyond the simple intention? For something to be well done, it seems, there must be a surplus in action; and the extravagance of formalities is yet another satisfaction for naive minds, ready to ask, even after singularly useless and interminable performances: "Is it over already?"

Hence, with each offensive advance of reflexion, man seems to try to free himself from the spontaneous urgings that took him naively outside of himself. He is ready to burn what he used to adore as soon as he thinks he has risen above it. What he seems to be looking for instinctively, is his own apotheosis. In order to reduce the object of his cult, in order to have no other religious duties than his human duties, has he not himself ascended the altar? And have we not witnessed, as instructive beginnings, the messianic coming of Reason or the attempt at a positive religion of Humanity?

— The ritual act, without admixture of any other, first appeared as the cult due exclusively to the idolized object; the ritual and the object were at once the form and the matter of superstition. This means that superstitious action, like an entirely superfluous and yet necessary luxury, had no rationale other than to reconcile to man the mysterious power on which he depends. But as the idol humanizes itself, ritual comes to be added, like a perfect form, to all common actions that are 313 the very stuff of human life. It remains for us to discover how, instead of juxtaposing itself by a positive cult to other distinct acts, superstition more subtly and less visibly insinuates itself into all the forms of practice, thought, science, metaphysics, art, natural morality; so that, precisely where it seems dead, for lack of any apparent object and positive cult, it comes back to life more imperceptibly and more imperiously.

III

In its effort to fulfill itself and to give its work a character of complete sufficiency, the human will ends up looking for the complement it requires in incomplete action itself. Rather than have recourse to magic formulas or consecrative ceremonies, it avails itself directly of its perfection, as if acts were not self-sufficient and complete because they are religious, but religious and divine because they are fulfilled and complete, because they are "moral or human."

Thus, out of the mystery which lives on at the heart of action in the most inward part of consciousness and which surpasses any given reality, we fashion an ideal that seems to be more and more identified with human action itself. In a reversal of perspective, religion, instead of appearing as the end, is taken as a means. Instead of weighing acts according to how they come under a ritual observance, we claim to judge religious forms according to the value of the actions themselves. Instead of orienting man toward an exterior and higher object, we try to redirect his action toward his consciousness and his thought. And the consequence of this inversion is, in a way, to reduce the three terms of superstitious action to two. It is to suppress the transcendent object of cult in order to place man in the presence of the mystery he bears in his own consciousness. It is to look for the end of adoration within the adorer himself, as if that were the true cult in spirit and in truth and the only way to remove from human life the defaming label of superstition. Thus, apparently left to itself and reduced simply to its expression, action perhaps henceforth will be sufficient to itself in its full independence.
314   And was that not the original wish of willing? To obtain that the phenomenon be so rich and so ample that it would absorb all and subsist alone.

In order to give the moral order a solid foundation and to make it a self-sufficient whole, has it not seemed enough to some to consider duties as originally independent of all metaphysical notions and all compromises with sensibility, but yet solidary with postulates so that, in acting well, we would be accomplishing, mysteriously no doubt but surely, the presumptive will of the perfect legislator, and so that finally morality itself constitutes the true cult? All duties and only duties seem to be religious. In claiming that God placed us in the world to act according to his will and not to offer him harrangues or compliments, one concludes with Kant: "Everything that man thinks he can do to make himself pleasing to God other than maintain a good conduct is pure superstition." What does this mean, if not that human action, by its own strength, pretends to assimilate, even to the point of exhausting it, all that knowledge cannot attain or that the will cannot fully embrace?

And when the metaphysician, claiming to house within his thought the infinite object he is seeking, imagines that, through his conceptions and through his precepts, through his systems and through his natural religion, he will lay hold of the transcendent Being, conquer and master it in some way, is he not idolatrous in his own fashion, as if he were cornering the living truth within a tenuous network of thoughts; as if, through the honor he renders his god in affirming and defining it, he were subordinating it entirely; as if, penetrating into the intimacy of infinite power, wisdom, and sanctity, because he has forged himself an ideal of perfection, he were about to participate in it himself and become in reality precisely that which he has declared to be inaccessible, that which has no other meaning in his consciousness than to be incommunicable and mysterious? Does he not transform the metaphysical phenomenon, which he has interiorly at his disposal, into a substance, into a Being which he thinks he has at his disposal exteriorly? That is still to succumb, then, to the strange pretention of capturing and using God with only human strength; it is to want this absolute to be at once outside of action in order to become its conclusion and inside action so that action may be sufficient unto itself. The divine can neither be placed in nor displaced from what man does by it, and yet he likes to maintain that 315 it is there, and there of his own doing alone. Even when he condescends to prescribe special acts toward the first being which his reason acknowledges, he thinks that prayer and adoration proceed from his thought alone and from his own will; and these actions, which he calls religious, are, like the others, rid of all parasitic form and all obscure and sacramental rite. His superstition is to make believe that he has none and to think he lives by clear ideas and rational practices; he is triumphant in the thought that he has dislodged the old dogmas. That too is a faith, and how credulous and dogmatic a one!

Idols still, the Unknowable, universal solidarity, the social organism, the country, love, art, science, as soon as passion enters into a heart and persuades it to find enough to satisfy it in them, as soon as it consecrates to them the powers of tenderness and dedication, as if man had at last found in them his all. If the evolutionist, raising his conceptions above individual or political outlooks, considers that conforming to the whole of nature through knowledge of cosmic laws is what is best for him, if the socialist consecrates his thoughts, which he judges to be salutary, to a work which he judges supremely important, if the scientist believes he is advancing toward the fulness of truth and working to become the magician, the priest, and the soothsayer of a future already present, do they not all attribute to the employment of their life and the virtue of their effort a plenitude and a perfection that we must also call superstitious? For in the state of their consciousness there are, out of three parts to be viewed, two parts that are the result of a desire rather than the expression of a reality. What they do undoubtedly contains meaning and importance; but on this real foundation they add a double fiction, — the vain conviction of the sovereign and, so to speak, sacred character of the object to which they are piously dedicated, — the proud pretense of rendering it an appropriate cult; as if both the end and the result of their acts merited that life should be lived as they make it to be. Thus, for many, it is science itself that becomes the fetish, and they sometimes consent to play before the people a role of magician: in presenting to simple folk learned words, mysterious phrases, scientific symbols designed to satisfy among the ignorant the long-lived desire for the marvelous, they propose an object of faith where, for their part, they pretend to find full clarity and where they give off to others as obscure what is luminous in their eyes, knowing full well that beyond this circumscribed light they too encounter darkness and an unknown; so that, perhaps unknown to themselves, they persuade the credulous that all the obscurity is already clarity for themselves, causing their science to be adored as the unveiled mystery and the permanent miracle.

316

Thus, at the very point where acts seem most rigorously determined and where life seems reduced to the dryness of geometric contours, in the most scientific conception of human existence one could imagine for one self, whence all feeling, all impulse of faith, all appearance of superstition is banished intentionally and in fact, there subsists a huge postulate. And the more this conception and these actions seem positive, it must be said, the more ingenuousness and illusion they reveal in those who are so little clearsighted and yet sufficiently enlightened by their own ardor for them to see written in themselves and in the universe only the glory, the power, and the divinity of science. One does not find the divine anywhere when one does not bear it within oneself. But one cannot suppress it everywhere except by concentrating it in oneself and by substituting a new credulity for the absent faith.

IV

Inasmuch as every conviction, even a negative one, and every form of free thinking is still a superstition, it is no wonder, then, that criticism always pushes its point forward. Through a protestation against the austere cult of a moral imperative veiled like Isis, against the metaphysical idol of systems equal to the universe, against the tyrannical devotion of a Science which sometimes joins to the credulous temerity of a child the insolence of an upstart, there arises in many contemporary minds what has been called *the new mysticism*. New, indeed, because it claims to remain grounded on science itself and on all the negations of modern criticism without denying anyone of them; new, because, sympathetic to all superstitions of the past, curious about popular beliefs, rites, sacramental forms, literal practices to which it even submits at times, it thinks it represents a step forward in what it rightly calls irreligion, even while remaining more religious than the most orthodox devotion. And as if henceforth this fine gold of the true secular piety were purified of all alloys, the impious mystic melts into one single aspiration the feeling, the cult, and the very object of his adoration. It is the mystery of his action and the fervor of his heart that he offers incense to. He too is pietistic in his own way.

How then does such a wonder come to be? And by what subtlety of feelings does one flatter oneself for having discovered the entrance to the always open chapel, where everyone ascends the altar, where the enigma is unveiled, and rest for the will is finally found? The religious disposition of the new mystics seems to be composed, like a light perfume, of the following two essences: there is no act where one does not feel something like an intoxication and a salutary exaltation, as if under the breath of the infinite passing over the soul; there is no act where one does not sense that the object of devotion, the result of the effort, is chimerical, finite, null. It is because it is vain, because it is disappointing to act, that it is beautiful, disinterested, and pious to do so. The more the act is void of any object, it seems, the more also is developed a consciousness satisfied with a subjective sufficiency and plenitude. The naive believer projected his love and his all outside; through analysis, can we not keep our cult within us and, in order to adore nothing, adore ourselves? Not only does the exquisite individual in his divine sovereignty not want to hold himself to any special act of any natural religion, but for him there is no longer any special rule in any act; by reason of the infinite variety of circumstances and feelings he goes through, no criterion of conduct is imposed on him. So that, if what he does matters little to him, at least acting, and again acting, is the great virtue, the inexhaustible source of feeling, the cult; the cult without object, without belief, without ritual, without priesthood, without anything else, the Cult. And is it not the same feeling which, in a less subtle and more generous form, inspires those secular apostles, those preachers of piety and devotion, whose Creed and Decalogue is summed up in a word: Action?

Acting for the sake of acting becomes, then, the superstition of those who want no other. What is the meaning of this singular devotion? And is this subtle disposition grounded in the truth of the feelings experienced? — In action, no matter how much we try to restrict it to what science teaches man about himself or the universe, what is best remains refractory to all analysis. We have succeeded in unmasking the vanity of everything else; but as vain as the ends of an activity that is always disappointed and always rising again may be, action itself remains wrapped as in a cloud of incense that conceals its brutal poverty and its nullity. Every act, every work limps, falls short, is imperfect. But acting reveals this mystery of powerlessness that contains the infinite aspiration of the heart. Far then from trying to ground itself on the sufficiency of anything whatsoever, the will overcomes the insufficiency of everything; it adores what escapes and surpasses it forever; it is divine, while it is living, loving, producing, expending itself, even fruitlessly. After all the superstitious acts that claimed to hold and fix the absolute, there survives only the superstition of action and faith in becoming, better still, the love of what can neither be made nor touched, of what is not and will not be real. We wanted to concentrate all the reality of things into human action and have it participate in the solidity of all that is, seemingly, without it. But on the contrary, is not action the dream that devours the substance of phenomena, the pit where all appearance of existence is swallowed up? And could it be that we have followed this long course of scientific inquiry only to return to the point of departure, the void?

V

It is a great service to man, the greatest of all, to cause all superstitions to vanish from before his eyes successively, but in order to obtain in him the pure sense of religious expectation. How important it is not to let fall by the wayside the benefit of this relentless Criticism, not to let the great flow of the mysticism that is rising again in our day deviate, not to let the effort of doubtlessly sincere generosity fall back into the emptiness of illusory satisfactions that would hold back wills and abort their *élan*! In the work of destructive thought, there is a profound religious sense. Hence, instead of repressing this movement, we must with all our might keep it from stopping prematurely. Nothing is more true, nothing is more necessary than to look, almost to the point of pride and naïveté, upon the metaphysician fascinated with his constructions, upon the artist in love with his work, the devotee of the moral ideal, or the apostle of action for the sake of action, as savage fetishists: in each instance, it is the same pretention and the same presumption. All are equally persuaded they can make their god without God. To lay bare the nothingness of such human effort is to do a work of pious impiety.

For if he stays only with his negative conclusions, if he takes satisfaction in them, with the hope of having confiscated and as it were dissolved the divine, if he is triumphant for having dug within himself an abyss deep enough to bury, once and for all, his action and all things, the impious critic is not yet impious enough. He still retains the superstition of not having any; he remains an idolater. He is the one who, in spite of his air of being a forerunner and beacon, remains backward and wrapped in darkness. We must, therefore, penetrate further and puncture this last idol, the only one man could still cling to in order to convince himself that he is fully self-sufficient. If there is in superstitious action, alongside the changing and perishable illusion, a sincere and invincible movement of the will, we must be careful, in analysing it, not to take the illusory for the real and the real for the illusory.

In crossing the immense field of the phenomenon, man has only gained the advantage of opening the way more clearly for a mystery that outlives the apparently complete use of all his powers. This surplus does not have to be added to willed action; it is already there; and in positing it, the will whence proceeds the act requires its use. In vain do we try to consecrate it in a ritual to the fictitious object of an idolatrous cult. In vain do we try to seal it up in each one of the actions which we mark with a sacred character, or to deposit it like a heavy encumbrance in some one of the phenomena whose emptiness this hidden need had made us sense. In vain, as consciousness renounces the illusory ambition of confiscating it, do we want to adore only the unknowable and the inaccessible. From all these attempts, there follows only this doubly imperious conclusion: it is impossible not to recognize the insufficiency of the whole natural order and not to feel an ulterior need; it is impossible to find within oneself something to satisfy this religious need. *It is necessary*; and *it is impracticable*. Those are, in brutal form, the conclusions of the determinism of human action.

But in this crisis that might be termed desperate, how easy it is, through the perhaps unconscious perfidy of a reverse interpretation, to pervert this double forced finding. It is this sophism, hidden under all the 320 forms of superstition as well as those of impiety, whose crude subtlety we must finally lay bare. Instead of admitting that man is powerless to bring about any sort of satisfaction for his necessary need for the divine, one concludes that all religious satisfaction is necessarily powerless to satisfy an illusory need.

Once it has broken through to the falsity of all idols and all superstitions, it is a subtle temptation for pride, always avid for self-sufficiency, to glory in knowing the human infirmity it acknowledges. By a singular sort of illusion, one ends up being content with a weakness one has to be quite powerful to feel and quite enlightened to discern; one remains satisfied with not being able to satisfy oneself. And, while one looks down from on high on all those who have narrowed their vision or imprisoned their life within some particular formula, one also pauses to consider them. This human action whose insufficiency we felt only because we willed it to be self-sufficient in the end, we finally will to be insufficient because we judge that that is the only way for us to restrict ourselves to it and find self-sufficiency in it. Can the equivocation be sorted out? Are we aware of the circle in which we get caught by an arbitrary and vicious decree? Can we feel rising again, through an inconsequence, the mortal conflict between two wills? And can we not see into what form of refined intolerance we are on the verge of falling under pretext of indifference and tolerance? If the despotism of clear ideas and scientific certitudes is frightening because it seems to leave no shadowy refuge for those it envelops with its light, it still does not succeed in violating the sanctuary of the surrounding mystery. Hence the tyranny of obscurity is more to be feared, because it weighs in the night upon those who think themselves secure; it prevents them, not from seeing a protective penumbra at the limit of their science, but from stepping out of the darkness and from ever hoping that a light will shine in the abyss whence their thought and their action come and into which they fall back.

What do we really know about this abyss? And if one thinks he knows, what is the mechanism of this faith in forced blindness? Even mystical irreligiousness is also a superstition from the moment when, from the real powerlessness of the human will and the absurd devotions of fetishism, from the false mysticism of science, or from the imaginings of theosophy, it concludes to the impossibility of any ulterior revelation. A powerlessness can be observed, but not an impossibility. There is perhaps more credulity and intolerance hidden in sectarian negation than in violent fanaticism. And, to leave nothing unsaid, there is, in fact, consciousness of powerlessness only through a notion of possibility. The claim of man to restrict himself to phenomena and to be self-sufficient is therefore radically illogical. In making the claim he belies it and goes beyond it. To base oneself on weak and incomplete action in order to admit the irremediable weakness of action, to erect a fact into a definitive and exclusive truth, is, without seeming to tamper with it, to denature it. In the order of phenomena, there is no contradiction or exclusion, no possibility or impossibility; there are simply determinate facts. But the moment that, from these facts, one claims to draw a negation bearing on the very possibility of other facts, one abandons science and facts. The most impious are still superstitious.

In the very name of determinism, there is only one inevitable conclusion, and this is it in its severity, without addition or subtraction: through his voluntary action man surpasses the phenomena; he cannot equal his own exigencies; he has within himself more than he can use by himself; he does not succeed, through his strength alone, in placing in his willed action all that lies at the principle of his voluntary activity. Thus, whether he pretends to get along without all religion or he makes himself one to his own liking, he does not exceed his right any less or satisfy any more his necessary need and his voluntary exigencies.

All attempts to bring human action to completion fail; and it is impossible for human action not to seek to complete itself and to be self-sufficient. It has to, it cannot. On the one hand, it is a necessity to clear away all strategems that, starting from man and coming from the most inward sanctuary of his heart, have as their ridiculous and pitiable object to lay hold of the divine. On the other hand, the sense of powerlessness as well as of the need man has for an infinite fulfilment remains incurable. Hence, as much as every natural religion is artificial, the expectation of some religion remains no less natural.

What an inextricable difficulty the human will has gotten itself caught in and backed itself into. Call to mind now all the conclusions that already close off every escape route. Impossible not to raise the problem. Impossible to find refuge in nothingness; for us it is no longer. Impossible to be content with the "something" in which we tried to enclose ourselves. Where can we go? The phenomenon does not suffice man; we cannot restrict ourselves to it, or deny it. Will we find, through a solution that seems necessary and yet inaccessible, a salvation?

322

From the preceding inquiry whose result seems quite negative there will necessarily follow the most positive of conclusions. We have purified the science of phenomena from all alloys, we have rid it of all ontology only to arrive, by a sort of method of residues, at making manifest what in action is no longer merely a phenomenon. There is something else in it that has to be defined. And this reality of action is not only a *fact* that one observes directly; if it has a scientific value, it is because it is a *necessity*, resulting from the total determinism of thought and life. To have given determinism all of its due is to have eliminated the illusory difficulties whose confusion of questions has often encumbered philosophy, but it is also to bring everything back to the highest option that is the great and the one business of man.

Part IV

The Necessary Being of Action

How the terms of the problem of human destiny are inevitably and voluntarily posited

323   In vain do we try to restrict voluntary action to what depends on the will itself. The immense order of phenomena where man's life spreads itself out seems to have been exhausted and human willing is not. The pretention it has of being self-sufficient aborts, but not out of penury. It aborts because in what we have willed and done up to now, that which wills and acts remains always higher than what is willed and done.

But from this very observation do we not see a strange conflict arise, and what might be called an *antiboly?*[1] Man claimed to get along by himself and to find in the natural order his self-sufficiency and his all. He 324 does not succeed at it; he does not succeed either in stopping or in going beyond. Nor can he go back either, since the least he was able to will is this natural order of phenomena, this *something* in which he discovers simply, not a reason for not wanting, but an imperious reason for wanting more.

What is the meaning, what is the necessary effect of this crisis which, in one form or another, secretly arises in every human consciousness? — In every human consciousness, inevitably there arises the sense that the

---

1. This word, *antiboly*, which means what we might call a clash (*entre-choc*), expresses here the apparently double and irreconcilable movement of the human will. What the term antinomy signifies from the static viewpoint of the understanding, antiboly sums up from the dynamic viewpoint of action. But in this analogy itself essential differences are to be noted. The antinomies are resolved in fact; and since it is a question there only of heterogeneous and solidary phenomena, the terms, apparently incompatible to the eye of the understanding, are really correlative and simultaneous. That will no longer be the case here: the terms of the alternative, simultaneously intelligible, exclude one another in fact, because henceforth it is a question not of what appears, but of what is. This is to say that we will inevitably be led to the affirmation of being, inevitably brought to posit an alternative in the face of it, inevitably obliged to opt between two decisions each of which radically excludes the other.

will is not its principle, nor its rule, nor its own end. And there are many ways to lead man to notice it, even if it be the powerlessness he finds himself in to be self-sufficient and to escape the necessity of willing. It had seemed that we cannot be in spite of ourselves; and yet behold man feels, to the point of anguish, that he is not the author of himself nor his own master. The all for him is not merely to accept the beautiful ordering of the universe or to ratify the determinism of his own actions; he still has to accept himself; he has to will, no longer what he wills, no longer life and the use he makes of it, but what in him produces it, criticizes it, and judges it.

Will it be possible to explain and justify this apparent tyranny, to resolve this conflict, and to offer the will a necessary alternative, but one such that, on whatever side the option stops, there can never be a disavowal?

I

THE CONFLICT

FIRST MOMENT
The Will Contradicted and Vanquished

The apparent abortion of willed action

325   It is hard to say whether it is a simple banality or an intolerable paradox to maintain that man aspires to be fully what he wills, and that he absolutely cannot be in spite of himself. — A worn-out truth, if we mean by that the illusory grandeur of the ambitious, the flatteries or the inward condolences of a solitary self-love that thinks everything is owed to it. — A strange challenge to common sense, when we claim that in effect the will is only to the extent that it produces and ratifies itself somehow, to the extent that it penetrates, dominates, and even creates its own organs of expression. And yet, it is this paradox that the natural history of action has justified, since, by simply willing, man posits and adopts a huge multitude of necessary conditions; and, on the contrary, it is this banal truth that seemingly will, if we reflect on it ever so little, disconcert the voluntary plan of our life.

    We would will to be self-sufficient; we cannot be. Against the determinism of willed action seems to rise an opposed determinism, one stronger and more evident still. We have only to follow everyday lan-

326 guage to recognize it: the will does not seem to have willed itself; in what it wants it perpetually encounters invincible obstacles and odious sufferings; in what it does, incurable weaknesses or faults whose consequences it cannot repair insinuate themselves; and death, by itself, sums up all these teachings. Before we will and in all that we will, then, there inevitably subsists something which, seemingly, we do not will.

    Hence it is not simply a new determinism which we must oppose to the determinism of willed action. It is a prior and more profound determinism, a determinism that precedes, envelops and surpasses our personal initiative. Consequently, nothing is yet accomplished if the difficulty that arises now cannot be resolved. For it is a question of what in ourselves is the principle of our own will, of what outside ourselves reveals to us that this principle does not seem to be ours, since we are overcome in life and overcome in death. How, then, does this disappointing contradiction raise its head in our consciousness where, it seemed, nothing could come up that was not the expression of a hidden will and a kind of extract of inward initiative or of spontaneous action? — But before explaining this inevitable fact by connecting it to its origins, our first task is to observe it well.

I

Suppose that man does everything as he wills it, obtains what he covets, vivifies the universe according to his liking, organizes and produces as he wishes the total ordering of conditions on which he rests his life: it remains that this will itself has not been posited or determined as it is by him. And even if, in the use he makes of it, he finds nothing to vex him, still he discovers deep within himself, this primordial contradiction: he wills, but he did not will to will.

It is not enough, indeed, that the crossing should be favorable: why am I embarked? Is there not in this an unexplainable constraint which corrupts, down to its source, all human action, even the most felicitous? Does a noble and generous heart accept even the greatest of goods, if it is imposed? To be sure, most men do not have enough penetration nor perhaps enough pride to sense all the strangeness of this problem. Nevertheless all have a vivid sense of not belonging to themselves. They know that they do not find within themselves either the origin, or the subsistence, or the end of their action. And it is for them troubling to think of it.

It is true that the bewitchment of trifles is very powerful; it is true that in the judgment of the senses or in the eyes of science, the universe is vast enough, populated enough, curious enough to deceive, but only those who want to be deceived. What a sophism of accumulation we often like to commit and, after we have felt the insufficiency of each detail, how quick we are to persuade ourselves that at least the sum is satisfying! That is when a hundred thousand nothings seem to add up to something. Surely we need an extreme subtlety of mind to see distinctly the wretched brevity of human learning, joys, and successes, or to assign with precision the limit for all that seems so ample to childish eyes. But we need a greater subtlety still to imagine that one can be content with it; and we

327

do not succeed in doing so, without making of this very contentment and this ironic egoism a new idol.

It has been the merit of a clearsighted criticism to have laid bare the vanity of the apparent satisfactions that all the variety of human superstitions has to offer an avid consciousness. What does it profit man to gain the universe? All that he has does not suffice him, and seems as nothing to him once he has it, because he does not suffice unto himself, because he does not possess himself. And everything he adds to this nourishment that makes him hungry is hollow meat: he is disgusted with his idols as he raises them to the summit of his life; he sets them up only to smash them down, as if he knew in advance that his hand would place this crown only through a sacrilegious temerity. But just as the patient, even when he is hopeless, still wants to do something to get better, how many people accept being duped and do not want to know that they know! These willful illusions that survive the most illuminating disappointments, these sometimes heroic sacrifices one makes for the sake of honor, of camaraderie, of human solidarity, of *esprit de corps*, of proprieties, even when one otherwise knows that one makes them only routinely, in boredom, for nothing: all that is touching, but it is nonsense. There is only one admission to be taken from it, always the same: the human will cannot keep itself to itself, because it does not come entirely from itself. No matter how wide the circle, action always makes it explode. It does not have the power to limit itself.

328 In its abstract form: "the will is forced to will itself," the problem may appear abstract or futile; in the truth of life, it is nevertheless the great tyranny which seems to weigh on the human heart and which is the principle of its most profound distress. At the source of our acts, some mysterious unknown escapes us; it is like a seed of suffering, of oppression, of death, sown in our very will. We did not will what in us is the principal thing; we have the invincible feeling of bearing a yoke and of not belonging to ourselves. We have been able, it is true, to adopt all the rest and take it upon ourselves, but all the rest is as nothing in comparison with what we will; less than nothing, it is pain as long as the will has not adopted, understood and taken itself into itself.

II

To be sure, the lesson of satiety is perhaps more conclusive than any other: inserted into action, the universe does not fill it; to draw close to the end is to draw away from desire; and the will, crossing in a leap all the seeming satisfactions it meets, finds itself afterward before a more unfathomable emptiness. But all do not seem equally able to understand this lesson. How few would see clearly, if we had to experience everything, penetrate into everything, in order to receive the great light of disgust and of detachment! It is not possible, but also it is not necessary to exhaust the world in order to feel that it does not quench our thirst. A keener bitterness, a more brutal and immediate warning educates us to the abusive contradictions we are exposed to. This lesson is suffering, the suffering which flows inexhaustibly from our poor human substance, and which has instinctively forced so many eyes to turn upward, so many arms to stretch out toward a liberator.

It is true that certain obstacles can be surmounted, certain oppositions conquered, certain griefs understood, accepted and used as the salutary prod for an activity that manages to make them enter into the voluntary plan of a happy life. But in spite of all possible energy and notwithstanding the most cunning tactics, how often pain flares up to the point where man is forced to regret he was born! As for that suffering which breaks up a life without killing or which kills it without stripping it of its wonder, there is no satisfying explanation and no possible deduction: it is the scandal of reason. What can the abstract formulas we delude ourselves with matter, or the general theories we fortify ourselves with! What an unfathomable difference between what we know and what we feel! We may well accept and foresee fatigue, being fed up with work, the reversals of fortune, the betrayals of life; we still remain always surprised and crushed by them because they strike elsewhere than we had feared, otherwise than we had expected. To know these things intellectually is one thing; the cruel thing is to suffer the disappointment and the hurt of the powerless will: "So, it is impossible; well then, we can change nothing; never again!"—Evil, suffering are not, any more than death, just facts for positive observation to see, nor consequences that flow from reason, nor means secretly willed by man. On the contrary, they are the poignant opposition of fact to reason, a conflict of the real with a will whose first movement is to hate it and to revolt.

And it is not only from the outside that these abusive contradictions arise, but also from the inside. How can we speak of freedom? Weak in the presence of seduction, soft when it comes to initiative, without strength to resist, if we want to discern good from evil, we fall into error; if we try to do good, we falter; if we set out to combat evil, we are vanquished. Not only do we have to undergo what we do not will; in addition, we do not truly will what we will. Before finding fault with others, let the will then find fault with itself! It feels spoiled to the marrow, without knowing how. What it lacks is the thought of willing and doing what it willed to do and think. And while the resolutions vanish as if

329

evaporated without trace, a parasitic life organizes itself within us that supplants personal initiative. Pierced by an insect, the leaf is forced to produce an abundance of sap to surround and nourish its enemy: this is the image of passion, which absorbs and devours the best substance of the soul.

330 Whether we undergo what we do not will, or do not do all that we will, or do what we do not will and end up willing it, we never quite escape this humiliating and painful fatality. Through the facts themselves and through our own acts, it reveals to us what we do not will; it forces us to notice what remains for us to will, so that we may will all the phenomena, more still, so that we may will the very will that produces them as they are, often in spite of ourselves. By eliminating what seems in conformity with our inward desires, it brings forward that which, whether favorable or contrary to the profound aspirations of man, is equally imposed on him, without his having yet consented to it.

III

Where this subjection is perhaps marked still more cruelly, is in the impossibility of remedying our acts and cleansing their unavoidable blemishes. — "What! That which I had the strength to do, I lack the strength to undo?" No. — "What! That which I was too weak to avoid doing, I will remain unable to erase entirely?" Yes.

It would be truly convenient indeed to disavow by a decree, to compensate by an act, what an act has produced, as if, after having tasted its advantages, we only had to spit out the dry pulp. — Not only would that be unjust: it is impossible. What I did, I never did alone: outside, and inside myself, the past is forever.

Outside, indeed, our works, like children detached from ourselves, act in turn without our leave. Children die, but acts live on; they are indestructible. We would like to persuade ourselves that we have done nothing reprehensible or detrimental, or to hope that good might come from evil itself through a convenient arrangement, and that felicitous compensations or courageous expiations will reestablish all things to perfection. The desire is an illusion. There is a kind of fault that is irreparable; and what most dread to believe is true nevertheless: action is indelible; no indemnification is ever an absolute reparation; no expiation, no penalty piled up on one side of the balance ever raises the other side; the consequences unfold to infinity, in space and time, as if to reveal the interior energy of action through the visible extent of its effects. Who has not felt, even to the point of anguish, the contradiction of a past that seems dead only to be sealed and irrevocable like a last will!

Inside, a fatality weighs on our conduct which, for being less obvious,   331
is all the more dreadful. The worst is not perhaps to be unable to change
our acts; it is that our acts change us, to the point that we can no longer
change ourselves. — We would prefer at times not to accept the advantageous consequences of a fault as a point of departure for the future. But
the corruptive effect of action is precisely to elicit new judgments and to
reverse the interior perspectives of conscience. — We would hope at times
to make a clean break from an embarrassing and tyrannical past that is
forever exposing us to new compromises by the very logic of disorder.
But, to go back and to suppress, along with the culpable urge, all the
brood of shameful desires that had hatched in the shadows, something
more than an egotistic fear or a velleity for wisdom and for uprightness
would be required. Who then is capable of this more radical rending
which exposes the depths of a conscience to the sunlight? There are
moments when the passions speak and decide, as if they left man only
with the right to be astonished at the criminal inspiration they reveal: the
revelation is often violent and sudden like a *coup d' etat*, but after what
long premeditation and with what imperceptible treacheries.

Hence, before, during, after our acts, there is dependence, constraint,
failure. This is the fund of servitude and weakness which the urgency of
action forces to come out: what we did not will, what we would no
longer will perhaps, we know we did and willed; the stain remains. And
what indeed is it to become stained, if not to mix together two hostile
wills, one that seems to start only from itself, and the other which brings
into the flow of action the impurity of an alien stream? If the powerlessness man feels in trying to bring the least of his acts to completion by
himself has led him to all sorts of superstition, the impossibility in which
he finds himself of having the sovereign say over his life and of purifying
himself, has inspired him with the whole variety of supplications, prayers,
and propitiatory sacrifices.

— If we had not first taken the measure of all the power of the human
will, if we had not run through the beautiful ordering of phenomena it
succeeds in organizing, it might seem that these observations are not
definitive, or that these contradictions are not insoluble, or that these
sentences are not without appeal. But after the analysis of action, there   332
is no loophole left: it is a fact, and the force of the fact is that it is determined by the scientific method of residues. Seeing all that we have been
able to do, we see precisely what we cannot do. And if we have demonstrated the power of the human will to the point of paradox, is it not to
convey the feeling, to the point of evidence, of the weakness of the human will? What we cannot do or undo at will, proves that we do not will,
with complete independence, even that which we succeed in producing
or healing. Hence, has not all this great effort man has expended in order

to raise himself toward *something* appeared to succeed at first only to fall back more miserably? Launched as a victorious conqueror, is the will condemned to fail by the very grandeur of its ambitions?

The disappointment would seem all the more incurable because the will aborts in this way, not for having failed to act or consent to everything which presented itself before it, but for having exhausted everything, for having lent itself to all experiences, for having faced up to the sufferings and stains of life. To act is well and good, for a while: it is a treatment and a kind of psychotherapy that revives a bit of confidence by giving the one who undergoes it the beautiful illusion of faith and a fruitful love. But after all, isn't it absurd and cruel in the end to live for the sake of living? No matter how much man looks within himself and without, in the infinite of science and of the universe; he is still alone, and he cannot remain alone. This felt powerlessness is not the effect of his ignorance; quite the contrary, the more he knows, the more he has, the more he is, the more acute also is his consciousness that he does not have, that he is not what he wills. One might say that by gobbling up all the satisfactions of the senses, of the mind, and of the heart, he is only deepening the abyss. By joy as well as by suffering, by success as well as by failure, by possession as well as by penury, he is forced to this cruel observation: whatever the will may have succeeded in attaining through its own strength, action is not yet equal to the willing from which it proceeds. The will has not yet willed itself entirely. The seeming abortions of action, the sufferings and failings that penetrate and weigh it down, the stains it cannot cleanse itself of, death and all the determinism of practical contradictions, only serve to reveal more imperiously this fundamental powerlessness.

SECOND MOMENT
The Will Affirmed and Maintained

The indestructibility of voluntary action

It is a fact: human pretentions are, on the whole, completely belied. 333
Whatever we may have gained of what we willed, from the viewpoint of
the very order of things willed, bankruptcy is inevitable. But this fact,
like every other, appears necessarily before consciousness only after a
more profound initiative; it is an effect that must be connected to its
cause through a bond of necessity, before we can see what its forced efficacity is, before we can understand how it too enters into the determinism of the will.

Three propositions sum up this necessary concatenation. —The sense
of the seeming abortion of our action is a fact only inasmuch as it implies
in us a will higher than the contradictions of life and the empirical
denials. —The presence within us of what is not willed brings to the fore
the willing will in all its purity. —And this internal mechanism only
manifests the necessity in which the will finds itself of willing itself and
positing itself. The being that we have, we undergo; but at the same time
we cannot fail to adopt it as something in complete accord with our will.

Thus, through the inevitable progress of an analysis that simply brings
to light a truth already living in us, we are led to will, no longer the object, no longer the fact, but the act and the very being of the will. It will   334
remain to be seen what this new necessity entails, what it supposes. Shall
we still be able to justify it to ourselves?

I

The experience of life and death, of the person and of its power, of
its action, its sufferings, and its failings, is not entirely empirical, nor
purely *a posteriori*: no, evil, pain and death are not entirely positive

facts, that is, belonging to those we can observe without first installing within them a hidden hypothesis or a desire against which reality, as it feels the resistance, produces the consciousness of a simple negation. They are facts only by way of contrast, by the effect of an internal opposition between the willed will and the willing will. Only this conflict explains within us the sense of a dependence, of a privation or an "inhibition," in a word, consciousness itself and reflexion; a consciousness no longer merely of phenomena that pass through me, but of myself through whom these phenomena pass; a consciousness of the phenomenon as phenomenon, i.e., of that which is not self-sufficient and cannot sustain itself alone.

To admit the insufficiency of every object offered to the will, to sense the infirmity of the human condition, to know death, is, then, to betray a higher pretension; those facts are possible, are real, are conscious only as a result of an antecedent initiative. Whoever raises the problem of being and of immortality already has the solution within him, through the hidden force of a kind of ontological argument, but an argument that is not based on a dialectic of ideas, an argument that simply develops the real and actual energy of human willing. It is not immortality, therefore, but death itself which goes against nature and whose notion has to be explained. We are not in space and time, rather space and time are in us. If death is a fact and an appearance, actions do not die; we observe, we understand the fact of dying only because we have the implicit certitude of living on.

Earlier it seemed that an exterior determinism, and hence one that is disconcerting and unintelligible, had risen up against the internal determinism of willed action. Now we begin to see how the one is tied to the other. The contradictions apparently most repugnant to the will, serve only to bring to light its invincible attachment to itself. In what it denies, it affirms itself and builds itself up indestructibly. Eliminate all that is willed, to leave only what is not willed: this rigorous method of elimination reveals more precisely what it is that wills, and it leaves willing with no other recourse but to will itself. This is what has to be well understood.

How careful we must be not to misunderstand the meaning of these necessary findings! To misunderstand them is not to suppress them or to prevent their effects; but a false interpretation of these effects themselves can pervert them by leading the reflected will astray in the supreme option to which it will soon inevitably be led. It is important, therefore, to understand properly the apparent abortion of action, and to show by what sequence of steps we arrive at observing this fact, this decisive fact whose inevitable consequences will remain for us to determine.

II

In its discouragement at not being able at first to attain what the conquering ardor of its ambition seemed to push it to, will the will, disappointed in all that it has willed, fall back into nothingness, as pessimism has imagined? But this nothingness which it seems at times to desire and to have forebodings of, is not (and it was in order to close off this false escape route that it was good to dissipate from the start all the feigned hope of the hopeless). But we saw that no true appetite covets this nothingness. But we have walled off this way of nothingness, without any turning back; and like an obstacle with infinite resistance, this rampart repels with its impenetrability the surge that strikes against it. In seeming to wish to lose itself in it, the will which, from the exhaustion of the phenomenon, feigns rushing into nothingness, rebounds back into itself. It finds there its own true being, whether it knows how to name it or not. The indestructible attachment of life to life, in spite of a character of apparent necessity, is the effect of a fundamental adherence of the will to its own nature. Only willing is strong enough to block the way for willing and to keep it from destroying itself.

No doubt, this is a way of speaking to the imagination. But behind these words which, while serving to focus the mind, seem to warp the natural approaches of thought by a sort of artificial precision, we must on the contrary extricate a more precise, a more certain, a more immediate action of the will, of a will that needs no complicated operations or learned dialectics or successive moments to arrive at this conclusion: "I will; and, if nothing of what is willed satisfies me, much more, if I will nothing of what is and of what I am, it is because I will myself, more than all that is and all that I am."

Indeed, is it because we do not immediately attain what we wish for that we cease desiring what we have desired? Not at all; we desire it more, we desire still more. All the beautiful order of phenomena where science ranges at ease, we have not found to be too much; we find that it is too little. And when painful contradictions tear from our hands what we thought we held, do they, in removing the nourishment, take away the appetite? Whether we embrace or despise the object put before desire, it is one and the same aspiration that arouses the yearning or the disgust. Apparent or provisional satisfactions may have masked this need; it was already. Trials unveil it. In what we will as in what we do not will, there is something we will above all else. In willed action, then, a real content is found whose amplitude reflexion has not yet equalled.

Seemingly quite negative conclusions: impossibility of stopping and of finding satisfaction by ourselves. But for this very reason, they are quite positive; what they mean is a necessity, not of going back, but of going forward. The surest testimony is the one which, deceived by a superficial appearance, in reality deposes against what it thinks it is establishing. Where one says: nothingness of the phenomenon, insufficiency of the phenomenon, abortion and meaninglessness of human action, we must translate: necessity and need for something else, for something in comparison with which the phenomenon seems only nothing. And reciprocally, to return to the language of appearances, it is this thing which appears to be nothing, since it is apart from phenomena. Without it, they would not be, without them, we would not know it.

Thus, it is all from one and the same willing that proceed the aim of trying out the phenomenon, the impossibility of restricting ourselves to it, the movement of contradiction which seems to cause action to abort, and the indestructibility of all these natural aspirations. In a word, all that we have willed up to now can no longer not be, nor can it remain simply what it is: and this double necessity, to all appearances contrary, is founded equally on one single aim, fully consequent with itself. And it is the unity of this determinism that makes it intelligible.

III

What depths are we not led to? Even if we willed nothing else, we will ourselves. And in willing ourselves, we ratify what causes all the rest to be for us. All the apparent constraints that seemed to weigh upon us one after the other, then, are justified and as though agreed to. But as necessity recedes before a will that takes it up and supports it, does it not reappear, beyond, more imperiously? Because determinism continues to develop its train, will we not fall again under the lash of a despotism more tyrannical than all? It is imposed on us that we should will ourselves, it is imposed on us that we should impose ourselves on ourselves.

We do not escape the need to take this very necessity into account. It has its forced repercussion and its natural expression in consciousness. We now have to sort out, then, how it reveals itself to thought. Indeed, from the conflict that stirs up every consciousness, there comes inevitably a supreme alternative, and this alternative will have to be resolved inevitably. It is all the way to this necessary question, all the way to its necessary solution, that science must follow the determinism of action.

No doubt, this tragic problem does not present itself to consciousness in this abstract form. But the manner of presenting the conflict that arises within us matters little, if it does arise in fact. Life is more subtle than any analysis, more logical than any dialectic. What we sense from the start, without having to be able to express it, is that the will is not content with any of the objects it has willed. There is always less in what is done or desired than in what is doing and desiring. The result seems like a caricature or a counterfeit of its real cause. The initial difficulty, therefore, remains in its entirety: is it possible to will ourselves and what is the true meaning of this necessary ambition? Torn between what I do 338 without willing it and what I will without doing it, I am always excluded from myself. How then get back into myself and put into my action what is already there undoubtedly, but unknown to me and beyond my grasp? How can we make the subject equal to the subject himself? For me to will myself fully, I have to will more than I have yet been able to find.

As I come up against the supreme necessity of the will, therefore, I have to determine what I will so that I may be able, in all fullness, *to will to will (vouloir vouloir)*. Yes, I have to will myself; but it is impossible for me to reach myself directly; from myself to myself, there is an abyss that nothing yet has been able to fill. There is no escape route for me to run away by, no passage for me to take forward by myself: what will come of this crisis?

Impossible to stop, impossible to go back, impossible to go forward alone: from this conflict that arises in every human consciousness inevitably comes forth the acknowledgement of the "one thing necessary" ("*l'unique nécessaire*"). Whether we know how to name it or not, this is the way where it is impossible not to pass. Yet here it is not a matter of finding a metaphysical definition for it; we have to study it, not to the extent that knowledge presumes to enter into it, but to the extent that *its action penetrates and promotes ours.* It too enters into the dynamism of action: through the presence of this thought which secretly stirs souls, voluntary life inevitably takes on a character of transcendence. The conflict, then, resolves itself into an alternative which, in the face of the contradictory terms of the dilemma, requires a supreme option and alone enables the will to will itself freely as it wishes to be forever.

THIRD MOMENT
The One Thing Necessary

The inevitable transcendence of human action

339   Let us see all in one glance the way we have travelled under the constraint of an inflexible determinism. It is impossible not to raise the problem of action; impossible to give it a negative solution; impossible to find ourselves as we will to be, either in ourselves or in others; in short, impossible to stop, to go back, or to go forward by ourselves. In my action there is something I have not yet been able to understand and equal, something which keeps it from falling back into nothingness and which is something only in being nothing of what I have willed up to now. What I have voluntarily posited, therefore, can neither surpass nor maintain itself. It is this conflict that explains the forced presence of a new affirmation in consciousness; and it is the reality of this necessary presence that makes possible in us the consciousness of this very conflict. There is a "one thing necessary." The entire movement of determinism brings us to this term, for it is from this term that the determinism itself begins, the whole meaning of which is to bring us back to it.

But let us make no mistake about it: in spite of a dialectical appearance, there is nothing in this argumentation, absolutely nothing, that is a deduction. What constitutes the strength of the proof is that it simply manifests the real expansion of the will. The demonstration here does not result from a logical construction of the understanding. It is not a matter of inventing anything whatsoever, nor of putting into voluntary 340 action what is supposedly not there yet; it is a matter of grasping precisely what is already there, what consequently is necessarily expressed to consciousness and is represented in it under whatever form it may be. It is an unknown to be discovered, but more by a complement in inventory than by a progress of discovery, more in view of an enrichment of active life than for a sterile satisfaction of the mind. The problem is to find out, not whether this "one thing necessary" is the abstract term of a reasoning

314

process, but whether it too will be able to enter into the development of willed action as a living truth.

Indeed, what importance is there in the idols, more or less purified, which human intelligence manages to propose for itself? It is not always because we give *being* a more precise formulation that we possess it better within ourselves. And perhaps it is better, perhaps even it is necessary to pursue it always without claiming to have found it in order not to cease attaining it by ceasing to look for it. *Amem non inveniendo invenire potius, quam inveniendo non invenire te* (I would prefer to find you by not finding rather than not to find you by finding)! The teachers of the interior life make the remark that, "in the acts of the will, when we think of the presence of this one thing necessary, we must show greater respect than if we were using the understanding through reflexion." More essential, indeed, than the conception by which we define it, is the way we are brought to propose it necessarily as an end for voluntary action; as a transcendent end, even while it is already in voluntary action. Without knowing its name or its nature, we can sense its approach and almost feel its contact, much as in silence and darkness we hear the step and touch the hand of a friend we have not yet recognized.

To be sure, the precision of metaphysical definitions is not vain; as we have seen, they have their own original efficacity and enter into the general dynamism of voluntary life. And yet it is not even the most distinct and the most exact conceptions that by themselves make us act and act well. Learned opinions and definitions are sometimes only labels or names we borrow so as to be able to speak of feelings we have never experienced. There is more to be done than to speculate on ideas that always fall short in one way or another. Let us set aside, then, what, in the work of thought, remains arbitrary, variable, and artificial. In every state of the soul, at every level of civilization, "a one necessary thing" presents itself, imposes itself on human consciousness; and it is the science of this language known to all which it is supremely important to determine.

It is not that we have to stop at an indefinable sense of the mystery, nor despair of grasping anything of it in thought, nor forbid ourselves from seeking any necessitating proof for it. Far from it. A proof that is only a logical argument always remains abstract and partial; it does not lead to being; it does not necessarily force thought up against real necessity. But a proof that results from the total movement of life, a proof that is action in its entirety will, on the contrary, have this binding power. To equal its spontaneous force with a dialectical presentation, then, we must leave the mind without any escape route. Indeed, it is proper to action to form a whole; through it, then, all the partial arguments will be united into a demonstrative synthesis. In their isolation, they remain sterile; by their unity, they are probative. Only on this condition will they imitate, will they stimulate, the movement of life. Having emerged from the dynamism of action, they will perforce keep its efficacity.

I

Strictly speaking, nothing is scientifically demonstrated unless its necessity has been established. To ground a real truth, it is not enough to suppose that it is, while showing that there is nothing to keep it from being. We have to suppose that it is not, while showing that it is impossible for it not to be. Once we have closed off all exits, the conclusion imposes itself.

Thus, it was necessary, from the beginning of this inquiry, to close off the way of nothingness once and for all. This idea of nothingness is not without the idea of something else. And the argument that might best be termed *ontological* is this counterproof that establishes the impossibility of absolute non-being, by grounding itself on the insufficiency of relative being.

Indeed, under what form does this thought of nothingness present itself to consciousness? Under the form of a negation. And what do we deny in order to affirm it? Everything that is an immediate object of knowledge and desire. That is to say that the greatness of all the rest serves only to bring out the incomparable excellence of this alleged nothingness. In aspiring to it, in acknowledging it, what we will and what we affirm is no longer what we do and what we think, but what we can neither do nor think, and what we still cannot keep from willing and affirming. Our science, our action is never such as a will limited only to phenomena would have it be. That is why, in the face of finished works and of defined words and thoughts, it seems that the true name of this unknown is "death and nothingness" rather than being and life. In order not to reduce it to determinations and symbols that would deny it in some way, we indicate what it is not, and not what it is, by saying truthfully that it is nothing, nothing of all that is. To such a degree is man filled with the imperious sense that, in his action, what is essential surpasses perceived or produced reality!

Here, then, affirmation is less correct and negation more true: negation penetrates further into the nature of this mystery present in our acts. Hence it is not without reason that mystics have spoken magnificently of nothingness, as of the profound spring from which life rises; that some

342

religious souls have kept the silence of adoration before the ineffable, in order not to denature it by their words, for no one is able or worthy to call it by its secret name; that the greatest minds have feared betraying this mysterious reality by trying to circumscribe it with a positive definition; and that loving hearts have thought they saw in atheism a form, the most respectful of all according to them, of modest and profound piety. Under all these veils is hidden a homage to being; it is nothingness that necessarily confesses it. Wherever we turn, we encounter it; and to flee from it is still a way of running toward it and falling into its hands. *Solus est qui frustra nunquam quaeri potest, nec cum inveniri non potest* (only it can never be sought in vain, not even when it cannot be found).

II

But this necessary admission has all its meaning and all its precision only through the complement of another lesson. The proof of being, grounded first on the totality of "what appears not to be," is decisive only if it rests at the same time on the totality of "what appears to be." For, how could the plenitude of nothingness and the necessity of being that hides within it be made evident, if not by using phenomena and experiencing their insufficiency? By unfolding into the universe, the will becomes more clearly conscious of itself and of its exigencies: nature, science, consciousness, social life, the metaphysical domain, the moral world have been for it only a series of means. It can neither give them up nor be satisfied with them; it uses them, then, as a launching pad. *Per ea quae non sunt et apparent, ad ea quae non apparent et sunt* (through what is not and appears, to what does not appear and is). 343

The proof of the "one thing necessary" thus borrows its force and its value from the whole order of phenomena. Without it, all is nothing and nothing cannot be. All that we will supposes that it is; all that we are requires that it be. The argument taken from universal contingency can then be formulated a thousand ways. This one thing necessary is found at the beginning and at the end of all the avenues man can enter; at the outcome of science and of the mind's curiosity, at the outcome of sincere and wounded passion, at the outcome of suffering and disgust, at the outcome of joy and recognition, everywhere, whether we descend into ourselves or ascend to the limits of metaphysical speculation, the same need re-appears. Nothing of what is known, possessed, done, is sufficient unto itself or is annihilated. Impossible to stay with it; impossible to do without it.

Thus understood, the argument *a contingentia* (from contingency) has a character quite other, a spring more powerful, than has been thought ordinarily. Instead of looking for the necessary outside the contingent, as an ulterior term, it manifests it within the contingent itself, as a reality already present. Instead of making it a transcendent but exterior support, it discovers that it is immanent at the very center of all that is. Instead of proving simply the impossibility of affirming the contingent alone, it proves the impossibility of denying the necessary that grounds it. Instead of saying, "Should at any moment nothing be, nothing will be eternally," it concludes, "From the moment something has been, eternally the one thing necessary is." Instead of resting on the fiction of a necessary ideal, it rests on the very necessity of the real.

We must not, then, claim that our acts are nothing and that phenomena are entirely empty. It would be to belie common experience. In what he does, in the life of the senses, in his acts and his pleasures, man feels at once a strange indigence and a more astonishing fulness. Don't try to tell him, then, that this life, this business that captivates him, even these delights he is fascinated with, are without consistency. We sense that in all these vanities there is already more than we know ourselves. And if, as we taste the phenomena, our appetite sometimes seems to grow without ever being satiated, it is because always, in willing and in order to will this little, we first will and still will something else.

Hence the entire order of nature is inevitably a guaranty of what surpasses it. The relative necessity of the contingent reveals the absolute necessity of the necessary. To be sure, in the conception of these phenomena that have, so to speak, their substance elsewhere than in themselves, in this imperfect form of existence whose definition we cannot bring to completion, there subsists a disconcerting ambiguity to the eye of reflexion: it seems that we possess enough being not to be able to get along without some; too much, to be detached from it; too little, to be content with it; more or less than we would hope, since we have it only to sense that we do not have it. But that is precisely the true character of the contingent: the contingent participates in the necessity of the real, without partaking of its privilege. What is exists necessarily while it is, even though by nature it is not anything necessary.

That is why visible things, human sciences, the phenomena of consciousness, the arts and works, *ea quae nec sunt, nec non esse possunt* (those things that neither are nor cannot not be), everything in us and outside of us requires the "one thing necessary." And if these shadows of being are a solid foundation to bear it, it is because the "one thing necessary" is itself their invisible support.

III

What then is this mysterious x that is neither nothingness nor phenomenon, though we cannot conceive the phenomenon or nothingness without including it in the thought that admits them? To find it, we cannot start from it, where we are not; we must start from ourselves, where it is.

In our knowledge, in our action, there subsists a constant disproportion between the object itself and thought, between the work and the will. Incessantly the conceived ideal is surpassed by the real operation, and incessantly the reality obtained is surpassed by an ever reviving ideal. One after the other, thought outstrips practice, and practice outstrips thought; the real and the ideal, therefore, must coincide, since this identity is given in fact; but it is given to us only to escape us no sooner than it is given. What a strange condition of life, this mutual and alternating propulsion of idea and action! Just as two movements of periodically unequal speed run apart and run together one after the other to coincide at one point, it seems that all our strivings oscillate around a point of coincidence where they never come to a halt, even though they go through it incessantly.

It is not from ourselves, then, that we draw either the light of our thought or the efficaciousness of our action. An energy hidden in the depth of consciousness, a truth that is more intimate than our own knowledge, a power that at every moment of our development furnishes the force, the scope, the clarity that is needed, all this is in us without being from us. We are necessarily led to conceive this real mystery only by discovering in it at the same time a power and a wisdom that surpass us infinitely.

Let the scope of this proof be properly understood, then. It gathers all that we have found, without or within ourselves, of intelligibility and intelligence, of movement and force, of truth and thought, in order to manifest its common principle. The admirable harmony of the visible universe, the perhaps more marvelous harmony of the sciences, the mechanism of consciousness, and all the beautiful ordering of human works, thus come to depend on this keystone, as if to prove its solidity. This argument too can then take a thousand diverse forms. But the essence of it is to reveal, in what moves, organizes, and knows itself, a common source of power and wisdom. If all the rest is summed up and grounded in our action and our thought, our thought and our action are grounded in and fecundate one another mutually only thanks to "the pure act of perfect thought."

Thus, like the cosmological argument, the teleological proof is re-

345

newed and confirmed through its union with the others. To present it in isolation, is to take away from it the best of its value. Every demonstration that does not equal its object and proves less than it should, is shaky; it is not to weaken it to impose on it a heavier task. To be probative, it must prove all that is to be proved. It is not enough to establish, by syllogism, the harmony of the means, the grandeur of the ends, and the necessity of a wise and intelligent cause to order the universe and thought. The true teleological proof goes further. It shows that the wisdom of things is not in things, that the wisdom of man is not in man. It is not limited to placing the work and the worker in the presence of one another, so as to guess at the presence and the aims of the one according to the qualities of the other; rather, it seeks to know how thought and action coincide and whence wisdom and power are united. For its point of departure it does not take only what is already realized, but also what is incessantly realizing and perfecting itself. It does not measure the Cause it affirms according to the dimension of the effects, but while recognizing it in them, it places it outside of them and finds in the relative beauty of things the very principle of all beauty.

Here then is how this argument, so rich in a variety of aspects, presents itself to reflexion in its abstract form. Neither can my thought equal my action, nor my action equal my thought. There is in me a disproportion between the efficient cause and the final cause; and yet neither the one nor the other can be in me what they already are without the permanent mediation of a perfect thought and a perfect action. All that is beauty and life in things, all that is light and power in man, contains, in its very imperfection and weakness, a sovereign perfection: thus will this triple relation be developed. — It is within us, it is in the real that we discover, as in an imperfect mirror, this inaccessible perfection. And yet, we can neither identify ourselves with it, nor can we identify it with ourselves.

— The force of this proof is to take its support in our most intimate experience. It is not by adding up our little qualities, not by extracting from things the beauty and power they manifest, not by abstracting or contrasting, that we discover "the one thing necessary," as if it were an ideal outside of ourselves and without roots in our life. Far from being a projection and like a fictitious extension of my thought and my activity, it is at the center of what I think and what I do; I surround it; and, to go from thought to action or from action to thought, to go from myself to myself, I pass through it incessantly. Thus, the order, the harmony, the wisdom that I discover in myself and in things, is not simply an effect starting from which a reasoning process would force me to go up toward a cause absent from its work; I cannot consider this harmony and this beauty as constituted and subsisting in itself; I do not make of them the premises of a deduction; I do not invoke any principle of causality; rather, I find in this imperfect wisdom of things and of my thought the presence and the necessary action of a perfect thought and a perfect power.

—And though I find this presence and this action in me, I cannot say they are mine. This "one thing necessary" has a reason for being only because we do not equal ourselves. To arrive at the equation of our voluntary action, we must look into ourselves all the way to the point where what is of us ceases. Just as the clarity of a look is seen only in the mirror of a clear look, so also consciousness knows itself only in the light of the life within its own life. There is at the bottom of my consciousness an *I* that is no longer *I*; I reflect my own image in it. I see myself only in it: its impenetrable mystery is like the foil that reflects light within me.

—But if it is within me more than I, still it is no more I than I am it. I do not equal myself because I do not equal it. The "one thing necessary," then, is not the obscure side of my thought, the invisible reverse side of my consciousness and my action, as if I were to see it only within myself and as if all its reality consisted only in the idea I have of it. I am necessarily brought to conceive it only because I am necessarily brought to acknowledge what is lacking to me in the very thing that I do: the absolute identity of the real and the ideal, of power and of wisdom, of being and of perfection, this is what it is in order for me to be what I am. A thought and a will without which there would be no thought and will in me and yet which neither my thought nor my will can comprehend, these are the solidary terms of the mystery that imposes itself in my consciousness. The only reason I have for affirming it, is that it is at once necessary and inaccessible to me; it is what cannot be made or thought by me, although I cannot do or think anything except through it. And if it remains inaccessible to me, it is not for lack of being or of clarity in it, but in me. It is therefore what I cannot be: all thought and all action. And I know it truly only insofar as it is incomprehensible to 348 me. Is it not true that, because of the abundance of a light whose rays break the contours of objects, there is at times more impenetrable depth, as in the splendor of the mysterious Orient, than in the midst of a darkness where we can at least flash on a light?

IV

Thus again the ontological argument will acquire a new meaning and forcefulness. It is not a matter of indifference in the dialectical presentation of proofs, to follow one order rather than another. With another order, we run the risk of seeing the idea of perfection as an arbitrarily constructed fiction without real foundation, whereas it is a quite vivid reality in our consciousness and it derives from our total action all the positive certitude there is already in us. For us, it is less a *look* than a *life*. It does not result from a speculation; it is tied to the entire movement of our thought and action. It is not something abstract, whence we could draw only something abstract, but an act that makes us act. It is not an ideal from which one may pretend to draw the real, but something real in which we find the ideal. We must not look in it, then, for the only thing that would ground an objection against it, a reality distinct from the ideal itself.

Thus, it is legitimate here, and only here, to identify the idea with being, because under this abstract identity we first place the identity of thought and action. So we must not say only that we go from the idea to being; we must say that first we find the idea in being and being in action. We discover within ourselves real perfection and we go on to ideal perfection. We go, so to speak, from ourselves to it, in order to go from it to it. To be sure, the ontological proof never has for us all the force it has in itself; for it is absolute only where there is a perfect idea of perfection itself, where essence is real and existence is ideal. Hence it is true that to reach "the one thing necessary," we do not grasp it in itself, where we are not; but we start from it within ourselves, where it is, in order to see better that it is by understanding a bit what it is. We are bound to affirm it to the extent that we have an idea of it: for this idea 349 itself is a reality. As we come to define better for ourselves what we are not, through a more complete experience and a more penetrating reflexion, we come to see more clearly that without which we would not be. To know it and to possess it more, is all one. The light wherein it sees me is also the one wherein I see it and wherein I see myself; for it is the light wherein it sees itself first.

Indeed, what does every attempt to penetrate the very mystery of perfection reveal? (For the ontological proof is only a play of entities if it does not have this daring and this necessary bearing). If perfection is a mystery to us, it is not because it is not known to us or because it might not know itself; far from it, it is because we necessarily conceive that it knows us and that it knows itself absolutely. Its obscurity is constituted in our eyes by an excess of light: while in our acts we sense an irremediable disproportion, we affirm, in its act, an immediate identity. It appears impenetrable to us through what we know of it. Its inaccessible interiority does not escape us in that it is alien to us, but in that it is more interior to us than our own interior. What is disconcerting to us in ourselves, is that we cannot equal ourselves; what is disconcerting to us in it, is the absolute equation of *being, knowing,* and *acting.* It is a subject in whom everything is subject, even the consciousness it has of itself, even the inward operation by which it realizes itself by finding a response equal to its call and a love corresponding to its own. And just as personality could not be solitary, as it is not *one* except by not being *alone,* to speak of this mysterious perfection as if existence in it differed from knowledge or knowledge from action, would be to lower it to the imperfections which, recognized in ourselves, forced us to pass over into it. It is more incomprehensible without the trinity than the trinity itself is incomprehensible to man. The trinity is the ontological argument transported into the absolute, where this proof is no longer a proof, but the truth itself and the life of being.

And it is not by diminishing this necessary truth or avoiding to define it precisely that we will make it acceptable to thought: it is all or nothing at all; and it is impossible that it be *nothing.* It is easier, it is more scientific, to acknowledge the maximum of the necessary truth than to be satisfied with a vague and indeterminate minimum. What is superstitious is to limit oneself to a partial argument or to a fragmentary conclusion. The notion of a first cause or a moral ideal, the idea of a metaphysical perfection or a pure act, all these conceptions of human reason, vain, false and idolatrous, if we consider them in isolation as abstract representations, are true, living and efficacious as soon as, in solidarity with one another, they are, no longer a game of the understanding, but a practical certitude. What the discursive labor of thought renders lengthy and leaves sterile, then, becomes immediate and practical, if, in the multiplicity of proofs, we find the means of presenting them all together. All together they are more simple and more direct than each taken separately: they are valid only by their synthetic unity; for it is by this concatenation itself that they reproduce the movement of life and sustain it, that they truly come from the teachings of action and return to action to teach it and vivify it.

It is in practice itself, then, that the certitude of "the one thing necessary" has its foundation. In what touches the total complexity of life, only action is necessarily complete and total as well. It bears on the whole; and that is why from it, and from it alone, arises the indisputable presence and the binding proof of Being. Dialectical subtleties, no matter how long and ingenious they may be, have no more bearing than a stone thrown at the sun by a child. And it is in an instant, in a single surge, by an immediate necessity that is made manifest is us *the one* that no reasoning could invent, because no deduction is equal to the plenitude of life in action; and he is the one who is this plenitude itself. Only the

350

total and concrete development of action reveals him in us then, not always under traits that might make him recognizable to the mind, but in a way which makes of him a concrete truth and which will render him efficacious, useful, and accessible to the will.

At the end, quickly reached, of what is finite, from the very first reflexion, we find ourselves in the presence of what the phenomenon and nothingness equally hide and manifest, in the face of one we can never speak of from memory as though of a stranger or of one who is absent, before the one for whom in all languages and in all consciousnesses there is a word and a feeling to recognize him by, God.

V

351   As soon as we touch on God, and as soon as, by the first reflexion that thrusts us toward Him, always present and always new, we awaken to the light of His presence, there is a kind of sudden stop; life seems held in suspense; and we do not proceed any further. — Yes; we do go further. Under whatever form it presents itself before consciousness, the thought of God is brought there by a determinism that forces it upon us: sprung necessarily from the dynamism of interior life, it necessarily has an effect; it has an immediate influence on the organization of our conduct. It is this necessary action of the necessary idea of God that we must determine: we shall see how the voluntary inevitably takes on a transcendent character, and how this necessity is the very expression of freedom. Thus, through the play of determinism, the conflict that has arisen in consciousness inevitably resolves itself into an alternative that presents the human will with a supreme option.

I. — The thought of God within us depends on our action in two ways. On the one hand, it is because in acting we find an infinite disproportion in ourselves that we are constrained to look to infinity for the equation of our action. On the other hand, it is because in affirming absolute perfection we do not ever arrive at equalling our own affirmation, that we are constrained to look for its complement and its commentary in action. The problem that action raises, only action can solve.

As soon as we think we know God enough, we no longer know him. To be sure, the instant of His appearance in consciousness resembles eternity so much that we fear entering into it wholly, with our eyes straining toward the flash that has shone only to make the night darker. But the mixture of shadow and clarity remains such that the presumption of the one who thinks he sees and the pretense of the one who feigns to ignore it are both equally confounded: against those who see too much, we must maintain that, in what we know and will, God remains what we can neither know nor do; against the willfully blind, we must maintain that, without dialectical complications or long studies, in the twinkling of an eye, for all, at any hour, God is the immediate certitude without which there is no other, the first clarity, the language known without having had to learn it. He is the only one that we cannot look for in vain, without ever being able to find him fully. *Nemo te quaerere valet, nisi qui prius invenerit: vis igitur inveniri ut quaeraris, quaeri ut inveniaris; potes quidem quaeri et inveniri, non tamen praeveniri* (No one can look for you unless he has already found you: hence you wish to be found so that people will look for you and to be looked for so that people will find you; for you can be looked for and found, not however preceded). 352

Hence the moment we seem to touch God through a trace of thought, He escapes us, if we do not keep Him, if we do not look for Him, through action. His immobility can be aimed at as a fixed goal only by a perpetual movement. Wherever we stop, He is not; wherever we walk forward, He is. It is a necessity always to go further, because He is always beyond. As soon as we no longer wonder at Him as at an inexpressible newness, and as soon as we look at Him from the outside as a matter for knowing or a simple occasion for speculative examination, without youth in our heart or loving anxiousness, it is done with: all we have in hand is phantom and idol. All that we have seen or felt of Him is only a means to go further. It is a road; therefore, we do not stop in it, otherwise it is no longer a road. To think of God is an action; yet we also do not act without cooperating with Him and without having Him collaborate with us by a sort of necessary *theergy* which integrates the part of the divine in the human operation, in order to achieve the equation of voluntary action in consciousness. And it is because action is a synthesis of man with God that it is in perpetual becoming, as if stirred by the inspiration of an infinite growth. Set within itself and content with itself, thought is a monster: its nature is to introduce into the unfolding of life a progressive dynamism. It is a fruit of life only to become a seed of new life. That is why the thought of the transcendent inevitably imposes a transcendent character on action.

And let us not imagine that, to insert this transcendent character into our lives, it is necessary to discern the presence or distinctly recognize the action of God in us. To acknowledge Him, to use Him, it is not indispensable to name or to define Him: we can even deny Him, without removing from our acts their necessary bearing. For in denying Him, we are only displacing the object of affirmation; but the reality of human acts is not touched, in its depth, by the superficial play of ideas and words. It is enough that, even masked and disguised, the universal good has secretly solicited the will, for the whole of life to be marked by this indelible impression. To hear its call or experience its contact, there is no need to stare at it. What inevitably arises in every human consciousness, what has in practice an inescapable efficacity, is not the conception of a speculative truth to be defined; it is the conviction, perhaps vague, but certain and imperious, of a destiny and an ulterior end to be attained. Indeed, it is not a question of a few details of conduct to be clarified or of partial decisions to be taken; it is the total character of the total life of each individual that each individual is led to worry about. An uneasiness, a natural aspiration toward what is better, the sense of having a role to fulfill, the quest for the meaning of life, these, then, are what mark human conduct with a necessary imprint. Whatever answer we give for the problem, the problem is raised. Man always places in his acts, no matter how obscurely he knows it, this character of transcendence. What he does, he never does simply for the sake of doing it.

Here, then, we are touching on the principle that vivifies the entire movement of life within us. There is no need to have resolved any metaphysical question to live, so to speak, metaphysically. The ontological argument is applicable to us as well! Thought and action unfold in us only because in the unfolding essence becomes real and existence ideal. We cannot deny it without lying to ourselves; and we do not truly deny it, because the lie changes nothing in the necessity of the truths it dissimulates. Henceforth, then, without attaching to speculative ignorances or errors any importance that they do not have by themselves, we must finally see what the necessary effect of God being present to man is. Under whatever form, clear or confused, consented to or repressed, acknowledged or anonymous, the truth of this presence reveals itself to consciousness, it has an influence that is certain. It is this higher dynamism that must be studied above all.

II. — Born, through the very impulse of determinism, of a conflict at the heart of human consciousness, the necessary thought of God, through a last step of determinism, resolves this conflict into an unavoidable alternative.

Because I am forced to conceive and to assign a higher term to my thought and my action, it is also a necessity for me to feel the need to equal my thought and my life to it. The idea of God (whether we know how to name Him or not) is the inevitable complement of human action; but human action also has as its inevitable ambition to reach and to use, to define and to realize in itself, this idea of perfection. What we know of God is this surplus of interior life that demands to be used: therefore, we cannot know God without wishing to become God in some way. The living thought we have of Him is and remains living only if it turns to practice, only if we live by it and nourish action with it. Here, as everywhere else, knowledge is never anything but a consequence and an origin of activity.

But in what embarrassment do we not find ourselves? Man feels an invincible need to capture God. It is because he cannot do so that he believes in Him and affirms Him; he believes in Him and affirms Him truly, only by using Him and putting Him effectively into practice. God's only reason for being for us is that He is what we cannot be ourselves or do with our own strength; and yet we appear to have being, will and action only in view of willing Him and becoming Him. It seems that He places Himself between us and ourselves, that He divides us even to the joints of our bones, and that, if we dare say, we have to pass over His body. And yet we have no action on Him: our will dies where He is born; our work ceases where His begins, and, to speak more correctly, His work seems to absorb all that is real in ours. What belongs to us, then, is to be without being; and yet we are forced to will to become what we can neither attain nor possess by ourselves. What a strange exigency. It is because I have the ambition of being infinitely that I feel my powerlessness: I did not make myself, I cannot do what I will, I am constrained to surpass myself; and at the same time, I can recognize this fundamental infirmity only by having a sense already of the means to overcome it, by the acknowledgement of an Other within me, by the substitution of another will for mine.

Thus, through the mechanism of the interior life, we are led to an alternative that sums up all the teachings of practice. Man, by himself, cannot be what he already is in spite of himself, what he claims to become voluntarily. Yes or no, will he will to live, even to the point of dying, so to speak, by consenting to be supplanted by God? Or else, will he pretend to be self-sufficient without God, profit by His necessary presence without making it voluntary, borrow from Him the strength to get along without Him, and will infinitely without willing the Infinite? To will and not to be able, to be able and not to will, that is the very option that presents itself to freedom: "to love oneself to the contempt of God, to love God to the contempt of self." Not that this tragic opposition is revealed to us with such sharpness and rigor, but if the thought that there is "something to be done with life" occurs to us, that is enough for even the most coarse to be called as well to resolve the great business of life, the one thing necessary.

The determinism of action, therefore, ends up raising an alternative in

355

human consciousness. And the usefulness of the preceding analyses is to show what the option of the will necessarily envelops. The insufficiency of these very analyses matter little: the importance of the choice does not depend on the explanation we try to give of it. It is enough that, in acting deliberately, we realize all these implicit conditions from the start. To have given determinism all its share is to have succeeded in determining precisely that of freedom: freedom is summed up completely in this very option, because the will is fully exercised only where the stakes are worthy of it. It is good to have analysed all the content of voluntary action; but this analysis itself must not hide from us the principle that brings it to a synthesis. The series of means is organized in consciousness only in view of this decisive question. All the movement of life leads up to this. The most rudimentary phenomenon would not be what it is for us without the link that ties it to this question. So, reciprocally, the knowledge of the least phenomenon has the role of making us rise, through the chain of determinism, to this free decision on which the destiny of each individual depends. The human will thus proposes for itself the series of means whose effect is to impose on it the exercise of its power. Hence, in this very necessity, it does not undergo anything that it has not willed.

To be sure, the alternative inevitably rises before consciousness, and there is one more necessity to declare oneself; but let us not be sidetracked. It is true, the option is imposed on us; but it is through it that we become what we will: whatever may result from it, we will have only ourselves to blame. Thus, in the last analysis, it is not freedom that is absorbed in determinism; it is the total determinism of human life that hangs from this supreme alternative: either exclude from ourselves any other will than our own, or hand ourselves over to the being that we are not as to the only salutary one. Man aspires to be a god: to be god without God and against God, to be god through God and with God, that is the dilemma. In the face of being, and only of being, the law of contradiction applies in all its rigor, and freedom exercises itself in all its force.

The necessity for man to opt only manifests his will to be and to be what he wills. Hence his action has a necessary being. But if he claims to find or to keep this being all to himself, it turns against him. If in the face of the alternative imposed on him, he does not orient his freedom toward a new form of life, he is lost. It is not necessary to know this higher life already to know that, if his acts repel it, he fails in his destiny. Not to be changed, for man, is the death of action. Hence he will be able to live only by being reborn, so to speak, in the labor of a new childbirth and by opening himself up to another action than his own. But whatever way the conflict may be resolved, the option of freedom will not eliminate what necessary being there is in willed action.

THE ALTERNATIVE

357   It is impossible that the development of voluntary action not come to an alternative. For option is the necessary form under which a will, imposed on itself, takes possession of itself, in order to will what it is by being what it wills. This necessity, then, is the consequence of a free initiative. And the very simple way in which popular consciousness conceives the problem of destiny as a choice, personal to each individual, between good and evil, between the order of God and the inclination of egoism, corresponds to the most profound drama of the interior life.

But what popular consciousness does not succeed in determining, what the science of action has served to bring to light, are the precise terms of the alternative. Through its inevitable expansion, the human will, even unknown to itself, has divine exigencies. Its wish is to attain and to conquer God; it gropes blindly to reach Him. And yet God has no reason for being, in our thought and in our action, except inasmuch as, inaccessible and inviolable in His mystery, He remains beyond our grasp. What is to be done, then? Shall we will to die to self, in order to live for him? But how? Or else, shall we not finally succeed in getting along without Him or, if need be, in placing Him at the service of man, to have Him for ourselves without being for Him?

And is it not strange that we should even be able to raise these ques-
358   tions? If in our willed actions "the one thing necessary" is always present, what room is left, then, in which man can opt? And if, whatever we do, whatever we know, our destiny unravels its divine thread, what then is the meaning of both the superficial intervention of our precarious decisions and the poor attempts of our science which strives to plumb the mystery of our lives, as if it were to anticipate the revelations of a supreme judgment? — But this latitude left to man is enough to terrify any thought courageous enough to take the measure of the abyss open before it. — But these decisions, as inefficacious as they appear, are efficacious enough to cut through the great and decisive business of life. — But this science of action, as presumptuous as it may be in raising the veil of pres-

ent responsibilities or future revelations, is enough to forestall surprises and justify the extremes of sanctions held in store for human actions.

There has to be an alternative, then; we have to declare ourselves. And the very necessity of action only manifests this free constraint. Hence, it is in and by human action that the problem of our destiny is resolved; and it is impossible that it not be resolved. On what sharp ridge are we not thrown? We cannot hold ourselves there? And, whichever way we go, to perdition or to salvation, it will have been willed.

FIRST OPTION
The Death of Action

359 Was it not man's ambition to suffice unto himself like a sovereign? Ready to acknowledge his dependence with regard to equals or lower beings, he accepts all natural chains as long as he does not have to recognize a master, to pray to a God. To be sure, he senses that his actions surpass the natural order, that there is in them more than a system of common phenomena and that his life has a meaning he cannot get rid of. But after all, doesn't this mystery of his own destiny belong to him like all the rest? Can he not restrict as he wishes the bearing of his conduct, renounce the honor of a vocation that is too high not to be irksome? Or if he is no longer in a position to say he does not will "the one thing necessary," if he cannot entirely ignore or forget that it is impossible to reject it or to suborn it like a dead idol, does he not pretend to use it as he wishes, to mete out its place for it, to give up the little it is his pleasure to give in order to get the whole he must have?

These desires and hopes have always worked upon human consciousness. Today they work more particularly on many souls emancipated from all faith, but not from all religious anxiety. Is it not the case that we would will everything about God, except God Himself? Is it not the case, after having excluded Him in order to enjoy everything without Him, that we would still will Him, almost in spite of Him? Is it not the 360 case that, whatever we do, it seems we have to be assured of a salvation in the end and be worthy of a happiness without which we do not will to conceive that being could truly be? This is the myth of the one who dared steal fire from the heavens and arrives at the final triumph without having repented. It is the old legend of the mortal who loved an immortal goddess in defiance of sacred prohibitions and who deifies himself, in spite of the gods whom he forces to recognize this divinity conquered against them. It is "the end of Satan," proclaimed as the means of having done with the Master and the dreaded Judge. — Artificial illusions which it is urgent to dissipate. Indeed, it matters little that we do not always

332

discern distinctly the necessary consequences of what we do: that is not what prevents them from unfolding justly. There is no need to name and define the faults committed, to know and to will them. The true science is the one that is efficacious in practice, as true freedom is the one that fixes the will in the great and decisive question: without God or through God.

To be self-sufficient, to limit oneself to what one wants and what one can, what is there in this pretention of man? How can he subsist while rejecting the principle of all subsistence? But how is it impossible for him to suppress within himself what he excludes from himself? How is it impossible for him to find, in what keeps his action from dying, the principle of a return to life? A being without Being, a voluntary destiny that one refuses to will, an undying death, that is the strange solution we must account for.

I

Voluntary action is made equal to itself in consciousness only inasmuch as we recognize in it the presence and the cooperation of "the one thing necessary." If we are not and can do nothing without Him, and if it is impossible for us to be nothing, how then explain that the will can acknowledge Him without accepting Him, or that it can deny itself without destroying itself? What is this astonishing mutilation? Or how can we understand that, even in what we can do without God and against God, it is still through Him that we do it? In what is voluntary, is there something, then, that can be not willed, in what is willed, something that can be not voluntary? — Yes, and it is this inward contradiction that is the very death of action.

Not to will all that we will and to persuade ourselves that we will it, 361 while we do not will it and we know it, such a disposition, subtle in the words that express it for reflexion, is quite simple and quite frequent, in the practice that inserts it into life. How many men seem to have little interest in anything absent! And is it not the great effort of modern thought to tend to justify this self-assurance of man in the face of his destiny? But let us go to the bottom of this pretention. Consciousness may well form a kind of second sincerity for itself by decreeing that it is secure, without emptiness and without anxiety. If we study the very way in which it persuades itself that it finds its repose, we will uncover the inner spring that keeps it from doing so. If we search out how it is possible for man to turn himself away from his destiny, we will find how it is impossible for him to escape it.

That the infinite power wrapped in voluntary action could be applied to and as it were used up in a finite term, should come as no surprise to us. It is more surprising, so to speak, that it should be able to find, under the symbol of the limited ends that solicit it, the infinite end it aspires to. We must keep in mind that the universal good cannot present itself to consciousness except under particular traits. To the extent that its presence moves the will, as the principle and efficient cause of a life avid to open itself out, the good truly keeps its infinitude; to the extent that, before thought, it proposes itself as an object to be conquered or as the final cause of action, it is no longer anything more than a partial and limited motive.

This is why the meaning of the movement that sweeps the human will along is ambiguous. What is finite, it seems, is this very God we must aim at; what is infinite, is the aspiration of the heart, it is that which starts from man, it is ourselves. But see the equivocation that action takes upon itself to dissipate: will one will to confiscate this great surge of sincerity in act and turn it back on oneself? Will one, on the contrary, through a free recognition, restore to this apparent finite of God its real infinitude and refer to Him this movement which seems to come from us, but which comes from Him to return to Him?

The option that seemed absurd and impossible, then, is only too easy. How readily, through the violence of passion or the proud perversion of the mind, is the will, so full of its borrowed power, exposed to take pleasure in itself and to limit itself! How easy it is to forget who is the One who hides under this inspiration of strength and of light! And yet He is there, present and veiled, in the feeling for what is better which ceaselessly elevates every life, in that obscure order of duty which needles egoism, even in the remorse which still maintains the rights of the ideal over moral degradation and the ruins of the heart. He is there, in those perpetual gifts of conscience, more than He is in the clearest conception we form of His essence. And that is why, to confiscate this first surge of sincerity for the benefit of man and his egotistic desires, is, while seeming to be an option between limited motives, to place in it immensity itself. In treating itself as limited, in adhering to objects whose insufficiency it has recognized, in looking in them for the infinite satisfaction that it covets, the will, so to speak, objectivizes itself in itself and subjectivizes itself in them. In judging their insufficiency to be sufficient, in finding them worthy of itself, it brings their infirmity into itself, it places its own infinity in them: it loses itself.

So be it, then, that instead of adoring God in God, man adores himself in his senses and in nature; so be it (to borrow the language of Spinoza), that finding in himself the infinite of the Substance that makes him be, he detaches this form of the infinite from the Substance itself to apply it to his own particular and limited being; the strangeness of this illogical option is all too readily explainable. And one does not need to have explained it to oneself to fall into it. Under the symbol of the most common motives and in the conflict of the most simple feelings, this great affair is decided for each one. What escapes consciousness is the abstract formulation, but not the concrete reality of the choice or the sense that, under these petty frivolities which we are toying with, there is a drama wherein we are at stake. Also, even if we suppose evil to be only a lesser good, without denaturing the inward truth, we can express, through a rigorous calculation, this dramatic alternative which no human life avoids resolving.

Here are two acts projected, which in the light of conscience I judge to be of unequal value. I don't know what the good is, but I see that one is better: it is a duty. I take note of this qualitative relation. Let it be 7 and 13. I opt for 7; it may be a pleasure, a gain whose easy attraction makes me reject 13, where I felt more difficulty, a necessary effort, a little sacrifice to be made, because what is better hardly ever comes without some struggle and some dedication. $7 - 13 = -6$. It seemed I had something in enjoying 7; and that is why the most empty and the most debt-ridden of lives still has a kind of vain feeling of fullness and abundance. But really, what I have is -6; the terrible and surprising and just bankruptcy of faulty action. From those who have not, even what they have will be taken away.

And in truth, if I choose either 13 or 7 with reflexion, I can place something more in it. It is a matter of certain and daily experience that, in an act that appears to us as good, as obligatory for us, there is something more than this little relative good. For if I love it and will it as I ought, I am ready to sacrifice it for something better, but not for the pleasure I find in it, since what appears better in itself is often more difficult and more irksome for us. It is not *this* good, then, which I will and which I do; it is that which it represents; something indeterminate which has no place in the world and no natural influence or sensible attraction, a nothing which, to use the language of mathematics, can be called the infinite (the infinite, which has no sign, and that is why it has to present itself to us through the mediation of a particular motive on which will depend the positive or negative character of the act); something which in everyone's conscience does not even have to be named to be duty. I took 7; and in this finite symbol I have compromised all that I am, all that I ought to be. In taking a condemned route, I have to answer for

363

what I refused to learn, neglected to try, disdained or dreaded to put in practice. The one who is voluptuous thinks he is not lacking in all generosity, that he is not falling into debt: $7 - 13 \infty = -\infty$. He must be told both that he has something and that he is losing everything. And the more he senses the miserable nothingness of what he loves, or the more passionate the ardor of the love he puts into it, the more also he abuses what indestructible force and light he has in him. From those who think they have, even what they do not have will be taken.

To be sure, the alternative does not present itself to all or always with the same clarity or with the same gravity. If, in the object that the will proposes for itself as an end, it undergoes the attraction of the mobile that sweeps it along, more than it considers or consents to an abuse of its infinite power, the option, even when perverse, remains venial. But the fault is serious, the reflexion deadly, when, in *this* particular good which we think little of, we have the sense of rejecting at the same time that of which it is only the expression, that which it is *good* to love and to do. If there seems to be more guilt in stealing a million than a penny, it is because instinctively we sense that, once moral reflexion has arisen, the violence of the temptation and the natural attraction of the motive are nothing in comparison with the power that governs action.

It is true that, through the imperceptible progress of perversion, man can come to the point of loving what he calls evil, for the sake of evil. Placing in the pleasure of revolting, or in the spite of a passion exalted by a consciousness of its illusion, the equivalent of all that he should will, he feels what is false and willed in independent action: and he grows all the more hardened with the stubborness of a pride which will not consent to belie itself or to admit its wrongfulness to itself even secretly. But it is not frequent, it is not necessary, in order for action to be struck with death, that one should come to such an abstract science or to such a formal love of evil.

And is not the scandal of thought even to entertain the hypothesis of a moral evil and of an infinite evil which an ignorant and limited man would commit, of an inexcusable evil, while in the weakness of the spirit, in the brevity of life, in the faintness of energy he has so many excuses? What then if we add that, should man refuse to surpass what is of man purely as man, he contracts a debt and one that he is forever incapable of paying off? Nevertheless, an ear must be given to this double assertion. — Wholly human virtue, though good in itself, does not have an infinite value; it is not worth enough for complete happiness; it does not bring man's destiny to its end. — The quite human fault and the mere pretention of not surpassing the human order contains an evil such that it justifies, not only the privation of the good, but the eternity of woe.

How urgent it is to shed light on this mystery, since so many darkened and temerarious souls are convinced of the two errors quite contrary to these two truths!

II

If it is possible to apply to a limited term the infinite tendency of the will, it remains impossible to destroy this aspect of infinity in doing so, impossible to suppress the force of the movement even where it is easy to twist its meaning, impossible to slip out from under the grandeur of human destiny, even as we fall short of it. Although one freely throws oneself at the object of desire to become like it, one does not restrict oneself to the size of the preferred idol; and the agent, even as he becomes what he does, keeps entire in his action the exigencies he does not satisfy.

365

The issue is not an optional surplus which we could give up by refusing the honor in order to avoid the pain, or the gain, so as not to risk the loss. And it is not just because we think ourselves secure in our conscience that we are truly so. No doubt, through a secret and subtle logic, we often seem to succeed in pacifying the restlessness of the heart, in drying up the flow of divine desires, and excluding from consciousness the most natural aspirations. But effort and study are required to do so, as in fixing our eyes carefully on a windowpane covered with light drawings, we half fail to see the distant prospect. And yet it is always this confused field of vision which serves as backdrop, which lights up these transparent trifles we try to see by themselves, and which we would not see if there were not beyond some depth and some brightness.

No doubt, moreover, after we have felt the emptiness of each of the experiences where we placed the whole of ourselves, after each disappointment of life, the vivid hope and the persevering illusion is reborn. And indeed, in this emptiness itself, all is not empty. Even the most vain of actions is for the will at least an occasion for it to experience its indestructible power. Also, what ingeniousness and agility are sometimes used to beguile the tedium of life and to hide from ourselves the inanity of the hours spent in "doing what we will"! If every detail is trivial, does it not seem that the whole is not? If each piece in the system seems false or ruinous, do we not manage to skip lightly enough from one to the other to keep the collapse from happening? Does not a conclusion legitimately grounded on a principle whose error we know finally seem solid and legitimate? — The ordinary deception of the sophism of accumulation or abstraction proves one thing only, that we will infinitely more than we find where we look, but that we look only where we would like to find. How many thus place what they will precisely where it could not be!

I can see why one can be indignant at the immense responsibility man is laden with, at the infinite weight of acts so lightly done that often one has not even placed on the scale their proximate consequences. What justice is there in what we don't know, in what we do almost without having willed it, in what is disproportionate? But it is this complaint that is the condemnation itself. Where does this cry of rebellion and this indignant appeal come from, if not from a heart enamored of light, since it protests against the darkness, in love with equity, since it sets itself up as judge of its judge? To love justice so much when one is unjust! And is it not in this boundless love of man for himself, for his reason, his right, and his happiness, that is found the spring for his voluntary acts and the principle of their eternal sanction?

Well then, would man thus commit himself without willing it and without knowing it, as if he could put the infinite in the finite and eternity in time? — But this excuse accuses him, because the disproportion he is complaining about is the reverse of the one he thinks he sees. It appears to him as a trap, but it harbors, so to speak, a favorable treatment.

Indeed, why speak of the fleeting brevity of time? The more one senses it is short and uncertain, the more it is strange to act as if it were not to end, as if it were all. It is only an appearance, so be it; only a form of human sensibility, so be it! That is why it is inexcusable to limit our desire to it and to tie up our action in it. Action does not come under the law of duration. If speculative critique has ruined the objective validity of time and space, the moral sense and the critique of life has long had, in fact, its *Transcendental Aesthetic*. Does not a good conscience find in a single effort the conclusions that rational analysis attains so laboriously? The man of duty is liberated from the deception of sensibility and from the illusions of time. And in return, is not putting off conversion to will that what we will presently should last forever?

What we will deliberately, what we do freely of our own bidding, we will and we do, not because time passes, but even though time seems to pass. Eternity is entirely in every instant. Just as intention has a universal bearing, it also has an atemporal ambition. To live as if we were never to die, to love time as if it were eternity, to wish to enjoy without end a passing pleasure, and to will to regret only that we cannot live forever as we are living, is there anything in this disposition of the will that mitigates its lack of reason and logic? Just because man gives himself to a pitiable short pleasure, he nonetheless keeps, in this gift itself, his eternal aspiration. What he does not manage to keep and to enjoy even for the duration of a lifetime, he still wills forever: *in suo aeterno peccat* (he sins in what is eternal about him).

Moreover, however far reaching the consequences of human actions may seem, there is in the unique and indivisible instant that produced them something to justify, no longer just their consequences in time, but infinitely more beyond. If these acts, thrown by a sudden decision into the huge machinery of universal determinism, prolong their reverberations in it; if they do not always stay entirely within the point of space and time where they are born; and if they seem at times amplified by the vast echo of the world, that is still only an inadequate image of their invisible extension. And this surprising immensity of their ramifications is a kind of salutary reminder which, through a visible symbol, at times rudely awakens reflexion by revealing to us what we already know, but always forget, namely, the immense bearing of voluntary action. Hence it is because man uses insufficient goods as if they were sufficient that he falls into debt infinitely. For what uses them in him is infinite; and his misfortune is to place, not time in eternity, but eternity in time. *Non cum tempore transit quod tempora transit: fugit hora, manent opera* (what passes through time does not pass with time: the hour runs out, but works remain).

Thus the deliberate and willed act naturalizes the absolute in the relative itself. Without knowing distinctly all that we do, we do more than we know and we know more than we do, in such wise however, that in this mixture of shadow and light in which our destiny is wrapped, a grace is still hidden. If the seriousness of the fault is veiled, the force of the help is more so. For if evil seems at first to be only a lesser good, it is in order that *the* good itself may also put on the particular traits and the attractive figure of a sensible motive, of a better act, of *one* relative good. But from these apparent relations, from these simple differences of degree, we must not conclude against the sincere acknowledgement of conscience: it keeps itself living and ardent, according to the observation of Carlyle, only inasmuch as it reminds us more or less of what we all more or less already know, namely that, under these approximations of knowledge, there is an absolutely infinite difference between a good man and an evil one. To be sure, in the middling area of the soul, there are superficial nuances that distinguish the common run of humanity. How can I admit a measureless responsibility in a boundless weakness? How can I believe in the infinite evil of this man whom I know and love, who is weak, illogical, and unhappy? But this is not to be believed, because the role of our human ignorance is not justice; it is indulgence and love. And yet, without judging anyone, — for the moral commandment "thou

368

shalt not judge" is absolute,—enter a bit more deeply, test hearts. See with your imagination this wretch who, without having given it any thought, would rather die of starvation than commit a crime: by the fine point of his soul this uncultured individual clings to eternal life. See this greedy man of affluence who, perhaps without scruple, deprives this same poor individual. What shares will be meted on the day of justice, and how there will be nothing arbitrary, nothing external, nothing excessive in the extremity of the avenging reprisals!

Nothing seemed more simple, nothing more natural or legitimate than to say to one's own will: "You will go no further; you will receive nothing higher; you will give nothing of what you have; you will not go out of yourself." And yet, this reserved and expectant attitude contains a voluntary negation and a positive privation, στερησις. In order to refuse all eminent gifts and keep ourselves to ourselves, we use precisely what we feign to do without. To look at it from the outside, *sub specie materiae* (under the aspect of matter), the act, thus subdued, no doubt appears moderate and perishable. But the great fault of man is to use his infinite power in order to limit himself. Only his will is strong enough to hold his will in check. And if the way can be blocked even for God, if man can exterminate Him and make it so that He will no longer be for man, it is because he uses Him against Him by first accepting what he needs to repel Him.

Man must not claim then that his responsibility is slight, under the pretext that he does nothing except what is slight and petty. What he is guilty of is precisely not willing anything, not doing anything except what is petty, his faintness of desire and love which does not suppress his proud susceptibility, his willing and not doing. One complains only where one would not want things to be as one knows them to be. And the one who attributes an absolute value to himself, who has an immense love for his well-being, lies to himself if he confines himself to mean pleasures. If, in the insatiable ambition of egoism, there is a mover with an infinite force, it is in order to launch man to infinity. The extent of the fault is measured by the energy of the movement more than by the end to which it tends; and the offense has a bearing only because the divine offended one is struck by the offender with all the power that is supposed to go to Him.

Therefore, it is not outside of man, but within him, that we must look for the secret judgment of eternity. Even when he is condemnable for having claimed to do without any law higher than his own decree, he is still his own law and condemnation. Judged by his own judgments, he is taken as the rule: not his thoughts, which are good at times in spite of him; not his words, which manifest an ordinarily illusory ideal; not even the appraisal he makes of others, although there he may often be defining impartially the practical application of impersonal laws whose universal and necessary force he recognizes at the same time as he perhaps exempts himself for his own account. What judges him is his very action: the internal vigor of his voluntary movement is what serves as measure and sanction for him.

III

But if it is possible for man to pervert the meaning and to limit the infinite tendency of his will, if it is impossible for him to suppress its boundless exigencies at the very moment he betrays them, and to exclude what he rejects, how can we understand nevertheless that, when his eyes are finally opened, he is not either converted or destroyed? Is it conceivable, is it necessary, that the full revelation of his obscure state does not change him and that his misfortune is to be forever unchanged?

This is precisely what proves the extent to which the veils that envelop human action leave its vigor intact and free. Remove the veils: that is when the will fixes itself of its own accord in its option, and when the contradiction into which it has fallen in refusing the superhuman life whose need it felt appears to it as its own work forever. It is not enough, then, to say: what justice would there be in keeping on falling as long as we could, and then to will these faults to go unpunished and to will to renounce them as soon as it would no longer be possible to commit them? Nor is it enough to understand the impossibility of a free return under the sudden burst of a compelling light: whoever has not willed when he could, will no longer be able to when he wills to. What we have to see is that the will itself, at bottom, is not converted and that, in revealing itself outside of time, action voluntarily remains for eternity what it is in time. *In suo temporis aeterno peccat homo: in suo aeternitatis aeterno luit* (Man sins in his eternity of time; he pays in his eternity of eternity). 370

To take advantage of the fact that all the natural order, even deprived of its fulfilment, cannot be annihilated, to look for a permanent satisfaction in what passes, to live off what dies, that is the deadly fault. The absolute and the infinite of a will which gives being to phenomena and makes of them a subsisting and indestructible reality insinuates itself into the free option. Man dies for having claimed to be content with duration and to limit himself to nature; it is not that he is not able to fill and surpass space or time: but he has so expanded this realm of the senses and of science that he could almost make believe he is at ease in it and can find in it a definitive home, that is, if he did not always, willy nilly, have to step out of it through the inevitable warning of conscience, the scandal of suffering and death. If dying to time teaches him what it is to live, it is because this life which does not pass away with time is exposed to a second death, the one that subsists forever. To do was the work of only an instant, to have done and to will is forever. *Quod factum est, factum non esse·non potest* (What is done cannot not have been done). This necessity reveals the presence of being in the phenomenon itself: that is why the law of contradiction applies to the past; for it is the law of being, and, under the appearances that come after one another in our knowledge, is hidden the action which fixes their permanent reality.

The issue, then, is no longer merely to make reparations for evil appearances, for the disorder of passing phenomena, for the evil committed in the natural order; it is no longer a question of this human impossibility. The issue is now about a reparation which is of another order, and, so to speak, a divine impossibility. Already, man has not been able to remedy the effects of acts that reverberate to infinity in his organism and in the universe. But to remedy the principle of his willed actions, to change its being and no longer just the phenomenon, how conceive that this is even possible? Look in wonder now on these presumptuous individuals who, to think themselves pure, virgin, full of merit and beauty before God and men, need only a flash of repentance, a better velleity, a vainglorious and sentimental two-penny alms, a bit of time to pass for the visible signs of their faults to disappear, a forgetfulness on their part, and a sort of pardon they have the nerve to bestow on their past, as if by regretting it they were doing a favor instead of asking for one! What man can do, he cannot undo. But what he cannot constitute, he can destroy alone.

Let it be understood once and for all, then: in voluntary action a secret nuptial takes place between the human will and the divine will. To be called to the life of reason and freedom, is to participate in the free necessity of God who cannot fail to will Himself. We too cannot fail to will ourselves: what we receive of being as our very own is such that it is impossible not to accept it. This gift, we cannot abuse, we cannot feign to refuse, except by already accepting it and, so to speak, by using God against God. Also, to reject His cooperation, to hand over our hearts and our works to the embrace of false goods is adultery. This union which constitutes us, this bond which we will from ourselves to Him as He willed it from Himself to us, we can violate without ever wanting to break it. Fearsome grandeur of man! He wills that God be no longer for him, and God is no longer for him. But, keeping the creative will always in his depths, he adheres to it so firmly that it becomes completely his.

His being remains without Being. And when God ratifies this solitary will, it is damnation. *Fiat voluntas tua, homo, in aeternum* (Your will be done, man, for eternity)!

To abuse the world, then, and to corrupt it, is nothing in comparison to the crime the perverted will charges itself with: to abuse God and to kill Him in man, to kill Him as far as man is in a position to do so, to strike at Him with a divine force. It would seem that what we cannot build up ourselves we cannot ruin by ourselves: but no; if the principle of the human fault is entirely in the guilty will, its destructive effect is not entirely limited to man. Action is a synthesis of man and God: neither God alone, nor man alone can change it, produce it, or annihilate it. To rectify it, a decree of omnipotence is not enough. Something else is needed. And, if we dare say, God necessarily has to die if man's crime is to be compensated for; God has to die voluntarily, if man's crime can be forgiven and destroyed. But, by himself, man can do nothing about it. His natural state is to be unchanged. And not to be changed, is the irremediable abortion of his destiny.

Is it clear what is entailed for man in the pretension of acting and living by his own strength alone, of walking, ascending, and rising again from a fall by himself and without aid, of being self-sufficient in his virtue as in his repentance and his expiation? To judge that one finds within oneself the truth necessary for one's conscience, the energy of one's action and the success of one's destiny, is not only to deprive oneself of a gratuitous and optional gift which, rejected and disdained, would still not compromise the happiness of an average life; no, it is, in truth, to give the lie to one's own aspiration and, under pretext of loving only oneself, to hate and to lose oneself. To lose oneself: is the force of the word understood? To lose oneself, without escaping from oneself. For, in killing forever the ambition for imperishable goods in itself, the will which has restricted itself to passing ends remains no less indestructible; and this immortal will which placed its all in ephemeral goods is as though dead as soon as it finally experiences their brute nullity. Its desire perishes; therefore, it will have willed for always what can never be: what it wills will escape it eternally and what it does not will will be eternally present to it.

To be without Being; to have one's center outside of oneself; to feel that all man's powers, turning against man, become hostile to him without being alien to him, is that not the consequence and the penalty of the self-sufficient pride of a solitary will which has placed its all where there is nothing to fill it? It is a just necessity that the man whose egoism has broken with universal life and with its principle be torn from the common stem. And, he will perish without end even to the roots of his

372

substance, because all that he will have loved will in a way be devoured and annihilated by the grandeur of his desire. Whoever has willed nothingness will have it and know it; but he who has willed it will not be destroyed forasmuch. And why not the total annihilation of those who are separated from life? Of course not! They have seen the light of reason; they keep their indelible will, they are human only by being inexterminable, they have mingled with life and acted in being. It is forever. Nothing in their state results from an external constraint: they persevere

373   in their own will, which is at once crime and punishment. They do not change. They are dead and what being they have is eternal. Like one living tied by both arms to a corpse, let them remain their own dead idol.

And if, in order to feed the imagination, we were to offer a symbol for the interior suffering which, turning the will against itself, rubs against all the wounded passions of the separated soul, we would no doubt be naturally inclined to a comparison with consuming fire. If pain is nothing else than the division of living things that cling to one another, what more intimate rending than that of a flame which, fueled, so to speak, by one's very vitals, never consumes what it tears apart without end! Image of the painful anarchy of a being decomposed in its inner parts, an enemy to itself and to all that is. And notwithstanding the present obscurity, which does not allow us any foretaste of the penetrating force in the final revelation, the wrath of avenging justice is already hidden in the actual state of the guilty one. Behind the mountains which he covers himself with, he knows enough, he wills enough, so that there will be no surprise, no iniquity, in the terrors of a judgment that will always remain the work of the first love.

In offering man an alternative and in imposing an option on him, the determinism of voluntary action has opened a double way. But whichever way the will goes, this determinism goes with it in order to make it produce all its consequences and to reveal to it its necessary being. We have just seen how man loses himself. Will he find a way to save himself? And where will he enter on this road of salvation? Indeed, if science cannot introduce him to this road or sustain him there, it must at least follow this new determinism which logically develops the necessary conditions of true life.

SECOND OPTION
The Life of Action

The substitutes and the preparations for perfect action

Action cannot stay enclosed in the natural order. It is not entirely within   374
it. And yet it cannot, of itself, surpass it. Its life is beyond its own power.
By his own strength, man does not succeed in giving back voluntarily in
his action all that is already there spontaneously. If he claims to limit
himself to what he can do, if he claims to draw from himself what he
does, he deprives himself of the very principle of his life. To restore the
plenitude of his original nature in willed action, must he not let the First
Cause take first place again in it? It is up to man to make way. What he
does not kill in himself, kills him; and his own self-will keeps him from
attaining his true will.

It is therefore a necessity for him to acknowledge his dependence
regarding this mysterious guest, to submit his own will to his. He has to
go that way. Otherwise, there is no way of solving the problem, this
problem which he raises and ratifies of his own will. He wills that we
should be demanding towards him, because that is the mark of the
grandeur of his nature, the response to the loving avidity of his call.
Hence his richness is a needy one, for nothing of what he has willed and
done is his for keeps, nor can it subsist if he does not find the possession
and the consistency of it in this God present and hidden at the heart of
every voluntary action. And what we have to call God here is a very con-   375
crete and practical feeling: to find Him, it is not our head that we must
break, but our heart. How then can He be freely installed in human life,
so that this immanence consented to of the transcendent may finally complete the reflected operation of the will by equalling what wills to what
is willed and posited in action?

In what comes from itself through reflexion, the human will senses the
irremediable insufficiency of its act as much as the invincible need to
bring it to completion. Reduced to its own resources alone, it can only
acknowledge its ignorance, its weakness and its desire, for it is true to

345

its infinite ambition only inasmuch as it recognizes its infinite powerlessness. What can be the practical and efficacious way of finally doing what we cannot do alone? And since the act cannot be brought to completion except if God gives Himself to us, how can we somehow substitute His action for ours? How, without even knowing if He has spoken, without knowing Him distinctly perhaps, can we participate in His secret mediation? How can we offer ourselves and open ourselves to the equivalents of perfect action, and prepare ourselves for a more clear revelation, if there be one, of human destiny? Is there, then, a death passing on to life?

I

What we judge good through personal lucidity or through teaching received, we must adhere to in mind, in heart and in action under pain of being condemned by our own judgment. All that is in conformity with conscience, even if conscience is involuntarily warped, requires of man a positive devotion. Thus it is that certain barbaric customs or superstitious rites can serve as matter for a good will and as a vehicle for a salutary inspiration. But with what reservations? The fact is that, in the particular act and in the finite symbol, the intention carries beyond the symbol and the act, so that as we discharge what we know, lacking anything better, we remain open, on the ready, docile for every more complete truth. To act according to the light and the strength we have, without setting limits on the generosity and the amplitude of desire, that is the disposition of a right will.

We must come back, then, to the practical rule which appeared from the start as the safeguard of active sincerity and the key to human destiny: to give ourselves and the universe to what we think is the good. 376 But now this rule has been justified and illumined; thus is resolved the apparent contradiction that treats duty at once as the triumph and the sacrifice of the will. On the one hand, indeed, we have acknowledged that all the hierarchy of natural goods simply expresses the most inward wish of human willing and that, to conform to it at all costs, is in the end to do what we sincerely will. On the other hand, it seems that there has to be a sacrifice and a kind of mortifying immolation, for one to be resolutely true to moral obligations, even when it is the most natural thing in the world and the most desirable.

To be more precise, the issue is not only to do all the good that we will, in the measure that we will it on our own through a movement of free complaisance, *bona omnino facere* (to do the good in every way). What is essential and painful is to do what we do well, that is, in a spirit of submission and detachment, to do it because we sense in it the order of a will to which ours has to subordinate itself, *bene omnia facere* (to do all things well). This explains why moral precepts appear much less as the formulation of our own will (though they are that in a very true sense) than as the expression of a sovereign authority which it is our first obligation to recognize as having a right over us. Indeed, upon reflection it is clear that, the more scientific morality will prove that it is in conformity with the true interests of man or that it results from the positive experiences accumulated by generations (which is true), the more it will remain necessary to clarify how, by an inclination toward evil, only man goes against his good by deviating from tried tradition.

If then, in what is the good and his good, he misconstrues his good by rejecting the good, it is because in reality he sees in it, with good reason, a will other than his own, and because, to accept it fully, he needs abnegation. To be sure, it is through a natural inclination that reason sees to its legitimate needs and interests, less because they are interests than because they are legitimate, that it harkens to generous sentiments, less because they flatter sensibility than because they are generous. All the hierarchy of these natural goods is like a ladder set up for the ascensions of the will. And yet, if we do only what charms us or what seems advantageous to us, we do not go far along the way of duty, or better still we do not truly enter upon it.

And neither do the men and the peoples enter upon it who maintain the dignity of their manners only with the consciousness of imposing their own obligations upon themselves. It is easier, in truth, to obey the law we make for ourselves and to bend our will before our will alone. But that is to remove from moral life all the necessary foundation of humility and abnegation which it needs.

To consult the immediate testimony of conscience, action is good when the will, to accomplish it, submits to an obligation that requires of it an effort and a kind of victory over itself. And this testimony is grounded, because actually there is no true good except where, in the place of all likings, all interests, all natural preferences of the will, we substitute a law, an order, an absolute authority, where we place in our act an initiative other than our own. *Unus est bonus Deus* (only God is good). Duty is duty only to the extent that, intentionally, we obey in it a divine commandment: a practical submission which, besides, is independent of metaphysical affirmations or negations. There is a way of serving God without naming or defining Him; and that is what "the Good" is.

Also moral disinterestedness is absolute, even for one who knows, scientifically, that his highest interest is in the good. For it is impossible

377

that, in conforming to the obligations of conscience, we not have the feeling of renouncing our will. It is impossible that, in obeying the law, we not seem to give up forever, without recourse and without exact equivalents, the fetching pleasures whose greatest charm perhaps lies in the illusion that, in setting them aside, we are closing ourselves off from this infinite world of enjoyments where man seems to be beholden only to himself. It is impossible that, in remaining at all costs faithful to the divine pact, we not lose, at the critical moment of decision and in the distress of an action that is often as painful as childbearing, the sense of working for ourselves, or even of working for an attentive and compassionate master, as if, deaf ourselves, we were obliged to sing for one deaf or one absent. To act for what is nothing in the eyes of the senses or even of the mind, that is the apparent folly reason requires when it goes as far as it should go.

Thus, whatever may be the natural value of the motive that solicits the will, it must in a way be muffled before a truly moral price is restored to it: a value that will be founded, no longer on the degree of conformity of this motive with our own will, but on its properly obligatory and imperative character. *Sta sine electione et elige* (take your stand without a choice and choose). There is only one way to reconcile contraries and to dominate opposed desires: it is to sacrifice the diverse alternatives, even the one we will choose; it is to come back to it only through a higher feeling than the natural attraction that was soliciting us. Otherwise, it would be too painful to have preferences, to be drained with sands of time, to feel a part of the beautiful and good reality running out between our fingers. We must have the merit of making everything equal, of loving everything, of seeing it as naught before the infinite good, in order to spread over all the sole presence of this absolute. Never to determine oneself through passion, even the passion for the good; whatever one desires, to hold oneself ready to do the contrary act, in order to come back, if it is good, to the primitive inclination only with a change of heart; to almost wish to take pleasure in everything we sacrifice and to find repugnance in everything we do, that is true and interior freedom.

In a sense, then, perfect and universal detachment attaches us quite purely to all, without ties and without disdain, for it makes us both quite indifferent to the particular forms of action and quite devoted to the great and supreme motive which alone communicates to all others and to the least its infinite value. What does a difference of degree matter in the eyes of God who destines us for Himself and with regard to whom all is good and all is evil according to whether we refer it to Him or withhold it from Him? It is not that we have to be absolutely disinterested regarding the natural content of human acts, for if these finite acts

378

have to express and realize the good that is not unless it is infinite, it is on the condition that we will do what is better, because the better serves as the passing and always changing garb for the good itself. In comparison with a good action, what is a billion or what is a cent? What is the whole world? We sense the answer well. And in all things must we not judge for ourselves as if it were for another, or as if it were a question of the affairs of state of Amenophis, a hundred thousand years and a hundred thousand leagues away, in the absolute, the universal, thus making action come down from the serene depths of eternity, as if we were dead?

The idea of the infinite, then, must become living in us; it must be willed and practiced there, act and reign there; in a way supplant us. It can do so at any time, and we owe that to it. Let us play our role, there- 379 fore, which is to get rid of our petty individual perspective in order to realize the absolute in ourselves and realize ourselves in the absolute and to set the universal in each particular form of our life, in order to give the relative and the particular an infinite value. Is not the free necessity that is the character of divine action also the ideal of human action? Human action must not leave outside of itself anything that constitutes man. It makes everything live in him. It rallies all his contrary tendencies. It raises him above the contingent oppositions that partition his consciousness. But it can restore this perfect simplicity only by suppressing self-will, in order to restore to the good which solicits it under particular traits its absolute and total character. He who is no longer self-willed always does his own will; and when we wanted nothing, it turns out that we have always done what we wanted.

The ever recurring temptation at the heart of the egoist is this proud or sensual murmur: "Do thus; you may, because you have a unique nature, because it is an extraordinary circumstance, because the common rules do not apply to you." A sophism of passion which the vain one listens to, always ready to post a plaque at each one of his steps and to have the world kneel before every beat of his heart. On the contrary, a good action is one which in the man himself surpasses and immolates man. Each time we fulfill a duty, we should feel that it takes our life, that it replaces our self-will, and that it raises up within us a new being. For we should die rather than not fulfill it; and, by living in order to perform it, there is already someone else living within us. Every act is like a will and testament. We shall have to take the time to die: it is as one dying that we must live, with that simplicity which goes straight to the essential and to the true.

Hence, there is nothing absolutely good and willed, except what we do not will of ourselves, what God wills in us and of us. But if in what

we will best, in the action most in conformity with our intimate wish, there is already a mortification, what will it be for all that thwarts, humiliates, and wounds our willing? If, in order to act well, we must suffer to be supplanted by a will in conformity with, it is true, but higher than ours, is it not the case that, in suffering itself, in all that is repugnant to our nature, there is need for a more courageous action so as to make
380 pain and death enter no less into the voluntary plan of life? But is it not also the case that this mortification is the true trial, the proof and the nourishment of a generous love? We do not love the good, unless we love for its sake what is least lovable. Where there is less of ourselves, there is more of the good.

II

If at the origin of good action there is a principle of renunciation, of passion and of death, it is not surprising that in all the unfolding of moral life we constantly encounter suffering and sacrifice. We have already seen how suffering serves to stimulate the development of the person, how it is a means of formation, a sign and an instrument of reparation or of progress; it keeps us from wanting the least in order to incline us to want the most. But to accept it in itself, to consent to it, to look for it, to love it, to make of it the mark and the very object of a generous and detached love, to place perfect action in painful passion, to be active even in dying, to make of each act a death and of death itself the act *par excellence*, that is the triumph of the will which is still disconcerting for nature and which in effect engenders in man a new and more than human life.

The heart of a man is measured by the acceptance he shows for suffering, for it is in him the imprint of One other than himself. Even when it comes from us to enter into consciousness like a sharp needle, it is always in spite of our spontaneous wish and the primitive effort of our willing. As foreseen as it may be, as resigned as we may be in submitting to its blows, as taken as we may be with its austere and vivifying charms, it remains nonetheless a stranger and an intruder. It is always something other than we expected. And caught in its grip, even the one who faces it, desires and loves it, cannot at the same time keep from hating it. It kills something in us to replace it with something that is not from us. And here is why it reveals this scandal of our freedom and our reason: we are not what we will, and to will all that we are, all that we are to be, we have to understand, to accept its lesson and its benefit.

381 Thus suffering is in us as a seed: through it something enters into us, without us, in spite of us. Let us receive it, then, even before knowing

what it is. The plowman throws down his most precious grain, he hides it in the earth, he disseminates it to the point that nothing of it seems to remain. But it is precisely because the seed is spread out that it remains, without the possibility of its being carried off. It rots to become fertile. Suffering is like this necessary decomposition for the birth of a work more full. He who has not suffered from something does not know and love it. And this teaching is summed up in a word, but one must have heart to understand it: the meaning of pain is to reveal to us what escapes egotistical knowledge and will; it is to be the way of effective love, because it detaches us from ourselves, in order to give us others and to solicit us to give ourselves to others.

For it does not effect in us its happy result without an active cooperation: it is a trial because it forces the secret dispositions of the will to manifest themselves. It spoils, sours, hardens those that it does not make more receptive and better. Upsetting the equilibrium of an indifferent life, it places us in a position to opt between that personal feeling which inclines us to close in on ourselves by violently excluding every intrusion and that goodness which opens itself up to fruitful sadness and to the seeds which the high waters of suffering bring.

But suffering is not just a trial. It is a proof of love and a renewal of interior life, like a refreshing bath for action. It keeps us from becoming acclimatized to this world and leaves us here with a kind of incurable discomfort. What does it really mean to become acclimatized, if not to find one's equilibrium in the restricted space where one lives away from home? Therefore, it will always be new to say: wherever we turn, we are ill at ease. And it is good to feel so; the worst thing would be not to suffer any more, as if an equilibrium had been found and the problem were already resolved. Undoubtedly, in the calm of an average life or in the recollection of speculation, life often seems to take care of itself. But in the face of a real grief, there are no beautiful theories that do not seem vain or absurd. As soon as we bring something living and suffering close to them, systems sound empty, thoughts remain ineffective. Suffering is what is new, unexplained, unknown, infinite, what cuts through life like a revealing sword.

Also there emerges a kind of reciprocity or, so to speak, a kind of identity between true love and active suffering. For without the education of pain we do not arrive at disinterested and courageous action. Love has the same effects in the soul as death in the body: it transports the one who loves into what he loves and what is loved into what is loving. To love, then, is to love to suffer because it is to love the joy and the action of others in ourselves: a pain that is itself lovable and dear, in which those who feel it acquiesce and which they would not give up for all the

382

sweetness of the universe. If to suffer is good for man, then, it is not by convention, but for a reason drawn from the depths of things. To understand well how pain effects infinite and true joy, will that not be to have resolved the supreme difficulty of life and stifled the worst scandal for human consciousness, by finally providing our will with the great relief of being able to ratify all? When we have the secret°of finding sweetness in bitterness itself, then all is sweet.

But that is not yet to say enough. If suffering is the test and the proof of a generous and valiant will, it is because suffering is also the effect and rather like the very act of love. For, if it is true that we are more where we love than where we are, where self-will is covered over and supplanted by a contrary will, it seems that every movement of personal interest will be, no longer a gain, but a loss, and that every apparent enrichment will become a real impoverishment. The sight of joys and feasting is painful to the heart in grief; to the one who loves the good more than his own good, any satisfaction that pleases too much is painful. We satisfy ourselves by depriving ourselves, never by satisfying ourselves.

Indeed, the equal anxiety of men in the most unequal of conditions is a truth full of instruction. As soon as a balance has been established in the state of a fortune or a soul, no matter how low or how high it is, people see only what is left to be desired, the least lack seems an infinite emptiness. And it is. If it becomes filled, the same impression re-appears more irritatingly: a proof that all the enjoyments and the possessions of the present are equally null in comparison with the good we wish for. How much more wise, then, to orient our aspirations contrariwise to those who look for these disappointing satisfactions! To love everything that calls to our attention our insatiable grandeur, to prefer the less to the more and privations that satisfy to pleasures that starve, to take pleasure in the sense of our lack, all that is painful, no doubt, but salutary. Suffering is the way forward and upward; and to advance greatly, it is enough to will to let ourselves be carried. Happiness is not what we have; it is that which we get along without and which we deprive ourselves of.

Moreover, even in the good we do, we must do as if it were not from us. Everywhere the sacrifice of self-will is the road of life for man. That by which we deprive ourselves is worth infinitely more than that of which we deprive ourselves. To practice this rigorous method of suppression is to set in evidence and at liberty that little surplus of strength in us which surpasses all natural powers. We do not acquire the infinite like a thing. We give it access into ourselves only through emptiness and mortification. And if our soul is in the least bit great or avid, we enjoy what we do not have better than what we have.

The mark of a sincere will and consistent with its primordial generosity, then, is to be content with nothing finite. Not only does it accept the suffering brought by the action of another like a gift which is painful and instructive; but by its own initiative and by dilating all its powers of love, it creates within itself a sort of voluntary passion and permanent death. Far from crouching as if to escape too many contacts by adapting to circumstances, it stretches out in order to be everywhere in narrow straits as though under a press. Man does not equal the fullness of his spontaneous aspiration through his deliberate intention except on the condition of annihilating his self-will by installing in himself a contrary and mortifying will. It is not that he stops feeling to the quick the wound in his nature enamored of independence; for, repeatedly cut off and repeatedly reborn, the secret roots of self-love cannot perish. Nor should we treat the enemy within with a kind of anger and violent harshness; for sacrifice, far from hardening the heart, often mollifies the feelings it represses. To do nothing of what we would choose, and to do so gracefully and gently, is to have within us a will other than our own; it is to be dead, but to be already risen again to life, and to draw the principle of action from its source.

Mortification, then, is the true metaphysical experiment, the one that touches on being itself. What dies is what hinders from seeing, from doing, from living; what survives is already what is reborn. To survive itself, that is the test of the good will. To be dead would be nothing, but to survive oneself, to feel stripped of one's inner complacencies and one's taste for independence, to be in this world as if not being in it, to find more ardor for all human tasks in detachment than one could find in passion, that is the masterpiece of man. So many people live as if they were never to die; it is an illusion. We must act as if we were dead; that is reality. As we take this infinite of death into account, how everything changes sign! And how little advanced is the philosophy itself of death! The fact is also that nothing can replace the practice of this method of voluntary suppressions. How few have experimented with it! How many would like to snatch from its clutches precisely what should be handed over to it, without dreaming that death can be and must be the act par excellence! Therein lies the secret of the holy terror which modern consciousness experiences, just as the ancient soul had felt it, at the approach, at the very thought, of the divine. If no one loves God without suffering, no one sees Him without dying. Nothing touches Him that is not reborn; for no will is good if it has not gone out of itself, in order to leave the whole place open to the total invasion of His will.

To be sure, it is not necessary, it is not even always useful, to know the reason and the benefit of this mysterious substitution which coura-

384

geously accepted suffering effects, which the generosity of a heart whose aspiration is limited by nothing finite obtains, which death faced up to or undergone with magnanimity brings to completion. What takes a long time to explain and is difficult to justify, in practice often requires only a simple effort to sum up and transform the whole of an existence. How little is required to find access to life! A slight act of dedication, under a quite common and sometimes childish form, and it is enough perhaps for the divine seed to take root in a soul, and for the problem of destiny to be resolved.

III

But to keep intact the modesty of conscience and that sincere generosity which is only a will perfectly consistent with itself, one last disposition remains essential. To do all we know and all we can about duty, even to the point of heroically shedding our blood, to suffer and die in order to acquire that without which no life is worth living, is good, and it is not enough. Once we have done everything as if expecting nothing from God, we still have to expect everything from God as if we had done nothing of ourselves. Let us be wary, then, of this secret presumption which is a supreme resurgence of self-will: willingly we persuade ourselves that human forces alone by virtue of some natural necessity, succeed in bringing the great work of salvation to consummation. No, they do not bring this great work to completion, for they do not even begin it.

To think that man's renunciation of his self-will is his own original work, to be persuaded finally that this abnegation is fully valid, expiatory and salutary, is always to come back to the first illusion. It is to lose sight of the truth of the living God and to treat Him still like an inert object, the work of men's hands and matter docile to their wills. It is to give Him to oneself and not to give oneself to Him.

We must, then, (and therein lies the difficulty of the narrow path that leads to life), ally these two practical dispositions: do all we can, as if we had only ourselves to count on; but at the same time be convinced that all we do, though necessary, is radically insufficient. The strength and the light we have cannot legitimately belong to us unless we first refer them back to their principle. In a sense, action has to be entirely from man, but it must first be willed as entirely from God. In this perfect synthesis of one with the other, one cannot say that the first part of the act comes from one and the second from the other. No, each has to act for the whole. There is a communion of two wills only on this condition: the one cannot do anything without the other. And action, a common work, proceeds nevertheless in its entirety from each.

It is not enough, then, to conceive of good desires and noble intentions, while waiting, in order to execute them, to be raised up by a
foreign inspiration. It is not enough for the will to be pregnant; it has to
have given birth. Let us not live in what we would like to do; for that
is what we do not do, and it is what we would never do. We must act,
even where pusillanimity is persuaded that it is impossible. No more than
we should without reservation trust the solidity of acts accomplished, for
what is of man in them is always ruinous, should we distrust future   386
works, because we must always expect a help and an almighty collaboration. It is one and the same feeling that inclines man to this circumspect
fear with regard to the past wherein he has placed himself, and to this
courageous initiative in the face of what is to come, where he must consider that another than himself is already present.

Before the problem of his destiny, then, the only attitude that is befit-
ting for man is to act as much as possible according to his lights and
strengths, but with the consciousness of not finding in himself the principle, the means and the end of his action, of never thinking that he has
reached the end, of always starting over with the spirit of a young soldier
and the timid ardor of a novice. Duty is to seek without tiring, for we
would not seek if we had not already found what we never attain in its
depths, what we lose as soon as we claim to restrict ourselves to it. In
acting for the better, therefore, we must still desire the good we know
nothing of and which we do not do. We must live with the sense that the
present is not a permanent dwelling, but a place of passage and a kind
of perpetual passing away. We must live with the fear of becoming too
adjusted to this dying life by enjoying a certain peace which it offers to
the tepid and the clever. To be sure, what we thus have to bear is like
the weight of a yoke. But this burden of moral life, difficult to face up
to, difficult to raise, grows lighter as we go forward, and it lightens all
the rest. *Onus cuncta exonerans* (a burden unburdening all things). In the
same way, far from being a weight for the bird, the feathers it bears, bear
it up.

But if man has to cast his acts thus beyond time and space, outside the
finite and outside himself, still that is not a lack of consistency in desire
nor the appetite of a patient who, always famished, cannot take anything
solid. For this permanent restlessness is good only to the extent that it
stimulates present activity, even as it never allows us to limit ourselves
to it. It is action itself that must give us, with the satiating nourishment,
this renascent vigor of health and this insatiable hunger which is the
mark of a healthy and integral will. Even in our desire for good desires,
we must push back outside of ourselves the origin of this voluntary
movement. Even when we are only asking to have something to give, this

prayer is not entirely from ourselves; and it is a prayer only inasmuch as the acknowledgement of this fact is at least implicit. For the absolute initiative of man, it is necessary to substitute, freely, since it is already there necessarily, the absolute initiative of God. It is not for us to give Him to ourselves, nor to give ourselves to ourselves; our role is to act so that God may be entirely in us as He is there perforce, and to find at the very principle of our consent to His sovereign action His efficacious presence. The true will of man is the divine willing. To acknowledge his fundamental passivity is, for man, the perfection of activity. To whoever recognizes that God does everything, God gives to have done everything; and it is true. Not to appropriate anything to oneself is the only method of acquiring the infinite. It is wherever we are no longer our own.

But here again, here especially, how this salutary disposition is independent of the abstract science we can have of it! For sincerity to remain whole, it is necessary and sufficient that, in acting as best we know how, we base ourselves, in desire and in intention, on the one, known or unknown, who alone can inspire, support, and perfect the beginning of a creature that we are. Whether to accomplish a good action or to remedy a voluntary failing, we do not have the strength to do or the means to expiate: we must therefore recognize it in order to remain in the truth. Truth is poured only into empty vessels. If they are called to the reward almost without labor, it is because the laborers of the last hour were not at first hired by anyone or for any task. Thus it is necessary that there remain in back of one's heart a little virgin nook where the unknown and desired guest touches the soul. He can give Himself only where room is made for Him. But, lacking all clarity about Him, how much uprightness and true generosity the sense of the need we have for His operation supposes! To call for Him thus even before knowing Him, we must have remained true to the sincerity of good willing to the end: a quite simple disposition that a single instant, a surge of the heart, is perhaps enough to produce, but which envelops the infinite.

It seemed that the supreme effort of the will was to sacrifice all that it has and all that it is. Yet now it appears that this effort itself is insufficient, once we attribute its merit to ourselves or admit its efficacity. No doubt, it is the sure and right way to love the invisible, to desire above all else what we renounce possessing in the present, to lose all in order to save what alone counts and deserves to be, to die, if necessary, in order to live, since it seems impossible to attain being without passing through death. This is man's acknowledgement of the absolute; it is the participation of the nothingness that we are in real life through an offering of apparent life. And yet all that is still nothing without the consciousness of the natural powerlessness, of the very impossibility for man to reach his necessary end by his own strength alone. Aristotle had a sense of this when he said: there is in man a life better than man; and it is not man who can sustain this life; something divine has to dwell in him.

Absolutely impossible and absolutely necessary for man, that is properly the notion of the supernatural. Man's action goes beyond man; and all the effort of his reason is to see that he cannot, that he must not restrict himself to it. A deeply felt expectation of an unknown messiah; a baptism of desire, which human science lacks the power to evoke, because this need itself is a gift. Science can show its necessity; it cannot give it birth. Indeed, if we have to found a real society and cooperate with God, how could we presume to succeed in doing so without recognizing that God remains the sovereign master of his gift and of his operation? A necessary admission, but one that ceases to be efficacious, if we do not call on the unknown mediator or if we close ourselves off from the revealed savior.

I show how the very idea of a Revelation enters into the interior development of human consciousness, so that, coming from the outside, it still cannot act inside except in virtue of a prior appropriateness. — I bring out to what characters this datum, external in appearance, owes its internal authority and credit. — Finally I show what is the utility of this Revelation: it has to serve and to have a practical efficacity, if we want the mysterious knowledge of the incomprehensible that has been revealed to have a meaning and to somehow humanize itself. It too, then, comes to take its place in the dynamism of action. It is not for human science to inquire as to whether it is real, nor even as to whether it is possible; science has to show, in the name of determinism, that it is necessary.

Part V
The Completion of Action

The end of human destiny

389 Action is not completed in the natural order. But is not the very name of the supernatural the scandal of reason? And is not the only attitude of the philosopher in the face of such an unknown to ignore it or, more resolutely and more frankly, to deny it? — No. To deny it or to ignore it, that is what is contrary to the philosophical spirit. Far from infringing on a reserved domain, we must show that there is no infringement possible. From this impossibility itself a necessary relation follows; and it is still up to rational science to study the absolute independence and the necessity of this higher order.

It is about the supernatural that it is especially right to repeat the statement of Aristotle about First Philosophy: "If we must not philosophize, we must still philosophize." One cannot exclude metaphysics except by a metaphysical critique. Can one then declare oneself against what, by hypothesis, is foreign to the philosophical order, without this peremptory judgment somehow exceeding philosophical competence? Two propositions go equally beyond the strict right of purely human science: "It is not." — "It is." Now, to show that it is impossible for philosophy to reject or to constitute by its forces alone a truth, an action, a life higher than nature, is still a work of philosophy. And yet this critique, to all
390 appearances so negative, which remains on the very terrain of those who claim to ignore what they in effect deny, necessarily has a very positive result. To establish that it is impossible to proffer on this subject a valid negation is actually to maintain, not that "it is" (faith being, by hypothesis, a gratuitous gift), but that "it is possible," since it is not possible to prove that it is impossible.

Besides, we must not think that the supposition of the supernatural is purely arbitrary. If it were, we would, by the very fact, be authorized to neglect it as an obviously fanciful fiction. But all that has gone before results in making us conscious of an incurable disproportion between the *élan* of the will and the human end of action. Also, in studying the condi-

358

tions for complete sincerity, in trying to determine the dispositions for a completely good and logical will, did we not get the sense that there was something perpetually under-stood (*sous-entendu*)? A proof, not that this inquiry was hiding an ulterior motive and artificial intentions, but that it was in correspondence with the secret movement of a consciousness which, going ahead of the slow pace of the investigation, already knows more than it pretends to know, and which gladly would be surprised to be living amidst truths, dogmas, ancient traditions whose meaning it had lost and which it rediscovers as if they were novelties.

That is not all: for this disposition which the sincere practice of life generates in the solitude of consciousness can still be encountered in living witness around us. Yes, there do remain witnesses, μαρτυρες, perhaps importunate and indiscreet, but whose state of soul has some claim on that sympathetic curiosity we have for so many others. For, living amid this historical and scientific civilization that is opposed to them in this age of criticism and naturalism, many at least know what is at issue. They hear the reproaches, they know the disdain of the high-minded. They too say the word that is said to them: *Stultitia et scandalum* (stupidity and scandal). If they do not take notice, they perhaps have reasons which it is as scientific to know as to know about a buddhist rite. And let one only ask himself if the motives he thinks he has for denying, are not precisely those that should make him affirm and will what he rejects and what he hates!

It would be strange, therefore, if it were scientific to exclude what it is not scientific to admit, as if the negative proof were not, of itself, more difficult to establish than the positive proof. For we would have to rely on an impossibility of fact to deny the simple logical possibility of the supernatural. We do not understand in its depth the least detail of the least customary fact. We do not even know what we do. And we would pretend to say: That is possible, that is not. In a sense, all is supernatural and nothing is, because in every act, better still, in every phenomenon, there subsists in what is known, an irreducible mystery. Sense experience is a mystery; and all believe in it, and we construct a science on the authority of the senses; then, we don't allow that there should be any other mystery than this one; as if, through what we know of it, we had determined and delimited what we do not know of it.

It would be strange if it were scientific to study the letter and the spirit of all cults except one. Did anyone judge that to criticize, as we did, all forms of superstition and all the fictions invented by human action to give itself the illusion of being completed, is to go beyond the rights of philosophy? No. Why, then, would it not be right for it to examine whether there is not one religious form which does not fall under these criticisms themselves and on which philosophy can no longer have any purchase? Not that it would be legitimate to pretend to discover, through reason alone, what has to be revealed in order for it to be known. But it is legitimate to push our investigation up to the point where we sense that we should desire interiorly something analogous to what dogmas propose from the outside. It is legitimate to consider these dogmas, assuredly not primarily as revealed, but as revealing; that is, to confront them with the profound exigencies of the will and to discover in them, if it is there, the image of our real needs and the awaited answer. It is legitimate to accept them, by way of hypothesis, as mathematicians do when they suppose a problem resolved and then verify the fictitious solution by way of analysis. Perhaps, in considering them thus we would be surprised at the human meaning of a doctrine which many judge unworthy of further examination and which they confuse (opposed reproaches whose very contradiction should provoke a bit of reflexion) with a dry formalism of practices, with an unction of mystical feelings, with a routine of sensible ceremonies, with a casuistic jurisprudence, with a mechanical discipline. We ought at least to interpret its spirit with the care we would bring to a Sanskrit text or a Mongolian custom.

392   Finally, it would be strange to oppose to the supernatural what is its only reason for being and its proper definition. Would it be at all, if it were only an object of study, a conquest of human effort, if it came under the jurisdiction of philosophy? Would it be at all, if it did not require of man anything that surpasses, disconcerts, and wounds his nature? Would it be, if the eminent gift which, by hypothesis, it brings to our consciousness were not so in conformity with the imperious exigencies of the will that this gift itself, far from being optional or supererogatory, becomes imposed on us as a duty?

Has the following accumulation of inconsequences been reflected on? — One might still admit readily enough that the natural order is not enough for man. But one would want the supernatural to enter into the natural order itself. — One claims that the very notion of revelation does not allow for rational discussion. And one cannot stand having this negative conclusion discussed: under pretext of respect, free inquiry refuses even to inquire. — One imposes a silent reserve on oneself regarding dogma which dogma does not ask for, which dogma condemns. And these respectful ones who do not want it to be criticized are the very ones in whose eyes it is a human invention. — One recognizes, with the clear-sightedness of a well-honed critique, the absolute inanity of all superstitious inventions, because what cannot come from man alone they make come from man. And in the presence of a doctrine that condemns all superstition by presenting itself as of superior origin, from this claim

which sets it apart, one finds new ground for complaint: one reproaches
it for being what one reproached the others for not being. — One confers
on superstitions themselves something of the internal value one takes
away from religion, as if at bottom all cults were equal, without noticing
that those who are not content with any purely natural form of action
are the very ones who know how to be content with faith and hold
themselves to it. For it is through one and the same feeling (*sentiment*)
that one rises to sense the need of faith, to find satisfaction in it, and to
love its exigencies. Those who await and receive the truth are those who
neither await nor receive any other. — One appears "on the verge of dying
for not being able to name what one adores." And if He names Himself,
one rends one's garments, shouting blasphemy; a strange craving which,
under the guise of a devouring appetite, hides a satiety, a disgust, a lack
of any generous hunger. When one loves the truth more than oneself,   393
does it cost to lower one's feeble thought before the infinity of what there
is to be believed? And therein lies the germ of a more serious inconsequence, the ordinary origin of all the others. — It seemed that the expansion of the heart was infinite, that its need for tenderness, for dedication,
and for merited happiness, the only kind it has any taste for, was insatiable; it seemed one was ready to suffer and die for love. But in the
face of the sensible and intellectual sacrifices that the egoism of pride or
pleasure must make for the sake of conscience, behold one revolts as if
it were tyranny and intolerance. The upright will has admitted that the
deadening of the senses alone, as an experimentation, can open the way
to a higher life, that nothing sensible must seduce us in what we will of
being, that, to receive the being we are waiting for, we must in a way
annihilate ourselves. And man crucifies out of hate the one who asks him
to be crucified out of love.

Is not the role of philosophy to straighten out the human will all the
way, by looking always in its action for what is truly in conformity to
its primitive aim? Also, without prejudging any properly religious question — that is of another order — it is necessary to set aside, through philosophy, the obstacles accumulated, wrongly to be sure, by a hostile partisan philosophy, not against the content of some dogmatic formula or
other, but against the very notion of revelation and the possibility, the
usefulness, of any defined dogma. They want philosophy to have its
proper and independent domain. Theology wants the same with and for
philosophy. Both the one and the other demand a separation of competences; they remain distinct from one another, but distinct in view of
an effective cooperation: *non adjutrix nisi libera: non libera nisi adjutrix
philosophia* (philosophy is not a helper unless it is free and not free unless
it is a helper). The fullness of philosophy consists, not in a presumptuous

self-sufficiency, but in the study of its own powerlessness and of the means which are offered from elsewhere to supply for its powerlessness. Yes or no, do these means correspond to its exigencies?

CHAPTER 1
The Notion of Dogmas and of Revealed Precepts and Philosophical Critique

If we had to think that revelation itself comes entirely from the outside 394 like a completely empirical datum, the very notion of a dogma or a revealed precept would be totally unintelligible. For, by hypothesis and by definition, revelation uses sensible and natural intermediaries only as a vehicle for the supernatural, which the senses and science are in no position to judge. Also, without as yet having to pronounce in the least on the value of what is called *revealed*, it is essential to study the mechanism and the genesis of this notion, a critique that philosophy has hardly begun.

I

Whether they be supernatural or not in their principle, it is not in sensible signs themselves that we must look for the origin of our idea of revelation. Through the development of practical activity and thanks to the effort of the will to equal itself to its own *élan* we saw how the need was born for an exterior correspondence and a necessary complement for our inner action.

Also, depending on the interior disposition of wills, the same revelatory signs produce opposite effects and provoke opposite interpretations. —To one who pretends to be self-sufficient, any doctrine or any discipline that proposes itself as being of supernatural origin seems a more odious monstrosity than any superstition; superstition, at least, is only the more or less avowed invention of man and a kind of enterprise of the will in the universal mystery. —To one who has felt a desire for the infinite, to one conscious of the needs of consciousness, but without having entered sincerely into the narrow path of passing through death to

395

life, about which we showed that it is the only road for a logical will, revelation, though perhaps awaited and called for, remains closed, scandalous, detestable from the moment it is not what we would wish it to be.

We must be quite clear as to the nature of the expressive symbols which alone can bring to man, from outside, the positive answer he is calling for: they could not be anything but signs with a double meaning, precisely because the sovereign originality of the interior life admits only what it has somehow digested and vivified. These signs, then, as striking as we may suppose them to be, could not have a necessitating efficaciousness. They can offer the infinite only under the guise of the finite. And that in itself constitutes, for more subtle minds, one of the most difficult obstacles to overcome, for it would seem almost natural to find the absolute in the suppression of the relative, and supernatural life in sensible death. But to recapture being under sensible species, to admit that a particular, contingent, and limited act should contain the universal and the infinite, to take from the series of phenomena one phenomenon that ceases belonging to the series entirely, that is the wonder. Spiritual grandeur has nothing of the brilliance that forces assent by imposing itself on the senses, nothing of that evidence that does violence to the understanding without making provision for the heart's entire freedom. What is visible to the eye, what is clear to thought seems to contradict and hide its invisible beauty. Hence it would be almost easier to believe in them without the sensible and reasonable in them: a peculiar test of the spirit, this mixture of light and shadow where, for lack of full clarity, it would seem that only full darkness would be possible.[1] And yet is that not the formal desire of the heart, is it not the constant invocation of the will? That the inaccessible make itself accessible, that is what we ask for; and if the wonder seems to be brought to consummation, we refuse to believe in it as a scandal too farfetched for reason.

That is why what subdues and illumines some is also what hardens and blinds others. *Signum contradictionis* (a sign of contradiction). There is found in it such a mixture of contraries that the ill-intentioned always find something in it against which to resist obstinately, and believers, something to guide and enlighten them. This is why sometimes a man too

396

---

1. Pascal felt this necessary struggle of light and darkness vividly: "I may well love total obscurity; but if God leads me into a half-obscure state, this little obscurity that is there displeases me; and because I do not find in it the merit of a complete obscurity, it does not please me. That is a fault, and a sign that I am making an idol of obscurity for myself, apart from God's order. But we must adore only His order." *Pensées*, ed. Havet, II, p. 116.

clearsighted for the common run appears enigmatic; and there is an apparent madness, like that of Hamlet, which is nothing but the forceful and raw expression, outside of banal conventions, of a penetrating reason. Signs, then, though necessary, are never sufficient. It is the interpretation, it is the interior need, that is everything, because upon this preparation depends whether the light will be blinding or whether the darkness will bring out the brilliance more vividly. For, to the one who knows how to hear, the mystery itself is a new illumination, since it proposes as obscure precisely what we want to surpass the capability of a limited view.

And as for miracles, which no science can say are impossible, since science pronounces only on the real and not on the possible, can miracles be anything else than a challenge to common reason, always ready to settle down in its routine customs? They are a provocation which satisfies or irritates hearts as well, according to the way they are disposed toward them. These sudden shocks are effective only inasmuch as one grasps, not the sensibly marvelous, what is that, but their symbolic sense. And what is this sense? No fact, however strange and disconcerting it may be, is impossible. The idea of fixed laws in nature is only an idol. Each phenomenon is a particular case and a unique solution. To go to the bottom of things, there is, no doubt, nothing more in the miracle than in the least of ordinary facts. But also there is nothing less in the most ordinary fact than in the miracle. And that is the meaning of those exceptional shocks that incite reflection to more general conclusions. What they reveal is that the divine is not just in what seems to surpass the accustomed powers of man and of nature, but everywhere, even where we readily think that man and nature are sufficient unto themselves. Miracles, then, are miraculous only in the eyes of those already prepared to recognize divine action in the most habitual of events and acts. Nature is so ample and so diverse that it is everywhere equivocal; and in striking souls, it gives off the sound we want it to give.

It is not, then, from revelation itself, (on the hypothesis that it is), nor from natural phenomena, (on the hypothesis that it is not), that the idea of revealed precepts or dogmas can come. It is from an interior initiative that this notion springs forth. But how could this quite subjective disposition recognize on the outside whether there actually is a nourishment prepared to calm this appetite for the divine? And after we have felt the unavoidable torment of the infinite, after we have summoned God to raise the veils of the world and to show himself, how can we discern this presence, if it is real? How can we recognize this authentic response, if it has truly spoken?

II

We may well ask God to reveal Himself. But most of the time man begins by setting his own conditions for this, as if he were seeking only to decree the apotheosis of his own desires. Wishing to follow an easier path off to the side, he demands that this path itself be the true way. Always, when we do not surrender to the divine will, we want God to will what man wills.

And yet, to believe in God, to desire Him, to call upon Him, all this necessary recognition from consciousness makes sense for us only inasmuch as we expect from Him what we are not, what we cannot be or do alone. If we do not want Him where He is, it is because we would want Him to be where He cannot be. Where can we find Him, then, if not where the will, by a sort of dispossession, is raised above itself? And as this abnegation is not without a hidden suffering, as this operation, to be supernatural, needs to crucify the complacencies of self-love, as it tends, according to the language of Saint Paul, to the division of the soul from the spirit even to the finest joints and the marrow of the bones, it is, then, one and the same characteristic of the divine which makes minds full of self or weak in courage reject it, and which reveals it to dedicated souls about whom we could say that they would not want a God who would not have jealous claims in their regard. For the great effort of the heart is to believe in God's love for man. And whoever has grasped why man can and wills to be divinely loved, as if he were the God of God Himself, is no longer surprised that the way of annihilation and mortification is the route of the fullness of love. Whoever is good requires that we be demanding toward him.

It is therefore only in an emptiness of the heart, it is in souls of silence and good will that a revelation makes itself effectively heard from the outside. It is worthy to be received only in virtue of what makes it contemptible and hateful to others. The sound of words and the sudden appearance of signs would undoubtedly be nothing, if there were not interiorly an intention of accepting the desired light, a sensitivity already prepared to judge of the divinity of the word heard. Men have always been on the alert to hear and to see, to receive what men cannot see and hear without dying. And if they have thought they could decipher this mortifying and vivifying word where it had not yet sounded, if they have closed the door on it when it claimed to be resounding, it is perhaps because they did not bear, purified within them, the sense of a higher life. The man of desire is rare; and he is the only one to be the measure of the truth given, the only one competent to discern its origin. To recognize it we must expect it to be, not as we would like it, but as it is.

And what can it be, what does it really have to be, if, in agreement with ourselves to the very end, we try to formulate, against ourselves, the ultimatum of our own will?

If there is any, divine revelation has to propose itself as independent of human initiative. It is necessary that it require an act of submission, a substitution of thought and of will, an admission from powerless reason; so that reason itself would judge it false as soon as it failed to require of us this unavoidable sacrifice. But this salutary disposition of obedience cannot be related back only to the effort of the human will; for the supernatural movement cannot proceed from ourselves. Even the *élan* of the search that brings us to God, then, has to be, in its principle, a gift. Without this indispensable mediation, we are nothing and we can do nothing. There is a revelation, therefore, given or received, only through a mediator: first and essential exigency.

And what we cannot conceive by ourselves we can still less consummate by ourselves; nothing that man brings to completion, nothing in the natural order of action, reaches its perfection and attains God; to make God the end of man according to the imperious need of our will, to become a cooperator with Him, to refer all life back to its source and its destiny, we need a help, an intercessor, a pontiff to be the act of our acts, the prayer of our prayer, and the offering of our gift. It is by Him alone that our will can equal itself to itself and hold on to everything in between, from its principle to its end: second and more essential exigency: *via et veritas* (the way and the truth), — above all *via* (the way).

And it is not only to believe and to act, to know and to do the truth, it is to remedy the inevitable deficiencies of action that a help is essential for man. What he does, even in the properly natural order, has infinite repercussions. And if he has done wrong, his failing always contains something absolutely irreparable. To annihilate evil, therefore, we need a power and an expiation of which we can never find in ourselves the smallest part. To destroy the past forever fixed! to give back life to dead action and to the perverted will! to remedy an outrage that wounds man and God! The mind boggles before the enormity of such a necessary task. To give, to preserve, and to restore life, we need a savior.

Supreme exigencies which man feels incapable of satisfying, whose necessity reason can see rather than understand their possibility, and which, simply to be conceived, already suppose an inspiration that does not come from man alone. But still (and here is one last demand of human consciousness), this initial inspiration must be given to all, as a sufficient minimum. Revelation, if it is, must, to be authentic, address itself prophetically to those who preceded it, symbolically and secretly to those who were not able to know it. It must be independent of times and places, truly universal and permanently efficacious, perpetuating itself not as something future or passed, but as the eternal present, multiple and successive in its application without ceasing to be one and fixed in its principle.

III

400   And yet, does not the greatest difficulty still subsist? We may well have shown how, through a quite subjective disposition, the thought of a possible revelation and the need for a real revelation is born. We were able to see how, from outside, it must present characteristics appropriate to the internal exigencies. But the essential is to understand in what way it acts and gives itself the proper guaranties for its credit. For even if theoretically we saw what these subjective dispositions and these objective conditions are, even if we discerned where and how a concordance is established between the two, this speculative knowledge would not yet be the one necessary to have, because, in order to be believed as it has to be believed, the revealed doctrine must itself furnish its reasons for belief and bring its own certitude, as a supernatural gift. If it has to be admitted, it can never be so inasmuch as it is clear to us and comes from us (besides, this clarity is never truly transparent); it can be accepted as it ought only inasmuch as it is communicated to us and remains mysterious in its depths.

Now that is the great and delicate problem: how to introduce into ourselves and make live there a thought, a life other than our own? And in what way can it be useful to affirm what remains impenetrable; what is there efficacious and salutary in confessing the revealed incomprehensible? How believe and what use is believing in what we cannot understand?

It is here, once again and especially, that the sovereign efficaciousness and the mediating power of action makes itself manifest. For, on the one hand, it is through the channel of action that the revealed truth penetrates deep into thought without losing anything of its supernatural integrity; and, on the other hand, if believing thought, as obscure as it remains amid the rays that faith fans out from its inaccessible center, has any meaning and value, it is because it ends up in action and finds in literal practice its commentary and its living reality. Let us consider for a moment this crucial explanation. Not that, for the examination, we should have to admit the formal truth of dogma; it will be enough to study, in the manner of mathematicians, the intrinsic relations and the

401   certain harmonies of a hypothesis whose necessity and coherence analysis

simply discovers in the very name of the determinism of human action.

Here then is the state of the difficulty. To bring nature to consummation and to close off man's aspiration, man and nature are not enough. But it is impossible for the complete deployment of voluntary action not to bring us before this gaping hole that separates us from what we will to be. It is impossible for us to fill the abyss, impossible for us not to want it to be filled, impossible for us not to conceive the necessity of a divine assistance. And yet it seems inconceivable for this operation to remain supernatural in becoming ours, or for it to be ours without ceasing to be supernatural. It should, it seems, come entirely from a source external to us; and it should be entirely immanent to us. By what opening, then, can this higher life insinuate itself into our life, if it is true that, in its very principle, it must be absolutely independent of our initiative? By what opening can we give it access? Through our thoughts? But we cannot believe without acting. Through our acts? But we cannot act without believing. And in this perfectly closed circle of the interior life, seemingly, there is no door prepared for the intrusion of a foreign operation. How then make this indispensable and inaccessible help come down into this void that remains wide open at the heart of our life?

The embarrassment has nothing fictitious about it and does not have to be defined to be felt. Even vaguely sensed, it has troubled to the point of anguish so many, ready, they say, had they known the road to Damascus, to run headlong into it. But they do know this road better than they think. For the regulated course of the interior life reveals to them, through a necessary dialectic, the precise conditions of a complete sincerity. Perhaps without knowing why, they sense that they must still act; and if they do not want to act without knowing why, it is possible, it is necessary for the science of action to make manifest to them the profound reason for this practical docility that seems imposed on them.

Even after he has silenced the last revolts of the senses and confessed his incapacity and his need, man does not have life in himself. He may be convinced of the excellence of dogma. He may even admit the possibility and the necessity of the supernatural, without forasmuch being converted to it, and without having faith, what is meant by the faith. He will not have it as long as he bases himself on his own thought and his own initiative, because to base himself on himself would be still to limit himself to that whose inadequacy he has recognized. It is here then that, to reintegrate into his willed operation all that is found at the principle itself of his voluntary aspiration, the generous unbeliever must take the decisive step of action. Why? Because he needs a gift. He still has to receive it; and action is the only receptacle that can contain it. If for the will to find its equation there has to be a synthesis of man and God, we

402

must not forget that the act in common which consecrates every alliance is, in a sense, entirely the work of each cooperator. Now man has before him acts which, by hypothesis, are purely of faith, acts which he has no natural reason to impose on himself and which are repugnant to his sense of himself because they demand of him a sort of disappropriation, acts which man purely as man would never accomplish for himself. And because of this he has a new reason to act: nature and man are not sufficient for him; hence he will act for what is nothing in nature and in man. Without faith, it is true, he would not produce these strange actions except as natural works. But in the last analysis, does he not have a natural reason to give it a try? Yes; if he is logical, he has to try; and the reason for this indispensable experiment is to bring to the desired contract man's full share, by acting for what is nothing in man, in order to see if all of God is revealed therein. We cannot know what is in question except by an effective experimentation. Therein resides a sufficient motive for action, a human motive that makes any systematic abstention inexcusable. To hold back on it is to hold back on oneself.

"But still, how could one act with confidence and without hypocrisy or servility by putting into practice what one does not believe in?"—Let us be reassured and make no mistake about it. One does not have faith; so be it. It is not by an effort of thought that one will ever get it. It does not directly touch the mind, and the mind touches it even less. But if what has gone before makes any sense, this human view, this human desire for what seems just and necessary is enough to authorize the very act it requires, an act natural in its intention; and in this action is perhaps hidden what the simple intention did not enclose yet, the presence of supernatural life which, if it is, will reveal itself to the man and which can reveal itself only in this way. If he sets all obstacles that clouded it aside, if he goes to the end of his sincerity, he will meet, in the voluntary operation, the certitude he wants. What scruple could hold him back? — The fear of desecrating what he does not believe in? But inasmuch as he does not believe in it before acting, he could not reproach himself for a natural act from the moment he admits its natural appropriateness. — The anxiety of not being sincere enough with himself? But have we not noted in the human order, this need to act in order to confirm and produce the will for a serious will? — The dread of the mystery he is approaching and of the light which may perhaps invade and subjugate him entirely after the action? But if he is fully sincere, isn't that what he must hope for? And that is why, quite exactly, the act is like the tollhouse and the gateway of faith: it supposes a total abdication of one's sense of oneself; it means the humble expectation of a truth that does not come from thought alone; it places into us a spirit other than our own. *Fac et videbis* (do and you will see).

Hence (however strange this rule of conduct may seem), whoever has understood the necessity, whoever has felt the need of faith, must, without having it, act as if he already had it, so that it may spring forth in his consciousness from the depths of this heroic action which submits the whole of the individual to the generosity of his *élan*. For it is not from thought that faith passes over into the heart, it is from practice that it draws down a divine light for the spirit. God acts in this action and that is why the thought that follows the act is richer by an infinity than that which precedes it. It has entered into a new world where no philosophical speculation can lead it or follow it.

At least, even while setting apart this supernatural given which is not at man's disposal for him either to insert in science or to use in practice, it remains necessary to posit this gift simply by way of hypothesis, in order to study, no longer just its abstract possibility or its preliminary conditions, but to define the natural cooperation and the conditional consequences that religious action requires and entails. For (it cannot be insisted upon enough), even supposing that this *theandric* action is founded entirely on the divine will, the human will remains coextensive to it. It is a gift, but a gift we acquire as if it were an earning.[1]

But if practice can arrive at faith, can faith arrive at practice itself? And does there not arise a supreme embarrassment under the form of this dilemma which seems to exclude faith from action or action from faith? If, indeed, even the act begun without conviction ends up with the light of a new belief, is not this belief, once it is received and possessed, a state

404

---

1. "Gratia liberum excitat arbitrium, cum seminat cogitatum; sanat, cum immutat affectum; roborat, ut perducat ad actum; servat, ne sentiat defectum. Sic autem ista cum libero arbitrio operatur, ut tantum illud in primo praeveniat, in ceteris comitetur; ad hoc utique praeveniens, ut jam sibi deinceps cooperetur. Ita tamen quod a sola gratia coeptum est, pariter ab utroque perficitur; ut mixtim, non singillatim; simul, non vicissim, per singulos profectus operentur. Non partim gratia, partim liberum arbitrium, sed totum singula opere individuo peragunt. Totum quidem hoc, et totum illa; sed ut totum in illo, sic totum in illa." (Grace stirs free will, when it plants the thought; heals it, when it changes the affection; strengthens it, to lead it to act; preserves it, lest it feel deficient. Yet that same grace so works with free will that it only goes before it at first and accompanies it in all the rest; indeed, it goes before so that thereafter free will may already cooperate with it. In such a way, nevertheless, that what was begun by grace alone is brought to perfection equally by each; so that mixed together, not singly, simultaneously, not successively, they act through every single step. It is not partially grace and partially free will that act, but both perform the whole, each by its individual work. Free will, indeed, does the whole, and grace does the whole, but as all is in free will, so all is from grace.) Saint Bernard, *Tractatus de Gratia et Libero Arbitrio*, ch. XIV, #47.

of security and of rest where it is enough to adore in spirit and in truth, without mixing the miseries of transitive action in with this higher life? Or else, if this faith is ever mysterious as a gift entirely from on high, in what way could the transcendent and incomprehensible dogma inspire acts capable of expressing it without denaturing it, and how could it enclose itself in the letter of a symbol, a rite, or a sacrament without changing the purity of the interior sense into idolatry?

A subtle and widespread error, born of an incomplete philosophy and a failure of the religious sense, which philosophy must dissipate through a more exact view of the dignity of human action and of its infinite capacity. For (simply by developing the regulated series of convergences founded on the very nature of action), it is, on the contrary, through practice that faith develops and is purified, as it is faith that inspires and transfigures all of man's practical life. From the letter to the spirit, from dogma to precept, there is a perpetual exchange and an intimate solidarity. The letter is the spirit in action. And if the mysteries seem purely speculative truths, nevertheless, through the reunion of one mystery with the other, are born quite practical truths. Dogmas are not only facts and ideas in acts, but also they are principles of action. This is what will be understood in studying the value of literal practice and the meaning of acts required by precept.

CHAPTER 2
The Value of Literal Practice
and the Conditions of Religious Action

That through the complete development of the human will and through a full generosity in action one could reach the avowal and the felt need for a truth higher than reason we have perhaps managed to understand and to admit. But that this faith could in turn become the principle of acts embodied in sensible nature, that the divine intervention should descend into the detail of practical life through material signs, that supernatural life should have a natural expression, no doubt at first seems unacceptable and unintelligible. To look for anything else in human acts than an imperfect symbol of God's pure act and to claim that the divine is, so to speak, entirely contained in the human without making it burst open, to believe that, under the particular determination of dogmas, rites and practices, the transcendent is immanent without losing anything of its infinity, is that not a form, and the most outrageous, of superstition and idolatry? — No: the way of adoring in spirit and in truth is to rise to a literal faithfulness and a practical submission. If the spirit demands and evokes the letter, the true letter inspires and vivifies the spirit.

To be sure, it is legitimate to speak about it here only as hypothetical; but it is necessary to do so, if it is true that this hypothetical gift must at one and the same time be acquired integrally and naturalized in human action. The same movement that forces us to conceive the idea of a religious action brings us, by the force of a logic we cannot escape, to determine the exigencies and as it were the requirements of this unavoidable conception. There is here, then, a new link in the chain of determinism. We have still to lay hold of it. Given what we know of voluntary action, it remains, by way of consequence, for us to define the indispensable condition for its completion. There is no need to know whether this condition is real or possible. On the side of man, it is not. The issue is to show that it is necessary. It is neither in a reality, nor in a possibility, but in a necessity that the complete study of the determinism of action ends up. Science òwes us nothing more nor less than the necessary. It is not for science to say whether the conditions it requires are really posited; but given that they are, its exigencies become absolute. It is for each one of us, then, to take this necessity into account; for this inevitable content of action determined by scientific analysis is that which, for reflexion, becomes moral exigencies and practical obligations.

Without any false respect, then, as well as without any temerity, it is appropriate to lead philosophy as far as it can go, as far as it has to go. It has too often abandoned a part, the highest, of its domain; that must be restored to it. In spite of the unaccustomed terms and the neglected questions that will be brought before it, let no one be mistaken about the properly philosophical aim that inspires this inquiry. And it is always this same thought: "how to make the willed end equal to the very principle of the voluntary aspiration?" For men can be brought to submission only by making them understand that it is the secret of their true independence. We must, therefore, aim at true independence to understand the secret of necessary submission. Moreover, even when it is a question of the supernatural, it is still a fundamentally human preoccupation and like a cry of nature that makes itself heard. The issue is to see how this notion of the supernatural is necessarily engendered, and how the supernatural seems necessary to the human will for action to reach its equation in consciousness. There is no question here of determining the content itself of Divine Revelation. In its principle, in its object and in its end, to be what it has to be if it is, Revelation must transcend the grasp of reason; and no effort of man purely as man could penetrate into its essence.[1] It would be to be radically ignorant of what it claims to be,

407

---

1. Perhaps, in order to reassure minds equally ready to fear that violence will be done to their free thought or to their belief, it would be useful to indicate in what precisely this Revelation claims to consist. How far reason has the right to go without being alarmed by any neighboring power, without alarming the authority that stands guard over and interprets the deposit of faith, one never knows well enough, to the common concern of both faith and reason. Lacking in this legitimate daring, reason, at the moment it claims to refuse all sharing, reduces itself and deprives itself of its entire sovereignty. Thanks to this necessary examination, faith, as it gains what natural preparation and what human support it needs, maintains its entire purity. If as soon as philosophy touches on the simple *notion* of the supernatural one dreads an abuse of power or a confusion of competences, it is because one knows nothing of the *essence* of this supernatural itself. Being above everything we can suspect or hope for, this mystery, far from dreading the encroachment of thought, opens up for it an infinite quarry, without thought ever being able to attain it. To be sure, in what faith proposes, all is not

therefore, to think that, in committing to rational examination what is still rational in the notion of the supernatural, we are encroaching on a reserved domain. The role of the philosopher is to establish that, fully consequent with our secret wish, we go all the way to literal practice; it is to express the inevitable exigencies of thought and as it were the natural prayer of the human will. Nothing more, but nothing less.

The question is as serious as it is delicate. If it appears very simple for man to put his justification into practice, how complex and difficult it is to justify this salutary practice. One can well understand still that practice should precede and prepare belief. But that the *act of faith* should inspire *faith in acts* is, for some of the consciousnesses most infatuated with the divine, the intolerable paradox. To be sure, they are infinitely right, these religious souls, in finding repugnant recipes and mechanical applications that profane their ineffable feeling. But if they are raised above niggardly superstitions, they are wrong nevertheless in not recognizing that the point they are happy to have reached is still only a middle ground and that there remains for them some progress to obtain. How I would wish to show them that the broadest and deepest faith finds its perfection in very precise acts, that this lowly and even humiliating practice alone preserves all the nobility and the purity of the interior cult, and that, if there is a letter where only death and corruption dwell, there is a necessary one that carries with it life and salvation.

inaccessible to our efforts; and in what reason can discover, there is a part covered and confirmed by revelation. But beyond all advances of human science and virtue, there is a truth impenetrable to any philosophical view, a good higher than any aspiration of the will. And this mystery, as faith proposes it, is as follows. Initiating us to the secret of His divine life, the hidden God reveals to us the divine processions, the generation of the Word by the Father, the spiration of the Spirit by the Father and the Son. Then, through love, he summons all men to a participation in His nature and in His happiness. Adopted by the Father, regenerated by the Son, anointed by the Holy Spirit, man is by grace what God is by nature, and, in time, the mystery of eternity is renewed. Man no longer says to God: "Master," but, "Father." And from this divine grace are born divine faculties. Faith illumines the intelligence to know the incomprehensible; charity dilates the will to embrace the infinite. No longer belonging to our nature, these operations go back all the way to the source whence they proceed. Heir of the Father, co-heir with the Son, united to the One and the Other by the Spirit, man contemplates God, loves Him, possesses Him. Without confusion of nature or person, he is God. The incommunicable has communicated Himself. So that, raised above all created or conceivable being, he who was not participates in the eternal privilege of the One who alone can say: "I am who am."

I

What we cannot know nor especially understand distinctly, we can do and put into practice. That is the usefulness, the eminent reason of action. It is not only the provisional vehicle to bring the coveted gift to consciousness. Its mediation is not passing, but permanent. It is the perpetual means for interior conversion and the instrument of the kingdom of faith. For, in a way that is incomprehensible, it makes the meaning of a still obscure faith flow to the very marrow of the bones, and it runs through the mysterious ways that bring to the light of reflexion the shrouded truths by which it is nourished. That is the secret of the value, that is the natural principle of the efficacity of literal practice. In short, to vivify the members, faith must act in them; and to vivify itself, it needs them to act on it. Always action gives more than it receives and receives more than it gives.

Just as no particular intention is brought to term without the operation which appears to determine it, but which actually completes and enriches it, so also moral and religious life is not perfected in man except by involving the whole of man. Here, no more than elsewhere is the sentiment independent of the organism where it expresses itself. Here as elsewhere, action is not only a consequence or a condition of the intention, but it adds an essential increase to it. It contains what are the grounds for the sentiment or the end of the tendency. To think that to adore in spirit and in truth is to abstain from all determinate practice, such is the error that resembles very much the illusion we fall into when we imagine that the real execution is only an accessory appendage and almost a deterioration of the ideal resolution. Of course, action seems to constrain the beautiful expansion of the interior life and to impoverish the richness of feeling. But that is so only in appearance. The necessity for a practical determination, far from drying up the liberality of the inward effusion, replenishes its source. Like the philosopher or the artist whose subservience to signs and forms prevents him from remaining complacent with confused intuitions, the religious soul finds a help against itself in the demanding rigor of the letter; under this constraint, it renews itself; and far from losing itself in a vague and floating aspiration after an infinite, it deepens and vivifies these sentiments it was afraid of profaning or killing, by projecting them out into the body of an act.

Also, in the simplicity of the most common practices, there is more infinite than in the haughtiest speculations or in the most exquisite feelings. And the humble person who acts according to the precepts of devotion he judges to be quite clear even though he does not comprehend them, has a much better sense of truth than all the theosophers of the world.

In the letter, this person has the spirit without any pretentions. The theosophers pretend to have it without the letter and do not have it. Who, then, gives proof of his spiritual fruitfulness, the one with the unction of speech, or the one who, even dryly, can do what he could not speak of? Yet it is the dialectician of interior feelings who glories in the abundance of his piety; and it is the one faithful to the letter who is reproached for having a devotion all for show. What is external still, are feelings, thoughts; what is most intimate, what manifests life best and transfigures, are works. What matter the fleeting marvels of dialectics or the ravishing emotions of conscience! There has to be a conclusion: it is action. *In actu perfectio* (perfection is in the act).

What is true of any particular intention, forced as it is to seek in the operation which realizes it a living commentary on it, is then even more true of the religious aspiration. Where else does it tend, if not to make 410 the whole man go into action and to produce in him the fullness of a new life, as if, to be completed, every action had to be a communion? Now this communion, necessarily desired, can be realized only in practice; for practice alone can tie together two orders that seemed incommunicable. And it is in acts alone that God, bearing the immensity of his gift, can gain a foothold within us. Human thought, always too narrow in some respect, once it becomes self-complacent, never has the breadth to contain all that it conceives and requires. But what escapes a limited outlook by the very expanse of truth and the variety of life, remains practicable. We cannot immediately understand the multiple aspects of all that is to be known; we can pass immediately to the practice of all that is to be done. To act only within the limits of the present clarity, and to restrict ourselves to the conception or the sense of the divine as we feel it, without seeking in life itself an immediate application for it, is to diminish ourselves. Through its tyranny, thought narrows action down; through its submission, action broadens thought out.

Let no one talk, then, of the servitude of the believer and the practicing communicant. The subjection he seems to live in is not a hindrance for his freedom; it is for him the means of managing to will all that he truly wills. What is enslaving is to think only with one's own light and to act only according to one's own judgment. Any man who no longer feels the need to renew and to surpass himself lacks life; to be attached to the narrow forms of one's thought is to be dead already. We must remain ever ready to destroy our fanciful or ruinous constructions, in order to be docile to contradictions. Without the ties of passion, of self-interest, or of habit, it is no doubt a suffering to be always rejuvenating our spirit in the letter, but it is the only means of maintaining all the discretion of conscience and total sincerity. To rest neither in doubt nor in certainty, never to be attached to truth as others are to their idols, to live in fear and freedom even while promising an invincible fidelity, to be always in dread of losing and to always be waiting for the light, to bear in one's heart the anguish of one in search along with the serenity and the credulous docility of a child, that is undoubtedly the way, not of slavery, but of liberation. Most apply themselves to see how right they are; we must apply ourselves to see in what we are wrong. How many think themselves religious, either because they cling to the conviction that they have purified the spirit of the letter, or because they are fascinated by some divine words with whose meaning they love to resonate! One would like everything to be clear for thought, and that there should be a unique center of perspective. There isn't any; that center is everywhere. But what we can't see clearly we can do fully. The true commentary is practice. Also, men do not have true disciples because they do not know how to appeal to the mysterious depths whence, through the manifold operation of submissive practice, the unity of free convictions rises. What is necessary, then, is to be attentive to what contradicts us, to go beyond the point where we would like to stop. In faith and in precepts, there are affirmations that seem to clash, prescriptions that seem to thwart us: that is why it is necessary and salutary for us to abide by them. If the external law continues to subsist, it is to warn us that, as long as it appears external to us and shatters within us some of the attachments of our reason or of our hearts, we are not yet at the center of truth and love. Far from holding us in, it forces us to spread out, to see in what our thought falls short and our will falters, to admit the contrary aspects of a truth larger than our knowledge, and to confer all the power of this perfect science mysteriously upon our action. The letter, incomprehensible and demanding, is the means of thinking and acting divinely.

Thus, the exigencies of human action and the conditions it requires to reach completion follow one another like a continuous chain. By the profound movement of his freedom man is led to will to ally himself with God and to form one synthesis with Him. Every act tends to become a communion. This synthesis could not be consummated except by action, the only receptacle big enough to contain the coveted gift. And not only can the alliance not be sealed, but it cannot persist or be strengthened except through literal practice. Faith, then, is not only an act and the effect of an act; by a natural necessity, it is in turn a principle of action. Just as, in the dynamism of reflexion, thought, which is the fruit of the experience of life, becomes itself a motive and a point of departure for an ulterior experience, so also faith, which could be called the divine experience within us, is the origin of an activity that concerns the whole man and makes him produce, through all his members, the belief he lives

by. For, if ideas are forces, it is not just by what is already clear about   412
them, but especially by what remains obscure about them; and it is by
penetrating into this penumbra that they obtain an additional light: by
throwing our thought into the obscurities of practice, we find, in the
clarity of practice, something to illumine the obscurities of thought.
Belief is sincere and living, then, only if, by reason of its very darkness,
it tends, through action, to win over the thoughts and energies which in
us are foreign and rebellious toward it. It is a total assimilation that must
be obtained, an assimilation of the whole organism to this principle of
a higher life.

In our little world, therefore, we have to cooperate in a sort of creation
by obtaining from all our powers that they believe, even to the intimate
depths of our organs. How can we effectively reach these dark energies,
how accomplish the work of reason and the will in this chaos, how produce man there and let God penetrate it, if not by practice? Literal practice must be like a ferment that leavens little by little, by an imperceptible
progress, all the weight of the members. Once we begin to entertain
within ourselves this vivifying force, a slow work of transsubstantiation
and conversion takes place in our carnal mass, in our desires and in our
appetites. Each act inspired by a thought of faith begins the generation
of a new man because it engenders God in man. Also, as the body
without soul is dead, dead also is the faith without works. And what is
it in faith that can actually die, if not its presence and its vivifying operation in the members? The member lives only in a close dependence. He
cannot raise himself to the dignity of the chief: his role is to act as the
chief orders, because that is his way of participating in the life of the
spirit. He does not think; he acts. And acting communicates to him the
essential of thought. This is his way of thinking and praying.

And it is not just to concert all of our interior life that literal practice
is necessary. For our action is pregnant with the universal life. It is not
only a function of the individual; it is a function of the great social body.
To foster circulation and unity in the city of souls, then, to regulate the
respiration of the universal life in us, there has to be cooperation and
edification. Edification, a beautiful word: it is never enough to act only
for self, we cannot do so; we have to build in others, become part of the   413
total work and fit ourselves into the edifice. If, through action, each finds
access into himself even to the hidden sources whence proceed feelings
and beliefs, through action also each finds in others the secret of common
thoughts and aspirations. It is thanks to this practical union that men,
causing their certitudes and their affections to rise from a depth they
know not, become attached to one another through a bond so powerful
and so gentle that they form only one spirit and one body. Yes, only

practice works this wonder of forming, with the diversity of *spirits*, a single *body*, because it uses and fashions that by which they are tied to one another. That is why there is unity of doctrine only as a result of a common discipline and a conformity of life. And that is why the dogmas and beliefs are teachings for thought only in view of becoming principles of action. This is the point we must come to in order to understand that intellectual union remains impossible among men, who nevertheless need it and need that it be free and total, impossible as long as it claims to remain independent of a discipline and a tradition; for a tradition and a discipline represent a constant interpretation of thought through acts, offering each individual, in the sanctified experience, something like an anticipated control, an authorized commentary, an impersonal verification of the truth it is for each one to resurrect in himself in order to take his place in the assembly of intelligent beings. Since we have to conspire with ourselves, with humanity, with the universe, for this communion, we need a literal practice. It is as it were the thought of this spiritual organism and the contribution of each member of this great body to the functions of the spirit.

As the analysis of the necessary relations and the natural exigencies of voluntary life leads us to define it, a double mystery is at work then in the action that comes from faith. It is through action that the divine takes hold in man, hides its presence there, insinuates into him a new thought and a new life. It is through action that the lowest and the most obscure parts which express the needs of the organism and the reverberations of the universe rise to faith and cooperate in the human and divine work that comes to completion in us. Without it the synthesis is not brought to perfection. For the whole body to be illumined, the eye has to be luminous; for the eye to be luminous, the body has to be active and sound.

II

414   The two following philosophical objections seem disposed of. "Religion," it was said, "is interior and cannot be contained in any form." Yes; the letter is necessary for the spirit. "Faith itself," it was further objected, "is valid only by reason of the feeling that inspires it, but not by reason of the formula that determines it while deforming it, nor by reason of acts that could not contain the immensity of the divine in its entirety." Yes; practice is necessary for faith. And yet these two objections contain a more profound truth than perhaps even those who fall back on them realize. To discover it will be to make manifest the error which they fall into. Here is how.

It is quite right to claim that works are indispensable for the interior sense: they ought to be vivifying for it. At the same time, it is also right to claim that the works which issue spontaneously from the interior sense are not equal to what they express and that to look for divine nourishment in human acts is to fall back into superstition; such human acts would be deadly for the religious sense. Thus some kind of practice is absolutely necessary for faith; and the practice born naturally from faith, to the extent that faith is a principle of action, remains radically inadequate and vain. To those who maintain that it is not our acts that sanctify, but we who sanctify our acts, we must answer that only action can be salutary. To those who maintain that their good works are fully salutary, we must answer that faith alone sanctifies.

To escape this apparent contradiction, some have imagined a hybrid compromise, but it is this middling and inconsequent solution that must be entirely rejected. Here is what it is. When they speak of faith and of the works indispensable for faith, there remains an ambiguity on the nature of this necessary relation. At one time, they consider practice as a natural consequence of the interior sense that inspires it. At another time, they recognize that, to have a living faith, we must act. In the first instance, they make action a necessary accessory to belief; in the second, they look on it as an integrating element, as an essential end, as an indispensable addition. By *works*, they mean either the natural consequence of an interior belief that manifests itself through the indeterminate spontaneity of practical proofs, or determinate acts accomplished for their own sake and which keep their original meaning. It is readily admitted that the most intimate sense of the divine needs to express itself in acts; but since none of these acts seems equal to faith itself, then some would like them, unlike other acts, not to be an end for intention nor a progress for the agent; they would hope to set up a category apart for them, as if religious life were to escape the common laws of life. And yet it is to avoid any derogation from nature that they are led to derogate from religious life in this way. In short, they would pretend to believe in the acts of religious life without ever acting out of its faith.

But in the course of this entire science of practice, it has come out constantly that action is something new and heterogeneous in relation to its own conditions. This scientific truth is once again confirmed here. It is not possible to consider religious practice as a subalternate appendage and as an arbitrary or accidental accessory to the feeling that inspires it. To believe that this feeling is the whole of true religion, to judge that works will gush forth from the heart as it is moved to do so, to slip out from under the discipline of a literal practice, is to betray both science and conscience. Hence it is vain to try to maintain this false position, as if one could say at one and the same time both that faith is all the more living when it is active and that to make these actions a means of believing is to depreciate or ruin faith. The pious enemies of the letter are not fully consistent, neither where they are wrong, nor when they are right. While recognizing the necessity of a practice, we must recognize the absolute inanity of all human practice, without ever sacrificing either one of these affirmations to the other. They seem incompatible, but we are invincibly brought to them; and it is from this very incompatibility that the inevitable solution to the problem emerges.

On the one hand, no act naturally born of religious belief perfects or equals its dignity. On the other hand, faith is possible only under the species of a defined letter and through the efficacity of a practical submission; and the true infinite could be immanent only in action; it is therefore a necessity for this action itself to be the object of a positive precept, and for it to start, no longer from the movement of our nature, but from the divine order. We must refer the determination of it to an authority distinct from ourselves, even when we are conscious of acquiring, at the cost of docility, a truer autonomy. What is in accord with our will is that this action be prescribed to us. We must arrive at the point of this avowal to satisfy the proper exigencies of minds most rightly hostile to superstitious devotions and to be more consistent than they with their own principles. And thus these truths, no longer opposed, but linked together in the logic of the most upright religious sense, fall into agreement: no faith without practice, no practice naturally equal to faith; no revealed truth without also prescribed acts.

If, then, as much by the impenetrable shadows it presents as by the light it brings above any other, faith is naturally the necessary source of a practice, this natural exigency is not enough to determine the particular nature or the precise form of the acts necessary to seal the necessary alliance and the perfect union man aspires to. In order for these ritual acts not to be reduced to an idolatrous fiction or for them to equal the faith whose vivifying expression they must be, it is required that they be, not an invention of man and the always imperfect effect of a natural movement, but the expression of positive precepts and the original imitation of dogma divinely transcribed into distinct commandments. It is not enough for them to become vehicles of the transcendent. They have to contain its real presence and be its immanent truth. *Caro verbum facta* (the Word made Flesh). Derived from dogma, the discipline and the authority of the positive prescriptions become themselves original dogmas. A practice is necessary; and any practice not given as a supernatural order is superstitious. It is nothing if it is not all.

Thus, the action which is supposed to contain the presence and com-

416

municate the reality of religious life could not, any more than faith could, start from human initiative. If the very letter of dogma is, by definition, divine thought incarnate in a sensible sign, the positive precept, however arbitrary its formula may appear, must no less contain a will other than man's. In spite of the determinate, relative, mutable character of the acts it prescribes, this practical dogmatism offers to the one who submits to it the means of cooperating with the author of the precept. And the human will is fully consequent with itself only if it reaches and consents to this need for an effective submission. To shy away from acts under pretext that they are an external and demeaning constraint is to fail the spirit that secretly demands this elevating submission. 417

In literal practice, therefore, the human act is identical with the divine act; and under the cover of the letter the fullness of a new spirit is insinuated. Indeed, we must not say that certain actions can take on an *absolute* value, in the *measure* that they offer a symbolic representation of the depth of things or that they realize, in facts, the relations which most faithfully express the real mystery of truth and the good. Besides, wouldn't that be a contradiction in terms? There is no approximate or symbolic absolute. No; the religious act cannot be a symbol: either it is or it is not a reality. For the essential relations of man with the absolute to be established in a precise way, they have to be defined absolutely and in this divine commerce there has to be a gift and a consecration which cannot come from us. If the good cannot be realized in man except through finite acts, still by a supernatural condescendence this finite itself must be given as the garb, better still, as the very body of the transcendent. If God does not place Himself therein for man to find Him there and nourish himself thereby, man will not place him there.

To be sure, practice does not work either through blind magic or through brute mechanism; there are dead acts, without spirit and without soul, external devotion, as vain as or worse than any other superstition. To be sure again, in the absence of any ritual form or of any recognized precept, there are vivifying acts that compensate for not knowing a more clear revelation, acts inspired by nothing sensible, egotistic, or presumptuous and which call for the unknown gift. But if literal practice is neither a pure formality for those who have to submit to it, nor an essential condition of salvation for those unable to be taught by it, still it is to the secret efficaciousness of a real mediation that our will, even unknown to itself, owes its ability to complete itself. It is possible even to ignore it without ceasing to profit by it and without sinning against the spirit. But this admirable extension of mercy to those who maintain a true generosity in their refusal of a literal practice does not do away with the complete truth in which they participate without seeing 418 it. The man of desire in a way finds in positive precepts as many experiences all prepared, as many hypotheses to be verified, where the fullness of truth is confirmed and gives itself over to those who have not turned away either their eyes or their hands. Properly understood, practice, in appearance the most arbitrary and the most difficult to bear for nature, is nothing else than a perfect conformity with the exigencies of freedom. We must not, therefore, turn into objections against dogma or discipline the consequences that follow from the simple supposition that they are.

In a word, there is an infinite present in all our voluntary actions and this infinite we cannot by ourselves grasp by our reflexion nor reproduce by our human effort. For us to grasp and produce it as we will it, therefore, this secret principle of all action must give itself to us under the very form through which we can enter into communion with it; we have to receive and possess it in our smallness. We must have the infinite as finite; and it is not for us to limit it; otherwise we would be lowering it to our size. It is up to this infinite alone to bring itself within our comprehension and to condescend to our littleness in order to exalt us and broaden us to its immensity. Once again, the reality of this gift, it is true, remains beyond the grasp of man and of philosophy; but it is reason's essential work to see its necessity and to determine the natural harmonies that regulate the concatenation of the supernatural truths themselves. If the symbolic acts whose object is to realize in man the perfect life and to make the will equal to itself in consciousness came from man alone, they could not but be temerarious and superstitious. That is why we are always tempted to be surprised and almost scandalized at the sight of a contingent sign that claims to express the necessary reality, of a relative and transient act that presents itself as absolute, of *something* that is supposed to contain *all*. It would be better, it seems, if it were *nothing* apparent. But if, as reason itself requires, the precept comes from a source other than the will of man, then the surprise should cease: infinite greatness can accommodate itself to our infinite smallness; the divine is more than universal, it is particular at each point and wholly in each. If it gives itself to all, like the manna which satisfied all tastes, it is under the most accessible and the most humble form, because in this sublime degradation its goodness and its dignity require that it be not just half condescending. The more negligible the symbol will be for the senses, the more it will meet the exigencies of reason and of the heart. Its brightness can only be that of a point, like the star whose ray, apart from a thin line of light, seems to leave the Ocean in darkness and yet illumines the immensity of the waves, since, no matter where we look from, the eye is led to its brightness.

Thus, in religious practice, the ordinary relations of thought and action have to be at once preserved, completed, and reversed: — preserved, for it remains true that belief, in order to be vivid and sincere, in order to sink into the members and assimilate the organism to itself, needs to manifest itself through practical works; — completed, for it is in the positive precept, and only there, that there is, by hypothesis, a perfect equation between the spirit and the literal form wherein it expresses itself; — reversed even, for, unlike habitual acts, where thought precedes the sensible operations and imperfectly penetrates the organism that realizes it on the outside, here it is the sensible sign that obscurely contains the light whose invisible center thought seeks to discover little by little. And that is what we must now understand well.

III

Action is prescribed only if, in what is to be done, it contains the reality of what is to be believed. Heterogeneous with regard to us, practice and dogma are in themselves identical; and their role is to make identical in us the truth known and the life attained; it is to bring to thought and to the will the unity of the ideal and the real; it is to reintegrate into man, who freely constitutes his personality, the integrity of the cause that creates him and vivifies him, a restoration which is possible only if the human will, whence the movement of personal life proceeds as from an efficient cause, assimilates itself to the end conceived and willed as the term of our destiny.

Hence, whereas, in the natural order, the material operation which translates the intention only extends the domain of the will and benefits thought only in the measure that it reconciles to it the still blind powers of life, here it is the operation itself which becomes nourishment and light   420
for the spirit; for it is the divine willing which shines forth through the obscurity of the sensible sign. The perfect food, therefore, which alone is capable of vivifying a thought and a will animated by faith, resides in the formal command, the ritual act, the sacramental material. What is visible and material in literal practice is not as such put into practice; one is not guided herein according to phenomena. Moreover, under the sensible wrapping that serves to give action a purchase, we touch, we possess the reality which the senses do not reach. Even in keeping its natural aspect and laws, the act takes place entirely in the absolute. It seems that in obeying the precept we make the eminent truth which it expresses come down into us. That is true; but we also transform and raise into that truth the act it prescribes. The literal precept is, so to speak, more

living and more spiritual than the spirit it takes hold of. We absorb it into ourselves, and it is the one that absorbs us into it.

The true letter, then, is the very reality of the spirit. It manifests its inaccessible life to us in its depth; it communicates it to us so that we may engender it and make it live in ourselves. Is it not through the body that generation takes place? A mystery impenetrable to the understanding is consummated there, the wonder of a fruitfulness which, through a very singular operation, puts the entire species into each living individual. In the same way, is it not through the revealing word and through a submissive practice that is inserted, diversely but wholly in each one of us, a thought and a life that is not from us? Has anyone given any thought to the strange power of the graft? All that is needed are a few living cells grafted onto the stem for this interior bonding to produce a physiological revolution that renews the sap of the wildling, and, suddenly, by a natural magic, fruitfulness takes the place of sterility. In the same way, the insertion of a thought of faith and of a sacramental operation into our viscera reforms and transfigures the functions of nature. Human sap is the food of supernatural life; but it is this latter life which grows fruitfully and blossoms out in us in order finally to bring forth full works.

And this comparison of the graft is still an imperfect one, for the enriched sap does not go back down to the roots so as to make the fruitfulness rise directly from them. Contrary to this, in the wondrous operation which, from two infinitely separated lives, forms a synthesis and a unique action through a double assimilation, literal practice insinuates the divine seed even into the most humble of functions. It associates the body to a life higher than that of the spirit. And it is from this sacramental matter, in which the living infinite seems annihilated and as though dead, that must rise again, through the effort of a good will, this life which is at once divine and human. We must all give ourselves birth by giving God birth in us, θεοτόκοι. And as if man had to be God in order to be fully human, there is enough within man that, in spite of his incomprehensible weakness, no other being can be greater than he. The gift which religious life brings him is so closely incorporated into his substance that human nature becomes capable of producing and creating in some way the One from whom it has everything, as if at one and the same time the donor wanted to have everything from the donee, and as if man, summoned finally to satisfy the infinite excess of his willing, became, according to the expression of Saint Thomas, "the God of his God."

To go to the end of the determinism of the exigencies of human action and of the chain of the relations necessary for the completion of our destiny, then, God has to offer Himself to us as if annihilated, so that we may restore to this apparent nothingness its fullness. In accordance with what we have to conceive and hope for, He makes Himself so small that we can hold Him, so weak that He needs us to lend Him our arms and our acts, so condescending that He hands Himself over to the ebb and flow of sensible life, so dispossessed that we have to return Him to Himself, so dead that we have to engender Him anew, as in the mysterious labor which brings forth living members from inert nourishment. It was the great temptation to become "like gods"; impossible dream. And yet man seems to have been given the ability to work a greater wonder: to be, we must, we can bring it about that God be for us and by us.

This is the point to which we must come for our will finally to find its equation, by bringing its end back to its principle. The act par excellence is a true communion and like a mutual generation of the two wills living in us. Is it possible for man's desires to be thus fulfilled or surpassed? Who has not wished to receive adoration and be the object of a cult? It is for reason to say that we do wish it, for faith to say whether we are such. We wish for more still, beyond, an excess of good which we do not know how to define; and this excess itself has to be promised to whoever has the generosity to will it. Is it promised or not? If every act must fecundate the soul as if for a divine conception, is not death itself the last, the complete, the eternal communion? Indeed, will not man need eternity to be able to receive and absorb God, this God whom man, in order to be and to live fully, needs to produce and to will, as he is known and willed by Him? It is not for us to satisfy these exigencies; it is for us to take cognizance of the capacity of the abyss prepared within us.

422

And under the strange rigorousness of the words we have had to use, let no one look for I know not what symbolic meaning, as if that were to be more precise or more tolerable or more profound still. No, those are not ideas to be interpreted, but acts to be put into practice. The true infinite is less in knowledge than in life; it is neither in facts, nor in sentiments, nor in ideas; it is in action. The apparent narrowness of practice is immensely more ample than the pretended breadth of speculation or all the mysticism of the heart. The spirit without the letter is no longer the spirit. Truth does not live in the abstract and universal form of thought: the only commentary that leaves it intact is the practice which renews in each intelligence the mystery of this conception and places all of it in each along with the richness of its contrary aspects. Heaven is, with scientific certainty, under our feet as well as above our heads; but since we still walk and live only on earth, it is in the down-to-earth of the act that, in spite of obstacles, we must find the heaven which extends beyond. We must take the letter literally, because only in it, and not in the interpretation we might give it, is hidden the secret of the operation it prescribes. The letter is not primarily a thought; it is above all practice. And if in its very obscurity there are clear and penetrating words like a loving glance, it is on the condition that they remain decisive and trenchant like the sword of action.

Thus is revealed little by little the integral ambition of the will which was looking for itself without knowing itself fully at first. It is in pretending to make itself effectively the equal of its own power that it ceases to find its sufficiency in itself alone. We wanted to do everything by ourselves, it seemed; and now, through this aim, we are led to recognize that we do nothing and that God alone, acting in us, grants us to be and to do what we will. Hence, when we will fully, it is Him, it is His will that we will. We ask that He be, that He sustain, complete, underpin all our operations; we belong to ourselves only to claim our dependence on Him and give ourselves back to Him; our true will is to have none other than His; and the triumph of our independence is in our submission. Submission and independence are equally real. For what we have to arrive at is that our willing be regulated by His, not His by ours. And when, through this free substitution, we recognize that He does everything in us, but through us and with us, then it is that He grants us to have done everything. We participate freely in His necessary freedom; in accepting that He be in us what He is in Himself, we gain being ourselves what He is Himself, *Ens a se* (Being from himself). We attain independence only through abnegation, but we have to attain it. What is impossible for the understanding and the effort of thought alone becomes a reality in practice; it is what joins together in a perfect synthesis two natures incompatible in appearance. Only wills can be wed in this way, so as to become, in a close cooperation, one and the same thing, *ut unum sint* (that they be one). That is why the power of manifesting love and acquiring God is attributed only to action.

All that has gone before are only conditions subordinate to action; to go to the end of these spiritual needs, it remains for us to justify them absolutely and to subordinate action to them. Now that we have considered everything, including the knowledge and the affirmation of being, as simple phenomena, we shall finally have to discover being itself in the phenomena. Hence we are reversing the ordinary terms of the problem; we are looking, not for what is under what appears, but in what appears for what is. A complete view of the exigencies implied by action reveals the secret of the exigencies it undergoes; and in taking cognizance of all that we require, we understand, we justify all that is required of us.

CHAPTER 3

The Bond of Knowledge and Action in Being

Can we push on still further and follow the advance of action, even   424
beyond this perfect form of religious practice which seems to close the
circle of human destiny? Yes, it is possible, it is necessary to do so. Under
the influence of this continuous determinism which develops the science
of action because it expresses the exigencies and the real expansion of the
will, one last effort of thought becomes inevitable, an effort which will
serve as a guaranty and a justification for all those that have preceded.
Far from all the rungs used to ascend to complete life having to be
discarded as passing means, man completes his role by grounding absolutely the universal reality with which action has been nourished, that
role which consists in becoming the real bond of things and conferring
upon them all the being they entail. But let no one be any more mistaken
about what is to follow than about what has gone before. The issue is
still to determine the necessary sequence of the needs of practice, even
to the point where, through the definition of its total conditions, the
truth of the relations required by action will be absolutely established.
How the idea of objective existence is inevitably formed within us; how
we invincibly affirm the very reality of the objects of our knowledge;
what is the necessary meaning of this objective existence precisely; under
what conditions this reality, inevitably conceived and affirmed, is in effect real, these questions initially only continue the movement of prac-   425
tical determinism. They seem to bear only on the internal relations which
make all phenomena solidary in our consciousness, but in the end these
phenomena themselves will be found to constitute the being of things.
The practical necessity of raising the ontological problem necessarily
leads us to the ontological solution of the practical problem.

Moreover, what had appeared up to now, in a regressive analysis, as
a series of necessary conditions and of means successively required to
constitute action little by little, henceforth, in a synthetic view, will reveal itself as a system of real truths and of beings simultaneously ordered.

We have considered all that is indispensable for the consummation of action; we must consider how action consummates and constitutes all the rest. What expressed simply a need of our will must acquire, before the understanding itself, an absolute truth. What has been up to now only a necessity of fact will be grounded in reason. What had been posited before thought only as means immanent to willing will be posited, outside the will, as ends immanent to thought. And whereas action had appeared first, and being, derived, it is truth and being which will appear first, but without their substance and their nature itself ceasing to be determined by action, which finds in them its rule as well as its sanction.

This necessary renewal of perspective, in leading us to define the exact value of all the preceding affirmations more precisely, will limit their bearing only in order to cast a better light on their properly scientific character. Not only are we ordinarily tempted to tie the knot too soon before having developed all the content of action, but we also run the risk of attributing to each of the successive observations an already metaphysical meaning which they do not have. Indeed, up to now, whatever else contrary habits of mind might have suggested to the reader, there has been a question only of means subordinate to action, without any question of erecting these practical conditions into real truths. — Even when we had to talk of Metaphysics, we had to consider in it only the element common to any conception of life and of things; and, prescinding from the variety as well as from the validity of systems, we saw only the necessity for man to form for himself an idea of the universe and of his destiny, the necessity for voluntary action to take on, under the impress of this inevitable conception, a new character, the principle of an original dynamism; that is why Metaphysics was treated in connection with the tiered forms of morality; it entered the lists only to confer a transcendent value on our acts. — Even when at a more advanced point in the development of action, we had to face up to the idea of God, we had to consider it only on a quite practical level: in showing that this conception, inevitably engendered in consciousness, forces us to affirm at least implicitly the living reality of this infinite perfection, there was no question of concluding to God's being from it; it was a question of observing that this necessary idea of the real God leads to the supreme alternative on which will depend whether God will really be or not be for us, which alone is absolutely important for us at first. To establish the efficaciousness of the God conceived as real and living, is not to prejudge the living reality of the God conceived. At that point, His truth is still entirely relative to human action as a practical means. The proofs of His existence that are given are renewed, therefore, not especially through the form of the argumentation, but by the spirit which inspires them and by the very nature of the conclusion. — Again, even when we had to speak of a supernatural, of a revealed dogma, and of a literal practice, we considered only a natural need of the will, without intending to ask whether this highest exigency has been met. — Finally, even when we shall have to determine the idea necessarily engendered within us of a subsistent reality, affirm the being of the objects of knowledge, and define the nature of this objective existence, we shall have to consider first only the inevitable sequence of the relations integrated in consciousness. The point is to constitute the science of the solidary appearances in its integrity. In spite of the apparent diversity of the links that make up the chain, all is continuous therein, all is of the same order; everywhere the same scientific relations, grounded on the same practical necessity.

This viewpoint appears to disconcert our habits of mind, but it is difficult to assume only because it requires us to return to the simple view of facts linked to one another without any sort of systematic prejudice. To explain the necessary generation of the notion of real existence, to show that we are inevitably led to affirm (whatever the value of this assertion may be otherwise) the reality of the objects of knowledge and the ends of action, to bring out how, through the mediation of this in- 427 evitable idea of objective existence, the needs of action are transformed into regulating ideas for it, to indicate what precise conception of being we are inevitably led to, and to determine the conditions which appear indispensable for this existence, so defined, to be realized in the way that we cannot keep from conceiving it: all this is not to step out of the determinism of phenomena, in spite of the renewal in perspective, but to manifest how, merely by thinking and acting, it is necessary for us to proceed as if this universal order were real and these obligations grounded. The role and the force of science is indeed to exclude all possibility of legitimate doubt and to constrain us, through the indirect way of necessity, to the admission of the truth which is in us before being in science, and which science attains only at the end while we live by it from the beginning.

— Now that the meaning of this new inquiry and the bearing of the solution to be found is defined, we must see how the question before us is engendered and organized. From the total solidarity of the phenomena, it follows both that it is impossible to arrive legitimately at the ontological problem before having run through all these interlocking links, and that it is impossible not to arrive at it after having developed the whole of this determinism of action. To raise the problem of knowledge and of being with a scientific precision and competence, we must previously have determined exactly the complete system of relations interposed between the two extreme terms. From the voluntary to the willed, from the ideal conceived to the real performed, from the efficient cause to the final cause, all the intermediaries must be passed through before we have the right to turn back and see, in the fleeting succession of the phenomena, the very solidity of being. But also, once thought has embraced the whole of the transient operations that little by little make the final cause immanent to the efficient cause, thought must necessarily make the entire series of its objects enter into the reality of the end that was already present from the very beginning.

A double consequence follows from this. — Since the inevitable determinism of action, embracing all the series of necessary means, forces us to this end, it follows that there is in us a certain knowledge of being which we cannot run away from; and even this knowledge, be it explicit or not, is coextensive with its object, whence it can be said that between being and knowing there is an absolute correspondence and a perfect reciprocity; it is impossible for man, however confusedly, not to form in effect this synthesis which the science of action has just analysed, and it is impossible for this synthesis, taking on an objective value in his eyes, not to really represent what is to be known and done. — On the other hand, since to attain the end we must pass through the alternative and decide the practical problem which presents itself to us as a question of life and death, it follows that between knowledge and being there subsists a radical heterogeneity, that between the sight and the possession of being the distance remains infinite, and that, if there is a necessary being of action, action does not necessarily have being in it. The universal nature of things, the human person, God, supernatural life, are undoubtedly conditions required by action and grounded in it. But action does not necessarily ground itself in God and does not inevitably realize all the conditions it posits itself.

Through this distinction, the problem of knowledge and being seems to take on a new meaning. Method and solution are transformed. — To think that we can arrive at being and legitimately affirm any reality whatsoever without having reached the very end of the series which extends from the first sensible intuition to the necessity of God and of religious practice, is to remain in illusion: we cannot stop at an object in the middle to make an absolute truth of it without falling into the idolatry of the understanding; every premature affirmation is illegitimate and, in the eyes of science, false, even when we will have to come back to it later on, but by a different way, and with a different meaning. — To think, on the contrary, that human conduct is independent of all metaphysical views, that practice is sufficient unto itself, and that it is possible to live without any concern for being, is equally an error. Against the ancient doctrines according to which the will acts in conformity with an object, κατα λογον, to the point of being one with it, μετα λογου; against the modern doctrines according to which the will creates its own object for itself and goes forward, not on the road of science, but on that of belief,[1] we must maintain that knowledge and action are mutually autonomous   429 and subordinated, that between truth and being there is a fundamental identity and a fundamental heterogeneity, in a word, that there subsists a necessary presence of reality in thought without reality being necessarily present to thought. Even those who, in theory, have attributed the most decisive role in knowledge to the will, have not really been able, in effect, to take into account the diversity introduced into knowledge by the supreme option from which hangs every human life. While keeping the truth of being which will appear as a rule and a sanction above the variations of human freedom, we must, on the contrary, show that, according to whether we accept or reject the action of this truth in us, our being is totally changed. The Word shines in all, but all do not have it in them. It would be strange if the question of truth and being could be settled apart from the practical decision imposed on us by the alternative to which the whole movement of science has had no other reason but to lead us.

Knowledge, then, is living or dead according to whether being, whose necessary presence it bears within it, is there only as a dead weight or reigns there through the effect of a free adherence. Thus it is important to study this threefold aspect of the solution. (1) How does thought inevitably conceive the reality of all the objects that have appeared as means for the will or conditions for action? (2) What, in the inevitable conception of being, can we reject and what remains of this necessary reality in the thought which excludes it or in the will which runs away from it? (3) What does a free admission, a practical adherence add to the being necessarily conceived and the truth inevitably recognized? In short, how does perfect action bring to consummation all that had served to constitute it? Therefore, we must establish for thought the absolute truth of all the relations posited in fact by action. The conditions which action supposes in order to become adequate to its exigencies must be shown, inversely, to be a reality which requires of it what is required for it to become equal to itself. Thus, while maintaining a complete heterogeneity,   430

1. In saying that "the Christian does not live in the world of science, but in the world of faith," some have claimed that Kantianism has substituted once and for all the Christian spirit for the Hellenic spirit in metaphysics. It is a mistake. The Word is no less light than life. And as dogma teaches a distinction in the unity of the divine operations, so also in man the conception and the possession of real truth, though identical in one sense, remain distinct and, in fact, separable.

we must maintain a complete solidarity of knowledge and the being which is its object. In a sense, the truth of being imposes itself entirely from the outside; it has an iron sceptre. In another sense, it has issued entirely from the most intimate freedom; its yoke is quite voluntary. And these two aspects are, if not inseparable, at least correlative: they are equally grounded in the living truth which makes up all that is substantial in things and still constitutes what is positive in privative knowledge and real in the error that denies it.

I

The entire nature of things has appeared to me as the series of means I have to will, which I do will in effect to accomplish my destiny. But I still have to understand how it happens that this series of means appears to me as a real nature of things. For the mediating role of action to be fully explained, this double aspect must be fully justified.

The issue, then, is to explain why the sequence of the practical determinism, just as the science of action has unfolded it, takes on the character of a real truth and how this notion of objective existence is engendered. In doing so we will have defined what is inevitably present and inevitably affirmed in the most elementary of the assertions which posit the reality of an object before the understanding. For, if it is observed that we cannot either have the notion of a true existence or insure the truth of any existence without the entire determinism of the practical conditions being at least implicitly included in our knowledge, it will follow at once both that it is impossible not to erect the total series of these conditions into objects for thought, and that it is impossible, in spite of the complete heterogeneity of the links that make up the chain, to affirm the truth of one of these solidary objects without including in the same affirmation all the others.

To show how the idea of objective existence is engendered in us, to bring out how it applies to each of the terms of the total series, to seek how the value of the series grows with each term and how each term implies the entire series, will be to bring to light not only what is independent of the determinations of the will in knowledge, but also what subordinates the possession of truth and the meaning of being to the solution of the practical problem which this minimal necessary knowledge imposes on every human consciousness.

I. — Whatever we may think and whatever we may will, from the fact alone that we think and we will, the universal order of determinism follows. In vain does one try to deny it or to undo it. By the effort one

431

makes to destroy it or to escape it one posits it and ratifies it. There is a will prior and immanent to any derogation from the necessities of practice; there is an affirmation of being anterior and interior to any effort at even a complete negation. Whatever we may eventually have to include under these words, the subjective conditions of thought and action take on an objective aspect.

Also, although the universal determinism may be in us to the extent that every step taken by the human will spontaneously implies it, by the same token it always appears to us as independent of our positive power, of our deliberate will, and of our reflected thought. It is for us a nature in the sense that, even in ratifying this order by our present action, we are admitting its necessary presence in our action. Though it is tied to the most intimate productions of the subject (otherwise we would not know it), it is nonetheless *the object* in our eyes (otherwise we could not see in it a system of means and of ends for the will). And since the role of this determinism is precisely to impose an alternative on our freedom, the point is that, being able to accept it or to reject its exigencies, we are face to face with something that is no doubt ours through the spontaneous production of thought, but that is at the same time outside of us as an end for the willed operation. Thus we discover the mutual generation and the relations of notions which seem most different. The nature of things appears as an objective reality to us because it is imposed on us by the unity of the determinism and because it imposes a free option on us. These two truly solidary aspects of the problem are equally indispensable for any conception of real existence. To arrive at the simple *idea* of an objective subsistence, the notion must be certified by a double act of the understanding and the will.

Hence, to the extent that we cannot not posit this chain of necessities which are the condition of our practical activity, whatever it may be, we are invincibly led to attribute an objective existence to the total order   432
of things because, if we may so speak, this real truth of the objects of thought is drawn from the very substance of the will. And the question is resolved prior to the dialectical interplay of ideas, in a region where the most hyperbolic doubt does not reach, underneath the realm of the understanding, before the intervention of discursive thoughts, more deeply than the intellectual necessities can press down their yoke, at the very principle of our personal adherence to our nature, at the point where we will our very selves: we are incurably, things are incurably for us.

Nor must we ever forget, the issue is the integral series. Nothing is valid, in the system of things, except through the continuity and the unity of the total determinism. To propose the least idea of the whole to the understanding, we have to propose to the will, at least confusedly, the alternative which implies it in its entirety. Though distinct, never is the speculative use of thought independent of the practical employment of life. And, if at first the immense multiplicity of objects is wrapped in the abstract idea of objective existence and in the empty framework of a single determinism, it is because destiny is entirely subordinated to one and the same question, to the one thing necessary. The series of the efficient causes which, in furnishing the understanding with the intelligible chain of its objects, proposes for it the problem of being, is at once correlative and irreducible to the system of final causes which, by the hierarchy of the means offered to the will, bring us to resolve the problem of our being. This double unity of series and of system is therefore necessary for any thought we have of an object, that is, for any thought. And reciprocally, the simple idea of an objective existence implies the double law that forms one and the same determinism. In short, what is necessarily voluntary is conceived as real and independent of us, because it must be freely willed by us. Causality and finality, objects linked together before the understanding and ends ordered in the will, that is how being and thought are for one another. The idea of being is subjective, because we imply it in every act of the will; the idea of being has an objective meaning for us, because what is produced in us appears to us as a system of means and ends still external to our willing and our being; for without the assimilation of the objects and the possession of these ends we are not what we will to be. That is still only the simple abstract and general notion of objective existence. But already, to explain its necessary generation in consciousness, we must come to see that the intellectual problem of being is raised at the same time as the moral problem of our being.

433

II. — The idea of a determinism at once one and total is engendered in us inevitably. It is a series and it is a system. But it is not enough to conceive it so. Since we affirm the reality of the system, it is a necessity to affirm that of the objects which constitute it and without which it is not. Not only does the phenomenon which occupies a place in the series of causes and effects not subsist really in our thought if it does not occupy a place in the system of means and ends; but also it is not really for us, if it does not fill in the empty framework of simple possibility with its singular nature. The laws that govern the concrete, be it a law of convergence and harmony like that of finality, are still only abstractions. For the notion of objective existence to be in consciousness, this abstract conception has to be realized in concrete objects. That is how knowledge is solidary with the affirmation of a determinate reality. This affirmation is a fact, independent of the very value of the objects. The notion of objective knowledge and that of a real existence, though quite distinct, are tied together.

It is not enough, then, to look in the double bond of determinism and finality for the secret of our unavoidable belief in an external reality. The chain of determinism is only through what it ties together and determines. Not the system, but what it contains, but each of the original syntheses each of which contains the whole law, but the singular nature and the irreducible quality of the objects given in intuition, is that whose objective value has to be grounded: they have such a value, since this very determinism has to have one for us. Each term is supported by the complete series; the series is rich with the content of each term. Each middle link participates in the solidity of the whole and exists apart like a world. That is how, in the total solidarity and the universal continuity, every particular synthesis appears with a character of absolute heterogeneity and complete originality. That is how also every particular object can   434 become, for the will, the matter for an option and bring us to resolve the alternative which settles the issue of life.

From this follows the precise notion we should have of this determinism. The unity which the determinism establishes among its heterogeneous terms is neither exclusively that of an analytical logic, nor that of a mathematical construction, nor that of an experimental synthesis. It is the unity of the most complex of bonds, that of the causal bond. Two extreme ideas of causality have been formed. — Either some have seen in the chain of causes and effects a purely intelligible relation and a law of thought which can be deduced a priori, as if this determinism were reducible to the necessary connection of movements, and as if the mechanical explanation of nature and the mathematical deductions themselves had precisely the coherence and the sufficiency which we have established that they cannot claim. — Or others have seen in the sequence of invariable antecedents and consequents only an arbitrary relation and a succession of fact. Both of these conceptions equally have a place in a broader doctrine. It is true that the solidarity of all the terms in the series is a necessity for thought; it is true that each term is so new in relation to all others from which it depends as from its conditions that it is impossible to deduce it from them. And, if these two conceptions are equally grounded, it is because, instead of seeing in causality either a properly subjective truth or an exclusively empirical relation, we must push the inquiry further forward and discover there the necessary law which expresses ideally to thought the real chain of practical necessities whose exigencies the will itself ratifies. Whence the ambiguous character of the causal bond: to study its logical nature, we would have to go back to the point where the unity of the analytical use and the synthetic use of our thinking would be revealed.

On one side, we have the abstract idea of a reality subsisting in itself, on the other, the notion of the singular and concrete quality which determines the very idea of this determinism. Such is the double affirmation which the idea of the causal bond implies; and the elements of this synthesis are equally indispensable for the distinct knowledge of the least object, indeed for the performance of the least human act, since it is proper to human action always to be determined by the view of an object or an end.

Thus we draw closer and closer to this conclusion. The necessary idea we have of objective reality, though independent in us of what may be willed by us, has as its necessary effect to subordinate the possession of this reality itself to the use of our will. Whatever is inevitable in knowledge is implied in any voluntary step taken; this is why it is inevitable that this necessary knowledge, never restricting itself to the still purely subjective character it is clothed with, should put us in a position to act and make its objective bearing depend on willed action.

III. — From what precedes a triple consequence follows:

(1) Each of the successive objects which has appeared to us as a synthesis irreducible to its elementary conditions must be considered as it is, in its very originality, independently of the relations it sustains with all the rest. Its nature and its truth is to be what is heterogeneous about it and proper to it: as it is given to intuition, so it is; and what there is to be discovered in it ulteriorly or anteriorly, is the new object of an ulterior or anterior investigation which will reveal the distinct nature of other syntheses equally irreducible. For example, to try to represent for oneself under sensible phenomena other phenomena more true than they, is to be taken in by a mirage and to chase after shadows, while neglecting to take the reality given for what it is: what lies behind sensation is no longer sensation.

(2) But at the same time, each term, without ceasing to be heterogeneous with regard to all the others, is tied to them by a solidarity such that we cannot know and affirm one without implying them all. The objects linked together in this determinism, therefore, are neither more nor less real at one point of the series than at a neighboring point. We must not look for the secret of one in the other, nor must we think that one can be admitted without the other. All, equally real, are equally unstable and ambiguous.

(3) There is then no object whose reality we can conceive and affirm without having encompassed the total series by an act of thought, without in fact submitting to the exigencies of the alternative which it imposes on us, in short, without passing through the point where shines the light of the Being who illumines every reason and in whose presence every will has to declare itself. We have the idea of an objective reality, we affirm

the reality of objects; but to do so, we must implicitly raise the problem
of our destiny and subordinate all that we are and all that is for us to   436
an option. We arrive at being and at beings only by way of this alternative: according to the very way we decide upon it, it is inevitable that
the meaning of being should change. *The knowledge of being* implies the
necessity of the option; *being within knowledge* is not before, but after
the freedom of the choice.

II

In thinking and in acting we quite spontaneously posit before us a system of conditions and objects which remain independent of our deliberate intervention and take on a character of objective reality in our eyes.
What thus seems to elude our action, what we cannot avoid thinking and
affirming, is, in appearance, what is most real and most assuredly outside of ourselves. Think nothing of the sort: the idea of objective existence and the inevitable belief in the objects of representation still express only an internal necessity. It is in what we can accept or reject that
we must find the true reality of the objects imposed on knowledge. Once
again, it is not that we should attribute a bearing which it does not have
to this assertion; in affirming that the privative knowledge of being has
a positive reality, we are always still only unfolding the exigencies of
thought and of practice: it is, so to speak, to constitute the universal $\tau\alpha$
$\pi\rho o\varsigma$ $\delta o\xi\alpha\nu$ (that is according to opinion).

To show how all that the perspective of the spirit presents as objective
can be excluded, not in the measure that it is a subjective view of the real
object, but in the measure that it is a real truth for the subject himself;
to indicate how this exclusion, far from leaving things as they stand, suppresses the possession, but not the need and the knowledge of the reality
known; to explain, finally, how this privative knowledge draws from the
excluded being the very sanction of the act that rejects it; these are the
points we must now illuminate.

I. — The universal nature of things imposes itself on thought as a series
of objects and as a system of particular ends. This intellectual necessity
only expresses the conditions of our interior life. It puts us in a position
to determine our attitude in the face of what is spontaneous and voluntary in us without yet being willed there. The real truth of objects, their   437
being does not reside then in the inevitable representation we have of
them; it consists in what it depends on us to will or not to will in them.
For them to be in us, we must will them to be for us what they are in
themselves.

Now the reason for the total determinism was, as we saw, to bring us either to ratify the apparent necessities that weigh on our life, by subordinating them, along with our will itself, to the divine will which is the common principle of them all, or to reject, not, of course, the inevitable knowledge of this determinism, but the practical exigencies it proposes for us: to undergo intellectual necessities is not yet to get out of oneself; to accept or to reject practical exigencies is to receive within oneself or to eliminate from oneself the reality whence these necessities themselves flow. Now, to give it access, we must receive it in the measure, not that it is subordinate to us, but that we depend on it.

And since, in spite of the multiplicity of objects, the chain is single, at issue for us is the entire system, either to include or to exclude its real presence. Everything, then, depends on the attitude adopted in the face of the one thing necessary, since it is the principle of the entire series, and since the sequence of the total determinism results in bringing us back to it without fail. Without being, there are no other beings in us; with it, all will be present.

Thus, in closing ourselves off from the obligations which appeared to us as the vivifying conditions of voluntary action, we close off at the same time access to, we deprive ourselves of the possession of the reality known, without forasmuch suppressing the knowledge of the reality. This is what must be properly understood.

II. — It seems strange that the knowledge of reality, though coextensive with the reality which has to be present to knowledge, should be radically distinct from reality, and that there should arise a properly intellectual difference between the necessary knowledge and the involuntary knowledge of a truth whose object is identical. Yet there is no distinction that is better grounded or more worthy of consideration.

What is necessary in the notion which we have of objective truth has the certain effect of presenting us with an inevitable alternative. It is impossible, then, for things to remain as they stand. The knowledge which, before the option, was simply subjective and propulsive becomes, after it, privative and constitutive of being. Without changing objects, it changes in nature. It keeps all that is necessary in it; it loses all that should have been voluntary. In clinging to what it was, it perverts the meaning of the dynamism which was in it, which was itself; but it does not suppress its effects: the dynamism tended toward being in order to fill knowledge with the reality which knowledge presented for a free adherence; it still tends toward being, but in order to empty knowledge of this reality which knowledge continues to require by a necessary exigency.

And what results from this voluntary privation is indeed an intellectual difference between these two knowledges, positive and negative, which a first look would judge identical because, except for the sign, they coincide on all points and have the same scope. The first knowledge, indeed the one which necessarily raises the problem and provides us with an integral view of the universal order, though often confused and reduced, is still only a representation of the object in the subject; or more exactly (in order to sharply underline the origin of subjective truth), it is only the production by man of the idea that the objects of his thought and the conditions of his action are inevitably real. The second of these knowledges, the one that follows the determination freely made in the face of this reality necessarily conceived, is no longer only a subjective disposition; rather than raise the practical problem, it translates the solution of it into our thought; rather than placing us in the presence of what is to be done, it gathers from what is done what is. It is then truly an objective knowledge, even when it is reduced to recording the deficit of action. For, that which, before the option has been consummated, is still only a view of the mind, becomes, after it, consciousness of a real lacuna and, if one can so speak, of a positive privation.

III. — Hence we see what is inevitably objective in our knowledge. Even when we claim to hold ourselves to what is necessarily present to thought and still purely subjective, the truth denied and excluded is being. After we have cut back all that can be not willed, there remains more in thought then than was simply necessary. For one who repels and rejects it, truth assuredly is not as it is for one who feeds on it, but it still is; though entirely different in the one and in the other, its rule is no more impaired in the one than in the other.

Thus the entire distinction and the entire solidarity of knowledge and being is maintained. — The distinction is complete: it is brought into evidence by this method of suppressions which seems to leave truth apart 439 from reality to the point of opposing them to one another; for, if thought inevitably proposes to us the universal order of things, this representation of reality is independent of the act on which will depend whether reality itself will be or not be for us and in us. — The solidarity is also complete: for, if willing resolves the problem raised by the understanding, reciprocally the nature of the solution, that is, the very meaning of being and the way the truth is in us, will be tied to the option of the will. We cannot say, therefore, either that thought and action are independent or that they are subordinate. Intimately united, they are original in relation to one another, like truth and reality themselves.

Also they are mutually for one another a rule and a sanction. In the man who acts as if beings were without Being and who accepts the means without directing them toward his end, the will continues to produce the exigency for all the being which knowledge requires, and knowledge shows the will all the necessary being it excludes: knowledge affirms the infinite we need to the one who has negated it, but in order to refuse all that it affirms to the negator. Above the errors and the deviations of every nature subsists a truth which, bearing within itself its own light, is its own proof; a truth which, with all the precision and all the rigor of necessity, maintains its sovereign rights over every reason and every freedom.

To the question, "what is the minimum of being which subsists in the man who has cut off from being all that can be not willed," we must therefore answer: in him, the subjective knowledge of the truth remains whole and positive; the objective knowledge of reality is whole also, but negative. The sanction lies at once in what he knows of real being and in what he does not know of it. For in knowing what is to be known, he knows equally that the real possession of what he has deprived himself of would have brought him an infinite surplus of clarity and joy. It is this surplus then which remains to be defined; for the privation is real only by contrast with true possession, and it is always proper to action to keep within itself something of the contraries between which it has opted, something even of those it has excluded. But always also the synthesis it forms is original; and never is the knowledge of contraries identical. If the subjective knowledge of truth, though coextensive with the privative knowledge of reality, has appeared as quite different from it, the complete knowledge which unites the whole possession of the real with the vision of the true, will differ from both the one and the other, even though both the one and the other subsist only in being related to this perfect completion.

440

III

For the truth to really reside in the knowledge we have of it, we must, regarding what is necessary in truth, will what is capable of not being willed, and make the free adherence which truth demands equal to what it imposes of inevitable clarity. Perhaps it will seem that this is to perpetrate a confusion of competences and to attribute a character which is no longer properly intellectual to knowledge, since this character seems subordinate to a voluntary act. Let us make no mistake about this. There is no question, by willing, of making reality subsist in us because an arbitrary decree might have created it in us; it is a question, by willing, of making it be in us because it is and as it is in itself. This act of the will does not make truth depend on us; it makes us depend on it. It is the role of the necessary knowledge which precedes and prepares the option, to be an inflexible rule; but once that which is necessarily voluntary about it is freely willed, it does not for that reason cease to be a knowledge. Quite the contrary, it gains thereby in bearing, really present within it, the being of which it still had only the representation. What was simply an idea of the object becomes, in truth, objective certitude and real possession.[1]

Since knowledge needs to be completed and as it were filled by a free adherence which, without changing its nature, changes its bearing, what then must be admitted into ourselves so as to put it in knowledge? How does this plenitude of the object insinuate itself into us? If to know others   441 truly we have to give ourselves to them, how is this the means of giving them to ourselves and giving ourselves to ourselves? Whence is it that, far from being a cause of confusion, the universal union appears as the condition for the real distinction of beings? How can and must the appearances themselves which distinguish them be absolutely grounded? In what sense is the determinism of phenomena subsistent? How, finally, does everything, even what seems able to be seen only from the outside, have to be reintegrated into being and serve to constitute true objective existence? It is the meaning of these questions which we must look for now: to understand them well will be to resolve them, because it will be simply to observe the necessary sequence of the relations which make them arise one from the other, by taking them from one provisional step to the next all the way to the definitive solution. Indeed, the issue is to see how this entire determinism, spontaneously produced and implied by every voluntary operation, how this determinism which has to be accepted and willed by what is most intimate in ourselves, nonetheless finds between these two subjective terms its own proper consistency and a truly objective reality, without ceasing to be ours: this is the only way of saving what knowledge must draw at once from itself and from being, and of reconciling the necessary originality of thought with the necessary authority of truth.

I. — The universal order is real in our knowledge only to the extent that we fully accept what is necessary about it. Now we cannot accept everything, we cannot accept ourselves without going through "the one thing necessary," where we saw precisely the principle of the total determinism. If our self-will keeps us from arriving at our true will, nothing can

1. Here again it is important to remain on guard against any misunderstanding. In speaking of the real possession of being in knowledge, we do not claim to go beyond the facts; we are merely observing that in acting as if it were, we know differently than if we did as if it were not. This is the positive difference that has to be defined precisely by determining what really objective existence is for us.

be in us really as long as we have not given up this solitude of egoism by a substitution of the divine willing for a self-love that loses all in wanting to gain all. We must, therefore, understand this double truth: we cannot arrive at God, affirm Him truly, do as if he were and make Him be in reality, have Him for ourselves, except by belonging to Him and by sacrificing all the rest to Him: all the rest communicates with us only through this mediator, and the only way of obtaining the all in all is to begin by a one on one with Him. No, we cannot belong to ourselves or to others without first belonging to Him. *Dimitte omnia et invenies omnia* (Give up everything and you will find everything.)

To know God really, then, is to bear in us His spirit, His will, His love. *Nequaquam plene cognoscitur nisi cum perfecte diligitur* (He is 442 never known fully except when he is perfectly loved.) If He offers Himself to man under a form of annihilation, man cannot offer himself to Him except by annihilating himself as well, in order to restore to God his divine privilege. Sacrifice is the solution to the metaphysical problem through the experimental method. And if, in the whole course of its development, action has appeared as a new source of light, also in the very end itself the knowledge which follows the perfect act of abnegation must contain a fuller revelation of being. Action sees being no longer from the outside; it has grasped it, it possesses it, it finds it within itself. True philosophy is the sanctity of reason. The will alienates us and assimilates us to its end; the understanding assimilates its object to us and acquires it for us. That is why, in giving ourselves to God through total dedication, we can see better into Him; the purity of interior detachment is the organ of perfect vision. We cannot see Him without having Him, not have Him without loving Him, not love Him without bringing Him the homage of all that He is, so as to find in all things only His will and His presence. What He is, we will Him to be, no matter what it costs us; and in that way what He is in Himself, He becomes in us.

Moreover, in trying to attain anything whatsoever directly, we go the wrong way. Impossible to really reach another being, impossible to reach our own selves without going through this one thing necessary, who must become our only will. We cannot arrive at our interior consistency except by not separating ourselves from Him; to be *one*, to be, I must not remain *alone*. I need all others; and yet, in the strict sense of the terms, in all the world there is only He and I to deal immediately with one another. Alone with Him alone; others have nothing to do with it. All the determinism of the conditions which favor or impede my life matters little; what matters is to capture within me its source and to bear, no longer its exterior constraint, but its intimate truth and action. What pleases me in the determinism, what displeases me, all, then, must be referred back to the first cause of all; and nothing strikes me, nothing penetrates me, nothing moves me, except what proceeds from that cause. Even what, on the outside, can be contrary to the divine willing is, within me, only divine permission and decision. I communicate only with God. And that is why the word of physical separation which begins at the embrace of friends taking leave of one another, an embrace that is always distant even in the closest grip, is the word *adieu*.

But also this is the word of the true and the only union, the one which even absence consecrates, because it reveals, through the suppression of the apparent ties, the solidity of the real bond. If we arrive at God only by offering up all that is not He, we find in Him the true reality of all that is not God. We never appear before Him alone, because in the acknowledgement which truly recognizes Him we include the homage and the gift of the entire universe; but we never find Him alone, because after having sacrificed to Being all the beings that would not be without Him, we acquire in Him all the beings that are through Being. The illusion of a detachment without compensation provides the truth and the joy of a possession without exception. Hence we must now grasp how the universal union is consummated in us, before seeing how we owe it to this total communion to be ourselves and to remain distinct in the incommunicable singularity of the human person.

II. — A profound understanding of the feelings of others always has as its cause or as its effect a bond of affection. A truth of common experience, but which touches the depth of our nature. Being is love; hence we know nothing if we do not love. And that is why charity is the organ of perfect knowledge: what is in another, it puts within us; and turning the illusion of egoism around, so to speak, it initiates us to the secret of every egoism confronting us. To the extent that things are, they act, they make us undergo (*pâtir*): to accept this undergoing (*passion*), to receive it actively, is to be within ourselves what they are within themselves. To exclude ourselves from ourselves by abnegation, is then to engender universal life within ourselves. And it is easy to explain this: what imposes itself on knowledge necessarily is still only appearance; and each being keeps to himself in his depth the intimate truth of his singular being. There is within me something which others cannot lay hold of and which raises me above the entire order of phenomena. There is within others, if they are as I am, something which I cannot lay hold of and which is only if it is inaccessible to me. I am not for them as I am for myself; they are not for me as they are for themselves. Egoism is disconcerted by the very thought of so many antagonistic egoisms; and, notwithstanding all the clarity of our science, we remain wrapped in solitude and obscurity. Only charity, by placing itself at the heart of all, lives above appearances,

communicates itself even to the interior of substances and completely resolves the problem of knowledge and being. It has the marvelous privilege of appropriating, without despoiling anyone of what belongs to him
and simply by participating in intention in the good of others, all the life
and action which they have.

And how can we give act and being to other ourselves? How do "other
and self" become identical in the absolute? How are others within us and
for us what they are within themselves and for themselves, if not when
we become for ourselves what we are for them and when they become
for us what they are for themselves? Hence an exact justice which considers in the person only his impersonal character and his abstract human
dignity is not enough. By making ourselves, so to speak, the impersonal
object and the devoted means at the service of others, we must go as far
as the sort of love which fixes on particularities so often offensive in the
individual. Each one in all save in himself, that is the motto of charity,
which grants to others the indulgent tenderness it refuses itself and which,
not content with being good toward them, accepts equally both their in-
gratitude, because it triumphs in doing good to the one who is not good,
and their goodness, because it triumphs still in becoming obliged to them
and in practicing the art of receiving, more difficult and perhaps better
than the science of giving. For we reproach others for being egoists only
if we are egoists; and we suffer in them only from our own miseries; there
is even an extreme desire for perfection in others which is the sign of a
lack of perfection in ourselves. Forgetting others for ourselves and ourselves for them, we must judge ourselves as another, others as ourself.
How often, in order to blame them, we put them in our place without
putting ourselves in theirs! To be all to all is to have broadened oneself
to the point of no longer having any particularities and any defects. To
love people without illusion is to give them all without asking anything
of them, without expecting anything of them, without refusing anything
good in them. Universal life is not the abstract sum of the impersonal
forms of thought and being; it is composed of all the variety of consciousnesses and sensibilities. To possess it in oneself, therefore, is to be an
egoist in all and to convert the martyrdom of life in common into felicity.
Rational happiness is the happiness of others; and to exert a good action
on them, is to make them act well.

The truth of love also extends to sense life, to bodies that suffer, even
to brute matter. We do not love men, we do not know them, if we restrict
ourselves to a haughty lofty mercy which, under pretext of making them
rise to it, does not go down to them. The man we must understand and
love is this physical wretchedness and this moral wretchedness which
seem to leave him no longer a man. And let no one imagine that there

is in this only a question of feelings. We are always inclined to forget that we are not free to perform a sort of *triage* in the universal determinism and to accept one part of it while rejecting the other. We cannot comprehend any of it within ourselves, unless we first go through all its exigencies. To love one man, to know him, as it is necessary to love him, we must love all men in intention and, as need arises, in fact; love them as they are, without waiting for them to be as they ought to be. In order to give them being in ourselves, it is a necessity to make ourselves voluntarily patient of their real action. In this action, everything concurs; consequently in it either nothing will be real or all will be real, even what is most individual and sensible about it. It is this sensible reality itself which, as we saw, is the universal bond of solidarity. So, the broadest love is the most precise; to bear the whole of humanity in our hearts, we must devote ourselves quite particularly and quite closely to some humble work of mercy; charity is not true and, if we may so speak, it is not scientific, except on this condition. It is universal, and it always fixes on what is unique.

Otherwise by what right and in the name of what virtue could one sacrifice his life to save one life or lose one man to preserve one man? In the passing life we save for another by giving it up for ourselves, we gain within ourselves the life that does not pass. In this body which we snatch from destruction, we render a cult to the indestructible charity which engages all the members of humanity together. For every form of man which goes by, we must feel that we ought to be ready to die for the least of the little ones; death is the triumph of love and access to life; it becomes like a duty; and duty is nothing else but death. This passion is more active and generous still when it is caused by moral woes: and how can we claim that love is self-interested and mercenary when it urges the merciful one to love so painfully those who pervert themselves, when it leads him to die, if necessary, for the one who has lost his way, as if this voluntary death were the only way of knowing those who separate themselves from life, of adhering still to those who cut themselves off   446 from human communion? Men go out only to those who suffer from their own evils, because it is only by such as these that they are known. Love and the science of men are all one.

Thus, according to a beautiful saying of Leibniz, "to love all men, to love God, is the same thing," because He is the only one lovable in all and everywhere, and because we cannot know any man without embracing them all in one and the same charity. They really unite with one another only through the ardor of a fire which the whole world could not kindle. Hence this circle is justified: without this active love of the members of humanity for one another, there is no God for man; he who does not love his brother does not have life within him: but also in vain would we try to group spirits in a family by rejecting the Father of spirits, to betray the exigencies of reason, to cover over this great emptiness by the exaltation of other sentiments; at the bottom of things, in the common practice of life, in the secret logic of consciousnesses, without God there is no man for man. There is, then, an intimate solidarity between these sentiments, between these acts that are so different; to adore in spirit and in truth one on one with God; to render a cult to the body of humanity in each of its members as if it were the body of God living at each point of the universal organism. And what is an organism in fact, if not the distinction at the same time as the union of the parts animated by one life, to the point that each cell has the honor of all the functions, since only the more humble ones make the more noble ones possible. Thus, in a society which, so to speak, has only one consciousness, each is in all through charity, all are in each through knowledge and action. And whereas in the order of appearances light foci are dispersed and lose their brightness and heat, here the rays are concentrated into new foci. The more we give, the more we have. What a boundless production of being and goodness there is, where the source is infinite and where its effusions, in fanning out, accumulate! Each for himself, each for another, each for all, each for each, all for all, all for each, all these loves come together and are reinforced when God is in all. And the knowledge we have of it is full of the reality it expresses.

But in grounding the most distant lives in this fashion, do we not expose personal consciousness to the risk of exploding and of losing itself in this universal confusion? Are not the limits of present knowledge and the tangible singularities of the individual the necessary conditions for the very distinction of persons? In erasing the boundaries of egoism and the mutual repugnances of sensibilities more impenetrable to one another than bodies themselves, are we not going to make disappear at the same time what has always seemed to be "the principle of individuation"? — No. Far from being a cause of confusion, this universal communion becomes the only means of possession and perfect distinction. It is the only way of realizing the human person and, through that, to constitute all the rest. It remains for us to justify the absolute truth of this mediating role of action.

III. — The problem that now imposes itself on us is a strange one. It is not enough to possess necessary knowledge and the idea of an objective reality. It is not enough to have voluntarily brought this real truth within ourselves, nor to have placed ourselves in others through an action which, in communicating to others all that we are, brings us back all that they are. It is necessary still that they be in themselves and that we remain in ourselves. And these two conditions are solidary. For if we do not realize ourselves except by participating in what they are, we are real and distinct only to the extent that they are also real and distinct. It is a necessity, then, to ground the external reality of external objects, so that seen from the outside the things outside will have a real consistency. The truth of the objective outside is indispensable for maintaining the subjective inside of beings. Here we are inevitably led to look for the objective reality of things, not in an ever fleeting underneath, not in one of the aspects which they assume for the senses or for the understanding, not in their metaphysical essence or in the intimacy of that incommunicable life where we penetrate in loving them, but in all of this at once. Their being is the very unity of this multiple appearance and the simultaneous diversity of these universally solidary phenomena. Of the terms which the science of action has just gone through in a continuous progress, none is either less or more solid than the other, as long as the relation which unites them all has not itself been erected into a reality. Through the analysis of this objective knowledge which seems to place us in possession of reality, we are led to reintegrate into it all the appearing of things, and to confer upon all the forms of knowledge and action, upon the illusions and errors themselves which seem to deprive us of being, a substantial truth. This appearing objective is the common element that forms the unity of the collection.   448

We must therefore establish the proper certitude of the totality of the appearing determinism of phenomena by considering, no longer what necessary knowledge it imposes on us, but what reality it contains in itself. It must be what it appears to be, and what is necessary, objective, exterior, despotic about it, must remain so. Everything hangs together in it: if everything were not real in it, nothing would be so. We must therefore go to the end of these exigencies by showing, no longer that mediating action is a fact necessary for the constitution of the entire order of things, but that the mediation of action is itself a truth, that it is real independently of the realities whose relation it constitutes in our knowledge, and that these realities themselves subsist only because the mediation has an intrinsic reality. This is to say that all the transitory conditions of action, whose apparent constraint has been reduced to being only a form of our most intimate willing, must become an absolute necessity and a definitive rule for the will itself. In short, we must confer upon the phenomenon all the "being in itself" it entails: it is a necessity for it to have such a being; otherwise, lacking this small piece, all that has been accomplished would become nothing once again; the whole order of nature would be dispersed; even personality would vanish, and nothing of what we have conceived would be conceivable: the solidity of the entire system is concerned in the consistency of the least phenomenon.

And if, by looking below at the most elementary conditions of action, the real truth of the phenomenon must be grounded for all the rest to be, by looking above, this same necessity is revealed more clearly still. Below it would be annihilation; above, the absorption of every distinct being into the divine immensity: and as if the little individual which consciousness shows us in ourselves were only a passing illusion, as if, once the veil of the sensible mystery were torn by death, the narrow limits of the person itself were to fall away forever, the legend of Christopher, crushed under the burden which seemed so light, would be the symbol of our overwhelming destiny. But no. Far from being a hindrance and a confinement, individual determinations are for man the condition and the means of his immense dilation: if he has a divine vocation, if, at the heart of the infinite itself, he must remain a distinct person, it is not by ceasing to be an individual, it is on condition of remaining such. *Omne individuum ineffabile* (every individual is ineffable). The true infinite is not in the abstract universal, it is in the concrete singular. Precisely by this is made manifest in all its greatness the role of what has been called the letter and matter, of all that constitutes the sensible of operation, of what composes, properly speaking, action, the body of action. For it is through this matter that the truth of the overwhelming infinite is intimately communicated to each individual; and it is through it that each one is protected against being overwhelmed by the infinite truth. To reach man, God must go through all of nature and offer Himself to him under the most brute of material species. To reach God, man must go through all of nature and find Him under the veil where He hides Himself only to be accessible. Thus the whole natural order comes between God and man as a bond and as an obstacle, as a necessary means of union and as a necessary means of distinction. And when, through a double convergence, each having gone all the way to meet the other, God and man have met, this natural order remains in the embrace of their mutual grasp, becoming thus for man the seal of his intimate adherence to his author and the seal of his inalienable personality. How then can this mediating relation also be itself realized?

Now then that the importance of the problem is manifest we cannot fail to note the whole of its difficulty and even its strangeness. From the first intuition on, the question of the real truth of the sensible phenomenon was, it seemed, an insoluble one. The moment we press immediate perception, something else than it comes out of it. What science extracts from it is no longer, never any longer, what sense perceives in it. Let not analysis try to fathom that abyss which separates the quality given from the property supposed; it gets lost in the process. In fixing on the intuitive

449

datum, it remains prisoner to the subjective phenomenon. In pursuing the rational element which it thinks it grasps in it, it never succeeds in coming back to the concrete datum. It has to turn the appearances away, χαιρειν εαν (bid them farewell), and the sensible no longer exists as sensible; it even seems inconceivable for the sensible to be; what it would be for it to be, is not comprehensible at first. And what we have just said about the sensible fact, must be repeated about every other object of knowledge for each term in the total series of things. No more than the sensible intuitions, do the conceptions of the understanding warrant being erected into realities by the understanding itself. Each order of phenomena calls for a critique which pushes the center of perspective further back. And yet if only one stone is lacking, the entire edifice is ruinous; it is therefore this relative, this apppearing of the phenomenon itself which, in order to complete the total restitution of the determinism of action, it is necessary to raise to the level of the being and the absolute which it entails.

450

IV

Simply by determining the sequence of relations connected in consciousness under the constraint of practical necessities, we are thus led to find, where one would hardly think of finding it, the definition of objective reality. Instead of pretending to apply to an ever evasive term an arbitrary and indeterminate notion of real existence, we must see at what precise point and in what defined sense this notion has its necessary application. Instead of placing reality in objects always unable to contain it, we must place them in it. Instead of looking for what is outside of what appears, we must take what appears to be what is. The first step to take, then, is to understand what it is *to be*, once we speak of objective existence. Then it will remain to be seen how it is possible to conceive what this being might be, and what are the necessary and sufficient conditions for a solution able to satisfy all the exigencies of the problem.

I. — On the one hand, the entire order of phenomena, to the extent that we have a necessary knowledge of it, is implied in every human action; and the idea itself we have of its objective existence is engendered within. Thereby, this necessary knowledge is subjective. — On the other hand, this total determinism of thought and of nature, to the extent that action looks for its nourishment and its ends in it, is reintegrated into the will of which it had appeared to be a spontaneous production. Thereby as well, this knowledge and this voluntary possession of the object is still subjective. Now it is between these subjective elements that what is properly and really objective finds its place. How so?

What is subjective in the first production of knowledge is not identical
with what is subjective in the final possession of acquired truth. On both
sides, undoubtedly, the fecundity of thought and the generative initiative
without which there is nothing in us are revealed. But from the first to
the last there comes into play as a means or as an obstacle the integral
series of the things whose immense interconnection the science of action
has just unraveled. What rises from the depth of our voluntary aspiration, is what we must assimilate through a practical adherence; to will
it for ourselves means that it is not from us; and action, in tending to
make subjective the reality which a first subjective view of the object proposed, determines what is properly objective in our knowledge. The difference between these two subjective terms, is precisely the real object;
and for this word to have a meaning, it has to be applied to those heterogeneous and solidary syntheses which appeared to us as natural intermediaries between what we will, because we are not there yet, and what
we are to be, because we shall have willed it. Of themselves, these two
terms are irreducible one to the other; what unites them inevitably has
for us a proper reality.

No matter how we analyse objective existence, then, under the form
in which it is ncessarily conceived, we will never be able to situate it anywhere else but there. It is a necessity, for us, that objective existence be;
and the necessity has to be such: in the spontaneous conviction of every
man, it has no other meaning. Truth and being cannot be in what is not
known, and not even knowable; what is knowable has to be what is.
How does what is known as objective subsist objectively as it is affirmed
and willed subjectively? That is the point to be elucidated. In every form
of knowledge is found this double element, the internal production of
thought appearing as an object, the object appearing as an external principle of perception and as an end for action. In every series of phenomena
is revealed this same duality of subjective initiative and of external passivity. Everywhere, an analogous mixture of produced knowledge and
knowledge undergone. And that is where, precisely in what has seemed
to be the ruin of every objective affirmation, the secret of all real existence of objects taken as objects will be found.

It was a discovery to have noted, as Kant did, that even the sensible
intuition, which was thought to be all a posteriori, supposes an a priori,
and that by reason of this subjective initiative, it is impossible to raise the
mechanism of nature to the absolute or to realize it outside of thought
in the same way as it is in thought. It is another discovery still to take
away from this critical conclusion the absolute value it maintains only
by an inconsequence, as if it were legitimate to use the understanding
against the sensibility when we use the sensibility against the understand-

ing. To suppose differences of nature and of solidity between the heterogeneous phenomena of which the chain of determinism is composed, to oppose the diverse faculties one to the other, to underscore some radical differences between the various results of their labor, all that is a remainder of idolatry. Grounded to the extent that they go against every attempt to locate objective reality here or there in a term of the series of human knowledges, the pretentions of Kantianism are illegitimate to the extent that, content with going against this artificial attempt, they erect into a true and positive solution of a real problem the negative critique of a fictitious problem. True in what it denies, criticism is false in what it affirms. Fallen are the chimerical questions that held it up, fallen is the system that destroys them. This doctrine itself also conspires with those it combats, by admitting that we must try to deposit the encumbering idea of real existence into a term, always pushed back, of the series of things; as if being, chased little by little from sensible intuition into the conceptions of the understanding or from the noumenon into the mystery of moral truths, had to be always elsewhere than where we are. Things are all equally unrealizable when we want to put reality into things as a thing distinct from them, and all equally real when we can see under what conditions they are all reintegrated together into being. Truth, then, is at once more rich and more simple than the philosophers have conceived it; and here it is now, quite in conformity with the popular sense.

All that we have called sense data, positive truths, subjective science, organic growth, social expansion, moral and metaphysical conceptions, certitude of the one thing necessary, murderous or vivifying option, supernatural completion of action, affirmation of the real objects of thought and of the conditions of practice, all are still only phenomena by the same right. If we consider any one of them apart, none can be realized. All call for a critique which brings us beyond what they are, without our being able to confine ourselves to them, without our being able to get along without them. Neither space or duration, nor scientific 453 symbolism, nor individual life, nor social organism, nor moral order, nor metaphysical constructions, can be erected separately into subsistent realities. It would be like saying that society can live without the family. What the *Transcendental Aesthetic* is for the intuitions of the senses, an analogous critique must be for scientific symbols or for rational conceptions or for the laws of ethics. Each order of phenomena is equally original as a distinct synthesis, transcendent with regard to those that are its antecedent conditions, irreducible to those it seems subordinate to as to its consequents, solidary with all, finding in none its total explanation, having its reality neither in itself nor in any other. To pretend to discover in one of the links of the determinism the solidity of the whole chain because the other links lack consistency, is a search that makes no sense. For the popular judgment, what is, is neither this nor that; it is all this and all that; and the people are right. There are no privileged orders; the sensible phenomenon, for example, is pregnant with all the explanations and all the ulterior knowledge which it seems at first to exclude, but which it actually implies; each order of truths seems to constitute a sufficient whole and form a determinism exclusive of every other; but these determinisms are all connected and make up only one. Thus in the perception of the least fact is already contained the metaphysical or moral problem. Reality, then, is not in any one of the terms more than it is in the others, nor in the one without the others; it resides in the multiplicity of the reciprocal relations which joins them all together; it is this complexus itself. Located in the series, our knowledge undergoes and produces things, as mediator; what it undergoes, what it produces, what it is, that, from its particular viewpoint, is what constitutes objective existence.

Thus, however strange this exigency may seem, objects must be what they seem, and their reality must consist, not in I know not what inaccessible hinterground, but in what is precisely determined and exactly knowable. They have seemed to serve as intermediaries: it is this relation, it is this mediating role which constitutes their being and which makes up their absolute truth. To be, for objects, is to subsist as they are known and willed by us, independent of the failings of human action and knowledge. The determinism of scientific appearances must, in truth, be the order of real objects, and its external despotism must be grounded in the intimacy of being. What is through us must still be without us and in spite of us. And what subjective idealism presents as the true expression of existence, must, in effect, be the matter of a truly objective realism. Things are not because we make them be; but they are such as we make them be, and such as they make us be. It is this double aspect of the solution which remains to be elucidated.

II. — Before determining all the indispensable conditions for the existence of things, it is necessary to see how that existence is conceivable. Defined as it has just been defined, is it not impossible? Without initially going to the point of saying that things are such as we make them be, without ourselves and in spite of ourselves, is it intelligible for them to be through us and for us, such as we know them to be? To take a particular example in the series of things, can the reality of the sensible phenomenon be the sensible phenomenon itself? How then understand that we are what we know and that what we know is?

In a word that has to be explained, the reality of the phenomenon is

454

included between those two rays of which it is the point of convergence and which, in coming together in us, constitute it in itself. Things are, because the senses and reason see them, and see them in common, without this double gaze, which, each by itself, seems to penetrate them completely, being confused in them. To know is to be what we know, to produce it, to have it, to become it in itself. *Sumus quod videmus* (we are what we see). Matter has being only if being becomes matter itself, if what is inner word and life in itself is really flesh. Hence what abstraction distinguishes in sensible reality must remain indissolubly united: we can show its irreducible aspects, we cannot disjoin its solidary facets. And, precisely, it is because it is not possible either to separate them or to reunite them that between these two known appearances there subsists what is their support and their bond, what makes up their solid truth. We act in them and on them, they act on us and in us. The knowledge, active and passive, which we have of them, is, according to what we have to conceive, the double ground of the phenomenon, sensible and real.

This is why it is equally right to say that these phenomena consist in what is immediately grasped by intuition, and that they consist in what our senses do not perceive of them. On the one hand, science is an admirable work, which, as it goes down from abstraction to abstraction to the most simple relations and to the most universal unity of natural laws, strips the world of its sensible masks. In matter itself it manifests what is intelligible, accessible to the conquests of thought, independent of place and duration, obedient to the spirit, that which, at the limit and in perfect knowledge, is only creative thought; it tends to bring the universe back to the divine intuition of its author. On the other hand, science is an admirable work which, as it determines more precisely the original characters of the syntheses directly perceived, brings out more clearly the definite reality of the sensible qualities and species, to the point of being able to say that the facts of experience are what experimental science reveals them to be; that they have, in this sensible knowledge, a rational truth; that the phenomena, as phenomena, possess a certain consistency; in a word, that things are far more profound than we know at second glance, since at the same time they are really such as we know them synthetically through a first look. And these two aspects are both real only to the extent that, irreducible to one another, they are bound together in the unity of one and the same act of the will, in the perception of one and the same sensibility and one and the same reason.

Therefore, it is because reason is immanent to the sensible and the sensible is immanent to reason that these phenomena have their own subsistence. They are, because reason sees them and penetrates the secret of their production. They are, because the senses undergo them and

455

become passive to their action. Their being consists precisely in what makes up the synthetic unity of this double existence. Thus, for example, a landscape is only a state of soul; and the objective harmony of the lines and colors is certain. Thus, pain is only the consciousness of being pain; and pain is the state itself the apperception of which causes the conscious suffering. Thus, the universe is only my representation; and it is the preliminary condition and the scientific truth of the sensible knowledge I have of it. The phenomenon, therefore, has, in what perceives it, the very reality of this substantial bond which constitutes the synthesis of the elements; for things which do not exist for themselves and which are *in themselves* only for others able to perceive them have the property of being at once known and sensed; this is what belongs to them: we are in them through rational consciousness, which, thanks to its character of universality, enfolds them and defines their relations according to the intelligible order of their production; they are in us through sense perception, which, thanks to its singular character, individualizes and qualifies them. Hence we have an absolute knowledge of the relative as relative; and that is why the relative *is*. It is, without our having to look behind the phenomenon for an explanation which would denature it. It is as it appears in the whole sequence of its heterogeneous but solidary manifestations. Through the diversity of its aspects, it is ambiguous; and it is this ambiguity which makes up its real truth. Its multiple phenomenon is its very being.

It is not enough, then, to say that the being of sensible things is to be perceived, unless we add that the perceiver as well is through the perceived. To be objective is therefore to be produced and undergone by a subject, for to exert a real action on a real being is to be real. Thus, for things to be truly, they must act; for them to act, they must be perceived and known. For, not perceiving themselves directly, since they are not causes of themselves, they must be perceived by one capable of acting on them. Produced and undergone, their being is to be active and passive *in uno* (in one and the same), and, mediately, *in se* (in themselves). Inserted as a necessary term in the series, thought, whence things depend, must also in one sense depend on them, so that they will not be reduced to it. We must therefore understand how objective knowledge, though indispensable and identical to objective existence, remains distinct from it, and how thought itself, in function of which we have just expressed the reality of the rest, is in turn only a middle term which can be expressed in function of the others.

III.—Such then is the unaccustomed but necessary order of questions that is revealed, the very order which corresponds to the immediate beliefs and the natural steps of thought. We conceive, we inevitably affirm an objective existence; subsequently, we must determine in what it can consist and how it is possible for it to be realized, how it is necessarily realized in our eyes, since it has to be realized for us. True, this is to reverse the usual terms of the problem. But the question of being is not preliminary, it is final; and perhaps it is good, before searching, to know   457 what we are truly looking for, without claiming to find reality outside the real. Far from striving ingeniously, then, but in vain, to see how what is can be given, we must show how what is given is. In claiming to make objects gravitate around thought, criticism had placed itself away from the center as if to consider this spectacle from the outside; and if it has attended especially to the centripetal movement which brings all things back to the subject, it is because it remained still located on the outside, as if to justify the usefulness of its effort and the novelty of its perspective: every subjectivist doctrine starts from a realist prejudice, contraries being always only the extremes of the same species. A fully consequent idealism makes all the distinctions which separate it from realism disappear and suppresses what is artificial in the poorly phrased question it claimed to be resolving.

The true difficulty, then, is to understand how what we know is real in the way that we know it, without our particular knowledge being absolutely essential to the relations that seem nevertheless to exist only in function of it. If it is necessary for us to conceive and affirm objective existence, this need inevitably provokes its expression; also we must see what, according to the very exigencies of our thought, is necessary for this existence to be necessarily realized, even without our thought; for this thought, in order to be truly, requires that these conditions with which it is solidary be subsistent as well. It is no longer simply a question of the sensible phenomenon, but of all phenomena, positive or metaphysical or moral or religious truths, every form of reality conceived in the multiple unity of one and the same determinism.

Undoubtedly, we have already begun to understand how it is possible for an object to be an object. To be, and to be in oneself, through another, therein resides the mystery of objective existence, the mystery of every borrowed existence which does not have its source in itself and which yet does not cease to subsist. But it is no longer enough to conceive the possibility of this existence. We must see how it is real and necessarily real: under what conditions can knowledge and will be creative of their object? Whence is it that we must reverse the terms of the relation, and say that the things which are such as we know them are known such as they are? How is that which is appearance in us reality in things, so that

458 objective truth must exercise its power over us and reign exteriorly without our ever being able to accuse it of being imposed on us from the outside?

To begin with, it is a necessity that the whole order of things, such as the science of action has little by little unfolded it before reflected knowledge, should have in its totality the same objective value: one link could not be less solid, less necessary, less real in it than any other. And in spite of the extreme diversity of the elements which compose the series, all, sense intuition or positive truths as well as the conditions of individual, social, or religious life, participate in one and the same hypothetical necessity. All, the affirmation of the living God as well as the most brute physical phenomenon, are still only forms of the same interior need. All, consequently, equally need by right to be grounded absolutely; and none can be without the other. The knowledge itself which seems to contain them and produce them all in us is also, in its turn, only a subordinate and necessary term with the others. That is why, in feigning to suppress our individual consciousness, we do not suppress the idea of consciousness, because in appearing to support the rest, it is supported by all the rest. With my thought, I cannot abolish thought, nor even conceive that it be abolished; no matter how much I suppose the absence of my person, invincibly I let the impersonal subsist in me, that is, the necessity of at least one person outside of myself, to support all that is, or all that can be, of his thought and of his will. Thus there subsists in us a necessary and impersonal truth which is ours at the moment we judge it to be independent of us, and which is independent of us at the moment we recognize that we have no thought of our own except by its presence in us. To confer an objective value upon the determinism of objects, which yet had existence only to the extent that they are required by action, is to attribute to each of the syntheses which compose it its own reality. Now it is possible to do that only if we do not make exception of any of the solidary parts of the whole, and only if we place our own thought within the series by the same title as every other contingent phenomenon. Things are without me, as they are through me and as I am through them. Also, from the moment the total series has taken on this character of objectivity, the necessity of this exterior determinism ceases to be con-

459 ditional and becomes absolute: the roles are as though reversed; from being required for the development of the will, objective truth becomes requiring and dominating.

And, for this multiplicity of objects to subsist truly, there is then yet another necessity that their indefinitely varied aspects be perceived as if by so many centers of perspective, which, from a particular viewpoint, bring this very diversity back to unity. Whence the repetition and the multiplication of sensibilities, everywhere diffused, which, in contributing each its singular share to the infinite richness of nature and to the free interplay of divine wisdom in the organization of universal history, prepare the necessary work of final concentration. For, in order that things perceived may be perceived such as they are, a perceptive or passive knowledge is not enough; there has to be a rational and productive knowledge. Nor is a rational and productive knowledge enough; there has to be a perceptive and passive knowledge. The reality of things consists in mediating between this double aspect. They are, then, on the condition that their multiple heterogeneity acts on whoever perceives and undergoes them; they are, on the condition that these multiple and passive perceptions, reduced to the unity of a thought able to embrace them all, be grounded in a will which, in producing them such as they are, accepts them such as they appear. What we undergo passively, we become and we make be only by making this passion active and voluntary.

The objective reality of beings is therefore tied to the action of a being who, in seeing, makes what he sees be, and who, in willing, becomes himself what he knows. If things are because God sees them, they are at first only passive of His creative action and as though nonexistent in themselves. But if things are active and truly real, if they subsist under their objective aspect, in short, if they are, it is because the divine eye sees them through the eye of the creature itself, no longer insofar as He creates them, but insofar as they are created and their author makes Himself passive of their proper action. They do not consist in an abstract and intelligible possibility of perception; their living reality depends on there being, joined to universal science and the divine omnipresence, a knowledge, at once total and singular, of all the partial syntheses garnered by all the disseminated sensibilities and reasons. Things, then, are what they are, phenomenal and real, only to the extent that, passive and active, they have initiative and power over their very cause, thus meeting their principle and the end of their unfolding in one and the same center, from which they draw the original unity of their borrowed action and in which they find the final unity of the synthetic perceptions of which they are the antecedent condition. 460

Thus, the total determinism is essential to each of the derived existences; and to the total determinism is essential the consenting thought which envelops it entirely and singularly in the unity of a voluntary action and passion. The Cartesian criterion of divine veracity furnished only an appearance of foundation for real truth: in order that what is known should be, it is not enough that a real being should know, this being has to be what is to be known, so that this known may have being. Beings are, but not without the being who sees them and makes them, no more than they can see themselves without his light and his presence. This, then, is to go further both than any realism and any idealism: for, where some claimed to find the truth of objective existence already, under the name of metaphysics and ontology, we must still see only determinate and solidary phenomena; where some thought to encounter only unrealizable phenomena, we must be able to find already the solidity of the being who sees them and makes them all what they are, from the richest forms of thought and life to the most brute facts. The alleged *thing in itself* is still a phenomenon; and it is the phenomenon which becomes truly *thing in itself*: a double advantage, to thus reduce to science what seemed foreign to the order of positive facts, and to bring to being what seemed foreign to the order of absolute reality.

The reality of the phenomenon and, with it, the total system and the very commonwealth of spirits would vanish without this double tie of the relative to the absolute and of the absolute to the relative. Not that the relative is in the least necessary; it is real only to the extent that it receives from the absolute the gift of being cause within the absolute itself: a conditional necessity which takes nothing away from the sovereign independence of the first cause, but which simply manifests to what condescendence on its part the existence of the secondary causes is subordinated. *Quod sciebat ab aeterno per divinitatem, aliter temporali didicit experimento per carnem* (what He knew from eternity through divinity, He learned in temporal experience through the flesh). That is the point to which we must come in order to see, if not the entire reason and the true end, at least the means taken by creative love in the gratuitous gift of being to others than Being. Moreover, without this view, we will never be able to ground the existence of anything whatsoever. Passive in its depth, nature must, in order to be, have a true action, and this action has to find its perfect consistency in the voluntary passion of a being able to confer on his knowledge an absolute character. Perhaps, destined to receive the divine life within himself, man might have been able to play this role of universal bond and to suffice for this creative mediation, because this immanence of God within us would be as the magnetic center which would tie all things together, like a bundle of needles invisibly bound together by a powerful magnet. But also in order that, in spite of everything, the mediation might be total, permanent, voluntary, in a word, such as to insure the reality of everything which undoubtedly was able not to be, but which, being as it is, requires a divine witness, perhaps a Mediator was needed who would make himself patient of this integral reality and who would be like the *Amen* of the universe, *"testis verus et fidelis qui est principium creaturae Dei"* (a true and faithful witness who is the principle of God's creature). Perhaps it was necessary

461

that, having become flesh himself, he should become, through a passion at once necessary and voluntary, the reality of the determinism appearing in nature and the forced knowledge of objective phenomena, the reality of the voluntary failings and the privative knowledge which is their sanction, the reality of religious action and of the sublime destiny held in store for man fully consequent with his own willing. He it is who is the measure of all things.

V

All that precedes only expresses the inevitable exigencies of thought and practice. That is why it is a system of scientific relations before appearing as a chain of real truths. In thinking and in acting, we imply this immense organism of necessary relations. To lay them out before reflexion is simply to unveil what we cannot help admitting in order to think, and affirming in order to act. Without always noting it distinctly, always we are inevitably brought to conceive the idea of objective existence, to posit the reality of objects conceived and ends sought, to suppose the conditions required for this reality to subsist. For, not being able to do as if it were not, we cannot not include in our action the indispensable conditions for it to be. And reciprocally, what cannot not be immanent in thought, we cannot not tend to make immanent to ourselves through practice. The circle is closed. It is this last link whose soldarity we still have to show, precisely because, by reason of its unique situation between the two ends of the chain which it holds, it plays a distinctive role. For while it is, so to speak, conditioned by practice, it conditions practice in turn. We are constrained by a subjective necessity to establish its real truth; and this truth will in effect be invested with all the objective reality that the most confident thought could affirm, with a reality such that the most defiant exigencies of the critical mind cannot touch or weaken it.

The complete exposition of the subjective necessities does not leave outside of them any support for doubt or negation. When all the conditions of thought and action are defined, when all the content of life has been reintegrated into consciousness, willy-nilly we *must* (*il faut*) think that it is; this is why we *ought to* (*nous devons*) do as if it were. The role of science seems entirely negative; in the speculative order, it is so; but in the practical order, it is entirely positive. Whence the character of ambiguity and the uneasy feeling which in the course of this study has reappeared at each successive stage. Impossible not to take each new level into account, as if it were definitive, since it is a certain truth for action;

462

impossible to restrict ourselves to it, since it is only a provisional stop and a partial relation for thought. Hence we could never insist too much both on the fixity and the instability, on the importance and the inadequacy of each of the progressive syntheses which we have had incessantly to constitute and surpass. Thus it is impossible for the natural order to be, and impossible for it not to be: the great test for man is that, willing infinitely, he would often like the infinite not to be. Thus, on the other hand, it is impossible for the supernatural order to be without the natural order, for which it is necessary, and impossible for it not to be, since the natural order in its entirety guarantees it in requiring it. Solidarity of the scientific conditions, which translates into a system of real truths.

463   The theoretical impossibility of doubt, therefore, entails the practical affirmation of reality at the very moment when the practical possibility of negation seems to entail the theoretical impossibility of certitude. But moral obligations themselves are only a necessity suspended in appearance; sooner or later what must be will be, for it is what already is; and the deviations, the faults, the illusory phenomena, will remain grounded forever in the truth which will reveal the present error and failure. The knowledge of the unavoidable, then, indicates what we have to avoid. In understanding even what ought not to be, without falsehood and evil ever ceasing to subsist, the sight of what is brings out what ought to be. Duty is what is; but what is also includes every derogation from duty. Thus is justified, without dualism, the radical distinction between evil and good, and, without monism, the total reintegration of the false and the true in being. For science, what difference could be found between what appears to be forever and what is? And how could a distinction be made between reality itself and an invincible and permanent illusion or, so to speak, an eternal appearance? For practice, it is quite otherwise: in doing as if it were, only practice possesses what is, if it is truly. Let no one then ever claim to have found in a theory, no matter how perfect, a deceitful equivalent for what is. We do not solve the problem of life without living; and never does speaking or proving dispense with doing and being. Hence we see justified absolutely, by science itself, the role of action: the science of practice establishes that there is no substitute for action.

Thus, it is a necessity to suppose the necessity of the natural order, of the supernatural order, and of the divine intermediary who makes up their bond and their subsistence. It is a necessity again that we are not able either to look for a confirmation of this truth elsewhere than in effective practice, or to fail to encounter it there. Let us suppose that action has given us this confirmation. Then the link which closes the chain is perfectly attached. The two ends had to be joined, they are; the necessity

of the total determinism had to be taken up into a free act of will, it is entirely; the mediating role of action had to be absolutely justified and grounded, it is; this mediation had to be a principle of unity and distinction, it is: we are beings in Being. Appearances themselves, duration, all the inconsistent forms of individual life, far from being abolished, participate in the absolute truth of the divine knowledge of the Mediator.   464
Time is what it is only when it is past, when it enters into eternity; but it is, because it remains eternally true that its mobile and fleeting apparition is known under the form of succession. The human person seems to pass, but his acts are beyond what passes. And thus, without ceasing to touch the banks of time, man uses and enjoys eternity at the same time as the perpetual renewal of duration: from the viewpoint in which he seems enclosed in order to remain a distinct individual, he uses and enjoys universality at the same time as the singularity of his personal life. Called to see all things in the unity of the divine plan, through the eyes of the Mediator, called to see himself in the permanent act of liberality and to love himself in loving the perpetual charity from which he has his being, he is this very act of his author, and he produces it in himself as it is in Him. Through his willing which has not always been, he is united to the will which has always been. He has had a beginning; and it is this limit which forever remains his distinctive mark; but once appearances open up, without vanishing, to reveal all things in their universal reason to him, he participates in the truth of creative love. He is only immortal; he has eternal life.

By simply observing the sequence of the exigencies of human action, and by requiring what reality it supposes to constitute itself, we find ourselves then in the presence of the inevitable term from which hangs, whether we know it or not, all the development of life and thought. But this last link depends on all the others only to make them all depend on it. What we require in order to act is first required of us. To be sure, what goes before, what accompanies, what follows our own decision, is in conformity with the most profound movement of our freedom. But also all the sensible, scientific, intellectual, moral, and religious conditions of human life find their principle and their authority above us. That is why, although they are spontaneously implied in us, we have to recognize them through a free effort; and that is why, even though we can revolt against them, they do not cease to be realized in us. To justify this exterior subsistence of the truth interior to man, there has to be a kind of metaphysics to the second power, in order to ground, not only what   465
a first metaphysics, still quite subjective, falsely presented to us as the very reality of being, whereas it was simply a view of the mind or a specu-

lative phenomenon, but also all the determinism of nature, of life, and of thought. Thus, as long as it is in the making, science has only to describe and record the inevitable, it has nothing imperious about it; but once it is done, it commands and, by the ascendency alone of what is, it exercises its judicature. Once the chain has been linked together, all the determinism which had appeared as the phenomenon of the human will in the understanding then appears henceforth at the same time as an absolute reality which the understanding imposes on the will. Consequently, to the truth of the primacy of action, *Im Anfang war die That*, "in the beginning was Action," corresponds the great affirmation of the equal primacy of truth: "*In principio erat Verbum*" (In the beginning was the Word). This reign of truth is entirely outside of us; it will never be disarmed of its iron sceptre; but also this reign of truth is entirely within us, since we produce all its despotic exigencies in ourselves. Nothing, in human destiny, is tyrannical; nothing, in being, is involuntary; nothing, in truly objective knowledge, which does not come from the depths of thought, this is indeed the solution to the problem of action; and so the common knot of science, of metaphysics, and of morality is tightened. From the least of our acts, from the least of facts, it is enough to draw out what is there to be found, in order to encounter the inevitable presence, not only of an abstract first cause, but of the sole author and the true consummator of all concrete reality. Down to the last detail of the last imperceptible phenomenon, mediating action makes up the truth and the being of all that is. And it would be strange indeed to be able to explain anything apart from Him without Whom nothing has been made, without Whom all that has been made falls back into nothingness.

Conclusion

Man's need is to equal himself, so that nothing of what he is may remain alien or contrary to his willing, and nothing of what he wills may remain inaccessible or denied to his being. To act is to seek this agreement of knowing, willing and being, and to contribute in producing it or in compromising it. Action is the double movement which bears being to the end it is aiming at as to a new perfection, and which reintegrates the final cause into the efficient cause. In the fullness of its mediating role, it is a return of the absolute to the absolute; the relative which it contains and sustains between these two terms, it absolves. To absolve, is to give truth and being to what does not have it of itself.

The role of action, then, is to develop being and to constitute it. To be sure, it determines it and even appears to exhaust it, as if effort were an impoverishment of life, and as if the execution depreciated the intention without ever making the real the equal of the ideal. But we must rise above this appearance. It is true that, to the extent that the agent is passive of his own operation and of the activity of the forces which he makes concur in his work, he suffers in action itself a kind of deterioration; and the intention keeps within itself something which the execution does not at first produce. Nevertheless the action performed brings back to the being who conceived and willed it a new richness which was not yet either in his conception or in his resolution. Not all that was simply ideal in the intention eludes action; at least a part is realized in it; and this real is heterogeneous with regard to this ideal. That is why, after having acted, we are other, we know otherwise, we will in another way than before; and that is why the original increase merits to be studied, more than the tendency itself which yet seemed to prepare and already contain it in its entirety. Action is the between-two and like the passage through which the efficient cause, which still has only the idea of the final cause, *intellectu et appetitu* (in intelligence and appetite), reaches the final cause, which is incorporated little by little into the efficient cause in order to communicate to it the perfection it was aspiring to, *re* (in reality). It appears to exhaust us; it fills us. It seems to go out of us; but what emanates thus from our most intimate depth brings back to us what is outside of us as an end to be attained, and makes immanent to us the total series of means through which we tend from our principle to our end. To give of self, then, is to gain more than what we give; and the most sacrificial or far ranging life is also the most intense.

Again, it is true that the effects of action vary infinitely and are even opposed according to the use man makes of his freedom before the alternative, of which it can be said that it is the business of his life and the one thing necessary. But the issue is not first to regulate and to judge action; the issue is to observe what it is and, so to speak, to take the measure of its scope from one extremity to the other of its real development. This complete view of what it is, is enough to make manifest what it ought to be; and the authority of the law which imposes itself on it arises precisely from the fact that science does not start from law itself, but, without having looked for it, arrives at it through the inevitable ascendency of what is. In running away from it, we still posit this rule which is not just an ideal, but which is already a truth, which is the truth itself. For it is by reason of the reality which is in them that errors follow upon one another, and that in running through all of them we arrive at the full reality which envelops and judges them all.

Also the study of action has as a necessary result to justify the very terms of the problem which imposes itself on all, by explaining completely the primitive ambition of man, and to determine the law of human life, simply by observing what is. *Veritas norma sui* (truth is its own norm). There is no exhortation or instruction to equal this view of the inevitable. To communicate to man the great and salutary concern for his destiny, science has only to uncover for him what he does; it has only 469 to measure impassibly the ample spread of the terms between which he oscillates. Without any ontological or deontological preoccupation, without any effort at persuasion, with the tranquil assurance of a charity more contained for being more pressing, we have only to let the necessary truth unfold in spite of all resistances. We must have enough confidence in it to look for nothing more than its presence alone. Far from trying to prop it up with a doctrine that supports it, we must oppose to it all those who refuse to recognize it, so that it may reign, in spite of all, in all, and so that it may dominate or include even those who seem to ignore it or exclude it. What is, is what ought to be and what will be.

To do the science of practice, then, and to find the equation of action is not just to develop, before reflected thought, all the content of spontaneous consciousness; better still, it is to indicate the means of reintegrating into the willed operation all that is at the principle of the voluntary operation. It is not a question of partial knowledge or of a moral reflexion, apt, to be sure, to illumine good will, but without any demonstrative character; it is a question of a total science, able to embrace the universal determinism of action and to follow its continuous deployment which bears its necessary consequences out to the infinite: from thought to practice and from practice to thought, the circle must be closed in science because it is closed in life. Thereby is determined with a new precision this double relation of knowledge and action. On the one hand, human acts unfold their consequences and impose them on us justly, without our having to know all their content distinctly in order to be responsible for them, without having the clear revelation of their often forgotten or misconstrued bearing change them essentially, without any ulterior knowledge modifying their value through the sanction it brings to them. On the other hand, the little interior light which follows action, which accompanies it and prepares it, is enough to guide it and to animate its immense organism, like the rudder, which, little as it is, and placed in the rear of a vessel, directs it in its forward motion.

This is why, to resolve the problem, there are apparently two methods, indirect and direct, scientific and practical; but these two methods must come together. This is why the word *destiny* has two meanings; but these two meanings are equally legitimate. This equivocal word designates the   470 necessary development of life, independent of man's intervention in the web of events which unfold in him and outside of him; and at the same time it designates the personal way through which we arrive at our last ends according to our use of life and the employment of our will. — Hence it is indispensable to show that there is a logic of action, and that the interconnection of voluntary operations falls under a rigorous determinism. — And it is indispensable to show that practical experimentation includes a sufficient clarity; that it substitutes for science, without science substituting for it; that it offers an exactness, scientific in its own way, even when this moral discipline is destitute of any theoretical justification. To face this double aspect of the problem, to bring out the unity of the solution, is the object of this conclusion.

I

Since it is in life itself that we must find the law of life, and since it is enough to reveal to action all that it is to judge it, this double truth will find its confirmation. On the one hand, all the possible forms of action are in fact compatible; the science of action takes them all in; in the real, there are no contradictories, there are only contraries whose opposed developments are tied together by one and the same determinism. On the other hand, under these diversely compatible forms of action is found a principle of contradiction which, in the fact itself, preserves the right, and absolutely decides the meaning of being. Hence compatibility and exclusion, this is the profound meaning of the law of contradiction which has to be elucidated. It makes truth reign in error without abolishing the error; it introduces the absolute of being into the phenomenon without suppressing the relative of the phenomenon.

Everywhere, in the natural history of action, it has been possible to eliminate the variable to consider only the common character and the trait essential to every development of human activity. Setting aside the premature assessments and the often rash judgments we make on the quality of acts, we had to study them all without qualifying any one of them. This is to say that, under the contingent and arbitrary forms of life, there is always a necessary sequence and a kind of rigid skeleton on which are founded the most supple and the most varied movements. Perhaps it has seemed that many chapters of this book, especially those that come at the end, surpass the order of reason, or that they do not have the impersonal and universal value, nor the compelling necessity of science. No doubt, in appearance, we can provisionally elude the consequences of this determinism of practice. But, down deep, we do not escape them. And the force of a true Critique of Life must be to find, underneath the superficial and temporary deviations, this hidden logic of action whose laws are no less rigorous than those of the abstract sciences.

But to say this is not enough. For, all the laws of thought, all the particular forms of logic, fall into this concrete determinism of practice, of which they are only a detached aspect. The logic of action is not a partial discipline; it is truly the General Logic, the one in which all the other scientific disciplines find their ground and their agreement. To develop all its content, we would, through a searching analysis of the conditions which the will imposes on itself, have to determine the very springs of human destiny. About such an enterprise, which would require a distinct treatise, we can only say a few words here, to the extent that the knowledge of this necessity inherent in action has a practical interest.

If it is true that the will undergoes nothing which it does not ratify and is nothing which it does not will, it is no less true that the conditions it needs to be what it wills are rigorously interconnected under the secret inspiration of its own aim. It is no less true that this necessity, which has its source in us, is independent of us and has its principle outside of us in real truth. Thus, for being voluntary in their origin, the laws of thought and of life are no less necessary and imposed in their application as well as in their first institution. —But precisely because they express the unavoidable truth, and precisely because they are grounded in a secret initiative of the will, they keep, in their very necessity, a character which it is essential for us to bring to light: the particular forms of logic have the right to exclude or the duty to ignore what escapes their grasp; the Logic of Action, being total, must, in a sense, include and allow for precisely what it condemns and eliminates.

For, unlike the abstract science of thought which isolates ideas and proceeds by complete inclusion or exclusion, the concrete reality of life perpetually reconciles contraries. What, from a speculative viewpoint, is incompatible and formally contradictory, comes together, in fact, in such a way as to constitute new syntheses distinct from their elements; and, as in a mechanism of associated parts, all the movements produce their compensating effect. Nothing is more important, in the entire study of human action, than this solidarity of what we do with what we do not do. There is no act which does not sum up the adverse tendencies and does not form a system with those which are overcome as well as with those which overcome. The motives which are contradictory before thought remain solidary in action. — Inversely, in the order of phenomena, there is never any formal contradiction, because the particular propositions which enunciate the given facts are never contradictory. And yet the law of contradiction applies to the real past. Thus, while from a formal viewpoint conciliation is impossible, from the real viewpoint it is contradiction that is impossible; and while future contingents are compatible in thought, past acts are incompatible in reality. Further still, we can never realize anything but contraries; and yet the law of contradiction governs our completed acts. Never are contradictories given in fact; and yet, in acting, we imply, in our acts which appear to bear simply on contraries, the contradictory that we do not realize. How can we escape from these embarrassments?

It is action which, serving as a link between these opposing forms of thought and life, insinuates the law of contradiction into the heart of things even as it perpetually effectuates an experimental synthesis of contraries. How does it arrive at this? Phenomena, taken simply for what they are, never contradict one another, being always heterogeneous and solidary. If then the law of contradiction applies to the past, it is because the *act* which is underneath the appearing *fact* has introduced into the phenomenon something other than the phenomenon, even something other than the possible. The entire movement of the interior life culminates in the necessary affirmation of being, because this movement is grounded on this necessity itself. The alternative which imposes itself on every human consciousness and which alone places us, in practice itself, in the face of the contradictories, only reveals the interplay of this internal dynamism. On the other hand, since the will, in opting according to the conditions it imposes on its own development, does not suppress the term of the alternative it rejects, the result is that, whatever it has chosen,

472

473

it keeps within it the presence of the excluded term as an element of the synthesis it forms. What it deprives itself of, στερησις, is not absolutely outside of it. This is why the sacrifice which it can make of phenomena, through mortification, is only apparent; and this is why, on the other hand, when it sets aside the importunities of duty or the exigencies of the "one thing necessary," it loses itself, but without annihilating itself forasmuch. Never do we escape the necessity of implying the contradictories and never do we realize one only by eliminating the other; through renunciation, we gain twice; through exclusive enjoyment, we lose twice: the phenomenon, though alien to the law of contradiction, is such that in it we have to opt between the contradictories, acquire what we seem to sacrifice liberally, and lose what we seem to hang on to avariciously.

The logical problem, then, is only an aspect of the problem of action. Not only is practice grounded in a dialectic whose rigorous exactness can be shown, but also the most abstract laws of the understanding have their full meaning only in relation to the concrete development of life. Moreover, a complete study of the mechanism of thought and practice would lead us to tie together the diverse particular forms of a still fragmentary logic at the same time as to bring out into the open the internal spring which sets everything in motion in us and which promotes our destiny. The usefulness of such a study would be two-fold; for it would finally constitute that general set of *Canons* for the human spirit of which formal logic and the methodology of the diverse sciences offer only samples; and at the same time it would make the solution of the moral problem benefit from all the rigor found in the most abstract and the most exact of sciences. It is the role of the logic of action to determine thus the chain of necessities which compose the drama of life and lead it inevitably to its *dénouement.* By manifesting the scientific character of this enchainment, it must, by the very fact, have a certain efficacity: it establishes that the solution is inevitable and necessarily bears on the whole; it shows that any practice founded on an incomplete theory is presumptuous, but that complete theory inevitably leads to practice, since only action can resolve the problem raised by action; it indicates the extreme terms in which the *élan* of the human will can culminate; it inserts, between the first given and these ultimate solutions of the problem, the entire series of necessary intermediaries; but it does not claim to realize, through a simple view, the solution which belongs only to effective practice. Far from it: speculation must remedy the dangers of speculation, by proving that it gives consciousness a light, not just to glow, but to go forward. Knowing does not dispense with doing; doing can dispense with knowing. If life is an enigma even for the clever, all that is needed is a completely good will for even the simplest of people to read it fluently.

It matters little for them to know what they do, as long as they do what they know. The sincerity of conscience and the discernment of vivifying truths depend more on acts than on thoughts; for it is never quite enough to do what we think good, it still has to be good to think that we have to do it. The logic of action seeks only to find an itinerary which would allow the intelligence of the learned to slowly and surely attain the heights of the humble and the little ones; it brings them to a point of departure. But the light it sheds on the road does not dispense anyone from the effort that remains necessary to climb to those heights.

II

It may have seemed that a *Science of Practice* should formulate rules of conduct, exhort consciences to the good, and teach us efficaciously what we have to do. But what we have had to go against is precisely the pretension of every morality which presumes to resolve the problem of life without going beyond that honest mediocrity of edifying instruction. A true science of human destiny is not to be had at such a low price; and action is too complex to let itself be led in that way. Between the rectitude of the man who, without discussion, without compromising with his conscience, preserves at that price the privilege of an infallible simplicity, and the integral knowledge of the necessary and sufficient conditions which action requires, there is no doubt room for a delicate art of salutary exhortations or for the reflexions of the moralist, but there   475
is no room for a truly scientific solution to the moral problem. It was with a very deliberate purpose that we had to renounce all moralizing instruction, in order to prescind from the variety which the free initiative of consciousness brings into life, and in order to determine simply what is unavoidable and necessary in the total deployment of human action. In comparison with the final teaching which this method prepares, all the rest is of secondary importance. To show the illusory and superstitious character of every attempt made to directly ground a self-sufficient morality and to constitute an autonomous science, has been the conclusion of such an inquiry. There is no closed conception of duty which is valid by itself and which constitutes the good through strictly formal precepts. There is no speculative truth whose adequate grasp would constitute the perfect life. Neither the ethical problem nor the metaphysical problem could ever be resolved alone. There is no morality outside of truth; but the truth understood is not, by itself alone, morality itself. The secret of life is higher than Kant or Spinoza saw it.

Perhaps this result seems entirely negative: "action is not self-sufficient;

man does not find within himself his rule and his end." But this is why the result is supremely important: it does away with illusions which, for being often generous, reasoned, tenacious, are nonetheless illusions. Is it useless, then, to establish that we are taking the wrong road in hoping that morality can be grounded as a science without surpassing the natural order or the phenomenon of duty or even metaphysical conceptions? Is it useless to show that every effort made by man to restrict himself to this way of thinking and of living is superstitious? Is it useless to determine under what conditions the practice of life can become certain and properly scientific? These are only prolegomena to morality, since it is not a question of determining the content of any precept; at any rate this inquiry has one interest which the most beautiful and the most precise formulations of our duties do not offer: it indicates the one road which we have to travel for the good to be the good, the necessary dispositions for the knowledge of duty to be something more than a vain theory, the required conditions for the very practice of the natural virtues to become efficacious and fully salutary. It may seem harsh to bunch together under a common reproach of superstition, one faithful to duty and a fetishistic savage; but it would be unjust to the former only to the extent that he himself would be unjust to the latter. Both can be equally close to or equally far from the truth, because the grossest of acts can serve as a vehicle for the good. But if one claims to be satisfied with the partial knowledge one has arrived at, if, profiting by the little light one already has, one closes oneself off from all new clarity and all new exigency, there is usurpation on the part of an incompetent thought, there is a perversion of sincerity. While full of admiration and tenderness for all the generous ones, wherever they come from, who go forward and devote themselves to a work of personal and social salvation, still (without ever suspecting anyone because the secret of consciences escapes us) we could not arm with enough inflexible severity toward themselves all those presumptuous people who come to a stop and stop others along the road on which we must always go forward without ever boasting of having arrived. To distinguish themselves from the fetishistic savage, they have only pride in addition; and when they think they are discovering for themselves and spreading the first and the last word of salvation, rather than acting, they are only getting agitated.

Hence there is no intermediary between the *science of practice* and that *practical science* which is grounded, not on a theoretical reflexion, but on a cultivation of the practical sense through practice itself. The role of the first is to prevent people from supplanting or mutilating the second. We do not have to know all that we do, in order to do it knowingly. Thought that is efficacious is not necessarily a complete system of analytical abstractions, πραξις μετα λογου (practice following thought); it is a concrete synthesis which, in each interior disposition, can sum up for consciousness all the labor of life, λογος μετα πραξεως (thought following practice). Even unaccompanied by a theoretical justification, action bears within it a sufficient certitude; it constitutes a conclusive method; it is an experimentation, in the most scientific sense of the word: a rigorous and demonstrative experimentation which substitutes for speculative study and for which nothing substitutes. The understanding confirms the practical method by showing that it does not even need to be confirmed. The conclusion of a science of action, then, must not be: "Here is what should be thought or believed or done"; what is that? It must be to actually act. That is everything, everything lies therein.

Thus there is a direct way which starts from the point to which the indirect method of science results in bringing us. For the issue is not a problem to be resolved if we can, but a project to be realized if we will. A solution is always inevitable; that is why it is more urgent to prepare it than to foresee it. With regard to this necessary end, foresight is optional, preparation is obligatory. To prepare for it by opening up the way which is not cleared ahead of time, by doing the truth before seeing it clearly, by filling ourselves with reality in order to deserve light, that is the science which is always accessible and alone indispensable for whoever has no other. Asceticism is a true science, and the only science for directing consciences: it illumines those who exercise themselves in it, and enables them to enlighten others, through the perfection of a tact which communicates to this interior touch of practice all the precision of sight. Also, by a reversal of perspective, we would now have to regard the series of practical necessities as a system of moral obligations, and to transcribe the conclusions of the logic of action into the dictates of conscience. That would be the object of a distinct study. Suffice it to indicate, along with the difference of viewpoints, the convergence of these two methods, speculative and empirical. For in this empiricism of duty are wrapped all the elements of the true science of practice.

The complete theory of action concluded to practice. — Practice, for its part, must culminate in the complete knowledge of the profound reasons which justify or condemn it. Precepts are like hypotheses whose truth we have to verify; and the obscure clarity of conscience is destined to become, through faithful practice, the full light of science.

The determinism of action appeared to the downward look of analytical reflexion as a series of necessary means and constraining relations. — To the eye of moral conscience, it appears as a ladder of ends which solicit good will and permit the exercise of freedom in the alternative from which the whole destiny of man is suspended.

Through a quite speculative anticipation, the science of action sought to foresee the consequences of practice, and to propose before present knowledge the future revelation of its immense content. — Through a quite practical effort, moral experimentation prepares what it does not

478   foresee and, busying itself with filling actual life with all possible reality, it sows the future in the present.

The logic of action showed the perpetual conciliation of contraries in the order of phenomena, up to the final contradiction which imposes an inevitable option on the will. — In practice, what was conciliation of contraries, becomes sacrifice and mortification; what was alternative and necessary contradiction, becomes total gain or loss freely consummated. For in sacrificing the apparent goods, we acquire the real good, and we have preserved even what seemed to be mortified; but in becoming attached to the life that passes, we lose it at the same time as we lose the one that does not pass.

Speculative science, as perfect as one might suppose it, was limited to showing the solidarity of heterogeneous phenomena and the relative originality of the successive syntheses which it studies, but without producing and, consequently, without ever knowing the force which, like a spark of life, effects the combination of the elements. — Practice, for its part, perpetually effects this wonder. Hence it is the very substance of what is known and the realizing truth of the universal order. It is in practice that sense data, in spite of their inconsistency, that scientific symbolism, in spite of its incoherence, that the dynamism of subjective life, in spite of the instability which perpetually upsets its equilibrium, that the organic and social phenomena, in spite of the determinism which never forms a synthesis except to make of it an element of ulterior syntheses, that all the forms of science and life, find their common reason for being. Being is never in the idea separated from action; and metaphysics itself, considered first under its speculative aspect, is true then only inasmuch as, like a rung in the system of phenomena, it enters into the general dynamism of life. Action grounds the reality of the ideal and moral order; it contains the real presence of what, without it, knowledge can simply represent, but of what, with it and through it, is vivifying truth.

Thus practice bears within itself its proper certitude and its true light: a light which undoubtedly is not of another nature than that of speculative vision, but which differs from it as two aspects of the same landscape differ, according to whether the sun is before or behind the beholder; the view is clearer where the light is less dazzling, and a reflexion guides us better than the center of the light. Similarly, as the brightness of con-

479   sciousness comes from action to beam ahead along the path we have to

walk, it illuminates the way better for the traveler who goes forward without looking back toward the source whence it comes; to look in the direction of the source is to see it as more abundant, but it is perhaps to see one's own way less well. Science is good, but in order to lead us beyond what it already knows. Whatever theoretical knowledge we may have of moral obligations, it is always new and instructive, it is never simply scientific to practice them. The perfection of science, though identical with the perfection of life, never is a substitute for it. Practice is never simply a surrogate, provisional and approximate, for the use of those who cannot live by their thought because they cannot even think of their life. Practice is neither the affair of sentiment or of generous inspiration without logical rigor, nor is it simply a theorem in act. What it bears within it, though quite accessible to knowledge, is infinitely more than knowledge.

— It has been claimed at times that true experience consists in experimenting with everything. Wrong: there is an experience which impoverishes life and reduces the knowledge of being in us; on the contrary, submission to mortifying duty gives to the man of sacrifice a universal competence and an interior richness which cannot be acquired otherwise. — It has been claimed that thought alone bears within it the true infinite, that action limits it in determining it, and that the French, for example, have too much of a bent for action, too much love for clarity, to have a philosophic head. Wrong again: in the most humble of practices and in acts submitted to the stringency of an austere rule, there is a fuller sense of life, more amplitude of thought, and more sense of mystery than in all metaphysical epics. — It has been claimed that the letter ends up killing the spirit, that all defined dogma is fatal for the freedom of thought, that literal practice is lethal to the sense of the living God. Wrong: the spirit is vivified only by the letter; the positive cult and the act following a quite clear obligation are the very functions of the divine life within us. This religious sense, this consciousness of the national genius in France, this character of generosity and active dedication, this love of clarity and decision, along with this great sense of mystery, are inseparable. We must not abandon anything of this heritage, lest we lose everything.

Thus, practical science, as different as it is from the science of practice, knows how to benefit from the latter's cooperation and knows equally well how to get along without it. Their solidarity is such that the complete knowledge of our acts will be the sanction of these acts themselves, and that the full revelation of what we have willed and done must fix the will forever. Their independence is such that this full revelation could not in any way modify the nature of acts performed by the obscure light of conscience, and that all the science of voluntary works and of their con-

480

sequences has to leave intact the will that persists in them. We will these acts just as we know them; we shall know them just as we will them. In reversing itself, the relation will not change; the reciprocity is perfect. But if it is knowledge which must bring the future sanction, it is practice which is the present obligation.

III

In order to resolve the human problem, the Critique of life cannot not resolve the universal problem. It determines the common knot of science, of morality and of metaphysics. It fixes the relations between knowledge and reality. It defines the meaning of being. It finds this vital point, at the intersection of knowing and willing, in action. Far from looking for being behind what is known and willed, in a middling term or in a fictitious substrate, it suppresses all occult reality, to find, in a mediation which makes the two terms equal without confusing them, the real truth of all that is. Things are known as they are, and they are as they are known; it is the unity of this double aspect which makes up their true being: this is the only way of reconciling objective existence and the very reality of the objects of experience with the primacy of the spirit and the sovereign originality of the interior life. To study the total determinism of knowledge and the entire order of phenomena, is the role of complete science. To show that this necessary knowledge has an absolute truth, to seek in what sense and under what conditions the known existence is really objective, is the role of metaphysics. To trace out, for the ascent of the will, the itinerary which leads from the primitive aspiration and necessary knowledge to the voluntary possession of being by transforming the system of necessities into a hierarchy of obligations, this is the role of morality. The critique of action serves as prolegomena to this triple study. In finding the point where it ties in, each one of them profits by recovering the independence of its development. — Without any pretense here of running through the three ways which open before us, suffice it to indicate what profit there is in having arrived at the point of convergence where, by turning around, we see them diverge.

I. — Since it is not in a substrate hidden behind each phenomenon that we must look for the reality of what is known, it follows that all ontological questions must first be put aside in the study of things, and that between the objects of knowledge there can be no contradiction. There is none where there is no being to serve in some way as resisting core or as impenetrable foundation. On the contrary, if we had to suppose some hidden foundation in phenomena distinct from them, or if we affirmed that they are the only and the true reality, it would be impossible not to transform into a formal opposition their certain heterogeneity, and not to erect the determinism which makes them solidary into an absolute. Whence arise difficulties that are insoluble, because they are artificial. Is there really any one single doctrine which, in the examination of the phenomena themselves, has escaped the ontological temptation? Is there one which has not presented affirmations or negations that were premature, incompetent, misplaced? What proves this is that, instead of considering these objects of knowledge as they appear, that is, as heterogeneous and solidary, they have been regarded as exclusive of one another, incompatible, burdened with antinomies. Now, how can one judge them to be so, if not because one insinuates into them a secret principle of contradiction which is appropriate for them only to the extent that one attributes being to them? Even phenomenism succumbs to this temptation in pretending to restrict itself to phenomena, as if that were all there is, and in judging them to be exclusive of all other reality. Even criticism is subject to this metaphysical vertigo in seeing irreducible oppositions where there is only heterogeneity. Even positivism is inconsistent with its principle in excluding, in the name of certain sciences which it invests by this very pretention with an objective value, an entire segment of our knowledge which is no less positive than the other, since we saw that all knowledge enters into one and the same determinism. By falling thus into such illusions with regard to the phenomenon as well as with regard to real being, and   482 by peopling the intellectual world with idols, all these doctrines have seen the difficulty where it is not, for failing to have seen it where it is. Contrary to one another, they are simply species of the same false genus: for Philosophy to deserve this proper name, it must be a doctrine other than the others and it must determine precisely, in what is controvertible, what is not controvertible; for this is what enters into the field of science.

Thus it is that, where systems have ordinarily spent themselves in vain debates, philosophy no longer finds any matter for discussions, because it simply brings to them the habits of the scientific spirit which does not speculate on any of its proper objects. To be scientific, the study of any phenomena whatsoever does not have to scrutinize their nature; far from that, it needs to be detached from this sterile curiosity. It takes these phenomena for what they are, without presupposing any restriction, without insinuating into this word any meaning foreign to what it denotes. Each synthesis appears original, heterogeneous, irreducible to its own conditions: hence for each distinct order there has to be a distinct study. Each order of phenomena is tied to the whole system by a continuous determinism: hence it is impossible for science to restrict itself to one point and to exclude any of the solidary objects which compose one and the same universe, one and the same problem. But instead of looking into a new order of facts for the explanation or the reality of a foregoing order, science reserves for a further inquiry the further objects which the necessary sequence of its investigations proposes for it: constantly drawn beyond itself, so to speak, it protects itself against the mirage which proposes every new unknown along the way as the secret of the known; it concentrates on each link of the chain as if it were alone, and does not think of finding in the positive sciences, for example, the truth of sense intuitions. Each order has its truth and as it were its own solidity; its objective value will consist, not in what it is not, but in what it is. That is why science peaceably takes possession of each order, without fear that one, to the exclusion of others, will claim to render an account of all things and exhaust truth and being by itself. Kant noted that between the thesis and the antithesis of his last antinomies there is no opposition, as in the case of two lines which, without being parallel, still do not meet if they are drawn on different planes. We must be more radical: among the solidary objects studied by science in the same plane of determinism, there is never any conflict, because the solidity of being is still lacking there. But if we succeed in first withdrawing being from everywhere in order to open everything up to scientific knowledge, it is precisely because we are otherwise led to reinstate it everywhere, by making of the phenomenon itself a metaphysical truth.

To take phenomena for what they are, neither more nor less, is a reservation that seems the most natural thing in the world; but to make such a reservation, it was necessary to have already risen to a higher conception: and, in making it, philosophy is led to renew the meaning of its inquiries; it reintegrates into the part of its domain where the great peace of science reigns most of the questions over which it had been lost in controversies without possible solution. It is useful, then, to consider for a moment what illusions we are exposed to, in order to see how many difficulties or ruinous divisions it is easy to circumvent. We escape them on the simple condition that we exclude from the study of the determinism of action every ulterior preoccupation. Granted, there always has to be an ulterior problem; but it is for lack of having discovered it where it is that many have been inclined to place it everywhere where it is not.

—Some are inclined to look for truth itself and for real being in sense data. —But thought has to be on guard against this false mysticism; it must take these sense data not as a reality exclusive of every other, but in the way they appear as a system of symbols to be deciphered. And, seeing what effort of reflexion has been necessary to free ourselves from the spirit of fascination with the senses, it is easy to appreciate the strength of this illusion.

—Some are inclined to look for the one secret of reality in the positive sciences, and to turn the conclusions they arrive at against everything that surpasses their range: do we not see certain minds, quite penetrated as they are by Kantian criticism, attribute a metaphysical value to scientific symbols, and treat the foundations of mathematics as if it were an issue of ontology?—But let us not forget, the positive sciences are only a coherent symbolism; and if we find in them a means of action, nevertheless we can never attribute to the phenomena which they bind together nor to the results which they obtain, I will not say an objective bearing, but simply a subjective value such that we could draw from it   484 any argument whatsoever against any other subjective truth. The positive sciences do not enable anyone to exclude or to deny anything whatsoever, either outside ourselves or inside ourselves. The contingency of necessary relations is the first of positive truths.

—Some are inclined to look for the very expression of life in the determinism of consciousness, and to believe that this internal dynamism excludes all that is not automatism and necessity.—But this automatism is once again an idol if one judges it to be the true and the last word about things: far from being absolute and exclusive, it is relative to freedom. Between scientific determinism and psychological determinism, there is the same relation as between psychological determinism and freedom itself. They seem to repel one another; actually they call for one another. Automatism of ideas and free choice are two solidary phenomena. Freedom cannot be denied in the name of the interior or exterior determinism of science, because, reciprocally, science is determined in the name of the freedom which is the soul of intellectual life and of scientific knowledge. The psychology which is apparently the most positive is still only mental alchemy as long as it insinuates into its research positivistic preoccupations. To ask the psychophysicist if he is a monadist or the psychologist if he excludes free choice, is to astonish him more than we would surprise the chemist if we were to ask today whether he is a partisan of phlogiston.

—Some are inclined, once freedom has been admitted, to look in it for the one spring of human action, as if one had either to reject it absolutely or to affirm it exclusively.—But no more than we should deny it in the name of the antecedent determinism must we deny, in its name, the determinism consequent on action. One of the essential results of the science of action is precisely to bring fully into light the necessary consequences of the phenomenon of freedom, prescinding from the variations of human conduct that cannot be determined. From the very fact that we will, there results an immense concatenation of new phenomena which little by little compose the very framework of the moral life. Thus defined, freedom does not break the series, it enters into it. And the strongest paradox which has perhaps been justified by this study, is to study the determinism of free actions, without impairing in the least the determinate use of freedom itself.

485 — Some are inclined to subordinate the autonomy of the will to heteronomy or heteronomy to autonomy, as if here again there were incompatibility. — But the scientific concatenation of the phenomena of consciousness manifests the mutual subordination and the solidarity of these two aspects. Through a progressive alternation, freedom is by turns a means and an end. The goal it seeks as an exterior end enters into the series of intermediaries which enable it to find itself; the rule which appears imposed on it, is still contained in its first aim, without ceasing to be offered to it as a true heteronomy.

— Some are inclined to consider as definitive and exclusive all the partial ends successively attained by action, as if the required sacrifices were without possible compensations, as if the syntheses constituted had absolute consistency and sufficiency, as if each new group of phenomena, absorbing everything, left no more room for anything else. — But these apparent sacrifices procure a real enrichment; but each of these ends obtained is itself only a means in the series of the advances of the will; but the social affections and duties, far from excluding one another, support and complement one another. Each synthesis is new with regard to its elements; it does not suppress them in surpassing them, it is not compromised in preserving them.

— Some are inclined, it is the great idol of the mind, to erect into an absolute the total system of phenomena and to confer upon universal conceptions, under whatever form they are organized in thought, a meaning such that there remains nothing to be added to them. Little as they may differ among themselves, these conceptions themselves seem to exclude one another: they are irreconcilable metaphysical systems. — But neither are they absolute truth, nor are they exclusive of one another. Forming diverse degrees in the general development of thought and in the dynamism of life, they too are solidary, like steps laid out in tiers. The naturalist solutions have their role and their certain efficaciousness; the idealist conceptions have theirs. Both the one and the other have their truth only to the extent that, tied to the development of action, they accept its teachings, shed light on its march forward, and prepare its progress.

— Some are inclined to attribute an absolute value to practice founded on only the witness of conscience, illuminated by only the light of reason,
486 supported by only the effort of good will; as if, by themselves, moral phenomena, cutting themselves off from all the others, had a divine suffi-

ciency, touched on the depth of things, worked out salvation, and made every ulterior search superfluous. — But this pretention is only one more idol: the truth is that, without stopping at what we do not know, we must act according to the duty we do know; the error is to judge that this forward march cannot and should not lead to any new light, and that reason is exclusive of a higher order, whereas it is solidary with it.

All these questions, which make up the ordinary object of passionate discussions, which raise contradictions, which absorb all the substance of metaphysics, must be left in the neutral zone of science, without introducing into them prematurely, as a ferment of discord, any preoccupation alien to the study of heterogeneous and solidary phenomena. It is simply a question of unraveling the complete chain of determinism. And where there is only something necessary, there is no being; where there is no being, there is no contradiction.

II. — But it is possible to conquer for science the neutral zone where peace should reign only by holding in reserve the secret principle of divisions, only by knowing how to look for objective existence solely where it can be, only by finding being solely where it is. The necessary knowledge of truth is still only a means of acquiring or losing the possession of reality. Although this objective knowledge should be identical with its object, there is still between the knowledge and the object all the difference that can separate possession from privation: hence being and knowing are as distinct and as alike as possible. And objective existence consists in that which, in this necessary identity, can and must be freely accepted to constitute voluntary identity. The reality of objects known is therefore grounded, not on a kind of duplicate underlying matter, not in the necessary form of their phenomenon; it is grounded in what imposes upon us an inevitable option; it is realized in the mediating action which enables them to be what they appear to be. Their existence is in them, then, since they are as they are known, and outside of them, since they are known as they are. Independent of the use we make of them, protected from human caprice, all of them susceptible of being studied with the impartiality of science, things therefore are all subordinated to 487 the great and decisive question of the use of life: their reason for being is to raise this problem for us; it is in the solution to the problem that they find their reason for being. *Omnia propter unum* (all for one purpose). Metaphysics is controverted, but not controvertible; it is so because the science of what is, without being dependent, is solidary with the will for what is. That is its originality.

Here then is the precise point around which all the battles are fought, the only sign of contradiction which must never disappear, which does not arise only as a result of a misunderstanding or a passing ignorance, which will never abandon consciences to the shame of being at rest. It is the one thing we have to do. In order not to see it everywhere where it is not, we must see it only where it is. It lies not in the fictitious oppositions between positivism and idealism, nor even in the struggles between nature and morality. It lies entirely in this necessary conflict which rises at the heart of the human will and which imposes on it the necessity to opt practically between the terms of an unavoidable alternative, an alternative such that man either tries to remain master of himself and to keep himself entirely within himself, or hands himself over to the divine order more or less obscurely revealed to his consciousness.

Being and life, then, are not for us in what is to be thought, nor even to be believed, nor even to be practised, but in what is actually practised. Man and philosophy must, so to speak, be decentered, so that this vital center may be placed where it really is, not in the objects attained by the senses, not in the ends which desire strives for, not in intellectual speculations, not in moral prescriptions, but in action: for it is through action that the questions of the relations between man and God are inevitably decided in fact. Thus, as the critique of life displaces and raises thought's center of perspective little by little, it displaces and raises the center of equilibrium of practice. In order to find the equation of action, it is called on to embrace and surpass the whole natural order. Without introducing any constraint or any postulate from the outside, and solely through the energy of the spring internal to the human will, the critique of life forces man to open himself to the gift of a higher life, or, if he closes himself up within himself, to pronounce his own condemnation.

III. — All the determinism of action, then, has the role of making a conflict rise inevitably, because the entire being of things and the entire fate of our being, hangs from the unavoidable duty to resolve it voluntarily. Even the conception we have of God is at first only an effect of this internal dynamism and a spring destined to push the determinism of consciousness to the point where we must opt. The solution to the problem is therefore grounded on the totality of human experience and science; but this whole natural order is only a means of accomplishing a higher destiny. Failing to arrive at it, the best ordered life remains like a frame well prepared, but empty. Every doctrine which does not reach the one thing necesary, every separated philosophy, will remain deceived by false appearances. It will be a doctrine, it will not be "Philosophy." It is to render Philosophy the best of services to put it in contact with this higher order, where it cannot enter in, but which it cannot ignore or exclude except by mutilating itself: if it does not go to the point of indicating its necessity, all the other questions it deals with lose their sense and their bond, it is no longer a *science*; every affirmation of objective existence is destitute of signification and grounding, it is no longer *metaphysical*; all practice remains deprived of salutary efficaciousness, it is no longer *moral*.

Thus is revealed the unity of the problem. It matters little that the speculative solution should be difficult to illuminate with a little light, if the practical solution is not put off or compromised by any obscurity. The clearest will is not always the most distinct, and the will which does not analyse its conditions is of the same nature as the one whose knowledge has penetrated the hidden reasons. Some recent doctrines have claimed to reduce everything in the universe to an obscure and irrational *willing*; the designation is not deserved. It is in a will, not reasoned at first, but able to be reasoned, that we must look for the anticipated secret of our being. The issue is the profound drama of our lives: there is nothing fictitious or external either in the question or in the solution itself. Every human life is an exquisite logic, which incorrect formulations can envelop in illusions or shackles, but which always clears them away in the end, often without having examined them. Simply to unfold the interior content of our acts is already to be quite powerful; for it is to rely on a spring which, slowly perhaps but surely, produces its effects little by little. The science of action has as its object to manifest the power of this internal mover. Whether it considers the deviation which propels the will away from its center forever, or whether it contemplates the marvelous way in which man, by a sort of demise from life, acquires the gift of God, always it finds within the intimate willing of each the principle of the destiny of each. The force of the proofs which it uses therefore depends on the fact that each one bears them within himself. Its ambition is to uncover for us what we like to hide from ourselves: not that it can truly anticipate the revelations to come; but it can at least unveil the dissimulations of the present. If knowledge is not man's end all and be all, it is enough, in man, to make him recognize his way.

—Perhaps it seems that to look for the end of action beyond given reality and to go in the direction of a good that is not to be found in nature, is to be mystical. —Perhaps it seems that to recognize for the will the necessity of surpassing itself, is to commit *a petitio principii* and to suppose the need for the infinite which is in question. —Perhaps it seems that to claim to procure for man the infinite satisfactions which he dreams of, is to fail in philosophic wisdom, since the ambition and the honor of philosophy has always been, it seems, to curb the blind *élan* of human desires.

Let us not be mistaken then. —We had to consider action, not to put in it what would not be there, not to interpret it, not to give it a direction, but to observe what it is, whether we know it or ignore it, whether we

489

will it expressly or not. It is an issue, not of simple tendencies, but of concrete acts, not of what might or should be, but of the real, of what is
done and willed. Only the analysis of the will, by revealing to us what
we must ratify in order to will even our own will, has shown us through
what conditions we must pass inevitably: to will the infinite, no, that is
not a point of departure, but a point of arrival for scientific inquiry. But
is it a point of departure and a principle for the spontaneous activity of
life? That is the question. If this need is in us, how can we make it not
be there, how escape the necessity of recognizing it? All we can try to do,
is to suppose that it is not, is to do as if it were not, is to will infinitely
without willing the infinite. And that is the origin of the negative character of the method which alone seemed to have the rigor of science: to
evade with all one's strength the conclusions one will be led to, to look
for all escape routes, is that to introduce a secret postulate? — And from
490 all these attempts there follows only a system of connected affirmations
which constrain us little by little to posit before reflected thought the end
which was already present at the origin of the movement by which we
were running away from it. Like Descartes, who had feigned new reasons
for doubting, we had to make some strange moral attitudes enter into the
domain of philosophical doctrines, and to start from further back in
order to go further forward than others had gone, from the frame of
mind of the aesthete to the devotion of the Grey Nun. But the Methodical
Doubt was the singular disposition of a single mind; we have to accept
all the diversity of human consciousnesses and to make even those who
feign not to set out at all go forward. The Methodical Doubt was limited
to an intellectual, a partial, an artificial difficulty; the issue is the vital
question, the total question. From the Methodical Doubt one emerged
as from a fiction; we have to remain in action as in reality. Thus, what
was only the problem of the understanding, becomes the problem of the
will; it is no longer only the Cartesian question, but the Kantian question
which we had to resolve anew by defining the relation of knowing, doing, and being; still more, it is the problem of pessimism concerning the
value of life, and concerning the agreement of our willing with the universal conditions of knowledge and existence; and more finally, it is the
philosophical problem in its entirety, since at issue is the relation of the
natural order with the supernatural itself and the indictment of separated
philosophy. — To remove the contradiction which people have always
sensed between the principle and the end of voluntary aspiration, human
wisdom has long since indicated the following solution: "Instead of trying in vain to make the willed end equal to the infinite principle of desire,
can we not regulate the desire according to the object and limit the aspiration?" Yes, we can and we do so, but at what cost? For what we reject

is not suppressed; and in this systematic abdication is found once again, as a principle of condemnation and death, the hidden contradiction that seemed removed. — Hence there is neither mysticism nor *petitio principii*, but a look at the real content of voluntary action, a disclosure of what the would-be wisdom of abstention contains and prepares, a justification, against a vain and temerarious science, of the great folly of living and dying, if need be, to save one's soul.

We do not escape what we will, even when it seems that we do not will it. All the mystery of life comes from this superficial disagreement between apparent desires and the sincere aspiration of the primitive willing. Nothing, whether in the inevitable conditions of our life, or in the personal use of our strength, or in the sometimes unforeseen consequences of our acts, is tyrannically imposed on us. What being we receive is identical with what we will of it, without our ever ceasing to will what we cannot lose of it. Hence it is the very meaning of being which we find defined. Like a two-edged sword, action resolves, in opposed directions, the question of life or death which imposes itself on all; and the syntheses it effectuates, always with the same elements, the solutions it arrives at, are so extreme that they surpass either all that the darkest of pessimisms has conceived or all that the most daring optimism has dreamed of: precisely in this does the grandeur and the goodness of our destiny reside. There is, in the first foundation of the human will, a first outline of being, which can no longer cease to be, but which, deprived of its completion, is worth less than if it were not. And for this beginning to find completion, the human will must receive perfection from a more than human hand. Man can gain his being only by denying it in some way, in order to refer it back to its principle and to its true end. To renounce what he has which is proper to himself, and to annihilate this nothingness which he is, is to receive that full life which he aspires to, but whose source he does not have within himself. His way of contributing to creating himself is to consent to the invasion of all that is prior life and higher will than his own. To will all that we will, in full sincerity of heart, is to place the action and the being of God within ourselves. No doubt, it is hard to do this, because we do not feel how this will is preeminently our own. But we must give all for all; life has a divine price; and in spite of its proud or sensual weaknesses, humanity is generous enough to belong more to whoever will demand more of it.

This work of life and salvation, science can show its necessity: it does not bring it to completion, it does not even begin to do so. Human action must prepare it and cooperate in it: it does not have the initiative for it, nor does it bring about its success; it is not digging the riverbed that fills it with water. Rational critique and moral practice have a certain

491

role of clearing out and of preparing the way, but the living source is elsewhere than in them. Even after we have posited, by way of a necessary hypothesis, the supernatural order as a scientific postulate, we must be on guard against thinking that we could prove its real truth through the development of its consequences or through its internal appropriatenesses. To affirm that it is, is an avowal which never comes from us alone. It is enough, therefore, to set aside everything that would falsely make it seem impossible, to show everything that makes it justly necessary, to prove that it can neither be established nor excluded by philosophy, and yet that man could not dispense with it without fault or without loss. If we cannot entirely demonstrate it before reason, we cannot any more competently deny it without having had an experience of it; and once one has had an experience of it, one finds in the experience itself only reasons to affirm it: this is why education can communicate it, through submissive practice, like an experimental truth; let us not do as if it were not, it will be for us. It is the total concern of life which is at stake; in everything else, it is possible to abstain or to be evasive, because the affirmations or the negations, always mixed with some alloy, remain relative. But before this *yes* without any *no*, and here alone, all is decided absolutely. There is no middle ground or neutrality: not to do as if it were true, is to do as if it were false. It is for philosophy to show the necessity of posing the alternative: "*Is it or is it not?*" For philosophy to make known that only this unique and universal question which embraces the entire destiny of man imposes itself on all with this absolute rigor. "Is it or is it not?" For philosophy to prove that we cannot, in practice, not pronounce for or against this supernatural: "Is it or is it not?" For philosophy, once again, to examine the consequences of one solution or the other and to measure their immense disparity. But philosophy can go no further, nor can it say, in its own name alone, whether it be or not. But if it is permitted to add one word, only one, which goes beyond the domain of human science and the competence of philosophy, the only word able, in the face of Christianity, to express that part of certitude, the best part, which cannot be communicated because it arises only from the intimacy of totally personal action, one word which would itself be an action, it must be said: "It is."